Committee of Inquiry into Dublin Metropolitan Police

Dublin Metropolitan Police

Minutes of Evidence

Committee of Inquiry into Dublin Metropolitan Police

Dublin Metropolitan Police
Minutes of Evidence

ISBN/EAN: 9783742817785

Manufactured in Europe, USA, Canada, Australia, Japa

Cover: Foto ©ninafisch / pixelio.de

Manufactured and distributed by brebook publishing software
(www.brebook.com)

Committee of Inquiry into Dublin Metropolitan Police

Dublin Metropolitan Police

DUBLIN METROPOLITAN POLICE.

EVIDENCE

TAKEN BEFORE THE

COMMITTEE OF INQUIRY:

1882-83.

With APPENDIX and MAPS.

[In continuation of Command Paper No. 3576.]

Presented to both Houses of Parliament by Command of Her Majesty.
1883.

INDEX TO EVIDENCE.

[3110]

LIST OF WITNESSES.

DUBLIN METROPOLITAN POLICE.

EVIDENCE

TAKEN BEFORE THE

COMMITTEE OF INQUIRY.

FIRST DAY.—19TH SEPTEMBER, 18[illegible].

Present:

Mr. J. W. O'DONNELL, Chairman; Mr. GEORGE MORRIS, D.L., Local Government Board; and Mr. R. W. A. HOLMES, Treasury Remembrancer.

Mr. FRANCIS M. HUME, examined.

1. *Mr. Holmes.*—What is your present position in the force?—Secretary and Accountant.

2. How long have you filled that position?—About eleven years.

3–6. Did you occupy any other position in the force before your present position?—Oh, yes; that of Chief Clerk.

7. What is that paper that you have in your hand?—This is a statement or return showing the authorised strength of the Dublin metropolitan police force and the present actual strength of the force, with the numbers, rates of pay, and allowances of the respective ranks.

8. Well, that Return will, of course, be printed. It will be in the appendix to our Report, and will form part of your evidence?—Just so.

9. *Mr. Morris.*—What is the present strength of the force?—The present strength of the force is 1,106.

10. *Chairman.*—Is that all told?—Yes; all told; officers and all.

11. *Mr. Holmes.*—That is the authorised strength of the force?—Yes.

12. Is that "authorised" strength authorised by Act of Parliament or by Treasury sanction?—It is authorised by vote of Parliament with Treasury sanction.

13. What do you mean when you say "authorised" strength of the force—is that the fixed strength of the force?—You know the force has varied slightly from time to time, and slight additions have been made as exigencies arose, but no material increase of the force has taken place since it was extended in 1840.

14. *Chairman.*—The only alterations that have been made are the additions to the number?—Yes, slight additions to the number.

15. *Mr. Holmes.*—Do the numbers vary each year according to the vote of Parliament, or is it under special arrangement with the Treasury?—Well, you know, the numbers might vary slightly occasionally. For instance, if any exigency arose, application would be made to the Treasury for authority to add so many men to the strength of the force—ten, twelve, fifteen men, as the occasion might require, and then, as a matter of course, in framing the estimate for the succeeding year, that addition would be included in the strength.

16. *Mr. Morris.*—What is the actual strength at the present time?—There are at present ten vacancies.

Mr. Francis [illegible].

[illegible]

17. Then there are 1,178 men now in the force?—Yes, 1,176.

18. *Chairman.*—There are only two short?—Yes.

19. *Mr. Holmes.*—Will you now kindly state the various ranks in the force and the number of men in each rank?—Yes.

20. Beginning with the highest?—The chief superintendent is the chief officer of the force under the Commissioners, so far as the force is concerned. There is one chief superintendent, and then there are six ordinary superintendents.

21. *Chairman.*—There are seven in all?—There are seven in all.

22. Including Kingstown?—Yes; including Kingstown—A, B, C, D, E, F, and G. The "G" is the detective division. Of inspectors of the first-class there are 7; of the second-class 8, and of the third-class, 16. Of acting inspectors there are 35; sergeants, 66; acting sergeants, 46. Then of constables—of what is called the first rate—there are [illegible] first-class constables. Then, of what is called the second rate, there are 118; of the third rate, 389; and of the fourth rate, 161. That completes the force, and then the ordinary number of supernumeraries is 40.

23. What are the supernumeraries?—The supernumeraries are men in training at the depôt to become constables.

24. *Chairman.*—When a man first joins he becomes a supernumerary?—Yes; he is called a supernumerary—meaning a recruit.

25-26. *Mr. Holmes.*—Then there are four different grades of constable?—We have, strictly speaking, only three classes, but the second class has two rates—a first rate and a second rate.

27. You say that when a man first joins he is called a supernumerary?—Yes.

28. How long does he remain in that position?—The period varies from six weeks to two months, or perhaps over that.

29. According to his ability in learning the drill and the duties?—Yes, and the exigencies of the service, as it might sometimes be necessary to appoint recruits constables at a somewhat earlier period than usual.

30. What is the pay of a supernumerary?—15s. 6d. a-week.

31. *Mr. Morris.*—The chief superintendent—what does he get?—His salary is [illegible]. Then the other superintendents, they begin at [illegible], advancing by [illegible] a-year to the maximum of [illegible]. Of course, having regard to the annual increments, all the superintendents are not under the same scale of pay at the same time; for instance, at the present moment one is in receipt of [illegible], one at [illegible], and three are at [illegible], the maximum. Then a first-class inspector has [illegible] a-year.

32-33. *Mr. Holmes.*—Is that a fixed salary?—Yes, that is a fixed salary. Then the second-class has [illegible] and the third-class [illegible]. Then the acting inspectors receive [illegible] 17s. 3d. Their weekly pay is [illegible] 16s. 6d.; it is given here in this Return. The sergeants receive [illegible] 11s. 11d., or 1l. 13s. 6d. per week; the acting sergeants [illegible] 14s. 6d., and the constables of the first rate [illegible] 13s. 9d., that is weekly 1l. 8s. 6d. That 1l. 8s. 6d. includes 6d. weekly allowance for boots and for [illegible] uniform.

34. You have stated that that payment includes a weekly allowance for boots; is that allowance given to all the men in the force?—That is an allowance given to all the men, from acting inspector downwards.

35. *Mr. Morris.*—Well, the second-class constables—what do they get?—[illegible] 13s. 11d., or weekly, 1l. 6s. 9d., and the third rate receive [illegible] 13s. 9d.

36. *Chairman.*—The 6d. that you say is allowed to the men for boots, from the class of acting inspector downwards, is that inclusive—from acting inspector inclusive?—Inclusive from acting inspector downwards—from acting inspector to fourth rate constable.

37. *Mr. Morris.*—The third-class has [illegible] 13s. 9d.?—Yes.

38. And the fourth rate?—[illegible] 13s. 3d., or a-week, 1l. 5s. 6d., including the 6d.

39. And the third-class, how much is it weekly?—The third-class is 1l. 6s. 9d.

40. *Mr. Holmes.*—How much is it a-week?—1l. 6s. 9d. The supernumeraries receive 15s. 6d. a-week, or [illegible] a-year.

41. On their becoming fourth class constables their wages go from 15s. 6d. a-week to 1l. 5s. 6d.?—Yes, quite so. That is the rate fixed.

42. When were those rates fixed?—From the 1st December, 1872.

43. *Chairman.*—Is that because that supernumeraries go from 15s. 6d. to 1l. 5s. 6d.?—Yes, that is so with supernumeraries. While the supernumerary is in training he is allowed to receive 15s. 6d. a-week, and on becoming a fourth rate constable he gets 1l. 5s. 6d.

44. The first immediate rise from supernumerary to fourth-class constable is from 15s. 6d. to 1l. 5s. 6d.?

45. *Mr. Holmes.*—Taking the average then, how soon does a recruit become a fourth rate constable?—Well, I know that Captain Talbot has been very anxious to make the men as perfect in their knowledge of police duties as possible before sending them out into the street, and Captain Talbot thinks that a period of some three months would not be too much to have them in training.

46. And where are the recruits trained?—At Kevin Street depôt.

47. *Chairman.*—Who is in charge of that depôt?—There is an inspector in charge of the recruits there.

48-9. *Mr. Holmes.*—Is that what they call the school?—There is a school there; and Inspector Thorpe is the inspector. I should mention, before perhaps you go further, that the rates I have given out are those pertaining to the general force. In the detective branch the rates are somewhat different.

50. Will you kindly state the strength of the detective force? I think you said that Division "G" is the detective force?—Yes, the strength is 44.

51. *Mr. Morris.*—What are the letters that apply to all the others?—A, B, C, D, E, and F.

52. Those six first letters apply to the general force?—Yes. The "G" Division is the detective Division. The Superintendent's yearly pay is [illegible].

53. Of the G Division?—Yes. Then the inspectors have [illegible]; the acting inspector [illegible] 14s. 7d.

54. *Mr. Holmes.*—That compares with [illegible] 17s. 3d., the rate paid in the other divisions to acting inspectors?—Yes, quite so. We have another rate of acting inspector in the G Division. He receives [illegible] 1s. 6d. Then the sergeant in the G Division has the same rate of pay as in the general force, [illegible] 13s. 1d.

55. Why is he not paid more when the acting inspector is?—Well, that rate was fixed. I rather think the duties of an acting inspector of the G Division are somewhat more important than the duties of an ordinary acting inspector.

56. And it is not so with the sergeant?—Not I should say to the same extent. However, there are only four sergeants in the G Division. There are thirteen acting inspectors, and the object evidently was to have the higher ranks better paid, because the higher a man's rank, the more important the nature of his duties. Of acting sergeants there are six, and they have in the G Division [illegible] 6s. 6d. A constable of the first rate has [illegible] 4s. 3d.

57. Do the gradations of constable come into the G Division?—Yes. There are first and second rates in the G Division, [illegible] 4s. 3d. and [illegible] 6s. 1d.

58. Are there third rate constables in the G Division?—No; there is no rank below that of second rate constable.

59. I see there are seven divisions, and omitting the chief superintendent, seven superintendents?—Yes.

60. I suppose there is a superintendent for each division?—Yes.

61. In which division is the chief superintendent?—The chief superintendent was formerly over the B Division, but latterly the B Division has an officer that may be said to be the acting superintendent. He is called the inspector in charge of the B Division. Now he (the chief superintendent) exercises a general supervision over the five superintendents, and the inspector in charge of the B Division. But practically it may be said that the chief superintendent is the superintendent of the B Division.

62. Now, in reference to the B Division; is there anything peculiar in that division that should make the chief superintendent be identified with it?—Well, the B Division is the division in which the Castle is situated; it is called the B, or Castle Division, and he belongs to and has charge of a division in which a large number of men are concentrated.

63. *Chairman.*—Has the chief superintendent apartments in the Castle-Yard?—Yes, he has a house there.

64. *Mr. Holmes.*—Then those ordinary superintendents are superintendents of each of the other divisions, excluding the B Division?—Yes, excluding that division in which there is an inspector in charge.

65. *Mr. Morris.*—It is better now to go back a little. What are the allowances in addition to pay in the A, B, C, D, E, and F Divisions. What allowances do the men get in addition to their pay?—Shall I begin with the superintendents?

66. *Mr. Holmes.*—Yes, I think so?—Well, the yearly allowances to the superintendents amount to 150*l.*—those who are not provided with quarters. The chief superintendent is provided with a free house and his allowances amount to 105*l.*

67. What is his allowance intended to meet?—It is intended to meet the following: 5*l.* for a horse. He purchases his own horse, and he is allowed, in consideration of the purchase, 5*l.* per annum.

68. *Chairman.*—By way of interest on the purchase money?—No.

69. For wear and tear?—Yes, for wear and tear. He purchases his own horse, because it is found more economical to let the superintendent purchase his own horse and allow him 5*l.* a-year.

70. *Mr. Morris.*—For the deterioration of the horse?—Yes, just so. Well, for forage, he is allowed 44*l.* per annum, and for a groom he is allowed 15*l.* more. And then for clothing he is allowed 10*l.*,—that is for uniform clothing. If the superintendent is not provided with an office and stable, he is allowed 20*l.* a-year in addition.

71. *Mr. Holmes.*—But the chief superintendent's allowance is only 105*l.*?—Yes. In addition, there are two superintendents of Divisions D and E, and in consideration of the large extent of these districts, and as one horse would not be sufficient, they are allowed at the rate of 1*s.* per day for car hire, which brings their total allowances up to 168*l.* 5*s.*

72. They are allowed 1*s.* a-day besides their allowance for a horse?—Yes, 1*s.* a-day besides their allowance for a horse, and in order to meet their expenditure on car hire. The superintendent of the F Division has 105*l.* a-year and free quarters. Therefore he is not allowed the 20*l.* a-year for an office and stable. Inspectors of the first-class, they are allowed 32*l.* a-year—26*l.* for lodgings and 6*l.* for uniform clothing—which makes their total salary or income 162*l.* The inspectors of the second-class have the same allowances as those of the first-class, in fact, all the three classes of inspectors have the same allowances of 32*l.* per annum.

73. *Chairman.*—What do you say that the 32*l.* is supposed to cover?—26*l.* for lodgings, and 6*l.* for uniform clothing.

74. Then they buy their own uniform?—They provide themselves with their own uniform, and so do the superintendents, and they are allowed in consideration of doing so, the superintendents 10*l.*, and the inspectors 6*l.* per annum.

75–7. *Mr. Holmes.*—Is the lodging allowance given irrespective of whether the men are married or single?—Yes; quite so. Then the allowances given to acting inspectors come to 34*s.* 6*d.* a year.

78. Why is their allowance so small?—As acting inspectors the same allowances are granted to them as to all the other ranks in the service—all the other ranks downwards.

79. *Chairman.*—What is that sum intended to meet?—There are 32*s.* in lieu of boots, and 2*s.* 6*d.* for lining uniform clothing.

80. Then from acting inspectors downwards I understand you to say that the only allowance given is 34*s.* 6*d.*?—Yes.

81. Is that inclusive of the 6*d.* per week?—Yes; it comes to that in the year.

82. *Mr. Holmes.*—Have you finished with the allowances now?—Yes, with the allowances for the general force. Then the allowances to the superintendent of the G Division are the same as the allowances to the other superintendents, 150*l.*, as he is not provided with quarters. The allowance for the inspector ordinarily is 32*l.*, the same as in the case of an ordinary inspector, but the present inspector is provided with quarters, and he only draws 6*l.* for uniform. Then the rates to the acting inspector in the G Division—the normal rate of allowance is 6*l.* 16*s.* 2*d.*, and so on with all the other grades, that is 32*s.* a-year for boots, and 2*s.* a-week in lieu of uniform clothing.

83–85. And what have the rest?—The rest have all the same. The reason of the difference in the allowance in reference to uniform is this: in the G Division they are allowed 32*s.* a-year in lieu of boots, and then in lieu of uniform clothing, and as compensation for wearing their own plain clothes, they are allowed 2*s.* a-week.

86. Which brings up the allowance to 6*l.* 16*s.* 2*d.*?—Yes.

87–8. Then as a rule the "G" men do not appear in uniform?—No. At assizes of course they do wear their uniform, and before the Judges they may appear in uniform, and other special occasions.

89. Now you have finished with allowances?—Yes.

90. And the difference in the case of the "G" men, as compared with the general force, is as between 6*l.* 16*s.* 2*d.* and 34*s.* 6*d.*?—Yes. Then in the case of the small troop, the men of the troop are allowed 6*d.* per week for spurs and gloves.

91. What division is that?—That is attached to the A Division.

92. The troopers are attached to the A Division?—Yes.

93. How many are there?—There are twenty-four horses—seventeen for the troop and seven for the police prisoners' vans.

94. These are what are called the mounted constables?—Yes. Perhaps I might add that the inspector of the horse police gets a special allowance of 12*l.* for uniform, instead of the 6*l.* given to the other ordinary inspectors, his uniform being subject to greater wear and tear. He is allowed 12*l.* instead of 6*l.*

95. Will you now tell us what is the extent of the Dublin metropolitan police area?—It is 34 square miles, and the population of the district (census 1881) 349,049.

96. Extending from what point? Give its boundaries?—It may be said to extend from Killiney at the south side to Annesley Bridge at the north side of the city.

97. Does it not go further?—The metropolitan police area terminates with the sea at Annesley Bridge, but, of course, it includes Terenure, south-westward.

98. Would you kindly put in writing, for the Committee, the exact boundaries of the Dublin metropolitan police area, and show the boundaries as defined by Act of Parliament, and the situation of the various divisions?—Yes. In fact, you know the district may be said, for all practical purposes, to be divided into six divisions.

99. Could you tell us how many barracks there are

Mr. Francis M. [illegible]

15 Sept., 1882.

[illegible] 22 Sept., 1880.

in the whole of the police area?—I think it would be better for me to put that in writing also, because I would then be more accurate.

100. And when you do so, would you give us the number of men in each barrack?—Yes.

101. Is there any allowance for lodgings given to the rank and file?—There is a deduction made from the pay of the rank and file who are provided with quarters.

102. *Mr. Morris.*—Take the thirty-eight acting inspectors—are they provided with lodgings or with barrack accommodation?—Well, you know that would all depend upon whether they are married or unmarried men. Married men, as a rule, do not generally reside in barracks. I think it would be much better to bring that also into the Return. We will give you the actual number of men in each barrack, and we will state the ranks, and whether they are married or single, as the case may be. I may mention that there is an officer called a divisional staff sergeant, who has charge of the barracks, and who might be called the barrack sergeant; he is generally provided with quarters, because he has to be there at all hours.

103. Well, with the exception of the barrack sergeant, are all the rest of the men who are provided with barrack accommodation constables?—Oh no, they are not. Unmarried acting inspectors might be provided with barrack accommodation; so might unmarried sergeants, acting sergeants, as well as the several rates of unmarried constables.

104. Can you tell us now, from memory, what is the usual number of men accommodated in a barrack?—Really, I could not say. I know the great majority of the men, as a matter of course, are accommodated in barracks.

105. And do they pay anything for barrack accommodation?—Yes, they do. That is, of course, the barrack accommodation includes lodging, bedding, and firing, and everything in that way. A fourth rate constable is charged 6d. per week, and the others are charged 1s. 2d. per week.

106. For what?—For what is called lodging and fuel.

107. That is deducted from their pay?—Yes.

108. To meet the expense of lodging and fuel?—Yes.

109. Then, in point of fact, they are supposed to pay, and they are charged rent for barrack accommodation?—Quite so.

110. And they have to pay for their own fuel?—No.

111. They are charged?—Just so; but the 1s. 2d. includes both lodging and fuel, except to the fourth rate constable, who is charged but 6d. per week.

112–113. *Mr. Holmes.*—Then there is no allowance given to the men to meet the cost of the fuel consumed in the guard-room?—Oh no. The fuel consumed at the guard-room is provided by the Board of Works. The deductions in respect of fuel are for cooking their food and so on.

114. And the Board of Works provides the fuel consumed at the guard-room?—Oh, certainly. The men have nothing to pay for the fuel consumed in the guard-room. Anything required for the public service, and not what might be called for the individual use of the men, as a matter of course, is provided by the public. But in stormy or wet weather in winter coal is provided free of charge to the men in barracks, to warm and keep dry their sleeping rooms.

115. How much of that 1s. 2d. is in respect of lodgings, and how much in respect of fuel?—In the proportions of 6d. and 8d.—6d. for lodging and 8d. for fuel.

116. *Chairman.*—Those who pay that are entitled to cook their own food?—As a matter of course.

117. There is a cook in the barracks?—Yes; quite so. There is a mess at the barracks.

118. *Mr. Holmes.*—Necessarily is there?—As a general rule there is a mess.

119. *Mr. Morris.*—I suppose they settle that among themselves?—Yes.

120. In the case of those men who live out of barracks there is no allowance made to them for lodgings?—None, except to superintendents and inspectors.

121. And there is no deduction made for lodgings at all?—No. As a matter of fact, formerly, before the increase of pay in 1872, an inspector provided with quarters had a deduction made from his pay of 2s. 11d. per month, but when the Treasury granted 20l. a-year in lieu of lodgings, that deduction, as a matter of course, was abolished.

122. *Mr. Holmes.*—How long does a man remain in the fourth rate as a constable before he gets promotion?—Somewhere about one year.

123. How is promotion regulated in the force?—Promotion is regulated according to the advanced class. It is better to read out the statement concerning that from the Commissioners' Regulations.

124. We don't want to go into particulars about the Regulations. State generally how is promotion regulated?—Well, promotion is regulated in this way:—A number of select men are selected, and they undergo a kind of competitive examination, and their names, as they succeed in passing, are placed on this advanced class, and from this advanced class promotions are made from time to time.

125. Before you enter into an explanation in reference to this, will you tell us what prospects a man has of rising in the force after he has been made a fourth rate constable. How long does he remain in that grade before he becomes a third rate constable?—Give us the history of a man when he joins the force, beginning below and going up? A man gets to what is called the second rate in about a year.

126. Begin with the fourth rate?—In the fourth rate a man must remain in that, say, about a year.

127. *Chairman.*—Does time alone remove him from that grade? Does period of service?—As a general rule it does, because being a junior rate a man will generally get to the second rate of the second-class in about a year.

128. There are two rates of pay in the second-class?—Quite so.

129. What is the difference in the amounts of those?—From 1l. 6s. 6d. to 1l. 8s. 9d. In about six and a-half years a man gets to the first rate of the second-class, and then in about eight and a-half years a man becomes a first-class constable. It takes one year to the second rate of the second class. It takes six and a-half years to reach the first rate of the second class—about that; and it takes eight and a-half years to reach the first-class.

130. Including the previous six and a-half?—Yes, including the previous period of his service. A man gets to the rank of acting sergeant in about ten years, and the rank of sergeant in about thirteen years, and to the rank of acting inspector in about fifteen years, and to the rank of inspector in about twenty years. But there might be, and often are, exceptional cases of intelligence and merit justifying promotion in much shorter periods. It affords pleasure to the Chief Commissioner to make such promotions.

131. How does a constable get promotion to those different ranks?—I say the Commissioners have what is called this advanced class, and that forms the nucleus of all promotions. (The witness then read the reference to the advanced class from the printed Regulations of the Commissioners at p. 233, under the head of "School.")

132. *Mr. Holmes.*—Then, as I understand you, the advanced class is composed only of first and second-rate constables?—That is the general rule, but Captain Talbot occasionally admits men of the third rate—clever, intelligent men—so as to encourage merit and afford every opportunity for promotion to clever men in the service.

133. Then, in order to become an acting sergeant, a constable must be put into the advanced class, and must pass an examination?—Quite

Mr. Francis M. Shade.

13 Sept., 1882.

134. But a man can rise from the rank of a fourth-rate constable to that of a first rate constable without being put into that class or any class, or having to pass any examination?—Quite so, in special cases of merit, or length of service, &c. I would, however, very much prefer leaving this matter to Captain Talbot, as it is more within his province than mine. It is Captain Talbot who makes the promotions, and it is under his supervision that these examinations take place.

135. *Mr Morris.*—I would wish to have a Return of the average annual amount of fines inflicted upon each individual grade, but I don't want the names of the individuals?—I will furnish you with such a Return. You are anxious to have a Return of the number of candidates who presented themselves from 1873 to 1882, and the number admitted, and the number rejected?

136. *Chairman.*—Yes?—I will read the particulars you require from the Return I hold in my hand, which is headed "Dublin Metropolitan Police. Return of the number of removals from the force from all causes from 1873 to 1882." The years go from 1873 to 1882—that is, a portion of 1882. In 1873 the deaths were 12; the pensioned, 30; discharged with gratuity, 15; voluntary resignations, 75; compulsory resignations, none; dismissals, 27; discharged unfit for further duty, being under five years' service, none; total, 160. In 1874 the deaths were 6; pensioned, 24, discharged with gratuity, 9; voluntary resignations, 16; compulsory resignations, none; dismissals, 35; discharged unfit for further duty, being under five years' service, 1; total, 91. In 1875 the deaths were 5; pensioned, 23; discharged with gratuity, 10; voluntary resignations, 21; compulsory resignations, none; dismissals, 29; discharged unfit for further duty, being under five years' service, none; total, 88.

137. *Mr. Holmes.*—I suppose the large number of resignations in 1873 was due to the low rates of pay?—No doubt, to a very considerable extent, in 1873, because, I may say, so much so that at that time the force had very considerably dwindled down, owing to the difficulty of getting recruits, through, as it was then believed, the very low and inadequate rates of pay.

138. Witness proceeded.—In 1875 there were 5 deaths; 10 pensioned; 13 discharged with gratuity; 26 voluntary resignations; no compulsory resignations; dismissals, 50; unfit for further duty, being under five years' service, none; total, 115.

139. What is the difference between dismissal and compulsory resignation?—Well, there is this difference, dismissal means that the case was of a much worse complexion than that of a compulsory resignation, in which there generally are some mitigating or extenuating circumstances. That is another matter that Captain Talbot can much better explain than I can. In 1876 there were 7 deaths; 10 pensioned; 4 were discharged with gratuity; 31 voluntary resignations; no compulsory resignations, 63 dismissals; unfit for further duty, under five years' service, 1; total, 116.

140. What is the meaning of "discharged with gratuity"?—That is a man returned unfit for further service, and who has not served a sufficient period to get a pension. In 1877 there were 8 deaths; 20 pensioned; 9 discharged with gratuity; 27 voluntary resignations; 41 dismissals; 2 discharged unfit for further duty, service being under five years; total, 110. In 1878 there were 11 deaths; 10 pensioned; 6 discharged with gratuity; 29 voluntary resignations; no compulsory resignations; 48 dismissals; 6 unfit for duty, service being under five years; total, 172.

141. The number of deaths was rather higher than the average in that year?—Yes, 11 in that year, but there were 12 deaths in 1872. In 1879 there were 10 deaths; 6 pensioned; 7 discharged with gratuity; 16 voluntary resignations; 3 compulsory resignations; 27 dismissals; 3 discharged unfit for further duty, service being under five years; making a total of 72. In 1880 there were 6 deaths; 17 pensioned; 7 discharged with gratuity; 23 voluntary resignations; 5 compulsory resignations; 45 dismissals; 3 discharged unfit for further duty, service being under five years, making a total of 106. In 1881 there were 11 deaths; 10 pensioned; 9 discharged with gratuity; 19 voluntary resignations; 3 compulsory resignations; 24 dismissals; 3 discharged unfit for further duty, service being under five years; making a total of 79. In 1882, up to the present time, there have been 7 deaths; 16 pensioned; 8 discharged with gratuity; 56 voluntary resignations; 7 compulsory resignations; 27 dismissals; 1 unfit for duty, service being under five years; and that makes a total of 122 up to the 11th September, 1882.

142–143. The number of voluntary resignations appears to be very large?—Very large. Two causes have been assigned: one is that the scale of pensions to which these men, the men appointed under the Act of 1867, are entitled, is not sufficiently large to induce them to continue in the service. That is stated.

144. That cause ought to have had effect before this year. The men surely were aware of the alteration in the scale of pensions before this year?—Yes; but you know it very often happens that men do not think of these things until they have been some three, four, or five years in the service, or longer perhaps than those periods. But perhaps from that up to seven years or so a man begins to look at his prospects. However, that is one cause which has been assigned. Another is that very encouraging accounts came home from Australia which induced, it is stated, very many of these men to resign, in the hope of bettering their condition in Australia. I may add there is a note at the bottom of the Return to which I have been referring, which states that of the number dismissed in 1882 there are seventeen men included who attended the meeting in contravention of orders.

145. *Chairman.*—What is the total number dismissed including these?—Twenty-seven for 1882.

146. *Mr Morris.*—I should like to have a schedule of the pensions that these men would be entitled to?—Yes; you can have that. I have not yet, however, given you the information you asked me for yesterday, as to the number of candidates who presented themselves from 1873 to 1882.

147. *Chairman.*—Will you give us now the number of recruits that joined the force from 1873?—The total number admitted from 1873 to the 11th September, 1882, was 1,368.

148–149. *Mr. Holmes.*—Can you give us the number in each year?—Yes; in 1873 there were 140; in 1873, 233, in 1874, 100; in 1875, 141; in 1876, 164; in 1877, 173; in 1878, 183; in 1879, 111; in 1880, 101; in 1881, 93; and up to the 11th September, 1882, 149; making a total of 1,368. We can give you the number rejected also. In 1873 the number rejected, that is, the number not found physically fit or otherwise for the service, was 10; in 1873 it was 70, because with the increase of pay there was a large influx of recruits. Before that it was almost impossible to get recruits, although we advertised very generally throughout the provinces; yet, strange to say, before the increase of pay took place it was almost impossible to get recruits. In 1874 the number rejected was 103; in 1875, 131; in 1876, 150, in 1877, 138; in 1878, 213; in 1879, 153; in 1880, 128; in 1881, 100; and up to the 11th September, 1882, 56; making a total of 1,330.

150. I suppose the rejections were in consequence of physical defects?—Yes, in consequence of physical defects, men having varicose veins, or perhaps not sufficiently stalwart or strong for the police service.

151. Will you please tell us from what classes of the community recruits are usually drawn?—As a general rule they are farmers' sons and labourers. Of course there are some exceptions. A good man presenting himself, and well recommended, and possessing all the physical requirements, would not be rejected, although not from those classes.

Mr. Francis [illegible]

[illegible] Sept. 18[illegible].

142. *Chairman.*—That is a good man from any other class?—Yes, from any other class.

143. Or any other locality?—Yes, just so. I may mention that the present Chief Commissioner is most anxious to recruit as intelligent men as possible, and we have a form of "conditions." If you will allow me I will read it.

144. *Mr. Holmes.*—Do many of the recruits come from the labouring classes?—Oh yes.

145. What proportion do they bear to the farming classes?—I could not answer that question off-hand, but I could let you know. I think the great majority of our recruits are returned as labourers—that is, they so describe themselves.

146. From what parts of the country do most of the recruits come?—Principally from the home counties—from Wicklow, Meath, Kildare, Westmeath; but, then, as a matter of fact, every other county is represented in the force.

147. But they principally come from the home counties?—Yes.

148. And the men are taken principally from the labouring classes?—Yes.

149. That is, they give that designation of their position or calling?—Yes, they are principally labourers.

150. *Chairman.*—Do you inquire into the fact?—Oh yes. As soon as the recruit presents himself and gives the designation of "labourer," we inquire whether he has been so employed or not. We send down to the constabulary and inquire as to the character, antecedents, relations, and all these things concerning the recruit. This (in my hand) is a quotation from the paper we have called "Qualifications and Conditions for Candidates." [The witness then read the document referred to, beginning with the words "Some degree," and ending with words "gain promotion."]

161. When a man calls himself a labourer do you ask what class of labour he has been doing?—Captain Talbot, or Colonel Connolly, has the recruit before him, and he asks him all these questions—who his father was, how he has been employed, and so on. I would say this is more a matter for Captain Talbot to give you information upon than myself. I wish to add that the Return from which I have quoted shows that 2,815 men presented themselves for admission into the force, of whom 1,585 were admitted, and 1,230 rejected.

162. *Mr. Morris.*—Now as to the pensions; can you give us any information on that point?—Yes.

163. First, I would ask you, suppose a man is fined during the time of his service as a policeman, does that fine afterwards militate against his pension?—No, except in cases of drunkenness or frequent drunken reports; but ordinary breaches of discipline, for which small fines had been inflicted, do not count at all. At the same time the man's character and all his reports are given in the special "form," and every circumstance for and against is carefully weighed in order to fulfil the requirements of the law before his pension is settled. The Acts that regulate pensions in relation to the Dublin metropolitan police are two. The first Act is the 10 & 11 Vict., cap. 108, passed on the 22nd July, 1847.

164. *Mr. Holmes.*—What is the scale of pensions under that Act?—For appointments before the Act was passed—for those men who were actually appointed to the force before the Act was passed, and who were actually serving in the force before the Act became law, after fifteen years' service and under twenty years, a pension not exceeding two-thirds of their annual pay is prescribed.

165. Are there any men now in the force who joined before that date, because if there are not you need not tell us anything about that scale?—There are some men in the force that joined prior to that date. The chief superintendent and two superintendents are the only men now serving who joined before the Act. As a matter of fact the chief superintendent is one of them. Of course we could give you the exact number of those men if you wished it. There has been, however, no time to get in to go into that matter. After twenty years' service the law provided a pension not exceeding full pay. However, on considering the matter at the proper time, in the administration of that and the other sections of the Act, the spirit of the Act, and not the letter, was generally had regard to, and as a rule the Commissioners required the men, before they got the full-pay pension, to serve for twenty-five years, and on this ground: that if you gave a man his full pay immediately on the completion of twenty years, no inducement would exist to men to continue in the force, and it might have the effect of encouraging others to retire, because a man might naturally say, "I am entitled to my full-pay pension after twenty years' service, and if I get that pension I will take it and go away." These scales only apply to men before the Act of 1847 was passed. Of course, in any case in which a man's health was really broken down, and the man was of excellent character, he would be granted his full pay as a matter of right. The section of the Act prescribing two-thirds of salary as a pension after fifteen and under twenty years' service was also administered in a modified manner to carry out the spirit of the section. The number of men who joined the force after the passing of the 1847 Act (22nd July, 1847), up to the passing of the 1867 Act (12th August, 1867), and serving on the 14th September, 1882, was 831; the number appointed under the Act of 1867, and serving on the 14th September, 1882, was 608.

166. Now, in reference to the next Act regulating pensions?—That Act made a distinction between appointments before the Act and after the Act. Now, this is the scale for appointments after the Act. After fifteen and under twenty years' service, half of salary; then after twenty and under twenty-five years, not exceeding two-thirds; then after twenty-five years' service and under thirty years' service, not exceeding three-fourths; and after thirty years' service, not exceeding full pay. After thirty years' service a man became entitled to full pay. I was now speaking of the Act of 1847 as to appointments to the force after the Act was passed.

167. *Mr. Holmes.*—And that scale applies to all men who joined the force prior to 1867?—Yes.

168. *Mr. Morris.*—And after 1847?—Yes; between the dates of the 22nd July, 1847, and the 12th August, 1867.

169. *Mr. Holmes.*—And is that scale of pensions applicable to the new and increased rates of pay?—Quite so. Perhaps it is as well to mention that this Act of 1847 provided that in the case of those appointments made after the Act was passed, a deduction of 2 per cent. was to be made from the salary in consideration of superannuation. That was abolished by the Act of 1867. That 2 per cent. had been deducted for very many years from the pay, and amounted to a considerable sum annually.

170. That sum formed a fund to pay the pensions?—It didn't exactly form a fund. A deduction was made from the salary, out of the pay, in fact.

171. The deduction so made was made applicable to the payment of the pensions?—It might be said it went indirectly towards it. It was so much paid to the Crown.

172. *Chairman.*—As a kind of indemnity to the Crown?—Just so. That deduction is, as I have already said, abolished.

173. *Mr. Holmes.*—The men who joined the force prior to 1867, and retired on full pension, as a matter of course they attained thirty years' service?—Certainly.

174–175. How long are they required to remain in the service before they can retire?—I will tell you. No man is obliged to remain in the service after he is 60 years of age. He may then retire as a matter of course, and his pension would be computed according to his period of service, but before 60 no man

Mr. [illegible] H. Hinds.

13 Sept., 1882.

can retire except upon a medical certificate. That is under the special Police Act of the 10th and 11th Vict., the 1857 Act.

176. *Mr. Morris.*—Now, we may come to the Act of 1867; how are the pensions regulated under that Act?—That is the 30th and 31st Vict., cap. 95, passed on the 12th August, 1867. That provides that on the completion of fifteen years' service, fifteen-fiftieths of the pay may be granted, or, shortly speaking, three-tenths.

177. But a man cannot claim it?—No, certainly not, except upon a medical certificate. A medical certificate is, as a rule, an indispensable factor in the arrangement of pensions. For each successive year after fifteen years up to thirty years service completed, one-fiftieth of the pay for each such year.

178. Added?—Just so. Then there is this proviso after thirty years' service, or if the person has attained the age of 60 years, a pension may be given of thirty-fiftieths or a larger proportion in cases of extraordinary merit or good conduct.

179. Is that in the Act?—Yes, that is in the Act; but for injuries received in the actual performance of duty, a pension is given in proportion to the injury received, but not exceeding full pay. However, the general rule in the service is that if a man receives an injury in the execution of his duty disqualifying him from further service, entitling him, in the opinion of the medical officer, he generally gets his full pay as pension.

180. That is in the present and existing Act?—Yes; there is also a similar provision in the Act of 1857. Personal injuries are always considered to constitute an exceptional case.

181-2. *Mr. Holmes.*—Have any men retired under the Act of 1867?—No; none as yet.

183. *Mr. Morris.*—So I understand you, a man may be kept, and cannot himself voluntarily retire from the force on pension, without the leave of the Commissioners, until he is 60 years of age, unless through illness. Is that so?—Yes; quite so.

184-91. He cannot voluntarily retire?—Certainly not.

192. Might I ask you, Mr. Hinds, in your opinion, and from your knowledge of the force, whether the men complain more of the scale of pension or of their scale of pay?—So far as I can gather, their complaint—that is, of the junior men—is altogether in reference to the scale of pensions under this Act. It is said that it is scarcely fair that a man, serving twenty-five years' service under this Act of 1867, should be superannuated on a much lower pension than a man who had served the same period under the Act of 1857. However, it is to be borne in mind that it was clearly the intention of the Legislature that the Act of 1857 should cease to be operative in regard to all men appointed from the passing of the Act of 1867.

193. *Mr. Holmes.*—In other words, that the scale of pensions prior to 1867 should not be applicable to the rates of pay after 1867?—Quite so; the Act of 1867 prescribed a new scale.

194. That is clearly the intention of the Act?—Yes. That is clearly the intention, because this new Act was passed.

195. As I presume you have now disposed of the subject of pensions, will you proceed to tell us what is the annual cost of maintaining the police force; also how much of that is contributed from the Imperial funds?—The estimate for 1882-83, the year ending the 31st March, 1883, for the Dublin metropolitan police force comes to 183,817*l*.

196-7. How much of that is borne by Imperial taxation?—Well, the local revenue amounts to somewhere about 52,000*l*. or 53,000*l*. I should say that 53,000*l*. is contributed by local taxation, and the balance is, as a matter of course, provided. The total expenditure is voted by Parliament in the first instance, and then the local revenue is paid into the Imperial Exchequer in aid.

198. *Mr. Morris.*—That would leave about 83,000*l*. How is the local taxation defrayed? How is it raised?—It is raised from the police tax, which is assessed at 8*d*. in the £ as the principal source.

199. Under what Act?—Under the Act 1st Vict., cap. 25. That Act was passed in the year 1837.

200. That is upon the rateable value of property in Dublin?—In Dublin and the remainder of the metropolitan police district.

201. *Chairman.*—What area is embraced by the Metropolitan police district?—39 square miles, and the whole of that district is subject to the police tax.

202. *Mr. Holmes.*—And is that the only source of local taxation?—No.

203. Tell us what other source there is?—In addition to that we have the carriage rates—the rates on carriage licences.

204. Will you tell us first how much is raised by the tax of 8*d*. in the £?—The tax of 8*d*. in the £, for the year to 31st March, 1882, amounted to 37,011*l*. 8*s*. 5*d*.; carriage licence rates, &c., 5,558*l*. 14*s*. Then what is called publicans' levy, under 6 & 7 Wm. IV, 1836.

205. *Mr. Morris.*—What is that for?—On the renewal of his licence, a sum of 10*s*. is paid by each publican to the police fund. Then the fees, fines, and penalties in the police courts amounted to 5,788*l*. 1*s*. 6*d*. for the same year.

206. I suppose that varies every year?—Oh yes; it varies very considerably. Of course, if there is a large decrease in the number of drunkards, or in the number of arrests, a necessary decrease in the amount of fines realised would be the result. Then there is the duty upon pawnbrokers' licences. They pay annually 10*l*. (Irish) direct to the police fund, and the amount to the 31st March last was 1,615*l*. 8*s*. 8*d*.

207-209. *Mr. Holmes.*—Now the amount derived from the local taxation of 8*d*. in the £ increases, of course, with the increase in value of the rateable property?—Clearly, there is no doubt about that.

210. *Mr. Morris.*—And the other contributions—the carriage licences, publicans' fees, fines, and pawnbrokers' licences—they vary every year?—Yes.

211. *Mr. Holmes.*—And can you give us a Return of the amount derived from local taxation during the last ten years?—Certainly.

212. Have you got that before you?—No, not for the last ten years; but we can give you that, of course. I should add that there is a small miscellaneous source of income which I have not yet mentioned. It is derived from forfeited property, sale of cast uniforms, bedding, &c.; it amounted in the year to 3,951*l*. 8*s*. 11*d*.

213. When I ask you for a Return for the last ten years of the amount derived from local taxation—that refers to the amount derived from the 8*d*. in the £ rate?—Quite so. I may observe that the proceeds of that tax vary, but since the present Collector-General came into office every exertion has been used to make it productive.

214-215. The number of unoccupied houses varies very much?—Yes. I was stating that the present Collector-General has made great efforts to get in arrears, and has endeavoured to get fair points affecting the tax settled. He has certainly left nothing undone to make the police tax as productive as possible, so I have noticed.

216. *Chairman.*—You have been connected with the Dublin metropolitan police since the formation of the present force?—Well, not exactly from the formation, but from some time afterwards.

217. Has there ever been any civilian Commissioner?—Oh, certainly.

218. Kindly mention one.—Mr. O'Ferrall was a civilian.

219. Any other?—The original Commissioners were Mr. O'Ferrall, who was a barrister, and Major Cottor. Major Cottor died, not in my time, and Colonel Browne succeeded him, and after some years—when Colonel Browne had served twenty years, he

Superintendent John Ward.

19 Sept., 1882.

223. *Chairman.*—What is your name?—John Ward.

224. How long have you been in the force?—On the 16th December, 1852, I joined.

225. *Mr. Morris.*—What position do you hold?—That of superintendent.

226. Chief superintendent?—No; the chief superintendent desires me to appear here for him, and the other superintendents also deputs me to appear for them, and to state their views to the Commission.

227. You joined in 1852, and worked yourself up to your present position?—Yes.

228. *Mr. Holmes.*—Beginning at the lowest rank, you have graduated until you are now a superintendent?—Yes.

229. Of what division?—I am superintendent of the D Division.

230. How many years have you been a superintendent?—Ten years last June. In June 1872 I was promoted.

231. How long were you in the various ranks; kindly give us a history of your promotion?—I may tell you—of course it may be irrelevant to this inquiry—that my father was a friend of Colonel Browne's. He was the Commissioner then.

232. *Chairman.*—Your father was in the army, I believe?—Yes, he was a captain in the army; and after I was in the force a fortnight or so I was put into the depôt in Kevin Street. I was promoted sergeant in five years, and I was promoted inspector in about eight years.

233. *Mr. Holmes.*—From the time you joined the force?—Yes; and I remained as inspector from then until 1872, when I was promoted superintendent.

234. And you are ten years and three months a superintendent?—Yes; from June 1872.

235. What is your present pay?—£250. The superintendent of the D division, and the superintendent of the E division, have 10d, 8d., or 1s. a day extra, as car hire.

236. What area is comprised by the D division?—I could not say the area, but I could give you the distances between the different boundaries. I take from Capel Street out to [illegible]; I suppose that is a distance of 3½ miles.

237. *Chairman.*—You take one side of Capel Street?—One side only. I take, if I may call it so, the Four Courts side of Capel Street, and extend out to Chapelizod and Finglas.

238. *Mr. Holmes.*—How many barracks are there in that division?—I have what are called out-stations. Of these I have four and two town stations.

239. By stations you mean barracks where the men are?—Yes. Of stations proper I have only two, although I have the charge of all the Park, and of the barracks and police surrounding the Park.

240. How many stations have you that are barracks?—Only two barracks—Manor Street and Green Street. The others we call out-stations.

241. That is outside the municipal boundary?—Yes outside the municipal boundary.

242. *Chairman.*—How many out-stations have you?—Four, not including the two I have given you. I have six altogether.

243. Two stations with barracks, and two without barracks in town?—No; I have two stations in town; these are Green Street and Bridewell Lane. Green Street station is a barrack as well as a station. Manor Street is a barrack, but not a station. Bridewell Lane is a station and not a barrack; and then the others are at the Park Gate, Chapelizod, [illegible], Glasnevin, and Cabra.

244. *Mr. Morris.*—As I take it, to put it shortly, you have six places to superintend in your district?—I have seven.

245. *Chairman.*—In two of which there are barracks?—Yes, Sir.

246. You have seven stations?—I have seven stations—out-stations, stations and barracks.

247. *Mr. Holmes.*—What are the out-stations outside the municipal boundary?—Well, there are no charges taken up there. For instance, if a prisoner was charged at [illegible] he would have to be brought to Bridewell Lane. Though four of them are outside the municipal boundary, they are within the police district.

248. What is the difference between a station and a barrack?—A station is supposed to be where we take charges; a barrack is supposed to be where men reside, but where no charges are taken; but as I have already said, Green Street station is a barrack as well as a station, because men reside in it.

249. How many men do you superintend?—I have 168 men. I will give you the number of men that I have charge of. I have 9 inspectors, 6 acting inspectors, 10 sergeants, 14 acting sergeants, and 128 men.

250. How many men are usually accommodated in a barrack?—Well, I think in Green Street there are accommodated on an average, sometimes we have more sometimes less, 54 men, and we have accommodation for 42 in Manor Street.

251. And the rest are in the out-stations?—Yes; the lodgers are engaged at the out-stations. I can give you the exact number at the out-stations if you wish.

252–253. Kindly do so; these are barracks?—Yes. At the Park Gate there is 1 sergeant and 9 constables; at Chapelizod 1 sergeant and 2 acting sergeants, and 9 constables; at [illegible] I have 1 sergeant, 3 acting sergeants, and 20 constables. That body of men does all the Viceregal duty. Then at Cabra I have 1 sergeant, 2 acting sergeants, and 5 constables. At Glasnevin, 1 sergeant, 2 acting sergeants, and 13 men; those are the out-stations. According as I want the men from those stations I draft them in. I strengthen my men according to circumstances from the other stations, as I may require them; but the numbers I have read out to you are the standing numbers for those stations.

254–255. Where are your head-quarters?—I call Green Street my principal station.

256. There are five barracks outside the city and two inside?—Yes, Manor Street and Green Street.

257. How often do you inspect these stations?—Twice a-day. The out-stations we are only supposed to visit once a-week, but I visit them sometimes once and sometimes twice a-week.

258. How often do you inspect each station, that is, the stations proper?—Bridewell Lane and Green Street I inspect twice a day, except circumstances arise to prevent me. My inspection, as a general rule, however, is twice a-day for each station.

259. And you inspect the out-stations once a-week?—Yes, perhaps oftener.

260. Is your pay fixed, or does it go up by increments?—That is my fixed salary at present, 250*l.* I commenced at 225*l.* and by increments of 5*l.* in five years it was brought up to 250*l.*

261. So that you are now at your maximum?—Yes.

262. As superintendent of the D Division, I understand you get 1*s.* a-day for car hire?—Yes, which, of course, if I was transferred to any other division I would lose.

263. What other allowances do you get?—Altogether my allowances are, irrespective of the 18*l.* 5*s.* for car hire. I will give you them in detail.

264. Please do so.—I am allowed 50*l.* a-year for a horse, 10*l.* a-year for clothing.

265. By clothing, you mean uniform?—Yes. 45*l.* a-year for the keep of a horse, and 5*l.* a-year for a man, and we purchase our own horse on being promoted. We are allowed 5*l.* yearly for the wear and tear of that horse; and I think all these sums will come to 135*l.*

266. You say you are allowed 5*l.* for the wear and tear of a horse when you are promoted?—Yes, each year.

267. When is an officer supposed to require to have a horse?—The very moment you are promoted to the position of superintendent you provide yourself with a horse.

268. The officers below the superintendent do not provide themselves with horses?—No; they are not allowed horses.

269. *Chairman.*—As a matter of fact, are there not only two stations in which charges are taken in your division?—Yes, Bridewell Lane and Green Street.

270. Manor Street is purely a barrack?—Yes. If a prisoner were taken in any of the out-stations that I have enumerated, he would have to be brought in to either of those stations,—Green Street or Bridewell Lane.

271. Now do you wish to give us any information in reference to your case—the case of the members of the force whose rank you represent?—I may say that a list of the matters has been made out by the superintendents in which changes are sought.

272. Is that on behalf of the superintendents?—Yes; only on behalf of the superintendents.

273-274. *Mr. Morris.*—Have you made it out in writing?—Yes; I have. This morning I gave a copy of it through the chief superintendent to Captain Talbot, and I presume it will be forwarded to you.

275. *Mr. Holmes.*—You have made a copy of it?—Yes.

276. Will you have any objection to hand it in?—Well, I could hardly give you that. This is merely a rough copy I kept. The captain, I presume, will give you the copy we sent him, or a copy of it. This is merely a note I kept of it to guide me in my evidence.

277. And the evidence you now give is a statement made by you on your own behalf and on the behalf of the other superintendents—the superintendents of all the divisions, and sent through Superintendent Corr to the Chief Commissioner?—Yes.

278. And has it his approval?—I cannot say whether it has or not.

279. Well, upon that question I hope you will clearly understand that the Government wish the officers and the men to say all that they like to say. We do not wish to fetter you in any way. We only ask that the men shall not bring any personal charges, and I have no doubt their good sense will prevent them from doing so. But we want the officers and men to state as fully and as freely as possible all their grounds of complaint?—I may tell you that so far as the superintendents are concerned, we do not intend to enter into any matter except pay, pensions, and allowances. I think I may state that on behalf of the other men of my rank, and on my own behalf, we are anxious to keep within our own limits, and not to enter into any matter except it concerns ourselves as superintendents, and consequent upon that determination, a document of this sort was drafted and was submitted to the superintendents, all of whom signed that document as I read it to-day.

280. Then you represent the seven superintendents?—No, sir; because the G Division are not identified with us in the views to which we give expression in this document. I would much rather the chief superintendent had been here, but he deputed me to represent him, and said he had every confidence in me to put forward the views of the superintendents. The first proposition that is here is this. The chief superintendent's salary—the net salary paid to him—of course I am giving the net salary—is 300*l.* a-year. Before we go any farther, I think it is right to state that what the superintendents would wish, if it were possible, would be to get a certain status. I really do not know what my status is in comparing myself with an officer of the Royal Irish Constabulary. We are called a chief force, and I believe, from the amount of duties that we have to perform, and the number of the inhabitants in our districts, and the amount of crime, and all that sort of thing that we have to deal with—I believe, from all these things—in fact, I am perfectly satisfied of it—that the duties of a superintendent of the Dublin metropolitan police are at least equal to, if not greater and more severe than, those of the county inspectors throughout Ireland. It is stated, of course, that the crime of Dublin is equal to that of all Ireland, and the duties that we have to perform, and the number of the inhabitants in our different divisions—all these things, I think, entitle us to get some standing, and to know what position we hold.

281. *Chairman.*—Is it status in reference to the constabulary?—Yes, and it is upon their lines we would wish to go for an increase.

282. *Mr. Holmes.*—You refer to the population. Can you tell me the population of the division of which you are superintendent?—As a rough guess I should say somewhere about 61,000. I take the census of the city of Dublin for that, and I divide it into four, and it leaves about 62,000, and I should say about 61,000 for my division.

283. *Chairman.*—As I understand you, what you mean by status is to be placed on the lines of the constabulary as regards rank, pay, allowances, and pension?—Exactly. I simply state that on the grounds of our duties and the extensive character of the supervision that we have to exercise. Well, the chief superintendent is at 300*l.*, that is his pay. He thinks that in proportion to the duties, which are very severe—that is being chief superintendent—I know his duties pretty well—he is about the hardest worked man in the service, and can never leave his post; he thinks he is entitled to begin at 400*l.*, and rise to 500*l.* by increments of 20*l.*

284-285. You are comparing the chief superintendent to the county inspector?—No, I am going higher than the county inspector, for the simple reason that the chief superintendent, I look upon it, has harder and more difficult duties to discharge than the county inspector, whose salary commences at 260*l.* and goes up to 350*l.* by increments of 20*l.* by the new Constabulary Act.

286. You seek the increase by reason of the greater duties of the superintendent-in-chief as compared with the county inspector?—Yes, they are unremitting.

287. *Mr. Morris.*—As far as the chief superintendent is concerned, you suggest that his salary should

Superintendent John Wood.

11 Sept., 1882.

Superintendent John Ward.

18 Sept., 1882.

commencing at 300*l*., I take it, and be increased until it stops at 350*l*. a-year?—Yes.

288. What are the principal duties of the chief superintendent?—The chief superintendent has to supervise all Returns that come in from the divisional superintendents; through his clerks he has to do that. He has to supervise the statistics.

289. What Returns do you allude to?—Our "states" in the morning. Everything that occurs in the division has to be put on what is called the "morning state," which is returned by the different divisions. He has several clerks in the chief superintendent's office. He is responsible for the statistics. There is a Department called the Statistical Department. He supervises that.

290. When you say there is a Department called the Statistical Department. Do you mean in each division?—No. There is one general statistical office, and they take what they want from our Returns as they come in. That belongs to the chief superintendent exclusively. We keep our own statistics for certain purposes in our own office.

291. I presume he has a staff under him to do that?—Certainly.

292. Now kindly resume the statement of his duties.—He has to patrol all the divisions once a-month. He has to go through each division on uncertain nights once in the month.

293. *Chairman.*—Once in the month on uncertain nights?—Yes.

294. He does not give notice of his coming?—Certainly not. The chief superintendent goes through each of the four town divisions in the same way.

295. What are the four town divisions?—A, B, C, and D.

296. Some of those are within, and others partially without, the municipal boundary?—Yes; C and D are partially without.

297. How often does he superintend the out divisions?—As to patrolling, he does not superintend those at all; but he has to visit every barrack and station in the whole police district once a-month. Those are the general duties that the chief superintendent has to perform; but there are a whole lot of minor details, the result of which is that I know he is never out of his office.

298. If there was a fire in your division, you would communicate with the chief superintendent?—Yes; he would have to come to it.

299. And in all cases of fire the chief superintendent must be communicated with by the superintendent of whatever division it may occur in, and he must be present at that fire?—Yes, quite so. In fact, he superintends, I need not say, the other superintendents. If it was a chimney, I would send word that it was a fire of only a trivial nature, and that he need not come. But if there appeared any likelihood of its going ahead, we would send for him. Those are the general matters that he has to attend to.

300. He has a great deal of official work?—Yes.

301. *Chairman.*—Besides what you say, there are a great many other matters of a minor nature that come into the duties of his office?—Yes; as long as the Commissioners are in their office he must be in his. He deals with statistical reports, ordinary reports, publichouse cases, licensing cases.

302. In fact, he is the constant referee of the Commissioners?—Yes, he is the referee.

303. *Mr. Holmes.*—What staff has he?—In his own office he has one clerk as chief superintendent. In the Statistical Department I think there are four clerks; and then in the superintendent's—like my own office, as it were, which is quite different from the statistical office, or what is called the chief superintendent's office—he has two clerks. I think he has seven clerks divided among these different offices.

304. *Chairman.*—I take it as counter-distinguished from your duties, he has the general superintendence of the whole city?—He has.

305. And of all the other superintendents?—Yes; and of the whole district within the metropolitan police area. He has to inspect all the barracks through the Dublin police force, including Dalkey, Killiney, and those places, once a-month; but for the night patrol, he only attends the four divisions I have named.

306. *Mr. Holmes.*—How many hours is the chief superintendent occupied throughout the day on official work, and otherwise in superintending the force?—I might answer for the chief superintendent as well as myself. I consider myself always on duty, and I never leave my own house without mentioning where I am going, or where I can be found, for I never can tell the moment that I may be called upon. And I know the chief superintendent to be in his office in the Lower Castle Yard from about 10 o'clock in the morning up to 6 or 7 o'clock in the evening, and latterly until 2 o'clock in the morning; but that, of course, is exceptional.

307. *Chairman.*—I understand you to say that he has the general superintendency of the whole metropolitan police district, and the visiting of the barracks; does that visiting extend to all the out-lying barracks?—Every one; Dalkey, Killiney, Kingstown, and so on.

308. *Mr. Morris.*—Then as to the salaries that you and the other superintendents of your class and grade then receive; what do you suggest as a fair and just remuneration for your services?—We ask for 300*l*.

309. To commence at 300*l*.?—Yes; to commence at 300*l*., and to go up by increments of 10*l*. to 400*l*.; for that is not equal to the salary that the county inspector at present gets under the new régime, but we have a reason for one particular thing for which we ask you, to have a ... to the class at which we would wish to commence. I having twenty-nine years' service, and some of the superintendents having thirty and some forty years' service, if these men were only given 300*l*. a-year, it would not benefit them, going away at the end of thirty years' service. It would not give them anything in the shape of extra pay for extra work for the last four years, and it would be only a benefit to those coming after us; and consequently, instead of asking 450*l*., which the county inspector gets, we only ask for 300*l*., but that our increments shall date back a certain number of years, in order that we may receive a salary in proportion to our services. For instance, if I was given 300*l*. and discharged to-morrow, of course I would not benefit anything by that 300*l*. a-year to a certain extent.

310. *Mr. Holmes.*—What you mean is this. You assume that 300*l*. a-year is to be the minimum salary of your rank in the future, but that in consequence of your having been for some years in the position of superintendent, you wish to be given, in addition, so many years' increments of 10*l*.?—Yes.

311. *Chairman.*—Some nominal number of years?—Yes. We wish that the divisional superintendents should commence at 300*l*., going up by increments of 10*l*. to 400*l*., and a portion of the emoluments allowed to the pension as well, because the Royal Irish Constabulary have now got emoluments granted to them of house rent, and that reckoned on their salaries. We desire that each superintendent should get a proportionate allowance to his pension according to the number of years he has served. In other words, a portion of the emoluments allowed and the pension, the same as granted to the Royal Irish Constabulary. They are allowed according to the Act, for house rent and servant, a proportionate amount. The entire house rent does not amount to more than one-sixth of the total amount allowed.

312. *Mr. Holmes.*—That is to say, in your case you receive 30*l*. allowance for a house. You would like one-sixth of that to be included in your pay for the purposes of pension?—I think the way the Act reads is this: Supposing I have 150*l*. a-year, I would get one-sixth of that as allowance to provide the price of a house, provided the price of the house did not exceed one-sixth of the whole; at all events, you will see that in the Act. This is a matter that will go purely to benefit the superintendents that may come after us.

This is for the house allowance. For the horse we seek to have an allowance of 50*l.* a-year.

313. *Mr. Morris.*—Instead of 30*l.*?—Yes, that is so. The county inspector has something about 53*l.* a-year. We seek 50*l.* a-year for a horse. I may tell you that I myself am paying 55*l.* a-year in Bloomington Street at the present time. Then we have 10*l.* a-year for clothing. We ask to have that increased to 12*l.* Then this is a matter that only can touch upon superintendents that are made after us. I believe that in the constabulary, on the promotion of a cadet to the rank of sub-inspector, he is allowed money for a horse; he is granted an allowance of 30*l.* for the purchase of a horse. We ask that the same allowance may be given us. That would not be any loss to the Government, because I have drawn 30*l.* for my horse. I have drawn 3*l.* a-year since my promotion, and that is 30*l.* in ten years, as a superintendent.

314. You mean that you would wish the county down?—Yes; and then that does away with the 3*l.* a-year.

315. And an annual allowance?—Yes, Sir. It comes to the same thing, of course, under the present system of keeping horses. It can only affect succeeding superintendents, because in any case it could not be done in any other way than at present, because we do not expect to get the 30*l.* Then, under the Act that I am under, the superintendents all at thirty years were entitled to full pay on retirement. The periods at which these different pensions and their increases commenced, I will now give. They commenced at fifteen years. There is half-pay granted at fifteen years, two-thirds at twenty, three-fourths at twenty-five, and full pay at thirty years and after.

316. *Mr. Morris.*—That is under the Act of 1847?—Yes. That is the Act that we are under. What we ask for is that, whatever the pay is at the time the pension commences, that one-thirtieth of that pay be allowed for each year, or, in other words, that we should get fifteen-thirtieths for fifteen years, and there would be nothing then between that period and twenty years, when the same proportion would be added.

317. *Mr. Holmes.*—Surely you consider that the scale of pensions under which you can retire is a very favourable scale?—Yes; but supposing we were entitled to two-thirds of our salary at twenty-five years' service, and supposing we served twenty-four years and eleven months, to which we would be entitled if we served another month, we would lose that.

318. But you must remember that the scale is exceptionally favourable?—Yes; that is, the Act of Parliament; but if we were under the 4th and 5th William, but that is going home. I may tell you that twenty-five years in the police force is nearly quite sufficient for a man.

319. *Mr. Holmes.*—But you are aware that under the General Superannuation Act of 1859, an ordinary civil servant must serve forty years before he gets two-thirds of his salary, whereas if you serve twenty-five years you get three-fourths, and if you serve twenty years, you get two-thirds?—Yes.

320. But your scale of pension is so exceptionally favourable that surely you would be very sanguine if you thought that the Legislature would make it still better?—No, Sir. As far as that is concerned, if "the labourer is worthy of his hire" at the end of twenty-five years, I think he ought to be worthy of his hire at the end of twenty-four years and eleven months. I want you perfectly to understand that point. I may tell you that there are numbers of men that endeavour to reach these different points of pension, and by doing so they injure themselves very materially.

321. But remember, too, that it was not the intention of Parliament that the old scale of pension should apply to the new and increased rates of pay, and that you are uncommonly fortunate in being allowed to retire under the old scale of pension applicable to the new and increased rates of pay?—Quite so. Still, we do not interfere with the existing rates, and we are only putting this forward. I am sure the Government never intended to work everything out of a man, but that he should have some few years after his work is over. The next proposition is a pension for the widow and children if the husband be killed in service, and the next is a gratuity in case of sudden death.

322. If an officer or a constable of the force were killed on duty and left a wife and children, would the wife and children receive anything?—I think not. I think not, as a matter of right; it might be done, and it has been done, I believe.

323. *Chairman.*—What occurred in the case of the constable Daly, who was killed while on duty in Moore Street—did his widow get nothing?—No, she did not. There were, however, circumstances in that case which prevented her receiving anything. I believe the constable was married without leave. I do not know of any case in which a pension was given under such circumstances. The next matter we ask is a gratuity in case of sudden death. Under existing circumstances, if a man served thirty years and died suddenly, his widow would not be entitled to anything.

324. *Mr. Holmes.*—Do you mean to say that she would be entitled to no gratuity in case of sudden death?—Yes.

325. And why should there be a difference between a sudden death and a lingering illness?—Well, there are certain forms to be gone through; a number of papers have to be signed. A man has to be attested sick, and the man has to put his signature to the document before it becomes legal. If he dropped down dead, all these things could not be done, of course. As far as the superintendents have gone into this matter, that is all on the subject of pensions that they wish to bring forward. That is what I have come here for the purpose of laying before you.

326. You have said everything you wished to say on the subject of pensions?—Yes. Upon the subject of allowances I wish to refer you to the Constabulary Act of 1883 as the basis of our claim. That Act of the 18th August, 1883, provides that "for the purpose of calculating the amount of any pension which may be granted under this Act the term 'salary' shall include all allowances for lodging, house rent, and servant, provided that the allowance in respect of lodging or house rent shall not exceed one-sixth of the actual salary and other emoluments."

327. But are you aware that an officer of the Royal Irish Constabulary retiring under that Act retires under the Superannuation Act of 1859, and that he must serve forty years before he can get his two-thirds, whereas you now can retire upon three-fourths?—Yes; but I am also aware that an officer who joins in the same year that I joined has all my advantages. In the constabulary an officer who joined in the same year that I joined goes away on his full pay after thirty years—just as I myself—and he gets these allowances as well; and that is exactly what we ask for.

328. *Chairman.*—The constabulary officer is better than you by reason of the granting of these allowances?—Yes. All the constabulary officers have just the same rate of pensions as we get.

329. *Mr. Holmes.*—You are not correct in stating that an officer in the constabulary of your standing can retire on full pay after thirty years; under the Act of 1847 he must have served forty years?—I was not aware of that.

330. And are you aware that under that Act the pension was calculated on the pay only, and not upon allowances?—No, I was not.

331. *Mr. Morris.*—I want to ask you one general question as regards the body of police and the dissatisfaction of the police lately. Do you, in your opinion, knowing the men as well as you do from the position you hold,—do you consider that the two grievances that they complain most of to be excessive duty and want of sufficient retiring allowance?—I believe the great cause of complaint is the retiring allowance.

332. The pension?—Yes.

333. You believe that to be their real ground of complaint?—Yes; because I may tell you that young men when they join the service never much calculate on

Superintendent John Wood.

17 Sept., 1889.

the pension they are entitled to, but after they come to be a year or two in the service—

335. In fact, when they become married men?—Yes, or before that; and when they read of the grievances of which constabulary pensioners complain—as to the way in which some of these have been treated—that of course, influences their minds, and they do not care for stopping in the service if they can get employment elsewhere. I can give you an instance of one of my sergeants who joined three days before the new Act came into operation in 1867. He was discharged lately, ill-health, but he got a pension of 48*l*.—half-pay. If he joined three days later he would only have got 34*l*. He would have then retired under the Act of 1867, but if he had retired under the Act of 1867, it would have made a difference of somewhere about 10*l*. a year in his pension.

336. And do you think that that has led to the men who joined since 1867 being discontented?—I believe so.

337. *Mr. Holmes.*—So far as you know, do men when they join the force know that there is a different scale of pension for men who joined before 1867 and those who joined after 1867?—Yes, because there is a form which shows what the pensions are.

338. And are they aware of the pension before they join?—Yes.

339. Then they have no ground for being dissatisfied?—When recruits join they don't look at pension, but it is only a few years after they serve that they find out that the pension is only so much.

340. And they have always been informed immediately upon joining the force of the rate of pension under which they entered?—I may tell you that I had charge of the depôt, where all the recruits came, for a number of years and during all that time I know they were perfectly instructed as to the pensions they were entitled to on leaving the force. Of course I cannot answer for what has happened since, but I believe that course to be still followed.

341. And then they joined the force with their eyes open?—Certainly.

342. *Mr. Morris.*—As a man having such large experience of the force, would you not think that the question that would arise, and that ought properly to be considered, would be whether the pension that they now retire on under the Act of 1867 is a fair and just pension, not comparing it with anything—whether that is a fair and just allowance for the man for a certain number of years' service?—That is a difficult question to answer. Of course all the Civil Servants—and I have a son who is a clerk in the War Office—they all retire on the same. I would not certainly say it should be made exceptional for one body of men.

343. One other question I wish to ask you, and it is a question I am anxious about, owing to your lengthened experience of the force, is it your experience that the men are more frequently drunk; that there is a larger number of cases of drunkenness in the force now in comparison with some years ago?—I believe we have less cases of drunkenness now—proportionately less—than we ever had; but up to within—well, I will say eighteen months or two years—I think that drunkenness was somewhat on the increase, but latterly we have decreased wonderfully in that regard in the force.

344. *Chairman.*—Do you mean to say that there is no general dissatisfaction among the men as to the number and amount of the force?—Oh, yes; there is dissatisfaction about the force.

345. *Mr. Morris.*—Is there dissatisfaction at the number of the force?—Yes, I believe there is.

346. *Chairman.*—Has there been any complaint about their not being furnished with the constabulary in the gratuity?—There is dissatisfaction over that. They consider that the duties they performed for the last three years or so were far and away more severe than those of some of the constabulary; for instance, the constabulary of the north and east of Ireland. They have had very little, comparatively speaking, to do. Of course, those in the south and west had something, but, all through, the Dublin police had extra duty to perform.

347. When you say extra duty, do you mean to say extra hours?—Yes, extra hours.

348. Now, surely the city was not affected by the general state of the country, was it?—Oh, yes; and they were put upon extra duty at all events. The number of hours that a man has to do duty by day is nine hours one day and eight hours the other. Well, I have known instances of men being fourteen and sixteen hours on duty. If, for instance, a meeting was held at the Rotunda, although I belong to the D Division, and have nothing to do with the Rotunda so far as my divisional duties are concerned, my men ought to be kept in reserve until that meeting was over, and the people had dispersed late at night. Though the men might not be called upon to act, they would be deprived of their freedom and relief from duty, and that must, of course, be regarded as an extra duty.

349. But still, meetings in the Rotunda are few and far between?—A meeting in the Phœnix Park, a meeting taking place in Dublin, no matter where it may be, affects the extent of the duty of some portion of the men at all events.

350. Does the general condition of the city impose additional duties upon the force?—It certainly does.

351. Within what period?—Since the meetings began to be held—that is the Land League meetings, meetings in the Phœnix Park, the State trials—from that time, and ever since, there has been extra duty imposed upon the men of the police force.

352. Was it of a severe kind?—Well, in some cases it was not only severe but dangerous. I may tell you that I got my own head cut open in Sackville Street, and the other portions of the extra duty may be simply remaining in the station-house.

353. *Mr. Holmes.*—Do you mean to say that there was so much time withdrawn from the leisure of the constables by doing the additional duty?—Quite so.

354. *Mr. Morris.*—I suppose you refer now to the occasion of the riots in Sackville Street when Mr. Parnell and others were imprisoned, and events of that kind that grew out of the land agitation?—Yes.

355. *Chairman.*—And the State trials here, and so on?—Yes. I need not tell you that Dublin is the city of excitement where a thing of that sort occurs that we must all be on the qui vive.

356. *Mr. Morris.*—And you think that that imposed some duty upon the men, and made them be more frequently confined to barracks in order to have them ready for active service if required?—Yes; I am certain of it.

357. And abridged their own time?—Quite so. The extra duties that I have to perform, and also my men, at the present moment of a [illegible] nature, require my men to be at different posts for uncertain lengths of time, and to be longer on duty; therefore they are required to perform extra duty.

358. To the abridgement of their own proper time?—Yes, everything of this sort is an abridgement of their own proper time, because they get no pay for it.

359–363. *Mr. Holmes.*—In ordinary times when a man is off duty is he allowed to go where he likes and do what he likes?—He is not allowed under any circumstances to dress in plain clothes without leave, or to go into a public-house; but he is perfectly free to leave barracks and go amongst his friends during the hours he is off duty.

364. From whom does he get leave to dress in plain clothes?—The officer in the station.

365. That may be a sergeant?—Yes. The man goes and says "I want liberty for plain clothes, sergeant." The other replies "certainly," and he and the man go into the station, and he puts his name down in a book for leave for plain clothes, and I initial it. There is no prevention of, or obstruction given to, the wearing of plain clothes. The officer on duty who gives the leave is always supposed to be an inspector or an acting inspector, but if any difficulty arose, I mean in the way of refusal of leave, then an inspector or a sergeant would act in the matter.

366. Are you aware that in the constabulary a man off duty is not allowed to go more than a quarter of a mile from his barracks?—No such rule exists in the Dublin metropolitan police. Our men can go through the metropolitan police district when off duty.

367. *Chairman.*—It is your experience of the duties of the men, extra and ordinary, within the last two or three years, that there has been a great increase of those duties?—No doubt.

368. And all the labours imposed on the men have been an abridgment of their own time?—Yes, a great increase of duty.

369. And I also understand that every facility is afforded to the men when off duty to dress in plain clothes and to enjoy themselves, provided they avoid the public-house?—Certainly.

370. And apply for permission for plain clothes?—Yes, there is no restriction on that. The public-house is the only house they are prohibited from going in.

371. *Mr. Holmes.*—I see that Dr. Nedley—in the valuable Returns he prepared for Lord Meath's Commission—states that in some of the barracks in London there are lavatories, libraries and billiard-rooms, and places where hot and cold baths are always ready; that the members of the London force are always provided with attractions and comforts of that kind. Are the barracks in Dublin provided with any such accommodation for the men?—Yes.

372. Or with such conveniences for the men?—Yes. My two barracks at Manor Street and Green Street both have baths in them.

373. And have they reading-rooms?—There are no reading-rooms.

374. Don't you think it would be very desirable that every large barrack should have a reading-room?—I do believe it necessary. I may add, however, that the sites of our barracks were, I think, all chosen for the simple purpose of keeping them out of the principal streets, and having them in the lanes and such thoroughfares; and the consequence is, that we are very much tied up for room. Manor Street barrack is, however, a very good barrack. The newspapers are got by the men themselves, but we have nothing in it in the shape of a reading-room. We have, however, baths and a ball-alley in Manor Street.

375. Each barrack has a canteen?—There is no canteen; but the man in charge of the mess has a barrel of porter, and he supplies the men with whatever liquor of that sort they may require.

376. And they can get a proper amount of drink without going into the public-house?—Yes.

377. That is as far as porter is concerned?—Yes.

378. *Mr. Morris.*—And ale?—Yes; they can get ale if they like.

379. *Chairman.*—But whiskey is excluded?—Yes. There is one thing I had omitted to mention as one of the changes that we would seek, and that is, that we would be allowed to retire on full pay after twenty-five years' service. I believe it is rumoured that there will be a Bill brought in for England one of these days, and that the time for retirement on full pay will be twenty-five years.

380. *Mr. Holmes.*—Are you aware that the scale of pensions under which the London men retire now is the same as the scale since 1867 in Dublin, from fifteen years up to twenty years?—Yes.

381–382. In London the scale then goes up by two-fiftieths instead of one-fiftieth from twenty to twenty-five years, so that in London a man could retire after twenty-five years' service upon the same pension as that on which a man can retire here after thirty years' service?—Yes.

383. Then in London, after twenty-five years' service, the increment drops from two-fiftieths to one-fiftieth up to twenty-eight years' service, at which period it stops, and the pension has reached its maximum, namely, thirty-three-fiftieths, which is as nearly as may be two-thirds of the pay. That is the scale of pensions that now obtains for the London men, and I believe that scale will be ultimately applied to the whole of England and Scotland?—I believed the officers who joined the police force of London prior to 1841 could retire after twenty-four years' service.

384. Do you not think it would be difficult to have a more favourable scale for the Dublin police?—Of course it would be; but then the consideration is whether or not it is a fair thing to ask. I am almost satisfied that the doctors would go in for twenty-five years' service for the force and then retirement.

[The Committee then adjourned.]

Second Day.—18th September, 1882.

Present:

Mr. J. W. O'Donnell, Mr. George Morris, D.L., and Mr. R. W. A. Holmes.

Superintendent William Armstrong, F Division, Dublin Metropolitan Police, continued.

386. *Chairman.*—Your name?—William Armstrong.

387. What is your position in the force?—That of superintendent.

388. Of what division?—Of the F Division.

389. When did you enter the force?—I entered the force in October 1848, and I am the oldest member of it except one.

390. And when were you appointed Superintendent?—Thirteen years ago. It will be thirteen years next October I think.

391. What is the extent of your division?—The F Division extends from Merrion Gates to down below Killiney Railway Station, and from the sea up to a place called Kilternan.

392. Have you any idea of the extent of the area in miles?—Well, in square miles it would be something about 20.

393. How many police stations have you in your division?—Five.

394. And how many barracks?—The barracks and stations are nearly altogether—very conveniently; in fact we have no station that is not a barrack as well.

Superintendent W. Armstrong.

13 Sept., 1882.

395. How many men are allotted to that division?—160 altogether.

396. Kindly now give us the ranks of the men under you and the different stations under your charge?—I have 2 inspectors at present; 2 are under me, but 1 is away; I have 4 acting inspectors, 12 sergeants, and 113 constables; altogether, 130, I think.

397. All told, including yourself?—No, not including myself.

398. What is the average number to each barrack?—They vary according to the district. I have at the present time 40 in Kingstown, 30 in Blackrock and Booterstown, 29 in Dalkey, and the remainder at Kill of the Grange. The district now contains, I suppose, a population of 40,000 people; whereas in 1841, when the police were first started, Kingstown had only a population of 7,000, while it has now 20,000.

399. Has the police force been increased since that time?—Not to the extent of a single man; but I believe lessened. I should say it was nearly the same.

400. Mr. Morris.—You are sure there has been no increase of the police force since then?—Since the force was first formed the population has gone on increasing, and the men have had their pay increased, but the number of the men has remained the same as at the formation of the service.

401. Chairman.—You have signed a Memorial that has been prepared?—Yes.

402. Will now be good enough to tell us of what you complain, or what you would wish to state in reference to that Memorial, and commence with each head separately in the order in which the requirements appear in the Memorial?—I will do so, Sir.

403. Mr. Morris.—We wish to leave you to yourself to tell your own story?—Yes.

404. Mr. Holmes.—And state them in what appears to you to be the order of their importance?—I think the first main thing that we ask for is, and is what I think would be the order of importance, to improve the last Police Act that expounds the pensions—the Act of 1867—and restore the men if it could be done, to the operation of the 10 & 11 Vict., which gave two-thirds of the pay after fifteen years' service, and full pay after twenty years' service. That I think would be the only way of providing for that grievance. As for myself, it does not concern me, for I am under that Act of the 10 & 11 Vict., and could retire on my full pay.

405. Mr. Holmes.—In point of fact, you ask that the men who have joined the force since 1867 should be put in the same position as regards pension as the men who joined the force prior to that date?—Yes, that would be satisfactory. It is all those young men who have struck who are under that 1867 Act.

406. Do you know whether the men who have joined the force since 1867 were made aware, upon joining, that the scale of pensions was altered?—I do not think they understand it. I know there is a printed circular which shows them that they get a certain pension, but then when they find their comrades going frequently away, in consequence of being dissatisfied with that rate of pension, it makes them, too, dissatisfied upon a consideration of their position.

407. Superintendent Ward told us yesterday that the men upon joining were made aware of all the conditions of service?—They get a printed letter, it is true.

408. But that is merely a formal matter, and is given to all men when they join?—Yes; but they never think anything seriously about pension until they are four or five years in the service. They only think of the present, and they only begin to think of the future when they see other people going away.

409. Do you think, if the men who joined the Dublin force since 1867 were aware that the London metropolitan police are not made at good a scale as the men who joined the Dublin force before 1867—do you, I say, think that they would still ask to be put in a better position than the London men?—I have asked about that myself, and I have been given to understand that the London men do not go in for making the police service a permanent occupation, but that they leave it for other situations. There are so many things open to men in London, and the police service is made a stepping stone to other appointments. Here, however, when a man joins the Dublin police, he makes it his occupation for life.

410. Chairman.—Their livelihood for life?—Yes, he does that. But the London man is in a different position, and he speculates in other ways.

411. Mr. Holmes.—In reference to the general question. Do you expect that the Government would put the Dublin police force in a better position than the police forces of England and Scotland generally as regards pensions?—I would not expect that; but I would expect that they would go as near London as possible, that is, in reference to pay. I do not know what their position is in reference to pensions. I think they were under the 2 & 3 Vict. at their formation. I simply wish to show you the dissatisfaction that has arisen in reference to the last Act. I think the other things might be considered fair enough. I do not think the men complain very much of the pay, but they do of the reductions and fines.

412. Have you anything further to add in reference to the pension and superannuation questions, with regard to the men?—No.

413. Mr. Morris.—Before you leave this subject I wish to ask you, did the men complain of not being given a gratuity, similar to what the Royal Irish Constabulary got?—Indeed, they did. That was the very first thing that set all this going—that they did not get the three months' pay. They were dissatisfied with the Act of 1867 before that, and then when the gratuity was given to the Royal Irish Constabulary, and not to them, it set this whole movement going, for they said they were neglected, although their duties had been so excessively increased of late years. In support of that last assertion I may refer you to the Blue Book, which will show you that upwards of 340 members of the force were assaulted during the years 1880 and 1881, and in many cases dangerously assaulted. This shows that nearly every man in the street has been beaten during 1880 and 1881, and some of them several times; and they are of the nature of assaults that are never spoken of. They never, under these circumstances, bring forward a charge of assault, but confine themselves to the original charge for which the prisoner was arrested.

414. Mr. Holmes.—These are, I presume, the ordinary assaults which a policeman must expect?—Yes; but they are very dangerous ones; indeed, one man lost his life.

415. Chairman.—Has there been an increase in the number of severe assaults according to the last Return?—Yes.

416. An increase of the average number?—Yes.

417. Of aggravated assaults?—Yes; the number of those assaults has been higher than for the preceding years.

418. Mr. Holmes.—Have you anything to add to what you have already said on the subject of pensions?—In reference to that I can only refer you to the 10 & 11 Vict., and what we would ask you to consider would be to include certain allowances, the same as are provided for in the other force, to include an allowance for the officers, superintendents and inspectors.

419. You are now speaking on behalf of the superintendents?—And the inspectors have no allowances, too; they have house rent.

420. But the inspectors will speak for themselves?—The allowances I would like to have included would be those for house rent, lodging, and servant.

421. You want to have the pension calculated upon your allowances as well as your salary?—Yes.

422-423. Do the men wish that the Act of 1867 should be repealed, and the Act of 1847 restored?—Yes. That last Act has made them very much dissatisfied.

424. Are there any superintendents in the force who have joined since 1867?—I think not.

Super-intendent W. Armstrong.

15 Sept., 1882.

425. As you are simply representing the superintendents, you ought, for the purposes of the question of pension, to confine yourself, if you have anything further to say on that subject, to the Act of 1847?—We are all satisfied with the Act of 1847. It is a very good one, and we do not complain of it at all.

426. *Chairman.*—All the superintendents are under the Act of 1847?—I think so.

427. All of them?—Well, there is one as to whom I am not certain. I don't know whether Superintendent Reeve-... is under the Act of 1847 or not.

428. But all the others are under it?—I think so.

429. Then your contention is that the allowances should be included in the pension?—Yes.

430. *Mr. Morris.*—Then you have no further evidence to offer on behalf of the superintendents on the subject of pension?—No, Sir.

431. *Mr. Holmes.*—Would you now state what is the next matter that you wish to bring under our notice?—Well, in the matter of extra duty the other officers may have more to tell you than I have; but I will give you a list of the extra duties performed since 1879. We have had to attend to forty-nine troop-ships in Kingstown Harbour. Every day my men had to stop there. Then we had the torchlight procession.

432. Are you speaking of Kingstown only?—Yes. We had the O'Connell procession, and then we had the burning of the Solway, where there were five persons burnt. That was in October 1881, and our men had to carry the bodies on shore, and had to attend the inquest, and see them buried. We had the arrival of Mr. Gladstone, the Duke of Edinburgh, and the Chief Secretaries, and we are called upon, even those men who are in bed, to turn out on those occasions. We had the opening of the new Town Hall, and also the general election. During the general election I had fifty of my men absent in Dublin for twenty-four hours, and at the end of that time they had to walk home to Kingstown.

433. *Mr. Holmes.*—Surely those are extra duties which the members of any police force are liable to perform?—I am explaining the nature of the extra duties, as they are over and above ordinary ones, but we must perform them, and continue to do so, and we wish to show you that we have done so. We had also fires, and our men are greatly taxed at fires, because we have no fire brigade in Kingstown. We had evictions, Land League sales and meetings. We had all these things to look after, as well as agricultural agitation, and we thus had a great deal of bother. I believe we have twenty-four gentlemen under armed police protection. We have police protecting 6 gentlemen in Kingstown, 6 in Blackrock, and 13 in Dalkey—24 persons in all—that we must keep under our eye. The police must not allow them out of their view. I have the names of those gentlemen. Within the last two or three years we have had that extra duty to do. It is a more responsible thing to keep a watch over those gentlemen, with people waiting whose intent it is to shoot them.

434. Of the extra duties which you have just enumerated, it appears to me that the only class that can be considered to be of an abnormal character, were those in connection with the Land League meetings. In reference to any other of the extra duties that you have named, surely the police force might justly be called upon to perform them at any time?—Quite so. Of course the general elections we would always have to attend.

435. *Chairman.*—But you also included police protection?—Yes I did. That is the protection of gentlemen who have come from the country, and who could not live in their own places.

436. *Mr. Morris.*—Does a policeman expect that his duties should be drawn out and defined according to hard and fast lines when he joins, and that he should not be called upon to do anything else but those duties?—Well, in these cases a man has to wait until he is fully relieved on the spot, because he or his successor in the duty must always have the place in view, and the consequence is that a man has to be out later than he ought to be. If he was on an ordinary beat he would be able to come home half an hour earlier; but as it is, he has to stay with his loaded revolver until he gives it up to the man who relieves him.

437. How many Land League meetings have you attended in your district?—I think in my district we had only two—in fact, we put an end to the rest of them by telling the people who went to them that they would be arrested.

438. Has the Land League agitation increased the duties of the men in your district?—Yes.

439. In what respect?—We had to have six men in a hut at Dalkey, and we have to keep men in it to protect the gentleman living there, or else he would be killed.

440. It then comes to this: that the increased duties are caused by protection?—Yes; and instead of having the men to patrol the usual beats the number is doubled.

441. How many men have you on that duty?—Twenty-four.

442. Are they withdrawn from their ordinary duty?—Well, they patrol a small circle.

443. Do the duties, practically in reference to protection, withdraw them from their ordinary duties?—It withdraws them from the area they would have to patrol.

444. Does it add to their duties?—It does.

445. *Mr. Holmes.*—How many men do you say are employed in your district on protection duty?—6 in Kingstown, 6 in Blackrock, and 13 in Dalkey—that is 24 in all. Then there are men employed on what is called "special attention" duty. I have 12 so employed. There are 24 men who have a very short area to patrol, and who must keep the place that they are "on" in view continuously night and day. And there is "special attention" duty, which consists of going into places, paying attention to houses at night, and into demesnes—we have twelve occupied in that way.

446. *Chairman.*—That is thirty-six?—Yes.

447. That duty is shared in, I suppose, by the full force of the men; they take it in turn?—I generally pull them off for a month. They take the duty a month about.

448. *Mr. Holmes.*—Surely those are the only duties that you can properly call extra duties?—Yes; at the time of the regatta we have a great deal of extra duty.

449. *Mr. Morris.*—Has there not been a regatta in Kingstown for the last twenty-five or thirty years?—Yes.

450. Then how do you put forward that as an extra duty—the labour in connection with a regatta existing as you tell me for twenty-five years?—Well, the labour has increased greatly of late years. We have to see that 10,000 or 12,000 persons get safely away by the railway.

451. Have you not had the same duty to discharge for several years?—We have.

452. And why do you put it forward as an extra duty now?—It has been always an extra duty.

453. Has it not been the same for the last five years as it has for the last fifteen?—It has, for the last twelve years.

454. Would you allow me to ask you did any of the men who were on protection duty, either protecting land, crops, or gentlemen, receive anything in the shape of an extra allowance or extra pay?—No, Sir.

455. No extra pay for that duty?—None whatever.

456. They are paid as if they were employed on any other ordinary duty as policemen?—Yes; they have the same pay.

457. I presume they are about the same time on that duty as they would be engaged in their ordinary duty?—Yes; perhaps a little longer waiting to be relieved—perhaps an hour longer.

458. *Chairman.*—Have you anything to say on behalf of the other superintendents whom you represent?—I have a short statement given to me by the other officers with regard to pay. The chief superintendent

Superintendent W. Armstrong.

13 Sept., 1882.

has given it to me to represent that his salary should begin at 160*l.* and rise by increments of 10*l.* a year to 200*l.*

459. *Mr. Morris.*—You have all agreed, I suppose, upon making the suggestions that Superintendent Ward laid before us yesterday, as to the improvement of your own pay?—Yes, Sir. He was made up for that purpose. I did not think I should be here at all, and I made no preparations.

460. You were, I suppose, in Dublin previous to commencing your duty in Kingstown?—No; I was promoted in Kingstown.

461. But previous to being promoted in Kingstown, I presume you were on duty in Dublin?—Yes; I was an Inspector in Dublin.

462. Do you consider that the Kingstown police of the F Division have heavier duties to discharge and more work to do than the police on duty in the city in the back streets of Dublin?—I think not, not so much, because we have only two police courts there in the week, whereas they have them here every day.

463. I suppose that arises from a large proportion of the population being resident gentry, and traders, and people of that class?—Yes.

464. And the large increase in population, I presume, has been of that class?—Yes. I wish to mention that a man engaged on protection duty has to remain, no matter how remote his place of duty may be, until he is relieved by another station-house officer, and the man relieved has then to walk home, being perhaps half an hour each way, whereas if he was on ordinary duty he could finish his beat at the point nearest to the police station, and get off in time.

465. Is that not the case with ordinary beat work, that the officer must wait until he is relieved?—Yes; but he gets to the nearest end of the beat to home.

466. *Mr. Holmes.*—Can you state how many voluntary resignations, and how many dismissals there were in your division during the last year?—I have not got the Return showing that, but from my recollection I would say that perhaps about a dozen resigned. I do not know that any were dismissed. I do not think I had a man dismissed for the last twelve months.

467. Can you tell me why these twelve men resigned?—I asked, myself, why they resigned. I asked each one that did resign that question. Three only gave me a reason for doing so. One stated that his father, mother, and sister were going to Australia, and that he wished to accompany them. In the case of the two others, the reason was that their brother had written from Sydney for them.

468. Were they men who had only recently joined the force?—They were men who joined under the last Act.

469. Who joined since 1867?—Yes; since 1867.

470. *Chairman.*—Have any of the men complained to you of their pensions being reduced by reason of fines or black marks against them?—They have not complained to me. I have not had any complaints of that class in my division, but I have heard of such complaints through town.

471. I suppose you conferred with Superintendent Ward and agree with him in the propositions he brought before us?—Yes.

472. *Mr. Morris.*—As you have such considerable experience in the police force, I should like to obtain your opinion upon this one fact. Do you think that drunkenness amongst the members of the police force in Dublin has increased or decreased within the last seven years?—Well, I think it has decreased within the last two or three years, but before that I believe there had been a great many cases; but I may say that, as far as my division is concerned, I had very little of it.

473. You concur in Superintendent Ward's statements in reference to pay and allowances?—Yes, I do. There is no use my repeating those statements, because you have them already.

474. Have you anything else to add?—I have nothing further to add.

Superintendent JOHN MALLON, G (Detective) Division, Dublin Metropolitan Police, examined.

Superintendent John Mallon.

13 Sept., 1882.

475. *Chairman.*—What is your name?—John Mallon.

476. How long have you been in the police force?—Twenty-three years and nine months.

477. Did you fill any position as an officer before you were appointed to your present position?—I came to the G Division in 1862 as clerk to the superintendent, and graduated in it until I attained the rank of superintendent in 1874.

478. And you have been since superintendent?—Yes.

479. Was any Memorial presented on behalf of your department?—Yes.

480. Have you got that Memorial?—I have not; but its terms is about the same as the one from other branches of the service.

481. We would feel obliged by your telling your own story in reference to the matters contained in the Memorial. You are, we presume, representing yourself and your whole division. Will you now kindly state fully what you desire, and the strength and the nature of the duties of your department?—Our headquarters are at Exchange Court. The division consists of the superintendent, the inspector, 12 acting inspectors, 4 sergeants, 6 acting sergeants, and 18 constables—in all, 54. Well, then, the duties of the division are of a much more responsible character than the ordinary duties of the police service. As a general rule the ordinary duties of the service are merely routine, but ours are technical, and the responsibilities are greater. For instance, all confidential inquiries are made by our department. Then the supervision of convicts released in the Dublin metropolitan police district is exclusively carried on by the G Division.

482. *Mr. Holmes.*—That is ticket-of-leave men?—Yes. At present we have in the district 217 men of that class—men whose original sentences have expired. In the case of a good number of them, of course, their original sentences have expired, but, nevertheless, we are obliged to keep up the supervision still. Then we have the supervision of public vehicles of the city. That is attached to the G Division. We have 1,085 hack cars, 774 cabs, and 140 stage carriages, and between 3,000 and 4,000 drivers and conductors, and, it may be said, that the supervision of that number of vehicles, and of the drivers and conductors, is exclusively thrown upon us. One thing is quite certain—that we have to inquire into the character of all the applicants to become owners of public vehicles, and drivers, and conductors, and the average applications would be from three to four each day, so that that entails a good deal of labour. Then we have fifty-seven pawn-offices in the city, and the supervision of pawn-offices is exclusively thrown upon the G Division. It is a very responsible and a very dangerous duty, because you are brought into contact with disease, and you are liable to get disease. For instance, during a small-pox epidemic, or when fever becomes prevalent, it is not at all unreasonable to suppose that, notwithstanding all the supervision exercised by the Public Health Committee, that wearing apparel, and, perhaps, bedclothes, are brought into pawn and pawned, and our men are obliged every day to search the pawn-offices for those things. And then all the duties that were created by the recent agitation—that class of duty was all thrown upon us. There has been extra duty thrown upon us lately, within the last three years, in consequence of the state of the country.

483. *Chairman.*—Has that been to any large extent?—Yes; very large. For instance, during three years I have been hardly able to have one meal of food at my own house, even on Sundays.

484. *Mr. Holmes.*—With reference to the supervision of ticket of leave men or other criminals, what do you call them?—Licence-holders, supervisees. They are generally called "people under supervision."

485. With reference to your duties in connexion with the supervision of criminals, do they require the members of the force to visit the houses where those criminals live in order to ascertain their whereabouts and to have a daily watch over them?—They certainly do. We keep a record of the names, and once each month the male convicts and licence-holders are supposed to report themselves at the Detective Office. Then, in the case of absentees, we are obliged to know why they were absent, and then those who do report themselves with regularity, we are obliged to inquire about. There is a good deal more risk attached to the performance of that duty than there is about ordinary duty, as you are brought into the haunts of crime and you are brought into contact with dangerous fellows.

486. *Mr. Morris.*—I think, as well as I can gather from your evidence, that nearly all the duties that you have mentioned are the ordinary duties of your branch of the service, with the exception of the extra duty which has been thrown on you for the last three years in connection with the Land League agitation. Is that so?—Yes; in a natural state of affairs, there would be only the ordinary duties of the detective branch.

487. But there has been, as I gather from you, in the last three years, in connection with the Land League agitation, much more of duty of one kind or another thrown upon you than formerly?—Very much more; because the detective department in Dublin suffered particularly from that, as questions arising in the country would be referred to us, and the ordinary police would never know anything about them.

488. *Mr. Holmes.*—Now you have shown us that the duties of the detective force are of a highly responsible, dangerous, and confidential character?—Yes.

489. What have you to say on the subject of pay?—I, in common with the men of the department, complain that our salaries are not as large as the salaries of a detective department elsewhere.

490. When you say "elsewhere," to what place do you refer?—To the London metropolis or Liverpool, or even the Royal Irish Constabulary. For instance, Mr. French is the detective director. He is a sub-inspector, and he has salary and allowances; and, in addition to that, he has a special allowance of 100*l.* a-year because he is detective director. I have not a farthing of any special allowance made to me as superintendent.

491. *Mr. Morris.*—Is your salary as superintendent of the detective force the same as an ordinary superintendent of the other force?—The same.

492. Is the pay of the detective force all through the different grades exactly the same?—It is not.

493. *Chairman.*—Have you the same pay and the same allowances as any other ordinary superintendent?—Yes.

494. *Mr. Morris.*—Will you now explain the pay that these men receive, and what you and they consider you ought to receive. I think that would be the way to put it. First, as regards yourself?—Yes.

495. *Mr. Holmes.*—Allow me, before you proceed, to ask you this question. You have just stated that your pay as the superintendent of the detective division is the same as that of the other superintendents?—Yes.

496. Are you correct in that statement?—Yes, my salary is 230*l.*

497. Don't the others commence at 200*l.* and go up to 250*l.*?—Yes.

498. But you got 230*l.*?—Yes, there is no gradation in my case.

499. Then your pay is better than that of the other superintendents?—It would be better for the first four or five years.

500. There is this distinction between you and the others, that you got 230*l.* at once, whereas the others begin at 200*l.* and go up to the maximum by 5*l.* a-year to 250*l.*?—Yes.

501. *Mr. Morris.*—What change would you expect, in every spirit of fair play, to be made in your position and salary?—I could not propose terms for myself, but I would expect, considering the nature of the duties to be performed, that I, or whoever is superintendent of the department, should have a special allowance, the same as the detective director of the Royal Irish Constabulary, or as the superintendent of the detective department in Liverpool, or the chief of the detective department at Scotland Yard. For instance, the superintendent of the detective department in Scotland Yard, that is the chief superintendent, his salary commences at 450*l.*, and increases to 550*l.* by annual increments of 10*l.* a-year.

502. *Mr. Holmes.*—Take the superintendent of the detective force of Liverpool, do you know what his salary is?—I do not exactly know what his salary is. I think it is about 450*l.* That would be the maximum. I could not say for certain, but he is the chief superintendent as well.

503. Would you now state specifically what you ask for yourself?—I should say an allowance corresponding to the allowance of the detective director of the Royal Irish Constabulary.

504. State what it is.—He gets 100*l.* a-year in addition to his salary as a sub-inspector.

505. What is his salary?—250*l.*, that is a first-class sub-inspector.

506. Then, in point of fact, you ask for an addition of 100*l.* a-year to your present salary?—Yes.

507. What allowances have you in addition to your pay?—I have the same allowances as the other superintendents, 13*l.*

508. Do you ask for this addition as an addition to your pay, or as an additional allowance?—In addition to the pay.

509. In addition to the pay, I presume by reason of your holding the special office of superintendent of the detective division?—Yes.

510. Will you now kindly proceed with the next matter you wish to bring under our notice?—Well, the inspector has 180*l.* a-year salary.

511. *Mr. Morris.*—That is 50*l.* a year more than a first-class inspector outside?—Yes.

512. *Mr. Holmes.*—What is your proposition as regards him?—Well, I believe his salary ought to be increased, say to 200*l.*, because in the absence of the superintendent, either on leave or through illness, which must occur, his duties would be thrown on him. Then we have 13 acting inspectors; 3 of these have 2*l.* 1*s.* 7*d.* per week, that is 4*s.* 11*d.* more than an acting inspector on the street. We have 10 acting inspectors who have 2*l.* 7*d.*, that is including all allowances, and that is 3*s.* 11*d.* more than the men on the street.

513. Dealing with these inspectors first, what do you propose for them?—What I propose for them is that there would be an increase of an additional inspector appointed, because we have thirteen acting inspectors, and in selecting men for the division, there is an inflexible rule adopted that no man who has been reported for intemperance is eligible for admission into the division; or no man that has been reported for insubordination or impertinence is eligible, so that in the selection of men those who are admitted are supposed to be more intelligent and better trained than the men employed on ordinary duty. Yet they do not get promotion. There is only one superintendentship and one inspectorship open to these thirteen men. They naturally feel discontented, and it is not advisable to allow them to take promotion elsewhere, and to leave the G Division on a large scale. It would be to my mind of service for an acting inspector of the G Division to go out as inspector because he would bring the detective elements with him outside; but, at the same time, a policeman trained in the department, and leaving it, is a greater loss to the department than it would

Superintendent John Mallon.

12 Sept., 1882.

Superintendent John Mallon.

13 Sept., 18[illegible].

he is a division outside, because no amount of book-learning will make a man a good detective. The knowledge must grow upon him, and it is in the police-court and at the Commission Court, giving evidence and listening to other constables giving evidence, and perhaps having got three or four smart cross-examinations—it is only then that he begins to see the value of evidence and the necessity of taking care in bringing a case forward before a magistrate or a judge. Well, in our department, the moral character of a man is of infinite importance, because if a man was untruthful he would be a dangerous man to have in the department, or if he was corrupt. So that there is no allowance made for the special qualities that are essentially necessary to make a good honest police officer.

604. What do you propose with regard to the acting inspectors?—If there was an additional inspector appointed in the G Division, and the allowance for plain clothes increased, it would be a greater inducement for the better class of men to come to the department. For instance, the allowance for plain clothes with us is only 4s. 11d. for three, and 3s. 11d. for the other but acting inspectors. The sergeants have only 3s. 11d., the acting sergeants, 3s. 11d., and the first-class constables, 3s. 11d., and the second-class constables, 3s. 11d. Whereas in London the constables are allowed 7s. per week.

605. For plain clothes?—Yes.

606. *Chairman.*—As a rule, don't the men of the G Division in Dublin always go in plain clothes?—Always.

607. Except when attending Commissions or other Courts?—Certainly; but they have not appeared in uniform at the Commission of late.

608. *Mr. Holmes.*—What would you consider a reasonable allowance to give to the various grades to provide them with plain clothes?—Well, the men dress very much alike, and I would therefore make no distinction as to clothes. I would say if they got as the London constables get, 7s. per week, it would be a fair allowance.

609. That is 18l. 4s. a-year?—Yes.

610. Is not that a rather large sum for plain clothes?—I dare say that would be a set-off against other expenses that they are obliged to incur, and that they have no legitimate means of charging. That is a question that has created dissatisfaction in the department.

611. There are certain other miscellaneous expenses which they cannot charge, but which they must defray?—Yes. I have talked very freely with the men, and we have compared their incomes with the incomes of men in nearly the same class of civilian life, and they say that it would improve their case very much if they made no exorbitant demand, or if they went beyond the mark. They are all perfectly satisfied. The things they complain of on the whole, are the allowance for clothes and the shortness of their pensions.

612. They are satisfied with their normal rates of pay?—They would expect some little increase, but they would have no idea of making any exorbitant demand. For instance, at Scotland Yard—the system which is the basis of our department—they have a chief superintendent with 800l. a-year; three chief inspectors with 350l. a-year. There are all those things there; but then our men could not, as a matter of course, expect to be placed on exactly the same footing, because in point of importance our duties would not take rank with the duties imposed upon the people of Scotland Yard. There is a disparity between the wealth of the two cities, and so on.

613. Have you now dealt with the question of pay?—Yes, as far as I know.

614. *Mr. Morris.*—As regards the question of pension after service, have you anything to offer as to that?—Well, the men of our department feel as the rest of the force do, that the pension of men joining after 1867 is small.

615. They wish, I presume, to have that pension improved?—Yes, to have that pension improved.

616. *Mr. Holmes.*—Now, tell me; do you think that the men in your division who joined since 1867 were made aware upon joining that they were under a different scale of pensions from that enjoyed by the men who joined before 1867?—They were perfectly well aware of that.

617. They were perfectly well aware upon joining?—Perfectly well aware.

618. Are you aware of the scale of pensions that obtains in London, under which the men of the London metropolitan police force are pensioned?—I believe the scale of pensions is the same as the scale of pensions to be given to our men who joined since 1867, and upon that I believe that our men would be more favourably considered, because in London they are obliged to pay 2½ per cent. to the Superannuation Fund.

619. You are not quite correct there. The London scale of pensions is more favourable than the Dublin scale of pensions since 1867. The London scale is the same as the Dublin scale from fifteen years' service to twenty years' service, namely, at fifteen years' service, fifteen-fiftieths of the salary, rising one-fiftieth each year until twenty years' service is attained, when it reaches twenty-fiftieths; but from twenty to twenty-five years' service the London scale goes up by yearly increments of two-fiftieths instead of one-fiftieth, so that at twenty-five years' service the London man would be in as good a position as the Dublin man after thirty. From twenty-five years' service to twenty-eight years' service the London scale drops to one-fiftieth, at which, when it attains thirty-three-fiftieths, as nearly as may be two-thirds of a man's salary, it stops. I presume that the men who have joined the Dublin force since 1867 could hardly expect that the Dublin force should be put in a better position than the London men as regards pension?—I do not think they would expect it.

620. You think they would be reasonably satisfied if the same scale of pension were extended to Dublin?—That is my opinion; but I am not authorized to give their opinion in reference to that. The important thing that the men complain about is the small allowance for plain clothes, because whatever they wear is their own plain clothes, and they are only allowed 3s. 11d. a-week to the men of the constables, and yet there is a uniform supplied to the police outside which is not supplied to us.

621. Do I understand you to say that the members of the detective force are not supplied with uniforms?—They are not.

622. Are they never supposed to wear uniform?—We were accustomed to wear uniform only when appearing before the Judges and the Recorder. And then it was generally felt that a man appearing in a blue uniform only occasionally was more liable to cold, especially in winter. Indeed, it was found that in winter they did catch cold, owing to the fact that their uniforms having been lying up for three and four months, got damp, and then Mr. Anderson, the Crown Solicitor, kindly interfered and said it was not necessary that they should appear in uniform, as that when members of the Royal Irish Constabulary came to Dublin they did not appear in uniform except when giving evidence in their own case, and that the London men, when they came here, always appeared in plain clothes.

623. How long has the uniform been withdrawn?—There has been no uniform supplied within the last six years, and you might have seen them without uniform for the last three years.

624. *Mr. Morris.*—Continuing the grievance of the men of the G Division, they amount to this, that they complain that for the last three years their work has been largely increased, and that they have received no consideration for it similar to that which was given to the men of the Royal Irish Constabulary?—Quite so.

625. And the men of the G Division also complain that the allowance made to them for clothes is not sufficient?—Yes.

626. And they would also like to have their retiring pensions, at all events, upon the same footing as the detective force in London?—Yes, the same as the police force in London.

627. These are what you consider the three principal grounds of complaint?—Yes, and the want of opportunity for further promotion.

628. These are the four grounds which, in your opinion, your division complains of?—Yes.

629. *Mr. Holmes.*—Have you anything else to say on the subject of pay or of pensions?—I have nothing else to say; nothing occurs to me, so far as I am personally concerned, in reference to my pay and allowances. I would be more interested in the men with smaller salaries. It is most necessary and essential that the subordinate grades in our department should be [illegible]. We stand on a different footing to the men outside, because the superintendent and every officer in our department are like one man. There are no distinctions of duty there. For every single case that is taken up by the G Division the superintendent is responsible. He takes the whole responsibility for the conduct of the case right through. A constable of the G Division, if he was dissatisfied, might be a very mischievous man, and my object for the good of the public service, and in my own interest, would be that the men in the subordinate grades should be better provided for.

630. *Mr. Morris.*—Have many of your men been fined?—No, Sir; we have not had any fines. When a man in our department commits himself it is a very serious thing; but we have had only two or three cases of punishment.

631. *Mr. Holmes.*—Within the last year have there been any voluntary resignations in your department?—Certainly.

632. But no men have been dismissed or punished?—Yes; no men have been dismissed or punished.

633. Would you kindly explain how the men are selected for your division?—They are generally selected for our division by watching the men giving evidence before the magistrate. For instance, if a man appeared before a magistrate, and conducted a case with ability, and deported himself properly, when a vacancy would occur in the department I would ask him if he would have any wish to come to us. It is by selection.

Chief Superintendent John Mallon.

18 Sept., 1882.

634. No man below the rank of a second class constable is, I suppose, eligible for your division, is that the case?—No, Sir, that is not the case now. We will take them if they are only twelve months in the service, provided they exhibit the necessary qualities.

635. There is no limit of service?—At present there is no limit of service.

636. *Chairman.*—As I take it there is no special training required, except the mode in which a man deports himself and gives evidence in Court?—Yes. First of all we send them to attend the carriage duty, then take them from carriage duty to pawn-office duty, and by the time they finish pawn-office duty they are pretty well up. The carriage duty gives them the knack of making inquiries. People coming up to Dublin to the railway stations, or coming in by boat, forget luggage in cabs, and that sort of thing, and they report their losses as a matter of course to the police, and a carriage man is sent to inquire about it, and he turns up the luggage at once.

637. Then, because a man shows sharpness in these different matters he is selected?—Yes. A man would be at least seven or eight years at carriage and pawn-office duties before he would have any case of importance, and even then a junior man is always sent along with a senior—the two are always sent together.

638. Have you anything else to bring before us on any other subject?—I have not, Sir.

Superintendent Thomas Byrne, A Division Dublin Metropolitan Police, examined.

Superintendent Thomas Byrne.

18 Sept., 1882.

639. *Chairman.*—What is your name?—Thomas Byrne.

640. What position in the Dublin metropolitan police do you occupy?—I am superintendent of the Dublin metropolitan police, and have charge of the A Division.

641. How long have you been in the force?—Thirty years and nine months.

642. When were you appointed a superintendent?—On the 1st March, 1868.

643. Would you kindly tell us what is the extent of the area of the A Division?—I should say, including the Kilmainham township, something about 5 square miles—between 4 and 5 square miles I should think.

644. How many stations have you in your division?—I have three stations.

645. How many barracks?—Four barracks. I have Chancery Lane, Newmarket, and Kilmainham—three stations were charges are taken. I have also Kilmainham barracks, and at James' Street there has been a small barrack, and Kevin Street barracks, and also another barrack at Clarke's Court, attached to the Chancery Lane station, in my district.

646. How many men have you under you?—203 men in all.

647. *Mr. Holmes.*—Be good enough to state their various grades, from inspector to constable, and give the number in each rank?—I cannot tell exactly the number in each rank. I have 6 inspectors, 7 acting inspectors, and I have the remainder in sergeants and 164 constables. The difference between 164 and 203 is made up by men whose ranks range from acting sergeant to inspector.

648. *Chairman.*—Have you conferred with Superintendent Ward in reference to the Memorial presented here?—I have, Sir.

649. Do you coincide with his views?—I do, Sir.

650. Have you anything to add to what he stated?—I have nothing to add. There is one point in reference to the question of pensions, about the contribution, that I would wish to say a word about, for that is under the Act which was in force when I joined.

651. *Mr. Holmes.*—Before you deal with that do I understand you to say that you agree with the views of Superintendent Ward as regards the matter of pay and allowances?—Yes.

652. And it is your wish that the superintendents of the Dublin metropolitan police should be put in the same position as county inspectors of the Royal Irish Constabulary as regards pay and allowances?—Certainly.

653. Will you tell me why you consider that you should be put in the same position as the county inspectors?—I will explain why I think so, and I will be as brief as I can. In the first place, the number of men of all ranks that are under me is 203, and I have 10 [illegible] and mounted men. The cash that passed through my hands for the past year, and which I was obliged to check in small sums varying from 6d. to 10s., amounted to 17,[illegible]l. 1s. 7d. The population of my district, taking it roughly, is 68,[illegible], and that is the population of a district which is the home of all the [illegible] and [illegible] in Ireland. The number I have stated includes the population of the Kilmainham township. That is a population not included in any division. I have over 65,000 inhabitants in my division.

654. Ought you not rather to compare yourself with the sub-inspector, remembering that the county inspector is responsible to the Inspector-General only, whereas, if I understand your position rightly, the chief superintendent of the Dublin metropolitan police is your immediate superior?—He is, Sir; but then at the same time our reports are made to the Commissioners. He is merely the medium for the transmission

Superintendent Tomalty[illegible].

10 Sept., 18[illegible].

of them. I make my reports direct to the Commissioner, but they must pass through the chief superintendent. Notwithstanding that, however, they are directed to the Commissioner, and I am responsible to him for my reports.

655. But is it not the fact that the chief superintendent exercises a certain amount of supervision over all the other superintendents?—He does.

656. *Chairman.*—Do you regard him as your superior officer?—Certainly.

657. *Mr. Holmes.*—There is this difference, that the county inspector is responsible only to the Inspector-General, whereas your immediate superior officer is the chief superintendent. Therefore it seems to me that your position is more analogous to that of the sub-inspectors than to that of the county inspectors?—Although the chief superintendent is the intermediary for purposes of centralisation, through which our reports pass, they are directed to the Commissioner, and the chief superintendent makes no note or comment on them.

658. Well, does he not superintend your districts at intervals?—Yes, he does, at night. Once a month he goes round and inspects the barracks and books.

659. *Chairman.*—You said to me just now that he was your superior officer. In what respect is he your superior officer?—Well, if he found an irregularity in my division or district he would be bound to report it to the Commissioner, and then I would be answerable for that to the Commissioner. Of course we look upon the chief superintendent as our superior officer. I consider that I could not be insubordinate to him in any way.

660. Do you consider yourself responsible, in the first instance, to the chief superintendent?—No, Sir, I do not. I am responsible to the Commissioner. The number of prisoners arrested and charged in my district for the year 1891 was 4,789. I had to take those charges and classify them for the Judge's Returns and everything else. The number of publicans in my division is 294; of spirit grocers and beer dealers, about 25. There is a change of ownership in reference to those places in each year of 60 on an average, each case entailing on the superintendent a personal inspection of the premises, and he is held responsible; and when they go before the magistrates, and the Crown Solicitor, and eventually when they go before the Recorder, the superintendent must see that all the requirements they put upon the licensed person are carried out. He must also see assignments; that is a portion of his duty.

661. Has this class of business increased much within the last two years?—It has in that way for the superintendents. Heretofore we were not held responsible for those things—the inspectors generally did them—but the Act of Parliament—the Licensing Laws now render it necessary that the first step to be taken in matters of this kind is that, that the superintendent is served with a notice. That is now required by law.

662. *Chairman.*—But as a matter of fact, those duties have increased?—Yes, they have.

663. *Mr. Holmes.*—Do you still adhere to Superintendent Ward's proposition that superintendents should be put in the same position as regards pay as the county inspectors?—I do, Sir, and for this reason. The county inspectors—I am just taking the average—have between twenty-five and twenty-seven stations; of course, there are forty in some counties, having about five men to each as a general rule. That would leave him about the same number of men to control as I have. Then I have to see to the men's requisitions, inspect their men-books, which entails labour on the superintendent in his district. For instance, when I was an inspector in Rathmines, I had the whole of the Rathmines township and portion of the Pembroke township, whereas the sub-inspector had only a small portion of Rathfarnham and portion of Tallaght.

664. Have you now said all you wish to say on the subject of pay?—Yes, Sir, I have, because we are entirely agreed on the subject, and we were in conference in reference to what Mr. Ward submitted to you.

665. Do you agree with him on the subject of pension?—I do, Sir.

666. *Mr. Morris.*—Superintendent Ward stated that in calculating the pension, he ought to include in that calculation some of the allowances that are made to you. Do you concur in that?—I concur in that also.

667. *Chairman.*—That is, that the amount of the allowance should be included in the amount of the pension?—Yes, a certain portion of it.

668. *Mr. Morris.*—As to the men under your charge, I wish to know from you, candidly, openly, and fairly, do you consider that drunkenness amongst the men is on the increase?—Oh no; it has decreased considerably.

669. *Chairman.*—Within what period?—Within, I am certain, twelve months. I will say twelve months in my division. It has also decreased generally throughout the force.

670. *Mr. Holmes.*—How many voluntary resignations were there in your division during the last year, and how many men in your division were dismissed during the same period?—I could not exactly tell that.

671. Will you tell us how many hours a policeman is on duty during the day?—He goes on at 6 in the morning, and is relieved at 9. He goes on also at 6 in the day, and is relieved at 9. Then his business is done. That is one "day relief."

672. Is he engaged on day duty for a month at a time?—Yes.

673. Then he gets off at 9 at night?—Yes. There is another "relief" goes on at 9 in the morning, and is relieved at 1 in the afternoon. He goes on again at 7 in the evening, and is relieved at 9. The day men all go off at 9 o'clock at night. The time occupied by the day relief is eight hours one day and nine hours another.

674. *Chairman.*—Is he master of his own time except for those eight hours?—He is not master of his own time.

675. Unless called upon?—He is. Of course, then he has to attend to prisoners, and that sort of thing.

676. Will you now kindly give us an outline of the duty of a night man?—Now in the case of the night men, the first relief comes on at 9 o'clock P.M., and he is off at 5 A.M.

677. When is he on again?—At half-past 10 on the following night.

678. And then he on duty from 5 o'clock one morning until half-past 10 that night?—Yes. On alternate nights he parades at 9 o'clock. There are two night reliefs, a single and a double, and when the men of the single relief go off duty at 5 A.M., the men of the double relief extend their hours, so as to cover the ground vacated by the men who went off at 5 o'clock, and remain on duty until 6 A.M., when they are relieved by the day men.

679. Do the men go on turns?—Yes, they do [illegible]. One night relief comes on at 9 P.M., and is off at 5 A.M., and the other comes on at 10.30 P.M., and is off at 6 A.M.; so that that gives the constable six hours one night, and seven and a-half hours another night.

680. *Mr. Morris.*—Do I understand you to say that the average duty of a policeman for two months is that he is about seven hours out of the twenty-four on night duty one month?—Yes.

681. And that he has about eight hours and a-half day duty for the next month?—Yes, that is a plain way of putting it.

682. Of course he has extra duty to discharge if called upon, in connection with charges and that sort of thing?—I can give you the whole of the extra duties since the [illegible] trials.

683. *Chairman.*—I want to ask you this. Can men employ their time as they please when off duty, or are they bound to attend classes or anything of that sort?—In the drill seasons they are bound to attend

drill, but we have no drill this summer. Circumstances arose, the effect of which were that there could be no drill.

684. Do they drill when off duty?—In their own time they parade for drill; but we have only drill during the summer months.

685. *Mr. Morris.*—As I understand it, you agreed entirely with Superintendent Ward that for the last three years, owing to the matters that grew out of the Land League agitation, you had much extra duty to discharge, and that your men felt aggrieved that they did not get some extra pay, such as that given to the Royal Irish Constabulary, in consideration of their extra duties?—The very question. They have no time to themselves—no time that they can call their own; and the men felt it when the kindred force got it and they did not get it.

686. *Chairman.*—What was the cause that principally contributed, in your opinion, to the recent agitation in the police force?—What led to it, and what was the primary cause of it, was that our men felt aggrieved that they did not get what their brother officers got in the sister force.

687. *Mr. Holmes.*—Under ordinary circumstances, and as an ordinary rule, when a constable is off duty can he call the time his own?—Yes, Sir.

688. But, of course, that time was considerably interfered with by the extra duties cast upon him by the Land League agitation?—Yes, Sir.

Superintendent [illegible].

13 Sept., 1882.

[The Committee then adjourned to next day.]

Third Day.—14th September, 1882.

Present:

Mr. J. W. O'Donnell, Mr. George Morris, D.L., and Mr. R. W. A. Holmes.

Mr. Robert Walker, District Superintendent, London Metropolitan Police, examined.

689. *Chairman.*—Your name, Sir?—Robert Walker.

690. What rank do you hold?—I am one of the two district superintendents of the London Metropolitan Police.

691. Are you still a district superintendent?—Yes.

692. How long have you been in the force?—Forty-four years and six months.

693. And how long have you held your present office?—I am in the fourteenth year of my present rank. I have held my present rank since the appointment was created.

694. *Mr. Holmes.*—We wish to be favoured with your evidence upon the main facts in connection with the London metropolitan police force as regards pay, allowances, deductions, pensions, and generally with regard to the organization of that force. Will you kindly tell us first what is the strength of the metropolitan police force, and will you also tell us the various ranks and grades of which that force is constituted?—I have before me the Commissioner's Return which is presented to Parliament for the year 1881—a Return showing the authorised strength of the metropolitan divisions on the 31st December, 1881. In London, and within the 15 miles circuit of our police duties, the total strength was 10,496. Her Majesty's dockyards are also under police care, and that service increases the total strength to 11,254. I may mention that the dockyards are Woolwich, Sheerness, Portsmouth, Plymouth (Devonport), and Pembroke—five.

695. Perhaps now you will kindly give us the various grades?—Before I give details of the grades, perhaps you will permit me to hand in a copy of a Return just made showing the grades and pay. (*Return handed in.*)

696. This Return will, of course, appear as part of your evidence; it will be printed either in the Appendix or in your evidence, as may be most convenient. Now will you be good enough to give us details of the grades?—This Return shows at a glance the number of officers on the 1st April last, the rate of pay, their annual allowances or benefits besides pay, and the maximum pay, and in the column on the right the allowances.

697. What is the extent of the London metropolitan area?—[illegible] square miles.

698–699. It includes all that is usually known as London, with the exception of the City of London?—Yes, with the exception of the City. The population of the metropolitan police district is now estimated at 4,793,657 souls.

700. *Mr. Holmes.*—What is the annual cost of maintaining this police force; how is it defrayed?—I will answer the last question first, if you will permit me. The rateable value of the metropolitan police area for 1880–81 was [illegible].

701. And upon that what does the police tax amount to in the £?—The tax is hardly a question for the Commissioner of Police. It rests with the Receiver of Police, and appears in his Reports. I am not at the moment able to answer that question.

702. I wanted to know what proportion of the cost of the maintenance of the police force was contributed from local sources, contributed by local taxation, as distinct from the Imperial quota?—I am not just now able to answer that question. It does not appear in the Commissioners' Report.

703. Can you tell us the number of barracks within the metropolitan police area proper, and, approximately, the average number of men accommodated in those barracks?—The number of barracks is 168, and the number of police residents paying rent in the various barracks is, according to size, from five to sixty men.

704. Are all single men accommodated?—No. Four-fifths of the single men are accommodated in barracks as near as possible.

705. Is it the case that there are blocks of buildings attached to most of the police barracks to accommodate married men and also single men who cannot be accommodated in the barrack?—Only in two cases are there blocks of buildings prepared for the police as yet.

706. Where are they?—In the M and N Divisions.

Mr. R. Walker.

14 Sept., 1882.

Mr. R. Walters.

16 Sept., 1902.

707. In what parts of London are they situated?—At Southwark and Paddington.

708. Is it the intention to provide all barracks with similar blocks of buildings?—The difficulty of obtaining sites has been the principal reason for delay. Then again, the expense would be so great, and the small charge for rent would be almost ineffectual towards paying a moderate interest for advances from the Treasury. These have been the principal causes of [illegible] during the fifty years that the force has been in existence.

709–710. Are the barracks and the blocks of buildings erected at the expense of Imperial taxation or at the cost of the ratepayers?—At the expense of the police funds. Will you allow me to add one word with regard to the barrack system for the police—for married police particularly? During the late Commissioner's (Sir Richard Mayne's) period of office, it was held by him to be of greater advantage to the public to have the married police living over the entire district than in concentrating them in barracks.

711. *Mr. Morris.*—To have them diffused over the entire district?—Yes. It was considered by the Commissioner that having bodies of single men living in police station-houses, who were ready at all times for any emergency, was of sufficient advantage in cases of fire, tumult, or the like for the aid of the police on duty; and, therefore, that by having the married police in private lodgings scattered over their divisions, they could observe, give information, and would be of greater service in restraining petty disorders when the police on duty were absent; that was the view taken.

712. *Chairman.*—In fact, they did the duties of policemen by way of prevention?—Yes.

713. *Mr. Holmes.*—You used the phrase just now, "police station-house." Does that refer to a barrack?—Yes; we do not know the word "barrack."

714. You call them station-houses?—Yes; we call them station-houses.

715. In the Return of rates of pay—I will begin with the last class—I see that in the case of a third-class constable, his maximum rate of pay is [illegible] 11s. 6d.?—Yes; he has [illegible] per week.

716. He receives that upon becoming an effective member of the force?—Within fourteen days of his joining the force.

717. Taking that as the maximum pay, what allowance does he receive in addition?—If he is a married man, nothing.

718. Take the case of a single man first?—He receives no allowance, except his uniform, of course.

719. Are boots included in the uniform?—Yes.

720. Are the boots supplied as in the case of the army?—By contract.

721. By contract?—Quite so, and always have been, I may add.

722. As he receives no allowance, will you tell me what deductions there are from the maximum pay of [illegible] 11s. 6d.?—1s. per week for lodging-money.

723. Then you say he is provided with accommodation in the section-house?—Yes; beds and all articles for his use, for kitchen use, and the like, are included in that 1s.

724. Then it includes fuel for kitchen purposes?—Yes. Lodging and kitchen coal allowance.

725. Is that the only deduction that is made from his pay?—That is the only deduction that is made from his pay. All that he requires—if I may add this—is just to provide himself with food, and that is done in messes, and the servants who cater for the constables are paid privately by the police out of their own funds.

726. Then practically, a third-class constable has [illegible], as stated?—He has [illegible], less superannuation.

727. Now we will go to the case of married men. First of all, may I ask you whether a man can get married when he likes, or is the leave to marry limited to men who have passed a certain period of service?—He can get married when he thinks fit.

728. Do married men get any allowance in addition to their pay?—They receive an allowance for coals as stated in the Return on the right-hand column. Sergeants and constables receive coals or a money allowance instead of 6d. per week.

729. Why do the married men receive an allowance for fuel, when the single men have to pay for their fuel?—The single men are provided with coals.

730. But there is, I understand you to say, a deduction of 1s. per week to cover rent and fuel?—Yes. The 1s. per week is for lodging and fuel.

731. Then the single man has to pay for lodging and fuel?—Yes.

732. But you have just told me that a married man gets an allowance of 6d. a week for fuel?—Yes.

733. Why should the married man be in a better position than the single man in regard to that allowance?—That is a very wide question. I should add that there is an allowance of [illegible] per week for fuel to single men living out of the station-house. A constable in barracks has to conform to regulations. Then to rise, and then exactly to go to bed, but to be in the station-house within certain hours. The object of that is, that in case of a demand for additional assistance in the streets, a single man may always be at hand and be ready to turn out when called upon. That is what the married constable does not suffer from. During the period that he is off duty, except on great occasions or emergencies, the married man is never called out into the streets. It is only the single men's services that are sought, and therefore we place the single constable in a better position than the married one, by reason of having to submit to these regulations.

734. *Chairman.*—Does any portion of the 1s. go to the supplying of fuel in the section-house, or does the Government supply it?—The Government supplies an allowance of so many pounds of coals a week for firing.

735. There is, then, no deduction from the constable in the section-house?—Yes. The fuel is provided.

736. The 1s. is for rent?—Yes. The married police living in stations have to provide their own fuel; the single men living in them is provided with fuel.

737. *Mr. Holmes.*—What you have told us with regard to the pay, allowances, and deductions, in the case of third-class constables, applies also to the first and second-class constables?—Quite so; there is no difference.

738. Is there any difference with respect to the sergeants?—Single sergeants are upon the same footing as single constables. The married sergeants stand upon the same basis as the married police, and upon the same rates.

739. As regards lodging?—Yes.

740. The same deduction of 1s. per week is made from the sergeant's pay as from the constable's?—The same, when living in the section-house.

741. We have now dealt with sergeants and constables, and come to the grade of inspectors. Will you kindly give us any information in your possession as to the pay, allowances, and duties of the inspectors of that grade of the service?—Would you allow me to point out an important matter connected with the constables before proceeding to the higher rank?

742. Certainly; we shall be very glad if you do so?—The second-class receive [illegible] per week after three years' service.

743. A man is in the third-class for three years before he gets into the second?—Yes, before he gets into the second, and after three years' service he receives [illegible] per week.

744. Then he is certain to rise to the second-class after three years' service if he conducts himself properly?—Quite so. And after eight years' total service he is advanced to 1l. 10s. per week, which places him in the first class, conduct being good. The total service is eight years.

745. Then after eight years' service a man is in receipt of 30s. a week?—Yes, conduct being good.

746. Subject, of course, to the deduction of 1s.?—Quite so, if he is living in the section-house.

747. *Chairman.*—That runs throughout the force?—Yes.

ent.—Will you now tell us how long stable before he gets into the rank he constable rises by tenure and good a sergeant? but there is no fixed

ris.—With whom does that selection by the superintendent?—The district gether with the divisional superinten-

—Has he to pass any examination Yes.

man.—What is the nature of that ex- n Educational Board in Whitehall officers recommended for the superior , of inspector, of superintendent, and to education the officer is either sent advanced.

any preparatory school, or means of ion the use of which is compulsory they can go up for that examination? eld in every station-house two after- for sergeants and constables under a id for by the Government. It is ers of those ranks to attend school a certificate from the school-master of reading, writing, and cyphering to first three rules, and so on. The books certain forms, filled up by the rintendent. I may mention that 1d. arged to the pupils while they attend

nother deduction?—Yes. That is for then the constable is perfect in the and the forms are submitted to the hey pass to the district superinten- on to the Commissioner, who relieves their attendance and pay.

ertificate of his competency?—Yes.

—As I take it, promotion amongst ne rank, is without examination or merely based on conduct and fitness? until relegated to school. The school- , relieves the constable of the small nth. The constable must, however, till the sergeant he is relieved by the school-master. He could be relieved in the higher examinations is sat by by the Educational Board, who deal pon education and recommend him to as fit to pass his examination.

is.—How are the men promoted from constables to the rank of third-class is the list made out, and by whom?— made, in the first place, by the super- d by his inspectors. The Commis- Orders," as it is termed, directs the be sent in the names of so many con- otion to the rank of sergeant. Each n the twenty divisions of police ntendent places himself at once in commun- inspectors to find out the fittest men . The qualifications then—and the important points in the police service s of a constable to rise are evidently his superior officers. His habits, his y of conduct, and fitness for his rank a man very speedily forward where the names of the three or five best re submitted by the superintendent to as being fit to pass the examination al Board, these officers recommended obtained the approval of the school- ing been relieved from the education men go up in two batches for ex- lly in two batches—and a report is h man's case from the Educational e different levels of examination, and d through each level, and whether he and having been considered fit, they on a list, and promoted according to

757. *Mr Holmes.*—In point of fact, those men go up and qualify?—Yes. Mr. R. Walker

758. *Chairman.*—And when they qualify they are put upon the list, and promoted according to seniority?—Yes. Amongst the sergeants promoted from one of the grades it always goes by seniority, and more frequently second-class sergeants, as well as constables, are promoted. 14 Sept., 18[illegible]

759. *Mr. Morris.*—Then I presume that, no matter how well educated a man may be, unless his conduct is good, and his fitness for the office ascertained, he is not recommended for promotion?—He is not.

760. Is sobriety included as a mark of good conduct?—Yes, in the first class. Sobriety is considered one of the principal recommendations for advancement.

761. *Mr. Holmes.*—How often are those examinations held? Are they postponed until there are a certain number of vacancies in the class of sergeant?—That is so. When there are a certain number of vacancies, and the previous recommendations are all advanced, the Commissioner then requires additional names for his book to pass the examination.

762. How many competitors are there usually for one vacancy?—It is not done by competition. The names of those who have passed best are entered according to length of service, and the oldest approved constable passes first to the superior grade. Usually twenty-five or thirty men go up for examination at a time. The men are required to attend school one hour twice in each week, as their duties may allow.

763. As we have now arrived at the rank of sergeant, will you deal with that rank as you have done with that of constable, and show us how a man rises in the various classes?—On the promotion of a constable to the rank of sergeant he is transferred to a new division, and there his superintendent sends him to any part of the division where the vacancy may occur. It may be many miles from town, or it may be in the very centre of town. He is considered to be fit to go anywhere to pursue his new rank. That is the object.

764. And the place is left to the discretion of the superintendent?—Of his new superintendent. On promotion he enters into the third class, and receives 1*l.* 14*s.* per week. After two years he is advanced to 1*l.* 16*s.* per week, and after five years from the date of promotion to 1*l.* 18*s.* per week. The clerk sergeants receive 2*s.* per week.

765. *Chairman.*—What are they?—They perform duties under the superintendent in the divisional office.

766. Are they confined to any one grade of sergeant?—They are recommended according to fitness.

767. *Mr. Holmes.*—Have they to pass an examination?—Yes.

768. A special examination?—Yes, a special examination.

769. Qualifying them, of course?—Yes.

770. Your observations as to the third grade of sergeants applies equally to the two other grades, first and second?—There is no difference.

771. They receive additional pay and there is no other difference?—Yes, that is all. Their duties are alike.

772. How are promotions made in the different grades of sergeant?—By length of service.

773. *Chairman.*—We have now dealt with the rank of sergeant. Will you tell us how promotion is made from that rank to the rank of inspector, beginning at the third-class inspector?—When vacancies occur in rank of inspector, the Commissioner, as in the former case, directs the superintendents to send in the names of sergeants fit and capable of passing to the superior grade of inspector.

774. *Chairman.*—Must they be from the first class?—They are not required to be in any class, but they are more frequently in the second class than the first, being usually younger men. The superintendents select the fittest sergeants and send in the names to the Commissioner. It is the duty, then, of the district superintendent to see the officers upon the Returns

Mr R. Walker. 14 Sept., 1868.

submitted by the superintendents, to examine them, judge of their fitness, and approve of their being sent forward for promotion. That is the duty of the district superintendent, as well as of the officers of the men recommended. The inspectors are then tested by the same Educational Board, but in a higher grade of examination than that of sergeants, and if they are found fit, in the usual way they are put upon the list and promoted according to seniority to be third-class inspectors. They receive on promotion 2l. 5s. per week, and they are advanced on recommendation to the second class.

775. *Mr. Holms.*—Once they get into the list of third-class inspectors they generally go up as a matter of course?—Yes. They are advanced on recommendation to the second class, their pay being then 2l. 12s. 6d. per week. They are advanced upon the recommendation of their superintendent to the Commissioner, and usually after five years' service in the third class. But a considerable proportion of third-class inspectors never reach the second class.

776. Why?—Usually their advanced age prevents them. Then second-class inspectors are advanced as vacancies occur to the first class, and their pay is then 3l. 2s. 6d. per week.

777. When does that occur?—Usually, in four years.

778. *Mr. Moran.*—Then how are they promoted from the second class to the first class? Is it by seniority or selection again?—They are promoted as vacancies occur—usually, after four years.

779. From second to first?—Yes. That is one—if I may be allowed to say so—one of the drawbacks of our service. The second-class inspectors remain until vacancies occur. I may be permitted to say that I have urged upon the Commissioner the desirableness of placing the whole police force upon the footing of advance by years, excepting the single grade of third-class inspectors. And with reference to the second-class inspectors, the Commissioner has been pleased to state that, at the close of this year, he will, if funds allow, place the second-class inspectors upon the same footing as constables and sergeants, and advance them by length of service in their rank, and thus the whole force will be upon the same footing—rising by years, excepting the third-class inspectors. When a man attains the rank of second class inspector, he can reach the highest grade of the service. But promotion to the first class at the present moment is as vacancies occur, but shortly, I hope, it will be by time—after four years' service in the second.

780. *Chairman.*—There is no promotion, unless there be a vacancy, to the first class?—No.

781. *Mr. Moran.*—Now, having reached the rank of a first-class inspector, from whom is the selection made to become a chief inspector?—The rank of chief inspector is obtained by the selection of the district superintendent, and his recommendation to the Commissioner.

782. And in all cases is he selected from the first, or second, or third class of inspectors?—Always from the first.

783. I perceive in this printed Return that you have handed in that you have given the pay of the inspectors as they rise?—Yes.

784. Then how does the chief inspector rise to be a superintendent?—On the recommendation of the district superintendent to the Commissioner.

785. And from what class is he generally selected?—From the chief inspectors only.

786. And is that by seniority in the service, or by selection for his fitness by the superintendent?—By the selection for fitness by the superintendent.

787. *Chairman.*—There is only one chief inspector?—In each division.

788. *Mr. Holms.*—You told us some days ago that there are twenty divisions, but from the Return you have handed in it would appear that there are thirty-one chief inspectors?—Any of the chief inspectors over the number of twenty are confined to the chief duties within the radius of the Commissioner's office.

789. *Chairman.*—In other words, twenty are on active service and eleven are engaged in connexion with the administrative duties of the service?—Yes; eleven are engaged on administrative duties.

790. *Mr. Holms.*—Is there a superintendent for each division?—Yes.

791. And the four superintendents over and above the number of divisions are also, I suppose, engaged in administrative duties?—They are superintendents of the detective and dockyard branches. The chief superintendent, Mr. Williamson, of the detective branch, constitutes the first of those officers; and the three other officers are connected with the dockyards.

792. *Mr. Moran.*—And the remaining twenty form the superintendents of the divisions?—Yes.

793. *Mr. Holms.*—I presume the men who form the detective force are better paid in all the grades than the men of the corresponding ranks of the general force?—Quite so. They are all drawn by fitness from the other grades of the police service.

794. *Mr. Moran.*—Then from the superintendents are the two district superintendents selected also?—Fourteen years ago, when the four district superintendents were selected, I was the only officer who had been in the ranks of the police. The three other officers were Colonel Pearson, Captain Baynes, and Mr. Howard from the Indian service. I held the rank for some years of chief superintendent, and that was the principal ground for my appointment as one of the district superintendents.

795. Then do I understand you to state that the two district superintendents are not always appointed from the body of superintendents?—Yes. I am the only instance where a district superintendent has been appointed from the ranks of the police.

796. *Mr. Holms.*—Then, in fact, the appointment of district superintendents, as hitherto carried out, has not been given as promotion to the police, except in your case?—It has not. After the district superintendents whom I have mentioned were appointed—at the close of last year, and on the occasion of the retirement of Captain Harris, one of the Assistant Commissioners—one of the district superintendents, namely Colonel Pearson, was advanced to the position of Assistant Commissioner, and about the same time Captain Baynes died, leaving Mr. Howard and myself as the remaining two. The Commissioner then recommended to the Secretary of State that the whole metropolitan police district should be divided into two portions—into two districts, a first and a second—and that the two remaining district superintendents should undertake the duties that had been carried out for thirteen years by four district superintendents. That recommendation was adopted, and exists at this moment.

797. Do you think the present system of promotion works well?—I do not think it could work better for the advantage of the police service at large.

798. In your opinion, it would not be desirable to give the posts of superintendent and chief inspector to men outside the force?—Certainly not.

799. *Chairman.*—Has there ever been a civilian Commissioner in London?—No.

800. I see there is a note in the margin of the printed Return as follows: "A reserve is attached to each division, A to Y, with a weekly allowance of 4s., 2s., and 1s. 6d. respectively to inspectors, police sergeants, and police constables." What is the meaning of that?—A reserve of selected men exists in each of the twenty divisions of usually thirty or forty police, according to the divisional strength. There is an inspector placed over those men, and so many sergeants, according to the number of constables, and those officers receive the weekly sums stated in the note to which you have referred; i.e. the inspectors, 4s. the sergeants, and 1s. 6d. each constable, while upon the reserve. It is a mark of advancement for good conduct and general fitness, a selection that is thought much of in the service by the men wearing what is called the "double letters," A R, B R, C R, and so on, meaning A Reserve, B Reserve, and C Reserve.

Mr. E. Walker.

14 Sept., 1882.

601. In fact, it is a kind of step in the service?—Precisely; but not giving a man any advantage for rising to a superior grade. They must be steady, smart, sober men; and these men, therefore, forming the reserve are sent out on all special occasions, Her Majesty's drawing-rooms, levées, state balls, race meetings, and so on. All the special duties are carried out by the "reserve" men without touching the men of the rank and file.

602. *Chairman.*—I think it is important that we should now have some information respecting the detective branch of the service. Am I to understand that this Return, headed "Criminal Investigation Department," applies to the detective force?—Yes. That Return contains the particulars of their ranks and pay.

603. *Mr. Morris.*—Then am I to understand that the detective force is drawn and selected from the general body of the police?—Yes.

604. How are they selected?—At the request of the Director of Criminal Investigation to the Commissioner of Police for additional men in his branch. The Commissioner of Police requests the superintendents to select the names of sergeants or constables whom they consider best adapted for detective duties, and which have been shown by aptitude in the pursuit of criminals, or in following up investigations.

605. *Chairman.*—In fact, it is a kind of requisition to the Chief Commissioner?—It is, Sir.

606. *Mr. Morris.*—Do I understand you to say that if a sergeant of the regular force shows aptitude for the duties of the detective branch, he may be selected and at once appointed a sergeant in the detective force?—At once.

607. Filling the same position and the same grade?—Yes, and in the grade and with the pay of first, second, or third class sergeants; but he would usually enter as a third-class sergeant. He must enter, I should state, in the lowest rank, and proceed by fitness to the superior ranks or as vacancies occur. The real system is this: Officers from their aptitude in following crime become very speedily known at head-quarters. They are frequently seen at the various Criminal Courts and often receive marked approval from the Judges. The Director of Criminal Investigation is not slow in taking note of the career and worth of each officer, and when he has vacancies, appealing to the Commissioner of Police to know if Police Constable Jones or Sergeant Smith could not be transferred into his grade in the detective branch, he having a vacancy for sergeant or constable, as the case may be. And therefore the Director, who is thoroughly acquainted with all that relates to crime carried out in the divisions, has his eye always upon the fittest men to enter his branch, and it is not usually left to the superintendent, I may here remark, to select his men, but he has to send the sergeant or constable to the Director to pass for a short period on probation, and then to be drafted into the detective service.

608. In fact, as I understand you, there is a requisition furnished by the Director of Criminal Investigations for certain eligible men?—Yes. Having known the detective police from the inception of the branch, I may be permitted to say that the talent of following up crime is a peculiar one, and requires peculiar abilities, but improved by training—largely improved by training—and therefore, as to the number shown here in this Return, they are really the best criminal officers that the metropolitan police can supply.

609. May I ask you this question? Supposing the Director of the Criminal Investigation Department sees a man in the first class of sergeants whom he thinks it would be desirable to get into the detective branch of the service does that man become a first-class sergeant in the detective branch?—No. He would enter upon the lowest rate of pay of the rank that he fills in it.

610. And then he is promoted according to merit and aptitude?—No. Usually as vacancies occur, and by seniority.

611. *Mr. Holmes.*—I see the rates of pay are so arranged that no injustice would be done by the change. For instance, the pay of a first-class sergeant in the general force is 90*l.* 1*s.* 6*d.* a-year, while the pay of a third-class sergeant in the detective branch is 100*l.* a-year?—Yes. It is a small rise at first, but with great hope beyond.

612. Do any of the men of the detective branch of the service receive any peculiar allowance?—Yes, for clothing.

613. Only for clothing?—Yes, only for clothing.

614. I see you give in the Return the amounts of the allowance they get for clothing?—Yes.

615. But how do you reconcile this; the chief superintendent and inspectors receive an allowance for plain clothes of 15*l.* per annum, the sergeants 10*l.* per annum, and the constables 7*s.* a-week? Why, the last-named allowance comes to 18*l.* 4*s.* a-year. Is the larger allowance given to the constables in consideration of the fact that the higher grades receive so much better pay?—Quite so. The constables are not able to afford garments that will suit the peculiar duties they have to follow; sometimes requiring very superior clothing and changes of clothing.

616. *Chairman.*—They require different outfits, in fact?—Yes.

617. *Mr. Holmes.*—Is the same deduction made from their pay as in the ranks of the general force when they reside in the section-house?—No. They never reside in the section-house. No section house is attached to the criminal branch. It would be unwise to bring that force into close connection with the working police. You will see from the first "remark" on the printed Return that it is an important element. Four superintendents receive a good service allowance of 25*l.* per annum in addition to their pay, and all superintendents receive 11*l.* per annum for the supply of uniform. These are advantages for the highest grade of police officers.

618. Are the men of the detective branch required to wear uniform?—Never.

619. *Chairman.*—They always appear in plain clothes?—Always.

620. *Mr. Holmes.*—Is there any allowance for house rent given to the superior officers?—There is no allowance for house rent given to any rank of police.

621. Is there any allowance for a horse?—No; horses are supplied where required.

622. Only where required?—Only where required. For instance, the superintendents of the exterior districts going to the extent of the 16-mile circle, have a horse and light cart allowed them, with an attendant groom. All relating to the horse and cart are supplied by the Government.

623. They do not receive a special allowance?—They do not receive any special allowance for that; but as I have said, they are supplied with horse, cart, harness, and groom. The district superintendents, if I may be permitted to remark for myself, have each one horse and a groom supplied by the Government, and an allowance of 50*l.* per annum for expenses, as shown in the Return I have placed before you.

624. Is that allowance over and above the horse and groom?—Yes. The superintendent is at liberty to select his own groom, who accompanies him in his cart when paying the men at his various stations, and for his protection.

625. *Chairman.*—What are the regulations as to marriage in the force? Can men marry when they please?—Yes.

626. Do they require to have the consent of their superiors?—Yes; the consent of their superintendents.

627. And if a man marries without consent is he in default?—He would be reported; but I have never known an instance where anything more than an admonition has followed from marrying contrary to orders. The practice is, when a man wishes to marry, he submits a written request to the superintendent, which enables the constable to leave the section-house and live in private apartments.

[illegible] Walker.

14 Sept., 18[illegible].

828. And that is the reason for the adoption of that course?—Yes, that is the reason; and the constable, on his marriage, submits his marriage certificate to show that he is not living in adultery.

829. As a matter of fact, there is no refusal, no prohibition, or no penalty for marrying?—No, we rather prefer it.

830. *Mr. Holmes.*—You prefer it, I suppose, because a married man becomes, as it were, wedded to the force?—Yes.

831. *Mr. Morris.*—Would you now be good enough to give some account of the duties performed by the various officers of police, with the average number of hours that the constables are on duty, and any other information that you think would be useful as bearing on the present inquiry?—Constables, on joining the service are placed, for the first month, upon a short probation at the police station-houses, there to learn the system of duty that they will afterwards have to carry out. After that time they pass into the ranks, usually for duty by night. The police duty is carried out by two bodies of constables appointed for day and night duty month by month. The duty by night being the principal duty, when the largest amount of protection has to be given, commences at 9·45 P.M. and ends at 6 A.M., that is eight and a quarter hours. The day duty is performed in two reliefs. The day duty portion is divided into two bodies of men, equal in strength. The first half of the day duty commences at 5·45 A.M., and the relief ends at 10 A.M. The second portion of the day duty relief takes up the duty at 9·45 A.M. and is relieved at 2 P.M. The first section again commences at 1·45 and ends at 6; and the second portion takes up the duty at 5·45 and ends at 10 P.M., when they are relieved by the night duty men.

832. The night duty is, unlike the day, done at one stretch?—Yes, it is done in one stretch, while the day duty gives four hours right on to the day police, usually about one-third of the strength, two-thirds being upon night duty, and one-third upon day duty.

833. Do the men at night walk in couples?—In very few instances.

834. *Chairman.*—Even in the crowded parts of London?—No, they do not.

835. *Mr. Holmes.*—When a man is off duty, in the course of the day and night shifts, is he at liberty to go where he likes and do what he pleases until his next duty comes on?—He is neither at liberty to go where he likes nor to do what he pleases. He must conform to the police rule, and always be ready to be found when wanted. He must not follow any occupation. During his hours of rest he must rest to prepare for his next tour of duty. No man must leave his division without a special leave.

836. *Chairman.*—You say that no man can have any other occupation?—He is not to follow any other occupation, according to the conditions.

837. Can policemen's wives follow any occupation or small trade?—They cannot keep a shop. Objection would not be taken to a constable's wife going out to a day's work—to washing or cleaning—but no trade or occupation must be followed at the constable's house.

838. *Mr. Holmes.*—Surely a constable's wife would be allowed to work as a dressmaker?—There would not be the least objection to that. Many constables' wives work at dressmaking in their houses to help their husbands.

839. But she is not permitted to carry on any occupation beyond that?—No ostensible occupation.

840. Nothing that would bring her husband in contact with the public, or subject him to the influence of the public?—Quite so. The constable must live as a private person.

841. And the only relaxation in reference to the prohibition of an occupation is that the wife may work as a dressmaker, or may follow some similar employment?—But nothing at the constable's house that would exhibit trade.

842. But she may work at home?—The constable must not have any shop or ostensible calling in his house.

843. *Chairman.*—Will you now kindly proceed to give us details of the duty in other grades of the service?—The sergeants follow in the same grade of night duty and day duty by turns.

844. *Mr. Morris.*—Can any of the constables or sergeants, during the time they are off duty, dress in plain clothes without leave?—Yes. For many years the members of the police force were never allowed to appear in plain clothes except under the sanction of their officers; but when the present Commissioner came, the sanction was given that the police might, when off duty, appear in plain clothes where they chose.

845. *Mr. Holmes.*—And is a constable now required to have a suit of plain clothes?—Always.

846. He is required to do so?—Yes, he is required to do so; but there is no inspection of his plain clothes the same as his uniform.

847. Is there a regulation that he should have plain clothes?—It is understood that he should have plain clothes, in order that he should be able to make private inquiries.

848. *Mr. Morris.*—Now, going a step higher, what are the duties of the inspectors?—The duties of the inspectors are equally divided between the station and patrolling. Their hours are by day and by night, as with the rest of the police, but their hours are from 9 P.M. until 6 A.M. and from 9 A.M. until 9 P.M., leaving three hours in the morning to be performed by sergeants, taken, according to fitness, from the street duties.

849. In other words, he does twelve hours day duty, and he does nine hours' night duty?—Yes, Sir.

850. That is, turn about?—Month about.

851. *Chairman.*—The inspectors' duties you say are always in the station?—In the station is their principal duty. There are always two inspectors, one in and one out, and who relieve each other according to the size of the sub-division. They are out four hours if it be a large one, or three hours if it be small.

852. In other words, there is one inspector always on duty at each station, and there is another inspector always patrolling in the circuit for twenty-one hours out of the twenty-four?—Yes.

853. The three other hours being done by sergeants?—Yes.

854. *Mr. Holmes.*—How many stations are there usually in an inspector's district?—Only one station in his district. The inspectors are all confined to separate stations—in other words, to separate sub-divisions. The constable has a beat, the sergeant a section, and the inspector a sub-division; and the sub-division contains the police-station, where the inspector performs duty, and where all the police attached to that station parade. There are four inspectors attached to each large station—two upon day duty and two upon night duty—one in and one out; and in the less important stations two inspectors and two station sergeants perform the duty—one of each rank together.

855. Now would you kindly inform us as to the duties of the superintendents?—The duties of superintendents are left to their own judgment. No hours of duty are laid down for them. They are simply in charge, to be in their offices when required, and to visit their stations as they think necessary.

856. *Mr. Morris.*—Would you now deal with the subject of fines inflicted on the members of the force for breaches of discipline, and so on? Who has the authority to fine a man for either misconduct, breach of discipline or drunkenness?—The superintendents are allowed to fine the constables to the extent of two days' pay.

857. *Chairman.*—Is that the maximum amount for any offence?—Yes, for any offence.

858. *Mr. Morris.*—Can he fine the sergeants?—No.

859. His authority is confined to the constables?—Yes, in the matter of fines and stoppages.

860. Who has authority to fine the sergeants?—The district superintendent.

861. And who has authority to fine the inspectors?—The Commissioner.

862. *Mr. Holmes.*—And is it in every case limited to

two days' pay?—The district superintendent can fine to the extent of four days' pay. That is the maximum.

863. That is in the case of the sergeants or constables?—Two days' pay by the superintendents for the constables, but the district superintendents can fine four days' pay in the ranks of sergeants and constables. All fines from an inspector must be by the Commissioner, to whom the district superintendent appeals in the cases of serious charges against the inspectors.

864. You have there told us that the superintendent can fine the constables two days' pay, but that the district superintendent can fine men of that rank four days' pay. In what cases does the district superintendent intervene?—The superintendent, when he thinks fit, appeals to his district superintendent in cases of serious charges against the men upon his morning report.

865. And he then takes the case in hand?—Yes.

866. Do these fines militate against the man's pensions hereafter—are they taken into account, and is there a certain rate of money deducted from the pension after a man has quitted the service in respect of the fines which were levied when he was in the service?—Misconduct is always taken into account, but no deduction is made on account of fines.

867. The infliction and levying of the fine, then, is the measure of the punishment, and there it ends?—No; the man whose misconduct has been frequent and grave during his service would, when retired, suffer in pension.

868. *Chairman.*—May I ask you in what case of misconduct does the district superintendent consider it fit to appeal to the Commissioner?—When the charge is very serious against a constable, and one affecting his honesty, his truthfulness, or his general fitness for the service, the district superintendent then appeals to the Commissioner, and gives a recommendation, or a statement of his opinion with reference to the charge, and possibly with reference to the constable's unfitness for continuing in the service. The offence is then sent before the Commissioner at once, to be dealt with by him, and that settlement is final—for either retaining in the service, dismissal, a higher fine upon the constable than the district superintendent may have inflicted, or, it may be, some other punishment.

869. Are sergeants ever reduced, as a punishment, again to the position of constable?—Only by the Commissioner.

870. But such punishment is inflicted by the Commissioner?—Yes; by the Commissioner only.

871. *Mr Holmes.*—Would a man be reduced in rank for drunkenness?—He would, as a sergeant.

872. *Chairman.*—He would be reduced?—Yes.

873. *Mr Holmes.*—He would be fined and reduced?—Yes, and reduced, it might be, to a lower rank than a first-class constable, if his conduct has been such as to merit severe punishment.

874. *Chairman.*—But whether the fine be high or low, or be the degradation great or small, it ends the punishment, and it is not brought into account as affecting the man's pension?—A man receives a pension in the rank he ends his police career in, and his conduct must have been bad if his pension is affected.

875. *Mr. Holmes.*—Do the men undergo any drill while they are off duty—do the constables, sergeants, and inspectors undergo drill?—The police, before they enter the ranks or become police at all, are for fourteen days under drill and instruction.

876. But when they attain the ranks of constables, sergeants, and inspectors, do they undergo drill?—The police are drilled for five months in the year. They are brought out one day every week for one hour's drill.

877. Does that apply to all the members of the force, or to only a certain specified number of them?—All the members of the police force off duty go out upon occasions of drill.

878. Of all grades?—Yes, and in uniform.

879. *Mr Harrel.*—And is that hour that they are being drilled taken from the number of hours they would be otherwise doing duty?—They are allowed this hour from their next tour of night duty.

880. *Chairman.*—They are drilled for five months one day in the week, and one hour on each day?—Yes, weather permitting. When there is no drill, then, of course, the hour is not given, but if there be they are allowed an hour from their next tour of duty.

Mr. R. Walker.

14 Sept., 1882.

881. Now, there is a matter in reference to which, having a good deal of experience of the police courts here, I am anxious to have some information from you. May I ask you to what hour a man who has been on night duty, and who may have to attend the police court with a charge—to what hour may he be detained in the police court?—A man having one or more charges may be able to return in two or three hours at most, when they are allowed "time off" for such attendance.

882. How many charges would you consider an average at a police court?—Twenty charges, I should think, would be the maximum at Bow Street. That is not taking into account the summonses, remanded cases, and the like.

883. I am only speaking of charges in which the night men would be engaged?—Yes. Nothing has been said as yet of reduction in class in consequence of misconduct, a very common occurrence with us. A district superintendent can reduce in class, but a superintendent cannot. The Commissioner can reduce two classes, I can only reduce one for misconduct; and my reduction must be for a fixed period—three, six, or twelve months. The Commissioner might reduce for two years, or beyond that time.

884. The Commissioner has not the power to degrade beyond the two years?—I won't say he has not the power, but the Commissioner usually degrades for a long period, after which the man rests by rotation to his former grade from which he has been removed.

885. Would he go to the bottom of his former grade, or take his former position?—He would go to the bottom of his former grade. The Commissioner reviews such reductions every time, and, it may be, extends them. I mean that the Commissioner assumes that power.

886. In fact, has an appellate jurisdiction over yours?—Yes, to lengthen my period, or, in fact, to change my decision altogether.

887. *Mr. Harrel.*—Or to vary your decision?—Yes. Or the officer may appeal from my decision to the Commissioner, who may confirm it or otherwise. If the man prefers to be seen by the Commissioner, he is at liberty to do so.

888. The Commissioner assumes the settlement, and his decision is final?—Yes, it is final. There is no appeal from the Commissioner.

889. *Mr. Harrel.*—What inducements in the way of amusement or occupation have the police—without going into minute particulars—to occupy their time, and to give them legitimate recreation, so as to induce them to avoid as much as possible the public-house in London—attached to the barracks, or in any other way?—A police library was established many years ago, and is added to occasionally, for the amusement of both the married and single police. Books are issued weekly, on pay-day, to the officers. That is one source, but there are a number of sources of amusement open to the police. In the police stations there is a reading-room and a billiard-room—if the police station be a large one—supplied at the cost of the police funds, for the amusement of both single and married men who choose to go there.

890. *Mr. Holmes.*—And at whose expense is the library maintained?—The library is maintained at 1d. per month from each man.

891. Is that contribution compulsory?—Yes, that is compulsory.

892. And the reading room at the barracks, at whose expense is that maintained?—That is maintained at the expense of the Commissioner, I mean as far as the tables and chairs are concerned, but each constable provides his own stationery.

893. How do you mean that it is maintained at the expense of the Commissioner?—I mean at the public

Mr. F. Walker.

10 Sept., 1892.

cost. The billiard-rooms, bagatelle-boards, and all the sundry matters are supplied at the public cost.

894. *Mr. Morris.*—And are there canteens attached to any of the barracks?—No canteens.

895. And from what source do the men get their drink who live in barracks?—Usually by a neighbouring publican sending in one of his waiters at meal-times with ale or porter and the men can get it as they choose to pay for it there and then.

896. Can they supply themselves with liquor between meal times?—They can, but not in the section-houses. No drinking is allowed in any of what we call the public rooms—the library, or reading and billiard-rooms.

897. *Mr. Holmes.*—Is it the case that all the stations or section-houses are furnished with libraries, reading-rooms, and billiard-rooms?—Only where there are ten constables resident. We give a reading-room for ten, and a billiard-room for twenty men where the space admits. The Commissioner will supply a billiard table for twenty men.

898. But in every section-house they are supplied with a library for the men, and a reading-room and billiard-room are provided for twenty men if the space permits?—Yes. And the library room is used for the instruction of the men, where the schoolmaster comes to teach.

899. *Mr. Morris.*—May I ask you, while on this subject, is it one of the rules of the force that the police in London should not enter a public-house, even in plain clothes?—When off duty, there is no order to the contrary.

900. *Mr. Holmes.*—Then do I understand you to say, Mr. Walker, that a police constable when off duty, and in plain clothes or uniform, is at liberty to go into a public-house?—Yes; but not in uniform. He has no liberty to go there except for necessary refreshment. There is no police law against his going into a public-house in uniform, or, in fact, anywhere.

901. *Mr. Morris.*—But I presume that, whether in uniform or plain clothes, if he is found in a state of intoxication he is punished in some shape for it?—He is brought immediately to the nearest police station by his comrades or a sergeant who may see him, and kept there until sober, and punished on the following day.

902. In fact, he is treated as an ordinary drunkard?—Yes; except that, instead of being sent before a higher tribunal, he is dealt with by his own superiors.

903. *Mr. Holmes.*—Do you think that the advantages provided for a man in the section-house tend to make the men content with their life there, and to wean them from frequenting the public-house?—To make them better men, superior men, sufficient men in their condition of life—certainly.

904. Do I understand you to say that the libraries, reading-rooms, and billiard-tables are supplied at the cost of the public with the exception of the deduction of 1d. per month from the pay of the men for the purposes of the library?—Yes, for the purchase of library books. There are no men allowed to play for money in the billiard-room, and no drink is allowed there, as I have already said.

905. *Mr. Morris.*—I should like to know from you on account of your long experience in the force, and without entering into particulars or statistics, do you think that in the police force in London drunkenness amongst the men is on the increase or on the decrease?—It is on the decrease, certainly on the decrease.

906. *Mr. Holmes.*—Do you think that the duties imposed upon the police under the Licensing Acts are compatible with their being allowed to enter public-houses, for instance, would not publicans endeavour to bribe the police not to enforce the law too strictly as regards the closing of public-houses, by supplying them with drink gratis?—There are two points in the question you have put to me; the matter of going into a public-house, and the probability of bribing the police to look over any infringement of the law by the publican. To the first I should say, the police of London have always been able to enter a public-house when off duty, not only in uniform, but in plain clothes. If it were known that a constable was in the habit of frequenting a public-house when off duty, his superintendent would admonish him in the first place, and if that failed to effect the necessary object, the superintendent would remove him from one to another division. But where a constable shows that drink has taken a hold upon him that constable is then brought before the district superintendent, and, it may be, the Commissioner, to be dealt with under a heavier scale. As to the second part of the question, the cases are few that come before the magistrates where an attempt is made by the publican to bribe the police. Whenever a constable is found inside a public-house on duty with his armlet on, a summons is immediately taken out against the publican, and the constable is put into the witness box.

907. You would not, then, be in favour of restricting the police from entering a public-house?—No, certainly not.

908. And I dare say you think it would be very difficult to enforce such a rule?—It would be impossible.

909. And that it is not judicious to make a rule that is sure to be frequently broken?—Certainly not. I may add that the London metropolitan police do not, as a body, frequent public-houses, and a constable in uniform is seldom seen at a public-house. If it was found that a constable had received drink from a publican without payment, that constable would be reported and heavily fined. The constable is not allowed, when on duty, to take drink at the public-house, except by the authority of his inspector or sergeant, standing by. He can be allowed to take refreshment at the door, his inspector or sergeant giving the permission, and standing by. He may ask a glass of ale, and he says, "Please, sergeant, can I have a glass of ale?" The sergeant replies, "Yes, certainly." At the public-house the constable may knock, have his glass of ale, drink it outside the door, and pass on. But for that same glass of ale drunk outside the door without leave the constable would be brought upon the report sheet and fined, probably a day's pay; and if a constable enters a public-house on duty a fine of not less than 5s. is inflicted, or two days' pay.

910. That is without permission?—Yes. No policeman on duty can enter a public-house, except in the discharge of his duty; and to take drink at once places the constable on a defaulter, and is not tolerated.

[The Committee then adjourned until next day.]

FOURTH DAY.—15TH SEPTEMBER, 1882.

Present:

MR. J. W. O'DONNELL, MR. GEORGE MORRIS, D.L., and MR. H. W. A. HOLMES.

Examination of MR. ROBERT WALKER, *District Superintendent, London Metropolitan Police, resumed.*

Mr. R. Walker. — 15 Sept., 1882.

911. CHAIRMAN.—Are there stoppages from the men for illness?—Yes; 1s. per day when sick.

912. Whether in the course of nature or by his own imprudence?—If by his own imprudence, such as a report for venereal disease, he is struck off pay altogether until well; in cases of common sickness, however, of constables, 1s. per day is deducted from their pay, and in return they receive medical aid.

913. *Mr. Holmes.*—That deduction is supposed, I imagine, merely to pay the expense of medical attendance and medicine?—Yes, of medical attendance and medicine, which he receives free at his own house, or in the section-house, as the case may be, the latter being in the case of a single man.

914. What is the usual course as regards pensions in reference to men permanently disabled, having incurred injuries in the discharge of their duties?—In cases where a constable is permanently injured and under fifteen years' service, that is, not entitled to pension, he is brought before a Board consisting of one of the Assistant Commissioners, one District Superintendent, and the superintendent of the division to which the constable is attached. That Board has the constable before them, and the result of that Board is to recommend a certain pension for twelve months, when the constable is to be examined at the end of a year from the date at which he receives the pension as to his fitness to resume duty, and in every case at the expiration of one year he is to be re-examined again. That rule has reference to constables under fifteen years' service. The result is that he receives his pension on the recommendation of a Board of superior officers.

915. What may be the scale of pension; is it in reference to his period of service?—Yes; and with reference principally to how far he may be able to support himself or to add to his support when he leaves the police.

916. Then a man permanently disabled gets a pension to enable him to live?—Yes.

917. CHAIRMAN.—I wish to ask you a question in reference to recommendations; in the case of a magistrate or Judge recommending a party for special merit or for a reward, what does the reward consist of in London; is it a money payment, or is it a mark that adds to his promotion?—It may be both; it may be a money payment direct from the Commissioner or an entry upon what we term the "Defaulter Sheet" of a commendation as it is called—a commendation to be kept in view in the future.

918. As regards his promotion?—Yes, as regards his advancement.

919. My experience as a magistrate was heretofore that the man recommended for special services for special merit received a pecuniary gratuity or a pecuniary reward; but I understand that latterly such rewards have been discontinued, and that the special service goes to the future promotion of the man?—That is not the case in London. We give money always, and such rewards act as an inducement to bring a man forward for promotion.

920. In one case I recommended the present inspector of carriages for a reward for special services, and he got 10l.?—Quite so; that is our plan.

921. *Mr. Holmes.*—It has been asserted by Constabulary witnesses examined before the other Committee (the Royal Irish Constabulary Inquiry Committee), of which I am a member, that the police in London are in the habit of receiving "tips" from the public for services rendered by them—such as, for instance, calling persons in the morning—and that the amount which a policeman receives from this source comes to a considerable sum at the end of the year; is this the case?—It is not the case; no money is allowed to be taken by a constable for any service for special duty, unless it passes through the hands of his superiors, but in no case is it allowed or granted for calling persons up in the morning.

922. And is that considered part of a policeman's duty?—Yes, quite so; to serve the inhabitants to the utmost of our power. Neither in money nor in kind do the police receive what might be termed "bribes."

923. Am I quite correct in assuming that the Government supply the station-houses with all the fuel that is requisite, not only for the guard-room, but for kitchen purposes?—Quite so.

924. And that the men are at no expense under the head of fuel?—At no expense for fuel; but it may happen in the smaller section-houses, at distant parts where the allowance for fire is too small, that the police have to purchase coal to supplement the allowance.

925. What is the allowance during the winter months?—If you will permit me to say it, the coals for the single men are kept separate from those required for the station and reading-room fires, at all stations where there is cellarage to admit of its being done; coals are not supplied for the use of married and single men living out of the section-houses. A money allowance in lieu of coals is substituted, namely, to married men, 4d. a-week; to single men, 3½d. per week.

926. But I am dealing now with the station-house fuel?—The following are the regulated allowances for police living in the section-houses: 40 lbs. weekly to each married man during the year, and 40 lbs. weekly to each single man during winter, and 20 lbs. weekly to each single man during summer. For office, station, and reading-room fires, 280 lbs. weekly in winter, and for the charge, reserve, and inspector's room at each inspector's station, 140 lbs., or half, weekly in summer. For the charge-room at each sergeant's station (a less important one), 200 lbs. weekly in winter and 100 lbs. weekly in summer, and for the superintendent's office—as much.

927. Don't you think that the allowance of 4d. a-week to married men who do not live in the section-house is a very small one, and, in fact, quite inadequate?—Quite inadequate.

928. Do the men complain of it?—They do not.

929. How came it to be fixed at so small a sum as 4d.?—It was upon the estimated cost of coals provided for the police generally.

930. But surely an allowance of 4d. a-week only amounts to 17s. 4d. a-year, which, at the price of coal in London, would not be sufficient to purchase a ton?—No, being the present cost of coals as paid to the contractor.

931. I do not understand you?—That is to say, a contractor supplies all the coals for the police service

Mr. E. Walker.

22 Sept., 1888.

at the lowest market rate; and it is expected that the police will be able to furnish themselves with coals at a similar rate in their lodgings as that paid to the contractor.

932. Yes, but a family would have more than a ton of coal in the year?—It is totally inadequate, I know.

933. *Chairman.*—At the present price of coals in London—say that you would get them at from 18s. to 19s. a ton—what would you say would be a fair average allowance?—1s. per week all the year round for one fire.

934. *Mr. Morris.*—Can you tell me whether the police force as a rule—taking the whole body, particularly the sergeants and constables, and the lower grades—whether they are at present and have been in a contented or discontented state in London?—No discontentment exists in the London metropolitan police on the subject of pay, allowances, or general government. The only question at this moment that causes irritation throughout the London police is on the subject of pensions.

935. And they would like, I suppose, to have the scale of pensions improved?—In order to obtain from the sergeants and constables freedom in the expression of opinion with regard to what they would wish as to pensions, the Commissioner has allowed them to meet in the several section-houses, where delegates came from various divisions, and to talk over the question and come to an understanding as to what their wishes are as regards pension, and these the Commissioner promises to submit to the Secretary of State.

936. *Mr. Holmes.*—Then in point of fact the question of pensions is practically an open one in London at the present moment?—Yes, perfectly open.

937. *Chairman.*—You say that the men discussed the question at the several stations, and at meetings at which delegates from the different divisions were present?—Yes, and by permission of the Commissioner himself.

938-947. *Mr. Holmes.*—Now that you have touched upon the subject of pensions, will you be good enough to tell us what is the present scale of pensions for the London police?—On fifteen years' service completed a pension of fifteen-fiftieths of the pay may be granted, and for each year of service completed up to twenty years an additional fiftieth of the pay; from twenty to twenty-five years completed, two-fiftieths for each year, and from twenty-five years one-fiftieth for each year to twenty-eight years complete, when the pension will be two-thirds of the pay.

948. Are the men satisfied with this scale?—They are not, and they strongly wish that the original scale of pensions may be gone back to—those which were granted previous to 1862.

949. And what was the original scale of pensions?—I refer to the scale of pensions granted to police who joined the service prior to 1862—of pensions for life, after fifteen years' service, fifteen-thirtieths of salary.

950. *Mr. Morris.*—That is one-half?—Yes. After twenty years' service, sixteen-thirtieths; after twenty-one years' service, seventeen-thirtieths; after twenty-two years' service, eighteen-thirtieths; after twenty-three years' service, nineteen-thirtieths; and after twenty-four years' service, twenty-thirtieths—two-thirds of the pay.

951. *Mr. Holmes.*—Was that the maximum?—Yes, that was the maximum; and no pension to exceed two-thirds of full pay except for injury on duty.

952. Under what Act was that?—Under the original Act of 1840.

953. *Mr. Morris.*—Might I ask you upon this particular point—if a man served twenty-four years under the old scale was he entitled to retire as by right, or had he to serve still further on in case he was in good health?—There is no entitling to retire in any grade of the police known under 60 years of age.

954. And am I to understand also that the police force in London, although they are now seeking to improve their present scale of pensions, do not ask any improvements as to retiring at a younger age than 60 as a right?—Their hope is that they may be allowed to retire after twenty years' service without the surgeon's medical certificate.

955. *Chairman.*—As a right?—Yes.

956. And now no man under 60 can retire without a medical certificate?—Yes.

957. And without the concurrence of his superiors?—Yes.

958. *Mr. Holmes.*—Do you not think that, unless a policeman has attained the higher ranks of the force, at 60 years of age he is hardly likely to be fit for his work at that age?—The instances are few where constables, sergeants, or inspectors ever reach the age of 60 in the police.

959. Do I understand you to say that they break down before that period?—I do not think at this moment that any officer of the three lower grades has reached the age of 60 years; 55 years or 50 are the times for giving way.

960. Then in your opinion would 50 years be a better limit for retirement than 60 years?—Yes, I think so. That is my personal opinion.

961. And that it would be reasonable to allow a man to retire either after thirty years' service or having attained the age of 50 years?—Yes, certainly, 60 is out of the question.

962. You have now given us the existing scale of pensions, and also the scale that was in force before 1862?—Quite so.

963. I presume that the men who entered the force since 1862 are somewhat discontented at finding that they are not in as good a position as the men who entered before 1862?—They are discontented.

964. *Mr. Morris.*—On that particular point?—That is the only point upon which discontent exists.

965. Do the men who joined the force since 1862 wish that the scale of pensions that applied before 1862 should be applied to them?—They would be glad to obtain the scale laid down in one of the papers that I have placed before you—the amended pension scale under the Act of 1840.

966. Would they be content with that scale?—Yes, but they would be still better satisfied with that which existed from the 13th January, 1840—of fifteen years' and twenty years' service.

967. Will you kindly state what that scale is?—Yes. Half-pay for fifteen years' service, two-thirds for twenty years' service—upon a medical certificate of unfitness in both cases.

968. And full pay—when?—There is no full pay on retirement known to the London metropolitan police, and I hope there never will be.

969. Then at no period of the existence of the London metropolitan police force could a man retire upon full pay?—Only upon injury. Full pay would only be granted in a case of disablement by injury while in the service.

970. *Chairman.*—And that is an exceptional case?—Yes, quite an exceptional case.

971. *Mr. Morris.*—Do you consider, Mr. Walker, from your long experience in the force, that it would be advisable, in the reverse, to grant, after any number of years' service, full pay on retirement?—I do not think it would be advisable to grant it.

972. As a retiring pension?—I do not.

973. You don't consider that it would be for the advantage of the force?—Certainly not.

974. Would you very shortly state your reasons for coming to that conclusion?—My principal reason is that it would induce men to remain in the service longer than they are fit for the duties.

975. Then you consider that it would be a greater inducement for men to retire, getting two-thirds of their pay after a certain number of years as a maximum pension, in order to always have some young men coming into the force and promotion going on?—Certainly.

976. You consider that that would be for the best advantage of the police force?—I do.

977. Do you consider that a man after thirty years' service should not receive more than two-thirds of his pay as pension?—I consider that two-thirds ought to be the maximum of pension in any case. I should be very glad, as the chief officer in the service, to see the members of the police force able to retire by right on completing twenty-four years' service, irrespective of age.

978. And then obtain two-thirds of their pay?—Yes, and then obtain two-thirds of their pay.

979. *Mr. Holmes*.—Is it not the case that there is a deduction of 2½ per cent. made from the pay of all the ranks to provide for a pension fund?—2½ per cent. and 2 per cent., according to rank.

980. (*Chairman*.—Still?)—Yes, still; 2½ per cent. from the pay of superintendents and first and second-class inspectors, and 2 per cent. from the pay of third-class inspectors and sergeants and constables.

981. *Mr. Holmes*.—And that deduction is intended to provide a pension fund?—It goes towards a pension fund, but never provides for such a fund.

982. To what extent does it go?—Oh, to a very small extent, the rest being supplemented from the Consolidated Fund.

983. Would you consider it advisable to abolish this deduction?—No, I would not.

984. You would not abolish the payment of that small percentage towards the Pension Fund?—No, I would not. It is the strongest incentive to keep men in the police, the weekly deduction of a small item from their pay to induce them to look forward to pension.

985. In other words, if they were dismissed from the force they would forfeit, I understand, that small reduction entirely?—It is, in a case such as you mention, entirely forfeited.

986. *Mr. Morris*.—With reference to the Return as to pensions that you have handed in, so I understand it—but I would like to have this perfectly clear—the Return is the amended pension scale under the Act of 1840?—Yes.

987. It was amended, I understand, by the Home Secretary, on the recommendation of Sir Richard Mayne?—Yes, and remained in force until 1862.

988. And all men who joined the force prior to 1862 were under the original Act?—Yes.

989. How came it to be amended by Sir Richard Mayne?—He recommended a change in the granting of pensions, and he amended the scale in consequence of so many men leaving the force when they reached twenty years' service. At that period they became pensioners, and were of no further use to the service.

990. *Mr. Holmes*.—Is it not the case that the men of the force in London now are extremely dissatisfied with the present scale of pensions, and that they are doing all they can to have it amended?—With the present scale of pensions the men are extremely dissatisfied—that is, with the existing scale.

991. And they have been permitted by the Chief Commissioner to meet with a view to discussing their grievances?—Yes, in the police-stations.

992. *Mr. Morris*.—There is one matter that I should like much to have some information upon. In almost the very first part of your evidence you stated that the police force amounted, in round numbers, to 10,500 men. I think 10,494 was the number you gave?—Yes, 10,494.

993. Have you any way of forming an estimate, or have you with you any information by which you could give us a Return—going back, I should like to have it for ten years—of the annual number of voluntary resignations in the force each year, and the number each year of dismissals from the force? Is there any way by which you could furnish such a Return as that?—The Return in the Commissioner's Report shows the number of men who have resigned, and the assigned causes of resignation, during the years 1877, 1878, 1879, 1880, and 1881—for five years.

994. Can you hand in that Return?—I can.

995. *Mr. Holmes*.—What page of the Commissioner's Report is it, might I ask?—Page 13, Return No. 6, of the Commissioner's last Report. I can send you from my office the number of resignations and dismissals for ten years readily.

996. If you could, it would be of service to us, as I think we have the like Return for ten years of the Dublin force, and we would wish to have the same information as to your force?—Quite so.

997. From what class of the community is the police force for the most part recruited; is the London police force recruited from farmers, labourers, or tradesmen?—May I speak personally?

998. Certainly.—On Tuesday morning last I inspected sixty-five young men volunteering for the metropolitan police. They were natives of England, Ireland, and Scotland. The youngest was an Irish lad 18 years of age; the oldest, 32 years of age, had just left the army.

999. What classes did they belong to?—The labouring classes; in every case a labourer. "What description of labour?" was my invariable question to every man as he came up. There was every description that you could mention. Indoor labourer as hired servant, outdoor labourer upon the farm, or gardener, or other occupation, but "labourer" universally.

1000. And that applies generally to the whole force, and not merely to your experience of Tuesday last?—Every week in the year the same question is put by the District Superintendent to the young men summoned for examination.

1001. Am I to understand that a very large proportion of the London metropolitan police is recruited from the labouring classes?—Yes, and from the country.

1002. But from the labouring classes?—From the labouring classes almost entirely; but that was not the case in the earlier years of the metropolitan police. Sons of gentlemen entered the service, men of good breeding, good education, and in a superior grade of society, and particularly from Ireland, volunteered for the metropolitan police; that was for the first fifteen years of the police.

1003. And the recruits are usually drawn from the country, and not from London?—There are very few drawn from the metropolis.

1004. And I suppose that the pay they receive in the force is very much larger than the wages they were in the habit of receiving?—Very much larger.

1005. At what period, may I ask, were the present rates of pay fixed?—Within the last seven years.

1006. Was it by Act of Parliament that they were then fixed?—No, by the Home Secretary.

1007. Do police pensioners easily find employment after they have left the force?—It is a curious fact that pensioners are seldom heard of except when they come quarterly for their pensions. They fall back into private life, either to live upon their pensions or to add to them in a manner that does not come under the notice of the police; they do not appeal to their superior officers for help to get bread except in rare cases.

1008. And do you not think that a mercantile house would be glad to have the services of a retired policeman as a hall-porter or in some position of trust and responsibility?—Yes; pensioners readily find employment when, owing to their appearance and manner, they can be brought into the position of hall-porters.

1009. Do the married men of the force complain that they do not receive a lodging allowance?—Before the present scale of pay was granted, the married police were very desirous of receiving a lodging allowance. The present scale of pay, however, appears to have met that claim in a great measure. The grounds of refusal would be the difficulty of meeting a claim for additional pay from the single men, they probably thinking themselves aggrieved by a married officer receiving an additional

Mr. R. Walker.

15 Sept., 1875.

rule to themselves; and the Commissioner, with all willingness to meet such a claim on the part of the married men, felt that it would raise another claim that it would be very difficult to set aside; and, further, that by giving a lodging allowance to the married police it would induce many more marriages than would be advisable for the good of the service.

1010. But, then, I understood you to say, at an earlier part of your evidence, that you rather wished the men to marry, because it wedded them to the force?—After ten years' service we prefer men marrying, for this reason, that men when they reach that period of service hardly get on comfortably with the young men who are drafted into our section-houses.

1011. Do you think that this would be expedient—to allow men to marry when they like, but not to give them any lodging allowance until after ten years in the force? Would not that induce men to put off marrying until they saved a little money, and induce habits of prudence and so forth, and at the same time keep men in the force?—Personally, I object to a lodging allowance for married men. I think it is better to give pay for the whole service, and leave the married man to fight his own battle upon the rate that he enters and obtains by good conduct. A badly-conducted married constable would still receive the allowance, and that would be contrary to the interests of the service. You can see that quite readily.

1012. And there, too, the rates of pay are fixed, not with a view to enabling a man to marry, but with a view to enabling a man to live comfortably, and it is his own look-out if he marries, and he must count the cost of such a step?—The rates of pay are fixed to enable them to live comfortably and to retain them in the service.

1013. Do many men remain constables all their lives?—Many men remain constables to the end of their career.

1014. What percentage of the class?—It is impossible to tell.

1015. And you think that, as a rule, the men in all grades can, with common prudence, live comfortably within their pay?—Yes, they can live comfortably; and if there be periods of special trouble—loss of wife, loss of children, or other calamity—the invariable rule is to appeal to their brother officers for help, which is willingly and readily given.

1016. Now, tell me, is it within your experience that men in the classes of constables save money while single?—When they reach the second class, but not before, they begin to save; they begin to take advantage of the Post Office Savings Bank, and it is a daily occurrence for the Post Office letter to come to one or other of the single men in the sections.

1017. That is to say, they begin to save when their weekly wages amount to 27s. per week?—They begin to save then; they cannot spend it, unless they are spendthrifts.

1018. But with the legitimate expenditure of a policeman, and making himself happy and comfortable, he can save money when he becomes a second-class constable?—Yes; a constable in the section-house has one meal per diem with his fellows, that is his dinner. He provides himself with the materials for his breakfast, for his tea, for his supper—these being retained in his own locker—bread, butter, bacon, tea, coffee, and so on. But his dinner is provided for him out of the mess, the general mess of the house, regulated by a mess-caterer, each of the senior officers taking it in turn, month about, who regulate the supplies, are responsible for their payment, for the mess-books, &c., are inspected by the inspector, and are tested by the superintendent, and laid before me every time I visit each section-house. The fact is that the 7s. or 8s. per week for the dinner is all that comes out of the constable's pocket, excepting the materials for his breakfast, tea, and supper.

1019. And what does it come to on an average per week for breakfast, tea, and supper?—6s., or it may be 6s.

1020. Then the total cost for food would amount to from 13s. to 14s. per week?—14s. per week at the outside.

1021. Then the constable who lives in the section-house has nothing further to pay under the head of board and lodging, except 1s. a-week which is deducted from his pay for rent?—Quite so, and those who cater are paid out of the men's pockets.

1022. Does the 1s. a-week for rent and station-house purposes include the caterer?—Not "station-house purposes." The deduction has nothing to do with station-house purposes; the deduction is made by the Government for his lodging, for his bed, and for his fuel. I mean that it goes into police funds, the 1s. per week that he pays, and for this he is provided with lodging, bed, firing, and the cooking of his food.

1023. Is he also provided with a servant? Does that deduction also go to pay the wages of a servant for cleaning the station-house?—The servant who makes his bed and cleans his room is paid for by the Government. The mess money includes the cost of cooking, service, and food.

1024. By service you mean the catering?—Yes.

1025. You have just told us that the cost of living in the section-house comes to about 13s. to 14s. a-week. Can you tell us what the average cost of lodgings is for single men living out of section-houses?—A single man living, as he can, out of the section-house pays 3s. 6d. per week.

1026. Then the single man who is not accommodated in the section-house is in a worse position than the man who is accommodated there?—He has to pay for everything.

1027. Is the 1s. a week stopped from a single man not living in the section-house?—No; he is in a much worse position than his fellow who lives in the section-house, and he consequently prays week after week that there may be a vacancy in the section-house, and that he may be taken in.

1028. Because then he would have to pay only 1s. per week?—Yes, he would have to pay only 1s. there, and he would have many comforts.

1029. The difference between 1s. and 3s. 6d. is very important to him?—Yes; it comes upon a young man very hard, and is apt to induce him to leave the police quickly, as many young men do before the end of three months, because they are sent to live at a coffee-house, or as best they can, which, to a single young man from the country, is anything but comfortable.

1030. I ask your opinion in reference to this; do you think, as a matter of your own personal opinion, that a single man who cannot be accommodated in the section-house ought to receive a fair lodging allowance?—It would raise a claim from the married police very difficult to be evaded; and, besides that, if a young single man got a lodging allowance he would sooner stay out of the section-house.

1031. No; because, so long as he remained single, he would get the lodging allowance. It is his own look-out if he marries?—Quite so.

1032. Do you now think that a single man ought to get a lodging allowance?—No; because then he would object to come into the section-house.

1033. I thought you said he prayed for the opportunity to go in?—Yes, so he does now, but if you granted him a lodging allowance he would not. By giving him an allowance it would be an inducement for him to stop out of the section-house, as allowing him greater freedom, and relieving him from calls for special action at fires and the like.

1034. Are the lodgings of the married and single men inspected by the police?—The lodgings of the married police are frequently inspected by the inspector, and the lodgings of the single police are inspected daily by the inspector, weekly by the superintendent, and quarterly by the District Superintendents, throughout the service. I would wish to be permitted to say, in concluding my evidence before this Committee, that I only hope that my visit to the metropolis will be of some service to my brother officers of the Dublin metropolitan police, whom I consider the finest body of police in Great Britain. Personally, having been in every great city of England and Scotland, and upon great State occasions, where I have seen the best officers of police called out, I can say that I have seen no such body of men anywhere as I have met with in the streets of Dublin. Mr. E. Walker. 16 Sept., 1882.

Inspector T. Kavanagh, A Division, Dublin Metropolitan Police, examined.

1035. *Chairman.*—Kindly give us your name?—Thomas Kavanagh.

1036. How long have you been in the force?—Just twenty-five years.

1037. How long are you an inspector?—About four years.

1038. What division are you attached to?—I belong to a sub-division of the A Division.

1039. Is it the same division you have been in since your appointment?—It is.

1040. What are your duties as an inspector?—I may preface my evidence by saying that I am deputed to represent the inspectors of the A Division before the Committee. My duties are to take charges—all the charges that come into the station against people, to supervise them, and to have a knowledge of the law bearing on each case, to see that the proper witnesses are in attendance before the magistrate, and that the case is properly conducted.

1041. *Mr. Holmes.*—Do you attend at the police-court to see that the case is properly conducted?—If possible, it is our business to attend at the police-court to see that the case is properly conducted.

1042. *Chairman.*—What is your station?—Chancery Lane.

1043. What are your hours of attendance there?—My hours are from 10 in the morning until 8 in the evening, but I am often there until 11 o'clock at night. That is the nominal tour of duty; that is, when I am on day duty. Then every second week I am on night duty, and then I go on at 8 o'clock at night, and, generally, I go off at 3 o'clock in the morning, and every alternate morning I go off at 10 o'clock. I go on at 8 o'clock one night, and go off at 3; and I go on at 8 o'clock another night, and go off at 10 o'clock the next morning.

1044. *Mr. Holmes.*—Are your duties entirely confined to the station-house, or have you outside duties?—Yes, I go out at a quarter-past 8 every second night that I am on night duty, and I patrol the sub-division, visit the constables and sergeants, and see that they are quite correct.

1045. What is the extent of your sub-division?—The extent of my sub-division is about 8 square miles.

1046. What main streets are comprised in it?—The only main streets are Christchurch Place, Castle Street, Bride Street, Heytesbury Street, and the South Circular Road. We have a number of low streets in the division that require constant supervision.

1047. Have you anything to add to your account of the duties?—We have to supervise all summons complaints when brought in by the constables, to see that they are proper to go before the magistrate, and to initial them.

1048. *Mr. Morris.*—Have you power to fine a constable?—Oh, no, Sir. We have to see after—I believe in my division there are something like 100 public-houses, twenty spirit grocers and beer dealers, and we have quite a number of unlicensed houses to supervise. We have to see that proper summonses are taken out against them under the proper Act of Parliament that bears on the case.

1049. *Mr. Holmes.*—What do you mean by unlicensed houses?—What we call "night" houses.

1050. Are these illicit houses?—Yes. We have to have warrants out for them.

1051. And is it specially your duty, as an inspector, to see to the public-houses?—It is; and I have to make very careful inquiries about the character of each applicant for a licence. I have to attend before the magistrate in every case to give the character of the party applying for the licence. If there is a summons heard against him, I have to attend when the case is heard, and give the character of the house. Inspector T. Kavanagh. 16 Sept., 82.

1052. Do you appear before the Recorder at the Licensing Sessions?—Yes; and to make out a proper list of the names of persons seeking transfers and new licences.

1053. And it is practically upon the information you give that the authorities act?—Practically so, and each case involves about three special reports, rendering necessary very delicate inquiries.

1054. *Mr. Morris.*—Are you a first, second, or third-class inspector?—I am a third-class inspector.

1055. How many classes of inspectors are there?—Three.

1056. *Mr. Holmes.*—What is your pay as a third-class inspector?—My pay is 137*l.*

1057. Is that the fixed rate, or does it commence at that?—It commences at that, with 20*l.* for a house and 5*l.* for uniform.

1058. When do you say your pay is increased?—When you become a second-class inspector.

1059. Will you now kindly bring before us the propositions which you are anxious to advance on your own behalf, and on behalf of the inspectors whom you are deputed to represent—introducing them in, as you regard them, the order of their importance?—I am authorised to ask an increase of pay.

1060. Before you proceed to state the amount of the increase you now look for, will you tell us what your pay was before the last increase was given to the force—what was your pay as a third-class inspector?—I was not an inspector at that time, but I am acquainted with the pay at that time.

1061. You are aware, I suppose, that there was a large increase in the pay after 1873?—I am aware of that.

1062. *Chairman.*—What increase of pay do you suggest, and why do you suggest it?—I am asked to seek an increase of pay for third-class inspectors. We would ask an increase of 13*l.* a-year, which would make the salary 150*l.*

1063. *Mr. Holmes.*—On what ground do you ask for that increase?—Well, Sir, we can be at no other business whatever, and when we retire we must live upon our pension, as we will not get employment in this country.

1064. You want the pay increased in order that when you retire the pension may be proportionately increased?—Yes, that; and I may add, the present pay we have is scarcely sufficient to keep ourselves and our families respectable, because we must be respectable, we must turn out respectably; we cannot associate with low persons, and we must live in respectable localities.

1065. Do you know what a third-class inspector gets in London?—I think it is something about 117*l.* 5*s.* 6*d.* a-year.

1067. And on what ground do you ask to be put in a still better position than a third-class inspector in London, remembering that you are now 137*l.* a-year

Inspector T. [illegible]

15 Sept., 1882.

better?—Well, the inspectors in London generally rise to a higher position than we can attain to, their prospects are better, and they are generally drafted to other forces in the Colonies, and so forth.

1068. *Mr. Morris.*—Now, are you aware of that fact yourself, or is it one of those chimerical ideas that are afloat in Ireland, about the green hills far away, and so on? Are you aware of a single case such as you mention?—I could not name cases of the kind.

1069. *Mr. Holmes.*—In order to compare your prospects with the men in London, will you tell me the rates of pay given to first and second-class inspectors in Dublin?—The rate of pay of a first-class inspector is 162*l.*, with the same allowances as a third-class inspector gets.

1070. And what has a second-class inspector?—150*l.*

1071. And have not they an allowance too?—Yes, the same allowance.

1072. Are you aware that the inspectors in London have no allowances in addition to their pay?—I am not aware of it. I did not make myself up on that point.

1073. Counting the allowance for lodging, your pay amounts to 157*l.* a-year?—It does.

1074. On looking over a Return which was handed in by Mr. Walker, District Superintendent of the London metropolitan police, I find that 157*l.* a-year is nearly as much as the amount of pay given to 118 of the first-class inspectors in London. The pay given to 118 first-class inspectors in London amounts to 162*l.* 11*s.* Now, with that knowledge, are you still prepared to ask for so large an addition to your pay as you have just mentioned?—Well, I would be glad to get it. The officers of the A Division agreed to ask this.

1075. I am sure that the inspectors of the Dublin metropolitan police force are as respectable as they undoubtedly are a most intelligent body of men, and, that being so, do you think, if they were fully aware of the rates of pay in London, and that they were in a better position, as it would turn out, than the corresponding ranks there—do you think they would still press for an improvement in their position as regards pay—confining yourself to that head for the present?—Well, I must say that I do not think we would base our claims at all upon the London inspectors.

1076. Then upon what grounds do you seek it?—In consequence of the rise of pay lately given to the officers of the Royal Irish Constabulary.

1077. Now, with what class in the Royal Irish Constabulary do you inspectors compare yourselves?—With the sub-inspectors. Our duties are much more severe than theirs.

1078. How many men have you authority over in your position of inspector?—I have about eighty-two.

1079. *Chairman.*—In your sub-division?—Yes.

1080. *Mr. Holmes.*—And what is the extent of your authority?—I can report them for offences. I have no power to fine them, but I can recommend them to my superiors as being worthy of promotion for good conduct and efficiency in the discharge of their duties.

1081. *Mr. Morris.*—You have general supervision over the men under your charge?—Yes.

1082. Upon what grounds do you ask an increase of pay?—Well, the population of my district exceeds that of any five sub-inspectors' districts.

1083. Have you taken the trouble to make a calculation, that you speak so accurately?—I did not make a calculation, nor have I one here with me.

1084. Is there any other reason?—And between 2,000 and 3,000 charges pass through my hands—charges taken for all classes. My hours of duty are longer than that of the Constabulary.

1085. How can you say that?—We have to be on duty night and day; they never do any night duty.

1086. How do you know that?—I know it from members of the force. They have to go on patrol—

1087-1088. You are now comparing yourselves with the sub-inspectors?—I do not want to compare myself with them in status.

1089. Supposing you were retiring, I presume you would retire under the old pension?—I would, Sir.

1090. *Chairman.*—Now having done with pay, will you please proceed with the next head? Have you anything to complain of as to retiring under the old pension system?—I wish to state that we would seek an increase of house-rent to 40*l.*; we have 20*l.* at present.

1091. *Mr. Morris.*—Besides the 15*l.* already mentioned?—Yes.

1092. Would you seek any increase in the uniform allowance?—Yes, Sir. Our present allowance for uniform is 8*l.*; we want it increased to 15*l.*

1093. *Mr. Holmes.*—In point of fact, you ask to receive under the head of pay and allowances 235*l.* a-year?—Yes.

1094. *Mr. Morris.*—Are you aware that the superintendents in London—whose position is a grade higher than yours—are only allowed 11*l.* a-year for uniform?—I am not; but I know this much, that it costs me more than 13*l.* for uniform.

1095. *Chairman.*—Well now, if you have dealt with the question of pay and allowances sufficiently, would you take up the next subject—that of the compensation you seek for extra duty for the last three years?—We seek compensation for the last three years' extra duty.

1096. *Mr. Holmes.*—How much do you ask?—Three months' pay.

1097. The same as was given to the Royal Irish Constabulary?—Yes.

1098. *Mr. Morris.*—Do you consider that that would be a fair allowance to be made for the extra work?—I think it would.

1099. Is it your opinion that very much extra work was thrown upon yourself, and upon the men under and above you, in consequence of the agitation in connexion with the Land League, and the meetings, processions, and everything of that sort?—Yes.

1100. Within the last three years?—Yes.

1101. Were the men out of pocket by reason of these extra duties in consequence of the state of the country?—I think they were.

1102. *Mr. Holmes.*—How?—Well, they would be kept out so long that they could not get home to their dinners, and they might have to get refreshments.

1103. Are you aware that perhaps the chief reason that this sum of money was granted to the Constabulary was in order to recoup them for the serious pecuniary losses they had to incur during that period?—Yes.

1104. Don't you think, therefore, that in order to entitle yourself to a similar allowance you would have to show, in the first instance, that you were seriously out of pocket?—I cannot say that the men were seriously out of pocket.

1105. You are of course aware that in many parts of the country, in the most disturbed districts, the Constabulary had a very great deal of extra duty of a very painful character to perform?—They had, of course.

1106. That they were exposed to a deal of rough treatment to which the police in Dublin, except on one or two occasions, were not exposed?—Well, we are exposed to more rough treatment than any other force in the United Kingdom.

1107. As a general rule?—Yes.

1108. *Chairman.*—Do you think that assaults and other injuries inflicted on the police, were greater in number during the last three years than previously?—Yes.

1109. And were your duties more onerous—more severe?—Yes, a great deal more severe. Why, in consequence of these meetings we would have to call men out before their regular hour of duty would commence, and keep them out, and the result of that would often be that a man was out the whole day and portion of the night.

1110. *Mr. Holmes.*—Were those duties required of the force generally?—They were. The reason of that was, and is, that we are not able to meet a strain when it comes upon us. We must depend upon the men of our division, and therefore we must put increased duty on them.

1111. Within the last three years was any addition made to the strength of the police to meet this extra work?—None whatever.

1112. Do you think that the men seriously took to heart the fact that they were left out in the cold in reference to the gratuity for extra duty?—They did.

1113. And then you think that it had a very serious effect upon their minds?—Yes.

1114. *Chairman.*—And still affects them?—Yes.

1115. It contributed, in your opinion, to the present discontent?—Yes, Sir.

1116. That it was the main fact in bringing about the present discontent?—Yes.

1117. *Mr. Holmes.*—You are clearly of that opinion?—I am clearly of that opinion.

1118. *Chairman.*—What is the next topic you wish to deal with?—Our next complaint is in respect to officers dying in the service before signing for their gratuity.

1119. *Mr. Holmes.*—You must explain that, as we are quite ignorant of what you mean?—The gratuity is that you are allowed a month's pay for each year's service if you are struck off.

1120. Do you mean that if a man is obliged through ill-health to leave the force before he has completed fifteen years' service he then gets a gratuity equal to one month's pay for each year of service?—Yes, that is so.

1121. Would you now explain what happens in the event of the man not signing for that gratuity?—If a man dies after his gratuity paper is made out, without having signed that paper, the gratuity is forfeited.

1122. *Mr. Morris.*—In other words, you would wish that the widow or orphans of the man who died should obtain that gratuity which he would have got if he had lived to complete the customary formalities?—Yes, quite so. We also wish that if a married officer is killed or dies in the service through injuries received in the discharge of his duties, his wife should be entitled to a pension as long as she remains single, and also his children.

1123. *Chairman.*—Equal, I suppose, to what he would have got had he retired through ill-health?—I would leave that to the Government. I would not dictate the amount or proportion. And we would wish to have that man's children provided for up to the age of 16 years.

1124. *Mr. Morris.*—By some allowance?—Yes, Sir; we feel that very much, because we are men who never have any means to fall back on.

1125. *Mr. Holmes.*—If a married officer was killed upon duty, would any gratuity be given to his family?—Well, they may get a gratuity.

1126. *Mr. Morris.*—But you would wish to have that a rule of the force?—Yes, I should wish to have that the rule.

1127. And you consider that such a rule would be for the benefit of the police force and also for the benefit of the public service?—I do.

1128. *Chairman.*—What other view have you to place before us?—I wish now to deal with the question of pensions, and with regard to the rate of pensions under which men are who joined the force, like myself, before 1867. I wish to say that we desire an increment of one-thirtieth of pay and house-allowance for each year's service, in addition to periodical periods of fifteen, twenty, and twenty-five years, and up to thirty years' service, when a man shall be allowed to retire on the full pay of his rank. This applies to the men under the 1867 Act, of which there are now 337 remaining in the force.

1129. *Mr. Holmes.*—Are you not aware that the men who joined the force before 1867 are under an exceptionally favourable scale of pensions?—We do not complain of the pensions, but we complain of this: if, for instance, I serve twenty-nine years and eleven months, I am only pensioned for twenty-five years.

1130. You would get three-fourths of your pay?—Yes.

1131. Are you aware that no other branch of the Civil Service can get more than two-thirds of their pay?—I am.

1132. And that in the general body of the Civil Service a man must have served forty years, and be over 60 years of age, to entitle him to that two-thirds?—Yes, but, as I said before, when we leave the service we must live on the pension we got; we cannot increase it by any means. The fact of being a policeman will entirely preclude one from getting any other employment.

1133. Is it not the case that after twenty years' service a man who had joined the force before 1867 can, if incapacitated, get two-thirds of his pay?—Yes.

1134. Is not two-thirds of their pay after twenty years' service a very liberal rate of pension, bearing in mind what I have just said, that an ordinary member of the Civil Service can only get two-thirds after forty years' service, and after he has attained the age of 60 years?—I know that; but, as I said before, we cannot supplement our pensions by employment. We cannot get it, and if I retired to-morrow I should have to retire on a pension for twenty years' service.

1135. Then in point of fact you are not satisfied with the extremely and exceptionally favourable scale of pensions under which you are entitled to retire?—I don't think you should say I am not satisfied.

1136. Well, you wish to improve what is already so good?—Yes.

1137. Are you aware—and if not I may mention it to you as a fact—that the highest rate of pension under which a member of the London metropolitan police force can retire is only two-thirds of his pay?—I am.

1138. Are you aware that the members of the London police force never could retire upon full pay, or even upon three-fourths of their pay; that the most they could retire upon at any time since the force was formed was two-thirds of their pay?—I am not.

1139. Now that I have made you aware of that fact, do you still ask to have your exceptionally favourable scale of pensions further improved?—I do, and for this reason; that when a police officer or constable retires in London, there is a situation open for him, and he can supplement his pension by employment. It is a passport to good employment to be a member of the police force in London. It is quite the reverse in the case of a member of the Dublin metropolitan police.

1140. Is it not the case that a pensioner of the police in Dublin finds it very easy to get employment? Are there not many cases of pensioners being employed as hall-porters and messengers in houses of business, and obtaining such like employment?—That had been the case up to about three years ago, but many of them had to leave since then.

1141. Why; are you stating this from your own knowledge?—Yes.

1142. That many pensioners who had been employed were obliged to leave their employment?—Yes.

1143. Why?—For no cause in life other than the fact that they were ex-policemen.

1144. Then do you state as a fact within your own knowledge that pensioners from the police force in Dublin have within the last three years been obliged to leave their employment simply because they were policemen at one time, and because of the hostility felt towards the police?—I am not aware of that, that is, I could not state a case except one, but that is over three years ago. But there are others who could state cases.

Inspector E. Kavanagh.

15 Sept., 1882.

Inspector T. Kavanagh. — 15 Sept., 1882.

1145. But you cannot make that statement of your own knowledge?—No.

1146. Do you seriously believe that policemen now would find it difficult, if not impossible, to get employment because they belonged to the police force?—That is the fact.

1147. And you earnestly believe that?—Yes; I know myself that it is very difficult for a policeman to get a house to live in.

1148. At present in Dublin?—Yes, at present in Dublin.

1149. But you don't think that the present feelings of the public towards the police are likely to continue?—I hope not, but I'm afraid they will.

1150. Prior to the last three years, surely, good relations existed between the people and the police?—Well, I could not say good relations—I would not say good relations. I would like to add as another reason why I ask for an increase of pay that the cost of living is higher in Dublin than in London. House-rent is much dearer; you would pay more for the same class of house in Dublin than in London, and besides that a superintendent can let portion of his house in London, a privilege that we are debarred from in Dublin.

1151. Are you not allowed to let part of your house?—We could not let an inch.

1152. Are you forbidden to do it?—Yes; we take a big house, and we must keep it whether we are able to furnish it or not.

1153. You cannot sublet any portion of it?—No, we cannot sublet any portion of it.

1154. As regards that last statement of yours, that superintendents of police in London are at liberty to let portions of their houses, we have no knowledge of that, but we shall ascertain from Mr. Walker how the facts are in reference to that?—I am led to believe that they can, whereas we cannot. I would also like to add, before concluding my evidence, and to state on behalf of myself and of the men who joined the force before 1867, that we think we should be allowed to retire after thirty years' service without a medical certificate.

1155. *Chairman*.—Have you anything further to lay before us?—No, Sir.

[The Committee then adjourned until next day.]

FIFTH DAY.—16TH SEPTEMBER, 1882.

Present:

MR. J. W. O'DONNELL, MR. GEORGE MORRIS, D.L., and MR. R. W. A. HOLMES.

District Superintendent ROBERT WALKER, London Metropolitan Police, recalled.

Mr R. Walker. — 16 Sept., 1882.

1156. *Chairman*.—I wish to ask you what are the average fines in the London metropolitan police for ordinary and trivial breaches of discipline, not involving serious criminality, insubordination, or serious breaches of discipline?—The usual course is for the superintendent to reprimand and admonish.

1157. In the first instance?—Yes, in the first instance. If a repetition of the neglect follows he will fine 1s., seldom more.

1158. Then the first offence is only a shilling?—The first offence is always a reprimand and caution, the second is a small fine, usually to the extent of 1s.

1159. *Mr. Holmes*.—Is that the case even if the first offence be drunkenness?—The first offence of drunkenness is always met by a fine of 5s.

1160. *Chairman*.—Without any reprimand?—With a reprimand. The first offence of drunkenness is always fined 5s., or less.

1161. In ordinary breaches of discipline of a trivial nature the course usually is to reprimand, and if there is a second offence—a similar offence, a mere trifling breach of discipline, the first penalty is 1s.?—Yes.

1162. But in a case of drunkenness, for the first offence the punishment or penalty is 5s. fine and reprimand?—Yes, and a reprimand always accompanies the fine. The second offence of drunkenness usually entails the loss of two days' pay.

1163. In all grades?—We, as a rule, never find drunkenness in any other grade than that of constable. Drunkenness in the case of a sergeant would, in all probability, bring reduction of rank, unless his conduct had been for many years good. If a man is reported for drunkenness he is sent before the district superintendent—usually sent before the district superintendent, the superintendent having no power to punish a first drunken report without making remission. The district superintendent deals with the constable according to his general character. A fine of three days' pay always follows a second or third drunken report, along with a reprimand and strong caution as to the future. If the conduct of the constable has not been generally good the district superintendent may fine him four days' pay, the full extent of his power to punish.

1164.—*Mr. Holmes*.—Then the limit of the punishment that the district superintendent can impose is a fine of four days' pay?—Yes, four days' pay. In case the constable has suffered by [illegible] in the face or the like so as to unfit him for duty, he is suspended until reported by the divisional surgeon fit to resume duty, and then he comes up upon the original report.

1165. Does his pay go on during that time?—Suspension of course stops the pay during suspension, and he comes up to be dealt with upon the original report. A step beyond that still. A long-continued course of misconduct, the constable being in either the second or first grades of his rank, is followed by reduction of class, imposed by the district superintendent, but which must be approved by the Commissioner afterwards.

1166. You mean habitual drunkenness?—Yes, habitual drunkenness, and lately the Commissioner has directed that in no case shall a constable be reduced without the district superintendent or the Assistant Commissioner fixing the period to be reduced.

1167. In all cases that has to be done?—Yes, from six months to two years.

1168. *Chairman.*—Are those fines recorded as against the man's pension?—They are recorded against the man, and they may affect his pension.

1169. As a rule, do they?—As a rule, they do not.

1170. *Mr. Morris.*—It depends upon the class of offences, I suppose, for which the fine is inflicted, whether it militates against his pension or not; if it is a very serious offence it does, I suppose?—Yes. All reports are recorded.

1171. Supposing a man oversleeps himself and is not in time at the police-court; or, supposing a man forgets any particular documents, these are all previous of discipline for breaches of which he is pulled up, or may be fined, but in no case of those cases would there be any difference in the man's pension, I suppose?—If he fails to attend at the proper time for duty, the inspector on duty cautions first, and there is no record. If he repeats that twice or three times he appears before the superintendent, who reprimands and cautions again; but if the neglect goes on the superintendent then fines, and that is recorded against him upon his defaulter's sheet, and goes to the end of his police career. Every entry upon the morning report—the daily morning report—affecting a constable, and proved against him, is entered upon the defaulter's sheet, and is carried along with him to the end of his career if he be thirty years in the service.

1172. And does that affect his pension?—If the constable has not conducted himself well during the whole course of his police career, if he has been guilty of drunkenness, or, it might be, insubordination or serious misconduct, the Commissioner then exercise the right to reduce or recommend the reduction of the rate of the pension he would be otherwise entitled to according to his class or rank to the Secretary of State.

1173. That just comes, in terms, to this—that for serious offences he may be, and is, reduced; but for trivial offences, he is not?—Quite so; he is not reduced for trivial offences.

1174. For instance, one case of drunkenness in a man's career, or even two or three cases of drunkenness in a man's career, would not, in the end, bring about a reduction of his pension?—It would not.

1175. *Chairman.*—It must be for serious offences more than once committed?—Yes.

1176. *Mr. Holmes.*—But repeated cases of drunkenness would have that effect?—Yes. I may be permitted to say that our service is long-suffering. Within a week from this date a constable was brought before me for the tenth time for being drunk over a service of eighteen years, and still holding a first-class place.

1177. He was not reduced?—He had been reduced, but the periods of sobriety brought him up again from the third-rate again to the second, and from the second to the first, and he came before me on Monday last with the tenth report of drunkenness to answer for. He was, as I have said, a first-class constable. I fined the constable to the full extent of my power, and I took away his class for six months. For three years previously, or thereabouts, his conduct had been good and without report. I considered the punishment sufficient, making allowance for long service and for periods of sobriety, and the report of his officer that he was a good and efficient constable in the streets. When the report came before the Assistant Commissioner in the afternoon, as is customary, he sent for the district superintendent, and I appeared before him. "I don't feel satisfied with your decision in that case of drunkenness. I consider that the constable should be put back for a much longer period than six months. What do you say?" I gave my reasons for my judgment. "I think," said the Commissioner, "that he should be put back for two years, and I shall alter your decision to that," taking the pen up and altering my decision of six months to two years. That appeared in the Police Orders of that same evening, and, I have no doubt, very much to the constable's annoyance; the district superintendent having told him the period he was put back, and finding afterwards that it had been extended to four times the length.

1178. Now tell me, when this man retires, assuming that he conducts himself well during the rest of his career in the police, when he retires is it probable that that those cases of drunkenness will militate against his pension?—In this particular case, if the constable has been sober for two or three years, and has brought no disgrace upon himself, I do not believe that the Commissioner would lower the pension if he has remained to his discharge.

1179. If a man be reduced for any period, long or short, may he, by his subsequent good conduct, reinstate himself in his original grade?—Certainly. I do not think, from my point of view and past experience, that the Assistant Commissioner acted with due consideration towards this man; but the constable had no appeal.

1180. *Chairman.*—Can any person under your position in the force fine a man for those ordinary and trivial offences, or for such a case as you have just mentioned?—No; the superintendent can stop in the case of the first drunken report with caution, and the second he must refer to me. An inspector of police has no power to reprimand, much less fine, a man.

1181. In the case of a married man (with a wife and family) having been killed in the discharge of his duty, is there any provision made for his widow and children?—Yes, according to the Police Orders. For the children a separate sum, for the wife so much, and each child under 15 years of age a separate sum, so long as the wife remains a widow.

1182. Then you say in such a case as I put there is provision made for the widow and the children, as long as the woman remains a widow?—Yes, a very fair provision; not sufficient to maintain the widow without work, but, nevertheless, a sum probably equal to 20*l.* a-year for life, in a case in which the husband has lost his life in the discharge of his duty.

1183. *Mr. Morris.*—One of the inspectors who gave his evidence before us yesterday complained that when a man who has not completed fifteen years' service dies before the necessary forms had been gone through to enable him to receive the gratuity of one month's pay for each year of service, that in that event the gratuity is not paid, and the men of the Dublin force seem to think that when a man dies before the necessary forms have been completed that the gratuity which he would have received had the forms been properly complied with should be paid to his family. What is the case in the London police force with regard to a matter of this kind?—I certainly do not remember any case of a man dying between the recommendation and the return from the Home Office of the gratuity, but I have known instances where the widow has signed for such gratuity, but at what time the husband died I am not in a position to say, but I have seen the widow's signature for the gratuity that ought to have been received by the dead husband on its coming back from the Home Office. Say that a constable has been recommended for the gratuity by the surgeon-in-chief, who alone recommends, the papers would come to the Commissioner, they would be written out, sent over to the Home Office in due form, and be returned by the Home Office, and were the husband to die in the interval, the widow would receive the amount and sign for it.

1184. But supposing the husband dies before the recommendation has been sent forward, would the widow get the gratuity?—No. If the husband dies before the recommendation of the chief surgeon, the widow would not certainly receive any gratuity except the gratuity that every widow receives from the comrades, who subscribe 1*d.* each upon the death of each of their comrades, and which amounts

Mr. R. Walker.

16 Sept., 1882.

Mr. R. Walker. 16 Sept., 1882.

to 30*l*., and that is received by each widow; that 30*l*. has nothing, however, to do with any Government arrangement.

1185. Don't you think where a constable has conducted himself thoroughly well during his period in the force, and dies under fifteen years' service, before the recommendation has been forwarded to the Home Secretary—don't you think, in a case of that kind, it would be only just to give the gratuity which he would have been entitled to had the necessary forms been complied with to his widow, the non-compliance not having been through any fault of the deceased man's. What is your opinion as to the equity of such a case?—Clearly the equity would be to give the widow what the husband is entitled to.

1186. *Mr. Holmes.*—As we have the good fortune to have you again before us, I would like to ask you a few general questions. Having regard to the evidence given by the constabulary witnesses before the other Committee on the question of fuel and light and the cost of living, I wish to be quite sure that I understand the evidence which you have given on this question. Is it, then, the case that the London section-houses are provided with fuel and light both for public and private purposes, and entirely at the public cost?—Yes.

1187. Speaking generally, is the fuel which is supplied at the public cost sufficient to meet the requirements of the men?—Yes, in all the large stations, and only insufficient in small stations in the exterior districts.

1188. *Chairman.*—In out-of-the-way stations where a small number of men are located?—Yes.

1189. *Mr. Holmes.*—What rooms in the station-houses are supplied with fires?—The charge-room, the library, the reserve-room, and the kitchens (two), as a rule.

1190. Are the bed-rooms in which the men are sleeping supplied with fires in the winter months?—No.

1191. You told us that the cost of messing comes to about 3*s*. a-week; what expenses exactly are covered by this sum?—All that is purchased for the daily dinner, the cost of food and the cooking of the food, and the cleaning of the kitchens.

1192. The cost of the food, the payment of the cook, and the cleaning of the kitchen?—Yes.

1193. You also told us that the cost of the men's breakfasts and suppers comes to about 5*s*. or 6*s*. a-week; can you tell us whether the men take meat at those meals?—As a rule, the men take meat, but the men of the different countries have peculiarities in regard to the eating of meat. The Irishman does not, the Scotchman seldom, the Englishman always.

1194. But you think that the allowance of 5*s*. or 6*s*. a-week for these two meals of breakfast and supper is sufficient to provide them with meat, if they like it?—Yes, ample. The Irishman is the more saving of the three. The dinner, I may add, is so ample that many of the men cannot eat the quantity supplied to them, and they put a portion away into their lockers for supper.

1195. Reverting again to the subject of promotion, you have told us that a constable of the third-class rises to the second after three years?—Yes.

1196. And from the second to the first after five years?—Yes.

1197. Now, am I to understand that a constable who conducts himself properly is quite certain to rise from each class after the periods which you have named, or, in other words, that there are always a sufficient number of vacancies to enable promotion after such periods?—The rising by class has nothing to do with vacancies. Promotion is certain after those periods, there being no fixed number of constables in the class.

1198. Is there a fixed number of sergeants?—Yes, fixed by the Secretary of State.

1199. Then a man cannot be promoted from the rank of constable to that of sergeant until there is a vacancy?—Not until there is a vacancy in the case of a sergeant. The promotion above the rank of first-class constable depends upon the number of vacancies, and not upon the length of service. The number of each rank throughout the service is fixed—constables, sergeants, and inspectors—by the Secretary of State. The number of constables in each class is not fixed.

1200. Is the number in each class of sergeants fixed?—No; they pass to the grade according to time. Third-class rises to second, and second to first by time and conduct.

1201. Inspector Kavanagh told us yesterday that the inspectors of the Dublin force were not at liberty to let any portion of their houses to lodgers. Is that the case in London?—There is no such restriction in our service.

1202. *Chairman.*—They may let lodgings if they please?—They do, as a matter of fact.

1202*a*. *Mr. Holmes.*—Inspector Kavanagh, in giving an account of the duties of the inspectors in Dublin, told us that he had to take all the charges that came into the station against people, to supervise them and to have a knowledge of the law bearing on each case, to see that the proper witnesses are in attendance before the magistrate, and that the case is properly conducted. He has also, every second night that he is on duty, to patrol the sub-division, visit the constables and sergeants, and see that they are quite correct. His hours of duty are as follows:—day tour, 10 A.M. to 8 P.M., 10 hours; first night tour, 8 P.M. to 3 A.M., 7 hours; second night tour, 8 P.M. to 10 A.M., 14 hours; making an average tour of 10⅓ hours. Will you tell us how the duties in London compare?—The general duties are similar in London, certainly not less, and the hours of duty are nearly alike; the tours are: day tour, 9 A.M. to 9 P.M., 12 hours; night tour, 9 P.M. to 6 A.M., 9 hours; the average tour being 10½ hours.

1202*b*. Inspector Kavanagh also told us that the Dublin inspectors ought to be in a better position than the London ones on the ground that the latter could rise to a higher position, that their prospects are better, and that they get appointments in the Colonies; is this the case?—Certainly not; there are only some twenty-five superior places that several hundred of the past rank can aspire to, and as to the Colonies, I never knew an instance.

1202*c*. The same witness stated that the pension scale for the Dublin force should be more favourable than the London scale on the ground that when a police officer retires in London there is a situation open for him; it is a passport to good employment to be a member of the police force in London; is this so?—It is not so. In London a pensioner has to fight his way like other men, and, being "worn out," the labour capacity of our men is not great, consequently they can only obtain light employment, which means light wages.

Inspector William Thorpe, A Division, Dublin Metropolitan Police, examined.

(Inspector Peter Cox, B Division, Dublin Metropolitan Police, being also present.)

Inspector Wm. Thorpe. 16 Sept., 1882.

1203. *Chairman.*—What is your name?—William Thorpe.

1204. What is your rank in the Dublin metropolitan police?—I am a second-class inspector.

1205. Of what division?—The A Division.

1206. How long have you been in the service?—Nearly twenty-five years. I was examined before the Commission that sat in 1872. I was then a sergeant

n were you promoted to your present
ar years and a-half ago.
n do you wish to bring under our
is stating the various duties, duration
uding to your view, the order of their
I wish to bring under your notice the
e pay which we receive at present. I
year, and, in addition to that, I am
-year for rent, but I pay 30l. I used to
f was unable to continue it. I have
iform; that is all that I am allowed.
Holmes.—That is 178l. altogether?—
consequence of the rules of the force
pation and pensions, I am obliged, in
of my family, to pay all insurances,
s my salary considerably. There is no
e for us at present. Suppose I were to
doctor seeing me, my family could not
r. And, then, suppose I was to die in
f my family were to get what I should
, and not the Government, why, I need
pay so much insurance.
you aware that your pay as a second-
r, exclusive of allowances, is more than
second-class inspector in London?—I
London and Ireland differ materially in
For instance, suppose I was an in-
gdom, and left on pension, I would not
fficulty in getting employment for my
ve, I cannot; it is almost impossible.
t of passive coldness shown towards us
re that does not at all exist in London,
t of Ireland, or anywhere in the world.
wn relations are cold to us.
man.—Has that feeling been increased
s, indeed—very much.
to what period?—Within the last three
—since the commencement of the Land
tion. Of course, it must be borne in
are all men recruited from the rural

Holmes.—Are you aware that, between
d pay, the amount you receive from the
s about 5l. more than a second-class
London, who gets 164l. 14s. a-year, but
no allowance whatsoever?—Of course,
correct; but there are a great many
nection with that. For instance, it is
men having more suitable intelligence
o the rank of inspector while quite a
London.
we are dealing with second-class in-
man works for a long time in the
olitan police before he attains the rank

re talking about second-class inspectors.
ing your position with officers of the
London. I am asking you to consider
if a second-class inspector in London is
less than what you are getting, and
try and address an argument to us to
that your pay should be increased?—
t insufficient. I may state to you here
ran a shilling in debt until I rose to the
ector, and then it was caused by the
y uniform and the changing to lodgings
e position. I had to incur debt that I
wiped out yet, although I am four and
n inspector.
do not you think it would be very diffi-
se your pay, having regard to the fact
f the same class in London are actually
s?—Well, it may be easier to live in
in Ireland. Of course, I am not living
d I cannot say.
Morris.—You said just now that you
r your life. I suppose you are aware
ident person in every rank of life, who
mage and has a family, does the same
daily.
e is certainly nothing exceptional in

that?—There is this difference between men in London and ourselves, that there a man may have the members of his family employed, or engaged in a lucrative business, and that we cannot have. We are debarred by the rules of the service from engaging in any trade or following any calling while in the police.

1219. Surely, if you have a son that has attained sufficient age and can take employment, you do not mean to say that the rules of the force prevent him from earning a livelihood independently of you?—No, Sir; but I mean to say that there is a difficulty found, and a very great difficulty found, in Dublin in getting employment for that son, in consequence of his being the son of a policeman.

1220. But surely, if he was a capable fellow, and if you gave him a good education, would he not have the same chance of getting on in life in Dublin as anywhere else?—He would—in London.

1221. Are you not aware that all the Government offices—Customs, Excise, every Government Office, I believe, except the Foreign Office—is now open to public competition, and the tinker's son is on a level with the duke's son if he is able to pass the examination?—That is so, no doubt; but it is the "if" that makes all the difference.

1222. Now, I would like to have an explanation from you as to that. You being an intelligent man, I would like to have an explanation from you of what you mean when you say that your son, through being the son of a policeman, is debarred from taking his place among the rank and file, when every class in the community, from the tinker to the duke, can compete for Government situations?—It requires means to educate a person for a Government situation. Where is the education to be got? I send some of my children to the public school in Marlborough Street, and I have to pay 10s. a quarter for each. Where four or five children are going to school, and this has to be paid for, and he has to educate them up to 17 or 18 years of age—until the time they would come to get a Government situation—it represents a lot of money.

1223. *Mr. Holmes.*—A second-class inspector in London would be in a worse position than you are in Dublin, as he would have a lower salary than you, and education is fully as dear?—I know nothing about the London police; I am only speaking of my own force.

1224. And you must remember that the examinations for these different Departments are actually held in Dublin?—I am aware of that; but what I want to put forward is this: how many men who are candidates, prepared at considerable expense, go up for the examination, fail, and are thrown out altogether. It is a risky thing.

1225. *Mr. Morris.*—Then, of course, that risk must attend everybody in the community as well as policemen or their sons?—Now, for instance, in the constabulary there is a rule made there for the officers' sons; they get a privilege in connection with the service, for they are admitted at special examinations, and they pass into the service as officers.

1226. *Chairman.*—Do you know that of your own knowledge?—I do, Sir. I know there is an examination of officers' sons held, and that they have special privileges as to age.

1227. *Mr. Holmes.*—Yes, but they have to pass a competitive examination?—They have, of course, Sir.

1228. *Chairman.*—Have you stated all that you wish to put before us on the question of pay?—I do not know that there is anything more that I have to say on that point. The only thing is, that I want if I can to get an addition to my pay, that is the fair meaning of it.

1229. *Mr. Holmes.*—Can you state what was the pay of a second-class inspector prior to 1873?—115l. a-year.

1230. Then there was an addition made to the pay of a second-class inspector at that time of 25l. a-year?—Yes, Sir.

Inspector Wm. Thorp.

16 Sept., 1882.

1831. Were the allowances increased under that Act?—Oh, yes.

1832. What was the allowance for house rent?—There was no fixed amount then for house rent for inspectors. It was according to the number in barracks and out of barracks. By that Commission the amount of allowance for rent was fixed for inspectors, and there was also an allowance granted at that time for clothing. There was no allowance for clothing up to that.

1833. You had to provide your own uniform up to 1872?—Yes; but at that time I was a sergeant.

1834. The change made in 1872 resulted in this. You got 35*l.* a-year as an addition to your pay, a fixed allowance for house rent of 20*l.*, and you got 8*l.* for uniform; whereas before that the allowance for house rent was uncertain, and you had no allowance for uniform?—That is the fact, Sir.

1835. Don't you think that the change made in 1872 was very considerably to your advantage?—Yes; certainly.

1836. And I am sure you were quite satisfied at that time?—I was not an inspector.

1837. But the inspectors generally were satisfied?—They appeared very glad to get it.

1838. Do you think the cost of living has increased since 1872?—I could hardly give an opinion upon that. The only thing I know is, that the cost of living is very great, and that I pay 10*d.* and 11*d.* a pound for meat.

1839. *Mr. Morris.*—I think you said you paid at one time 45*l.* a-year for your house?—Yes.

1840. Are you restricted by the rules of the force from making anything by letting lodgings?—Oh, certainly.

1841. *Chairman.* Are you not allowed to let any portion of your house in lodgings?—Certainly not.

1842. It would be contrary to rule?—Yes, contrary to rule. Another thing I may mention is, that when I held the house at 45*l.* a-year I had to enter into an agreement for three years, or otherwise I would not get it for less than 50*l.* We are prohibited by the rules of the force from sub-letting any portion of our houses.

1843. *Mr. Holmes.*—Do you think that the men would consider it a boon to be allowed to sub-let?—Some of them would. They would take respectable houses if they could let portions to respectable tenants. It would be a considerable boon; I have no doubt about that, I know it.

1844. They would be able to get a better class of houses?—Yes.

1845. Are you obliged to reside in your division?—Yes, Sir; that is the rule of the service, that each man shall reside within his division.

1846. As regards the allowance given to the Royal Irish Constabulary for extra duty, I presume you agree with Inspector Kavanagh, who gave evidence here, and also Superintendent Ward, that the men of the Dublin metropolitan police feel it to be a grievance that they got no allowance of a similar kind?—Certainly.

1847. *Chairman.* You agree with the views they put forward on this subject?—Yes, I do. We did a lot of extra duty, and we got nothing for it.

1848. And the result was much discontent at not being included in the grant of that gratuity?—Yes; it sprang up rather suddenly with us.

1849. You agree that it was a grievance, and that they felt it severely?—Yes.

1850. *Mr. Holmes.*—Don't you think that the constabulary in the disturbed parts of Ireland were much more entitled to be considered by the Government in relation to compensation for extra duty than the Dublin metropolitan police?—Oh, no, Sir, I do not, and I will explain the reason why. The extra duties of the constabulary commenced somewhat earlier than ours did. They were engaged at the Land League duties, if I may so put it, somewhat earlier than we were; but later on the brunt of it came upon us all here in connexion with the State trials, the demonstrations of one description or another, protection duty, and all these things, and we have a good deal of it even still, up to the present time, and the only difference with regard to the constabulary and ourselves, if there can be a difference, was in point of time, for the constabulary duties may be said to have commenced a little earlier than ours.

1851. Are you aware that many members of the constabulary force were very seriously out of pocket by having to pay a great deal for their lodgings and food when absent from their stations, and that this 180,000*l.* was intended in a great degree to reimburse them for their actual loss?—Certainly.

1852. Can you say that the men of the Dublin metropolitan police force were at any loss by the performance of that duty?—I cannot; but I heard of one constabulary man who drew 27*l.* out of bank and expended it. I have not heard of any of our men drawing money out of bank to meet their expenses.

1853. *Mr. Morris.*—I presume that you consider that the staff of the Dublin metropolitan police who are quartered at Kingstown had quite as much to do as the Royal Irish Constabulary had, who were quartered at Bray, and who got a share of the gratuity?—No; but a good deal more.

1854. And I presume that the men of your force quartered at Kingstown had as good a right to get something of what was going as the Royal Irish Constabulary who were quartered at Bray?—They had a better right.

1855. *Chairman.*—Within the last three years has there been an increase of serious offences as regards the police, aggravated assaults on the police?—Oh, yes.

1856. You have now dealt with the question of pay. Have you anything else to add on that subject, and if not, proceed to the next matter that you wish to bring under our notice?—I wish now to allude to the subject of pensions, and the point I should like to advocate in reference to the question of pensions is this: that at thirty years' service a man would have the option of retiring without a medical certificate.

1857. *Mr. Holmes.*—You come of course under the favourable scale?—I do, Sir.

1858. Will you state what that scale is?—I am entitled to half my pay in whatever grade I am at fifteen years' service, two-thirds at twenty years, three-fourths at twenty-five years, and full pay at thirty years, provided I am returned unfit by the medical board.

1859. Don't you consider that a very favourable scale of pensions?—I do, Sir. And another thing I would like; I would not at all object to the medical certificate up to the thirty years, but that a man should after thirty years' service be free to leave and go away without passing through a medical ordeal if he so desire it. Many of us, I speak for myself and those whose opinions I know, have a great dislike to be on the sick list, if we can possibly keep off it. We have a dislike to going to hospitals, and we would almost do anything sooner than go on the sick report or go into hospital, and then at the end of our service to have to go under the ordeal of a medical examination, perhaps having to take medicine when we do not consider we want it, we feel to be a great hardship.

1860. *Mr. Morris.*—Is it your experience that after thirty years in the police force there is not much left in a man for active service?—Not very much. He is a very fortunate man that is worth much. As a rule, they are completely worn out.

1861. *Chairman.*—What you suggest is, that an alteration of the law should take place?—What I would suggest is, that a man at the end of thirty years' service should retire without a medical certificate; but I would not have any compulsion.

1862. *Mr. Holmes.*—Inspector Kavanagh did not approve even of that favourable scale of pensions; he wished to have annual increments given between fifteen and twenty, twenty and twenty-five, and twenty-five and thirty years' service. Are you prepared to put forward the fact that they are not given

Inspector Wm. [illegible].

18 Sept., 18[illegible].

as a grievance?—Oh, it is not a grievance. I would like to have them, though.

1862. You are not, then, prepared to go as far as Inspector Kavanagh is on the subject of pensions?—No. It is quite new to me.

1863. *Chairman.*—Would you now kindly proceed to refer to the next subject that you wish to bring before us?—I wish now to refer to a matter that bears on the subject of pensions. Assuming that I have got twenty-five years' service and that I should die, my idea on the point is this, that my wife and my children, if alive—if I have a wife or children—that they should get some moiety of the pension I would be entitled to at twenty-five years' service, that they should get some moiety of it, say, at least one-third, so long as my wife should remain a widow; that she should enjoy that moiety of the pension, but in the event of her marrying that it should be stopped; that if I had any children depending on me, that they should also be entitled to a moiety.

1864. Do you mean in addition to the moiety to the wife?—Yes.

1865. But in that way you might get the whole of the pension?—I am going to limit it to a certain extent, that in no case the pension allowed to the wife and children is to exceed three-fourths of what I would be entitled to, and that the allowance to the children should cease on each of them arriving at the age of 16 years.

1866. And how would you apportion it?—I would leave that in the hands of the Commissioner of Police.

1867. *Mr. Holmes.*—You are aware that you are now starting a new doctrine on the subject of pensions?—It may be new.

1868. You are aware that the meaning of "pension" is, that it is a retiring allowance given to a man—to the man himself—upon leaving the service?—I think also that it cannot be considered an extravagant demand to say that if I should die the Government should not get the benefit of my pension, but that my family should get the benefit—some benefit, at all events, in the end.

1869. The pension is intended to reward a man for his service to the State, independently of whether he is a married or a single man?—I am aware of that.

1870. And you now say that his family is to be considered?—I wish my family to have what I have earned in the service; that it should not die with me, but that it should go to the benefit of my family, and not to the Government.

1871. You are only entitled to the pension on leaving the force; it is to reward you for a long period of service to the State?—Would you allow me to put it this way? we have always, under the Act of Parliament, had compensation for fifteen years' service. Well, supposing I have fifteen years' service, and anything should happen to me, and I should die without the doctor seeing me and giving me the formal certificate, the fifteen years' compensation to which I would be entitled goes into the hands of the Treasury, instead of into my wife's hands, or the hands of my next of kin.

1872. You mean that your wife should not lose the money to which you would have been entitled if the necessary formalities had been completed before your death?—Yes, certainly, that is the point; and I suppose there must be an Act of Parliament for it.

1873. *Mr. Morris.*—Before we leave this point, let me remind you of one thing. Take, for instance, the case of officers serving in the Indian army; I suppose you are aware that their widows and children, if the officers die, get some pension?—Well, I have heard they do.

1874. But are you aware that during their lifetime those officers are obliged to contribute an annual sum towards that widows' and orphans' fund?—I am not aware of that, Sir.

1875. But you think that, no matter how small a prudent man's salary may be, if he wants to leave something to his wife or to his children, it would be but fair that he should contribute even a small quota during his lifetime to aid a fund for that purpose?—Certainly, I think it would be a most proper thing to do.

1876. Then, in your opinion, it would be better for the force if a fund was formed, the Treasury contributing part of it, and the men contributing partly, by subscription, for the purpose of creating a fund for the benefit of the widows and children of men who die in the service; is that the way you wish to put it?—I think it would be a very good institution, but the present state of things is deplorable.

1877. That is, as regards the widow and children surviving?—Yes.

1878. *Mr. Holmes.*—Would the men be willing to submit to a deduction from their pay to go towards creating a fund for widows and orphans?—I think they would, and I think it would be calculated to keep the service together.

1879. *Chairman.*—Is there any other point you wish to advert to?—I wish to refer to another matter in connexion with pensions, where a man dies without the medical officer giving the necessary certificate under fifteen years' service. I consider it a grievance that the gratuity to which he would have been entitled had the necessary forms been complied with should not upon his death, without such forms having been complied with, be given to his wife or children.

1880. We have now dealt with the questions of pay and pension; what other subjects do you wish to bring under our observation?—I think I have touched on everything that concerns myself, and, beyond any information I can give in reference to the service generally, I do not know that I have anything to add. Here is a statement of one case of what I refer to. Constable William McKee, 129 A, joined the service on the 5th January, 1863, and died of small-pox on the 1st March, 1877, having thus served for fourteen years and two months. His compensation papers were made out; the amount, over 70*l.*, was approved by Government, and the cheque was filled; but he died before his signature could be obtained. His two orphans were sent to an industrial school, and a third died shortly after his death. A long correspondence took place between the Chief Commissioner and the Treasury, and after many months a final reply was given stating that deceased's widow could not get the compensation.

1881. Has there been any increase within the past three years in the number of aggravated assaults on the police?—Oh, yes, there has been an increase of very serious and aggravated assaults. There is, and has been, an increase in the violence shown towards us, and there has been a bitterness exhibited towards us within the last three years that was never before so strongly marked. I would just like to add before closing my evidence in reference to the question of promotion, that, although my pay is, I am aware, higher than that of a second-class inspector in London, a man in London can attain to the position of an inspector at a much earlier period of life than he could possibly attain the same position in the Dublin metropolitan police, and therefore has an opportunity of doing more for his family than the man in Dublin has. In London many public offices are filled, and in the Colonies and elsewhere officers from the London metropolitan police get important appointments. I do not know, as to the last statement, that it relates a matter of fact, but I know what I have stated there by common report.

1882. *Mr. Holmes.*—Upon this question of promotion, how long is a constable in the fourth class before he rises to the third?—About one year—the time is an average of about one year.

1883. How long is he in the third class before he rises to the second?—About four years.

1884. And how long is he in the second class before he rises to the first?—About two years.

1885. Then on an average a man attains the posi-

Inspector Wm. Thorpe.

16 Sept., [illegible].

1285. Is a first-class constable after seven years' service?—Yes, Sir, that is about the average.

1286. Does promotion in the rank of constable depend upon a vacancy, or is it quite certain that after a given period the constable will rise from one class to another?—It is quite certain.

1287. The period, then, is that in which the constable must remain in each class?—No, it depends upon vacancies.

1288. It is only an average, then, that you have given—a man might have longer service than seven years, and still might not be in the position of a first-class constable?—Yes.

1289. Or a man might attain the position of a first-class constable at an earlier period than seven years?—Well, it is possible.

1290. But on an average it takes seven years?—Yes.

1291. What is the weekly pay of a first-class constable?—[illegible]s., and then there is an allowance of [illegible] for boots. I wish to add that I have no fault to find with reference to the discipline of the force.

Inspector Patrick Orr, continued.

Inspector Patk. Orr.

16 Sept., [illegible].

1292. *Chairman.*—You have been present and heard the evidence given and the statements made by Inspector Thorpe, who has just been examined?—Yes.

1293. Do you concur in that evidence?—Yes; and I desire to say that my opinions entirely coincide with those expressed by Inspector Thorpe. One thing I wish, if I may be permitted, to add, is that there has been a great deal of talk about the administration of discipline in the service.

1294. *Mr. Holmes.*—Yes; what are your views in reference to that?—What I would wish to say is, that I am entirely satisfied with the way in which the force is disciplined. I have over twenty-seven years' service, and I wish to say that everything seemed to go on fair and right during that period.

1295. You have no complaint to make on the subject of discipline?—None whatever; and to support that view I may mention that during that twenty-seven years I have not been punished, and I have got everything that I was entitled to.

1296. As you have touched upon the question of discipline, I would like to ask you, is there not a rule in the force forbidding policemen to enter public-houses either on duty or off duty?—Yes, and a wholesome one; it could not be done without.

1297. Will you tell me why you think that rule should be insisted upon?—My reason for that would be, that I think it would be abused by the police if they were to be allowed to enter public-houses. I would allow it to a certain extent, but if they were allowed to go into public-houses indiscriminately they would mix with the people, and rows would in all likelihood follow, and that would cause trouble and injury both to themselves and to the service. I think that in the men's own interests it is a wholesome rule, and it is a rule that has been carried out, in my opinion, with satisfactory results during my period of service; it is no new change.

1298. Do you think that if the police were allowed to go into public-houses, that the fact that they were so allowed would tend to interfere with the due performance of their duties under the Licensing Acts?—Not much; I think not.

1299. You don't think publicans would be tempted to try to bribe the police, in order that they might wink at infringements of the law, by supplying them with drink gratis?—I am sure it is a fact that publicans would be inclined to try and bribe the police in order that they might break the law.

1300. And that the men would be hardly able to resist the temptation?—No; I think the men are very strict, and that it would not be easy to bring about undue familiarity between them and the publicans, or at least such among them as would be inclined to encourage it.

1301. *Mr. Harris.*—Is it true that the men complain as a body that they are not allowed to enter public-houses when off duty and in plain clothes?—Some of them do.

1302. But generally they do not?—It has been always the rule, and it has never been brought out as a complaint.

1303. Would you enforce it strictly?—I think I would; I think it is for the benefit of the men themselves.

1304. *Mr. Holmes.*—Is the rule frequently broken?—Not frequently; but it has been broken; time after time it has been broken. The officers are not anxious to interfere with the men off duty and in plain clothes. It has occurred occasionally, however, that men going into public-houses and having some whisky and water while on duty were seen coming out and were reported.

1305. But if a man was not on duty and did that would he be reported?—He is subject to the discipline, because it is against the Commissioner's rules.

1306. Would you object to a man entering a public-house under such circumstances?—No, in plain clothes I would not so much object; but I must say I would not give them the privilege at all. There are a great many officers in the service who differ with me in that opinion, but I really think it would be for the advantage of the service not to give that privilege.

1307. Even off duty and in plain clothes?—I certainly think it would not.

1308. You still object to the permission?—Yes.

[The Commission adjourned until the following Monday.]

SIXTH DAY.—16TH SEPTEMBER, 1882.

PRESENT:

MR. J. W. O'DONNELL, MR. GEORGE MORRIS, D.L., and MR. R. W. A. HOLMES.

District Superintendent ROBERT WALKER, London Metropolitan Police, recalled.

1809. *Chairman.*—At what age do candidates generally enter the police force in London; what is the average age?—From 20 to 24 years, excepting in the case of army men.

1810. What is the prevailing opinion amongst the majority of the superior officers of the force in London as regards the time when men should be allowed to retire without a medical certificate?—Twenty-four years.

1811. That it should be optional with the man to retire after that service?—Yes.

1812. *Mr. Holmes.*—Is that your individual opinion, or do you only state the prevailing opinion?—Yes, that is my opinion, and also the prevailing opinion, with which I agree.

1813. At what rate of pension?—Two-thirds; for I think that amount of pension is the utmost that a police officer can claim after twenty-four years' service; two-thirds of his pay as pension when he retires.

1814. Without the medical certificate?—Yes.

1815. That would enable a man who joined the force at 20 years of age to retire at 44?—Yes.

1816. Or if he joined at 24, to retire at 48?—Yes, he has then seen his best.

1817. You think so?—Yes.

1818. You think a man has seen his best at 48 years of age?—Yes; even after twenty years' service men fall in the limbs from rheumatism.

1819. Do you think that if the men are given the option of retiring after twenty-four years' service upon their maximum pension they would generally avail themselves of that power, and leave the force after twenty-four years' service?—I don't think that they would, provided that the pension was secured to them, come what may, excepting in cases of proceedings against them for felony or other serious crime.

Mr. R. Walker.

16 Sept., 1882.

Inspector JOHN DOHERTY, G Division, Dublin Metropolitan Police, examined.

(Inspectors Richard Fogarty, Patrick John Mackie, and Thomas Mealy present during the examination of this witness.)

1820. *Chairman.*—What is your name?—John Doherty.

1821. How long have you been in the force?—For twenty-eight years and five months.

1822. What is your position?—Third-class inspector.

1823. How long have you been an inspector?—About two and [illegible] years; two years last March.

1824. Where are you stationed?—At Store Street station, where I have been for the last six months. Prior to that time I was stationed at College Street.

1825–1827. In giving evidence before us, may I ask you how many of the men of your rank you represent? Do you represent the whole of them?—I am one of those elected at a meeting of inspectors to give evidence before this Commission.

1828. *Chairman.*—What is the first subject with which you desire to deal?—The first thing we want is under the head of pay. We want for third-class inspectors a rise from 107*l.* a-year to 130*l.*; for second-class inspectors we want a rise from 110*l.* to 140*l.*, and for first-class from 130*l.* to 150*l.* We want 30*l.* a-year allowed for house-rent, in addition, instead of 20*l.*, which is the present allowance, and we want 12*l.* for uniform instead of 8*l.*, what we have at present for each of those ranks. The grounds on which we base our claim for this pay are these, first, in view of the recent rise of pay given to the officers of the Royal Irish Constabulary; secondly, on account of the arduous duties that we have to perform, the long hours that we have to continue on duty, the important business that we have to transact, and also on account of the fact that we have to deal with a criminal population—we being the inspectors of the metropolitan police of the City of Dublin—and to deal with more serious crimes and more indictable offences that pass through our hands than pass through the hands of every other officer of police in all Ireland put together. The statistics will show that. We have additional duties cast upon us by the Prevention of Crimes Act, and cast upon us as inspectors solely. There is no other rank to which the duty can attach—in[illegible] way to the execution of warrants. We have also duties as to property, we have the licensing business to attend to, and special reports, Government and others, also, then the military business all goes through our hands. Whoever may get these things, they all go to the inspector to make his inquiry and report. These reports are almost always made after our long dreary tour of duty made, and we think that we ought to be paid for this extra work. We have no one to assist us, no clerk—no one to assist us. We have to do it by ourselves, make our own inquiries, and make our own reports, and to perform our duty the same as an ordinary inspector in the station along with that. Comparing ourselves with the London metropolitan police, we are in this position that they are not in. They are in a rich city, surrounded by friends, by rich merchants, by people who will give them employment, and who are not hostile to them, and who will also give their children employment.

1829. *Mr. Holmes.*—Do you refer now to the case when they leave the service?—I refer to the case when they leave the force, and to our families while we are in the force. I mean to say this; that I am a married man, and I have a number of children growing, and who would be able to earn, and if I was in London I would get plenty of employment for them, whereas here it is impossible.

1830. Do you mean to say that the great bulk of

Inspector John Doherty.

16 Sept., 1882.

Inspector John Doherty.

13 Sept., 1883.

bring the children of police officers would prevent them getting employment?—I mean to say this, that we have seen cases where one of our children would not be allowed into a shop; we have plenty of cases of that kind.

1831. *Chairman.*—Within what time has that state of things existed; recently?—Yes, and for a long time.

1832. And simply because the father was a policeman?—Quite so; and they have been turned out of employment on that account; the men objected to being employed with them.

1833. Can you give us an instance in which such an event happened?—I can, and a very recent one. A constable in the G Division sent his son to a most respectable brass-founder to have him bound to learn the trade of a brass-founder or plumber, I don't know which. When he entered the establishment the men objected to work with the boy in consequence of his father being a policeman, and he had to leave the establishment, and he has got no trade since.

1834. *Mr. Holmes.*—But that hostile feeling against the police has only sprung up within the last two or three years?—Yes, more particularly during that time.

1835. Do you mean that it has intensified during that time?—Yes, it has intensified very much.

1836. But did it exist prior to the troubled times?—Not so much. It came into this city largely with Fenianism, and remained ever since; we are isolated from society in consequence of that to a great extent; we meet with every sort of employment that would suit the children of our men, but they cannot do it.

1837. The employers, I understand you to convey, are willing enough to take them, but the fellow-workmen won't allow them to do the work?—Yes.

1838. *Chairman.*—Does that extend to policemen on pension?—Oh, yes, Sir; scarcely any of them get anything in the way of employment except on a railway or something like that; some small thing.

1839. *Mr. Holmes.*—You seek an increase in your pay for two reasons; first of all you compare yourselves with the officers of the Royal Irish Constabulary?—Yes.

1840. With what officers?—With the sub-inspectors; we hold a relative rank in the metropolitan police.

1841. Are you aware that each class of inspector in Dublin is considerably better paid than the corresponding class in London?—I am not.

1842. I will just mention to you the rates. A third-class inspector in Dublin receives, with his house allowance, 157*l.* a-year. A London inspector of the third class receives 117*l.* &c.; he has no allowance; he is supplied with his uniform; and I did not, in comparing you with him, include your allowance for uniform. The second-class inspector in Dublin has 176*l.*, while the second-class inspector in London has 144*l.* 14*s.*, and no allowance. A first-class inspector in Dublin has, with his allowance for house-rent, 196*l.*, and a first-class inspector in London has 162*l.* 18*s.*, and no allowance. So that you see a first-class inspector in Dublin is considerably better paid than a first-class inspector in London. Now, although your pay is less, I believe, than the amount the sub-inspectors receive in the Royal Irish Constabulary, don't you think you should compare yourselves more with the corresponding officers of the London metropolitan police force?—No, Sir, the two countries are quite different, and for the very reason I am just after stating to you, which is a most serious one.

1843. But don't you foresee a great deal of difficulty in improving your position as regards pay, bearing in mind what I have just told you?—I do, Sir; I see some difficulty. I see some difficulty if you say, "There is the London metropolitan police force, and there is our force established on the same footing; why should there be a difference of pay?" But then, if you look at the duties we perform and the duties they perform; the city they are in and the city we are in; the prospects of our families and of our men both in and out of the service—I say that if you look at these things, you will perceive that we are placed in so much worse a position that we ought to be paid for it.

1844. Are your duties more arduous as regards them than the duties of the London police?—Yes, much more, usually, because there are less officers of my rank here to perform the duties. Yet we have not one-half the number of men that they have, in proportion, and we have to deal with a most turbulent population, and nearly every man in London—nearly every man in London is a policeman. The people there all assist the police.

1845. *Mr. Morris.*—In fact, you consider that your life is more in danger here than in the same position in London?—There is no doubt about it. We have occasionally to face violent mobs. Not long ago I had to face a mob of that kind, and I got a blow of a stone in the back of my head that cut me to the bone. I suppose you would scarcely ever meet the danger we have to encounter in London. Then I had, not long since, to take command of a large body of men during the disturbance, and to patrol up and down Dame Street. Showers of stones hailed on us for hours during the time we were out there, and several of the men were struck. You would never see that in London. We had also a week's riots in Sackville Street, when we were stoned and struck several times, I and the men.

1846. *Mr. Holmes.*—What do you mean by saying you have duties to perform in connexion with the military?—We have even to pay some of the pensioners. All complaints that they make about anything we have to prepare private and confidential reports upon.

1847. The inspectors have nothing to say to the paying of pensioners?—We have to see after all the reserve men.

1848. In what way?—We have to go round and warn them in, and see that they are sent in.

1849. Have not the London police to do the same?—I don't know. It is a duty I didn't care to mention, it is so small.

1850. Do you know whether the inspectors in London have clerks to assist them?—I don't know; I have never been in London in my life.

1851. *Mr. Morris.*—Have you any further observations to offer under the head of pay?—I think not.

1852. You have just mentioned that you had duty to perform in connexion with the Prevention of Crime Act and the Licensing Acts. You are of course aware that the first-mentioned Act is a temporary one?—Yes.

1853. You are aware that the police in London also have duties to discharge in connexion with the Licensing Acts?—Yes; but not such large duties as we have. We have over 1,000 public-houses.

1854. How do you make that out? There are more public-houses in London than in Dublin?—I will tell you. We go on duty at 8 o'clock at night, and we go off at 10 o'clock the next morning. I am engaged both in and out of the station—if I am not walking about outside, I am writing inside. Well, some publican wants, say, a transfer of a licence, or something like that, that I have to attend the magistrate's office about. There is no sleep for me. When I go home at half-past 10 o'clock, I have to go over immediately afterwards to the magistrate's office, to meet the publicans there, with scarcely time to get my breakfast. I sit there until I find my applicant and his attorney in Court, and then have to wait the convenience of the magistrate. There may be some important case going on, and I often had to stop in the Police Court two or three hours. Then there may be a postponement for an hour applied for, or something of that description, or, if there is not, nevertheless I am often there from two to three hours. I go home, and I am home perhaps about 3 or 4 o'clock, with time to get no sleep and no rest, for I have to be out for duty that night at 8 o'clock again. I say that

to be paid for. I question
house in London have to do
I they would do it for one

n by increasing your hous-
rather higher ?—No; I think
that our numbers are quite
nd properly.
any suggestion as to how
oved ?—Yes; but I should
s proper place, and when
d of "tour of duty."
Kindly proceed with the
h to lay before us ?—We
r the house be increased
to explain the reason why
enormous rents that are
e City of Dublin, entirely
. we find that we can get
me that the Commissioners
nough for us to live in—for
years I have been looking for
suitable house to reside in ;
a-year. I could get nothing
ything that would be suit-

you not select a house
the sanction of the Com-
a house, but if I do select
idered suitable, I will find
other district before very
use for which I am paying
ot at all suitable.
ved that if the full amount
e so as to pay and house-rent,
uld be in receipt of 220l.

fected that there would be
han a third-class inspector

but that would result in a
tween the rates of pay of
ere ought to be a com-
re is actually a considerable
d-class inspectors and the
London. Our third-class
., without allowances; the
er I find has only 117l.
e inspectors here have more
n than the inspectors in
ady remunerated for such
her pay which they now
entirely unchanged within
s or thereabouts. Our long
and considerably more duty

portance of the state of the
pline of the service; both,
ng to us.
ine of discipline been drawn
e years ?—Well, I may tell
own up, from the smallest
ase, the Commissioner gets
intendent of the division to
nt hands the matter over to
The inspector is the man
on it—he has to go and
d send his report forward ;
s, I may add, are prepared
ay by the inspector. The
tive officer.
pector always to do these
h.
e with him before—what
here were not so many of
The complaints were fewer,
nd the matters for special
ns, the collection of the
laced upon us, and special
ports have to be prepared

1367. *Chairman.*—Have you any further reference to make to the subject of pay ?—Nothing.

1368. Be good enough to proceed to the next branch of your evidence ?—Now I come to the matter of uniform. We are allowed 8l. a-year each for uniform. We say that that sum is wholly insufficient. In my own case, the first year I was promoted I paid 41l. and upwards, when I was only allowed 8l. per year.

1369. *Mr. Holmes.*—How long does a uniform last ?—A jacket such as I am now wearing lasts for one year.

1370. I suppose your outfit is not so expensive in subsequent years as it is in the first year of promotion ?—No.

1371. What do you pay in subsequent years ?—It costs 13l. a-year to keep up one's uniform.

1372. How do you account for your statement that you paid 41l. during the first year of your promotion ?—Well, I paid 31l. for the uniform as it originally was; then there was some change in the uniform in reference to this jacket, and I had to get a whole lot of other things that cost me 10l. odd, and the fact is that my total outlay was 41l. 16s.

1373. Are you aware that a superintendent in London receives only 11l. a-year for uniform, which I presume, as it is that of a superintendent, is more expensive than yours ?—I will show you that you are under a misapprehension about that. The superintendent is nearly always in plain clothes, except when he appears before the Commissioners, or on some other important day. We are always wearing this expensive uniform. Inspectors are always in uniform on duty, superintendents are not. The cost of uniform would do a superintendent for his life. A superintendent makes money on his uniform; we lose on it.

1374. When you speak of a superintendent, you mean a superintendent in Dublin ?—Yes. I would wish, if you will allow me, to give the price of the articles that we require every year. We wear out each year one patrol-jacket, the contract price of which is 3l. 16s.; two pairs of trousers at 3 guineas each pair; that is the very least we can pay for them, that is the contract price given to Messrs. Ireland on the Quay. A cape, 18s. One topcoat might be used, but I think would be scarcely used in two years, so we will put down 3l. 10s. for that; three pairs of boots at 1l. each pair; and then the repairing of these would cost something more, but we will say 1l., and then we have one office-jacket, 1 guinea.

1375. What does the total come to ?—14l. 15s. We are not taking into account helmets, belts, gloves, or what they call a dress suit, the jacket alone of which cost me 6 guineas.

1376. How long does a dress suit last ?—About three years.

1377. Upon what occasions have you to use it ?—At Castle balls, levées, for special purposes, reviews, and matters of that kind. We are not taking those things into account.

1378. Do you know when this allowance of 8l. was fixed ?—In 1873, at the time the last increase of pay was granted. These amounts are wholly insufficient.

1379. *Chairman.*—Have you anything further to add as to the allowance for uniform ?—No, Sir.

1380. Well, please proceed to deal with the next subject upon which you wish to give evidence ?—The next point is under the head of pensions. Every member of the service should, in our opinion, be granted half-pay for fifteen years' service. This is what we want; one-thirtieth of his pay additional for every year served up to thirty years, when he should be entitled to full pay and allowance for house only. We do not ask the uniform allowance; we do not want that.

1381. *Mr. Holmes.*—I suppose all the inspectors now present, including yourself, come, so far as pension is concerned, under the Act of 1847 ?—Yes.

1382. Are you aware that you are under a very favourable scale ?—Yes; it is more favourable than

Inspector
John Doherty.

13 Sept., 1888.

Inspector John Doherty. — 18th Sept., 1882.

under the Act by the provisions of which those who joined the force after us are pensioned.

1883. Are you aware that at no period in the history of the police force in London could a policeman retire on more than two-thirds of his pay; that that was always the maximum?—I was not aware of that. But we would be very willing to change places with them, for then there would be a fine opening for us to get employment when we would leave the force.

1884. Don't you see that there would be considerable difficulty in giving the force here a better scale of pensions than the London men, or the men of the police forces of England and Scotland?—The two countries are so wholly different from Ireland, and the spirit displayed towards the police there and that shown here is so different, that I venture to think there could be no comparison.

1885. But looking at it from an Imperial point of view, and from the view that must be taken by the Imperial Legislature, don't you think it would be a very difficult thing to put the Dublin men in a far better position than the men of England and Scotland; and don't you think that the most that could be done would be to give the men here the same scale of pensions as that given to the men in the countries I have named?—There is an apparent difficulty in it. But you must take the circumstances of the two countries into consideration, and you must take this also into consideration—that the Government have now given a much more liberal scale of pay and pension to the officers of the Royal Irish Constabulary than the officers of the rural English police forces receive.

1886. Are you aware that the officers of the Royal Irish Constabulary by the recent Act are placed under the Superannuation Act of 1859, and are you aware that they will have to remain in the service for forty years before they can retire upon two-thirds of their pay?—And so they can, because their life is mere pleasure compared to ours.

1887. Now, as a reasonable man, and speaking only, I take it, for what you think would be fairly and justly extended to you, do you really think that the Government will still further improve the very favourable scale under which you men who joined the force before 1867 are at present?—I think myself, personally, that I would be quite satisfied with the Act of 1847, so far as the scale of pensions is concerned. For myself personally, I say that; but we entirely object to serve thirty years, and then only retire on a medical certificate. Every single thing that was in us is out of us long before thirty years' service is reached, and we have a great objection to going before the doctor and saying that we are sick, and striving to be released from further service in that way. I, personally, would be satisfied if I could retire after thirty years' service without the necessity of obtaining a medical certificate of unfitness to serve. If, however, there is any general change made in the pension scale, we merely put forward this as one that would, in our opinion, be a fair one.

1888. Speaking not for yourself, but for the men who joined after 1867, don't you think it would be next door to impossible to put the men in Dublin in a better position than the men in London?—I do not. The same thing would apply to the men as to us.

1889. Do you think that the English or the Irish tax-payer would acquiesce in such an arrangement as that? Do you think that the tax-payers of the United Kingdom would consent to the granting of such a demand as this?—As far as the tax-payers of the city of Dublin are concerned, I am well aware that they would be content to pay any additional sum that would give additional remuneration, such as would be reasonable and right, to the police force of their city. You must, of course, take a whole lot of things into consideration in calculating a matter of this description. And a distinction has been drawn between the Constabulary and the English police.

1890. In what respect?—Well, I believe that the officers of the Royal Irish Constabulary are better paid, and in a far better position, than the officers of any English rural or Scotch police force.

[At this stage the further examination of the witness was adjourned until next day.]

SEVENTH DAY.—19TH SEPTEMBER, 1882.

PRESENT:

MR. J. W. O'DONNELL, MR. GEORGE MORRIS, and MR. R. W. A. HOLMES.

Examination of Inspector Doherty, Dublin Metropolitan Police, resumed.

1891. *Mr. Holmes.*—You sought for an increase of pay yesterday on the ground that you should be compared with the sub-inspectors of the Royal Irish Constabulary, and that you should be paid as well. Are you aware that the pay of a third-class inspector of the Dublin police is higher than that of a third-class sub-inspector of the Royal Irish Constabulary?—I am; but we don't seek an increase of pay on the ground that we should be compared with the sub-inspectors of the Royal Irish Constabulary, for their system would be unsuitable to us in many ways, and they get their pay as a sort of encouragement, the same as would be held out to a set of boys on going into the depôt.

1892. You asked yesterday to be paid as well as the sub-inspectors, and I now say to you, are you aware that the pay of a third-class inspector in Dublin is higher than that of a third-class sub-inspector?—I am, Sir; but he is only on that grade for a few months, and it does not make much matter one way or the other.

1893. Do you not think that the duties of a sub-inspector of constabulary are more responsible than your duties?—No, Sir, not so responsible. He has not so many men under his control.

1894. Yes, but has he not to act on his own independent judgment more frequently than you?—No, not once for every one hundred times that I have.

1895. Have you not the Commissioner and superintendent at hand to consult?—No, I must act on my own responsibility in every case, and if I am not

Inspector John Doherty.

22 Sept., 1882.

present at any outrage I am sent for, and the responsibility placed upon my shoulders, and it is generally the same way with a sub-inspector of constabulary.

1396. Is it not the case that a sub-inspector of constabulary has to keep up a better appearance in life than you do; that his position requires him to do so, having to live in the country, and to dine and mix with the gentry of the neighbourhood in which he is stationed?—It is not. I have to keep up as good an appearance as him; I have to buy as expensive a uniform as he has; I have to live in as expensive a house as he has; I have to keep as select society as he has. Sub-inspectors have, it is true, to keep up a horse and servant, for which they get an allowance which we do not ask.

1397. *Chairman.*—Will you kindly proceed with your evidence at the point where it was interrupted by our adjournment last evening?—Yes, Sir; I wish to say, in reference to the subject of pension, that if the Pension Act of 1847 was fairly and properly administered, it would give entire satisfaction to the service; for instance, take three men of equal good character leaving the service——

1398. And of equal rank?—Yes, of equal service, equal rank, and equal good character; one gets his full pay, one is cut 12*l.* per year, another is cut 24*l.*

1399. Do you know of those instances?—I do, Sir.

1400. *Mr. Morris.*—Are there reasons given at the time for these curtailments, whether good or mistaken ones?—There are no reasons given, nor is there any appeal from the decision made. The thing is all a matter of discretion. It is said, "I think you are entitled to so-and-so," and the man, if he felt aggrieved, would have no satisfaction at all.

1401. *Mr. Holmes.*—Is this your evidence, that the whole service would be content with the Act of 1847 if properly and fairly administered?—Quite so.

1402-1403. That is, if there was security for pension?—Yes.

1404. When you allude to "the service," do you allude to the men who joined before 1867?—Yes; that would apply to the whole service, those who joined both before and after 1867. We had a notable case here, where a man with thirty years' service was reduced 7*l.* a-year. The man in whose case that happened is the first man who was ever successful in overcoming this system, and last week his Excellency granted that man his full retiring allowance.

1405. *Mr. Morris.*—We are aware of all the circumstances of that case?—The young men, as well as the old men, in the service, look narrowly to every pension that is given to both officers and men leaving the service; and, seeing an Act of Parliament like this administered in such a way, it has the most discouraging effects on them.

1406. Are you of opinion that the fact that a man has been fined for misconduct, breach of discipline, or drunkenness during his service in the force should not militate against his pension?—I am, indeed.

1407. That the fine or punishment inflicted should be sufficient at once, and an end put to the transaction?—Yes. More than that; it is the opinion of every man in the service that after some time—say, five years, or any other fixed period—these records should not be kept against men's characters, and continually used to their damage. Say a man goes drunk two or three times, and that he gets over it, he, in all probability, becomes a sober man; but those drunken records that he has been punished on are held over his head for a number of years, and continued against him until he is going out on his pension; in fact, they follow him to the grave. Some years ago in the service the reports were cancelled, after six months; when a man had a clean sheet for six months all previous reports were wiped out.

1408. *Mr. Holmes.*—And he would then get a clean bill of health?—Yes, Sir. This is a matter for consideration. I knew hundreds of men who were wild in their young days, but who afterwards turned out excellent men. In the constabulary they have a superior way of doing things. In the case of a man who is punished in the constabulary, he knows what he will get and what he may look forward to; he knows he will lose 1*l.* of his pension for every unfavourable record. That is satisfactory, because it is certain, and lies before a man.

1409. I can assure you, as a member of the present Constabulary Inquiry Committee, as a matter of fact, that the witnesses we have examined bring forward the same complaint that you are doing now—that their bad marks follow them to the grave?—They only follow them in a small way in pension, but they follow us in a much larger way in twenty-fives and thirties.

1410. *Chairman.*—Have you anything else to state on the present subject?—Nothing, I think, under that heading.

1411. What is your next head of request?—I now wish to make reference to the subject of gratuities; I mean for short service under the pension period. I am first instructed to say that every officer in the service incapacitated through ill-health, and after five years' service, should, in our opinion, be granted at the rate of one month's pay for each year's service up to ten years—we had that rule at one time,—and that between ten and fifteen years he should be entitled to two months' pay. We had that rule also formerly, but it was taken away. We claim that between fifteen years and the time of his being rendered unfit—no matter what the service may be—he should be entitled to three months' pay for each year served.

1412. *Mr. Holmes.* Was that also an old rule?—That was an old rule also, Sir, up to fifteen years, but it never went beyond it. When you worked up to fifteen years you were entitled to a pension.

1413. When were those rules abolished?—They were in existence from the time I joined the force up to two or three years ago. In the event of an officer of the service becoming seriously ill, and of his electing in the interests of his wife or next of kin to take compensation, we think it should be granted instead of pension; and should any member of the service die while serving without being returned unfit by the medical officer, and before he signs the paper for the gratuity—that his wife or next of kin should be granted the amount of the gratuity to which he would be entitled according to the foregoing scale. Now, we have several cases I may mention in the service of men being struck off without receiving gratuity. They are struck down with some disease; there is a difficulty in getting the doctor, and we think that the men ought, through no fault of their own, the little bit of square paper, should not militate against those men. At present, if the doctor delays in coming to a dying man, or if some of the police officials are not to be found, the very fact of the man not being able to sign the paper—it may be only a matter of a few minutes—is sufficient to cause the forfeiture of the gratuity, and his wife and children become paupers.

1414. *Mr. Morris.*—You are of opinion that the family of any man losing his life in the service while on duty should be compensated?—Yes, certainly.

1415. *Chairman.*—To the extent of the pension or gratuity to which that man would have been entitled?—Yes.

1416. What is the next item of your evidence?—I now wish to refer to that branch of my evidence which I may describe as being under the head of "Tour of duty." Up to the year 1877 the inspectors and acting inspectors doing station-house duty performed a tour of twenty-four hours on duty and twenty-four hours off duty. They went on at 10 o'clock one morning, and went off at 10 o'clock the next morning, performing duty during the whole twenty-four hours, and on every alternate day they went off at 6 A.M., doing in that day twenty hours' duty instead of the twenty-four.

1417. *Mr. Morris.*—So that the tour of twenty-four hours on and twenty-four hours off was every

Inspector John Doherty.

14 Sept., 1882.

alternate day?—Yes. That tour of duty, although without doubt very severe, I may say satisfied the officers of the service. They were quite willing to perform it, feeling that though it was a severe tour they had time for rest after going off duty between that morning and the following day, when they returned to duty at 10 o'clock. For no apparent cause that we could see, the authorities changed that tour of duty. They brought on the officers as usual at 10 o'clock in the morning, and made it a rule that they were to go off at 8 o'clock in the evening, but they took good care also to make it a rule that they were to clear up their day's work before they left their respective stations. The fact is, that the officers never got off at 8 o'clock; 10 and 11 o'clock and often 2 o'clock in the morning were the usual hours, and this arose from very troublesome cases often coming in at the worst time of the evening, between 7 and 8 o'clock. I myself often was on duty up till 2 and 3 o'clock in the morning.

1468. *Chairman.*—Do you mean to say that you were on duty until that hour, having been nominally put on from 10 A.M. until 8 P.M.?—Quite so. I was on duty until the hour I have mentioned with the exception of an hour and a-quarter for dinner, but no time for supper. That is the present tour of day duty.

1469. *Mr. Holmes.*—Don't you think the change was made in the interest of the men themselves, that probably the Commissioners thought that twenty-four hours was a very long stretch for a man to be on duty?—It was not, I regret to say, done in the interests of the men.

1470. Don't you think that that was the intention?—Well, I really could not tell you. The night-duty tour is even worse. The night-duty tour commences at 8 P.M. and is supposed to end for one of the officers at 10 A.M. the next day, and for the other at 8 o'clock in the morning. They take it alternately. One has a long night and the other a short night. That is the way they calculate it.

1471. *Chairman.*—That is seven and fourteen hours?—Yes, Sir. The inspector has to attend to his ordinary duty of taking charges, investigating complaints, receiving reports of robberies, burglaries, and all that sort of thing in the station during his tour of duty. He has to go out and patrol his sub-division the same as an acting inspector. He has at times whatever during his tour of duty to attend to his special reports of every description, or to write them out or make them up; and it frequently occurs that he has not even time within the given time to finish his ordinary duty without putting two or three hours, nearly always an hour extra, duty on him. And we get no compensation whatever for this. If an inspector going off duty at 10 o'clock in the morning happens to meet with any discipline case—say, for instance, the case of a drunken constable, or if he has to attend the magistrates' office, or if he has to attend drill—in place of going to his bed he has to go and attend to these duties, and he is often out of bed until 3 and 4 and 5 o'clock in the evening, and he has to return to his duty at 8 o'clock; and we always found it that the man who did the whole day's duty was a fresher man for continuing the duty than the man who was supposed to have gone off at 10 o'clock on that morning.

1472. Do you mean to say that though you were entitled to retire at 10 o'clock, the extra work would occupy you up to 7 o'clock in the evening?—Often up to 3 and 4 o'clock in the evening.

1473. But under the old system, you were quite certain of getting every second day to rest yourself?—Under that system a man had a night's rest; under the present system a man has no time to rest.

1474. *Mr. Holmes.*—Now, take the case of a man entitled to go off duty at 8 o'clock at night, but who does not actually get off duty until 2 o'clock in the morning; when does that man resume duty?—At 10 o'clock the same morning.

1475. Nominally, the interval of rest would be from 8 P.M. until 10 A.M., but owing to his having to remain to finish his work he would not get home until 2 o'clock in the morning?—Quite so. In the summer months during the drill season we are even in a worse position. Now, I will assume a case; I have to attend drill, we will say; I go off at, perhaps, 2 o'clock that morning after clearing up my work. I have to be at Kevin Street at 6 o'clock. I am drilled there for an hour and a-quarter, often an hour and a-half, and we leave that drill-square often not able to walk with the perspiration dripping off us.

1476. On how many days in the week does that happen?—Every second day with the exception of Saturday and Sunday, that is, during the summer season.

1477. When does it begin?—It begins in May and ends when the weather breaks, about October. We have some of it this year, I must, perhaps. I just walk home then and take off my day-duty uniform, dress in my night uniform, and I have just time to get to my station, take my tea, and I have fourteen hours before me that night of hard work, after getting that drilling in Kevin Street during the day, and with probably something before me to keep me out of my bed on the next day.

1478. Tell me, is the time that you are on drill included in your tour of duty, or is that not done?—It is included in my time off duty.

1479. It is an extra thing which breaks in upon your rest?—All get exemption from duty except the inspector and acting inspector, the station-house officers.

1480. *Mr. Holmes.*—The inspectors are the only class in the force who are not allowed to count their drill as part of their duty?—Yes, quite so. Constables for that term of drill of, say, one hour and a-half, are allowed four hours when on day duty and three hours when on night duty. When the tour of duty that I have described was imposed on us, after about six or eight months, seeing the unsatisfactory working of it, we remonstrated with the authorities, and asked liberty to resume our old tour of duty, hard and all as it was. Well, it was given us for a short period. But again this objectionable tour of duty was substituted after an interval of two months, and it continues in operation ever since.

1481. *Mr. Moran.*—Do you know of your own knowledge whether all the inspectors and acting inspectors agree in opinion with you upon the desire to resume the twenty-four hours' tour of duty, and can you tell me if there is a division of opinion amongst yourselves about it?—There is not any division of opinion amongst ourselves about it. We memorialized the Commissioner about a month ago, setting forth the errors of the tour of duty as well as we could, and respectfully asking him to consider the question of the tour of duty.

1482. Were the inspectors unanimous?—Well, forty-eight signed it. I think there were two or three who could not sign it because they were absent. Oh! we were all unanimous on the subject of the same tour of duty.

1483. When you say forty-eight signed it, that number includes the acting inspectors?—Yes, and there are some inspectors who are on staff appointments and not doing station-house duty, and it did not concern them. We memorialized the Commissioner to be good enough to give us back our old tour of duty, or some modification of the present tour of duty. For this present tour of duty ends at 8 o'clock, and we are precluded from going to evening service or going to church. We never can go out at 8 o'clock. Under the present tour of duty, that hour gets you always either in the office or in your bed. These things have been put to the Commissioner again and again. And again adverting to the Memorial, I should state that it is about a month ago we drew the attention of the Commissioner to the fact that there was no police supervision—no superior supervision over the police from 6 o'clock in the morning until 10 o'clock—whereas, under the old system, the inspector had supervision over the men until 10 o'clock in the morning for the whole twenty-four hours. They had to go occasional rounds at uncertain hours, which kept up the supervision until 10 o'clock in the morning. We also reminded him that burglaries had alarmingly increased, and that is a well-known fact, and is shown by the statistics. The officers—and I think one of them is now present—that presented that Memorial will tell you what was said about it. We pointed out these matters to the Commissioner, and he refused to consider them. Inspector Mooney will state the answer given by the Commissioner to the Memorial. We asked nothing, only our old tour of duty. We don't see why we should be compelled to perform more duty than the constables on the street are asked to perform. If our tour of duty was the same as that of the constables, we would be quite satisfied with it. There is a large question in that; you would not have officers to perform the duty; but with our old tour of duty we would be quite satisfied.

1434. Then, in your opinion, in order to lighten your duties it would be necessary to increase the number of inspectors, or to return to the old system?—Yes; or to return to the old system which worked so well for years.

1435. *Chairman.*—Will you now, if you have nothing further to add on the subject, kindly proceed to the next matter that you wish to bring before us?—I will now, with the permission of the Committee, refer to the question of "Leave of absence."

1436. What are the present regulations with regard to leave of absence?—Every inspector is nominally entitled to a month's leave of absence, every acting inspector to three weeks, every sergeant to three weeks, every constable to ten days, and every acting sergeant to fourteen days, but they do not get it.

1437. How is that?—I cannot tell you. We wish that every inspector should be entitled to one month's leave in each year and one day's leave in every month. We are entitled to that leave already under the present regulations of the service. Should the exigencies of the service preclude the Commissioner from granting such leave when applied for within the year, a month's extra pay should be granted. Now, I myself applied for leave for the last two years, and I got no leave.

1438. In either year?—Yes. I have twenty-eight years' service, and I think I only got leave four or five times during the whole of that period. If you apply for it, you cannot get it. I was refused on the ground of the Exhibition being open, but then other officers applied and were refused. We don't object to being refused when there is necessity; but I think when we cannot get our leave that we are entitled to, we ought to be paid for our extra duty.

1439. Is it a regulation of the service that an inspector should be entitled to a month's leave, or does it rest entirely with the Commissioner whether he can get it or not?—It is a regulation of the service.

1440. When you were refused it, were you paid your month's leave?—I have received a month's pay, but I have lost my leave. I am sure that if we were to be paid for the extra duty we perform instead of our leave we would get no extra pay, but we would get our leave instead.

1441. What further question do you wish to touch upon?—The next item is that of "Extra duty." We think that extra pay should be given for extra duty.

1442. *Mr. Holmes.*—Explain to us what you mean by extra duty?—Duty performed by inspectors or other officers after having performed the ordinary tour of duty laid down by the rules of the service.

1443. I presume, then, taking the case you mentioned some time ago, that if you are nominally entitled to go off duty at 8 o'clock, and then you are kept until 9 o'clock in the morning, that that extra time should be considered as extra duty, and that you should be paid therefor?—Quite so. I am sure they would then be very anxious to get me off duty at 8 o'clock, and would make some arrangements which would insure that being the case. If we do not have extra pay, we think that we should have time given for it. The meaning of that is, that if I perform extra duty I should be given relaxation for it; that more time should be given me in order to get rest. This would be more suitable to us than payment. We think that, if the tour of duty is to be broken into periods, eight hours is quite sufficient for any officer to be on duty. And we think that if officers perform extra duty, they should be at liberty to make arrangements themselves to go off duty, or to get somebody to take their place in order that they may be able to get proper relaxation for rest, without applying to the superintendent or other superior officer.

Inspector John Delaney.

10 Sept., 1882.

1444. Your proposition amounts to this: that whereas under the old system you were twenty-four hours on duty on alternate days, which amounted to eighty-four hours in the week, you now wish to have only fifty-six hours in the week?—I don't wish for that. I only say that if we are to be paid for extra duty, that eight hours should be the period fixed as that which we were bound to perform; and that anything over eight hours we should be paid for. I do not give preference to the eight hours' system over the twenty-four.

1445. Do you observe that the latter proposition is so much larger than the first proposition—the first proposition being that you were satisfied with twenty-four hours on duty and twenty-four hours off duty. Taking that at three times twenty-four and twelve hours, it gives eighty-four hours; you would be doing eighty-four hours' duty then?—Yes.

1446. Whereas the proposal that you should go on duty for eight hours out of the twenty-four, in the seven days, would only come to fifty-six hours?—I understand.

1447. Making a difference of twenty-eight hours in the duty?—Yes, quite so. But broken periods of a tour of duty cause the consumption of a deal of time and the expenditure of a great deal of labour by the officer. For each tour of duty he has to clean himself and his uniform, and to walk to the station and back. A man doing broken periods of service is practically no gainer in rest. It is all very well to theorise, but in practice that is so. A man performs more duty under the short-hours' system. Of course this all has reference to the present system, and is only suggested if the present tour of duty is continued. If two tours are given to a man it would make it much harder than if he was given one tour, because you make that man go home twice, which entails all the trouble I have already referred to. The plan seems very nice in theory, but when you reduce it to practice it is quite the reverse.

1448. You would prefer the old system with longer hours than the present with nominally shorter hours?—I would.

1449. *Chairman.*—The present system is nominally ten hours a-day?—Yes, ten hours when on day duty and fourteen hours when on night duty. I forgot to mention that, in this present tour of duty, we have a change every Friday which we had not before. We have to do eighteen hours' duty on the Friday; we get that for a treat on every Friday. Why they fix on Friday I don't know. There is a change of duty every week. We go on duty at 10 o'clock in the morning and we go off at 2 o'clock. We go on then at 8 o'clock, and remain on duty until 10 o'clock the next morning; we get that for a treat every Friday. We perform eighteen hours that day out of the twenty-four.

1450. *Mr. Morris.*—I wish to put to you one question in reference to this. As a man over twenty-eight years in the service, don't you consider that, even if you were off duty, from your position in connection with the police force, it would be necessary that your whereabouts should be known, and that you should be ready to be called upon in case of any

Inspector John Doherty.

29 Sept., 1882.

sudden necessity or emergency; don't you think, in fact, that, in case of an emergency, the whereabouts of all the men while off duty should be more or less known?—Yes, certainly. In case of an emergency we don't object to any amount of extra duty being put upon us, and without extra pay in those cases.

1451. What is the next question to which you wish to refer?—The next question is that of promotions to the rank of inspector.

1452. How many classes of inspectors are there?—Three, and the acting inspector.

1453. What do you ask for?—Every inspector, on being promoted to that rank, we think, should have his promotion approved of by his Excellency the Lord Lieutenant. That would give us a better status than we have now, and would give us some security for our rank.

1454. *Mr. Holmes.*—Who investigates charges against inspectors?—One or other of the Commissioners, under the present system. It is, however, a very rare thing to have a charge brought against an inspector.

1455. *Mr. Morris.*—Do you consider, putting aside altogether the question of the system at present adopted, that it would be better that some other person had the trial of cases against officers of the force than the Commissioner of Police, whoever he might be?—No, Sir; I would still like to see the Commissioner of Police trying cases of that kind.

1456. Who would you associate with him?—The superintendents of all the divisions used, up to a few years ago, to sit at the board when cases of discipline were being disposed of by the Commissioner.

1457. Then, as I understand you, you would wish such cases to be tried not by one individual Commissioner, but by a board consisting of him and some of the superintendents?—Quite so.

1458. As was the case heretofore?—Yes.

1459. With one of the Commissioners presiding?—Yes. That was always the case in Mr. O'Ferrall's and Colonel Lake's time.

1460. *Mr. Holmes.*—Would you be content if there was a return to the old system? Yes, quite so. The service came to perfection under the old system.

1461. Then, if you are content that a return should be made to the old system, you do not wish that the Lord Lieutenant should be saddled with those troublesome duties of approving of your promotions, and so on?—No; if our promotions and status are put into the hands of a board, certainly not; we would be quite content if there was a return to the old system. Those boards were held weekly. Now, however, the Commissioner sits daily, and we consider it unfair to be surprised by a charge being brought against us, of which we get no notice whatever until we are walked in before the Commissioner. We ought to get time to make a proper defence, to have legal assistance, if necessary, and the evidence given against us should be taken on oath.

1462. *Chairman.*—Have you to deal with any other question?—The next question is as to the power of dismissal. We think that no Commissioner, however just, ought to dismiss any member of the service without assigning a just cause for so doing; and to do so is, we think, against natural and constitutional justice.

1463. *Mr. Holmes.*—How is a man dismissed now; explain the procedure that is adopted?—You may be told that your services are no longer required, without any cause being assigned. I think that is unjust.

1464. Well, I presume that power is never exercised by the Commissioner unless there is very good cause?—We cannot say. We think he ought to show his cause. The power is, however, seldom exercised.

1465. *Mr. Morris.*—Do you consider that he should give a cause for telling a sub-constable that his services are no longer required?—I think so.

1466. As well as to the case of any other class?—I would not mind the case of a constable so much. But he has great experience of his officers; he has not that of the sub-constable. He may get a constable or recruit, and he may find out something that, in the opinion of the Commissioner, would render him unfit to be in the police service at all. I don't think the Commissioner in that case should be bound to say, "I have found out so-and-so against you." But in the case of an officer whose whole life has been spent in the service, I say that no Commissioner should have the power to dismiss him without assigning a reason. Upon the question of punishment we shall be quite content to leave that in the hands of the Commissioner, provided he is assisted by a board of superintendents, as I have already suggested.

1467. *Chairman.*—What further point do you desire to refer to?—Under the head of "Transfers," I wish to bring our views before you. We think that no inspector should be transferred from one division to another unless upon conviction of a corrupt offence, and a reason given why he should be removed from the district, unless all his expenses be paid, and in no case should a less sum than 10*l.* be allowed to inspectors. One inspector ought, in our opinion, to be at liberty to exchange with another subject to the approval of the Commissioner. The unnecessary transfer of officers inflicts great hardship on the officers as well as loss to the public. Now last January, in the cold weather, there were no less than eighteen of us, nearly every inspector, transferred in one night. There was no cause whatever shown for it, nor up to this can anyone see any reason for it. The only object that we could see in it was, that in the case of every inspector there was great care taken to put him as far away from his residence as possible, so that he had to shift his lodgings. Many of us had houses, and the greatest inconvenience was caused us. I had a house of my own purchasing and had a beautiful garden, and every comfort, but I was hurled out of it, and every one of my comrades had the same experience, more or less. We ask here for 10*l.* for lodgings, but that sum would not at all compensate us, if the system I have described were pursued to any extent.

1468. Is a man required to change his residence whenever he is transferred?—Yes; when transferred he must live in his district.

1469. *Mr. Holmes.*—The transfer of a man from one district to another involves a change of residence?—Yes, certainly, and the breaking up of your home.

1470. *Mr. Morris.*—Putting aside the transfer on the occasion you mention, whether any reason could be assigned for it or not, don't you think, for the good of the force, it is a wholesome rule that the inspector should live in his district?—Yes, I do; there is no question about that.

1471. *Mr. Holmes.*—Did none of the inspectors, upon the occasion to which you refer, remonstrate, or bring the matter under the notice of the Commissioner, or point out the hardship involved by the sudden change?—They did; and some of their children were sick with scarlatina and other diseases, and there was no relaxation of the order.

1472. When you receive notice of transfer are you required to leave your district at once, on the moment?—In this case we were directed to leave our houses at once, but we didn't do it, we could not do it; we could not get lodgings. Some left in a week, some in a month, and more went on where they were for months, and they were threatened every time, "If you are not out of that shortly, you will see what will happen." In the case of the men transferred that night the inspectors had to resume their duties at their new stations on the following morning. Transfers of this description are also against the public interest, as I will show you. This was at a time when the city was in a state of turmoil, in January last. We were all sent to new districts, where we knew nobody, where we didn't know the men, and where we were strangers to the people that would give us information about what was going on. The Arms Act had just been passed, and arms were being removed from place to place. It was under those circumstances that we were sent to new districts, and we were therefore like a lot of common fools.

1473. Now, do you really mean to say that none of you can assign a reason for the transfer of so many inspectors?—Not the slightest.

1474. Without any kind of notice or explanation?—No, Sir. We thought it was a harsh and arbitrary act, and without any reason whatever.

1475. *Chairman.*—And you got no notice?—No notice whatever.

1476. *Mr. Holmes.*—On the question of drill, may I ask do the inspectors drill, or are they drilled?—I drill and am drilled.

1477. Before you get the rank of inspector you have to pass an examination in drill?—You are drilled in the presence of the Assistant-Commissioner, and get a certificate, without which you cannot pass; and for every subsequent promotion you must go through a like examination, and get a like certificate.

1478. You have to do that in the rank of inspector?—In every rank; you might have a dozen of them.

1479. Are you drilled after your promotion?—Yes, Sir. Before concluding my evidence to-day I wish to make an observation with reference to my evidence yesterday. Now that we have been informed what the scale of pay is for the classes of inspectors in London, we think the demands we put forward yesterday for increase of pay were somewhat excessive, and we would propose the following scale instead:—For third-class inspectors, 150*l.* instead of 137*l.*; second-class, 175*l.* instead of 160*l.*; first-class, 200*l.* instead of 180*l.* We think the 40*l.* we asked for lodgings is a rather large demand.

1480. Supposing you were allowed to let lodgings, would you be content with your present allowance?—We would not; it is too small. We would be content with 30*l.*

1481. With regard to uniform, would you be content if the uniform was supplied to you as in London?—Quite so.

Inspector John Doherty.

14 Sept., 1882.

Inspector Richard Fogarty, Dublin Metropolitan Police, examined.

1482. *Chairman.*—You have listened to the evidence given, and the statements made by Inspector Doherty?—I have.

1483. Do you coincide with his views and with his evidence?—I do.

1484. Do you entirely coincide with what Inspector Doherty has stated?—I entirely concur in the views he has put forward.

Inspector R. Fogarty.

14 Sept., 1882.

Inspector Mollaly, Dublin Metropolitan Police, examined.

1485. *Chairman.*—You have heard the evidence of Inspector Doherty?—Yes.

1486. Do you coincide with the views to which he has given expression?—I entirely concur in the views which he has placed before the Committee on behalf of the inspectors of the service.

Inspector Mollaly.

14 Sept., 1882.

Inspector Manly, Dublin Metropolitan Police, examined.

1487. *Chairman.*—Do you entirely concur with the evidence given by Inspector Doherty, and the statements he has made?—Yes, Sir.

1488. You have heard him speak of the Memorial presented to the Commissioner with the view of inducing him to order a return back to the old tour of duty. Was it you who promoted that Memorial?—Yes; I got up this Memorial from the commencement, and we had it prepared a good while before we presented it. I was advised by my friends not to present it until after I received my promotion.

1489. *Mr. Morris.*—I presume you were then an acting inspector?—Yes. On the day that I was promoted I came down and wrote an explanation of the Memorial, and asked the Chief Superintendent to lay it before the Commissioner and to explain its points—to direct his attention to the fact that burglaries had increased at the rate of 183 per cent. since the introduction of the tour of duty four years ago, and that that increase had been mainly caused by the want of supervision of the inspectors and acting inspectors over the men at the time the burglaries were committed, because they were always committed between 3 and 6 o'clock in the morning. I was then brought before the Commissioner, who said he would not give the old tour that we were looking for—that he would not grant the old tour.

1490. During the time that you were an acting inspector, and before your promotion, could you state, from your own knowledge, that it was the wish of the large majority of the acting inspectors to have the old tour of duty reverted to?—I merely formulated our views. The moment I got it up every one of the station-house officers signed it who saw it with the exception of two or three.

1491. *Chairman.*—As regards that Memorial, it embraced all the views of the acting inspectors except two or three?—Yes. They all—forty-three station-house officers out of fifty-two inspectors and acting inspectors—signed it. In the case of the remainder of the fifty-two some of them were absent, and two or three had never gone under the old tour, and they did not understand it.

1492. Is there anything else you wish to speak about?—The case of Captain McFarland has been referred to here. I wish to explain it.

1493. We have been informed of the facts of that case.—Then I have nothing further to say.

Inspector Manly.

14 Sept., 1882.

Acting Inspector John Kelly, A Division, Dublin Metropolitan Police, examined.

1494. *Chairman.*—How long are you in the force?—Fifteen years and four months.

1495. How long have you been an acting inspector?—Just two years.

1496. Where are you stationed?—At Chancery Lane Station.

1497. What do you wish to bring under our notice, on your own behalf and on behalf of the other acting

Acting Inspector John Kelly.

14 Sept., 1882.

Acting Inspector John Kelly.

——

22 Sept., 1882.

inspectors?—Well, Sir, first of all, we think we ought to have extra pay for extra duty, and an increase in our weekly pay.

1498. *Mr. Holmes.*—Will you kindly state what your weekly pay is?—1*l.* 16*s.* 8*d.*

1499. What is that in the year?—95*l.* 17*s.* 8*d.* per annum.

1500. *Chairman.*—What increase do you suggest?—Well, Sir, we have come to the conclusion amongst ourselves that we would leave that to the gentlemen of the Committee, after they hear what we have to say on the subject. We would prefer leaving the extent of the increase to you.

1501. What case do you make for an increase?—The increased cost of living. The present pay is 1*l.* 16*s.* 8*d.*, and it will take a man at least 2*l.* 10*s.*—at least 50*s.* a-week—to live fairly.

1502. What was the pay of an acting inspector before the increase in 1878?—1*l.* 4*s.*

1503. *Mr. Holmes.*—Do you think the cost of living has increased since 1878?—It has, Sir.

1504. In what items?—Well, it is more difficult to get lodgings now; lodgings are dearer, and we must live in respectable lodgings now. We must have respectable lodgings, and we cannot live in low streets or back streets, and the state of the country and the state of the city has a good deal to do with it. We cannot live in tenement houses, with people who do not like us. I have made an estimate of what it will cost a married man, with, say, two or three children, to live—what it will take from him in the week. I have included all the items that are required or necessary for a family for a week, and the cost comes to 2*l.* 4*s.* 10½*d.*

1505. Kindly state what the items are?—Lodgings, 5*s.* per week; meat, 1½ lbs. per day, at 10*d.*, 10*s.* 6*d.* in the week, and I think I have reason [illegible] meat has increased enormously in price since 1872.

1506. But that is not the fact?—Well, I remember when we used to get meat at the Castle at 7*d.* and 7½*d.*, and we cannot get it for anything like that now. I know that I can get no steak under 1*s.* a lb. I know that is what I am paying at the present time.

1507. Is not 1½ lbs. of meat a-day a rather large allowance for one man?—I am giving that allowance to five persons—a man and his wife and three children. Well, tea and sugar I put down at 2*s.* 6*d.* weekly; butter, 2 lbs. per week, at 1*s.* 4*d.*, 2*s.* 8*d.*; bread, two loaves per day, 4*s.* 8*d.* per week; milk, 1 quart per day, 2*s.* 4*d.* weekly; potatoes, 2 stone, 1*s.* 4*d.*; coal, 3*s.* a-week—that is not even allowing two bags, because two bags would come to 3*s.* 8*d.*; school for children, 6*d.*; soap, 6*d.*; lamp oil, 10*d.*; fish, one day, 8*d.*; family requisites, clothes, boots, everything else necessary for a family, 5*s.*; and then 1½*d.* a-week, deducted from the pay for the band, makes in all 2*l.* 4*s.* 10½*d.*

1508-1513. Who pays for the band, as you have mentioned it?—The service. Gentlemen, I have a document (it is as short as we could possibly make it) containing an outline of the reasons for seeking an increase of pay, to our rank in particular. We consider that we have a better claim than any other rank or grade in the service for an increase of pay, inasmuch as we have more difficult and more onerous duties than any other men in the service, except the inspectors and superintendents—we come next. With your permission, I will read this document for you. It is as follows:—

"*Reasons in Support of Acting Inspectors' Claims for Increase of Pay.*

"The duty performed by an acting inspector is exactly the same as that done by the inspector, and in many stations, where there is but one inspector, the acting inspector in charge of the opposite tour has exactly the same responsibilities on him as his inspector. The acting inspector must be a man who, from his ordinary and technical education, can deal promptly with all cases arising in his sub-division, or coming in any way under his notice; must be equally competent with the inspector to give proper legal directions to those under him; must be able to report for the Commissioners' information on all matters requiring same; and, in fact, the efficiency of the sergeants and constables depends as much on the supervision, efficiency, and example of the acting inspector as on that of the inspector, who is oftentimes absent from the station duties at races, reviews, &c.; but the acting inspector never, from the date of his appointment to that rank until he either gets further promotion or retires on pension, is thus employed. Further, the acting inspector, from his position, being always in the station, is looked to by the public for advice and assistance at all times in dealing with, and disposing of, charges and complaints, either real or imaginary; and it frequently occurs that persons given into custody in the heat of temper would, if detained through inexperience or ignorance, involve the parties giving them into custody in serious consequences. And from the position the acting inspector occupies in the force and in the estimation of the public the rank is entirely underpaid, and not in proportion to the responsibilities or the services rendered to the public; and to maintain the efficiency and respectability of the rank it should be better paid.

"When compared with head constables of the Royal Irish Constabulary, and the general pay of that force and ours compared, the difference in the amounts given to equivalent ranks in both forces is not maintained between head constables and acting inspectors; and it will hardly be denied that acting inspectors undergo twice as much mental and physical labour as head constables; and even in our own service, no other rank performs the same number of hours of duty by day or night except inspectors—on an average ten or eleven per day and nearly twelve per night. At present, a man might be thus employed sixteen or eighteen years out of the thirty years of his service, and then be entitled to about 1*l.* per week to sustain a broken-down constitution." (This has reference, I may observe, to the men who joined the service before the 12th August, 1867.)

1514. How many acting inspectors are there?—Fifty-one in the service.

1515. Is there an acting inspector attached to every station-house?—There are two attached to all the principal stations.

1516. Are the acting inspectors and inspectors on duty at the same time in the station-house?—Yes, Sir.

1517. And what relation does the acting inspector bear to the inspector in the performance of duty?—They both go on the same tour together. One goes out on duty patrolling the sub-division and visiting the sergeants and constables, and the other remains in the station.

1518. Does the inspector also go out and patrol the sub-division?—Yes. The inspector goes out on the first morning of the week, and on the second morning of the week the acting inspector goes out. There are two who go on for day duty at 10 o'clock in the morning, an acting inspector and an inspector, and they are relieved by an acting inspector and an inspector at 6 o'clock in the evening.

1519. *Chairman.*—What do you mean by saying that the acting inspector is always in the station?—What I meant by that was, that the acting inspector is never sent on duty to races, reviews, exhibitions, or anything of that sort; not that we want to be sent on those duties, I merely mention the fact. Whereas in the case of the inspector, he is perhaps once or twice every week employed on special duty, which may be at races or reviews, or making special inquiries.

1520. What next do you wish to lay before us?—With regard to pensions, we would wish to be allowed to retire from the service after twenty-five years'

Acting Inspector John Kelly.

16 Sept., 1882.

service on full pay, three-fifths of pay at fifteen years' service, with one twenty-fifth added for each year from fifteen to twenty-five years.

1521. *Mr. Holmes.*—Then in point of fact, you are not satisfied with the scale of pensions under the Act of 1847?—No, Sir.

1522. But are you aware that that scale is the very best scale in existence, and that no other class of civil servants enjoys so good a scale?—Well, Sir, there are very few classes of civil servants that can be compared to the Dublin police, because we have to attend out in all weathers, and we have to encounter every class of criminal.

1523. But have not all police forces to do that?—Well, I am not aware that anyone has such severe and long hours of duty as we have.

1524. *Mr. Morris.*—But as I understand the question Mr. Holmes put to you, you do not seem to have comprehended its meaning. He has said that you, being under the scale of pensions provided by the Act of 1847, are better off than any other civil servant under Her Majesty, and then you answer that by saying that you are entitled to be better off. Without disputing that question with you, I wish to show you that Mr. Holmes is striving to impress upon you that you are already in that better position under the Act of 1847. Do you see the point now?—I do, Sir. I see it now.

1525. Well, what do you say in reply to that?—It is considered by the great body of the Dublin police that thirty years is too long to have to serve; that men are too worn out at thirty years' service. When the average is taken, it will be found that men who have spent thirty years in the service do not as a rule live much over ten or twelve years after retiring.

1526. Are you speaking on the authority of statistical Tables that have been made out, or is this mere hearsay?—I have no Tables.

1527. *Mr. Holmes.*—Are you aware that the London police never could retire upon full pay, and that the most they could ever get was two-thirds of their pay?—I am, Sir. I am aware of that.

1528. And you men now who joined the force in Dublin before 1867 can retire after thirty years' service upon your full pay, provided you are incapacitated?—Yes, Sir.

1529. Then do you not admit that the scale of pensions under which you can retire is an exceptionally favourable one?—Well, it is a good scale of pensions. I do admit that it is a good scale of pensions. But for all practical purposes, the London police cannot be compared with the Dublin police.

1530. *Chairman.*—In what way?—The London policeman is not looked upon in the same way as our men at all. Our men when they go out to do duty on the streets, unless there are two of them walking together—I am not now including in this reference very respectable streets—they are in great danger, and we have to have our men doubled, chiefly, of course, in the lower parts of Dublin, to save them from being badly treated. The London police I believe, too, have a great many advantages that we do not possess. They are allowed to have a house; and, if I am not misinformed, their wives and families are allowed to have some business to supplement their pay.

1531. In other words, you think that the life of a Dublin policeman is more hazardous, and is fraught with more wear and tear on his constitution, than that of a London policeman?—Yes, Sir; that is my argument. It is harder work, Sir.

1532. *Mr. Holmes.*—And that, therefore, you ought to be allowed to retire at twenty-five years' service, instead of thirty?—Yes, Sir.

1533. *Chairman.*—What other point is there on which you desire to lay your views before us?—Well, Sir, the next point is in reference to gratuity after three years' service under the Act of 1867.

1534. What do you suggest?—That after three years' service a man struck off from the service by the medical officer as not able to serve should be allowed one month's pay for each year; and from ten to fifteen years, a man struck off should be allowed two months' pay for each year.

1535. When you say "struck off," you mean unable to go on in consequence of unfitness through sickness?—Yes, Sir.

1536. Not struck off through misconduct?—No, Sir; we don't mean that. And in case a man dies in hospital, that his wife or children be allowed that compensation, although he may have been unable to sign the document that would, under ordinary circumstances, be presented to him for signature.

1537. Kindly proceed with the next matter?—We also ask that sick men be allowed full pay while sick, unless it is their own fault; that there be no stoppage from men while on the sick list unless it is their own fault.

1538. *Mr. Holmes.*—What is the deduction now made?—One shilling per day from the pay of men of all ranks up to that of Inspector.

1539. I suppose that deduction is made to pay the cost of medical attendance?—I don't know, Sir; I am not aware.

1540. Supposing a man did not go into hospital, and was treated at home for his illness, would the deduction be made then?—Yes Sir.

1541. *Mr. Morris.*—Does he receive the benefit of the police doctor gratis?—Oh, yes, Sir; he receives the benefit of the attendance of the doctor of the force.

1542. And does it include medicine?—Yes, Sir.

1543. *Chairman.*—And there is one shilling a-day stopped for that?—Yes.

1544. *Mr. Morris.*—Then you get something for the shilling a-day?—Yes, Sir. All our men consider that a man who is sick would want his full pay more than a man that would be in his health. For instance, a man with a wife and family with 1*l.* 8*s.* 2*d.* per week, if he falls sick, and has to lie at home for a week or a fortnight, and 7*s.* is deducted from his pay, that leaves him only 1*l.* 1*s.* 2*d.*, which is a very small sum to support his family and get nourishment for himself.

1545. *Mr. Holmes.*—If you knew that a similar deduction was made from the pay of the London police, for the purpose of meeting the cost of medical attendance, would you still ask that you should be relieved of the deduction?—I would, Sir, because I believe that it is not made for that purpose. I believe that the shilling is not stopped for the purpose of paying the doctor.

1546. For what purpose is it stopped?—I don't know. I am not able to answer that question.

1547. Is it to put a stop to malingering?—I think it has a tendency in that direction, although I am not able to say so positively, Sir.

1548. Do you think, if that was the object of the deduction, it has been effected?—I don't think it has.

1549. You don't think it does put a stop to malingering, then?—No, Sir.

1550. And that it, on the contrary, only bears hard upon the men that are really ill?—Yes, Sir.

1551. *Chairman.*—Have you any further statement to make?—Yes, Sir. We ask that officers and constables when transferred not on complaint or promotion should be allowed a reasonable sum to defray the expenses they are occasioned by the change.

1552. When they are transferred from one district to another?—Yes.

1553. And also that allowance should be given to all grades?—Yes, Sir.

1554. *Mr. Morris.*—Do you carry your opinion so far as that even a constable of the first, second, or third class should be paid for being transferred from one district to another?—Yes, Sir; if he is transferred for the good of the service.

1555. *Mr. Holmes.*—Are men in the rank of constable frequently transferred from one district to another?—No, Sir; not very often. The principal thing that we object to is that married men should be transferred unless for grave reasons, because

Acting Inspector Jones, Esq.

13 Sept., 1882.

frequent moving breaks up his little stock of furniture, and breaks up his establishment, and he has to go into a strange house; and perhaps from the unsanitary condition of the district or the house he is not very safe in moving from the one in which he is placed to another.

1556. In cases of men who are not transferred by reason of their misconduct, do they get reasonable notice that they are to be transferred?—Sometimes they get no notice, and some times they do.

1557. *Mr. Morris.*—It is uncertain?—Yes.

1558. *Chairman.*—Have you anything further to add?—Well, Sir, I wish to refer to the Pension Act of 1867.

1559. *Mr. Holmes.*—Are there any acting inspectors who have joined since 1867?—There are only two acting inspectors who have joined the service since 1867.

1560. What do you suggest on the subject of the Act of 1867?—A man holding my rank and who joined the service since 1867, after twenty-five years' service would be only taking as much as I am entitled to at fifteen years, namely, 66*l*. 13*s*. 7*d*.; that is, one-half.

1561. Are the men, as a rule, who joined the force since 1867, aware upon joining that they are under a different scale of pensions as compared with the men who joined before that year?—No, Sir; they do not understand it until they are two or three years in the service.

1562. Are they not told when joining the terms upon which pension is given?—Yes, they get a Circular.

1563. Does not that Circular tell them the scale of pensions they would be under?—It does, Sir.

1564–1565. *Mr. Morris.*—I presume they only practically realise their position when they see other men entitled to retire under an Act which is more favourable than theirs?—Exactly so, Sir; it is only then they begin to understand it.

1566. Was it a cause of dissatisfaction amongst the officers and men of the Dublin metropolitan police that they received nothing at the time that the Royal Irish Constabulary received a gratuity for their extra services during the last three years?—It was, Sir.

1567. *Chairman.*—Do you think that dissatisfaction led up to the recent crisis?—I do, Sir.

1568. *Mr. Holmes.*—Were the men of the Dublin police force aware that the constabulary in many districts were considerably out of pocket by the expenses they had to incur in the discharge of their duty in recent times?—They had to pay if they left their districts.

1569. That they had to pay a great deal for their night's lodging, and the extra cost of food, and that they were losers to a serious extent by reason of the disturbed times?—They were, Sir.

1570. Are the men of the Dublin metropolitan police aware of that fact?—They are, Sir. But they believed—the Dublin police believed—that the constabulary men are recouped for expenses incurred in travelling from one part of Ireland to another, that they are paid back again.

1571. As a matter of fact they were not, and as a matter of fact the allowances they got prior to the recent changes that have been made were not sufficient to meet those extra calls?—But they did get some expenses; they got some mileage expenses. But as a matter of fact, the men of our force "not receiving any of the 180,000*l*.," as they called it, was a cause of discontent among them.

1572. *Mr. Morris.*—I presume the police in Dublin are aware that the Royal Irish Constabulary quartered in the town of Belfast, and those that happened to be quartered in the town of Bray, received a share of that 180,000*l*.?—Yes, Sir.

1573. And I suppose the police in Dublin considered that they had quite as much extra duty to discharge as the Royal Irish Constabulary in Belfast or Bray in connection with the land agitation?—We consider, Sir, that we had more extra duty to discharge than they had.

1574. *Chairman.*—Have you anything further to add?—I am commissioned by the men to bring under your notice that the severity of fines inflicted within the last six or seven years was the cause of great discontent in the service.

1575. *Mr. Holmes.*—Specify any instances of that that you know of your own knowledge?—Yes, Sir. There were several men reported for not noticing a placard that was posted up in the city, and the fines went to over 60*l*.

1576. How much were men individually fined?—From 1*l*. to 30*s*. for not noticing and reporting this placard being up.

1577. And in your opinion, that was excessive?—Yes, Sir; it is not my individual opinion, it is the opinion of the service, so far as I know it.

1578. But you do not complain that there was a fine inflicted, or you do not think that the members of the service could complain if there was a fine inflicted for any breach of discipline. You only complain of the extent of that fine, that it was excessive?—I do not complain that there was a fine imposed for the breach of discipline, only that the fine was too high.

1579. In fact, you think the system of fining is too severely carried out?—Yes, Sir, that is the opinion of the service, and that is one of the causes of the discontent.

1580. *Mr. Morris.*—And you consider that for trifling breaches of discipline—I am altogether omitting drunkenness or insubordination—for small offences of discipline, the fines imposed are excessive, and the men of the force, as a body, complain of that also?—Yes, Sir.

1581. *Chairman.*—Is there anything else that you wish to add to your evidence?—Yes; the curtailment of pensions when men retire from the service is another cause of discontent. We expect, when retiring from the service, that we will get what we are entitled to by the Act of Parliament, and that it will be in no one's power to cut that, or to make it any smaller than what we ought to get.

1582. You complain of the reductions of the pensions; and from what cause?—Well, Sir, some of the best charactered men that were ever in the service have been cut in their pensions.

1583. *Mr. Holmes.*—Has any reason been assigned?—No reason has been assigned; we do not know what the pensions have been curtailed for.

1584. *Mr. Morris.*—Are you of opinion that when a constable or inspector or sergeant is fined for any offence, that that fine ought to be considered as a sufficient punishment without being carried over as a punishment to count against him when he becomes entitled to his pension?—Yes, Sir.

1585. *Chairman.*—That the punishment at the time should be final?—Yes, Sir.

1586. What is the present system? Are the fines recorded and taken into account in reduction of pension?—Yes, Sir, they are.

1587. *Mr. Morris.*—And you consider that a cause of grievance to the force?—I do, Sir.

1588. Is there any limit of time within which they will not be carried out?—No limit, Sir.

1589. Then if a man be fined for a violation of discipline, or even for drunkenness, and punished, that punishment will be still held over his head and affect his pension; is that so?—Yes, Sir.

1590. You know that to be the case?—Yes, Sir. A young man in the force might commit himself, and when he would get a cooler head he would be very sorry that he fell into such an error; and we consider that punishments for trifling offences committed in a man's youthful days should not be held over his head when he is an old man in the service.

1591. Do the force think that the fines inflicted for drunkenness are excessive?—Well, Sir, we do not much care what a man is fined for being drunk. Let him get off as best he can. Any man that gets drunk, let him be punished.

Acting Inspector James Downey, examined.

1602. *Chairman*.—You have heard the evidence of Acting Inspector Kelly?—I have.

1603. And do you concur in it?—Yes.

1604. Fully?—Yes.

Acting Inspector J. Downey.

19 Sept., 1882.

Acting Inspector Joseph Johnston, examined.

1605. *Chairman*.—You also have heard the evidence of Acting Inspector Kelly?—Yes, Sir.

1606. And do you also concur in the evidence, and the statements made by him?—I do.

Acting Inspector J. Johnston.

19 Sept., 1882.

[The Committee then adjourned until Thursday, September 21st.]

Eighth Day.—21st SEPTEMBER, 1882.

Present:

Mr. J. W. O'Donnell, Mr. George Morris, D.L., and Mr. R. W. A. Holmes.

Acting Inspector John Doran, Dublin Metropolitan Police, examined.

(Also present Acting Inspector John Shelley.)

1607. *Chairman*.—You have attended here to-day for the purpose of giving evidence on behalf of the men of your rank in the Dublin metropolitan police?—Yes.

1608. But I understand that you know the other men of your rank who have been already examined, and that you are aware of the nature of the evidence they gave?—Yes.

1609. And that you have full confidence in them and in the mode in which they laid the matters which you wish to bring under the notice of the Committee before us?—Yes. I have full confidence in the four men who were elected by their comrades to come here and give evidence.

1610. We have no objection to take your evidence beyond the fact that, if you have no fresh matter to

Acting Inspector John Doran.

21 Sept., 1882.

Acting Inspector John Dunne. 22 Sept., 1882.

present to our notice, it is undesirable to repeat evidence already given?—Although I attended here to offer my evidence, I was by no means certain that I would be required.

1611. *Mr. Holmes.*—May I ask you, do the acting inspectors receive a lodging allowance?—They do not.

1612. Are they supplied with uniform?—They are. The acting inspectors, you are already aware, have to perform the same duty as inspectors.

1613. We are aware of that, and I suppose there is really no doubt about it that your duties are precisely the same as those of the inspectors?—Yes, exactly the same as an inspector's.

1614. It is merely the first step to becoming an inspector?—Yes. You must be an acting inspector before you are an inspector.

1615. Have you the same responsibility as an inspector?—Well, just the same. I may mention that I was speaking last night to one of the acting inspectors who was examined here, and I could not think of anything I could add to the evidence he gave.

Acting Inspector JOHN SHELLEY, Dublin Metropolitan Police, examined.

Acting Inspector John Shelley. 22 Sept., 1882.

1616. *Chairman.*—You have heard the statements just made by Acting Inspector Dunne?—Yes.

1617. Do you concur in what he said?—Yes, and I may add that I also saw last night one of the acting inspectors examined before you on Tuesday, and I am satisfied that he represented everything that we desire to point out to you.

Sergeant JOHN DEMPSEY, Dublin Metropolitan Police, examined.

(Also present Sergeants Eugene M'Carthy, James Corrigan, and Henry Kilkenny, Dublin Metropolitan Police.)

Sergeant J. Dempsey. 22 Sept., 1882.

1618. *Chairman.*—How long have you been in the force?—Fifteen years and eight months.

1619. How long are you in your present rank?—For two years past.

1620. What is your present rank?—That of full sergeant.

1621. Where are you stationed?—Chancery Lane Station, in the A Division.

1622. What do you wish to bring under our notice affecting yourself and the other sergeants, kindly deal with the subject in what you consider the order of their importance?—First of all, we request that we may be granted three months pay, the same as the Royal Irish Constabulary, for extra duty performed during the last two years or two and a-half years.

1623. *Mr. Holmes.*—Please state the grounds of that request?—Well, on the 8th April, 1879, there was a conference of the Irish Members of Parliament, held in the Rotunda, and the Land League was established. At that time men had to be on duty either in the neighbourhood of where this meeting was held, or in their own stations, until late hours of the night—sometimes 12 o'clock, and more times 1 o'clock—along with doing their ordinary duty. For instance, when they should come off duty at 9 o'clock at night, the day men would be kept on until 12 o'clock that night or 1 o'clock the next morning, and then would have to resume duty at 6 o'clock on the same morning. And then again, the men who should go out at half-past 10 would be brought out at 9 P.M. I kept on duty until 6 o'clock in the morning.

1624. You are speaking for the sergeants now; were many of them so employed?—Yes, sergeants and constables. This refers to the whole working police force at that time. After the conference in the Rotunda in 1879, there were branches of the Land League formed through the city, and all those branches had meetings two and three times a week, and sometimes more. Those meetings had to be watched by the sergeants and men on the beats, and they would have to stop out, every man would be there, for the purpose. They would at other times have to stop on reserve at the station, and very frequently a couple would stop out watching those meetings.

1625. But did that entail extra duty?—Yes, Sir. If a meeting commenced in the evening, and a man should have gone off at 9 o'clock, he could not do so; but if that meeting were not over until 11 o'clock, he would have to stop on until it was over, and make his report at once, or else he could not go off duty. Then, in March 1880, we had the large Land League meeting in the Park.

1626. I think you had better speak generally?—And in the same year we had the State trials, and a great many were employed there, and got extra duty during the trial in which Mr. Parnell and others were traversers.

1627. *Chairman.*—I don't think that any duty imposed upon you in attending to trials or the Commission of Oyer and Terminer should be considered extra duty?—The State trials, which entailed an enormous amount of labour on the men, were not Commissions.

1628. Every State trial and Commission forms part of the administration of the law, and comes within the scope of the ordinary duty of a constable?—There was a great deal of extra duty imposed on the men.

1629. Yes, and upon the Judges, counsel, and every person engaged?—Oh, yes, Sir.

1630. Unless you put forward some substantial grievance, or indicate some substantial extra work not at all dependent upon Commissions or State trials, I don't think that evidence can strengthen your case?—Of course, where men would be done in the evenings after the trials, it is not exactly about being on duty in the four Courts they complain; they would naturally expect to be relieved from duty, but what they complain of is doing extra duty. The men were kept on reserve at the stations during that time, and during the late hours of the night, until such time as the city was quiet. I do not say that the mere fact of being on duty there was extra duty, but during the time those trials were going on officers and men were kept on reserve duty at the stations, or in many cases patrolling the streets until quietness was restored, sometimes at 1 o'clock in the morning, and sometimes longer.

1631. As I understand your answer, it is this, that you do not mean to say that it is the mere attendance at the Commission of which you com-

Sergeant J. Dempsey.

22 Sept., 188[illegible]

plain, but of the time you were afterwards detained on duty?—Yes, certainly; the time after the Commission was over. We would be kept until 12 o'clock at night before we could get off duty.

1632. *Mr. Holmes.*—Is it a fact that the state of the city during the last three years entailed constant extra duty upon the men?—It is so; a great deal of extra duty. As soon as the suspects began to be arrested, men were kept constantly going to the railway stations.

1633. Don't you think that that is comprised in the general answer you gave to the general question?—Well, I do not wish to press it, but I wish to show the amount of day duty done by the men, and how they were placed, and that when the suspects began to be arrested, men of the force were sent to all the railway stations, irrespective of whether they should or should not be on duty. Everywhere they were met or could be found; when a telegram came in advising of the arrival of suspects—and they came in very frequently—they were ordered to go to the railway station, and they would have to remain there until the train came in, and the prisoner or prisoners escorted to Kilmainham, or to some railway station, as the case might be.

1634. But surely suspects were not arrested every day in the year?—Indeed, they were coming in by every train, and we used to have them coming in to all the different stations.

1635. Are you aware that many members of the constabulary were seriously out of pocket by reason of the performance of their duties in the present state of the country, the men were ordered away at a moment's notice from their own barracks, perhaps to distant places, and had to pay heavy sums for their lodgings, and much more than the allowance they received would have enabled them to do; are you aware of that?—I am aware of it.

1636. Were the men of the Dublin metropolitan police force out of pocket by reason of the state of the country?—Well, I don't mean to say they were out of pocket much.

1637. Were they out of pocket at all; can you adduce a single case where a sergeant or constable of the Dublin metropolitan police force lost money by reason of the land agitation?—No, because any money they spent in car fare was refunded.

1638. Are you aware that it transpired in evidence before the late Committee of Inquiry into the Royal Irish Constabulary that many of the men who had saved money before the last three years were obliged to eat into their savings for the purpose of meeting these extra expenses; are you aware of that?—I am aware that the constabulary had to expend a great deal of money, but whether they were allowed it or not I am not aware. But in reference to the Dublin force, I may state that when men had to remain in the Castle barracks from Rathmines, as they often had to do, until 1 o'clock in the morning, it cost them a good deal for the refreshments that they required, owing to the extra duty they performed during such days and nights.

1639. *Chairman.*—Were not those refreshments paid for by the Government?—No, Sir. Any extra refreshments they required they paid for out of their own pocket, and they came to a good deal.

1640. *Mr. Morris.*—In fact, you wish to put it this way: that suppose you were stationed at Killiney you would be brought on this extra duty into Dublin. Is not that so? Were not some of the men who were doing duty at Killiney and Kingstown brought into Dublin to do extra duty during the agitation?—Yes.

1641. And of course, they were obliged, when on duty, to eat something?—Yes, Sir.

1642. And then the Royal Irish Constabulary, who were quartered at Bray, were not brought in at all?—No, Sir.

1643. And they had very little, if anything at all, to say to the Land League agitation, for it scarcely affected the neighbourhood of Bray; is not that so?—Yes, Sir.

1644. And yet they got the three months' pay as a gratuity?—Yes.

1645. And you consider it a hardship that the men quartered at Kingstown did not receive the same consideration?—Yes. But we contend that we have done more extra duty than the constabulary have done in any part of Ireland.

1646. Show us how that is so?—That has been done by the men as I have described it during the agitation. And then there is the additional consideration of all the men having to go out to Kilmainham Gaol from half-past 8 o'clock at night. Men had to go there from all the town divisions, and do duty from 9 o'clock at night until 7 o'clock the next morning, so that it would be half-past 7 o'clock or 8 o'clock by the time they would get home.

1647. And that was extra duty, beyond their ordinary duty?—Yes.

1648. *Mr. Holmes.*—Surely you don't consider your duties were as severe, or anything like as severe, as those performed during the agitation by the Royal Irish Constabulary in the counties of Kerry, Clare, Limerick, and Galway?—I would say they were much more severe. The constabulary had a good deal of duty, no doubt, to perform in connexion with many matters arising out of the agitation—Land League meetings, Sheriffs' sales, and things of that description; but it was nearly all on day duty that they had to do these things, whereas the principal part of our extra duty consisted of night duty, from half-past 8 until 7 o'clock the next morning, and in a great many instances they had to get refreshments, and we were a long time at Kilmainham before it was thought fit to supply refreshments to the men.

1649. Do the constables and sergeants of the Dublin metropolitan police feel it to be a grievance that they did not participate in the gratuity given to the constabulary?—I believe it to be the principal grievance. They look upon themselves as being as well, if not better, entitled to it than the constabulary, and they naturally expected they would be considered in reference to it.

1650. And was it a very sore disappointment to them when they found they were not?—Yes, it was a very sore disappointment to them.

1651. *Chairman.*—And you think that led to the recent crisis?—In a great measure, I believe it did.

1652. *Mr. Morris.*—In fact, you consider that the metropolitan police were passed over?—Well, to put it plainly, we considered that it was a slight upon us.

1653. *Chairman.*—Have you anything further to add on this topic?—Well, no. As far as extra duty is concerned, I think we have spoken enough about it.

1654. Well, what is the next matter you desire to bring under the notice of the Committee?—The next thing that we propose to bring under your notice is, that if you would be pleased to recommend that the pay of the sergeants and acting sergeants of the Dublin metropolitan police be increased according to their ranks in proportion to the increase of pay that the Government may be pleased to grant to the acting inspectors of the same service.

1655. *Mr. Holmes.*—How many classes of sergeants are there?—There are two; acting sergeants and sergeants.

1656. *Chairman.*—A man cannot pass to the grade of sergeant from constable without being an acting sergeant?—Yes, Sir.

1657. *Mr. Morris.*—Your pay as a sergeant is 89l. 15s. 11d.?—Yes.

1658. And do you suggest any reasonable increase?—I would be inclined to leave the amount in the hands of the authorities. What we want is this. We complain that the pay is small, in consequence of

Sergeant J. Gregory.

7 Sept., 1882.

the enormous expenditure we are under for living and rearing our families, particularly any of us who happen to be married and living out. House-rent and everything else is enormously dear, and after these expenses are met we have no money to meet the cost of clothing for ourselves or our families. We have no money to pay for the schooling of our children if we have any, and, in fact, we have not money enough to meet our necessities, and we live very humbly. Then we are circumstanced in a peculiar way with reference to house-rent. We are not allowed by our own authorities to live in humble places, for if we were allowed to live in humble places by the authorities, the inhabitants would not allow us to live in them; so that we have to go and live in respectable neighbourhoods, where, if the inhabitants do not associate with us, they let us alone at all events.

1659. What is your ordinary average rent per week?—7s. to 7s. 6d. for these small cottages that are built. Sometimes one might chance to get a house at a reasonable rent, one of these small cottages. But generally when a tenant is leaving one of them, the next that comes to occupy that cottage has to pay a higher rent. In fact, the landlords of those places make it a compliment to give a house to a policeman at all.

1660. Then, in point of fact, your house-rent is 20l. a-year?—Yes; in fact, it is very poor accommodation for that.

1661. Mr. *Holmes.*—What increase of pay do you suggest. It is better that we should know your views on the subject?—Well, I am not aware what increase the acting inspectors have been looking for; but at any time I remember throughout the service the difference between the pay of an acting inspector and a sergeant has been only from 1s. to 1s. 6d. a-week. Well, it was considered that the sergeants were entitled to higher pay in consequence of the duties that they have to perform, that they have to go through the same duties as an acting inspector. I am over two years a sergeant, and the duties I have had to perform for these two years have been the same as the duties performed by the acting inspectors. If the acting inspector is called away from the office the sergeant comes in and does his duty. An acting inspector may be called away for some hours on special duty, and the sergeant is then brought in and does his hour of duty the same as the acting inspector. He does the same amount of work beside him in the office, has the same hours, and is just as responsible in every shape and form as the acting inspector while he is there. I believe that the sergeants of the service would be satisfied that whatever increase the acting inspectors may get, that they will be just placed on the same footing in reference to the increase as they are at the present time.

1662. What is your weekly pay?—My weekly pay is 1l. 14s. 6d.

1663. Have you any allowances?—We have an allowance of 6d. per week for boots, or 1l. 16s. 6d. a-year for boots, getting uniform fitted and repaired, keeping ourselves in gloves, mufti clothes, stoppages for band, and repairs of boots.

1664. I suppose that allowance does not at all meet what it is intended?—It leaves a balance of 1l. 7s. 6d. that we are out of pocket, allowing two pairs of boots in the year, which would not do at all.

1665. Mr. *Morris.*—In fact, the allowances which are made to you amount to about half what it costs you?—Yes, about half.

1666. Mr. *Holmes.*—Are you aware that the London men are only supplied by the Government with two pairs of boots in the year?—I believe they are supplied with boots in that way.

1667. But you find that this allowance, which is intended to meet the cost of your boots, and the wear and tear of your uniform clothes, and your gloves, does not at all provide what it is intended it should provide?—It does not. We have to get our uniform fitted after we get it. Of course, we could not go out wearing it in the state in which we get it from the stores, and it costs from 7s. 6d. to 10s. to have fitted a tunic and two pairs of trousers in the year.

1668. *Chairman.*—And is the cost of fitting the clothes included in the 6d. a-week?—Yes, Sir.

1669. Mr. *Holmes.*—Instead of being provided with that allowance, would you prefer to be supplied with boots?—No; because I don't think the men would like it. They would not wear boots such as are supplied to the London men.

1670. Why? Do you think they give the men a slovenly appearance?—I cannot say, as I have never been in London.

1671. Then, how do you know that the men here would not wear such boots as are supplied to the London force?—From what I have heard from men who have been in the London service. They say our men would not wear those boots at all; that they are great heavy boots, that the leather is very hard; and that they talk the feet when going along the streets. It is not on the ground that they would be slovenly that our men would object to be served with those boots; they say simply that they would prefer the allowance. There are some persons whom it is very hard to fit with boots, and suppose such persons got those boots supplied to them by the Government, why they would bring corns or something else on their feet, and render those men useless for service for some time. They would not fit them at all.

1672. Mr. *Morris.*—In fact, you think it is a better plan to make an allowance to the constable than to supply the article?—Yes.

1673. Mr. *Holmes.*—What was the pay of a sergeant before the increase given in 1872?—1l. 5s. a-week.

1674. Do you think that the increase in pay then granted was regarded as a boon by the men, and were they satisfied with it?—They were.

1675. And do you think the cost of living has really increased since 1872?—Oh, it has. It has increased in many ways. There have been great difficulties thrown in the way of the police of late years, and those difficulties have been a great deal more serious than previously. For instance, the police cannot now allow their children to mix with any other children, and anything they have to pay for they have to get in the first-class houses, and pay the dearest cost.

1676. *Chairman.*—Why is that?—Because their wives and families cannot go into those houses where the general public resort.

1677. Why?—Because they would be insulted, and they have to go and live in neighbourhoods where their pay is not at all suitable for the purpose, in order that they may live in peace and quietness.

1678. They have to go and live in higher and wealthier neighbourhoods than their pay entitles them to resort to?—Yes; they have to go and live where clerks and people of that class of life would pass them by without notice, and not say anything to them, whereas, no policeman could go and live in any of the ordinary open streets.

1679. Mr. *Holmes.*—Has this state of things has only sprung into existence within the last three years?—Well, I would say within the last three years.

1680. Prior to the last three years a policeman did not experience anything of that kind?—Not so much.

1681. But did they experience it at all?—At any time a policeman cannot live as cheaply as the ordinary class of people can live in this city.

1682. Is that owing to the bad feeling of the people towards the police?—I believe it is, to a great extent.

1683. But did that bad feeling really exist before the last three years?—It was very seldom that a

Sergeant J. Dempsey.

21 Sept., 188[illegible]

good feeling existed on the part of the people towards the police at any time, as a matter of fact.

1684. Are you serious in saying that?—I am.

1685. And do you allude, in making that statement, to the Dublin metropolitan police?—I am alluding to any police.

1686. *Mr Harris.*—But that is only on the part of a certain class of people?—Yes, Sir. The class of people that the police have to mix up with.

1687. I believe, as evidence of that, that for many years in Dublin, when a policeman tries to do his duty in arresting a drunken or rowdy character, "the people," as they are called generally, are another rowdy character against him?—Yes; and they are attacked in very many cases by people that you would not at all expect would be guilty of that sort of thing.

1688. *Mr. Holmes.*—Do you mean to say that the small traders and shopkeepers with whom you would naturally be inclined to deal are not willing to deal with you because you are a policeman?—They would not deal fairly with you, on any consideration, because you are a policeman.

1689. And, therefore, you are obliged to go to the more expensive shops?—Yes.

1690. And that is an actual fact?—Yes, it is a fact.

1691. *Chairman.*—Have you anything further to add on the question of pay?—Nothing further to add on that point, Sir.

1692. What is the next matter that occurs to you as worthy of our attention?—The next point is, that we desire that the Pension Act of the 11th August, 1867, should be repealed, and that the members who joined the service since that be placed on the same scale of pensions as that laid down for the men who joined under the Act of 1847, and we wish that the Act of 1847 should be amended so as to enable members of the service to retire on full pay pension after twenty-five years' service.

1693. *Mr Holmes.*—You come under the old Act yourself?—Yes, Sir.

1694. When men join the Dublin police force are they, as a rule, aware of the change that was made in the scale of pensions by the Act of 1867?—Well, when young men are joining the police my experience of them is that they do not look at pension, because they never join the police with the intention of remaining very long. It is only after they come to be in the service four or five years that they get to like the police, and then they begin to think of making a home in the police for themselves after they begin to know the benefits they are likely to derive from being in the police and remaining in the police. Then in a similar way under the Act of 1867, as soon as men have served four or five years in the police, and when they become conversant with it and know the rules and regulations of it, they see that the Act only gives them a very small allowance for a pension after fifteen years, or, indeed, after twenty-five years, they are not inclined to stop much longer in the service; they emigrate and go away, because they know very well that, while they are in the police, their families cannot pursue any business, that they have to live exclusively on their pay, and that if they get broken down in their health at fifteen years, and that they were struck off the service, the pension they would get would not be able to keep themselves or their families at all.

1695. Going back to the scale of pensions under which you came—the scale of the Act of 1847—are you aware that that is an exceptionally favourable scale?—I am aware that the scale of 1847 is a favourable scale.

1696. But you are not satisfied with it; you want to amend it, do you not?—In a certain way, I do. In this way the Act of 1847 is a good Act, that a man is entitled to half-pay after fifteen years' service. After serving fifteen years, however, and a man is struck off through ill-health and directed to be pensioned, should that man have served nineteen and a-half years, and become broken down in health after that period, he would be only entitled to one-half of his pay as pension, whereas, if he had served another half-year, he would have got another quarter of his pension added.

1697. Don't you think that half-pay as pension after fifteen years' service is a very good pension?—It would be more favourable to others than it is to the police, because the chances of a man being broken down after fifteen or twenty years' service are innumerable in the police. And men get broken down after twenty years' service, and the small pension that is given to him is very little to keep him alive.

1698. Are you aware that at no time could men retire from the London police on full pay—that the most they could retire on was two-thirds?—I am aware that there is some such rule in the London police, but I do not think that our force would compare favourably with the London police.

1699. Why?—Because the London police can carry on their business in a very different way to that in which we have to carry on ours. They are backed up by the population; they are not opposed to them; and, besides that, a London policeman can keep a shop.

1700. It is not a fact that London policemen can keep shops, or their wives; but the latter can pursue certain callings. For instance, a policeman's wife can be a dressmaker, can do washing, or keep a laundry, but the police in London are not allowed to keep shops or trade in any way?—They are allowed to let lodgings, which is a very lucrative way of living; whereas here we are dismissed for that very thing alone.

1701. And would you consider it a boon if the police in Dublin were allowed to let part of their houses?—I would not, because it would not be easy to get suitable lodgers, and the police would want to keep apart altogether from those people. I would suggest the propriety of their living by themselves.

1702. Don't you think it would be a very difficult thing to obtain a better scale of pensions for the Dublin men than for the men of the other police forces of the United Kingdom?—It might be a difficult thing to have a better scale of pensions for the Dublin men, but from the way in which those men have to work in Dublin, and with all the obstacles that beset them, I think the Dublin men are entitled to a better scale of pension.

1703. Are you aware that there are certain ranks of the Dublin police that are better paid than some of the corresponding ranks of the London police force?—I am not aware of that.

1704. Then you may take it as a fact that the third-class of inspectors here are considerably better paid than the third-class inspectors in London?—But the inspectors here have to do infinitely more work than the inspectors in London.

1705. How do you know that?—I understand that an inspector in London never has to do any desk work at all—or scarcely any; whereas, an inspector here has to stand at his desk for fourteen hours at night, and work all the time as hard as he can. Now, there are over 600 men under the Act of 1867, and our present strength is only 1,134, so that there is comparatively a small number of men who are under the old Act of 1847; and, in fact, in two or three years hence we will have scarcely anyone at all under the old Act of 1847. The number of men under that Act will be very small indeed.

1706. Well, what do you intend to convey by that statement?—I mean to convey by that statement that the force can scarcely be kept up except the Act of 1870 is repealed. The present state of things is felt particularly by the men who have five years' service. I was speaking to some of those men yesterday, and they feel very strongly about the present rate of pensions; and if asked the reason why, one of those men will say, "Well, I have five years' service now (or, perhaps, six or eight, as the

Sergeant J. [illegible].

21 Sept., 1867.

cate might be), and if I remain here five years more I shall be completely broken down, and I shall have nothing for the latter end of my days. I had better seek my fortune somewhere else, and where I will get something for the latter end of my days."

1707. May I ask you, have many men, who were members of the force, emigrated recently?—A terrible lot; and their places cannot properly be filled for a long time to come. And there is a good deal of money lost upon training those men, because, when they emigrate, they are efficient public officers, having passed through the different classes; whereas, when fresh young men come to replace them, they have to be at the depôt for a considerable time, and fresh money has to be spent on training them there, and even then they must be inexperienced policemen for some years.

1708. You don't think those men are dissatisfied with their pay. It is not so much a question of their pay as of their pension?—Well, some consider that the pay is insufficient, but these terrible grievances as I believe, and that which caused the late discontent amongst them, was the question of pension.

1709. *Chairman.*—What do you propose in reference to pension after twenty-five years' service?—What I propose is, that the pension, after fifteen years—at which time they are entitled to half-pay under the Act of 1847—should be according to the Act of 1847, but that for each year they serve after that fractional parts of their pay should be granted to them as pension, instead of having fixed periods of years between each increment of pension.

1710. *Mr Holmes.*—But do you mean seriously to say that the constables of the Dublin metropolitan police consider that they are not sufficiently paid—the constables of the first, second, and third class?—I believe they do think that they are not sufficiently paid.

1711. Do you think they would consider themselves insufficiently paid if they were aware of the fact that the second and third class constables in Dublin are better paid than the second and third class constables in London?—I don't know.

1712. As a reasonable man, I ask you to answer me that question?—Well, there have been discontent caused in the service among the men in the ranks of constable in consequence of a system that was got up of late in the service of keeping them on the lowest grade—the fourth class—for a considerable period; and the position of a fourth-rate constable brings with it a very small allowance for a man to strive and manage to live on. He can barely live and feed himself, putting out of the question the possibility of his ever being able to save any money to put him in a position to go home and see his friends, if he was disposed to take the leave that he would be entitled to. He never could save any money on that pay.

1713. How long is a man usually in the fourth class in Dublin?—He would be usually in the fourth class for about nine months from the time he would leave the depôt; but of late a system of examination has been got up for men desiring to pass from fourth class to third; and if the men were not able to attend school in their own time to prepare for those examinations, they might be in the fourth class for years. I have known constables that were on the list of clerks, and they were kept in the fourth class for three years because they were not able to attend school, and make themselves up in the questions that would be asked them.

1714. What are the subjects of examination?—There would be sometimes questions asked in reference to duty, such as, "What is a cab?" Well, if the candidate was not able to describe what a cab was, according to the definition laid down by the examiner—indeed, the questions are sometimes more like conundrums than anything else—if the candidate was not able to guess the answer, he would lose his examination, and he would not get his rate. Others who were able to attend school, and be up in that description of questions, and clever at the guessing business, would get a place before such a man as I have described. I have known constables that were left in that way for three years, and who then emigrated out of the service, and those were smart, intelligent constables.

1715. Is there an examination from the third to the second grade?—Yes, from the third to the second, and from the second to the first.

1716. And, I presume, the subjects of examination are more difficult according as the classes go up?—Yes, Sir.

1717. Who are generally the examiners?—The examiners of late are all selected from the superintendents, and there is now a written examination. A programme is drawn out, and the papers in relation to the examination are transmitted, through the superintendent, to the Commissioner. The answers to the questions are written down, and they would then be subjected to some sort of scrutiny, and whatever marks the candidate got would be recorded, and upon his position in the list would depend his promotion.

1718. Who are the scrutineers?—I don't know.

1719. Don't you think it is a very useful thing for a police force to have a school and to have examinations, in order to fit men who may be very good policemen, but of indifferent acquirements, to rise to be officers?—I am very sure it is.

1720. Therefore, you do not give this evidence with a view to the abolition of the school system in the force?—By no means.

1721. Then it is not against the system of schooling, and of bettering a man's education, that you give this evidence; but it is because you think the system might be improved?—Quite so.

1722. *Chairman.*—You approve of the system of education; but there are, in your opinion, defects in the administration of it?—I believe so.

1723. *Mr Morris.*—And you consider, I presume, that many a man might be an excellent constable, sergeant, or the like, but that he might not be sufficiently educated to be fit to be promoted to the rank of inspector, whereas if he received some education while in the police service he might become a first-class inspector?—The sort of education a man would get in the school would not fit him for a very sufficient first-class inspector.

1724. *Mr Holmes.*—Would it not?—That is, the sort of education a man gets at present there.

1725–1730. Who are the schoolmasters—are they taken from the force?—An inspector is the schoolmaster, and he has a young man assisting him—a constable in the force.

1731. Presuming a man could rise with fair rapidity from one class to another, if he was a well-conducted man, are you prepared to say that the rates of pay in the fourth class of constables are insufficient, having regard to what I have already told you, that the second and third class constables in Dublin are better paid than the corresponding ranks in London?—I do not think they would be.

1732–1733. If the promotion, then, was certain and fairly rapid, the men would be fairly satisfied with the present rates of pay?—Well, they might be fairly satisfied with the pay; but I could not speak on that point very clearly. I may add that it takes a man here a year before he arrives at the second class, whereas in London it takes him only about three months.

1734. *Chairman.*—Do you wish to add anything further to your evidence?—It is my opinion that it is not so much the smallness of the pay of which the men complain as of other grievances that beset them in the service. For instance, men on small pay being fined for trivial offences, fined 30s. for not noticing a pane of glass broken, or for not noticing a knocker wrenched off a door on his beat, whether it was done before he came on duty or after he came off duty. If it was discovered afterwards, he would

Sergeant J. Dempsey.

21 Sept. 1882.

be sure to be brought up and fined 30s. or 1*l.* for such a thing as that; and very likely if it came for his turn for examination he would be deprived of his examination. Then, again, men get it into their minds that at the end of their service they have no certainty that they will get the pensions to which they are entitled, because they see other men struck off after twenty or thirty years' service, and seriously curtailed in their pensions on going out. I believe these things had a terrible effect on the minds of the men who resigned from the service, and had the effect of leaving the service in almost a demoralised state.

1735. *Mr. Holmes.*—Can you give us some instances in which fines are unduly inflicted?—I will give you one instance. I remember a case where there was a placard found posted through the city. It was in the spring of the year 1879, I think in the month of March, or else it was in the month of March 1880. But, whatever time it was posted, all the men that passed on that beat, both officers and men, for the twenty-four hours previously, until it was discovered by the men who discovered it, were brought down and fined for not seeing the placard; whether it was posted within their time of being on beat or not they did not trouble themselves to inquire into; but the men were fined according to their ranks, from 2*l.* to 30s.—the sergeants were fined 2*l.*; the acting sergeants, 30s.; and the constables, 30s.

1736. *Mr. Morris.*—What was the nature of the placard?—There was something in its nature which had reference to a meeting of Irishmen that was held in New York or some part of America some time previously, because I remember reading it in one of the weekly papers some short time before the raid was made about the placard business. It was on a Sunday morning that the placard was observed posted throughout the city and the suburbs. It was not discovered until between nine and ten o'clock on Sunday morning by the men on duty then.

1737. *Mr. Holmes.*—And did the fines on that occasion amount to the aggregate of 40*l.* or more?—Yes.

1738. But is it not a very important part of a policeman's duties that he should look about and observe everything that is going on?—A very important part.

1739. Supposing a policeman frequently erred in that respect, and did not observe what was going on, and allowed things to pass that ought to have been noticed, do you not think he should be punished in some way for that?—Yes, I know he should be punished.

1740. What kind of punishment would you suggest?—I could not suggest what kind of punishment, but I would consider that the punishment that should be meted out would be according to the character of the man in default. If he was a man constantly going about and seeing nothing, any man of common sense would scarcely think such a man fit to be a policeman.

1741. Is it a fact that if a policeman did not observe a knocker wrenched off a door he would be fined 20s.?—Well, they have been frequently fined up to 1*l.* at all events, and sergeants and acting sergeants up to 1*l.* 5s. and 25s. for that sort of thing. And then if a police constable was not observing a bunch of cabbage leaves that had been thrown on to the street, and if the sergeant came up afterwards and found that it had not been noticed, he would report the constable, who was pretty certain to be brought up and fined.

1742. For not noticing a cabbage leaf?—Yes.

1743. Would the fine in a case of that kind amount to 1*l.*?—In some cases that has been done.

1744. Do not talk of "some cases." As a general rule, would the fine in a case of that kind be so heavy as a 1*l.*?—As a general rule, it would; and at the same time, the man's beat might be so large that he would not have sufficient time to patrol the whole of it; and yet if that occurred in a certain part of the beat where he would not have had time to pass while doing his beat during his whole tour of duty, he would be fined 1*l.* or 30s. notwithstanding. That is a great grievance.

1745. Now, you are an intelligent man, having reached the position of sergeant in the police force. In other words, you complain that the fines at present inflicted for these offences are excessive?—Yes, that the fines are excessive, and together with that, that there has not been that painstaking in making inquiries as to the chances that the man had of seeing these things occur that there should be.

1746. You mean that there have not been proper inquiries made?—Yes; that there have been no proper inquiries made, and no explanation received from the men.

1747. *Mr. Morris.*—But I do not take you as objecting, as I understand you, to the system if it was properly administered?—By no means; discipline must be carried out.

1748. But you do not object to men being fined for breaches of discipline, on principle?—Certainly not.

1749. But your objection is that sufficient care is not taken in investigating each case before the fine is inflicted?—Quite so.

1750. In fact, that it is hastily done?—Yes; hastily done, Sir.

1751. *Mr. Holmes.*—And have you really no opportunity of explanation?—In many cases a man would be asked what he had got to say, but, before he would get time to say anything, he would be told to "shut up"—that he was only making his case worse.

1752. *Mr. Morris.*—Are there fines inflicted for drunkenness in the force?—Oh, yes.

1753. About how much is the fine generally for the first offence of drunkenness?—Well, for the first offence, a man generally might get off with 30s.

1754. Is that for being drunk on duty?—Yes. The fine would vary from 30s. to 3*l.*

1755. For the first offence?—Yes; and if he held any rank he would be reduced.

1756. That is for being drunk on duty?—Yes, for being drunk on or off duty.

1757. Are the fines inflicted the same on a man that is drunk when he is off duty as when he is on duty?—Just the same, but I would wish you to understand this, that drunkenness in the police is a thing unknown. It is not for being drunk that a man is fined; it is for being unfit for duty.

1758. Of course, when I put the question, I meant to convey that the constable was drunk and unfit for duty?—But this unfitness for duty would be to ordinary eyes scarcely perceptible in a man.

1759. As a matter of fact, of course, a policeman, from his very position as a peace officer, and one who has the looking after of other people, should be a particularly sober man—at all events, while on duty? That is your opinion, is it not?—Yes, Sir. I merely state that for the purpose of clearing up a point in reference to the matter of drunkenness, and to have a correct view put forward, because otherwise people might be under the impression that if a policeman was reported unfit for duty from the effects of liquor, that the liquor would be noticeable on the man in the street, while, as a matter of fact, such is not the case.

1760. What punishment is inflicted on a man for the second offence of being drunk?—I knew one case——

1761. There is no use in talking of one case. What is the average?—The average punishment is either reduction or a fine of 3*l.*

1762. For the second offence?—Yes.

1763. Is it not the fact that, up to two or three years ago, drunkenness was on the increase amongst the men of the metropolitan police force in Dublin, but that, for the last two years, it has considerably

Sergeant J. Dempsey.

21 Sept., 18[illegible].

decreased?—A number of men might be reported as being unfit for duty, but not for drunkenness.

1764. In the last two years?—Yes.

1765. But for the last two years has it been to so great an extent as before?—Oh, I believe the number of reports for that offence has decreased.

1766. The Inspectors who were examined before us stated that, according to the statistics for the last two years, the number of reported cases of drunkenness has decreased. Is that your opinion?—It is, Sir.

1767. *Chairman.*—In the case of a third report or conviction for drunkenness, what is the punishment?—Dismissal, as a rule.

1768. *Mr. Holmes.*—From any grade?—If a man holds rank, and he is reported once for being drunk, he is reduced; but if he is reported three times, he is dismissed.

1769. *Mr. Morris.*—And is it not your opinion that drunkenness in the police force, as a rule, should be severely dealt with?—It is, Sir.

1770. *Chairman.*—And is it a fact that a constable, after three convictions for drunkenness, is dismissed from the force?—It is a fact. They were dismissed for the second offence about two years ago. There was a number of constables dismissed for the second offence of drunkenness about two years ago, some of them men of long standing—of sixteen, seventeen, and eighteen years' service. There had not been a drunken report against some of them for ten years before, and in consequence of having that second drunken report against them they were dismissed.

1771. *Mr. Holmes.*—For what other breaches of discipline or good conduct are fines imposed?—Oh, for any imaginary thing. Walking slovenly in the streets, gossipping, speaking to comrades, speaking to any one if it was not a matter relating to duty—in fact, in innumerable cases are fines imposed; coming out of a public-house on or off duty, in plain clothes or in uniform. In fact, the fine on a man of not coming out of a public-house differs very little whether he is off or on duty, or on Commissioners' leave. If a man was on Commissioners' leave and in plain clothes, he might be punished just the same.

1772. If a man on Commissioners' leave went home to his native village or town, and was seen coming out of a public-house, would he be fined for that?—I do not know of an instance of that. The constabulary do not interfere with the Dublin police when on leave in the country; but if a man is reported coming out of a public-house in Dublin he is fined, and I have known men on Commissioners' leave in the city to have been reported for coming out of a public-house.

1773. *Mr. Morris.*—You were proceeding to allude to a number of matters a while ago under the head of extra duty that the police had been called upon to perform. I suppose you consider that all the members of the police force are liable to be called upon in cases of sudden emergency, such as a fire or a riot, at any hour of the day or night, and that, in fact, they ought to reside for that purpose where their whereabouts may be known?—Oh, yes.

1774. You don't put forward calls on emergency of that kind, such as a sudden riot or fire, as cases for extra pay or extra consideration?—Oh, not at all.

1775. *Mr. Holmes.*—By whom are these fines inflicted?—By the Commissioner or the Assistant-Commissioner. There is another thing, as far as discipline is concerned, that affects every man in the force, and which has caused great discontent, and it is this—that no matter who accuses a man, that party can assert what he likes, and the man has no redress, although he might be as innocent as it is possible to be. He may deny being guilty of the offence, but he won't be listened to.

1776. *Mr. Morris.*—From what you have stated to me privately, I think you are under the impression that there was a case in reference to discipline in which you considered that you were unfairly dealt with individually?—Yes, Sir, I do.

1777. And that the decision in that case was a mistake?—I don't know about the decision being a mistake, but I was wronged.

1778. You consider yourself that you were wrongly treated?—Yes, I was fined 5*l.*, and transferred, and kept out of my promotion of full sergeant for twelve months, and that leaves me that I am not an acting inspector to-day.

1779. Have you anything further to add?—Not on that point.

1780. *Chairman.*—Has it always been the custom or system in the police force that the Chief Commissioner or the two Commissioners should hear cases alone?—Well, the Commissioner generally hears cases alone—the Chief Commissioner, or the Assistant-Commissioner, or the two of them.

1781. Is that the same system as heretofore. Has that been always the custom?—Yes, with this exception, that previous to that a Board of Superintendents used to attend at the hearing of cases before the Commissioners.

1782. *Mr. Holmes.*—What do you call a "Board of Superintendents"?—The superintendents of all the divisions, the seven superintendents, used to sit.

1783. But did the seven superintendents and the Commissioner form a board?—Yes.

1784. For the investigation of charges brought against the police?—Yes.

1785. Would that be for the investigation of small trifling cases, or would it be for the investigation of serious charges?—Every sort of case. The Commissioners used to hold board days once a-week some time ago, but that has been changed, and any man who is reported is brought down on the day he is reported, or the following day, and the case is investigated. Say he is reported last night for a breach of discipline, he would be brought before the Commissioner to-day, but at the inquiry the superintendents are not present, except the superintendent of his division and the Chief Superintendent.

1786. The Chief Superintendent and the superintendent of his division are all that are present?—Yes, Sir.

1787. *Chairman.*—Do they form a board with the Commissioner?—No, Sir, they are simply brought in.

1788. Heretofore, did they take an active part in the inquiry?—Heretofore the superintendents attended the board, and they included, of course, the superintendent of the division that the man was in at the time, and the other superintendents that the man might have served under previous to the time of the committal of the offence which was the subject of the inquiry, and those superintendents might be asked as to the general character of the man when he was serving in their respective divisions.

1789. *Mr. Holmes.*—You said just now that there was a board of superintendents who used to attend at the hearing of these cases before the Commissioner; now, did those superintendents take an active part in the inquiry, or were they merely referees as to character?—They were sitting by.

1790. Did they take part in the inquiry?—I never heard them say anything except when they were asked a question touching a man in a particular case.

1791. Then what do you mean by saying there was a board of superintendents?—The superintendents used to assemble in the Commissioners' Court whenever they would be hearing these cases. The Commissioner, of course, decided the case himself, but he might be disposed to ask the superintendents a question touching on the case, or as to the man's conduct of a particular superintendent, or as to the general body.

1792. And now you mean to say that the Commissioners sit alone, and they are no longer assisted by or require the attendance of the superintendents? —They no longer require the attendance of the superintendents, except the particular superintendent of the man's division and the Chief Superintendent. And they also of course bring the man forward who states the case against the delinquent.

1793. *Mr. Morris.*—You are aware that there must be some person or number of persons to adjudicate upon complaints?—Oh, yes, Sir.

1794. Would you wish to suggest any better course than that the Commissioner, or the Commissioner and the Assistant-Commissioner, should be the tribunal to investigate the complaints against their own men?—I would not wish to suggest any other Court, with this exception.

1795. Mind you, I am not pointing to the present Commissioners, but to the system, because the present Commissioners will pass away, and so will you and I, and we are therefore, as I have said, going into the system, and I am in no way prejudiced concerning it. Have you any remedy to suggest in reference to the tribunal that should hear those complaints?—Not as the tribunal; but I think the men would be more satisfied if, in serious cases where a man would be accused of a breach of discipline and denied it, those cases were heard on sworn evidence.

1796. *Mr Holmes.*—Is not the present system of disposing of those cases practically the same as the former system, because if a man of the A Division is charged with an offence, the case is never gone into by the Commissioners, except the superintendent of the A Division and the Chief Superintendent are present?—No, Sir.

1797. Was not that formerly the case?—No; all the superintendents used to be in the Board-room at the time.

1798. But they took no part in the hearing of the case?—No part, except that the man against whom the case might be heard might have been in a different division from that in which he was when the offence was committed.

1799. And the superintendent of that division would be called upon as to character?—Yes, Sir.

1800. *Mr. Morris.*—Can you make any suggestion to us that we could consider, and having considered it, that we could either approve of it or disapprove of it, in recommending to his Excellency an improved tribunal for investigating complaints against the police?—No, I think the Commissioners have a right to be the proper people to hear complaints of breaches of discipline against the police.

1801. Would you like every serious case to be investigated by both Commissioners sitting together?—Yes, I would, Sir.

1802. Would you like the Chief Superintendent to be associated with them?—I would, Sir.

1803. *Chairman.*—As a Court?—Yes. What I mean is, that I would not like it to go outside the force itself.

1804. *Mr. Morris.*—Do you consider that it would be for the improvement of the force generally—from the fourth-class constable up to the superintendent, through all ranks, that a public inquiry with evidence on oath should be held into almost every complaint that was made. Do you think it would be for the improvement of the force to have such a Court, and open to the public. Or do you think it would be better to have the police force so arranged that their complaints could be in some way or another settled between themselves?—I think it would be better to have them settled between themselves.

1805. *Chairman.*—To have police cases tried by the police authorities only, and the inquiries not to be open to the public?—Yes, not to be open to the public.

1806. But you would prefer in serious cases that the evidence should be on oath?—I would.

1807. That is your opinion?—That is my individual opinion.

1808. And that the tribunal should consist of the two Commissioners and the Chief Superintendent? —Yes, with the exception of the seven superintendents being present in the Board-room.

1809. As reference for character?—Yes, quite so.

1810. *Mr Morris.*—Would you now kindly proceed, if there is any other topic that you desire to lay before us?—The next thing that we wish to lay before you refers to compensation to members of the service struck off in consequence of ill-health.

1811. You refer now to the question of gratuities? —Yes, Sir. We suggest that a member of the service struck off through ill-health after three years' service should receive at least two months' pay for each year served,—after three years and under ten—and that he should receive three months' pay for each year served after ten years.

1812. *Mr. Holmes.*—Up to fifteen years?—Up to any time.

1813. But is he not entitled to pension after fifteen years' service?—The reason we were looking for that in that way was, that in case a man died suddenly after fifteen years' service or after twenty or twenty-five years' service, his people would be entitled to receive the compensation that he would be entitled to receive if he was struck off through ill-health, and so far gone that there was no hope of recovery, a pension would be of no service to him then, and he would prefer to obtain the gratuity.

1814. *Chairman.*—What do you suggest?—That the gratuity I have mentioned should be given to his family in case a man died suddenly after serving fifteen or twenty years.

1815. *Mr. Holmes.*—Do you mean to say this: that if a man dropped down dead in the street after twenty-five years' service,—that in a case of that kind a gratuity of three months' pay for each year's service should be paid to his wife and children? —Yes, Sir.

1816. If he dropped down dead?—Yes, Sir. That would be for each year served after ten; two months' pay for each year served after three and up to ten. And we also ask that the wife and family might be permitted to receive the compensation in cases where the signature of the deceased could not be had.

1817. *Mr. Morris.*—You don't mean to say that if a man was unmarried the compensation should go to his brothers and first cousins?—I do.

1818. Take the case of an unmarried man dying. You do not think in a case of that kind the gratuity should be paid to his brothers and other family relatives?—I do not go so far as that; but I do say it should go to his parents if they required it, because in many cases an unmarried man might be, and often is, the sole support of his mother and father.

1819. *Chairman.*—What is the next matter to which you wish to refer?—We would wish that a sufficient sum, say, 7*l.*, would be allowed for burial, and not the small sum of 3*l.* 10*s.* 0*d.* which has heretofore been allowed, and which is entirely insufficient to bury respectably a member of the service, who dies in the service.

1820. *Mr Holmes.*—Under what head does that allowance come?—It is allowed by the Commissioner; it is charged out of the contingent fund; but his comrades have in many instances to make up an amount sufficient to procure respectable burial.

1821. To what ranks is that allowance limited?— To all ranks.

1822. Do you mean to say that if a superintendent or an inspector died a burial allowance would be given?—There would be no allowance at all

Sergeant J. Dempsey.

21 Sept., 1882.

Sergeant J. Pomeroy

21 Sept., 1872

given if he had a family able to bury him. It is only where a member of the service living in barracks and away from his friends dies that such an allowance is given. I do not know of any case where a married man was buried in that way.

1823. It is limited entirely to cases of single men dying in barracks?—I believe so.

1824. And I suppose only in the event of a single man leaving no means behind him?—Yes; and except he is buried in Dublin he would not get that 3*l.* 10*s.* 6*d.* at all.

1825. *Mr Morris.*—Are there many cases of that kind?—Yes, Sir. There were a great many cases within the last three or four years, and a good many cases in which men who were entitled to compensation died in hospital and did not get it because they did not sign for the compensation, and all they got was the 3*l.* 10*s.* 6*d.* to bury them.

1826. *Chairman.*—Have you anything further to add on this subject?—Nothing further on this subject.

1827. *Mr Morris.*—Is there any other subject you desire to touch upon?—We would wish that there should be no stoppages made from the pay of any member of the service who is on the sick report through no fault of his own, and that separate ward accommodation should be allowed to men who have to go to a public hospital.

1828. The stoppage, as I understand it, is 1*s.* per day?—Yes, the stoppage is 1*s.* a-day according to the laid-down scale.

1829. *Mr Holmes.*—And does that go towards a fund for providing a doctor and medicine for the force?—I don't know where it goes; it is stopped from his pay.

1830. Or is it for the purpose of preventing malingering in the force?—It is not; if a man was supposed to be malingering, he would not be supposed to get any pay.

1831. I mean, that might be one of the ways of preventing it?—That was the primary object of it, no doubt, but then there is something a great deal more serious than the stoppage of 1*s.* a-day from their pay.

1832. Explain that?—Because under the new regulation that has been made out, if a man is two months on the sick report half his pay is stopped; if half his pay is stopped because he is two months on the sick report it brings him very little, whether single or married.

1833. How long is that regulation in operation?—About five or six years; there was one case of that which occurred, and it appeared to be attended by great hardship. There was a sergeant in the service who appeared to be a very delicate man. He was on the sick report for six months, and half his pay was stopped; and then he was on the sick report again for twelve months, and half his pay was stopped, until ultimately he was struck off.

1834. Is it the fact if a man got a serious illness, like smallpox or scarlatina, in the discharge of his duty, that after two months one-half of his pay would be deducted?—Quite so.

1835. *Chairman.*—What is the next question?—The next question to which I wish to refer is under the head of lodgings; we wish the sergeants and acting sergeants not accommodated in barracks to be granted a sufficient sum, say, 20*l.* a-year, as lodging allowance.

1836. Whether married or single?—Yes; those who are not accommodated in barracks.

1837. Are there many single men not accommodated in Dublin in barracks?—I am not aware of any.

1838. But your claim applies to single and married men?—Yes.

1839. *Mr. Holmes.*—Are you aware that the men who are not accommodated in barracks in London are not given any lodging allowance?—No; but I understand they have blocks of houses in which they get accommodation at a very reasonable rent.

1840. Are you aware that in cases where the men cannot be accommodated, either at the station-houses or in the blocks of buildings, they do not get any lodging allowance?—No, I am not.

1841. Well, accepting that as a fact, would you still say that the men here should get a lodging allowance when the men in London are not given it?—Well, I think the men here have a right to a lodging allowance; the inspectors are granted a lodging allowance yearly, and there are other members of the service who have to live in as respectable places, and those persons, in addition to that, are subject to monthly inspections from the inspectors, and yet they have no lodging allowance.

1842. Taking the case of a second-class constable, do you think that a second-class constable here should get a lodging allowance when the second-class constable in London does not, I ask you that as a reasonable man?—It must be borne in mind that a second-class constable would be allowed to let lodgings, and that sort of thing.

1843. Now, is it likely that a second-class constable would have a house at all, would he not be in lodgings himself?—It would be quite possible for him to take a house, rent it himself, and let lodgings, and in that case live rent free.

1844. Don't you think that would be a very foolish speculation, to take a house when a man in that position is in receipt of only 70*l.* a-year?—I do not; there are men who have less than 70*l.* a-year, and they let lodgings, and by that means are under no rent.

1845. Would the sergeants and constables of the metropolitan police consider it a boon if they were allowed to let a portion of their houses in lodgings?—They would consider it a boon if they were not allowed a sum of money in lieu of lodgings. We would also ask for free barrack accommodation and coal.

1846. *Mr. Morris.*—What do you mean by free accommodation?—The men living in barracks have to pay for their lodgings.

1847. *Mr. Holmes.*—What deduction is made from their pay?—1*s.* 9*d.* a-week.

1848. *Chairman.*—Does that include coals?—Yes, Sir.

1849. *Mr. Holmes.*—Subject to the deduction which is at present made, are the barracks supplied with fuel and light free of expense to the men?—Yes, Sir.

1850. *Chairman.*—And for that deduction they get lodging?—Yes; the 1*s.* 9*d.* per week covers all, except that they might have to buy candles for the bedrooms.

1851. Does that deduction of 1*s.* 9*d.* cover the expense of barrack sergeants?—No; they have to pay for his services as well.

1852. *Mr. Holmes.*—Is there another deduction made for the services of the barrack sergeant?—Yes, Sir; 1*s.* a-week from the sergeants and first-class constables, and 10*d.* a-week, I believe, from the others.

1853. *Mr. Morris.*—And suppose you had to pay in any other place for it, could you, by any possibility, get attendance, fuel, lodging, house, everything at a lower rate than 2*s.* 9*d.* per week?—Not if they had to pay in isolated cases they would not. But in the case of men who all occupy one large room, where ten men sleep, to take 2*s.* 9*d.* from each of them for that room would amount to a nice thing at the end of a year.

1854. But don't you say that they get fire and attendance?—Yes, they do, of course.

1855. Is there any other place in the world where you could get such accommodation on cheaper terms than 2*s.* 9*d.* per week, the same accommodation as is now had in the barracks?—I don't think so.

1856. *Mr Holmes.*—Do the sergeants mean together, separately, or do they mess with the constables, in the barracks?—They mess separately.

1857. What does your mess bill come to in the week; I refer, of course, to the cost of your dinner alone?—5s. 3d. a-week.

1858. And what do your breakfasts and suppers come to in the week?—14s.

1859. Do you mean to say that your breakfasts and suppers come to more than your dinners?—I do, Sir.

1860. Is not that a very high estimate?—It is; but a man going out on night-duty wants nearly as much nourishment again as the man on day-duty. If you will allow me, I will hand in an estimate of the yearly cost of living for single men in barracks of all grades, and it amounts to 73*l.* 14*s.* 6*d.* That estimate is as follows:—

List of the Weekly and Annual Expenditure of a Dublin Police Sergeant living in Barracks.

Necessaries.	Weekly.	Yearly.
	£ s. d.	£ s. d.
[illegible]	0 0 11 / 0 0 4	[illegible]
Annual cost of living	—	[illegible]

1861. *Mr. Morris.*—You hand in that return, which includes the cost of living and necessaries?—Yes.

1862. Then, according to that estimate of yours, no man under the rank of a second-class sergeant can live within his pay?—No man can.

1863. Now, is it the fact, that no man in the force who belongs to any of the several ranks of constable can save money?—I believe it to be a positive fact—that is, if he gives himself the necessaries of life—that he cannot save money.

1864. Do the constables, as a matter of fact, save money?—I do not know of any at present to be saving.

1865. And is not a prudent constable able to save?—Not a farthing.

1866. Were you able to live within your pay as a constable?—I would have to do so. I could incur no debt. I would be dismissed for incurring one penny of debt.

1867. *Mr. Holmes.*—Don't you think that that estimate has been framed upon a very liberal scale?—A great many of us went at it, and we wanted is to set forth everything according to the most moderate terms we could think of.

1868. Would the men here in Dublin consider it a boon if the barracks were supplied with reading-rooms?—Yes, they would.

1869. And if they were made comfortable as a place of resort when off duty?—Yes.

1870. With libraries and reading-rooms?—Yes.

1871. Would they consider those a boon?—Yes, they would, Sir.

1872. Is there a billiard-table at Kevin Street barracks?—There is no billiard-table, but there is a skittle-alley. Not only do I think that the comforts you mention would be a boon, but I think they would be a great source of benefit to the health of the men as well.

1873. And you think they would serve to make them fond of their barrack life, and would be the means of inducing them to remain more in barracks when they are off duty?—I do, Sir. I might mention, while on that subject, that there is a library belonging to the police, and that there are branch libraries in the different stations—small presses of books, so that any member of the service wishing to borrow a book can do so, and bring it home to read.

1874. Do I understand you to say that there is a small library attached to each station?—Yes.

1875. *Chairman.*—Who pays the expense of that library?—Oh, the men have subscribed to it.

1876. *Mr. Holmes.*—What do they subscribe?—1*d.* a-week.

1877. But the men would think it a great boon if each barrack were supplied with a reading-room?—Oh, yes, they would.

1878. Upon an average, how many men are accommodated in the barracks in Dublin?—Well, from thirty-five to forty.

1879. *Chairman.*—Have you anything else to add?—We ask that for any extra duty performed, extra pay should be granted to the members of the service according to the stipulated scale of pay.

1880. What do you mean by extra duty?—Where men would be called upon to perform extra duty, such as extra duty they have been called upon to perform during the last couple of years, that they would be paid according to the stipulated scale of pay they have been receiving for the extra duty they perform.

1881. *Mr. Holmes.*—Is not a policeman supposed to be always ready to be employed?—Oh, yes. He is always supposed to be ready for duty, but it could not be expected that he would be always on duty. He has a great deal of duty to perform that is not looked upon as duty at all. For instance, a man after going off duty at night or going off at 6 o'clock in the morning might have to go and attend the police court, and be there half the day, and be kept there until 3 or 4 o'clock in the afternoon, and there is no consideration at all taken for that.

1882. And does it often happen that a man going off duty at 6 o'clock in the morning is obliged to follow his case to the police court, and is obliged to remain there until late in the afternoon?—Frequently. It frequently occurs also in the case of men while they are on day duty, that they rarely go through a month of day duty without having some summonses during the month, and, in a great many instances, those summonses come on for hearing during the time they are on night duty, so that when they go off duty in the morning, they have to go to the police court and attend to their summonses.

1883. If a man goes off duty at 6 o'clock in the morning, when would that man go on duty again?—At 9 o'clock at night.

1884. And that man might be kept in the police court until 4 o'clock in the afternoon?—Yes.

1885. So that he would only have from 4 o'clock until 9 o'clock to rest himself?—Yes.

1886. Does that frequently happen?—Yes; I might say it frequently happens.

1887. And for a case of that kind, I understand you to say that a man should receive extra pay?—No; not in that case.

1888. Then when should the extra pay be given?—Whenever they are called upon to perform extra duty similar to that performed within the last couple of years. Say, where men have to go up to Kilmainham Prison or the Viceregal Lodge, and remain there from 8 or 9 o'clock at night until 6 o'clock in the morning; whereas, the ordinary duty would not be more than six and a-half hours each night.

1889. Whereas, now they are—from what?—From nine and a-half to ten hours, and sometimes eleven hours before they get to their barracks.

Sergeant J. [illegible]

21 Sept., 1882.

1890. *Mr. Morris.*—Don't you think that in all the systems of police forces throughout the world, from time to time there will occasionally arise—in this country—where extra duty will be required of the men?—I am aware of that.

1891. Don't you think that merely paying a policeman so much for eight or nine hours' duty, as the case may be, and that then you are to take into account any extra hours he is on duty, and that he is to be paid at a certain additional rate for those extra hours. Don't you think that all that would complicate the accounts, and that it would always lead to a discussion, if a man was sent on extra duty, as to whether he should discharge that duty in one hour or two hours, and don't you think that if men were really liberally paid, it would be much better in the interests of the police and in the interests of the public that the arrangement should be as at present—that they should take the rough and smooth together?—Well, I think it would; but the Royal Irish Constabulary receive extra pay for extra duty where they are so many hours on duty; there any time they are on duty after a certain number of hours they receive extra pay here.

1892. *Mr. Holmes.*—Are you aware that that extra pay is not intended as extra remuneration, but to provide them with the means of living while they are absent from the barracks. Are you aware that it is in the nature of an allowance for lodging and food, and not remuneration at all?—I am not aware of it.

1893. *Chairman.*—Instead of extra pay for extra duty, as you would wish, the system in London, as I remember it, is to allow a kind of equivalent in rest to the constable for the extra duty performed wherever it can be done. Would that satisfy the men here?—It could not be done in Dublin. The police are not numerous enough.

1894. Have you anything now to add to your evidence? The next point is touching on leave, the annual leave to sergeants and acting sergeants. We would ask that the annual leave to sergeants and acting sergeants be one month in the year, and that, in addition thereto, they get two days' leave in each month, one of such days to be a Sunday; and, in case the exigencies of the service would not allow them to get three month's leave within the year, that they be paid for it if they have to work.

1895. That they should have either pay or leave?—Yes, Sir.

1896. *Mr. Morris.*—Then the two days in every other month would give them very nearly another month in the year?—Yes; I might say that the reason of the men pressing this so strongly is, that it is very difficult for them to get the leave they are entitled to at the present time. No matter who is entitled to leave, the sergeants and acting sergeants generally must be working.

1897. *Chairman.*—Kindly proceed to the next head of your evidence, if you have nothing to add on the question of leave?—The next matter is that we ask that, in case any officer of the service should be reduced from a higher to a lower grade, if his conduct remains good for three years after he is reduced, that he be restored to his former position. That was the system that was in the service in the days of the late Sir Henry Lake and Mr O'Farrell—that any officer who was reduced for any offence, or for any breach of discipline, they invariably restored him after three years if his conduct remained good, and it was a system that was found to give general satisfaction. But now, if an officer is reduced, no matter what the offence, be it trifling or serious, he is reduced finally; he is, in general, never restored to his former position.

1898. *Mr. Holmes.*—Do you mean to say that, when once a man has been reduced, he can never be promoted to his former rank?—Yes, except in very rare cases. I do not know of a case where a man was restored, after having been reduced, of late years.

1899. I suppose that is very disheartening to the men?—Yes, Sir, very. In some cases they get reckless, and they are dismissed from the service in a very short time afterwards; whereas, if the hope of being restored was held out to them, they would be all very good-charactered men, and men that would mind themselves in the service, and mind others that they might be put in charge of in the service during the time they might be in it, as has been done in many cases.

1900. The system had been that, if a man who was reduced conducted himself well for three or four years in the rank to which he had been reduced, he would then be reinstated to his former rank?—Yes.

1901. And that, you say, worked remarkably well?—Yes.

1902. Is there anything else you wish to state to us?—The next thing that we wish to draw your attention to is that, in consequence of the great danger of degradation or excessive fines to which the officers and constables expose themselves by entering hotels and public-houses to obtain refreshments, when relieved off duty and in plain clothes, or perhaps on annual or ordinary leave, we wish that attention would be drawn to the matter, with the view of rendering it no breach of discipline, and that a man will not be committing any offence if he be found coming out of a public-house or hotel in plain clothes and on leave, because the service consider it a very great hardship that, when a man goes out to meet his people, who may have come from the country, he is deterred from going into a refreshment-house with them without running the risk, if seen by an officer of the force, of being reported and punished almost as severely as a man coming out of a public-house on duty.

1903. You speak of a man off duty, on leave and in plain clothes?—Yes.

1904. *Mr Morris.*—But, in putting forward that view, you do not hold, I hope, that there should not be extreme strictness upon a man in uniform and on duty?—Oh, by no means.

1905. Your relaxation applies only to constables on leave and in plain clothes?—Yes.

1906. I may tell you that in London the police are allowed when off duty, whether in plain clothes or in uniform, to go into public-houses, but do you not think that, in a city like Dublin, where the people are so hostile at the present moment to the police, according to your own statement, that it would be in the interests of the police themselves not to allow them to go to public-houses, in order to prevent them getting into rows with the people?—I do not know that these men would think so, with the stringent discipline that is observed at the present time.

1907. But in the point of view that I have put, what is your opinion?—I believe it is right not to allow men in uniform to go into public-houses, nor to hold out any hope that they would be allowed to frequent public-houses when in uniform.

1908. Do not you think a policeman in plain clothes would be recognised in a small city like Dublin as a policeman?—He might be recognised, but people would not be as likely to fasten upon him in plain clothes as in uniform. And there is this much also in it, the police, as a rule, if they are going into places for refreshment, like to select respectable places, and they would not go into places where they would be likely to be insulted; but, so far as the present discipline of the service is concerned, it does not make any difference whether he was at the Shelbourne Hotel or the lowest public-house; he would be punished all the same.

1909. And you think, if permission was given to the police to go into public-houses in plain clothes, that they would not go into disreputable public-houses, but that they would only frequent those that would be respectable?—I think that would be so. I do not mean that it would be necessary to promulgate it to the service that they would be at liberty to go into respectable public-houses, but what I mean is, that it would give great satisfaction to the men if there was some relaxation of the present stringent code. I now wish to draw your attention to cases where a member of the service would lose his life in the execution of his duty—where he would be struck down by the assassin——

1910. *Mr. Holmes.*—Or by a blow of a stone or a brickbat?—Yes. We would ask that, in that case, his wife would be allowed by the Government the compensation allowance, for the purpose of supporting herself and her children.

1911. *Chairman.*—As long as she remained unmarried, I suppose?—Yes, Sir, certainly—a sum, say, of 25*l.* or 30*l.*; and that 5*l.* a-year be allowed to each of her children until they arrive at the age of 17 years.

1912. *Mr. Holmes.*—In addition to the allowance to herself?—Yes.

1913. *Chairman* (addressing *Sergeants* McCarthy, Kilkenny, and Corrigan).—You have each heard the evidence given on your behalf by Sergeant Dempsey?

Sergeant McCarthy.—We have.

1914. *Chairman.*—And do you concur in it?—I do.

1915. Do you concur in that evidence, Sergeant Kilkenny?

Sergeant Kilkenny.—I do.

1916. *Chairman.*—And do you also concur in it, Sergeant Corrigan?

Sergeant Corrigan.—I do, Sir, entirely.

Sergeant JOHN DEMPSEY re-examined.

Sergeant Dempsey.—There is an estimate of a married man's weekly expenditure that I would be glad to have inserted in the evidence.

1917. *Chairman.*—Certainly?—It is as follows:—

To Weekly Account of Married Men.

	£	s.	d.
House-rent, per week	0	7	6
Meat (9 lbs., at 10d. per lb.)	0	7	6
Fish, on Fridays	0	0	6
Potatoes (1½ stone, at 8d. per stone) ..	0	1	0
Bread (3 loaves per day, at 6½d.) ..	[illegible]	[illegible]	[illegible]
Butter (2 lbs. per week, at 1s. 4d. per lb.) ..	0	2	8
Tea (1 lb.)	0	3	0
Sugar (3 lbs.)	0	[illegible]	[illegible]
Milk (1 quart per day, at 4d. per quart) ..	0	2	4
Coals, per week	0	1	[illegible]
Sundry articles for household uses ..	0	3	6
Total	1	16	0
Allowance for boots, &c., 6d. per week ..	1	11	[illegible]
Two pairs of boots, at 18s. per pair ..	1	16	0
Repairs for ditto	0	10	0
Fitting and repairs to uniform	0	7	6
Three pairs white gloves, at 1s. per pair ..	0	3	0
One pair black ditto	0	1	[illegible]
Stoppages for band	0	4	4
Total	3	[illegible]	[illegible]
Deficit	1	[illegible]	[illegible]

1918. *Chairman.*—In a word, what do you consider to be the most serious grievances of which the men have reason to complain as a force, as a body?—The pension question, fines and discipline, and being debarred from receiving the three months' gratuity, the same as the Royal Irish Constabulary.

1919. You believe these are the burning questions to-day?—Yes.

1920. Speaking generally for the force, the three most burning questions are discipline, fines and pensions, and the non-payment of the additional gratuity of three months' pay, the same as the Royal Irish Constabulary?—Yes, Sir.

1921. *Mr. Morris.*—These are the three most important questions?—They are the three most important questions, I believe, to be considered in the whole case.

[The Committee then adjourned until next day.]

NINTH DAY.—22ND SEPTEMBER, 1882.

Sergeant [illegible]. — [illegible] Sept., 18[illegible]

to state those matters which you desire to bring under the notice of the Committee?—The first matter I wish to lay before you is, of course, the rate of pay—at least, I mean the three months' pay, or a gratuity for past extra work, the same as that granted to the Royal Irish Constabulary. That is the great present cause of discontent, and the remote cause is the system of heavy fines in the service. Of course, the immediate cause of the agitation was the three months' pay not being granted to our service.

1927. *Mr. Holmes.*—Why do you think that the Dublin police should have received a similar gratuity?—I will tell you, Sir. Because the principal portion of the work for the last three years was laid in Dublin. All in connection with the Land League. We had the Central Land League offices here, and we had branches all over the city, and the county too. We had two Land League meetings in Kingstown, and other meetings all over the city. Of course you have heard of these things. We had the Land League Convention, and a great deal to do with it, and we had the arrests, and we had meetings at the Phœnix Park, and at Harold's Cross, of labourers.

1928. I don't know whether you are aware of it, but a great many members of the Royal Irish Constabulary were severe losers by this agitation; that is to say, they were severely out of pocket. For instance, if a constable was ordered away from his barrack, he had to sleep out at night?—We had to do so too in some cases.

1929. The constable had to pay an exorbitant price for his board and for his lodging, and the result was that men who, prior to the agitation, had saved money, were obliged to make inroads into their savings for the purpose of meeting the charges upon them, and the principal justification for giving that 180,000*l.* was to recoup those men for their losses. Now, having stated that to you, will you tell me whether in Dublin the men were out of pocket by reason of the land agitation?—We were not exactly out of pocket, but there was any amount of extra duty imposed upon us, and the men think that for that extra duty they have a right to be compensated in some manner, and the newspapers stated that the constabulary were compensated for the extra duty performed, and not that that money was given to them to recoup them for the outlay of their own money. When we saw that the constabulary at Dundrum, and Bray, and Shankhill, and Stepaside [illegible], and they certainly did not do a great deal of extra duty, it caused much discontent. As far as regards the point of the constabulary men being out of pocket, the men who were transferred from place to place received travelling expenses of [illegible] 6*d.* a night while they were out, and, of course, we got no such thing at all. Our men came into Kingstown at 6 o'clock one morning from Dublin, from whence they had marched. They were out on that occasion for twenty-four hours, and they didn't get a penny at all for the extra duty. Then we have had meetings of Political Prisoners Aid Societies, the suspects had to be watched, we had to turn out our men for every train by which suspects arrived. No matter where those men were on duty, in every place they were sent, when a telegram came warning us that suspects were arriving at the Broadstone or Kingsbridge, all hands had to turn out. In Kingstown we had one eviction, three Sheriffs' sales, and we had the protection of a boycotted farm on the Barton estate.

1930. And it is your firm belief that the fact that the Dublin men did not participate in this gratuity was the principal cause of the discontent?—Yes, the immediate cause of the discontent; but there were remote causes, a good many of them.

1931. *Chairman.*—Now kindly proceed to the next question, if you have nothing further to say as to that?—Well, in reference to increase of pay, we found our claim for increase of pay on the increased cost of living.

1932. *Mr. Holmes.*—Is it solely upon that ground that you found it?—No.

1933. Because I will ask you, is it a fact that the cost of living has increased since 1872, when the last addition to your pay was made?—Oh, yes, it has increased since then. A policeman can incur no debts—at least he must pay them; and he is liable to be reported and punished for incurring debts. The difference between an acting inspector's and an inspector's pay and allowance is something like 70*l.* They claim an adequate increase of pay, and we, as sergeants, claim a proportionate increase of pay.

1934. As you have referred to the inspectors, are you aware that the third-class inspectors in Dublin are very much better paid than the third-class inspectors in London?—Yes. There is a class more of inspectors, I believe, in London than there is in Dublin. A London inspector is equal to our acting inspector.

1935. There are three classes of inspectors here, and there are three classes of inspectors in London. In addition, there is a class of acting inspectors here of which there are none in London?—Our acting inspectors are equal in the performance of their duties to the third class of inspectors in London. And then the sergeants have, I must say, to perform a great deal of extra duty annually that there is no account taken of at all, and I will just give you an idea of it.

1936. First of all, state what your duties are as sergeant?—Yes, I shall, Sir. The sergeant is responsible for the conduct and character of the men under his charge. He has to report any misconduct on their behalf, but at the same time not to take undue advantage of the men. If he sees them committing an act he is supposed to go on the spot and prevent it, and at once put a stop to the irregularity. He is not to become unduly familiar with them, and he is supposed to show them a good example in punctuality, and smartness, and knowledge of his duties. He has to parade at the station properly the men themselves, and form them into ranks for inspection. He is to report the parade sober and correct.

1937. *Chairman.*—Are these the ordinary duties of a sergeant?—Yes. He has to march out the men to their beats, see that they know their beats, and patrol them regularly. He has to visit the sections, and he is held responsible if any irregularity is taking place in the section.

1938. By the section you mean the section-house?—I mean by "the section," the section over which he is placed—the number of men, twelve, fourteen, or fifteen, as the case may be, that he has charge of. He is responsible for their acts in great measure I may tell you, Sir.

1939. *Mr. Holmes.*—Then I presume the sergeant is continually patrolling his section?—Yes; and he is as liable to make arrests as any constable on his beat. He has to stand at "attention," instead [illegible] and not to hold unnecessary conversation with them. In cases of a serious nature, such as felony or disturbance, he has to send for assistance to the station, and remain on the street himself. He has to afford information to strangers and others making inquiries.

1940. *Mr. Morris.*—Have not the constables to do that?—Well, yes, but you see there is a similarity between the duties of sergeants and constables. He has to watch suspicious vehicles by night; he has to make a daily inspection of all the vehicles on the stands; he is responsible for the good order of public-houses, and the proper closing of the same; and also of spirit grocers and beer dealers. He is also responsible that no night houses spring up in the section of which he has charge. He has to notice the gas lamps, and report their state weekly, and also of [illegible], fountains, street gratings, and down pipes. These are, I think, the principal things he has to attend to while on duty. He has then, when going off duty, to attend at the station to see that the men are dismissed, to receive their reports, and afterwards, if there are any inquiries to be made on the reports, he has to make those inquiries himself and report the facts in full.

1941. I thought it was the inspector's duty to receive the reports?—No, Sir. The inspectors go out and patrol the subdivision, and see that the sergeants are doing their duty; and they receive only reports at the time.

1942. I mean at the station-house; is it not the duty of the inspector to receive the reports, and not the sergeant?—He receives them from the sergeants. I must report to the inspector. The sergeant is to inspect the clothing and appointments of the constables under his charge every Saturday. That applies to the constables living in barracks and the married constables living out of barracks, and that inspection entails the expenditure of two hours' time weekly, that is, one hour in the barrack inspecting the appointments of the constables, and one hour inspecting the lodgings of the married men. That represents one hour's duty at least daily, extra, beyond the men themselves, and then two hours weekly, and that is in all equal to 469 hours annually, or two months and three days, nearly, in the year.

1943. *Mr. Holmes.*—What is the extent of a section?—The extent of a section might be about six or seven streets. The sergeant has also to go in and take his turn in the inspector's office, if the inspector has to go off, when on night duty, to make inquiries. The next day the sergeant often has to remain on duty until 3 o'clock, and then has to come in at 8 and remain on duty all night.

1944. I thought the acting inspector took the place of the inspector?—The sergeant replaces the inspector, and the acting inspector takes full charge.

1945. What was the pay of a sergeant before 1872?—1l. 6s. a-week, or 68l. a-year.

1946. And what is your present pay?—88l. 18s. 11d. a-year; that is, 1l. 14s. 6d. per week. For an increase of pay we ground our application and our claim to a proportionate increase of pay to what the acting inspectors may get, on the fact that we are very often called upon to perform the same duties.

1947. *Chairman.*—You are assuming that the acting inspectors will get an increase of pay?—We are.

1948. I don't think you have any right to assume that. You should, I think, put forward your own views, irrespective of that assumption?—Well, the London police sergeants are paid better than we are.

1949. *Mr. Holmes.*—Do you know what pay a first-class sergeant in London has?—104l.

1950. No, he has not. The pay of a first-class sergeant of the London metropolitan police is 99l. 1s. 8d.; that of a second-class sergeant, 92l. 17s. 2d.; and that of a third-class sergeant, 86l. 13s. 11d. So that your pay is better than that of a third-class sergeant in London, but not quite so good as that of the second-class sergeant there?—Yes, I know it is; but we have a different class of people to contend with. We have rougher characters, and the public, as a rule, are not so much inclined to come to our assistance as they would be in London.

1951. How many sergeants are there in the force in Dublin?—About seventy, Sir. The married men desire me to state that during this recent agitation many policemen's sons have been put out of employment in consequence of the agitation and the positions their fathers hold, and that they would want some extra salary to support and maintain those children while idle. They also wish me to say that they are desirous that they should be allowed some extra pay in order to educate their children for Government positions in the civil service, and for clerkships under the Government; and from a list I have made out here, I see that the sergeants at the present time are only able to spare 1s. 6d. a-week, all other things being considered, and taking the cost of living out of it.

1952. That is, married sergeants are only able to do that?—No, Sir, single sergeants; and you will see that by the bill of fare, by the list that I have been assisted in drawing up, that the men have given me, and which is not an exorbitant one. In it you will see that they did not allow themselves porter for dinner.

1953. Do you mean to say that a single sergeant cannot live within his pay?—No, Sir; I am telling you that I have 1s. 6d. a-week to spare.

1954. Are you aware that many bank clerks begin on a very much less salary?—I do not know that they do. I think they begin on 80l. or 90l. a-year, generally speaking.

1955. *Mr. Morris.*—Are you aware that very many bank clerks never get more than 100l. a-year, even when they are old men?—That may be so. I think the grounds I have mentioned are the principal ones on which the sergeants found their claim for increase of pay.

1956. Are you a married man?—No, Sir.

1957. Then you are living in barracks?—Yes.

1958. Now, without giving items, what does your weekly mess come to for three meals a-day, or about what?—About 7s. for the mess alone, for dinner alone.

1959. Now, what for breakfast and supper?—I have not made it up in that way; but we have made up weekly what the items would be. We have dinner, 8s., the amount that appears in our mess book; bread, four loaves in the week at 4d. each, would be 1s. 4d.; butter, 2 lbs. at 1s. 6d., 3s.; tea, ½ lb. at 3s., would be 1s.; sugar, 8d. I see rashers are included, 1½ lbs. at 1s. per lb., 1s. 6d.; milk, 1s. 2d.; oatmeal for supper and milk for it, 1s. 6d.; cooks and messenger, 1s. 4d. a-week. We pay our cooks 1s. 4d. a-week.

1960. What is the messenger. Is he the caterer?—Oh, no, Sir; we have a caterer appointed.

1961. What is the messenger?—The messenger is the man who goes for the sugar, butter, bread, and everything for us also in the morning. A little boy is employed for the purpose. These items are equal to 19s. 6d. a-week, or 50l. 14s. for our living alone.

1962. We had it in evidence here from Mr. Superintendent Walker, of the London metropolitan police, who brought over a Return that showed it, that in the case of the sergeants and constables in London living in barracks and eating meat, I think he said twice a-day, and sometimes three times a-day, that the mess account for those men is between 13s. and 14s. a-week at the outside?—Well, that may be, in consequence of the men messing in barracks for everything; I don't know whether they do or not.

1963. They only mess for dinner. Their breakfasts and suppers are separate?—Well, in that case, the cost of living in London must be cheaper than in Dublin, because we are prepared to satisfy you by books and other evidence that the sum I have named is the very lowest sum that we can live on.

1964. Taking your estimate of the cost of living at 19s. 6d. a-week, a man who is a sergeant would appear to have about 40l. a-year over?—But may I enumerate the other articles that are necessary for our maintenance during the year?

1965. Yes, certainly?—We have washing shirts, sheets, drawers, stockings, &c., at 8d. a-week, which amounts to 3l. 4s. a-year. Then there are tobacco, pipes, and matches, 1s. a-week, 2l. 12s. a-year.

1966. *Mr. Holmes.*—Surely you do not call tobacco a "necessary"?—Yes, you may put it down as such. It was allowed in 1872. Then there is soap, blacking, candles, and cleaning stuff, 6d. a-week, 1l. 6s. a-year. Then three pairs of boots at 1l. per pair, 3l. That is what I pay for them, and I will show you the bills if you like.

Sergeant R. Laughton.

22 Sept., 1882.

Sergeant S. Lambden.
—
25 Sept., 1888.

1967. Do you require three pairs of boots in the year?—Yes, Sir. We require two pairs of boots to work in, and one pair for Sundays.

1968. The London police are only supplied with two pairs?—But we are not supplied with any at all.

1969. *Mr. Morris.*—Would you be satisfied if you were supplied with boots?—Oh yes, Sir; but we would be better satisfied to have our own boots, because if we got the regulation boots they might not be good fits, and if they did not fit the men might go sick, and all that sort of thing occur. The cost of repairing boots would be 13s. 6d. a-year. Then three regulation shirts at 7s. 6d. each come to 1l. 2s. 6d. in the year; two undershirts at 6s. are 12s. They are warm shirts for winter and while on night duty. Two dress shirts at 6s. 6d. come to 13s.; two night shirts at 4s. 6d., 9s.; eight pairs of woollen socks at 1s. 6d. a-pair come to 12s.; collars, cuffs, studs, &c., 10s.; two scarfs at 2s. 6d., 5s.; three pairs of drawers at 3s. 6d. a-pair, 10s. 6d.; two pairs of suspenders at 2s. 6d., 5s.; six pocket-handkerchiefs at 9d. each, and two towels at 1s. each, 6s. 6d.; six pairs of white gloves at 10d. a-pair, and two pairs of black gloves at 1s. 6d. a-pair—in all, 8s.; average cost of plain clothes, hat, &c., per year, 5l.

1970. *Mr. Holmes.*—Are you aware that this estimate that you have given us of the cost of your clothes and washing amounts to 22l. 10s.?—Yes, Sir.

1971. Besides your uniform?—Yes, Sir.

1972. You have now given us an estimate of the cost of living and of the cost of clothes and washing, and the two items together come to 74l. 4s. a-year, which, deducted from your pay of 89l. 18s. 11d., leaves a sum of over 15l. a-year. How do you account for the balance?—But there are other items which you have not heard yet.

1973. Please state them?—The average cost of repairing and fitting uniform comes to 11s. Well, I may mention that we are allowed a little for fitting uniform; but it is not at all sufficient.

1974. But the 11s. represents, I suppose, the difference between what you are allowed and what you actually pay?—The 11s. represents the average cost of repairing and fitting uniform.

1975. Over what you are allowed?—No, including what we are allowed; that is, 11s. Well, brushes, cooking utensils, delft, knives and forks, &c., come to 5s. 6d. a-year. The average reduction per year during sickness, at fifteen days, 15s., being 1s. a-day. Duty book, memorandum books, stationery, and stamps, 12s. 6d. per year.

1976. Are you not supplied with your duty books?—No, Sir. The contributions to Church offerings, twice a-year, 10s. in all. Sundays at Church at 3d. each Sunday, 13s.; lodging and fuel, which is deducted from our pay, 1s. 3d. per week, 3l. 5s. a-year. Hair brushes, razors, hair-cutting, hair oil, &c., 16s.; bank-money (which is deducted from us weekly), at 1½d. per week; and 1d. a-week for library, 10s. 10d. in all yearly. One newspaper every day, 1d., 1l. 6s. a-year; coffee-money when on night duty, at 7d. per week, 15s. 6d. per year. That is for the coffee we get in the station. Then the average yearly cost of attending a comrade's funeral, or the funeral of a superannuated policeman, is 1l. 10s.; pocket-money weekly is 1s. 6d., or 4l. 6s. 6d. a-year, and that makes a total of 89l. 18s. 11d.

1977. Then, according to your estimate, it would appear that no one could live in the force under the pay of a sergeant without being in debt?—Well, taking into account the responsibility of the sergeant, or, at least, everything that the sergeant is supposed to show his men in the way of cleanliness, intelligence, dress, and smartness; everything he requires he must have, and if he gets everything he requires it will take his whole salary, 89l. 18s. 11d.

1978. *Mr. Morris.*—Don't you think it might with advantage be a part of his duty to teach his men economy as well?—Certainly.

1979. As well as extravagance?—Yes. He might show them a good example.

1980. *Mr. Holmes.*—Do you mean to tell us, as a matter of fact, that men below the rank of sergeant cannot live within their pay?—Well, of course, they are obliged to live within their pay, and in that case they have to sacrifice themselves, and do without many things they would require.

1981. Now take the case of a fourth-class constable, his pay is something like 15l. less than that of a sergeant's; according to your estimate it would be utterly impossible for a man in that rank to live in the force?—Utterly impossible.

1982. And do you think they are hopelessly in debt?—Yes.

1983. Is it a fact that they are hopelessly in debt?—It is a fact that a good many of them are very much in debt.

1984. Do the men, as a matter of fact, in the various grades of constable, and with the pay of constables, save money?—Well, yes; the senior constables do sometimes.

1985. Well, the pay of a senior constable is only 73l. 11s. 3d.?—Yes.

1986. You admit he can save money?—Yes, by using strategy.

1987. *Mr. Morris.*—Would you substitute "economy" for "strategy"?—Yes.

1988. *Mr. Holmes.*—Now, I ask you, as a reasonable man, don't you think that the estimate that you have just given us has been framed on a very high standard, that is to say, not framed for the rank of constable?—I daresay the constables themselves will bring a lighter estimate than this.

1989. Do you know of any cases of married sergeants being able to save money and live within their pay?—I do not.

1990. Do you not think it is probable that some of the married sergeants can not only live within their pay but save money?—I think it is improbable.

1991. *Mr. Morris.*—Unless their wives carried on some business?—But that is prohibited to us.

1992. *Chairman.*—What is the next subject you wish to give evidence upon?—The next thing is the repeal of the Pension Act of 1887.

1993. *Mr. Morris.*—You would come in under the Pension Act of 1887?—Yes, Sir. A great deal of the discontent existing at the present time has been caused by the knowledge of the low scale of pensions on which we shall have to retire.

1994. *Mr. Holmes.*—When you joined the force, may I ask you were you made aware that the scale of pensions had been changed?—I never knew a bit about pensions.

1995. Have you got the circular that was issued to you when you joined?—I have not got it here; but it was similar to the ones in existence at the present time.

1996. Does not that circular inform you of the scale of pensions under which the men joined?—No, Sir; that we would get pensions, that is all.

1997. As a matter of fact, you were not aware, when joining, that the scale of pensions for men joining under the Act of 1887 had been altered from what it was prior to that time?—Yes, Sir.

1998. *Chairman.*—Do you mean to say that the circular merely mentions that you will get pensions, but that it does not specify the amount of those pensions?—Yes, to the best of my remembrance.

1999. *Mr. Holmes.*—Are you aware that the men of the London metropolitan police force can only get two-thirds of their pay as the maximum of their pension after twenty-eight years' service?—I have learned about that, Sir, but I think they are under the same Act as ourselves.

2000. It is a different Act, and a little better. Do you think that the men here could be put under a better scale of pensions than the men in London?—No; nor I don't think that the men here want it; but still I should say they are better entitled to it.

2001. But why?—For this reason: When we retire from the force we are not recognised by our friends, we are old and unable to work, and we may have families depending upon us, and we must support ourselves out of our own pockets alone, for we will get no employment—at least in a good many cases. We have to walk about with our hands in our pockets, and think that the pension which we would be entitled to under the existing Act is not at all sufficient, or anything near it.

2002. What I ask you is, would you be satisfied if you were under the same scale of pensions as the London men, if you could get, say, two thirds of your pay after twenty-eight years' service?—No, we want to be placed on as good a footing as the men now serving in our force under the old Act.

2003. Are you aware that no other class of civil servants receive full pay on retirement as pension?—Yes, perfectly well aware.

2004. Don't you think there would be very considerable difficulty in putting the metropolitan police force in Ireland under an exceptionally favourable scale of pensions, and one differing not only from every class of civil servants, but from the kindred police forces of the United Kingdom?—I respectfully say that a civil servant's salary is entirely a wrong estimate for our salary. I will explain to you, if you will allow me, what I mean. A civil servant gets a salary of 150*l*., 200*l*., 300*l*., and sometimes 600*l*. a-year, while we who are sergeants in the police only get a small salary.

2005. But you may rise from the rank of sergeant?—Oh, we may be reduced. Civil servants get large salaries, and the fifteen-fiftieths of the salary of a civil servant as pension would be something handsome. On a civil servant's salary a man would be able to fill any position when retiring, whereas the fifteen-fiftieths of our salaries after fifteen years would be only something like 23*l*. of a pension, 23*l*. 10*s*. 6*d*. and a fraction for a sergeant. Well, it would be only about 23*l*., and now, surely, 23*l*. a-year would not be able to support a man and his family. After fifteen years we would be entitled to 23*l*.; after thirty years we would be entitled to 33*l*., so that that Act may answer well enough for civil servants, whereas it would not answer at all for us. Well, as a matter of fact, the good men are retiring from the service when they leave the Act under which they are serving. Those men are going away in batches; men who have served six, seven, and eight years. Those men who have got good characters, are getting on well in other forces. We have got letters showing that men who have left our service for the last twelve months, and went into forces in the Colonies, that some of those men are in receipt of 10*l*. 10*s*. a-month, that is, 7*s*. a-day.

2006. But having regard to the position which a man has to keep up who has 300*l*. a-year, we will say, don't you think he would feel the loss of one-third of his income as much as you would, having regard to the position you would have to keep up?—That may be, but the rate of pension allowed us would not be at all sufficient to support us, or go in any way near it, and the Royal Irish Constabulary are claiming the repeal of the Act of 1857, and that Act is one of the principal causes of discontent in the service at the present time.

2007. *Mr. Morris.*—When you compare your payment with the payments that is given to men who have resigned and emigrated to the Colonies, do you think that that is a fair comparison?—Yes, very fair.

2008. Don't you think that the rate of pay in the country in which we are living is a more equal comparison than that of the Colonies?—I do not think it at all.

2009. Do you think that because a man, a labouring man or a workman, gets 6*s*. a-day in New Zealand or in Australia, that that is a reason why I am to give in this country 6*s*. a-day for a labouring man if I can get one for 2*s*.?—Well, Sir, that is all very good, but the proof is positive that the good men are going—that the men who have served six, seven, and ten years in the service are resigning.

Sergeant S. Linklon.

23 Sept. 1882.

2010. But if good men can be got in their places, what then?—And worse men are coming into the force. There are men being taken into the police force at the present time who were dismissed from the service six years ago, and who have served their time in the army since. Men who were dismissed six and seven years ago have put in their time in the army, and are now being taken back into the police force.

2011. In making the comparison you have just instituted I do not suppose you would go to the length of saying that because a man gets 10*s*. a-day—we will say in San Francisco or New Zealand—a man in Dublin is entitled to get 10*s*. a-day also?—Well, no; but it is open for any young man who sees the world before him when he can get his passage to Australia for 13*l*., and who can save that by hook or by crook, as a sensible young man is entitled to do, it is open to him, I say, to start for the country where he can better himself.

2012. And don't you think it is quite right for him to do that?—Well, if he gets encouragement why should he not remain at home.

2013. *Mr. Holmes.*—But if the present pay is sufficient to attract into the service good men, do you think the Government are called upon to increase the pay?—The pay is not sufficient to attract good men at the present time, and good men are going and bad men are coming—army reserve men—men who I myself, when I was recruiting clerk under the chief superintendent, saw turned away from the gate—those men are now being taken on. I know that of my own knowledge.

2014. Do you attribute the fact of men leaving the force to discontent with the present rate of pay or the present scale of pension?—I attribute it in the first instance to the scale of pension, and in the second instance to the severe discipline which they are bound to submit to, as well as the heavy fines and other matters.

2015. *Chairman.*—It comes to this, that of your own knowledge you know that an inferior description of men are now being taken into the force?—Yes, Sir.

2016. What is the next item of your evidence?—We want optional retirement after twenty-five years' service.

2017. Without a medical certificate?—Yes, Sir, without a medical certificate; and compulsory retirement after thirty years' service, in order to preserve the efficiency of the force. The old members of the service want the Act of 1847.

2018. *Mr. Holmes.*—In what respect?—They want a year to be reckoned a fraction or part in computing their pensions, and they want no curtailment of their pensions.

2019. As you are not under the Act of 1847—as you have not the good fortune to be under that Act—don't you think the men who are ought to be thoroughly or well satisfied with the scale applicable to them?—I believe they are well satisfied with the scale, but they are dissatisfied with the curtailment of their pensions under it. As a matter of fact they are curtailed in any case where reports the men have had during their service stand against them.

2020. *Mr. Morris.*—Any bad marks that there are against them?—Yes, Sir; all reports are brought against them. The smallest thing goes against a man's record of character.

2021. *Chairman.*—I suppose it comes to this: you are satisfied with the law, but not with the administration of the law?—Yes.

2022. I understand that you now wish to refer to

Sergeant S. Lambton.

27 Sept., 1892.

the question of gratuities?—Yes. I am asked to state to you that we ask to have granted to us two months' pay as compensation after three years' service, and three months' for every year served after that as gratuity.

2023. Up to fifteen years?—No, sir. For every year afterwards served three months' pay as gratuity, because we have had cases in the service where men who were entitled to a pension and may have had sixteen years' service, died, and they would not get either pension or gratuity. Now we want it to be optional in such a case to take the gratuity to which he may be entitled, or the pension.

2024. *Mr. Holmes.*—In case of ill-health?—Yes, or being returned unfit for further service. To serve fifteen years and get merely the pension to which he would then be entitled, is a great hardship on a man.

2025. Surely in the case you have instanced a man will always take his pension sooner than a gratuity?—But if a man finds himself in danger of death, he will be glad to have a few pounds to leave to his family. In a case of sudden death we would wish, in the case of a single man, that his father or mother should receive the gratuity, or that the wife and family should receive it in the case of a married man without the signature of the deceased man. We could instance a number of cases that were very hard in which the widow was left in very great straits. In the case of Superintendent Davis, who died some time since, he was only given compensation on fifteen years' service, and he left a large family to be provided for. I may add that we want an allowance of 7*l.* at least for the funeral expenses of every man who dies while serving in the force in order to prevent the continuance of the system which is at present in existence that of making a special collection from the comrades of the deceased in order to provide for him decent burial. I think that concludes all I have to urge on the subject of gratuity.

2026. *Mr. Morris.*—Do you consider that it would lead to economy, and that it would furnish an incentive to men to remain in the force to provide for all the contingencies that you have mentioned, or that, if they were granted the requests you have put forward it would, perhaps, lead them to adopt a more reckless life?—No, Sir. On the contrary, it would induce smart and intelligent men to join the service, and to remain in it, and to regard it as their home.

2027. Do you think that the fact that a man's wife and family and next of kin as you have mentioned being so well provided for by the regulations which you propose would be an incentive to men to be more sparing during lifetime or more extravagant?—I am sure it would be an incentive to be more sparing and careful.

2028. Do you know of any other branch of the Civil Service in which a man's wife and family are provided for in case of death?—I know that the State provides for the widows and orphans of certain officers by giving them annuities and other compensation, whereas there is no such thing provided for the widows and orphans of policemen. And I may instance the case of Constable Daly, who was killed in Moore Street, where we had to make up a collection in the service for his widow.

2029. *Mr. Holmes.*—May I ask you to specify what officers' widows receive the annuities to which you allude?—I should say the widows of officers of the army and navy.

2030. *Mr. Morris.*—Are you aware that in India an officer serving in the Indian service is obliged out of his annual pay to contribute a considerable sum towards a fund for his widow and orphans?—Yes.

2031–2032. And do you consider that the State is bound to provide a sum and an independence for the next-of-kin or the wife and family of a member of the Dublin metropolitan police without his contributing during his lifetime one penny towards such a fund?—There are many men in the service at the present time who have contributed to a widow's fund, and we don't know what has become of it, the service does not know. Of course, young men in the service, such as I myself, did not contribute to such a fund.

2033. *Mr. Holmes.*—Don't you think that any man, whether a policeman or not, ought, as a prudent man, to deprive himself of some small amount of his income during his lifetime for the benefit of his wife and family?—I am sure our men would have no objection to contribute to a fund for that object.

2034. Would you be in favour of a fund being established to which the men should contribute something for the wives and families of deceased members of the force?—I would, Sir. I would be as glad to see it established in Dublin as I would be glad to see an hospital, such as the one at present existing in London—the Police Orphanage; and I would be glad also to see His Royal Highness the Prince of Wales visiting our annual Police Fête the same as in London, and I would have no objection to contribute to such a fund, and I am sure the service would have no objection. But I say that at the present time it is hard for me to answer a question on that point, seeing from the daily papers that the London police are agitating against being asked to subscribe to such a fund. There must be some hardship in connection with it, so I should not be inclined to bring such an incumbrance on our service when the other service is crying out against it.

2035. *Mr. Morris.*—Do you not think that it would have a very demoralising influence upon any body of men, whether in the public or any private service, that a Widows' and Orphans' Fund should be established, to which the men whose wives and children were to be benefited should contribute nothing?—I think some provision should be made for them.

2036. Without the husband during his lifetime denying himself a single thing or contributing towards that fund?—Now, as I have already said, the men would not object to contribute to such a fund.

2037. But your individual opinion I am anxious to learn; do you think such a plan would work well for any institution in the world either private or Governmental?—I think it would.

2038. Are you not aware that wherever there is a fund for the purpose of giving to the wife or family, or next of kin, as you have put it, are you not aware that in every such institution there is some contribution, be it small or be it large, from the man during his life?—I am, Sir.

2039. And then do you expect that the Dublin police are to be the exception to the rule?—No; I am sure that our men would not object to contribute to such a fund.

2040. Then would you be for making it compulsory in the service?—Well, yes; provided that the sum to be subscribed would not be an exorbitant one, and that the fund was properly administered. We are compelled to subscribe to a band fund, and why should we not subscribe to a widows' fund.

2041. What deduction is made from your pay to provide for the band fund?—1½*d.* per week from officers of all ranks under an acting inspector and sergeant.

2042. I suppose you are aware that all the clerks in the public banks contribute towards a fund for their widows and children in case of the husband's death?—I have heard of such a fund.

2043. As to the time of retirement, I should like to put one question to you. I think you fixed the date of retirement at twenty-five years' service?—Yes.

2044–2045. To be optional at that period, and after thirty years' compulsory?—Yes

2046. The pension, of course, being an increasing one up to thirty years?—I would object to such an arrangement on this ground There are many men who cannot advance in the service, and who have no means of advancing themselves, or at least who cannot advance themselves in the service, and they would be anxious to retire. When such men arrive at a certain rank, and when they have no further hopes of advancement, of course, if retirement were optional, any man who would see himself in such a position could retire

2047. But suppose his pension was increasing by the number of years served between twenty-five and thirty years, do you think there would be many men anxious to retire before they were thirty years in the service?—I don't think there would.

2048 On the whole view of the question, would you consider it a fair compromise if it was compulsory for a man to leave the service without any medical certificate or any other formality of the kind, after thirty years' service?—I would not, on the whole. It would not be fair to the service itself. In order to preserve the current of promotion, and to induce good men to come to the force, retirement should be optional after twenty-five years' service for men who find their further advancement barred

2049. *Mr Holmes.*—Before we leave this question, I wish to ask you is it not your opinion that the Civil Service, including, of course, the police, are in a much better position than other classes of the community in that, while they are in the service, their income is certain, and after they leave the service they are sure of a pension in their old age?—Yes, generally speaking, but not altogether. Business men can make their fortunes, and the humblest man can rise to the highest position, and may become Lord Mayor of Dublin. I don't think any member of the Civil Service is as well off at all as a successful business man.

2050. *Chairman.*—What is the next branch of your evidence?—The next matter that we desire to lay before the Committee is that we ask that no stoppage be made from the men's pay when on the sick reports. In some instances half their pay is stopped weekly, and that prevents those men from keeping themselves properly nourished and, in fact, supporting their families if they are married. We also ask for separate ward accommodation in the Dublin hospitals. Dr. Kedley, the chief medical officer of the force, has himself recommended that over and over again. Our men are subjected to very bad treatment in some of the hospitals, and they have to commingle with characters not at all suited to them

2051 *Mr. Holmes.*—Are the men now sent to different hospitals, or is there one hospital that they are generally sent to, as in the case of the Royal Irish Constabulary, who are sent to Steevens's Hospital?—They are sent to different hospitals, but they are sent to one hospital as a rule

2052. What hospital is that?—To the Hardwicke or Richmond Hospital But latterly, I must say, the doctor has been very good in that way; he has allowed our men to choose their own hospitals, because, I suppose, from what he has recommended in his Blue Book in reference to the treatment of the men had been subjected to in the hospitals, he thought it best to do so

2053. Are you speaking of Dr Kedley?—Yes. I wish now to state that we want a lodging allowance of 20*l.* a-year for married sergeants and acting sergeants, and we want free accommodation for single men who reside in barracks. There is now, as you are doubtless aware, 1*s.* 3*d.* stopped from our pay for lodging.

2054. Are you aware that in the London police force a lodging allowance is not given to married men, and furthermore, that single men who cannot be accommodated in barracks do not receive any lodging allowance?—Yes

2055. You are aware of it?—Yes; but I am also aware that in the London police the married men are provided with accommodation

2056 Only in very few cases?—I dare say in a few cases only; but our married men are subjected to great hardships under the present arrangement. They have to reside in transient houses and pay weekly rents. They have no certainty but that they will be transferred at any time or any day, and consequently they cannot take houses themselves. They are obliged to live in respectable houses, because their lodgings are inspected both weekly and monthly. Our inspectors receive at the present time 20*l.* for lodging allowance, and the sergeants go in for 20*l.* now.

2057. And why do you ask to receive as much as the inspectors are getting?—Because the inspectors at the present time are asking for an increase of their lodging allowance

2058. But are you certain that they will get it?—I am not quite certain; but it is our business to look for it.

2059. Are you aware that the pay of a third-class inspector in Dublin is 130*l.* a-year?—Yes

2060. And that in addition to that he gets 20*l.* a-year for lodging allowance; whereas in London the pay of a third-class inspector is only 117*l.* a-year, and he does not receive anything for lodging allowance, so that that allowance is a special boon given to the Dublin inspectors?—But, as I have already stated, our acting inspectors here—at least I understand so, and we have been told so—are equal in their rank and duties to the third-class inspectors in the London police, and although they are equal in position, owing to the duties they are called upon to perform, our acting inspectors are not equal in pay or allowances. The next point to which I wish to refer is that of extra pay for extra duty. It is not so much for the money that we are looking, or the receipt of extra pay for extra duty, but we make the claim in order to prevent our being subject to the performance of unnecessary extra duty

2061. What do you mean by "unnecessary extra duty?"—I mean a man being kept out on duty out of his turn The men are called in to do station work, and the amount of that work varies. We will say that it occurs twice every week that a sergeant has to go in and do station work The inspector has to go off duty at night at 12 o'clock, having come on duty at 8 o'clock. The sergeant has to come on immediately after and relieve him, and it very often happens that when the sergeant is called in at 12 o'clock at night he has to remain on duty until 10 o'clock the next morning If there were some preventative of unnecessary extra duty we would consider it a great boon. I mean this in particular either in case of fires or other emergencies I will explain what I mean The men have been frequently called out to fires just after going to bed after having been out all night. The sergeants and men have had to turn out to go to fires in the city and in the country; men who were out all night until 6 o'clock, and didn't get to bed until 7 o'clock, those men were turned out for fires, and before they got half-way to the place where the fire was said to be, they would get an order to return to barracks; that they were not required.

2062 *Mr Morris.*—Why do you call that unnecessary duty? Do you mean to tell me that the citizens of Dublin would ever listen to the proposition, or that this Committee should report that that should not be the case? The administration of the force, of which such a case as you have put is part, must be left to somebody, and do you mean to say that the citizens of Dublin would ever listen to us if we recommended that the police force—every man of them, whether off or on duty, whether in plain clothes or in uniform—should not turn out in cases of great

Sergeant S. Lawless.

29 Sept., 1882.

Sergeant A. [illegible]. — [illegible] Sept., [illegible].

emergency, such as the report of a fire or outbreak?—Certainly not. The men would not object to it if they were really wanted; but what they do object to is being turned out of bed, and then afterwards being told that they are not wanted.

2063. *Mr. Holmes.*—But suppose that instead of their services being unnecessary, it turned out that they happened to be of the most vital importance. You must see that this is one of those things that you will always have to leave to the discretion of those to whom is entrusted the administration of the force?—I mention it only in order that unnecessary labour might not be thrown upon us. In the case of men only getting to bed at 7 o'clock, it is very hard to turn them out when there are plenty of other men that could be turned out. What we urge is, that the night man should not be turned out unless in cases of great emergency.

2064. *Mr Morris.*—Surely such cases as you have alluded to are cases of great emergency?—But for a false alarm we think it very hard to be turned out.

2065. But instead of its being a false alarm, supposing it were a genuine one?—But that should be ascertained before we are sent for.

2066. How could it be ascertained? All the people in the place might be burned meanwhile. You will, I imagine, never get the citizens of Dublin to go with you in seeking for any change in that respect?—We do not ask it, but we want some preventative put upon it. If we got the pension point settled satisfactorily, we would not press the point of extra pay for extra duty. The next matter I wish to bring under your notice is the question of leave. We want one month's annual leave for sergeants, and also two days in each month, one of those days to be a Sunday. In case a man cannot be spared for his annual leave, we ask that he would be given a month's pay instead of it, and the argument for that is, that in the Civil Service they get four or six weeks' annual leave. They also get every Sunday and Bank holiday, and one half of every Saturday. I have been informed that the Royal Irish Constabulary receive one month's annual leave, four days quarterly, and one day in each month. Daily labourers, of course, have the fifty-two Sundays and all holidays, and in large cities and towns they receive half of every Saturday. Sunday's is the hardest duty a policeman has to perform. He has to clean his uniform and his trappings on every Sunday, the same as on Saturday, and he has to go to some place of worship besides performing his ordinary duty. He has to go to church in his own time, whereas the Royal Irish Constabulary are marched to church. Those are all the arguments I have to put forward in favour of annual and daily leave. We would like one day to be a Sunday in any case.

At this stage, Sergeant D'Arcy was examined.

Sergeant D'Arcy. — [illegible] Sept., [illegible].

2067. *Mr. Morris.*—I understand you wish to give evidence on the subject of the examination for promotion?—Yes, Sir. You are called on for medical inspection before you are allowed to go up to compete for the rank of acting inspector, and if you are rejected by the doctor you are passed over and sent away. In the course of four or four and a-half years afterwards you are informed you may then go up for a similar examination without having to pass any medical board. Meanwhile, thirty or forty men, who were your juniors, have passed over your head. You have then to go up for drill examination, and also for examination at the school for three days, and if you come out of Trinity College [illegible] for examination, you would not pass, except you attended that school at [illegible] Street. You are sure to be tripped either in the medical or drill inspection, and if you pass both of these inspections you are sure to be tripped up in school, unless you can attend it previously with regularity.

2068. How long were you supposed to attend school?—I was stationed at Blackrock and could not attend school. I was called upon for a medical examination, which I did not pass, and I consequently lost my promotion. At the end of four and a-half years I was allowed to go up for examination without any medical inspection. I then had to go up for drill examination, and I passed that. I was afterwards examined for three days in the school and was rejected.

2069. *[illegible].*—For what rank was this examination?—That of acting inspector; and men were then put before me who were only second-class constables, when I was a full sergeant. Several other men besides myself were also passed over some of nearly my own service.

2070. *Mr. Holmes.*—Does not that go to show that those younger men were better able to pass the requisite examination than you were?—No, Sir. The first knock down I got was being rejected by the doctor; but still I was allowed to serve.

2071. On the second occasion you were rejected on intellectual grounds?—Yes, after an interval of four and a-half years, and after forty men were passed over me. I was then allowed to compete without the medical examination.

2072. Do you think that if you had been allowed to compete in the literary examination the first time you would have passed?—I do, Sir. I was working in the inspector's office for eight years without a blot on my character. I have done the duty of an inspector and an acting inspector for those eight years, and as far as my officers and the Commissioners of Police were concerned, without any flaw whatever, though part of my time was spent in College Street, one of the busiest stations in Dublin.

inspector in the station, was well qualified to fill the rank of acting inspector, and that he would have passed the examination were it not for the school.

2076. In other words, Sergeant D'Arcy objects to the intellectual test ?—No, Sir, not exactly. He is satisfied to go for the examination in literary qualifications or in police duties, but he is dissatisfied with being put questions of a technical character under the Act of Parliament, which are inculcated in the school, and which he cannot answer unless he attends the school.

2077. But do his duties prevent him from attending it ?—Yes.

2078. Then his is a special grievance ?—Yes, but also it is a grievance with the other officers of the service.

2079. Is it not the case that all the other candidates are debarred by their duties from attending the school just as much as Sergeant D'Arcy ?—Yes it is, but all the other candidates sacrifice their rest in attending at Kevin Street for drill and school instruction, no matter how far away from Kevin Street their stations may be. They have to attend in their own time.

2080. But is that compulsory on them ?—No, it is not. It is optional; but if they want to advance themselves in the service they must attend.

2081. *Mr. Morris.*—Then you are in favour of abolishing the school ?—Yes.

2082. Both schools ?—The school altogether, under the existing system.

2083. Do you mean the school for drill and the school for literary requirements ?—We are in favour of the abolition of the school; but we are in favour of examinations, that is to say, let a man improve himself and come and pass the examination.

2084. *Mr. Holmes.*—As best he can ?—Yes, and if he does not pass the examination let him stop behind, let the examination be ever so severe.

2085. But the longer he remains at the school now, the sooner he is likely to obtain promotion ?—Quite so; certainly; because while he goes to the school he gets marks for attending.

2086. Then, as I understand you, you do not object to the examination, even though it be a difficult one; but you object to being required to attend school after performing your ordinary duties ?—Yes, independently of our ordinary duties.

2087. *Mr. Morris.*—And how would a man prepare himself for the examination for promotion to the rank of inspector, and from that of first-class constable to sergeant, and from being sergeant to inspector, if there was no school ?—By the practice and experience of the service, and by the natural improvement of the officers themselves.

2088. How is he to get his literary qualification—how is he to learn ?—He does not, at the present time, go to the school at all to learn literary qualifications; it is only police duties he learns there.

2089. Do you mean to say that there is no literary instruction given at the school ?—There is instruction of that kind given to the constables, but not to the superior officers. The officers are qualified already. They must have enough education to qualify them.

2090. *Chairman.*—Have you anything further to add ?—The next point is about entering public-houses and hotels when off duty and in plain clothes, and on leave.

2091. What do you wish to say on that question ?—It is a very hard point and a great grievance in the service for a sergeant to be subject to a fine of 5*l.* for entering a public-house when off duty and in plain clothes and on leave.

2092. *Mr. Holmes.*—When you say "subject to a fine of 5*l.*," you do not mean to say that that is the usual fine that is levied ?—Well, not the usual fine; but he is subject to a fine. He is subject to punishment in any case, and it is a hardship for a man to be prohibited from entering a hotel with his brother or father, who may have come from the country to see him. He cannot now enter either a public-house or a hotel. I do not want to insinuate, either, that the man should be allowed to get drunk or to associate with bad characters.

Sergeant
[illegible]

[illegible] Sept., 18[illegible].

2093. Does the present restriction extend to constables off duty and in plain clothes ?—Yes. Constable D'Arcy, 159 F.—he has since gone out of the service—was fined 30*s.* for entering a public-house while on Commissioners' leave. He was after getting Commissioners' leave, and he went into a spirit-grocer's shop, having, while on his way to the railway-station, stopped his cab, with his boxes on the top, at the door. He went in to get some wine and other things he wanted to bring to his sick mother in the country, and at the time, I believe, he took a glass of wine at the counter. However, he was reported by the sergeant for it, and he was afterwards brought up and fined 30*s.* for being in a public-house while off duty and on Commissioners' leave. Another sergeant went into a public-house off duty and in plain clothes, at Kingstown, with an acting inspector who was off duty, but in uniform. The two men were seen coming out of this public-house, and were reported for it. The sergeant was eventually fined 3*l.* and the acting inspector fined 7*l.* and transferred.

2094. For that offence only ?—Yes.

2095. What is the usual amount of fine inflicted in a case of drunkenness, it being the first offence ?—With regard to the fines altogether, I think they are not fairly dealt out.

2096. What is the usual amount of the fine inflicted for a first offence in the case of drunkenness when a constable is on duty ?—A man may get off with a caution for the first offence.

2097. *Mr. Morris.*—And do not you consider it a very heinous offence for a police constable, no matter what his rank is, to get drunk on duty ?—Certainly.

2098. And do you see any objection to a system that gives liberty and discretion to somebody over him to fine him very heavily for such an offence ?—I am not objecting to it at all, Sir.

2099. *Mr. Holmes.*—May I again ask you what is the usual amount of the fine imposed for a first offence of drunkenness ? Is the man who offends for the first time always let off with a caution ?—He is not, Sir. The average fine is 5*s.*; but some people are let off with a caution, and others have been fined up to 3*l.* for a first offence.

2100. *Mr. Morris.*—What would be the penalty for a second offence ?—The second offence may be dealt with in the very same manner, or a man may be reduced.

2101. *Mr. Holmes.*—And what is done in the case of the third offence ?—Well, in reference to the third offence, if a man happened to be reduced for a second offence, he would surely be dismissed for third. But there may be some instances in which he would get off with a fine.

2102. *Mr. Morris.*—Is it the Commissioner or the Assistant-Commissioner in all cases that inflicts these fines ?—Yes, the Commissioner or the Assistant-Commissioner inflicts these fines.

2103. *Mr. Holmes.*—Tell me, is the fine for a case of drunkenness ever so low as 5*s.* ?—No, I think not; not for any offence committed by a constable on duty, not to my knowledge; even when off duty it was never that. At the very least he would be fined 5*s.*, if he was not let off with a caution for the first offence, or for any other offence of drunkenness.

2104. Does it frequently happen that men are let off with a caution for the first offence ?—Well, I should say yes, but it is according to the character of the man.

2105. And then it would be only in a case of aggravated drunkenness, where the constable was unruly as well as drunk, that the fine would be inflicted at all ?—Oh, no. It has occurred in this

Sergeant, R. Lambert.
—
22 Sept., 1882.

service that a man has actually been put down for being drunk who had not tasted liquor, and that is the reason why drunkenness is so prevalent in the service. If a man is announced "unfit for duty from the effects of liquor," that is put down as "drunk." It has occurred more than once that a man who never took a drop of drink that day was reported as being "unfit for duty from the effects of liquor" when he came on his parade. Take the case of a man having to walk from the Castle to College Street. When he would get there, if he would be a little bit red in the face, or something brought him under the notice of the superior officer, or the man might not be well fixed, or he might have taken some slight quantity of drink for his dinner—a pint of porter it might be—well, that man would be ordered to fall out of the ranks, and he would be put down as being "unfit for duty from the effects of liquor." That man would be brought up and fined 20s., 30s., or 40s., according to whether it was his first, second, third, or fourth offence, or he might be reduced or dismissed?

2106. Do you consider that the Dublin metropolitan police have fallen to so low a stage of morality that an inspector would report a man for being drunk and get him fined, when he was not drunk or unfit for duty?—I am sorry to say that cases have arisen in the service where men who could prove on oath that they didn't drink more than one pint of porter, have been reported as being "unfit for duty from the effects of liquor"—

2107. And fined?—Yes, and fined.

2108. Are there many such cases?—I should say not many such cases, but there are cases of that kind.

2109. And do you consider that there are a sufficient number of cases of a similar nature occurring in the entire force to justify you in bringing this matter to be inquired into as a grievance?—Yes, not of course that particular case, but what I want to be understood is—

2110. Do you consider that a sufficient number of cases have occurred in the metropolitan police to make you regard it as important to bring this subject forward amongst the grievances of the force, concerning which we are holding this inquiry?—I should be sorry to say that.

2111. Well, then, if you do not consider it of sufficient importance, why do you bring it forward to be printed in a Blue Book, and read by the public?—For the purpose of having the unfitness defined—whether the man is drunk or whether he is sober.

2112. *Mr. Morris.*—Did you ever hear, in the whole course of your life, that it was almost impossible to define the various stages of drunkenness?—Of course I did, Sir.

2113. And do you consider that you could suggest any better remedy for the supervision of the force than that the inspector of his division should be the person entrusted to report a man as to whether he was sufficiently sober to go on duty or not? What method of action would you suggest to remedy that? Would you have the Commissioners at once sent for to hold an inquiry on the spot?—I would suggest that the opinion of the officers present and of the men on parade should be had as to whether the man was sober or whether he was drunk.

2114. Would you have a poll of the men present taken? Would you have a show of vote as to whether the man was or was not under the influence of liquor, and have the decision follow the opinion of the majority?—I am informed that that is the practice in the Royal Irish Constabulary.

2115. And do you think it would add to the discipline of the force to have the opinion of all the men in the barrack taken as to whether a particular man was drunk or sober?—Oh no; but of all the officers and men actually present for that parade of duty.

2116. *Chairman.*—What you have been saying in reference to fines applies to the offence of drunkenness only?—The point is that we should not be punished for entering hotels or public-houses with our private friends when off duty, in our own time; but I do not want to say that a man who enters a public-house on duty or in uniform should escape without punishment.

2117. What you mean is that casual visits of men to public-houses when off duty and in plain clothes should not be punished?—Yes, that they should not be liable to fine or punishment or even reports, because reports stand against you in your service for ever after.

2118. Do you think that if the police were allowed to enter public-houses when off duty or in plain clothes that there would be any danger of their coming into collision with the people?—I don't think there would.

2119. Do you think that the police might be trusted only to enter respectable public-houses?—I do, Sir, because the police are very respectable themselves, and would only go into such houses.

2120. Have you anything further to add on that point?—No, Sir; not on that point.

2121. Do you wish to add anything on any other point?—We would ask that in a case in which a fine of 10s. or more severe punishment is imposed, the evidence given should be sworn testimony. This point is brought forward in consequence of the excessive fines imposed in the service.

2122. *Mr. Morris.*—Would you have the Court open to the public?—No, Sir; I should say not.

2123. *Mr. Roberts.*—How is the investigation of alleged offences against discipline conducted now? Supposing a constable is charged with being drunk, how would the investigation be conducted and by whom?—It is conducted by the Commissioners of Police. The constable reported, the sergeant who has him reported, and the superintendent of the division enter the Commissioners' office. The report and evidence is gone into by the sergeant, the superintendent gives the man his character, and the Commissioners deal with the offence.

2124. *Mr. Morris.*—Is the man present?—Yes, I said so.

2125. And is he permitted to offer any explanation or excuse?—I am sorry to say, Sir, that in many cases he is not permitted, and even when he is, he is often told that he is not telling the truth, that he is not believed, and told to hold his tongue and not to say anything more. I could mention a case that occurred to myself, but perhaps, as it is too personal, I will not mention it. But in one case—in order to prove the excessiveness of the fines—I might refer you to orders of the 10th January, 1879, where thirty-four officers and men appear on the one sheet of orders.

2126. *Chairman.*—Was that in reference to the placard?—Yes, Sir. Fines amounting to £44, were inflicted that day.

2127. On what occasion were those fines inflicted?—On the 10th January, 1879, and in relation to a placard posted through Dublin on a Saturday night, and the officers and the constables of the service saw the placard, but neglected to report it, having seen the substance of the placard published in the daily papers on that very day or some days before.

2128. What was the nature of the placard?—It was held to be a seditious placard, or a placard of a seditious nature; but afterwards there was some understanding that it was not seditious. However, the fines were inflicted all the same. But I must qualify that. Of course, if you refer to the orders, you will see that there were other offences besides the placard on the same sheet of orders. Of course I shall include all the thirty-four officers and men; but there were other offences on the sheet.

2129. What were the other offences?—Ordinary small offences. If you ask for the sheet of orders you will see that.

Sergeant R. Lambkin.

22 Sept., 1882.

2130. Were there any offences of drunkenness?—Yes, I think there were some offences of that kind included. There were also some cases of neglect of duty as not noticing knockers wrenched off, or something of that kind.

2131. *Mr. Morris.*—Is there any other way, except by fining, to compel constables to do their duty?—Oh yes; reduction from one grade to another.

2132. Would not that be much more severe than fining?—It would be much more severe than fining; but we complain that the fines are excessive.

2133. That is what I want clearly to understand is your complaint: that the fines are excessive?—Yes.

2134. But you are not in favour of abolishing the system of fines for neglect of duty?—No, but of having some limit placed on the system.

2135. You are in favour of fines, but not of excessive ones?—Yes; but not excessive ones.

2136. *Mr. Holmes.*—Could you suggest any better system of holding inquiries into charges against the men in the force than the present system?—Yes. Formerly the superintendents of divisions had some voice or influence—at least I believe so—in determining the punishment that would be meted out to a man, and I think that if that system were reintroduced it would prove of service.

2137. You think that would be preferable to leaving the matter entirely to the discretion of one of the Commissioners?—Yes.

2138. You would have either one Commissioner or both Commissioners sitting together, and assisted by a Board of Superintendents?—One Commissioner would do, assisted by a Board of Superintendents, who should have a voice in the decision.

2139. And who would have a voice in meting out the punishment?—Yes. I may mention that what I refer to was always the case in Mr. O'Farrell's and Colonel Lake's time. It is only since then that the Board of Superintendents has been done away with.

2140. They took part in the proceedings?—Yes. When I say that the superintendents had a voice in the proceedings, I should explain that they had not a voice in the actual determination of the punishment to be awarded to the offender; but they had a great voice in giving a character to the man and an influence in the result—that the punishment should be light or heavy as the case may be.

2141. *Chairman.*—As I understand you the fact was this, that the superintendents sat at the investigation held by the Commissioner, and attended it, and they were referred to as to the character of the man whose case had been investigated?—Yes, and their united voice had weight with the Commissioner in giving his decision.

2142. In fact, they were referees of character as regarded the offender?—Yes, Sir.

2143. And you think it would be beneficial to the force if that system were revived?—Yes, Sir. I think it would; the solitary system does not work well.

2144. But I thought you told us that the superintendent of the man's division was also present?—I mean the solitary superintendent.

2145. You don't believe in the solitary superintendent?—No, Sir; because the superintendent may be a very hard man. There are some good superintendents, and others who are very hard.

2146. Surely the superintendent of the man's division should be the best judge of the man's character?—Quite so, but if he is a hard man, the others might mitigate his severity.

2147. How is it possible for the other superintendents to know anything about the man's character?—As a rule, the man has served in their divisions. The next point I wish to mention is a special grievance of the sergeants. They are responsible for the negligence of the constables, who may not notice matters on their beats, and for those cases of neglect the sergeants are liable to be fined more heavily than the constables themselves; and they feel that to be a great grievance.

2148. *Mr. Morris.*—Is that the grievance?—Yes, Sir.

2149. Do you think it a less offence for you to do anything wrong than a constable?—I do not. I think it is a greater.

2150. *Mr. Holmes.*—And ought not the punishment to be greater?—Yes. But with regard to this, I may explain it by saying that if a constable on his beat does not see that a knocker has been wrenched off during the night, and the constable who comes after him does not see the same thing, as soon as the fact is discovered the sergeant and constables on that beat for both reliefs are reported, and although the sergeant may not have been in the street in question at all, and although it may have been impossible for him to be there, he is reported, and the punishment inflicted on him is heavier than the punishment inflicted on the constable. There is another point to which I wish to direct the attention of the Committee, if you will allow me. It is with reference to gossiping on duty. I do not want to say that a man should not be reported for gossiping on duty; but I mean to say that a sergeant or constable should not be punished severely for speaking to a respectable person when on duty, as is at present the case.

2151. Now, is it the fact, that if I were to accost you while on duty, and you were to speak to me, and were reported for so doing, you would be punished?—Well, no, if I were able to give a satisfactory explanation to my officer, and told him all that you had been saying to me. But we will instance the case of a sergeant going round his section, and a respectable shop-keeper addresses him, bids him "good morning," and talks about the politics of the day, or anything of that kind, if an inspector sees him he is liable to be reported and punished severely for it, and liable to reduction. Now the sergeants in an especial manner are expected to make themselves agreeable to and acquainted with the people who reside in their sections, and unless they speak to the people, surely to goodness they cannot know anything at all about them.

2152. *Mr. Morris.*—Before you leave this subject, I wish to have it on record that if a sergeant or constable spends his time unnecessarily gossiping or talking about every subject in the world except his business, you do not object to his being fined?—Certainly not, and fined heavily.

2153. You don't, then, object to the system, but to the way in which it is at present carried out?—Yes. I object to the way in which it is carried out, because a man is liable to be reported for the most trifling thing, and that report stands against him for life. There is no redemption from it at all. We want some system to be introduced in the way of cancelling reports after three years, or on promotion to a superior rank, because it is a great drawback that if a man is reported at any time his previous character is looked into, and offences for which he may have been punished sixteen or twenty years ago are brought up against him.

2154. *Chairman.*—In a word, you want to have punishments fixed in the first instance?—Yes, fixed in the first instance, and reports cancelled after three years' good conduct or on promotion. The last point I wish to bring before you is this. Some old officers of the service wish me to state that the superannuated officers of our service get no recognition at all in the way of being appointed magistrates or justices of the peace in the Colonies or other places, the same as the officers of other services; and they think some of them, at least all the superior officers, are well fitted for such positions.

2155. *Mr. Morris.*—In fact, they would extend their sphere of duty from Dublin to the world at large?—Yes; that they should get some recognition from the Government.

Sergeant R. Leahive. — [illegible] Sept., 1882.

2156. More than a pension?—Yes. Ah, well, if it was only an honorary thing they would appreciate it. I understand that the London police officers get appointments as magistrates and justices of the peace out in the Colonies or other places. I am informed so, but I don't know it of my own knowledge. There is one other matter I would like to mention with reference to the clerks in the service—such as the staff-sergeants and the men in the magistrate's office. These are men employed on special duties, and they have no means of distinguishing themselves in the service otherwise than by the performance of their daily duties, and consequently no means of getting rewards. The Dublin clerks would ask that they be put on the same footing as the London police clerks, who are also sergeants, with regard to pay. They are paid 104l. a-year.

2157. *Chairman.*—Do you mean the office sergeants in the police-courts?—I mean the divisional clerk sergeants, the pay sergeants. They have no assistants, and no substitutes should they be sick or go on leave, so that it is more difficult for them to get leave.

2158. *Mr. Holmes.*—Do you know, as a matter of fact, that the London men to whom you refer are paid 104l. a-year?—I have seen it so stated in the Instruction Book of the London police. Formerly, these sergeants in the Dublin service, in lieu of the chances they would have if they were employed on outside duty, used to be put forward on an annual recommendation for a gratuity of 5l. in recognition of the meritorious performance of their duties in connexion with which so much money passes through their hands. That recommendation for a gratuity to these sergeants has been discontinued since December 1878. We ask to be put on the same footing as regards pay, and that we should get the 5l. annually as heretofore up to 1878. I am now talking about the divisional clerk sergeants alone. Before March 1878 the divisional clerk sergeant used to have an assistant; he has no assistant since that date.

2159. *Mr. Morris.*—Suppose the assistant was found to be unnecessary, is there any occasion why he should be kept there?—We do not ask for him now; but we ask for the recommendation of the grant of the annual sum as heretofore, especially when the duties have increased in many ways since the disestablishment of the assistant clerks.

2160. *Mr. Holmes.*—Are you a divisional clerk sergeant yourself? Yes, Sir. The staff-sergeants and the magistrates' court clerks—they have got the 5l. also, as well as the clerk sergeants. The clerk sergeants want to be placed on the same footing as the London clerk sergeants, and all want the 5l. annually, as heretofore. The warrant collectors also desire me to bring their case before you. The collectors of jurors' fines are entitled, by Act of Parliament, to some little remuneration for collecting the fines, and they do not get it.

2161. *Mr. Morris.*—While they are on that duty they are on no other duty?—Oh, they are; the warrant collector in Kingstown is the office sergeant. When his day's work is over in the office he has to go and execute the warrants, and in the case of jury warrants there is a special provision made in some Act of Parliament which says that the authorities are to recoup him for any expense he may incur, travelling or otherwise.

2162. *Chairman.*—And are they not recouped by Act of Parliament?—They are not, Sir.

2163. Would you and the police force generally approve of the system of management of the force that prevailed in Colonel Lake's and Mr. O'Ferrall's time of having one of the Commissioners a lawyer?—Yes.

2164. Or a civilian?—A lawyer or a civil servant of long standing who would understand law. A lawyer would, I think, be best suited to be above the head of the police, because he would be a man who is dealing every day with law.

2165. And lawyers are capable of weighing evidence?—Yes.

2166. *Mr. Holmes.*—And do you think that that would contribute more towards the satisfaction and contentment of the force than the system which exists at present?—Indeed, I do think it would, and every man in the force thinks with me.

2167. You think it would be better to have a civilian associated with a military man in the control of the force?—Yes, I think that would be conducive to its greater efficiency; it is the opinion of the whole of the service that the police force should not be governed by two military men.

2168. *Chairman.*—But that the old system should be revived, and the force governed by one civilian and one military man?—Yes, because, in the first place, it does not give satisfaction in this way; that there is too much drill, the men complain of that.

2169. *Mr. Morris.*—Suppose, now, we condense all your grievances and complaints into what are the things that you mainly complain of, and that you would wish to see remedied, would one be the three months' pay?—Yes.

2170. What are the most important?—The three months' pay or gratuity; the repeal of the Pension Act of 1867; the increase of pay, and an improved system of discipline.

2171. *Chairman.*—Have you anything further to state?—Nothing, except to thank the Committee for the patience with which they have heard me.

Sergeant D'Arcy re-examined.

Sergeant D'Arcy. — [illegible] Sept., 1882.

2172. *Chairman.*—How long are you in the force?—Twenty-four years next July.

2173. And how long have you been a sergeant?—Nine years on the [illegible] November next.

2174. You have been present during the examination of Sergeant Leahive, and you have heard the evidence he has given, and the statements he has made?—Yes.

2175. Do you concur in that evidence and in those statements?—Yes, Sir, entirely; in every respect.

[The Committee then adjourned until next day.]

TENTH DAY.—22ND SEPTEMBER, 1882.

Present:

MR. J. W. O'DONNELL, MR. GEORGE MORRIS, D.L., and MR. B. W. A. HOLMES.

Acting Sergeant WILLIAM DOWLING, Dublin Metropolitan Police, examined.

(Acting Sergeants Thomas Carew, Lawrence Boland, Michael Dixon, William Brewster, and John Culler, also present.)

2176. *Chairman.*—Your name?—William Dowling.

2177. How long are you in the force?—I joined on the 22nd December, 1869; I shall be thirteen years in the force next December.

2178. You are at present an acting sergeant?—Yes.

2179. How long have you been an acting sergeant?—Three years and nine months.

2180. Where are you stationed?—At Arbour Hill.

2181. You have been deputed to give evidence on behalf of the body at large?—Yes.

2182. Now kindly inform us what matters you desire to bring under the notice of the Committee?—The first grievance that we have to complain of is that we have not received any extra pay for the extra duty performed by us during the past three years.

2183. *Mr. Holmes.*—When you talk of "extra pay," I presume you refer to the gratuity which was distributed amongst the Royal Irish Constabulary?—Yes.

2184. When you talk of "extra pay" you allude to that gift?—Yes, I do.

2185. Will you please state the reasons why you think the police in Dublin should share in that gift?—We have performed during the last three years an enormous amount of extra duty in reference to the Land League agitation, and all the meetings that were held in connexion with it. In 1879 we commenced first at the meetings of the Land League, and upon all occasions of meetings we performed a lot of extra duty. In March 1880 there was a great monster Land League meeting in the Phœnix Park, and that entailed very severe duty on the men, for on the day on which the meeting was held the men in general had sixteen, and some seventeen, and some eighteen hours' duty between day and night. There was a general election in April 1880; then there were the State trials in December 1880 and January 1881, and for about three weeks or a month the men had thrown upon them an enormous amount of extra duty.

2186. *Chairman.*—But the same remark applies to the Commission and other trials?—Yes. Then Land League meetings were held at Harold's Cross Green several of them, and Land and Labour League meetings were held; and upon all occasions they entailed an amount of extra duty. Then the arrest of persons under the Coercion Act brought with it a lot of extra duty for us. We had to meet them at the different railway stations and escort them to the various prisons on many occasions that I need not enumerate. At all times that duty was performed cheerfully.

2187. That was in reference to the suspects?—Yes. We had to go and meet trains at different hours of the night at the Kingsbridge, Broadstone, and Amiens Street Terminí, and escort prisoners to other railway stations *en route* to county gaols, and also to Kilmainham. That had to be done so many times a-week, perhaps twice or thrice a-week. Then we had extra duty at Kilmainham Gaol during the whole time—since the first prisoners under the Coercion Act were placed there. There has been an average of about twenty-four men on duty there between inside and outside of the prison, and each of these men did eleven hours nightly. — Acting Sergeant W. Dowling. 22 Sept., 1882.

2188. Was that outside their ordinary duty?—Oh, no, Sir; but the man had to be longer on duty every night than the ordinary tour in consequence of being on that peculiar duty; and the men at home had to do extra duty to fill the places of those men who were so engaged. On the 25th September, 1881, there was a great torchlight procession for Parnell, and we had a very busy night in Dublin, and a lot of extra duty. Then there was the arrest of a number of prisoners. The riots in Sackville Street continued for about ten or twelve nights. In any case, they were the cause of much extra duty to us; and although we were not exactly on the streets during the whole of those nights, we were on reserve in the stations and under the very same discipline as if we were on the street during all that time. I believe that no less than seventy-seven constables were dressed in Jervis Street Hospital alone for injuries they received in those riots. Then, in reference to all the different murders in the city—upon each of these occasions, and for weeks afterwards, a large amount of extra duty was imposed upon us. Those are the principal things.

2189. *Mr. Holmes.*—Then it is your opinion that the state of the city during the last three years imposed upon the men continuous extra duty?—Yes, Sir.

2190. Not merely upon isolated occasions, but from day to day?—Yes; from day to day.

2191. Are you aware that many members of the Royal Irish Constabulary force were out of pocket by reason of the expense they were put to owing to the performance of their duties in the troubled times?—I believe so, Sir; but there have been a great number of them who have been put to no expense at all. I can illustrate that by saying that within three or ten minutes' walk of the station to which I myself belong, there are two constabulary stations—Ballybough and Drumcondra—and I am well aware that in those cases the men were never out of pocket, and had quiet and easy times, yet they received the three months' pay, while we, who were really doing the extra duty, received none at all.

2192. And you might say the same of the men who were stationed at Dundrum and Bray?—Yes; the same might be said of the men stationed all

Acting Sergeant W. Dowling.

22 Sept., 1882.

around the Dublin police district. Within ten minutes' walk of the station I belong to myself this thing has occurred: they have received the pay, and we have received none.

2193. And were you frequently drafted into Dublin to assist the men in the city?—We have been, Sir. We have been drafted from one part of the city to another, and upon every occasion that we have been drafted away, and we have been detained beyond a reasonable time, we were bound to get refreshments, so that if the constabulary were out of pocket certain expenses in their way, we also were in our way.

2194. *Mr. Morris.*—Is that all you have to say upon that branch of your evidence which relates to the allowance of the three months' pay for extra duty?—Yes.

2195. What is the next subject that you wish to bring before us?—It is that we ask a substantial increase of pay, Sir.

2196. What is your pay at present?—My pay is 1l. 12s. 6d. a-week.

2197. That comes to 84l. 14s. 8d. a-year?—Yes.

2198. And on what ground do you seek an increase?—In consequence of the increased price of provisions since the scale of pay was struck. In the matter of provisions our expenditure is very large, and we have to pay the very dearest price for everything.

2199. What provisions are dearer?—Well, for instance, beef is dearer. At the present time a man can get no beef under 11d. per lb. Under the contract in barracks they may get it for something less, but the married men outside have no such contract, and they have to pay the highest market price for it.

2200. *Mr. Holmes.*—Are you aware that the prices of provisions, according to the contract prices, with which we have been furnished, are lower now than in 1872?—I believe, Sir, that no matter what the contract price may be, one-half of the service—the married portion of it—have no benefit whatever from the contract prices. The expenses of men in barracks will be seen from an estimate which I furnish. We have gone as near as we can possibly go, and, living in barracks, a single man will be put to a much lower expenditure than a married man living outside.

2201. *Chairman.*—What do you say are the expenses of a man living in barracks?—76l. 17s. a-year.

2202. *Mr. Holmes.*—And what does that include, everything?—Yes, everything.

2203. *Chairman.*—His living and accessories?—Yes.

2204. *Mr. Holmes.*—Well, then according to that estimate, a single acting sergeant living in barracks would have about 8l. or 9l. a-year over and above his expenditure?—He would, Sir.

2205. He would be able to save that amount of money or about that?—Yes, by expending merely what we have marked out for him, which is at the very lowest scale we could devise.

2206. And by great economy?—Yes, by great economy, and by adopting the scale laid down in the estimate which has been framed on consultation amongst all the men.

2207. What is the estimate for the married man?—107l. 6s. 9d., the family consisting of himself, his wife, and, upon an average, four children. There are many members of the service who have eight children, and the items are here struck out at the very lowest scale, and when you come to examine them you will see that there is nothing included in them but the pure necessaries of life. I now hand in the two estimates for married and single men. There is included the cost of lodgings in the estimate for the married man. These estimates are as follows:—

Estimate of the Weekly and Annual Expenditure of a Dublin Metropolitan Police Sergeant living in Barracks.

Items.	Weekly.			Yearly.		
	s.	d.		£	s.	d.
Bread (1 loaf weekly)	[illegible]	[illegible]	[illegible]	[illegible]	[illegible]	[illegible]
[illegible]	[illegible]	[illegible]	[illegible]	[illegible]	[illegible]	[illegible]
[illegible]	[illegible]	[illegible]	[illegible]	[illegible]	[illegible]	[illegible]
[illegible]	[illegible]	[illegible]	[illegible]	[illegible]	[illegible]	[illegible]
[illegible]	[illegible]	[illegible]	[illegible]	[illegible]	[illegible]	[illegible]
[illegible]	[illegible]	[illegible]	[illegible]	[illegible]	[illegible]	[illegible]
[illegible]	[illegible]	[illegible]	[illegible]	[illegible]	[illegible]	[illegible]
[illegible]	[illegible]	[illegible]	[illegible]	[illegible]	[illegible]	[illegible]
[illegible]	[illegible]	[illegible]	[illegible]	[illegible]	[illegible]	[illegible]
[illegible]	[illegible]	[illegible]	[illegible]	[illegible]	[illegible]	[illegible]
[illegible]	[illegible]	[illegible]	[illegible]	[illegible]	[illegible]	[illegible]
[illegible]	[illegible]	[illegible]	[illegible]	[illegible]	[illegible]	[illegible]
[illegible]	[illegible]	[illegible]	[illegible]	[illegible]	[illegible]	[illegible]
[illegible]	[illegible]	[illegible]	[illegible]	[illegible]	[illegible]	[illegible]
[illegible]	[illegible]	[illegible]	[illegible]	[illegible]	[illegible]	[illegible]
[illegible]		[illegible]		[illegible]	[illegible]	[illegible]
[illegible]		[illegible]		[illegible]	[illegible]	[illegible]
[illegible]		[illegible]		[illegible]	[illegible]	[illegible]
[illegible]		[illegible]		[illegible]	[illegible]	[illegible]
[illegible]		[illegible]		[illegible]	[illegible]	[illegible]
[illegible]		[illegible]		[illegible]	[illegible]	[illegible]
[illegible]		[illegible]		[illegible]	[illegible]	[illegible]
[illegible]		[illegible]		[illegible]	[illegible]	[illegible]
[illegible]		[illegible]		[illegible]	[illegible]	[illegible]
Total	—			[illegible]	17	[illegible]

Estimated Cost of Living of a Married Acting Sergeant in the Dublin Metropolitan Police.

Details.	Weekly.			Yearly.		
	£	s.	d.	£	s.	d.
[illegible]	[illegible]	[illegible]	[illegible]	[illegible]	[illegible]	[illegible]
[illegible]	[illegible]	[illegible]	[illegible]	[illegible]	[illegible]	[illegible]
[illegible]	[illegible]	[illegible]	[illegible]	[illegible]	[illegible]	[illegible]
[illegible]	[illegible]	[illegible]	[illegible]	[illegible]	[illegible]	[illegible]
[illegible]	[illegible]	[illegible]	[illegible]	[illegible]	[illegible]	[illegible]
[illegible]	[illegible]	[illegible]	[illegible]	[illegible]	[illegible]	[illegible]
[illegible]	[illegible]	[illegible]	[illegible]	[illegible]	[illegible]	[illegible]
[illegible]	[illegible]	[illegible]	[illegible]	[illegible]	[illegible]	[illegible]
[illegible]	[illegible]	[illegible]	[illegible]	[illegible]	[illegible]	[illegible]
[illegible]	[illegible]	[illegible]	[illegible]	[illegible]	[illegible]	[illegible]
[illegible]	[illegible]	[illegible]	[illegible]	[illegible]	[illegible]	[illegible]
[illegible]	[illegible]	[illegible]	[illegible]	[illegible]	[illegible]	[illegible]
Total of weekly items	1	[illegible]	[illegible]	[illegible]	[illegible]	7
[illegible]		[illegible]		[illegible]	[illegible]	[illegible]
[illegible]		[illegible]		[illegible]	[illegible]	[illegible]
[illegible]		[illegible]		[illegible]	[illegible]	[illegible]
[illegible]		[illegible]		[illegible]	[illegible]	[illegible]
[illegible]		[illegible]		[illegible]	[illegible]	[illegible]
[illegible]		[illegible]		[illegible]	[illegible]	[illegible]
[illegible]		[illegible]		[illegible]	[illegible]	[illegible]
[illegible]		[illegible]		[illegible]	[illegible]	[illegible]
[illegible]		—		[illegible]	[illegible]	[illegible]
	1	[illegible]	[illegible]	[illegible]	[illegible]	[illegible]
[illegible]		—		[illegible]	[illegible]	[illegible]
		..		[illegible]	[illegible]	[illegible]

I wish to state that it is a great hardship and a great cause of complaint amongst the married men that lodgings are so dear in Dublin. They are far dearer in Dublin than in London. A policeman is bound to have respectable lodgings, for his lodgings are inspected monthly by the inspector or superintendent, and he is therefore bound to live in superior lodgings, and he will not get them in Dublin under high rates. An acting sergeant or a sergeant must pay 7s. weekly at the present time, and there is a great objection raised by people, even then, to having a policeman in the house at all, and in many cases, I myself for one, have been refused on two different occasions—we are refused accommodation altogether, on account of the fact of being a policeman.

2208. You are of course aware that the salaries of all civil servants are fixed, not with a view necessarily to enabling them to marry, but of enabling them to live, and if they choose to marry and bring a family into the world without having sufficient means and without looking about them, they must take the consequences like everyone else?—We are very well aware of that; we do not dispute that at all. We only ask that something reasonable, that some privileges would be allowed to us to enable us to rear our families respectably.

2209. Assuming that your pay is sufficient to keep you as a single man. Do you think it ought to be increased because you choose to marry?—No, Sir.

2210. Because it practically comes to that when you ask for a lodging allowance, and admit that you would not require it if you were a single man?—Well, it is a rule in some of the other police forces to grant it, or something equivalent to it. In London there is a rule where constables are provided with lodgings at a fixed rate, at a rate regulated by the Secretary of State. In London, lodgings are supplied to a constable for 3s. weekly, to a sergeant for 4s. weekly, and to an inspector for 5s 6d weekly.

2211. It is only in a very few cases that married men are accommodated in blocks of building, and when they are not so accommodated they must pay for their lodgings according to the rates that are going. They do not receive any lodging allowance?—No, Sir, I am aware of that.

2212. On the contrary, they are obliged to pay rent for their lodgings, even when accommodated in those blocks of houses?—Yes, I am aware of that. Some of the larger firms in Dublin provide lodgings for their employés. For instance, at the railway works at Inchicore the employes are supplied with lodgings at a cheap rate; at Guinness' brewery the workpeople are, to a great extent, supplied with lodgings, and a great many more of the large firms in Dublin make similar provision for their work-people.

2213. *Chairman.*—But I think these lodgings are paid for?—Yes, they are paid for, but at a reduced scale or at a reasonable rent.

2214. *Mr. Holmes.*—Then I presume the married men of the Dublin metropolitan police would be quite prepared to pay a reasonable rent if they were provided with accommodation similar to that provided for some of the married men in London?—We ask no more than that, Sir.

2215. *Mr. Morris.*—As a reasonable man, I ask you what in your opinion, and in the opinion of the other men who are with you here, is the increase of pay you would ask? I ask you that as a reasonable man, and putting aside all wild propositions?—We would ask 1s a-day as an increase in our pay.

2216. *Mr. Holmes.*—Then you, as an acting sergeant, would wish to have your pay raised from 84l 11s. 6d to 102l. a-year?—Yes, Sir.

2217. Are you aware that your pay would then be higher than that of a first-class sergeant in the London metropolitan police?—Yes, Sir; but I am also aware that at the present time there is a great amount of discontent caused in the London police by the same state of things. They are also asking for an increase of pay.

2218. *Chairman.*—How do you know that?—Well, I have seen a letter from one of them, and we have seen it in the public prints.

2219. *Mr. Morris.*—Do you think that in considering the question of what would be the proper pay to give you as an acting sergeant or as a constable in this country, the decision of the point should be regulated by what a man in a similar position would get either in California, or New Zealand, or in any part of the Colonies?—We do not expect that.

2220. But, rather, don't you think it should be regulated by the price at which labour is got in our own country?—Well, yes, Sir, we do not dispute that at all.

2221. You do not think, at least I presume you do not, that because a man of your class and position in Australia can get 10s. a-day in Australia, he is to get 10s. a-day in Dublin?—Oh, by no means.

2222. When as good a man is to be got for 5s.?—Oh, by no means; we do not ask that.

2223. *Mr. Holmes.*—Now is it, or is it not, your opinion that the present rates of pay are quite sufficient to attract to the force good men?—I believe not, Sir.

2224. Is it not a fact that there is no lack of recruits?—Well, as for recruits, there are some recruits coming, but there are also numbers of resignations—many of them resign afterwards, and the present scale of pay is not sufficient to give them contentment or to keep them in the force.

Acting Sergeant W. Dowling.

25 Sept., 1882.

2225. *Mr. Morris.*—Is it a fact that some of the men who have resigned and emigrated had resigned in the police force a sufficient time to get an amount of money as a gratuity for their service which enabled them to emigrate?—I do not believe that such a thing has been the fact.

2226. You do not think such a system as that has been adopted at all?—I do not think there is such a system in existence at all. We have instances where first-class men—men getting the first rate of pay—men seven and eight years in the service—have resigned and emigrated.

2227. *Mr. Holmes.*—Are you aware that several of the grades of the metropolitan police force in Dublin are better paid than the corresponding grades in London?—I am, Sir; but I am also aware that in some of the grades—the very grade I myself represent among them—we are not so well paid as the men doing the same duty as we do in London.

2228. *Mr. Morris.*—I suppose you found part of your reasons for claiming to be better paid in Ireland than the men in England on the fact that your duties are more onerous and more dangerous?—Yes, Sir, and more severe. I can just produce, if you wish, a Table showing the amount of duty for one year, according to the published Returns, that has been performed by the Dublin police. I wish to refer you to that. It is taken from the statistics contained in the Commissioners' Report published in 1877, an extract from the official Returns. It is as follows:—

TABLE showing the Number of Persons taken into Custody in the year 1877.

Offences			Number
[illegible]	[illegible]	Offences against the person [illegible]	[illegible]
[illegible]	[illegible]	[illegible]	[illegible]
[illegible]	[illegible]	[illegible]	[illegible]
[illegible]	[illegible]	Malicious [illegible] property	[illegible]
[illegible]	[illegible]	[illegible]	[illegible]
[illegible]	[illegible]	[illegible]	[illegible]
Total			17,[illegible]

2229. *Mr. Holmes.*—I think you said you obtained your present rank after you had been nine years in the force?—Yes, Sir.

2230. Don't you think the weekly pay of 1l 1s 6d. is very handsome pay for so short a period of service?—Thirteen years is long service. It is a long time in the Dublin police.

2231. You attained your rank in that time?—But then, at the present time, I think the pay is not sufficient for the duties that I have to perform.

2232. Is not a weekly wage of nearly 1l. 11s. a-week as high as almost the highest wages that are given to skilled labour?—No, an artisan at the present time receives 36s. a-week according to the rules of trade in Dublin, and he has other privileges, and a policeman has none.

2233. To what class of artisans do you refer?—To any—painters, carpenters, bricklayers, plasterers—any of the general working classes of trades. The trades' price of labour in Dublin is 36s. per week at the present time.

2234. That is a little more than 1s a-week in excess of your pay?—Yes, Sir; but for that he has only to work five and a-half days, whereas a policeman has to work seven days or seven nights, as the case may be.

2235. Are you not aware that his pay is precarious—that he may be getting 36s. one week and be out of employment the next; whereas your pay is certain and continuous. Are you not aware of that?—I am aware that if a tradesman conducts himself in a respectable manner—in the same manner as a

Acting Sergeant W. [illegible].

[illegible]

policeman is obliged to conduct himself—he would be never able one more idle than a policeman.

2236. Are you aware that he does not get a pension when he can work no longer?—I am.

2237. Are you not in a better position than the skilled artisan in that respect?—I am, but we have to provide ourselves with the necessaries of life, which renders our pay insufficient to keep us respectably.

2238. Then, according to that, I presume the pay of a respectable artisan is not sufficient?—But he has more privileges than we have. An artisan may keep a shop, and his wife may assist him in many ways. If she has any trade or business she may follow it, and he may live in worse lodgings than a policeman; and by that means we are not nearly so well off as the artisan.

2239. And he has, you say, only five and a-half days to work, and you have seven?—Yes; he has only half a day on Saturday, and no Sunday work.

2240. *Mr. Morris.*—But is it not the case that, in addition to your pay, you are practically provided with good lodgings gratis in the barracks?—That is not so. The men in the barracks have to pay 1s. 6d. a-week for their lodgings.

2241. *Mr. Holmes.*—May I ask you where you would get such lodgings for the same amount of money?—They have to pay the expenses of servants; they have to pay the cost of messenger, [illegible], and all things like that. They have to pay for all these things themselves in barracks.

2242. What does that make the lodgings and attendance amount to in the week?—2s. 6d.

2243. Where would he get about it so such lodgings in Dublin for that amount per week with attendance?—That is very true, no doubt; but in London there is only 1s. a-week stopped from the men of the metropolitan police force for all these things.

2244. *Chairman.*—Have you anything to add on this branch of your evidence?—No, Sir.

2245. What is the next subject which you wish should be considered by the Committee?—The next subject is that of pensions.

2246. Kindly state your views and the views of the men you represent fully as to that question?—The Pension Act of 1867 has created great discontent in the service, and the pension now granted is wholly insufficient to induce proper men to remain in the service, because, under no circumstances under the Act could a man ever obtain his full pay. Under the Act of 1867, thirty-fiftieths of his pay is the most that he could receive as pension, and that after thirty years' service. He then must be certified by a medical board to be unfit to further serve; and, indeed, after a service of thirty years in the Dublin police, he is unfit to serve in any place else, for he is not able to knock out any kind of a living, and that Act only provides him with something better than what a poor labouring man would have, so that, after his life of service in the force, he has nothing but poverty awaiting him in the end.

2247. *Mr. Holmes.*—Do you seriously assert that a man in the Dublin police on leaving the force should receive as pension the full rate of pay?—I do, Sir.

2248. But are you aware that there are no civil servants under the Crown who are pensioned at that rate?—Well, there are no civil servants under the Crown that deserve to be pensioned so liberally as do the police, because they are broken down. The service that a policeman renders to the country for his twenty-five years is very considerable. He does far more duty in twenty-five years than a civil servant does in fifty years. We can show, on a comparison of ours, with the duty of a civil servant, that the duties of a civil servant are very far less than ours.

2249. Are you aware that during the whole history of the London metropolitan police force at no period could a man retire on full pay pension as a man could here. Are you aware of that?—I have heard it, Sir.

2250. Well, you may accept it as a fact; are you aware that the most the men can or ever could get in the London metropolitan police force is two-thirds of their pay as pension?—I am.

2251. Do you think that the Dublin men could be put on a better scale of pension than the London men?—I believe it would be necessary to do it.

2252. Why?—To induce men, first and foremost, to remain in the force, it would be necessary to do it, and because the duties here in Dublin are so arduous that the men deserve it. When a man leaves the force in London he has every opportunity and every prospect that he will get some other situation that he may be able to fill. In Dublin, a superannuated policeman has very little chance of getting employment; every one's hand is against him. I have known men, and I know men at the present time, who have got their pensions, and they cannot get any employment. They must get something easy to do, or they would not be able for it at all, and that they cannot get in Dublin. When a man retires from the Dublin police he must live on the pension he gets.

2253. Was it always the case that the Dublin police pensioner found it impossible to get anything to do?—I don't think it was.

2254. What has caused the change?—There is a bitterness against the police at the present time existing, that is to say, amongst a certain class, not exactly amongst the employers themselves, but amongst the working hands—a feeling that they will not remain in an establishment where there are police pensioners or policemen about at all.

2255. Do you know that of your own knowledge?—Yes, I do, personally. Since the Phoenix Park riots in 1871 there has been a bitterness raised in Dublin against the police. It is only on the part of the working classes, and the working classes will not work with a policeman. I have known a pensioner who, after getting employment, had to leave that employment because the employer could not keep him, as the other people in the place would not work with him.

2256. And, as a matter of fact, you know that the hostile spirit commenced in 1871, on the occasion of the Park riots?—Yes.

2257. And has continued ever since?—Yes, and at the present time the bitterness is more intense than ever it was before.

2258. *Mr. Morris.*—In reference to the subject of retirement, don't you think it would be an improvement on the present system, at all events, and one that might lead to more contentment upon the subject of retirement, if a policeman were given the privilege of retiring, if he liked to do so, after thirty years' service, without any medical board or inspection, or any other formality?—I believe it would be a great privilege.

2259. It would be better than the present system?—Far better; but if after twenty-five years he was allowed to retire, if he wished it, without the necessity of being certified unfit, the men would greatly prefer it.

2260. You and the force would prefer twenty-five years?—Yes.

2261. But you think, at all events, it would be an improvement on the present system if a man was allowed to retire of his own accord after twenty-eight or thirty years' service upon whatever pension was awarded him?—I do, and I believe it would be of great service to the men.

2262. But you would prefer, and the force would prefer, a shorter period?—Yes.

2263. *Chairman.*—You contend that a man should be able to retire after twenty-five years' service on full pay?—That is what I ask.

2264. *Mr. Holmes.*—Assuming that you could retire after twenty-five years' service if you liked, and that you could get, after twenty-eight years' service, two-thirds of your pay, as the men can get in London who retire at that time, do you think that would satisfy the men even if their present pay was not increased ?—I don't think it would, Sir; I don't believe it would.

2265. *Chairman.*—What is the next subject that you wish to bring before us ?—It is in reference to the matter of gratuity; that is our next grievance. At present a man is entitled to receive one month's pay for each year he serves after five years, from five years up to ten, and two months' pay from ten to fourteen years, when the gratuity stops. He cannot receive it for more than fourteen years at any time, and there have been cases where even superintendents have been dying in the service, and they could not receive more than a gratuity for the fourteen years. That is a matter of great complaint amongst the members of the force, and they ask now respectfully that the period at which it can first be allowed be three years, as heretofore. It was, I should state, formerly three years in the service until 1867, when it was increased to five, and that they should get two months' pay for each year they serve.

2266. After three years ?—For the whole period of service.

2267. After three years ?—Yes; so that it would not stop at the fourteen years, but that for each year a man serves while in the force. And in case of sudden death we ask that the next-of-kin should receive that compensation without the deceased having to go through the formality of signing the papers which are now necessary to secure it.

2268. *Mr. Morris.*—Will you describe what you mean by the "next-of-kin" ?—Well, his wife and children, his father or mother; outside of whom we would not ask to go; I include the father or mother because in some cases a policeman is the sole support of his father and mother. At the present time, and according to the present regulations, the dying man must have signed his "compensation papers," as they are called, for if he dies without affixing his signature to them, the whole of the gratuity is lost. At the present time, if a man who is not entitled to a gratuity dies in the service, there is a sum of 8*l.* 10*s.* 6*d.* only allowed for his burial; that is totally insufficient. The next matter I wish to lay before you is our request that no stoppage be made from the pay of members of the service when on the sick report.

2269. *Mr. Holmes.*—Are you aware that that deduction is made from the pay of the London police and from the pay of the men of other police forces ?—I am aware of it. At the present time in any case where a man is sick in Dublin he has no means of support but his pay, while in other police forces they have something, because they are allowed more privileges than we have in Dublin.

2270. What do you mean by being "allowed more privileges" than the men in Dublin ?—I am informed and believe that the men in some of the borough forces in England who are policemen are allowed to have lodgers in their houses, and their wives are permitted to carry on business such as dressmaking. I do not, of course, say that they are allowed to keep shops.

2271. And by that means supplement the pay of their husbands ?—Yes, Sir. In Dublin a policeman has no privilege whatever; he is debarred from everything except his week's pay alone. Out of that he is obliged to provide everything. His wife, if she happens to be a dressmaker or milliner, is not allowed to carry on her business and supplement her husband's income in any way.

2272. *Chairman.*—What is the next item of your evidence ?—The sergeants and acting sergeants residing in barracks ask that they be granted the barracks free.

2273. *Mr. Holmes.*—You are, of course, aware that in London a deduction is made from the pay of the men for their barrack accommodation ?—I am, Sir. We also ask that for any extra duty we perform we will be allowed a reasonable amount of pay on the scale laid down.

2274. *Mr. Morris.*—That would be at so much an hour for extra duty ?—Yes, Sir; according to the scale of pay that we were in receipt of.

2275. This is a question I have put to the sergeants and inspectors, and it is a question I feel very strongly on. Do you think that the citizens of Dublin would be satisfied if the police were to be paid by the hour ?—We do not ask it, Sir, except in extreme cases. We do not ask it as an ordinary thing.

2276. Don't you think that the very nature of your profession and business as policemen entitle the citizens of Dublin, and the same rule would apply elsewhere, who are no doubt paying you well, to require that you should be at their service on all occasions and at all times in case of emergency—sudden outbreak, riots, fires, or anything of that kind ?—Oh, certainly, Sir; we do not mean to [illegible] anything else.

2277. Then, do you think that the discipline of a police force could be properly carried out were time to be measured in the way that you suggest ?—I am very well aware, Sir, that it could not be done, nor do we ask it to be done except in this way; we ask this pay, or at least some scale for the purpose of entitling us to payment, in order to show that it is not unnecessary to compel us to do extra duty; because we are under the impression that on some occasions our men ought not be asked to do the extra duty that is imposed upon them. It is not for the purpose of emolument that we ask this pay, but as a check that we would not be unnecessarily asked to do extra duty, and that our men would not be kept on extra duty without due occasion for it.

2278. Do you consider that such a check is necessary ?—I do, Sir.

2279. A sergeant yesterday gave evidence that on some occasions the alarm of fire was given, and that it was found that the fire was put out before the policemen who had been sent for arrived; that they were stopped on the way, and he looked upon it as a great grievance. Do you look upon it as a grievance ?—No, Sir. We do not look upon any such things as emergencies as grievances.

2280. When you say you should be paid extra pay for extra time, I presume you allude to a case similar to that of the skilled artisan, who is sometimes, if he is asked to work extra hours to hasten a job, paid so much an hour extra ?—We do not ask that.

2281. Then how would you ask to have the thing worked out ?—Where there is continuous extra duty for any time.

2282. Who is to be the judge of that continuous duty ?—We would leave that to the Commissioner. We do not, in asking for this, mean to include anything in the way of the ordinary duty of policemen; we do not mean that we should be paid for that; we only ask extra pay for continuous extra duty.

2283. Then, suppose, as an acting sergeant, you were sent to do some extra duty, and you took two hours to do it, and that, in the opinion of the Commissioner, superintendent, or inspector, you ought to have done it in half-an-hour, there would be at once a discussion as to the amount of extra pay you were to be allowed ?—We do not want hours or two hours at all. We want, that when there is a continuous run of extra duty for any length of time there would be some scale of regulations so that we would be paid for it.

2284. Don't you think that as a police force it would be better, suppose you were satisfied with your pay and pension, to have a system by which you could take on a whole the rough and smooth of your work ?—I do, Sir.

2285. And that they should be at all times ready when called upon, instead of looking for extra pay for extra duties ?—I do, Sir. I believe it would be a far better system.

2286. Do not you think that, in the end, it would lead to great confusion in the force if the proposition for payment for extra duty was adopted ?—I

Acting Sergeant W. Sterling.
—
25 Sept., 1882.

have no doubt it would. The reason I was asked to ask it was so that there might be some check—that instead of keeping men on extra duty when it is not necessary, that might be prevented.

2287 Who is to be the judge of what constitutes extra duty?—We would leave that in the hands of the Commissioner or Superintendent.

2288 Then I suppose it is at this very moment in the power of the Commissioners and Superintendents to define what constitutes extra duty?—But there is no extra pay for extra duty at the present time.

2289 *Mr. Holmes.*—You have been explaining, at some length, your views as to extra pay for extra duty to Mr Morris. May I ask you, do you think that this proposition of yours would be feasible—would be capable of being worked out?—Well, no, Sir—perhaps not; but I am quite certain that if the men were paid substantial weekly pay, and that they were contented with their weekly pay, that they would be satisfied to do extra duty without extra pay. Then we ask that the annual leave of sergeants and acting sergeants be increased to one month.

2290 What is it at present?—The acting sergeant is entitled to an annual leave of fourteen days, and the full sergeant to twenty-one days; and we ask that they be made evenly for the month. There is great difficulty sometimes in getting leave. I am also instructed to ask that, in lieu of leave being granted, we receive a month's pay. This is for the same purpose as the other; it is not for the purpose of getting the month's pay, but it is for the purpose of getting the leave. We ask the pay as a check, so that we will get the leave; because there are many times that we have been refused the leave, and we do not get the leave always as we expect it. We also ask that we get two days' leave in the month. At the present time we are entitled to one, if we get it, but very often we cannot be spared, and we do not get it. We ask that one of those days may be a Sunday. It is right, above all other days, for us to get a Sunday's leave. The next thing we ask is that no examination, medical or otherwise, be held on promotion from the rank of acting sergeant to that of sergeant, and that such promotion should go by seniority. Formerly in our force it was always the system that promotion from the rank of acting sergeant to that of full sergeant went by seniority, until the last four or five years. There was no such thing as examination, until the last four or five years, since the formation of the force. Since that time it has created a great amount of discontent in the rank of acting sergeant.

2291. Why was the change made?—I do not know.

2292. Was it not to secure greater efficiency in the rank of sergeant?—I believe that was the suggestion, Sir. Then there are also the divisional pay clerks to whom I wish to refer. The system of appointing divisional pay clerks we protest against. They were always chosen heretofore from the rank of acting sergeant, until the change that introduced the present system, and since that time they are made from the junior members of the service.

2293 *Mr Morris.*—Whom do you call the junior members of the service?—Men of twelve months' service. When a vacancy occurs they get into the office, and they are appointed acting sergeant after one month.

2294 *Chairman.*—Are you now referring to own stables?—Yes, Sir.

2295. Of what grade?—Of the third and fourth grade.

2296 Is it possible for a man who has been in the force twelve months to be made a pay clerk?—It is possible under the system, but the same thing has not occurred in such very short service.

2297. And would he become a full sergeant after another year?—He would.

2298. In other words, such a man would become a full sergeant after being a little more than two years in the force?—That is quite possible.

2299 And you wish that the divisional pay clerks should be selected entirely from men of the rank of acting sergeant?—Yes, as heretofore. For thirty-nine years that worked very satisfactorily, but for the last five or six years it has been changed, and it has created great complaint. The system of examinations, then, for promotion from the rank of acting sergeant to that of full sergeant debars old and experienced men, and leaves them acting sergeants, it might be, for the remainder of their time of service, and gives the preference to young, inexperienced men to get promotion over them; and we ask that promotion to the rank of sergeant be made by seniority.

2300. From the rank of acting sergeant?—Yes. The duties are exactly the same; there is no difference in the duties whatever of acting sergeant and sergeant; and it has always been the custom, for thirty-nine years, that the senior acting sergeant got the first vacancy for the rank of full sergeant, and that plan always worked satisfactorily. For the last five or six years that has been changed, and the change has created great dissatisfaction. After an acting sergeant obtains the rank of full sergeant, he can go out on the streets as a section sergeant again, and then he is eligible to compete for the rank of acting inspector; so that, by that means, all ranks of the service have an opportunity of advancement. But, if the present system was worked on, it would fill the higher grades of the service solely from clerks, so that the men on the streets would have no chance of promotion.

2301 *Mr Holmes.*—If a vacancy occurs in the rank of acting inspector, how is it filled?—It is filled by examination from the rank of full sergeants. There are so many full sergeants qualified for the examination, and the examination is carried on, and then the successful candidate first on the list gets the first vacancy.

2302 Is it not of great importance that acting inspectors should be men of ability and capacity?—Certainly.

2303. Don't you think that that proposition of yours, limiting promotion to the rank of sergeant entirely to seniority might shut out the ablest men from the rank of acting inspector?—I am quite certain that, generally, full sergeants are thoroughly competent for the rank of acting inspector. It has always been found so after thirty-nine years' experience, and there is only five or six years' experience of the new system, and it is for you to judge which has of the two worked most satisfactorily.

2304 *Chairman.*—What is the next point that you wish to refer to?—We would ask that, in case an officer in the service is reduced from a high rank of officers to a lower grade than that which he was at—we ask that the term of the reduction be limited, and not, as at present, final. Heretofore, the conditions were that when a man was reduced from a higher to a lower rank, he would be reinstated at the end of three years, if his conduct was good; and we ask to have the same system back again. There are some very good men reduced in the service, some very smart men reduced for trivial offences. If they are reduced to a lower grade altogether, they lose heart and courage in the service, and, in fact, they become useless members to a great extent. We ask that the reduction should not be final, but that the limit given to it be three years.

2305 What do you mean by final, not perpetual?—Yes. At the same time, I may add, when a man is reduced he has to go through the same ordeal as a recruit after he is reduced, and he may be reduced for very little. We ask that he should be reinstated to his former rank at any time not exceeding three years, if his conduct is good. The next ground of complaint that we have is a cause of great discontent, and that is the restriction then imposed

Acting Sergeant W. [illegible]

[illegible] Sept., 18[illegible]

by the Commissioner for very slight trivial offences. This has been one of the greatest causes of discontent in the service, and I may produce a few instances of what we complain of as an illustration. Knockers taken off doors, a pane of glass broken in a window, and things like that, it is nearly impossible for a policeman to avoid these escaping his attention. Sergeants of sections and men on the beats, they cannot detect them at all times, because a man may be walking about a couple of hours elsewhere, and these things may be done before you come back, and no matter how vigilant you may be, they may escape you. Nevertheless, if you are reported for them you are invariably fined, and the fines vary from 20s., 15s., to 10s., and 5s. to 7s. 6d., and sometimes they run even as high as 30s., and that for a pane of glass being broken on a man's beat, and no notice being taken and no report made of it. And even reductions have taken place in the rank of acting sergeant for trivial offences; for there is one instance where two acting sergeants were reduced for merely gossiping with each other. They were where the boundaries of their two districts met, and they simply stood for a while gossiping with each other, and they were reduced to the ranks and have remained in the ranks ever since.

2306. *Mr. Morris.*—But while you complain of these fines for irregularities on the part of the force as being excessive, I suppose you do not put it that there should not be some power given to fine policemen for neglect of duty?—I do not; but I mean to say that these cases were not in reality cases of neglect of duty; because on a dark winter's night a policeman going on his beat might find it very hard to observe these things.

2307. But how could you carry out discipline in the force unless you gave power to some man to punish, limiting, perhaps, his powers as to fining, for neglect of duty?—That is all we want.

2308. But the policeman complained of, or against whom the report is made, is not to be the judge?—No, Sir.

2309. Therefore, you must allow somebody to be the judge of whether the offence complained of does or does not amount to a neglect of duty?—Certainly, we agree with that. All that we want is a limit to the excessive fines. It is the excessive amount of them that we complain of.

2310. *Chairman.*—You approve of the system of fining but you disapprove of the excessive amounts of the fines?—We approve of the system of fining; we do not at all go against it.

2311. In fact, you believe that the discipline of the force could not be kept up without some fines for neglect of duty imposed by some person whose duty it was to be the judge of what that neglect of duty was?—Yes, Sir.

2312. But what you complain of is that the fines hitherto imposed in the administration of the business of the police force have been excessive for the offences which led to their infliction?—Yes, Sir; that is so.

2313. And that those punishments are kept over the man's heads?—Yes; they are registered as bad marks, and we ask that they should be all erased.

2314. After a certain lapse of time?—Yes. A man may commit an offence when he joins the service, and he may serve for thirty years, and on the last day, when he is going out of the force, his pension may be curtailed, on account of that old offence.

2315. And you consider that, for small breaches of discipline, if a man is fined, and gets a black mark, and his conduct afterwards is good for two or three years, that that mark should be erased?—Yes.

2316. And not affect his pension when he is leaving the force?—Yes, that is the principal thing.

2317. You wish that the fine or punishment, or whatever it may be, should be final at the time, and not be recorded against a man so as to affect his pension?—Yes.

2318. *Mr. Morris.*—Provided his conduct was afterwards good?—Yes. Another great cause of complaint is, that when men are off duty in plain clothes on leave, or meeting a friend, that it is an offence, and one for which we are punished very severely, to go into a public-house to get refreshment. We say nothing about men while in uniform and off duty; but I do not see that it should be any offence for me to go into a public-house with a friend while off duty and in plain clothes. We say that a man off duty and in plain clothes has a right to have the privileges of any other man, so that those privileges are nothing more than any respectable man would enjoy.

2319. *Mr. Holmes.*—Then you would claim that privilege to constables off duty and in plain clothes?—Yes, Sir; that is all we ask.

2320. *Mr. Morris.*—Do you consider that the relaxation of the present rule as regards allowing men to go into public-houses when in plain clothes and on leave would not be an encouragement to drink in the force?—I am quite certain it would be no encouragement whatever. It would be a great privilege if men could enjoy it with a little freedom, and I am quite certain that it would not lead to the encouragement of habits of drinking in the force in any way.

2321. But supposing a man went into a public-house in plain clothes, and off duty, and took a little drop too much, and that he had to go on duty immediately afterwards, and that he appeared in uniform with the signs of liquor on him—I suppose you would not go to the length of saying that it was any excuse for him that he took the drink while off duty?—I would not; but there is no fear of him going out on duty with the signs of drink upon him, and that is the reason why we ask this at all. And another great cause of complaint and ground of discontent in the service is the tribunal by which we are tried. We ask that something also be done with regard to that, and that when the offence is classed against us, and that we believe we are harshly treated, whether by mistake or otherwise, we would then ask that the investigation be one upon sworn testimony.

2322. What tribunal would you have?—We suggest that there would be a Board of Superintendents to try the case.

2323. *Mr. Holmes.*—Associated with the Commissioner, I presume?—Yes, Sir. That seven or six superintendents, as the case may be, should sit along with the Commissioner, and that if necessary, the accused may be sworn.

2324. And do you suggest that the superintendents should have a voice in the sentence?—I do, Sir.

2325. An equal voice with the Commissioner?—Yes.

2326. *Mr. Morris.*—And do you not think that that would interfere in any way with the other duties of the superintendents—listening to every complaint?—It was the system for thirty-nine years. The Board sat every Tuesday.

2327. And heard all complaints?—Yes.

2328. Trivial and important?—Yes.

2329. *Mr. Holmes.*—But is it a fact that the superintendents ever had a voice in the sentence?—They always sat with the Commissioner.

2330. Were they not always referees as to character?—That is all. They gave their opinions.

2331. *Chairman.*—They gave the best opinion they could to the Commissioner?—Yes.

2332. They did not take part in the proceedings so far as adjudicating upon them, but being referred to as to the character of the accused, they gave it?—Yes.

2333. *Mr. Holmes.*—Is not the present system practically the same as the old one, that is, when any charge is brought against a man of the A, B, C, D, or E Divisions, the superintendent of his own division is always present?—Yes; but there is this difference, that his own superintendent may not know anything at all about him, whereas if the other superintendents were there, they would understand all about him. We only ask that proper sworn testimony should be given. Of course, that would be only necessary in extreme cases, and where a man believes he is aggrieved.

2934. *Mr Morris.*—Would you have that inquiry open to the public?—No, Sir.

2935. Or would you prefer to have that inquiry amongst yourselves?—Yes, amongst ourselves; especially in cases where civilians report us. It is very often the case that civilians may run in bewildered, and allege that a policeman assaulted them, or some slight trifling case like that, and there have been cases that went before the Commissioner where the complainant was really the guilty party, and we ask that especially in cases of that sort there should be sworn testimony. We ask that there should be no examination for drill for the promotion to the rank of sergeant from acting sergeant. We ask for the privilege that officers of the force, when they take respectable houses, should have respectable lodgers, and that it would not be an offence for them to keep a respectable lodger or two. If it did not interfere with the work of the force in any way for a man having a couple of rooms to spare in a respectable house, we do not see why that power should not be given. The privilege is not allowed now, and we ask respectfully that it should be given. The next matter I wish to bring before the Committee is that of transfers—the transfer of a man from one division to another, sometimes as it is called, "for the good of the service." We ask in cases of that kind that a reasonable amount should be allowed, especially to married men.

2936. *Chairman.*—For expenses?—Yes, Sir. In cases of transfer by the Commissioner for the good of the service without consulting our own wishes. We ask that the families of policemen, such as their wives or daughters, might be allowed to carry on a respectable business, such as dressmaking, millinery, laundry work, and so on, in their own houses, without that being rendered a breach of discipline. Those are the principle things we have to say, Gentlemen.

2937. What do you mean by any examination for drill?—A man has to pass an examination for drill from the rank of acting sergeant to full sergeant.

2938. You would ask to have that dispensed with?—Yes, we ask to have that dispensed with as not necessary. There have been several men rejected for that, and it has debarred them from going up for the other examination, because they were not able to qualify for drill.

2939. *Mr. Morris* (addressing Sergeants Carew, Boland, Dunn, Brewster, and Cullen).—You, who are five other acting sergeants deputed to attend here on behalf of the men of your rank, have heard Acting Sergeant Dowling examined, and the evidence he has given very fully and clearly. Have any one of you anything to add? If not, state, do you concur in the evidence given by Acting Sergeant Dowling as representing your views?

Sergeant Carew.—We all concur.

(The remaining four men also stated that they concurred.)

2940. *Mr. Morris.*—You think he has fully and satisfactorily put the case as the representative of the men of your class?

Sergeant Carew.—Indeed, I think he did it just as well as it could be possibly put. We have nothing further to say.

[The Committee then adjourned until the following Monday.]

Eleventh Day.—25th September, 1882.

Present:

Mr. J. W. O'Donnell, Mr. George Morris, D.L., and Mr. H. W. A. Holmes.

Thomas Cox, First-class Constable, Dublin Metropolitan Police, examined.

(Also present: James Gibney, third-class constable; Michael M'Cormick, first-class constable; William Butler, third-class constable; Henry Stephens, third-class constable; and Lawrence Fogarty, first-class constable.)

2941. *Chairman.*—What is your name?—Thomas Cox.

2942. You are a first-class constable?—Yes, Sir.

2943. How long are you in the Dublin metropolitan police force?—Fifteen years next December.

2944. Where are you stationed?—In College Street.

2945. Will you now state the matters you wish to bring under the notice of the Committee, taking the various matters in what you consider to be the order of their importance?—The first grievance that we wish to bring under your notice is that of the three months' pay as gratuity to all ranks who joined previous to October 1879 as compensation for extra duty, and for expenses incurred in doing that extra duty. We ask for two months' gratuity to constables who joined previous to the 1st October, 1880, and for one month's gratuity to constables who joined previous to October 1881.

2946. *Mr. Holmes.*—I presume you make this claim in consequence of the three months' pay that was given to the Royal Irish Constabulary?—Yes. Because we consider that we have done a deal of extra duty as well as they, and we incurred some expenses in doing that extra duty.

2947. Well, now; when you say you incurred expense in doing extra duty, will you explain to the Committee how you incurred those expenses?—After doing our hour of duty, very often we would be told off to hurry over to the Bridewell, Arbour Street, or one of the other railway stations, to escort prisoners coming up, to bring them to the different prisons or to leave them at another railway station, in order that they might be conveyed to the prisons to which they were ultimately to be committed. In doing that, we should take cars over at our own expense, as we were usually left with so little time to meet the train. We had to pay for these cars out of our own pocket.

2348. Do you mean to say you were not repaid your fare afterwards?—No, we were not.

2349. And you were directed by the authorities to take cars?—Oh, no, we were not; but we took cars in order to be in time to meet the trains. In escorting the suspects we were supplied with cars, but not in going to the railway stations. I have very often had to do it myself in order to be in time.

2350. *Chairman.*—In order to be in time there?—In order to be in time to meet them.

2351. *Mr. Holmes.*—If you were ordered by the authorities to go to the railway stations, and were not given sufficient time to be there before the train arrived without driving there, surely in such a case as that, the authorities would have supplied you with the necessary car fare?—We never asked it. They supplied us with cars when escorting the suspects.

2352. *Chairman.*—But not in going to meet them?—Yes; but not in going to meet them.

2353. Did your other duties prevent you being in time?—Yes, Sir. Well, supposing I was on my way home to my dinner, having put in my full tour of duty from 2 to 6 o'clock, an order would come to me to go over to the Broadstone to meet the 6 o'clock train, and the result would be that at the time I should be either home or on my way home to get my dinner. I would have to take a car in order to be in time to meet the train, so as to escort the suspects coming by it.

2354. *Mr. Holmes.*—Are you aware that the members of the Royal Irish Constabulary were out of pocket by having to pay very high prices for their meals and night's lodging when absent on duty from their barracks?—I was under the impression, and so were we all, that they are allowed when absent from barracks at night.

2355. They are; but are you aware that the allowances were not sufficient to meet the extraordinary expenses to which they were put in the recent troubled times, and that many members of the constabulary force were seriously out of pocket by reason of their being obliged to pay more for their night's lodging and for their meals than the allowance enabled them to meet?—I am sure they were, and so were we, because when the authorities draft our men from one station to another, and from country stations and out-stations, and bring them in to Dublin, there is no provision made for giving them refreshments. They were kept on duty during a great portion of the night, and we often had to pay 6d. for a sandwich, and to pay also the messenger for bringing it.

2356. Were you yourself out of pocket by reason of these calls made upon you?—Yes, a good deal out of pocket, but I kept no accurate account of it.

2357. To what extent do you suppose you were out of pocket?—I could not say exactly, because I kept no accurate account of how much I was out of pocket.

2358. Can you state approximately how much you were out of pocket?—Well, I should say that any day I was absent and that I could not get home to my dinner I was out of pocket at least 6d. to get my lunch that day.

2359. But I mean on the whole, how much were you out of pocket within the last three years?—I could not say, on the whole.

2360. Were you a pound out of pocket?—I was more, a good deal more than a 1l. I was pounds out of pocket, but I could not say how many.

2361. *Chairman.*—You kept no account?—No, we were so harassed with extra duty that it distracted us very much. The extra duty was something very severe.

2362. Well, it was within 20l.?—Yes. I remember being on duty on one occasion for twenty-four hours at a stretch. One morning I left Chapelizod Station and came to Bridewell Lane and reported myself at 6 o'clock. I was on duty all that day and night and reported myself at Bridewell Lane at 6 o'clock the next morning when going off duty, and got to Chapelizod at 7 o'clock in the morning.

2363. And you were on duty all that time?—Yes; on duty all that time. I may say I was on my feet all that time with the exception of an hour or so that I was sitting down.

2364. Did that occur more than once?—No; I never was on so long a tour of duty as that, Sir. That was the longest tour I ever did without getting a rest.

2365. And did you take many tours much longer than the ordinary duty?—Oh, yes. The ordinary tour was the least duty that I would do.

2366. Did you take many tours that exceeded your ordinary duty?—Oh, yes, Sir. Since the commencement of the Land League agitation throughout Ireland, especially here in Dublin, we were greatly harassed by extra duty. We had to do our regular tour of duty on the streets, and then we had to keep ourselves in readiness at all times, and then turn out when called on, and we were called on very often.

2367. Have you anything further to say on the head of extra duty?—No, Sir.

2368. Then will you proceed to deal with the next head of your evidence?—Well, we would like an increase of pay adequate to the increased cost of living, say, 1s. a-day. It is very expensive for a man to live now to what it was some years ago, everything is so very dear, and our present scale of pay is not sufficient at all to enable us to live in that respectable style which we are supposed to aspire to. A man must always have a good suit of plain clothes, have at least two or three pairs of boots, and he pays a big price for them besides, from 14s. to 16s. per pair.

2369. Have you made out an estimate of your expenses?—Yes, I have. The cheapest way we can live, we would require three loaves of bread per week——

2370. *Mr. Holmes.*—Do you speak of living in barracks?—Yes.

2371. And are you alluding to single men?—Yes, Sir. Three loaves of bread per week would be 1s., and that would be 2l. 12s. in the year.

2372. We have already had a good deal of statistics of that kind, and really to save time, I think it would be better if you put the cost of living either at so much per week or so much per year, because we have been already furnished with three or four of these lists?—Shall I give the amount according to this scale, Sir?

2373. You can hand in the scale if you like?—Well, I will do so, Sir. It is as follows:—

LIST of the Weekly and Annual Expenditure of a Metropolitan Police Constable living in Barracks.

Items.	Weekly.	Yearly.
[illegible]	[illegible]	[illegible]
Total	—	[illegible]

2374. *Chairman.*—Then the total cost of living of a constable is 73l. 13s. 6d.?—Yes; 73l. 13s. 6d. it costs a constable who is a single man to live in barracks.

2375. And his ordinary clothing is included in that?—Yes; his plain clothes and all necessaries are included.

2376. *Mr. Holmes.*—What is your yearly pay?—73l. 8s.

2377. The amount, according to the statement of Mr. Hinds in his evidence, is 73l. 10s. 6d.?—There is

Metropolitan Constable Thomas Cox.

[illegible] Sept., 1882.

First-class Constable Thomas [illegible]. 24 Sept., 1882.

a sum of 1*l.* 14*s.* 8*d.*, which is an added allowance given for boot money.

2378. How much per week is your salary?—1*l.* 8*s.* a-week; but from the 1*l.* 8*s.* there is a good deal taken for lodging, barrack rent, money for paying mess, and all that sort of thing.

2379. Do you include that in your estimate?—Yes.

2380. According to your own estimate, you, as a first-class constable, would appear to be able to live within your pay and have a trifle over?—Yes; and have a couple of pounds over.

2381. As a matter of fact, what surplus do you have at the end of a year?—None.

2382. Are you aware that second and third-class constables in Dublin are better paid than the corresponding ranks in London?—I am not aware of that.

2383. Well, you may take it from me as a fact that they are. I have the London scale before me, and from it I find that while a second-class constable in Dublin has 71*l.* 13*s.* 11*d.*, a second-class constable in London has 70*l.* 1*s.* 11*d.* A third-class constable in Dublin appears to have 67*l.* 15*s.* 3*d.*, and a third-class constable in London has 64*l.* 11*s.* 6*d.* There is a fourth scale in Dublin to which there is no corresponding scale in London. Well, now having regard to what I have just stated, namely, that two of the ranks of constable in Dublin are better paid than the corresponding ranks in London, do you not see some grave objections to these demands of yours to have your pay increased?—But they are promoted sooner from one rank to another in London than the men are here; but moreover, men won't be in their service for more than three or four years until they are "first rate" there, whereas it will be seven before they are second here.

2384. Upon an average, how long does it take for a man who joins the force here, and who conducts himself well, to get from the lowest grade to the first grade of constable?—Between eight and nine years; about eight years and a-half.

2385. Do not many men attain the first rank within a much shorter period?—Yes, latterly, within the last few years.

2386. How is that?—Because they went to school since the school was opened. There were a number of men that there were facilities given to for attending the school, and who were able to attend school the entire time and of course that left them "well up" for the examinations, and when the examinations came off, they were able to walk over men's heads in those who hadn't any opportunity of going to school, because they took more marks.

2387. Then are you in favour of the school or against it as a system?—Well, I would say it would be of more good to the service to keep the school going, but I think that it should be left optional to the men whether they attended it or not.

2388. *Chairman.*—Is attendance at the school now compulsory?—It is not compulsory, except in the case of young men under six months' service. It is compulsory for them. But without going to the school you have no chance of promotion.

2389. *Mr. Morris.*—Don't you think it is a very useful thing for young men?—Yes, it is, for young men.

2390. Don't you think they might be at a worse place than school, though they are men?—Certainly.

2391. Is it necessary to pass an examination for each grade of constable?—Yes; but there was an order issued a short time since saying that there would be no more examinations for grades.

2392. In what subjects are the men examined?—On the routine of duty; they are examined in the geography of Ireland, in arithmetic, grammar, our duty, the Licensing Laws, and the Traffic Act.

2393. Don't you think that all those things are most useful for a young constable?—They are very necessary for a constable.

2394. You said that those who attended the school had had facilities given them for attending the school, and that others could not attend. Why could not the others attend?—Those whose duties gave them the opportunity of attending school they could attend school every day, whereas men having their regular tour of duty at an inconvenient time could not, nor could those who were stationed at Kingstown, Chapelizod, or [illegible], because they were stationed away from school and could not attend it.

2395. *Mr. Holmes.*—You said just now that you based your claim for an increase of pay on the ground that the cost of living had increased very much within the last few years. Are you quite sure of that?—Yes. I remember myself getting as good a [illegible] some for dinner in the [illegible] [illegible] getting as good a stew for 4*s.* 6*d.* as we have now for 6*s.* 6*d.*

2396. When did you only pay 4*s.* 6*d.* for your mess?—About ten years ago and some weeks only 4*s.*

2397. Was that before the increase that was given in your pay in 1874?—Yes; before the increase we had the meat very cheap, but it has got very dear latterly.

2398. *Mr. Morris.*—Do you think that is owing to the increase in price or to bad management?—It is owing to the increase in price. The prices of provisions, the prices of meat and of vegetables, and of everything else that we use, have increased.

2399. *Mr. Holmes.*—Assuming that the price of meat has gone up within the last ten years, have other articles of consumption gone up in price?—Yes.

2400. Are tea, sugar, butter, and eggs dearer?—Eggs are dearer, but tea and sugar are about the same price. Potatoes are dearer; we pay 10*s.* a cwt. for potatoes.

2401. Would you be surprised to hear that according to the returns that we have before us of the contract prices for certain Government Departments, in nearly every instance the prices of food were higher in 1872 than they were in 1882?—Well, I am not aware of that. We had the meat cheaper then than we have it now.

2402. *Chairman.*—Have you anything further to add on this subject?—No, Sir.

2403. Well, now proceed with the next question that you wish to give evidence upon?—That is in reference to the pension scale. We would like a pension of half-pay at fifteen years, three-fourths after twenty years, and full pay at twenty-five years; discharge to be granted after the last-named period if the man desires to leave the service. We also ask that a fractional part of the pension be granted for each year between fifteen and twenty, but that no fractional part should be given between twenty and twenty-five; that fractional part to be one twenty-fifth or one-thirtieth.

2404. *Mr. Holmes.*—Then it appears that you are not satisfied with the scale of pensions laid down before 1867; you want to have that scale of pensions improved?—We want to have the Pension Act of 1867 repealed, and that you would put us under the Act of 1847.

2405. Yes; but according to what you have just said to the Commission, you are not satisfied with the Act of 1847; you want to improve even that Act?—Yes; we would be satisfied with that if we got the fractional allowance for each year from fifteen to twenty.

2406. But you are asking to be allowed to retire, if I understand your evidence correctly, on full pay after twenty-five years' service. You are aware, I presume, that under the Act of 1847 a man cannot get full pay until after thirty years' service, and then only on a medical certificate of unfitness for duty. You are aware of that?—Yes.

2407. Then it does come to this, that you are not satisfied with even that scale of pensions, and you would like to have a better one?—We would like to have that changed so that we could retire on full pay at twenty-five years' service without the doctor's certificate.

2408. *Mr. Morris.*—Why don't you answer Mr. Holmes' question. Mr. Holmes says that you are not satisfied even with the Pension Act of 1847 unless it is improved for you, and then you give an answer that is not at all a direct one to the question put to you?—I am not satisfied with the Act of 1847, and the members of the force in general are not satisfied with it.

2409. *Mr. Holmes.*—And do you [illegible], as a [illegible]

Pensioner Constable Thomas Cox.

[illegible] Sept., [illegible]

men, seriously ask to have the extremely favourable scale of pensions, under the Act of 1847 improved?—Yes.

2410. And do you think that Parliament will listen to such a proposal for one moment?—Well, if favourably put before Parliament I believe it would.

2411. *Mr. Morris.*—And in saying what you do say, you are speaking the views of the constables as a body?—Yes.

2412. *Mr. Holmes.*—Are you aware that the most that the members of the metropolitan police force in London can get is two-thirds of their pay as pension?—I do not know the scale of pension that the London metropolitan police are entitled to.

2413. Are you aware that no class in the Civil Service can get more than two-thirds of pay as pension on retirement, and that a civil servant must serve forty years and be over sixty years of age before he is entitled to that two-thirds. Are you aware that that scale of pension, with its conditions, applies to every civil servant of Her Majesty's?—I was not aware of that.

2414. Now that you are aware of it, and also of the fact that the most a London policeman can get is two-thirds, are you still prepared to put forward such a demand?—Yes; the London police are not satisfied either, it appears.

2415. As I take it, you want an increment for each year between fifteen and twenty years' service, and between twenty and twenty-five years' service, to be added to the pension scale?—Yes.

2416. And the right to retire at twenty-five years' service?—Yes.

2417. Upon full pay?—Yes.

2418. Now I ask you as a reasonable man, do you think that it would be possible for Parliament to put the Dublin men, or the police forces of Ireland generally, under a better scale of pensions than the police forces of England and Scotland?—Yes, it would be possible for Parliament to do it.

2419. It would be possible to do anything; do you think it is likely?—It is not likely they will.

2420. Do you think it would be just?—It would be just. We have harder duties to do. We have a very hostile population to deal with. In London, or in any other city of England or Scotland, the populace are always willing to assist the police, but here in Dublin they will put against us, for even those persons who are inclined to assist the police are afraid, on account of the rougher elements, to interfere on our behalf.

2421. And these are some of the grounds on which you seek for better terms than the English and Scotch police?—Yes.

2422. *Chairman.*—What is the next head of your evidence?—We would like when a man is reduced from a higher to a lower grade of constable, that he would not be kept on the reduced scale, but that he would get his place at the end of three years in case he has a clean sheet, and has no reports against him for that period.

2423. You would not like to have the reduction permanent, but that the man should be reinstated at the end of three years if he was in the meantime well conducted?—Yes.

2424. *Mr. Holmes.*—For what breaches of discipline or other offences are men now degraded?—For drunkenness principally.

2425. *Mr. Morris.*—And don't you think that it is a very great and serious offence for a man, in the position of a sergeant or acting sergeant particularly, to get drunk?—I am sure it is a very serious offence to get drunk while on duty.

2426. And do not the members of the force generally consider it a very serious offence?—They consider, of course, that a man on duty has no right to get drunk.

2427. Does it ever happen that a man is degraded for the first offence of drunkenness?—Yes, for the first offence.

2428. Do you know that of your own knowledge?—Yes; of my own knowledge I know that.

2429. *Mr. Holmes.*—And had that man no other unfavourable records against him; was he a man of previous good character?—Yes, he was, for some years before that.

2430. And you state as a fact that this man was, to your own knowledge, degraded for a first offence of drunkenness?—Yes.

2431. *Mr. Morris.*—For being drunk on duty?—For being drunk on duty.

2432. Are there many cases in the year of men being drunk on duty?—No, not many cases; very few cases of being drunk on duty; but while off duty it is the very same offence, to being reported for being unfit for duty from the effects of liquor. Men are also punished for that.

2433. Don't you consider that even if a man is away for forty-eight hours on leave, and in plain clothes, when his hour for going on duty turns up, it is quite as bad to turn up in liquor to go on duty?—We admit it is bad; he has a right to be sober for duty.

2434. Do you think it would be possible to carry on the police force as a system in Dublin, or in any other city, unless the offence of drunkenness was considered a serious one, and was dealt with severely?—It would not be possible; discipline must be carried out, but in some cases it is carried out in a very stringent manner.

2435. And particularly on the question of being drunk?—Yes; the whole force are against drunkenness, and, as a rule, there is very little drunkenness in the service now; but if a man is on leave, we think it hard that he should be punished for taking refreshments in a public-house. I know two cases myself of men on leave and in plain clothes who were reported for being in respectable public-houses, and were severely fined for it.

2436. *Mr. Holmes.*—What was the amount of the fine?—In one case I know that the fine was 10s., and in another case 7s. 6d. They were young constables. I know of the case of two officers, one in plain clothes, off duty, and the other in uniform, off duty. They went into a respectable public-house, and were seen coming out. One was fined 7*l.*, and the other 5*l.*

2437. And you are personally aware of these cases?—Yes; I am aware of every case I am speaking of.

2438. What was the rank of the officers?—One was an acting inspector, and the other a full sergeant.

2439. *Chairman.*—What is the next question that you wish to bring before us?

Constable Lawrence Fogarty.—Might I be permitted to make a statement at this stage?

2440. *Chairman.*—Certainly.

Constable Fogarty.—I wish to remark that in reference to [illegible] I know of one case in which a man was reduced to the bottom of fourth rate, and fined.

2441. From what grade?—He was on fourth rate, but forward in fourth rate, and he was reduced back to the bottom of fourth rate and fined 20s. for smoking at 3 o'clock in the morning, and he on duty at the Kevin Street police barrack gate.

2442. He was on duty there?—Yes. I know of another case; the gaoler in Newmarket Police-station was fined 10s. for smoking in the reserve room.

2443. At night?—It was in the day time, Sir, about 12 o'clock in the day.

2444. *Mr. Morris.*—But still, although the fine may be excessive, you know if there is a rule it should be enforced?—Of course, the act was against discipline; but, at the same time, a caution in such a case, or a very nominal fine, would meet the case. I know of another case, one of knocker wrenching—a thing which has been very common in the city—in reference to which several men were fined for the one knocker, which was only valued at 1s. The men were fined as each man in his turn [illegible] to work the beat. For instance, the man who went off at 6 o'clock in the morning—I was the sufferer in that case, and indeed I got off with half-a-crown fine for not reporting it, because I only passed the place once. The next man on the beat—the man who relieved me—also missed noticing it, and he was fined 5s. The man who relieved him, from 9 to 3 o'clock in the middle of the day, was fined 10s., and

[illegible] Constable Thomas Cox. — [illegible] Sept., 1882.

the next man that followed him, from 2 o'clock in the afternoon until 9 o'clock at night, was also fined 10s. for the same breaches, so that the fines in that case amounted to 1l. 7s. 6d. for the one breaches.

9445. But don't you see if the constable on duty, whose business it is to protect the interests of the citizens, neglects his duty, he becomes useless, and would not be wanted at all. Don't you perceive that although that breach was only worth 1s., those men, one after another, according to the statement you have made, neglected their duty in not reporting it?—Yes; I agree to that, but I mean to say that the fines were very exorbitant in the matter.

9446. The fines were heavy, but I suppose you do not go the length of saying that they should not be fined?—I do not.

9447. But your evidence points to the fines as being excessive?—Yes.

9448. But you are not against the system of fining altogether?—Certainly not. We must uphold discipline, because we could not do without it.

9449. *Chairman.*—You approve of the system of fining, but you object to the excessive character of the fines?—Yes; nominal fines have as much effect, and even continuing frequently.

Examination of Constable Cox resumed.

9450. *Chairman.*—Would you be good enough to proceed with your evidence in relation to the next matter you wish to bring before the Committee?—When a report is investigated we would like to get a fair opportunity of defending ourselves, which we do not now get. A gentleman will write a letter of complaint to the effect that he saw a constable was absent from such and such a fixed point. He might say that "I saw that the constable was absent from the fixed point at the corner of Suffolk Street, and Nassau Street, and Grafton Street." A gentleman wrote once saying that he was near being run over by a tramway car, and there was no constable by. Well, the constable happened to be in the station, to which place he had occasion to go. It is the rule to report yourself to the officer on duty when you have occasion to go into the station, and you also report yourself going out, but notwithstanding the officer's reporting himself to the officer at the station, he was brought up on the strength of the gentleman's letter, and was fined 10s., although the gentleman did not appear himself at all.

9451. Do you know that of your own knowledge?—Yes; I know that of my own knowledge.

9452. Was the fact of his having reported himself to the officer in the station relied on by him?—Yes; but he was told that he had a right to be at his post.

9453. *Mr. Morris.*—And before that case was adjudicated upon was the book at the station looked at?—There is no entry made in the book at the station. If you are going in all you have to do is to report yourself; there is no entry made of it.

9454. And had they the officer or sergeant present to say that he did report himself?—Yes; and he did say it.

9455. And was the party who made the report there?—He was not there. He was not asked any questions. The constable was told he had a right to be there, and he was fined 10s.

9456. And did he refer to the report?—Yes, he did. Then there was a pane of glass broken in William Street in a house that was off the street—a small pane of glass. I saw eleven men, among them four acting sergeants, reported for not seeing that and reporting on it. They were not allowed to make any defence. The Commissioner who dealt with the case said—"If I were to ask each of you for an explanation you would all be willing to give faulty explanations, so I will take good care I will listen to no explanation, but deal with the case according to my own judgment."

9457. *Mr. Holmes.*—Were you present at the inquiry?—Yes, I was one of the parties fined. The acting sergeants were fined 1l. each, and the constables were fined 10s. each. Well, a smaller fine would have effected the neglect in that case; at least, we imagine that it would cover the neglect. I have seen a man who was at Westland Row on duty at half-past 8 o'clock in the morning reported for having one glove off. It was put down, "Walking the beat in a slovenly manner with one glove off at half-past 8 o'clock in the morning." That man was fined 1l. He was on the approved list for promotion at the time, and was in consequence of that punishment kept back for six months.

9458. You are quite certain of the facts of this case?—I am quite certain of them.

9459. You know them of your own knowledge?—I know them, because I am the man myself.

9460. Who reported you?—The acting sergeant on duty.

9461. *Chairman.*—In the case of the eleven men reported for not observing the broken pane of glass in William Street, were they allowed to make no defence?—They were allowed to make no defence. He said, "If I were to ask them for an explanation they would be giving me faulty explanations, and I will take good care I will listen to no explanation," and commencing first with the acting sergeants he fined them 1l. each in turn, and when he came to the constables he fined them 10s. each.

9462. *Mr. Holmes.*—You said just now that in addition to being fined 1l. you were kept back from promotion for six months?—Yes.

9463. To what rank was that?—To the rank of acting sergeant. That was in 1878.

9464. When were you reduced from acting sergeant?—In 1878 I got promotion, and last April 1881 I was reduced.

9465. Why were you reduced?—For going into the station ten minutes before my time was up on duty to warm my hands at the fire, the night being extremely cold.

9466. From the time you were made acting sergeant up to the time you had been reduced, were there any other complaints against you?—Yes, sir, there were.

9467. How many?—There were two.

9468. Previous to this?—Yes. There was one of them which arose in this way: I had to live in an outstation, and I locked the door at half-past 10 o'clock at night, and took the key and put it into my pocket; and some time between that and the morning I lost the key, and I could not tell where I lost it. However, I was fined 20s. for that.

9469. What was the other complaint?—The other complaint was for not reporting a stray sheep. The sheep lay down on the roadside, and I waited for some time to look for the owner of it. Meanwhile, another flock of sheep came up, and the sheep to which I refer got up and went away with them, and I thought it was all right, as I believed both flocks of sheep belonged to the same owner. I was fined 1l. for that. Those were the only two complaints.

9470. Will it be necessary for you to pass an examination before you get promotion to the rank of acting sergeant?—I will never get the opportunity again, except the three years' system is adopted.

9471. Do you mean to say that you have no hope of promotion?—Except through being well recommended by my superintendent. I might then get an opportunity. I might be put upon the advanced class then, and by going to school for two or three years I would be allowed to compete then, but it would be a great favour conferred upon me.

9472. And you would be obliged to pass another examination before you could become an acting sergeant again?—Yes.

9473. Although you have passed one before?—Yes.

At this stage of Constable Cox's examination,

Constable PATRICK HURLEY, 26 C, Second-class Constable, Dublin Metropolitan Police, was, at his own request, examined.

9474. *Chairman*.—The Committee understand that you are anxious to give evidence in relation to the question of discipline?—I wish to bring before the Committee my own case in order to illustrate the working of the system of discipline in the Dublin metropolitan police force. I was on duty this time twelve months in the Northern Divisional police-court as office constable, and one day, while the morning charges were going on before the late Dr. M'Blaine, two women came to the door of the Court, one of whom had a child in her arms, and she said that she appeared in a summons case. There was no summons going on at the time, and any summonses didn't come on for two hours and a-half afterwards. The women went away, and evidently proceeded round to the other door that leads into the Court, because they came into the Court through it. The woman who had been speaking to me came over to me and said, "26 C, I will report you;" and she commenced to speak so loudly that I was bound to remove her, while the charge that was being heard was going on, as she was interrupting the business of the Court. I put herself and the child out. About three weeks afterwards she made a letter report to the Commissioners, and the Commissioners brought me up before them. I brought the acting inspector on duty at the Court—Acting Inspector Crofton—to prove that I had done no harm, as well as a statement from Dr. M'Blaine—who said that the whole thing occurred under his eye—in which he said that he saw nothing in what I did beyond what I was supposed to do to enable me to keep order and regularity in the Court. Colonel Connolly there and then said, "I see my way through this. You, Acting Inspector Crofton, are too long there, and I will direct that you shall be removed; and as for you, 26 C, I will reduce you." He asked me for no statement whatever. Well, that day week I was brought up before Captain Talbot, and Captain Talbot reduced me there and then from first to second class constable; and nobody appeared to prosecute me at all. There was only the false statement of the letter of the woman, and the statements of that letter were not substantiated, either by her or anybody else.

9475. *Mr. Holmes*.—In what position of life was the woman?—She had a child with her, but I knew nothing about her or her business. She did not even before the Commissioner to substantiate the statements of her letter, and yet I was reduced from first to second rate, which reduction has brought with it a loss of 1*s*. 6*d*. per week, amounting to 3*l*. 18*s*. for the year; and it will be, on the 30th of this month, twelve months since I was reduced. I have been reduced, and I don't know when I may be called up again.

Second-class Constable P. Hurley. 26 Sept., 1882.

9476. Were you not called upon for an explanation?—I was not asked what I had to say for myself, and yet I was reduced.

9477. And no party appeared against you?—Quite so.

9478. *Mr. Morris*.—Were there any other black marks against you?—Well, there were some fines.

9479. For what offences?—There were one or two other offences against me. I think I was fined for being one morning for two or three minutes in a shed down at the North Wall when the inspector came up. I was fined another time for gossiping, and I was fined another time for having a glove off.

9480. About what fines were inflicted upon you on each of these occasions?—There was 2*d*. at one time.

9481. Were you fined for drunkenness at all?—No, Sir, never.

9482. What was the 2*d*. for?—That was for selling plain porter in the barracks instead of "X X."

9483. At the canteen?—Yes, Sir; in Kilmainham barracks.

9484. What were the amounts of the fines on the other occasions to which you refer?—I was fined 10*s*. for being in the shed. There was another case, but I forget what the amount is, as I didn't make a memorandum of it. There was another occasion when I was fined 7*s*. 6*d*. for a collision that occurred at the North Wall. I gave the names of both parties, but something subsequently occurred about it, and it appeared that there was one wrong address. I was reported for not making it an occurrence in the station-house, and I was fined 7*s*. 6*d*.

9485. Have you anything further to add about discipline?—No, Sir.

9486. *Chairman*.—You were told you were reduced because of the substance of the letter?—Yes.

9487. You were told you were reported for having put a woman out of Court?—Yes.

9488. And on the substance of the letter she wrote you were reduced?—Yes.

9489. And she didn't appear, nor did any other person, against you?—No, Sir; nor any other person.

9490. Do you wish to give evidence on any other point?—No, Sir; I am quite content to leave the rest to my comrades, who are now before you.

Examination of Constable Cox resumed.

9491. *Chairman*.—Will you now proceed with your evidence?—We would like full pay when we are sick. When any member of the force gets sick through no fault of his own we think he is entitled to full pay, because it is then that he wants his pay.

9492. *Mr. Holmes*.—The acting sergeants, sergeants, acting inspectors, and inspectors have gone very fully into that matter, and I suppose you agree with the views they have put forward?—Yes, certainly. I may mention that a man was severely injured, and was put on half-pay. I believe that man—Constable Stephen Gleeson—is injured for life, and he was put on half-pay.

9493. For how long?—I am not able to say. It is over twelve months since he was assaulted, and he is in hospital ever since, and he has only got half-pay now.

9494. And the men, I suppose, consider that a grievance?—Yes.

9495. *Chairman*.—Have you anything else to add with reference to that?—No, Sir, nothing. I may now say that the men would expect to be paid at the rate of 15*s*. per month when they are wearing plain clothes on duty. I refer to men who are employed on special duty.

First-class Constable Thomas Cox. 26 Sept., 1882.

9496. *Mr. Holmes*.—That would be 9*l*. a-year?—Yes, Sir. The longest term, except in the case of the sergeants, is three months. He will wear out a suit of clothes in three months, and he will get no suit under 4*l*. or 4*l*. 10*s*. I consider that 15*s*. a-month is not too much for plain clothes.

9497. Are policemen, other than those of the detective division, required to appear often in plain clothes?—Yes.

9498. How often, on an average, is a policeman required to appear in plain clothes?—Some men are very often in plain clothes. In the principal stations of each

First class Constable Thomas Cox.

26 Sept., 1882.

division there are two or three men on duty in plain clothes at all times of the night as well as day.

2499. *Chairman.*—In plain clothes?—Yes.

2500. But that is their own wish?—No; they are told to dress in plain clothes to do a certain duty.

2501. *Mr. Holmes.*—Is it not the fact that the great body of the men, other than the Detective Division, are not required to wear plain clothes?—Quite so, Sir. Only two or three in each division are required to do so. They are told off for a month at a time. There are three or four in some stations and some in others.

2502. And you only put forward that demand on behalf of those men, but not on behalf of the force generally?—Quite so.

2503. Only on behalf of those required to be on duty in plain clothes?—Yes.

2504. *Mr. Morris.*—Whenever a man is in plain clothes on duty that he should get 10s. a-month for the wear and tear of those clothes?—Yes.

2505. *Mr. Holmes.*—But don't you estimate the wear and tear at a very high figure?—No matter how good a man's suit of clothes may be, after he has knocked a month or two out of it, pulling and dragging prisoners about, it is no use. According to the rules of the service, you must have a respectable suit of plain clothes to be shown every Saturday with your other things.

2506. You must have one suit of plain clothes?—Yes.

2507. *Chairman.*—What is the next matter?—When men are transferred for the good of the service, and not for any misconduct, a reasonable allowance should be given to them to pay their expenses from one station to another. There is no allowance at all given at present. Supposing a man is sent from this to Rathborough he has to defray his own expenses, and to take a car or a cab, as the case may be. I think in the case of married constables they would be entitled to compensation for transfer, as they are put to great expense when they have to change their lodgings.

2508. What is the next matter you wish to deal with?—We would like all reports, no matter how black the sheet, after a period of three years to be cancelled, and that a man might be allowed to have a clean sheet. We would like to have fourteen days' leave in each year for each constable.

2509. *Mr. Holmes.*—What is the extent of the present leave?—Ten days. We would also like to have two days' leave in each month. We would also ask that a married constable if he has a house, should be permitted to let a portion of that house to respectable persons, so as that he would not have to pay a big rent for that house, or he could avoid living in a locality inhabited by bad character persons by that means.

2510. You think that that would not interfere with the discipline of the force, the independent action of the men, or the good order of the force?—I believe not.

2511. Is that the general opinion of the force?—Yes.

2512. That it would not in any way militate against the good order and regularity of the force?—Yes. By letting a portion of that house to some respectable persons it would serve him and help him to live rent free. According to the regulations of the force, at present married men must live in respectable lodgings. For instance, a married man won't be allowed to live in a low street or a backward street or place.

2513. Some of the men have gone the length of saying that they would not be safe in living in those streets?—The regulations of the service won't allow them, in the first place. I know several instances of that where men were compelled to leave under threat of a report to the Commissioners for not having suitable lodgings.

Constable Fogarty.—I myself had a cottage in a quiet neighbourhood; I had only two apartments, but I had it for 3s. a-week. I had to leave that.

2514. Why?—Because they considered that the two apartments were not sufficient for my family. I have a large family—a wife and nine children. I had to give that and take another cottage, and I had to pay 6s. a-week rent for that; that was an increased cost to me of 3s., but I was compelled to do that.

2515. Have you anything else to add?—I have nothing more to add, I think.

Examination of Constable Cox resumed.

2516. *Chairman.*—Would you kindly continue your evidence?—Yes, Sir. We would ask that when members of the force become incapacitated from ill-health that they would be allowed the following scale of gratuities—that is, two months' pay as gratuity for every year after three and up to ten years' service, and three months' pay for every year from eleven to fifteen years.

2517. That is the same scale as the acting sergeants put in, so to speak?—I don't know.

2518. Are there any reading-rooms in any of the stations or libraries in the barracks?—No, not in any of the stations, with the exception of this one and the Castle; there is one kept here.

2519. Are you in favour of having reading-rooms?—Oh, yes; but the men have very little time to spend in libraries or reading-rooms.

2520. *Mr. Holmes.*—Do you think that the men would consider it a boon if each of the barracks was supplied with a reading-room?—I think they would; but the way they have to do duty at present they have very little time. They go on duty at 6 o'clock in the morning, and go off at 2 o'clock, and by the time they get their breakfast and polish and clean up all their traps they have very little time to go to a reading-room, when they have to turn out for duty at 2 o'clock, and remain on duty until 6 o'clock. Next day they go out at 2 o'clock and go off at 6, and then they go out again at 2 o'clock; but if it was possible that they could be allowed two hours off every second evening, then they would have time to attend a library.

2521. *Chairman.*—You say you do not find fault with the system of fining or of reduction in proper cases; in other words, that you object to the administration of the law, but not to the law itself. Would you like to have any alteration in the tribunal?—We would like to have some alteration, so that the fines would not be so very severe. We should like that the several superintendents would have a voice in the matter.

2522. Do you mean that they should attend as referees?—Yes; and that if the accused denied the charge made against him, the witnesses should be sworn.

2523. You say the superintendents should attend when charges are investigated against the men, and that they should attend as referees of character, and that the old system which was in operation years ago should be revived?—Yes; and if the accused denies the charge, the investigation should be a sworn one.

2524. In serious cases?—Yes; a sworn investigation in serious cases.

2525. Is that all you have to say on that point?—Yes.

2526. Have you any other matter to bring before us?—Yes, Sir. With regard to going into public-houses when off duty and in plain clothes, we think a constable should be allowed to enjoy the same privilege that every other citizen can enjoy, of going into a respectable public-house for the purpose of taking refreshments. It would not lead to making a man a drunkard.

2527. The men would be in favour of obtaining liberty to enter public-houses when in plain clothes off duty?—I think they would.

2528. You do not think that that would lead to drunkenness in the force?—I think it would not.

2529. And that it would not lead to men coming on duty in a state unfit to do their duty?—No; I don't think it would.

2530. But you would not seek the permission when the men are in uniform?—The men are against going, whether on or off duty, into public-houses in uniform.

2531. *Mr. Morris.*—I presume that you are speaking, more or less, as the mouth of a substantial majority of the constables of the Dublin police—am I to understand that?—Yes, Sir.

2532. Presuming that, and making as short a

summary as I possibly can of the things that you and the force take the greatest interest in, it may be this, first you complain of not having got the gratuity the same as the Royal Irish Constabulary for your extra work during the last three unsettled years we have passed through in this country. Is not that so?—That is the first grievance.

2533. Then you wish to have an increase of pay; is that so?—Yes.

2534. Then you wish that the Pension Act of 1867 should be repealed?—Yes.

2535. And that you should be placed under a more favourable Pension Act than the former Act, that of 1847?—Yes.

2536. And you also complain that the fines and discipline in the force are too severe?—Yes.

2537. And that the punishments incidental to the carrying out of discipline, either in the way of reduction in grade or by fines, are too severely administered?—Yes.

2538. And, summing up all your grievances, they are comprised within the compass I have stated?—Yes.

2539. Under these four heads?—Yes.

Pensioned Constable Thomas Cox.

[illegible] Sept., [illegible]

Constable FOGARTY, examined.

2540. *Chairman.*—What matter do you wish to bring before us?—We are anxious that the compensation in the case of men dying suddenly in the service should not be lost. If a young man died suddenly in the service, and his people have no opportunity of obtaining his signature, we would ask that the compensation to which he would have been entitled should be paid to his relatives. Almost every man has some poor person belonging to him, who should, as his next-of-kin, be entitled to his compensation if he was entitled to compensation?

2541. Have you anything further to add?—I do not think I have anything further to add.

(Constables Gilmary, M'Cormick, Butler, Stephens, and Fogarty having been asked by the Chairman whether they concurred in the evidence given and the statements that they had heard made by Constable Cox, replied that they fully and thoroughly concurred in all that Constable Cox had stated.)

Constable Fogarty.

[illegible] Sept., [illegible]

Constable COX, re-examined.

2542. *Mr. Holmes.*—Before we part, may I ask you, do the men feel more on the subject of pay or that of pension?—They feel that without having the pension scale made something better than it is, they have no provision made for them in their old days. They feel that their present pay is little enough for them at twenty-five or thirty years' service.

2543. But the question of pension is the one they feel most strongly upon?—Yes.

2544. *Mr. Morris.*—At present, you can retire after thirty years' service on a medical certificate?—Yes; under the old Act.

2545. Don't you think that, no matter what the future scale of pension may be, it would be a fair compromise and arrangement in reference to retirement if the policeman was given the power to retire if he pleased, whether the authorities wished it or not, at twenty-five years' service?—Yes.

2546. What would you say to twenty-eight or thirty years?—Very few are able to come to that.

2547. Do you think that a man is so worn out after twenty-five years' service, that there is no more work left in him?—He is of no use.

2548. Is that a fact?—Yes.

2549. *Mr. Holmes.*—You all adhere to that?—Yes; we all adhere to that. I believe that the greatest question is that of the pension. I believe in reference to the resignation from the force within the last twelve months, that pension was the sole cause of those men—some of whom had splendid characters—going away.

2550. May I take it then, if the pension scale were improved, the men would be fairly satisfied with the present rates of pay, bearing in mind the fact that several ranks in Dublin are better paid than the corresponding ranks in London?—I believe that, if the pension scale were changed, so as that they could retire on full pay at twenty-five or thirty years' service, they would be satisfied with a small increase of wages.

2551. *Mr. Morris.*—Do you think that public opinion—sound public opinion, not theoretical public opinion—in the times in which we live at present, would sanction the granting of full pay allowance or pension after any number of years' service?—Oh, yes, I believe it would. Times would not change through the times. The public are the same now as they were twenty years ago.

2552. *Mr. Holmes.*—But are you aware that no class of the Civil Service receives full pay as pension?—Yes, Sir, you told me so.

2553. You were not aware of it before?—No.

2554. Well, to repeat my former question, now that you are aware of it, don't you see that there are great difficulties in the way of giving you what other civil servants do not get?—There are great difficulties, no doubt; but we have very hard and dangerous duties to do.

2555. That might be an argument for giving you a larger proportion of pension than any other civil servant of the Crown gets, no matter in what position or station, but still you would not go the length of arguing that it should be full pay?—It ought go so far, for when a man is old he requires full pay. It really is when he is 50 or 60 years of age that he would want something to keep him up in his old age.

2556. That is an observation applying to all classes and ranks of men?—Yes. The gentlemen of the Civil Service are not so hard-worked, and they can work as well at 60 years of age as they can at 30. In fact, they know their business better at the end of 60 years than at the commencement of their official life, and they generally have a better salary then, because their income rises with service.

2557. *Mr. Morris.*—But there is such a thing as promotion in your service too?—Oh, there is, but it is very slow.

First-class Constable Thomas Cox.

[illegible] Sept., [illegible]

Constable HENRY STEPHENS, examined.

2558. *Chairman.*—I understand you wish to add something to the evidence?—I wish, before leaving, to make one observation. I represent a body of men in the third grade of constables, and I wish to say, on their behalf and on my own, that we think that constables ought to get the third rate after six months' service;

First-class Constable H. Stephens.

[illegible] Sept., [illegible]

First-class Constable R. Stephens. 15 Sept., 1882.

that they ought to get the second rate after being four years and a-half on the previous grade; and first rate after a period of seven years' service.

2559. If there are no black marks against them in the meantime?—Yes, Sir; and without having to compete for it.

2560. Is there anything else you wish to add?—The majority of the men, in fact, the whole of them, say that they would like to have separate hospital accommodation. I do not think we have anything more to add to our evidence.

Constable Laurence Sheehan, Dublin Metropolitan Mounted Police, examined.

Constable L. Sheehan. 15 Sept., 1882.

2561. *Chairman.*—What is your name?—Laurence Sheehan.

2562. You belong to the mounted branch of the Dublin metropolitan police?—Yes.

2563. What grade do you fill?—That of first-class constable.

2564. What is the strength of the force of mounted men?—Twenty-eight, including the inspector. There are one sergeant, two acting sergeants, and then the inspector, and twenty-four men of the rank of constable.

2565. *Mr. Holmes.*—Do they belong to one grade of constables?—No, Sir; to different grades.

2566. *Chairman.*—Do they all belong to one division?—Yes; all to one division.

2567. The "A" Division?—Yes, Sir.

2568. How long have you been in the force?—Nine years and six months.

2569. *Mr. Holmes.*—What duties are performed by the mounted men as distinguished from the duties performed by the police force at large?—We have very often to perform duty twice and three times a-day. We have to attend banquets, balls, and such things as that, and get no extra pay for it, and then to attend to our horses and stable duties afterwards.

2570. *Mr. Harris.*—What are the special duties of the mounted men?—Patrolling of all sorts and escorting the Lord Mayor. In ordinary times we have to patrol from 6 o'clock until 11 o'clock at night; those are the ordinary duties.

2571. *Mr. Holmes.*—That is all you have got to do in ordinary times?—Yes, Sir.

2572. As mounted policemen?—Yes, Sir.

2573. How is your time occupied afterwards?—Well, if there are escorts wanted we have to attend to them.

2574. I am now speaking of ordinary quiet times?—We have to work in the stables during the day.

2575. *Chairman.*—You are not working all day in the stables?—Not all day.

2576. *Mr. Holmes.*—How long are you supposed to be on duty?—We go to the stables at 7 o'clock in the morning and work until 9 o'clock, and then we groom from 4 until 7 o'clock.

2577. In the evening?—Yes, Sir; and then we get an hour for our supper, and then we go out at 6 o'clock and remain on duty until 11 o'clock.

2578. What are you doing between 9 and 4 o'clock?—Nothing, Sir.

2579. Then it seems to me that you have very easy times of it?—Upon that duty we would, Sir.

2580. That was before the late troubles in this last year or two?—Yes, Sir.

2581. Have you been selected to represent the mounted men?—Yes.

2582. Are the mounted constables paid at the same rate as the force generally?—Just the same. They have 6d. per week more.

2583. For what?—Spurs and gloves.

2584. *Chairman.*—What grievances, if any, have you to bring before the Committee?—The fact of our doing extra duty and getting no extra pay for it.

2585. For the last three years?—It commenced with the State trials. We have often to go on mounted duty three and four times a-day, Sir. Our men expect to get 6d. a-day more than the infantry men for wear and tear of under clothing which is consumed while working in the stables. They have to attend banquets, balls, and the opera when it is here, and they get nothing for it, after being out on their own duty.

2586. *Mr. Harris.*—Has not that always been the duty of the men of your force for the last twenty-five years?—No, Sir.

2587. *Chairman.*—But probably if these extra duties were not thrown upon you sometimes, your ordinary duties would be extremely light, because you have told us that you are only expected to be on duty from 6 until 11 at night, and that you have the day to yourself from 9 to 4?—Yes.

2588. Don't you think it is only fair to impose upon you at odd times a little extra work without paying you anything extra for it?—But we have done a lot of extra duty since the State trials.

2589. *Mr. Harris.*—The point I wish to bring again before you is this: you stated that you are obliged to be on duty at the opera, and at balls and parties and banquets; is it not the case that a certain number of mounted men always attended on those occasions?—Yes, Sir, they used to attend, but we never received any extra pay for it.

2590. *Mr. Holmes.*—Is it not part of your ordinary duty to attend on all those occasions?—Well, it is, Sir.

2591. Then why do you expect to get extra pay for doing your ordinary duty?—We have performed such a lot of extra duty for the last three years that we expect to get something for it.

2592. What other matters do you wish to bring before us?—That is all, Sir. Of course, we go on the same footing as the other men as regards pension and extra pay.

2593. And do you understand the nature of the demands which the men have put forward?—Yes, Sir, I have heard what they are.

2594. Do you concur with them?—Yes, Sir.

2595. *Chairman.*—And do you look forward to being paid the three months' gratuity the same as the Royal Irish Constabulary?—Yes, Sir.

2596. By reason of the extra work thrown upon you for the last three years?—Yes, Sir.

2597. *Mr. Holmes.*—I think you said your rank was that of a first-class constable?—Yes, Sir.

2598. Are you aware that the pay of second and third class constables here is higher than that of second and third class constables in London?—No, Sir, I was not aware of that.

2599. Now that you are aware of it—for you may take it as a fact from me that it is so—are you still prepared to ask that the constables in Dublin should be better paid than the constables in London?—I don't know the duties of the constables in London.

2600. Assuming that they are required to be on duty for as long a time as you are during the day, and that their duties are as continuous, do you still think that you should be paid at a higher rate than the London men?—I should think so, Sir.

2601. But why—why should Dublin policemen be paid higher than London men, remembering that London is the capital of Great Britain and of the commercial world?—I should think we should get more.

2602. But why?—Well, I don't see why we shouldn't. I imagine the police there have not the same duties to perform that we have.

2603. They are not so unpopular?—No, Sir. All that we ask is for extra pay for extra duty, and 6d. a-day for the wear and tear of our under-clothing.

2604. *Mr. Harris.*—And the improvement of pension on retirement?—Yes. We are in the same position as that which the infantry have taken as regards that.

Twelfth Day.—26th September, 1882.

Present:

Mr. J. W. O'Donnell, Mr. George Morris, D.L., and Mr. R. W. A. Holmes.

Owen McNally, First-class Constable, Dublin Metropolitan Police, *examined*.

(Also present: *John Roland, First-class Constable, Dublin Metropolitan Police, 70 B; John Lawless, First-class Constable, Dublin Metropolitan Police, 71 B; Andrew Murphy, First-class Constable, Dublin Metropolitan Police, 160 F; Michael Nunn, First-class Constable, Dublin Metropolitan Police, 89 F; and Hugh Morgan, Third-class Constable, Dublin Metropolitan Police, 115 D.*)

Acting Sergeant Richard Chase, Dublin Metropolitan Mounted Police, was also present during the taking of the foregoing evidence.

9608. *Chairman.*—What is your name?—Owen McNally.

9609. What are you?—A first-class constable.

9610. How long have you been in the service?—I am in the (twentieth) year of my service.

9611. Were you ever reduced?—Yes, I was reduced from the rank of acting sergeant.

9612. Where are you stationed?—In Great Street police-station.

9613. Do you appear on behalf of the men of the several divisions who are now present?—Yes.

9614. Do you know what the constables who were examined yesterday brought under the notice of the Committee?—No, Sir; I know what they intended to bring before the Committee, but I do not know the nature of the evidence they actually gave.

9615. Well, would you now be good enough to state what you desire to bring forward for our consideration, and we would ask you to deal with the several heads of your evidence in what you regard as the order of their importance?—The first thing I would respectfully bring under your notice would be the gratuity of three months' pay for extra duty performed.

9616. You mean the same as the constabulary received?—Yes.

9617. You complain on behalf of the constables of the force of not having received a gratuity something like that given to the Royal Irish Constabulary?—Yes, and which, in my opinion, was the great cause of the late unhappy discontent in the force; a great deal of the discontent was attributable to that. I did not attend the meetings that were held, from fortunately having to attend the Commission in Green Street, but I endeavoured to dissuade all the men I saw from attending it.

9618. *Mr. Morris.*—I suppose you have just the same grounds of complaint as regards the non-receipt of that gratuity as the other men who represented the constables yesterday?—Yes; the very same.

9619. You have nothing additional to add?—No; just the extra duty performed.

9620. *Mr. Holmes.*—Then of all the questions you are going to bring before us you consider that the most important?—Yes. I think the gratuity the most important.

9621. The men feel the most keenly upon the question of gratuity?—Yes.

9622. Do those whom you represent seek a similar amount?—Yes, a similar amount, three months' pay as gratuity.

9623. The constables who were before us yesterday suggested that there should be a distinction made between the men who joined the force before October 1879 in this way: that they should get three months; the men who joined before October 1880, two months; and the men who joined before October 1881, one month's pay as gratuity. Do you agree with them in that?—I do, Sir.

9624. *Chairman.*—And do those whom you represent agree in that?—Yes.

9625. *Mr. Morris.*—You think there ought to be a distinction in the gratuity between the men who had the longer service in the troubled times, and the men who had the shorter service?—Yes, we do, Sir.

9626. Would you now deal with the next question you desire to bring under the notice of the Committee?—The next thing we wish to bring before you is that of young men who joined the service since the 12th August, 1867, being placed on such a low scale of pension. The Pension Act of the 12th August, 1867, has caused great discontent in the service. After a few years, when the men become fully aware of their position as regards pension, if they have been able to save any money, which is almost impossible, their inclination would be to emigrate or leave the service in consequence of the fact that there are no hopes held out to them of a retiring allowance.

9627. They can hardly say "no hopes." It may be that they consider them small hopes?—Well, then, there are small hopes. As an instance of that, I may point out to the Committee that a constable of my time in the service, at least under the Act under which I joined, at fifteen years' service would be entitled to 27*l.*, whereas under the Act of 1867 he would be entitled to only 22*l.* After twenty years' service I would be entitled to 36*l.*, whereas he would be only entitled to 22*l.*; at twenty-five years' service I would be entitled to 56*l.*, and he would be entitled to 37*l.*; and at thirty years' service I would be entitled to 75*l.*; whereas all he could get, all that he would be entitled to receive, would be 15*l.*

9628. *Mr. Holmes.*—That is assuming he had risen only to the rank of a first-class constable?—Yes, assuming he never rose beyond the rank of a first-class constable.

First-class Constable Owen McEvoy.

3rd Sept., 1882.

Assuming we get what we are entitled to by the Act of 1847 and the Act of 1867 on behalf of the men, I hold that after twenty-five years' service—I am speaking now as regards my own rank of constables—constables of the first-class ought to be entitled to five-sixths of their pension at twenty-five years' service, and not three-fourths as at present. They are entitled to half pay at fifteen years, fifteen-thirtieths at present, but we are of opinion that twenty-five thirtieths ought to be his pension, in other words, five-sixths of his pay, at twenty-five years, and not three-fourths as at present.

2629. Then, speaking for yourself and for the men who joined the force before 1867, you are not satisfied with the scale of pensions under which you came, and you wish to have that scale amended?—Do you mean the 1847 Act.

2630. Yes?—I do not at all attempt to touch that Act. I am talking of the 1867 Act, and think that, so far as the twenty-five years is concerned, the pension ought to be five-sixths of the pay.

2631. Then you wish to have the Act of 1867 amended in that respect?—I respectfully bring it before the Commission that the pension after that service ought to be five-sixths.

2632. You are not content with the Act of 1867, which goes by periods of five years?—No, Sir.

2633. And not by yearly increments?—Yes. We should prefer yearly increments from fifteen to twenty years, because when a man gets at nineteen years' service there is no difference in his pension from that which he would receive at fifteen years' service. There is no difference in the pension between fifteen and twenty years. At fifteen years he is entitled to 37*l.*, whereas he ought to get 47*l.* at nineteen years.

2634. Don't you think the pension of one-half of salary after fifteen years' service is a very good pension?—It is a very fair pension.

2635. And don't you think the pension of two-thirds after twenty years' service is also a very good pension?—A very fair pension.

2636. Then there is nothing unreasonable in not giving a yearly increment between the periods of fifteen and twenty years?—Nothing unreasonable, but we think it would be more satisfactory to the force if yearly increments were given between those periods.

2637. You still wish to have the Act of 1867 amended by giving yearly increments between the periods of five years?—Certainly so.

2638. But are you not aware that the Act of 1867 is a singularly favourable Act, and that it gives very good pensions to the men at the fixed periods you have mentioned?—I would call it a very fair Act of Parliament for those who joined under it, such as myself.

2639. Are you aware that the men of the London metropolitan police force can only get two-thirds of their pay as pension upon leaving the force?—I have heard so.

2640. And that rate is the most favourable they have under any circumstances?—I have heard so.

2641. Well, then, don't you think it would be somewhat difficult to put the Dublin men in a very much better position than the London men—I am referring to the men who joined the force since 1867—having regard to the fact that the most that the men can get in London is two-thirds of pay as pension—don't you think it would be very difficult to give the men here a better scale of pensions than that enjoyed by the men in London?—I would certainly say that the Dublin men would have more difficult and onerous duties to perform than the men in London. Besides, the London men, according to rumour, are not satisfied with their pension.

2642. *Chairman.*—On what grounds do you put forward the suggestion for the amendment of the Act of 1867?—We think that the scale of pensions should rise by annual increments.

2643. On what grounds do you want to have amended the Act of 1867; what reasons have you to urge for such a step?—Because it would be the means of causing more content in the service. Men at nineteen years' service only get the same as men at fifteen years; and men at twenty-four years' service only get the same pension as men going away at twenty years' service.

2644. *Mr. Holmes.*—But, for a man leaving the force at nineteen years' service, don't you consider a pension of one-half his pay is very good?—I would not.

2645. You would not?—Not at nineteen years.

2646. Are you aware that a man in the London force would to-day only get nineteen-fiftieths of his pay after nineteen years' service?—That would be in accordance with the Act of 1867, I presume.

2647. *Mr. Morris.*—What you consider, as I understand your meaning, is, that it is not fair to a man to retire, say at twenty-four years' service, on the same pension as that on which a man can retire at twenty years' service?—Exactly.

2648. In fact, that then he is spending his four years without getting anything additional for it?—Yes. If he retired at twenty years' service, another man should fill his place, and then the Government would be paying the pension that that man would draw at twenty years' service, and also paying the man to fill his place in the service, so that he ought to be paid for the four years by the increase being granted.

2649. *Mr. Holmes.*—But, surely, you are aware that the 1867 scale is an exceptionally favourable scale, and that no other class of the civil service ever had as favourable a scale as that?—That is the very reason why our men want to have amended the Act of 1847, and then it shall be placed on the same scale.

2650. You are not content with the Act of 1867—you want to amend the Act of 1867—don't you say that?—I do, Sir.

2651. Very well, then, I say to you, are you not aware that the Act of 1867 was exceptionally favourable Act?—Yes, with the amendment I suggest.

2652. But even as it stands?—I am not aware that it is so very favourable at all.

2653. Do you mean to say that you do not consider that two-thirds of your pay after twenty years' service is not a favourable scale?—It is a favourable scale, but I mean to say that at twenty-four years getting two-thirds of that pension is not a favourable scale, but that it ought to rise by annual increments. With reference to the Act of 1847, I would propose to have it amended as follows: half-pay at fifteen years' service, two-thirds pay at twenty years' service, and five-sixths at twenty-five years' service, full pay at thirty years' service, with optional retirement from the force at twenty-five years' service.

2654. Do you think that the men who joined the force since 1867 seriously expect that they will be put in a better position than the police forces in England and Scotland as regards pension?—They expect to be put on the scale, and on the footing as regards the scale of pension I have mentioned to you.

2655. *Mr. Morris.*—You have given us now a statement as to what the men expect as regards the amendment of the Act of 1867?—Yes, Sir.

2656. *Mr. Holmes.*—Do you know what the scale of pensions is for the London metropolitan police?—I have heard that the men cannot pass two-thirds.

2657. Are you aware that there was a Bill before Parliament last Session for the purpose of applying the London scale of pensions to the police forces of England and Scotland?—I have heard it rumoured.

2658. Supposing that that Bill became an Act, and that two-thirds was the most in the way of pension that could be given to the police forces of England and Scotland, do you think that Parliament would give a higher scale of pensions to the police forces in Ireland?—We would not expect to be put on a higher scale of pensions than the London metropolitan police, though certainly we have more arduous duties to perform.

2659. *Mr. Morris.*—And do you consider that the Dublin metropolitan police, having those more arduous and dangerous duties to perform, ought to get a better scale of pensions than the London police?—They ought. A constable in the Dublin metropolitan police has to perform very dangerous and arduous duties, and there are very few of the public who are inclined to take his part, whereas in London it is not so.

2660. *Mr. Holmes.*—Were the duties of the police in Dublin always more arduous, do you think, than the duties of the other police forces of the United Kingdom?—I think they were. I have particular cognisance myself that since 1863, but more especially since 1865, 1866, and 1867, that the duties were very arduous and very heavy.

2661. *Mr. Meade.*—You were there the Fenian movement in Ireland?—Yes, Sir, since the Fenian movement. I have been out very severe nights in 1866 and 1867, and in my opinion the duties of the London police were not at all nearly as severe as those of the metropolitan police in Dublin.

2662. As a matter of fact, I believe that very often since 1865 the police in Dublin were obliged in many streets to go in couples together?—They were doubled in the Fenian movement, Sir, and they have been doubled recently; but before that, in the interval, they were not doubled, and each man worked his beat singly.

2663. *Mr. Holmes.*—In the interval to which you allude, that is to say, the years between 1867 and 1877, do you think the duties of the Dublin metropolitan police force were more arduous than the London police in those years?—I do say that they were exceedingly far more arduous within the two periods I have mentioned.

2664. *Chairman.*—What is the next subject with which you wish to deal?—The next subject would be reductions. We wish no man to be reduced to the ranks for a longer period than three years, except under extraordinary circumstances; and, that the man so reduced shall, if he keep his previous good character, be promoted to his former rank.

2665. *Mr. Holmes.*—That he shall be reinstated?—Yes, that he shall be reinstated to his former rank, to be senior or junior on that rank according as the Commissioner thinks fit. He may be junior if the Commissioner thinks fit, or if he is a deserving man he could be made senior and placed at the top of the rank.

2666. For what class of offences are men reduced?—Drunkenness; being unfit for duty from the effects of liquor; having the appearance of drink.

2667. Do you know of any case where a man was reduced for his first offence?—I do, Sir. For a first offence in fourteen years I was reduced.

2668. You were reduced once previously, were you not?—Never before.

2669. After fourteen years' service?—Yes, Sir.

2670. Had you any unfavourable records for other matters?—For card playing (1); neglecting to deliver letters (2); and not being in my division although told to be in my division by a certain time (3). I was living in another division, and I was reported for not being in my division by a certain time. The inspector said he told me the time to be in my division; I denied it before the Commissioner. I was told that I had my house let furnished, and I said I would not forego my promotion, no matter how many houses I had. The inspector told the Commissioner that he had told me to be in my division.

2671. Do you mean stalls?—I was living in one division and doing duty in another. I distinctly told the Commissioner that if he were to dismiss me I would tell the truth—that I never was told one word about it, nor neither was I, and I was fined 10s. Those are all the reports that I ever had against me.

2672. Then you were not reduced for the first offence of drunkenness only. I presume the Commissioner took into account these previous unfavourable records?—I suppose so.

2673. If you had not had any unfavourable records I presume that the Commissioner would not have reduced you in rank for this first offence of drunkenness?—With that I do not concur; I think he would.

2674. You mentioned three or four different reports, were you punished in each of these cases?—I was fined 5s. for card playing in barracks; 3s. 6d. for not delivering letters in proper time—I was then assistant clerk; and 10s. for not being in my division. These are the fines. I may mention that on the day of my being reported unfit for duty I was at a [illegible] which was given in Mount Street Barracks by permission of the Commissioner of Police. The loss of my rest, and the fact of dancing over night had the effect to think the next day that I was not fit for duty, and I was brought into the station about half-past 11 o'clock in the day, and I was told by the chief superintendent on the next day that the surgeon would not be on my case for two hours, although it was my first offence for drunkenness.

Probationer Constable Owen McFetty.

24 Sept., 1882.

2675. How long was that after the previous offence for which you had been punished?—The card playing was about twelve months previous to the charge of being unfit for duty. The delivery of the letters was about eight or nine years before, and living in my division was only about three or four months, or five months previously.

2676. And does that reduction still continue?—Yes, Sir, since 1877. I was reduced in February 1877.

2677. And at the time you were reduced you were an acting sergeant?—Yes, Sir.

2678. Of course, putting aside your own case, as a matter of fact do not you consider that, in the case of any policeman, whether he be a constable or a sergeant, that being drunk, or having the sign of drink on him going on duty, is a very great breach of discipline?—Decidedly so; but we are of opinion that he ought to get the chance of promotion after three years of good conduct.

2679. But in the abstract you think it is a very great breach of discipline?—Decidedly so; we do not at all view it in any other light.

2680. And that it should be severely punished?—Decidedly so.

2681. *Chairman.*—But you think that the punishment in your case, and in that of others, is excessive?—Yes, Sir; we think that it is excessive. I then got on the advanced class in June 1880, the class from which acting sergeants may be made. That was three years and four or five months after being reduced, and I was employed at the collection of agricultural statistics in June 1880. I went out in the evening and I met a friend, and I went into a public-house and paid for two "halves of malt." I was reported for that and fined 5s., and in four or five nights afterwards orders came out removing me from the advanced class, although I was punished by the fine of 5s. four or five days previously for the same offence. I was removed from the advanced class either four or five days after being in that public-house with a civilian in uniform.

2682. *Mr. Holmes.*—You were off duty?—Yes, off duty in uniform.

2683. In uniform?—Yes.

2684. How were you off duty. I understand you to say that you were engaged collecting agricultural statistics?—Yes; but that was only during the agricultural hours, from 10 to 4 o'clock in the afternoon. This was afterwards.

2685. This was, then, after you had performed your duty?—Yes, although I was in public-houses in the course of my duty during the day in the collection of statistics—the carrying of a certain book for the purpose [illegible] the man so engaged. In the same month I was fined 15s., or rather in May 1880, for standing in Bull Lane at half-past 11 o'clock at night.

2686. I suppose, having now given us a list of the fines and punishments to which you have been subjected, you consider that these fines and punishments are excessive?—Quite so.

2687. While at the same time you fully admit that fines and punishments must follow from breaches of discipline?—Decidedly. Discipline cannot be kept up without the men being punished; but the infliction of smaller fines we think would act as a deterrent for breaches of discipline just as effectually as the infliction of a fine of 10s. for going into a public-house if you meet your brother or your father.

2688. *Mr. Harte.*—Do you think, for some of the other men have stated it, that when a man is reduced from the position of sergeant to that of constable, and that he finds he must never get up again, that it more or less has the effect of driving the man to desperation and makes him very reckless?—Precisely.

First class Constable Owen [illegible].

26 Sept., 18[illegible].

2689. Whereas if the hope were held out to him that after three years' good exemplary conduct he would get back to his former position, that it would make that man more anxious to do good, is that your view?—Yes, most men would be anxious, whereas they do not now take any interest in minding themselves after being reduced. They expect never to be thought of any more. It is all a new school whom the authorities intend to promote. There being no hope for a man reduced under such circumstances after nineteen or twenty years' service, he does not take the same interest in himself as he would otherwise.

2690. When these fines are inflicted, as much as say 1*l*., or over 1*l*., are they stopped weekly from the pay?—Yes, Sir.

2691. It is turned into instalments?—It is not drawn, it remains in bank as not drawn on the estimate.

2692. But how does the man pay it?—He never actually pays it. He gets his pay, less the stoppage for the fine.

2693. But surely, say a man was fined 5*l*., such a fine is not deducted all at once?—No; it is deducted from the pay at the rate of 11*s*. per week.

2694. At the rate of 11*s*. it is deducted until the full amount is cleared off?—Yes; he draws his pay minus the 11*s*.

2695. *Mr. Holmes.*—Do you mean to say that if a constable was fined 5*l*. there would be taken off his pay 11*s*. per week until that fine was paid?—Yes.

2696. That a constable's pay is reduced to that extent while the fine is being paid?—Yes, Sir; there are the Commissioner's orders, that 11*s*. is to be stopped from a first-class constable. Whilst on the punishments I would like to mention the case of an acting inspector and sergeant, who were reduced on the letter of a notorious brewdealer and night-house keeper for going into a public house at half-past 6 o'clock in the morning and paying for two glasses of whiskey while in uniform, both being off duty. The sergeant lost 5*s*. 6*d*. a-week, and the other man lost 7*s*. a-week.

2697–2705. How long did the reductions last?—One man is in the force still, and he is reduced still. That is up to six years ago. He has paid that 7*s*. a-week all that time. The other man got reckless, and he got reported for drink two or three times subsequent to this reduction, and he is since dismissed the service.

2706. Have you now said all that you desire to say on the subject of fines?—Yes.

2707. *Mr. Mayne.*—Before you leave the question of force, may I ask you, are you aware that there is a general complaint amongst the inhabitants—I am not saying whether rightly or wrongly—and there has been for a long time, that the police are not active enough—even in small matters, such as the regulation of the traffic, and so on?—I hope you will remember the vast extent of streets that have been brought into regulation for the last ten or fifteen years, while the force still consists of the same number of men. A great many men are employed on different special duties—such as for sanitary purposes, by the Board of Works, and are otherwise employed—and no addition has been made to the force. There are a great many complaints, but we must remember that a great many of them are unfounded.

2708. I merely ask you as to the fact—are you aware of these complaints?—Yes.

2709. Do you believe these complaints, as a rule, to be well founded or the reverse?—I do not believe them to be well founded.

2710. *Mr. Holmes.*—You said something about men being on special duties upon which they had not been heretofore engaged, and that, in consequence, the number of police in Dublin is insufficient for the proper discharge of their duties, and for the protection of the city?—I think they are insufficient.

2711. *Chairman.*—Proceed now, if you so desire, with the next subject in relation to which you wish to give evidence?—The next subject is that of promotion. If a man seeks promotion to the rank of acting sergeant, no matter what his qualifications are, he must first be considered to pass for the class called the "advanced class." When I joined, a man should be first class before he is allowed to compete, and I had to wait for three years until the list was exhausted. I was first for first class at the time of an examination held here for acting sergeant, and I cannot [illegible] the Commissioner, but he would not allow me to compete for the rank of acting sergeant, because I was not of the first class; and now second-class men are allowed up to compete for the rank of acting sergeant.

2712. The plan has been changed since?—Yes; and it is now going down to third rate, as if there were not men of intelligence on the first rate to be promoted to acting sergeants, without going down to junior men who have been but four or five years in the service.

2713. Is it to test the fitness and competency of new men for the rank that the examination is held?—Certainly, but what experience can a man of four or five years' service have compared with a man of nine or ten years' service.

2714. *Mr. Mayne.*—Don't you think that the natural average of intelligence which applies to all men applies to the police?—Yes, Sir, just the same.

2715. Don't you think that though many men would reach the position of first-class constable, you would find many other men in the third class who would be better men, both as soldiers and every other qualification?—It does not follow that the man should be better in intelligence in the third class.

2716. It does not follow, but, as a matter of fact, is it not often the case that you would find a third-class constable a better man than a man in the first class?—Yes.

2717. A more intelligent man, I mean?—Yes; but if a second-class man be promoted acting sergeant, he takes up the vacancy that a first class should have got, and the then second rate is deprived of a step up to the place filled by the first-class man. It deprives the senior man of the second rate, if he is a junior man of the same rate, who gets the acting sergeantship. It deprives the senior man of the second rate of 1*s*. 6*d*. a-week which he should have got if promotion was taken from the first class.

2718. *Chairman.*—What I understand you to say is that, instead of the vacancies for the rank of acting sergeant being thrown open to the first class only, they are now open to the second and third grades, provided the men pass the examination?—Yes, certainly, Sir.

2719. *Mr. Mayne.*—Then you would ask that in the promotion for the position of acting sergeant the men should be taken from the first-class constables?—Yes; or if the Commissioner took men from the second class constables. If the Commissioner promoted men from the second rate, constables ought to get their first rate after seven years, or after whatever period would be fixed by the Commissioner.

2720. Without examination?—Yes, without examination. The constable ought to get second and first rates without any examination. The public don't know rate a man is on the streets. He is supposed to have as much intelligence, and to know as well how to act on third rate as on first, and he ought to get his second rate when it comes to his turn, and also first rate when it comes to his turn.

2721. Would you have examinations for promotion after that?—Certainly I would have examination for promotion; but, in my opinion, the first examination is quite sufficient to this extent—that an acting sergeant ought to get the rank of full sergeant when it comes to his turn.

2722. For promotion from any class of constable to be made an acting sergeant you would be in favour of examination?—Decidedly.

2723. One examination?—Yes, one examination.

2724. And then he should attain the rank of a full sergeant without any further examinations?—Yes.

2725. And then you would have an examination for acting inspector?—Yes; I would hold another examination for acting inspector, because an officer of that rank has to do office duty, and he is supposed to be a superior class of man to the men in the street, and he has to take the inspector's place at different times.

Fourteenth Constable Owen McNally.

26 Sept., 1882.

With reference to the school and this advanced class, if a man does not keep up so many attendances at this school he is struck off the advanced class, and he does not get promotion at all, no matter what his qualifications are. He must keep up a certain number of attendances at the school to keep himself on this class, otherwise he cannot get promotion, though a man may think he has sufficient qualifications without attending school after doing his duty for so many hours. A great many police think they are well qualified for the position of an acting sergeant without attending school at all. But they are struck off the class, except that they have so many attendances in the month, and they cannot get an acting sergeantship there, because they are struck off the class from which acting sergeants are made. We find fault with that. The school is essentially necessary, in my opinion, for the education of the men who go there, but it ought not to be compulsory on men to go there.

2726. You consider school a useful institution to have?—Yes, and it ought to be frequented, and it would be frequented if men would get two hours off every second evening, from 7 to 9 o'clock, to attend school. They would gain a vast deal by attending the school, if they got two hours to do so—from 7 to 9.

2727. Don't you think that a man, anxious to forward himself, in any position or sphere of life, might go and get instruction when he was off duty out of his own time?—Decidedly, Sir; but if, in his opinion, he has sufficient qualification, I don't think he should be compelled to attend school.

2728. *Chairman.*—As I take it, if he does not attend school, he must study elsewhere?—Yes. What I mean is this. I don't want attendance at school to be a necessary condition to a man going in for an examination. I wish that attendance at school should be optional.

2729. What is the next matter you wish to bring before us?—I think that reports, when being investigated by the Commissioners—if the accused deny the charge or complaint—ought to be on sworn testimony, and that all evidence, for or against the accused—ought to be sworn testimony only.

2730. You would not have that in all cases?—I would have it in every case where a man denies the charge.

2731. *Mr. Morris.*—But I suppose that the inquiry should be held amongst yourselves, and not in an open public court?—Oh, yes; amongst ourselves, and not in an open public court.

2732. *Chairman.*—Do you wish for any alteration in the tribunal?—No alteration whatever; nor do we wish the public to know anything about our arrangements. That is the rule at present. They do not know anything about our arrangements, and a very proper and right rule it is, Sir.

2733. What is the next topic of your evidence?—We think that every man taking a house ought to be allowed to let a portion of it to respectable persons. If a man let one or two rooms to a gentleman, he might pay the rent for him, and that would help a man very much, in order that he might not have to be living in houses with persons antagonistic to his way of thinking.

2734. *Mr. Holmes.*—You are in favour of men being allowed to let lodgings?—Yes.

2735. *Chairman.*—Kindly proceed to the next branch of your evidence?—In reference to the question of gratuities, I wish to say that a number of members of the force die in the service before they are entitled to pension. We would like them to get a gratuity of two months' pay for each year served up to ten years, and afterwards that it should be optional with them to take either gratuity or pension. If the man gets better, and had obtained his gratuity, we ask that it may be optional with him to get it changed back into pension, provided he hands back the amount of the gratuity he gets to the Commissioner, whom we hope might be pleased to change it to the pension to which the man would be entitled.

2736. *Mr. Holmes.*—You make that suggestion with a view to enabling a man, who is not likely to recover, to leave something substantial to his family?—Exactly so, Sir. And then we would suggest that it is not necessary for a man to sign a certain receipt, which is at present in use. I believe it cannot be given, except the man's signature for the amount of the gratuity be attached to the recognised document. We hold that it ought to be given to the next-of-kin of the man on their making the statutory declaration that they are the next-of-kin, and entitled to the gratuity.

2737. *Mr. Morris.*—Define what you mean by the "next-of-kin"?—I would first say the wife and children; after that, I would say the father or mother. If the wife be alive, she and the children first, and I would certainly go as far as the brother or sister, in the event of there being no father or mother, but I would not go one single bit further. Now, with reference to burial expenses, we think that if a man die in the service before the completion of three years, the barrack sergeant ought to be handed a sum of 7*l.* for his funeral expenses.

2738. At present there is a small sum allowed for that purpose—2*l.* 12*s.* 6*d.* I think?—Yes, either 2*l.* 7*s.* 6*d.* or 2*l.* 12*s.* 6*d.*

2739. *Chairman.*—Do you wish to add anything on that subject?—No, Sir.

2740. Then be good enough to proceed with the next head of your evidence?—If men are transferred from one division to another, and not for misconduct, we think that a reasonable allowance ought to be given them, especially to married men to meet the expense of removal.

2741. *Mr. Holmes.*—Are men frequently transferred for the good of the service—I mean married men?—It is rarely occurred. It is very seldom; but it is done, though not very often.

2742. *Chairman.*—What further have you to state?—We think that men in plain clothes off duty ought not to be subject to the same stringent regulations as to discipline as men on duty or in uniform.

2743. *Mr. Holmes.*—Is that in reference to the question of entering a public-house?—Yes, or hotel, with a friend, not for the purpose of gambling; and, so long as they are in respectable company, they might be passed over by any officer seeing them when in plain clothes and off duty. We only wish to be allowed to go into a public-house off duty and in plain clothes; and, if in uniform, we hold that a man has no right to go in, or out of a public-house either on or off duty. But we think that even if a man did go into a public-house when off duty and in uniform, a small fine would be sufficient, and that he should not be subjected to the heavy fines which are now imposed.

2744. *Chairman.*—Have you any other matter to bring before the Commission?—We would also ask that a man should be paid 15*s.* a month in lieu of wearing his plain clothes while on duty, and we think that this allowance ought to apply to pensioners as well as other men. It does not at all become a man to be in uniform going to the butcher's and buying meat, or going to the market, to buy potatoes and all those things. We think, as regards pensioners, they ought to be allowed 15*s.* a month in lieu of wearing their plain clothes.

2745. *Mr. Holmes.*—When you say 15*s.* a month, you do not mean for every month in the year, but only for the month in which the man was obliged to wear plain clothes?—Yes, quite so. I may mention that there is an allowance of 10*s.* a-month at present to all men except pensioners. Where a man is employed in plain clothes now for a month he would get 10*s.*, and, as an instance, the importance of having men in plain clothes, I may remind you of the case on Grattan Bridge a night or two ago. If the officer was not in plain clothes that night the fellow who had the lead in his possession would not have gone near him. We would suggest that we should get 15*s.* a-month for wearing plain clothes during the time a man would be on duty wearing them; and that even if he was only employed for a fortnight in plain clothes, he should be paid at the rate of 15*s.* a-month.

2746. It is usual, then, for men who do not belong to the detective division to wear plain clothes?—Yes. A man may be employed to prevent the playing of points and lanes, or to watch certain places, or the like. There is always a certain number of men in plain clothes sent out from the different stations.

2747. The present allowance is 10s. a-month, and you wish it to be made 15s.?—Yes.

2748. Would not an allowance of 10s. per month, which is at the rate of 6d. a-day, be sufficient to provide a man with plain clothes?—Well, a man wants for a month or two on night duty is of very little use afterwards.

2749. *Chairman.*—Please state the next matter that you wish to bring before us?—Another matter is that the uniform material which is at present issued to the force is not as good as it used to be. We would also wish that the men would be allowed to keep any cast uniform clothing they like to keep, on paying the same price for it as would be offered at the auction. Some men do not care to keep their own old tunic, caps, or leggings, but if any man likes to keep any portion of his cast uniform let him pay the same rate for it as would be realized in the case of the man who does not like to keep it. We are of opinion that a man going on the sick report ought not to be charged 1s. a-day while sick through no fault of his own. I suppose I was not twenty days sick for the last twenty years. I was sick on Sunday just for the one day, and I am as sure as I am here that there will be 1s. stopped from my pay for that day.

2750. *Mr. Holmes.*—What substitute would you provide for that, and at the same time have a proper check on malingering?—Malingering should be fined, or if a man goes sick without a cause, if he brings it upon himself. The men of the Royal Irish Constabulary are ninety days sick before any money is stopped from them. They are ninety days without having their pay stopped, and here we are certain to have 1s. stopped for the second day. Sometimes the doctor might recommend to the Commissioner that a man should get his pay; but, as a rule, 1s. a-day is stopped.

2751. *Chairman.*—Have you any other proposition to urge on behalf of the men whom you represent?—We would certainly ask, with every confidence in the Commissioners, that they would be pleased to recommend us for a small increase of pay. We would not lay down any scale, and I would not go further than to say that a constable of the first class would get 4s. 6d. per day, or 31s. 6d. per week, and that it should tell in the pension; and that there should be no reduction at all in the pension on going out, and not as at present.

2752. What does he get now?—2*l.* 8s. 6d. per week. 1*l.* 8s. will only tell in the pension, and not 1*l.* 8s. 6d.

2753. The 6d. is the allowance for boots?—Yes, Sir.

2754. *Mr. Morris.*—You want to have that pay increased?—Yes, Sir. We want 4s. 6d. a-day, or 31s. 6d. per week, with good-conduct pay as follows:—After twenty years' service to get an additional 6d. a-day, making the pay 5s. a-day, or 35s. per week.

2755. *Mr. Holmes.*—Are you aware of the fact that third-class constables here are better paid than the corresponding ranks in London?—I am, Sir; but, in answer to that, I must remind you that the men in the London police get to first class after two years, or two and a-half years.

2756. Do you ask for an increase of the pay of the second class constable?—We would say 4s. 3d. per day, or 1*l.* 9s. 9d. per week. His present pay is 1*l.* 6s. 3d.

2757. And what do you say as to the third class?—We would hold that 4s. a-day should be his pay, or 28s. a week. His present pay is 1*l.* 0s. 6d., and we would not have any fourth rate at all. Men after six months in the depôt as recruits, we hold should be placed on the third class.

2758. You think that the fourth-rate constables ought to be abolished, and that there ought to be only third-class constables as the lowest rate?—Yes, Sir. And we also think that after the first six months they should get that rate. At present, during the six months they are in the depôt, they receive 2s. a-day. We think they should receive 21s. a-week for that first six months. They would not know the duty before then, and during that time we think that 21s. ought to be quite sufficient.

2759. But, bearing in mind that the constables here, on the whole, are as well paid as those in London, do not you see some difficulty in the way of the carrying out of your propositions, and of thus placing you in a better position than they?—We hope to see the London men put superior to us before long.

2760. *Chairman.*—Who hears at present the complaints against constables?—The Commissioner or Assistant-Commissioner.

2761. Has he any one attending with him?—The Chief Superintendent invariably attends.

2762. Does any person attend from the district in which the person accused happens to be doing duty?—Either the Superintendent of his division—of the division in which he is the accused—or, in his place, an inspector deputed by him.

2763. Do you suggest any alteration in that tribunal by having any other parties to attend?—I would like to have the Superintendent of each division to attend on a given day in each week, in order that there should be nothing done but that which his Superintendent hears, and the other men who know the character of the delinquent.

2764. And you would have them attend as referees of character in the case of the parties charged?—Yes, Sir; the same as in Mr. O'Ferrall's and Colonel Lake's time. They used to hold a Board every Tuesday at which the seven superintendents attended at 11 o'clock, when the delinquents were called up.

2765. The object of that was that the man charged might have been in all of the different divisions from time to time?—Exactly, Sir.

2766. *Mr. Morris.*—As I understand it the whole of your evidence summed up, is as follows: What you complain of, and what the men consider as grievances under which they are suffering are, first, not having received a superannuation somewhat similar to that given to the Royal Irish Constabulary for the last three years' extra work?—Yes, Sir.

2767. Then the next grievance you complain of is that of pensions?—Yes.

2768. And you particularly consider that the Pension Act of 1857 is not a sufficiently favourable one for the men?—I do, and it will never work. The 1857 Act will never work; the men will not remain in the force.

2769. You consider that the Act for pensions of 1857 should be amended upon a more favourable scale than it now is?—We do, Sir.

2770. That is your second cause of complaint?—Yes.

2771. And your third cause of complaint, as I understand you, is that fines, penalties, and reductions are too severely administered in the force?—Yes, and arrears.

2772. And under these three heads now you consider are stated the principal grievances of the Dublin metropolitan police force?—Yes, Sir, we do. I forgot to mention that if men get permission to marry, and do get married, they ought to be allowed lodging allowance.

2773. *Mr. Holmes.*—You are aware, of course, that no lodging allowance is given to the men in London?—I am aware also that the coast-guard service get it.

2774. *Chairman.*—Is there any other constable wishes to add anything to the evidence given by Constable McNally?

Constable Boland.—We have nothing to add, Sir.

2775. *Chairman.*—You have all heard the evidence given by Constable McNally?

Constable Boland.—We have, Sir.

2776. *Chairman.*—And do you concur in that evidence?

Constable Boland.—We do, Sir, entirely.

[Constables Lawless, Murphy, Moore, and Morgan also expressed their assent.]

2777. *Mr. Morris.*—And not one of you has anything further to add?

Constable Boland.—We have nothing further to add, Sir.

Acting Sergeant Richard Chase.

22 Sept., 1882.

2778. *Chairman.*—What is your name?—Richard Chase.

2779. You are an acting sergeant?—Yes.

2780. How many years service have you?—Eight years on the 19th of this month.

2781. Is there anything that specially relates to your branch of the service that the other constable has not mentioned? You need not repeat anything that he has referred to, but if there is anything you would wish to state that has reference to your special branch of the service—the mounted branch—be good enough now to state it?—I quite concur in all the evidence that has been given. With regard to our service, we claim three months' money on account of the extra duty that we have performed.

2782. Is there anything that relates to your branch that the other constable has omitted to state?—We had a great deal more extra work to perform since the agitation sprung up than we had before. For the last few years the mounted men have had a great deal more wear and tear on their shirts and under clothing. Their boots are more expensive than the foot men's boots, and there are other expenses that they are put to that bring their expenses to a great deal more than those of the foot men. We have a great deal more work in our own line than the foot men have, for after we are on duty a great many hours we have two or three hours' work to do when we go home.

2783. *Mr. Holmes.*—In what way?—In the stables and in our barracks.

2784. How long are you on duty during the day?—For different periods. Sometimes for three, four, and five hours, sometimes more.

2785. *Mr. Morris.*—On active duty?—Yes.

2786. What is the average of your time on active duty?—Taking one thing with another, about four hours a day. That is the outside work. Then when we go home we have an hour's grooming at our horses, and if the weather is fine we can manage our kits in an hour or an hour and a-half, and then we have to get our accoutrements cleaned up as well, but of course in wet weather there is double work.

2787. But taking your out-duty and your duty in stables together, how long are you on an average occupied—how many hours in the day are you upon an average occupied?—I did not make any average of it, but I could give you an outline of the duty that we perform.

2788. Speaking roughly?—I should say that we are from nine to ten hours a-day, sometimes more. But I should say that, taking the average, we are about ten hours a-day on duty.

2789. How do you make that out. You have told us that you are not more than four hours at outside work, and you do not seem to say that you are six hours at stable duty?—We are called up in the morning at half-past 6 o'clock for stables, and we are in stables very often until 10 o'clock. We very seldom get away before that for our breakfast. That is, cleaning up stables and horses and kits for the day's work. And then we go on duty at different periods of the day; it is very uncertain. We go on duty for three and four hours, sometimes more, and when we go home off outside duty we have our horses, stables, and accoutrements to clean up for the next day's work, and particularly for the last three years we have had to do two and three turns of duty a-day. Then we have to go out and do a turn of duty at night as well. Often three times have we to go on mounted duty during the day then, and especially was that the case during the sitting of the last Commission.

2790. Surely if the night is fine to do mounted duty must be a very pleasant occupation?—Yes, Sir; it is very pleasant recreation in fine weather, but it is not very pleasant on a winter's night, or a frosty night, to be out from 8 to 12 o'clock patrolling country roads, or out in Phoenix Park.

2791. But a policeman, as well as any other man, must take the rough and the smooth together?—We do not go in for anything else.

2792. But you do not mean seriously to say that the duties of the mounted men are more severe than those of the foot police?—We hold that we have more work to do than they have. Take the principle of the cavalry soldier, he is paid more pay than an infantry soldier. We have more wear on our shirts and drawers, and our boots are more expensive. We have to keep on very warm under-clothing in consequence of having to work in stables, and the riding is very severe on our drawers, and it will take two pairs of Wellington boots for each twelve months at 31s., and there is 12s. a pair for stable boots. We have to provide spurs and gloves; we are allowed 6d. a-week for those, but it is not enough. We have five articles of uniform to get filled.

2793. What are these articles?—Jacket, tunic, two pairs of overalls, and cape.

2794. And do you get the same allowance for fitting uniform and for boots that the other men get?—Yes, we do; and we also get 6d. a-week for spurs and gloves.

2795. And what do your spurs and gloves cost you in the year?—A pair of spurs when you buy them first costs 4s. 6d. You must have two pairs, for one pair would not be sufficient for your work. As for gloves, two pairs only do for the twelve months.

2796. What do you pay for your gloves?—3s. a-pair. You would not get good gloves for less money.

2797. Then the allowance amply provides for your expenditure in spurs and gloves?—Yes, the allowance will do for spurs and gloves.

2798. And it leaves a margin over?—It will not leave much of a margin over. But we have five articles of uniform to get fitted, while a foot policeman has only two. He has only his tunic and overalls, and he may have his great coat, but we have the five articles I have mentioned.

2799. Is it an increase of pay over the foot men that you desire?—Yes.

2800. What amount do you seek?—6d. a-day.

2801. Then the cavalry members of the police force expect 6d. a-day more than the foot men?—Yes, that is the metropolitan policemen.

2802. You seek an addition of 6d. to your present pay?—Yes.

2803. Have you anything else to add?—No, Sir; we concur with the foot men in everything they have put forward, and we claim the same allowance as the foot men for extra work and longer hours.

Chief Superintendent Richard Corr.

20 Sept., 1882.

2808. What do you wish to bring under our notice?—Well, as regards the extra duty performed by the men in the service since the 14th March, 1880, I wish to say that we had a great amount of extra duty from time to time. In the case of the day men, who should go off duty at 9 o'clock, we had to keep them on duty and out until 12 and 1 o'clock every night. They would have then to go on their regular reliefs in the morning at 6 and 9 o'clock. They were kept from 9 until 2 or 3 o'clock in the morning, the day men who ordinarily would be going off at 9 o'clock at night, we had often to keep them on reserve, or send them out in the street until the hours I have named.

2809. And you consider that for that they ought to receive the same consideration as the men of the Royal Irish Constabulary?—I do, Sir; and no men ever discharged their duty more cheerfully and willingly than they did from time to time. The riots in Sackville Street continued for some seven or eight days running, and much extra duty and danger was incurred by the men. The day men, who should under ordinary circumstances have gone off duty at 9 o'clock, we often had to keep on reserve, or to send them out in case of emergency after those band fellows, or to meetings in the Land League rooms in Sackville Street, and they had to be kept on duty until 12 or half-past 11 o'clock, as the case might be, and when the streets were perfectly quiet, and the people had gone away, we would let them off, but they would have to resume their regular duty the next morning, when one relief goes on duty at 6 o'clock and the other at 9 o'clock. That was from the 14th March, 1880, when the first Land League meeting took place in Beresford Place, until very recently.

2810. *Mr. Holmes.*—Were these extra duties continuous?—Oh, no, not continuous; but occasions would arise when meetings would take place and band fellows would go out at night, and we would have in consequence to keep these day men on duty.

2811. The duties were occasional for a number of years?—Yes; and previous to 1880 we had meetings out in the Park—societal meetings, and subsequently we had Land League meetings held there.

2812. *Mr. Morris.*—But you consider that from March 1880 there has been a good deal of extra duty performed by the force?—There has.

2813. *Chairman.*—Extra and dangerous duties?—Yes; there were nights in Sackville Street when the men were carrying their lives in their hands, when there were showers of stones coming in every direction. The two Commissioners were there every night during the whole week.

2814. *Mr. Holmes.*—And the men you say performed those duties cheerfully, and always without discontent?—No men in any force in the world could have performed their duties more cheerfully or more willingly than they did.

2815. *Chairman.*—What amount of gratuity would you recommend to the men for these extra duties?—Oh, well Sir, I would not wish to take the liberty or responsibility on myself of recommending any sum as compensation to the men.

2816. *Mr. Holmes.*—But what is your opinion?—I know the feeling of the men.

2817. What is the feeling of the men?—I know what the feeling of the men is, and from what I hear the same gratuity as the Royal Irish Constabulary got is what they are anxious to obtain. That is the feeling of the men.

2818. Some of the witnesses whom we have examined among the constables, in fact, all the constables have suggested that the men who joined the force before October 1879 should get three months' pay as gratuity for extra work; that the men who joined the force before October 1880 should get two months, and that the men who joined the force before October 1881 should get one month's extra pay as gratuity?—Well, I think that that would be a very fair distribution, very fair.

2819. *Chairman.*—What is the next question you would like to deal with?—That of pensions. The men who joined the service under the comparatively recent Act of 1867 are certainly not contented at all as regards the pension, and I am decidedly of opinion that the force will scarcely be kept recruited under that Act.

2820. *Mr. Holmes.*—But is it your opinion that the men who joined the force since 1867 should be put under the old scale of pensions of 1847. You are aware, I presume, that they ask that they should be so placed?—Yes.

2821. What is your opinion as to that request?—Well, my opinion is that from the discontented state of those young men who joined under the 1867 Act, that they will not be contented unless there is some improvement at all events made in their position as regards pension.

2822. But do you go to the extent of saying that the men who joined under the Act of 1867 should be given the benefits of the 1847 Act?—Well, I would not go that length.

2823. Are you aware of the scale of pensions for the London metropolitan police force?—Yes. I think that that would be a fair scale for the Dublin metropolitan police.

2824. Are you aware that there was a Bill before Parliament last Session, the intention of which was to extend to the whole of England and Scotland the scale of pension now in force in relation to the London metropolitan police,—are you aware of that?—Yes.

2825. After twenty-eight years' service, a man of the London metropolitan police force can retire upon two-thirds of his pay?—Yes.

2826. Do you think that if that scale was made applicable to the Dublin men it would satisfy them?—I think it would in great measure; I am sure it would. They cannot expect more, at all events, than the London force.

2827. *Mr. Morris.*—Before you leave that subject, may I ask you what is your opinion as to this point: If there was a change made in the service of the police to that effect, that, whatever pension he would be entitled to, he should, after twenty-eight years, have leave to retire if he chose from the service without the necessity of obtaining a medical certificate, and without having to go to hospital or to pretend to be ill, as they are at present obliged to do—is it your opinion that after twenty-eight years' service a man ought to have permission to retire from the force?—I would say that after thirty years' service a man ought to have permission to retire from the force.

2828. In your opinion, thirty years would be the limit?—Yes.

2829. And then you consider that whatever pension a man would be entitled to, that man should have permission to retire without a medical certificate?—Yes, on the full amount that he would be entitled to. But then you would lose some first-class men at thirty years' service. If they wish to remain in the service you will have, in the case of men of thirty years' service, first class men, men of intelligence, men on whom you can place every reliance and confidence.

2830. Don't you think that when a man has served thirty years in the police force, he should then be entitled, if he so chose, to retire upon whatever pension he is entitled to?—I am of that opinion.

2831. You would give him that privilege?—Yes, I would, decidedly.

2832. Are men physically fit after thirty years' service?—A great many are.

2833. Able to endure night work and to rough it?—They are.

2834. After thirty years' service?—They are. Some are and some are not. I suppose there is not severer duty in any force in the world than the duty which a man in the Dublin metropolitan police has to contend with from time to time. Being out from half-past 10 at night until 6 o'clock in the morning, during a cold winter's night, is very hard, with discipline to be kept up in addition.

2835. Don't you think that the more severe part of their service consists of dealing in some of the streets of Dublin with vicious characters to the danger of their lives?—Decidedly.

2536. Don't you think that that is more severe than the fact of walking about by night?—They have to walk about, and they have the roughs to contend with at all hours of the night. I attended the last Commission of Inquiry in 1872, and I made a recommendation with reference to married men. They are very badly situated as regards their lodgings. It is impossible to get respectable lodgings, and in some of the divisions the men have to go into such places as Townsend Street and Mark Street, and down filthy lanes. It is impossible for a man with four or five children to get into a respectable house. I recommended that if a plot of ground was taken in each division for the number of married men, where proper sanitary arrangements would be carried out, it would have a very good effect.

2537. And that they should be charged a moderate rent?—Yes; a moderate rent for that accommodation.

2538. *Mr. Holmes.*—But you are not in favour of giving a lodging allowance to married men?—No; I think if they got their quarters at a moderate rent, it would recoup the Government in a very short time.

2539. *Chairman.*—If they got good quarters at a moderate rent?—Yes.

2540. *Mr. Holmes.*—I suppose you are aware that in some of the London districts there are blocks of buildings, as we have been informed, attached to the police-stations, where married men are accommodated? You would like some such thing to be provided here?—I would.

2541. You think they would pay the Government the outlay?—I think so in a very short time.

2542. Some of the men have suggested that they should be allowed to let portions of their houses in lodgings. They say that if they were allowed to do that, they would be able to take a better class of house. Do you see any objection to that?—Well, the Commissioners did give the privilege to men taking respectable houses, and from time to time disputes arose between the tenants, which resulted in the Commissioners withdrawing the privilege altogether.

2543. *Chairman.*—That would occur in many instances?—Yes, Sir.

2544. *Mr. Morris.*—It is right to say that others of them did mention that they thought it would not be for the advantage of the force that they should have that privilege. There appeared to be a difference of opinion upon the question between the men themselves?—Yes; there is. I think if there were blocks of buildings in each division, it would have a very good and salutary effect on the whole service, and there would be this advantage, even over respectable houses, that the sanitary arrangements would be carried out.

2545. You have seen some of these buildings erected by the Company, called the Artisans Dwellings Company?—Yes; I have.

2546. I suppose you mean blocks of buildings similar somewhat to them?—Yes; similar to them.

2547. *Mr. Holmes.*—You are aware that in London the police-stations are fitted up with libraries and reading rooms for the use of the men?—Yes.

2548. Do you think that the men here would look upon those comforts as a boon?—Indeed, they would. The Commissioner has already supplied the different barracks with some books out of the library.

2549. On the whole, are you in favour of giving the privilege to married men who take houses to let lodgings, bearing in mind entirely the welfare of the force and its interests in the future?—It would certainly give the men a better opportunity of getting respectable houses if they got respectable tenants into their houses.

2550. But on a comprehensive view of the matter, and bearing in mind the welfare of the force and the interests of the public, would you prefer a system of having blocks of buildings at moderate rents supplied to the married men, rather than of giving them the privilege of taking houses and letting lodgings?—I would.

2551. *Chairman.*—What would you say to trying both arrangements until they have the blocks of houses completed?—Yes; I should think there would be no objection to that until their houses were completed.

2552. *Mr. Morris.*—Of course, in letting lodgings should it not be under the supervision of some officer to see that they got good tenants?—Yes.

2553. *Mr. Holmes.*—After what period of service are men allowed to marry?—Five years. If a constable got a respectable young woman and some handsome fortune with her, it has been the case that the Commissioners took the matter into consideration, and gave leave to marry at three years' service.

2554. Now, if they were accommodated with lodgings at moderate rents would you be for restricting them from marrying until after a longer period of service than at present?—I think five years would be a suitable limit.

2555. You are aware that in the constabulary they are not allowed to marry until after seven years?—Yes.

2556. While in London there is no restriction at all?—No.

2557. Don't you think that if married men were provided with accommodation at a moderate rent it would have the effect of encouraging more marriages than at present?—Well, it might. It might have some effect, but still, unless they had five years' service, they would be deterred from marrying. There are a great many of our men get married without any authority at all being obtained, and they keep it a secret for some years.

2558. *Chairman.*—If you have disposed of this topic, kindly proceed to the next matter upon which you desire to give evidence?—The late Sir Henry Lake appointed me chief superintendent in 1876, and I wish to call the attention of the Committee to the fact that I have duties imposed upon me that none of my predecessors ever had before.

2559. *Mr. Holmes.*—You are now speaking for yourself?—I am.

2560. And not for the force?—Yes. I have to inspect all the barracks in the city once a-month, and the barracks in the E and F Divisions once every two months.

2561. *Mr. Morris.*—Before you go into your duties, would you kindly mention the salary at which you were appointed first?—330*l.*

2562. With what allowances?—105*l.* as allowances.

2563. And what is your present salary?—The same.

2564. There has been no increase in your salary since your appointment?—No, Sir.

2565. Nor is there, I suppose, any scale upon which it goes up?—No.

2566. *Chairman.*—Have you any allowances besides the allowance of 105*l.*?—I have free quarters at the Castle.

2567. *Mr. Holmes.*—For what purpose is the allowance given?—There is a sum of 45*l.* a-year allowed for a man, 45*l.* a-year for forage, 10*l.* for uniform, and 5*l.* for wear and tear.

2568. Wear and tear of a horse?—Yes, Sir. The duty my predecessor never had to perform. I have to visit those barracks I have mentioned, and I have to patrol each town division once a-month. I go out at half past 9 o'clock at night, and I do not return until between 2 and 3 o'clock in the morning. That is done after my office hours. I am waiting on the Commissioners all day. Then I have to attend every fire that takes place in the city, which my predecessors never had to do. That is in pursuance of an Order written by the late Sir Henry Lake requesting me to attend. I often come in off my rounds at 3 o'clock in the morning, and I would not be half-an-hour in bed when I would be called up to a fire. That repeatedly occurred from time to time.

2569. What do you propose as to your salary?—I leave my case in your hands. You can deal with me as you think fit.

2570. You are aware that in London the superintendents, of whom there are twenty-three, get from 300*l.*, rising by 10*l.* a-year to 400*l.*?—Yes.

Chief Superintendent Mallon.

2d Sept., 1882.

2871. They receive no allowance except 10*l.* a-year for uniform, so that your pay, including your allowances, is the same—in fact, better—than the pay of a superintendent in London. Are you aware of that?—I am, Sir.

2872. What increase would you propose should be made to the pay of the chief superintendent in Dublin?—Well, I have 450*l.* a-year, pay and allowances, for which I go through a great deal of duty that my predecessors never had to perform. I think from my position here that I should be equal to the district superintendents in London.

2873. Do you mean in point of pay?—Mr. Walker joined the service the same year as I did, and he has 500*l.* a-year, I understand, now.

2874. Have you anything further to say in reference to your own case?—I have nothing further to say about myself. I leave my position in your hands, after forty-five years' service now on the 1st December. There is not a man in the service who joined the service at 200 strong but myself, for some years past.

2875. I should wish you to distinguish between your own individual case, of which we are thoroughly aware—and your long and your able service—and in fixing the salary we should wish your opinion as to what a man should get who would hold your office to-morrow, suppose you vacated it. What would be a proper salary for the chief superintendent, putting aside your own case?—It is a rather nice point for me to give an opinion upon, for those who would come after me would turn round and say that I was not very favourably disposed towards them.

2876. At all events, you consider that the present salary is rather low for the office?—Yes, it is.

2877. And that there ought to be a better salary, no matter who fills it?—Yes.

2878. What was the chief superintendent's salary before 1878?—[illegible] 10s. and allowances.

2879. *Chairman.*—Have you anything else to say on behalf of the force?—Well, I have not, Sir. Nothing else, I think.

2880. *Mr. Holmes.*—Do you think that the present pay, taking it all round, is fairly adequate?—The pay is very fair, but there is 1s. 6d. a-week stopped on the pay apart from the men.

2881. For what?—For lodging and fuel, for those living in barracks.

2882. And in your opinion ought that deduction to be discontinued?—Yes, I think it ought. I think the men should receive the full amount on the sheet.

2883. But if the unmarried man was to receive the full amount of his pay, and get, in addition to that, lodging and firing gratis, would you not be putting the unmarried man on an unfair footing if you charged the married men even a moderate amount for the accommodation to be given in those buildings of which you have been speaking?—Yes, that would be so.

2884. Are you aware that in London the police pay—I think it is 1s. a-week—single men pay 1s. a week for accommodation similar to that which the men get here?—Yes; but the men pay 1s. 6d. here.

2885. *Mr Morris.*—I should now like to ask you one or two questions as regards the police force generally. Are you aware whether or not there is an opinion in Dublin—rightly or wrongly—amongst a considerable body of inhabitants, that the police in Dublin are not quite as active in the detection of crime as they might be?—Well, Sir; I could not agree with that opinion. I think there is not a body of police in the British Empire more active in the discharge of their duty in detecting crime, and every other offence—disorderly conduct and drunkenness, and the like—than the Dublin metropolitan police are.

2886. *Mr. Holmes.*—Mr. Superintendent Corr, many of the witnesses whom we have already examined, have complained to us that the fines are very excessive, and that they are levied without sufficient inquiry, and that the men are not afforded an opportunity of vindicating their conduct or of answering the charges which have been brought against them. Have you any objection to give us your opinion on that matter?—Well, I will tell you, Sir, that there is no case that goes before the Commissioners that is not properly investigated by Colonel Connolly, who decides all these cases, unless, in his absence, the Chief Commissioner [illegible] very seldom. Every case that is brought forward gets a thorough investigation. Anything that the constable has to say in his defence is heard patiently, and I never knew an instance in which the system was the same, and I always attend the Board when these investigations take place. And, as regards heavy fines, I should tell you that there were a great many young men in the service who were addicted to drink, and there was nothing to put it down with the exception of heavy fines or dismissals. When you see a man with ten or twelve drunken reports against him, I think it is high time to get rid of him. That has been the cause of the infliction of heavy fines.

2887. *Mr. Morris.*—But what some of the witnesses who have been before us have complained of is that constable 141 B, or a man with any other number, is fined without the Commissioner requiring the presence of the accuser to substantiate the charge?—I never knew of an instance of the kind.

2888. What they say is that when a civilian writes a complaint to the Commissioner of Police, the man complained of is brought up before the Commissioner, and that he is fined without any further evidence than the hearing of his explanation and the reading of the civilian's letter?—I never knew an instance of the kind; not in my memory.

2889. *Mr. Holmes.*—What is the amount of the fine that is usually inflicted for the first offence of drunkenness?—For the first offence of drunkenness—if the constable is a well-conducted man—he gets a "stand over"—he is not fined at all. It is put in the defaulters' book as "stand over." While if he is brought up again, for drunkenness, that would appear as a second case against him, and then he would be fined perhaps 1*l.* or 10s.

2890. For the second case a fine of 20s.?—Well, generally 1*l.*

2891. Don't you think that a fine of 1*l.* for a second offence of drunkenness is a very severe fine?—Well, that is owing to the character of the man. Some of those young men have a great many reports for neglect of duty, &c.

2892. Don't you think that a moderate fine, accompanied by a reprimand and an admonition would accomplish the same purpose, or, perhaps, would be even more effectual in deterring men from offending again?—Well, it might, Sir, but I think the Commissioners give every case proper consideration.

2893. *Chairman.*—Is there any limit fixed to their degradation or reduction?—No, Sir. If a man is reduced he gets on again in regular rotation, perhaps, by examination.

2894. Do any of the reductions last for years?—Yes, in some instances.

2895. *Mr. Morris.*—I will put you a case. Suppose a man to be an acting sergeant, and that he is reduced for some offence to the position of a constable—I suppose that man's character to be thoroughly good for three years, and that there are no black marks against him of any kind during those three years—is he ever put back then to be an acting sergeant without having to undergo another examination, or has he to work up just the same as if he had never been promoted?—Yes; he would have to work up again.

2896. *Chairman.*—He is not reinstated in his former rank?—No.

2897. *Mr. Morris.*—And suppose a constable is reduced from being a first-class constable to being a second-class constable for any offence, is he left a second-class constable for the rest of his life unless he works up in the ordinary way?—Yes, unless he works up in the ordinary way.

2898. Do you think it would be an improvement in the force, and for the benefit of the force, and for the benefit of the men, supposing there was a rule that when a first-class constable was reduced, say for three years, or two years, or one year, and then if there was no mark against his character in the meantime, that he should go as a matter of course back again into the position of a first-class constable?—Yes; that would be an improvement.

7899. And for the benefit of the force?—Yes; it would give encouragement to those men who are reduced.

7900. Don't you think it would be an encouragement to a man to conduct himself well?—Yes, certainly.

7901. And do you think that the present system may sometimes lead to men losing heart and becoming more or less reckless?—Often, it does, for a man must go through the same steps as if he had never been reduced.

7902. And do you think it would be an improvement to the force or an encouragement to the men if a man was reduced from first to second or third-class constable, that after a given time, say one, two, or three years, with good conduct, he should go back to his former position—to be reinstated?—It would be a great encouragement after his reduction; it would be a great encouragement to his future conduct, and I would recommend the same to all ranks.

7903. *Chairman.*—As a matter of fact, don't these fines and reductions go in reducing the amount of a man's pension?—No.

7904. They do not?—No.

7905. Nor are they taken into account in regulating his pension?—No, not that I am aware of.

7906. *Mr. Holmes.*—They have never been taken into account?—In reference to the force as regards the pension, the position is left in the Commissioner's hands to recommend.

7907. *Chairman.*—Do what they call black marks—fines and reductions—do they operate in reducing a man's pension?—No, they do not. There are no black marks kept with us at all. None. Of course all reports are recorded and a reduction will tell against a man as regards his pay.

7908. *Mr. Morris.*—Suppose a man twenty years in the service as a first-class constable, never having reached a higher grade, and that during that twenty years that man has been frequently fined for offences; and suppose another man twenty years in the service—a man of the same service and of the same grade, a first-class constable, with no mark against him during that twenty years—is there any difference made in the pension that is given to these two men?—That lies with the Commissioner; that is entirely with the Commissioner.

7909. Does the Commissioner take these black marks or fines into account?—I think you had better ask him to answer that question.

7910. However, the exercise of discretion in such a matter as that rests with the Commissioner?—Yes. There is a Board of Superintendents always held on these pension papers, and they recommend as to the officer or constable, as the case may be, whether he served "with diligence and fidelity" during the period of his service, or did not.

7911. And I suppose naturally the Commissioner who has to sign that paper feels some hesitation in signing it if a man has not served with diligence and fidelity?—He has, of course.

7912. If the two men whom I have alluded to are entitled to the same pension after twenty years' service, do you think it would be for the good of the police force, for the good of the service, and for the benefit of the State, that a man's fine should be sufficient punishment, and that when he is retiring at the end of twenty years, having been punished perhaps ten years before that for being drunk, that punishment should not militate against him in reducing his pension?—Well, then there would be no inducement held out for the possession of an exemplary character in the service. If I am an exemplary character in the service, and if an unfortunate brother constable retires on the same pension, of what use is my character to me?

7913. Do not you think there is sufficient advantage in the fact that the man is punished at the time for the offence, whereas the exemplary character is not punished at all?—He is not, because he is not brought forward.

7914. But that is his benefit?—That is his benefit, of course.

7915. And there is a difference as that?—Of course there is, and the late Mr. O'Farrell, and the late Sir Henry Lake, always held that where one man is an exemplary character and retiring from the service, and another man retiring is of an indifferent character, that the bad-natured man should not be viewed in the same light as regards his pension.

Chief Superintendent Richard Corr.

2d Sept., 1882.

7916. And you can state of your own knowledge that these were the opinions of Mr. O'Farrell and Colonel Lake?—Yes, I can.

7917. *Mr. Holmes.*—Looking through the various ranks and the rates of pay, I see that there is a wide difference between the pay of acting inspectors and that of the third class of inspectors. I see that the pay of an acting inspector is 83*l.* 17*s.* 6*d.*, while the pay of a third-class inspector is 137*l.*, and he receives in addition an allowance of 20*l.* Now, may I ask you are not the duties of an acting inspector precisely the same as those of the inspector?—Precisely.

7918. Are they in every way as responsible?—In every way as responsible. There is no rank in the service that is more under paid than that of the acting inspector's. These officers are promoted according to their place on the seniority list, and according to the examination they are placed on that list. They are not sufficiently paid at all, taking into consideration the amount of the third-class inspector's pay, and his lodging money. He gets 6*d.* a-year only for uniform.

7919. Are you aware that, including their allowances, the third class inspectors in Dublin are considerably more highly paid than the corresponding third class in London?—I am not aware of that.

7920. Are you aware that in London there is no class of acting inspectors?—No.

7921. Is there any reason why there should be acting inspectors in Dublin?—In the case of the inspector and the acting inspector, the inspector goes out his rounds and leaves the acting inspector in the office to discharge the same duties as he has to discharge; he comes in, and then goes for an hour to dinner. On his return the acting inspector goes out on his rounds, and he has the same duties to perform and the same responsibilities as the inspector. You see there is very little difference between the pay of the rank of sergeant and that of acting inspector.

7922. *Chairman.*—All the duties and responsibilities of the acting inspector are equal to those of the inspectors?—Certainly, in every respect, Sir.

7923. *Mr. Holmes.*—Putting aside, however, for a moment the case of the acting inspectors, is it your opinion that all the other ranks are fairly well paid under the scale laid down in 1873?—Well, I think there ought to be a little improvement made as regards their pay.

7924. Are you aware that the second and third-class constables in Dublin are better paid than the corresponding ranks in London?—No, I am not aware of that; and as regards the lodging money for inspectors of 20*l.* a-year, I may mention that these officers get no kind of respectable house under 40*l.* a-year.

7925. But are you aware, as I have told you, that the third class inspectors here are much better paid than the corresponding classes in London, and if that is the case, as you may be assured it is, do not you think it would be somewhat unreasonable to increase their present pay?—If they are better paid than the third-class inspectors in London I think it would be unreasonable for the inspectors here to expect more than these officers in London have. I am quite clear on that.

7926. As you were not aware of the rates of pay given to the third class inspectors in London, I may mention to you that whereas the third class inspectors in Dublin receive 137*l.* a-year as pay, and 70*l.* in allowances, the third class of inspectors in London receives the sum of only 117*l.* 0*s.* 0*d.* as pay, with no allowances. In other words, the third-class inspector in Dublin receives 40*l.* a-year more than the third class inspector in London. Now that you are aware of that, do you think that it would be reasonable to increase the pay of the third-class inspectors here?—I do not think it would. I think they cannot expect it at all events.

U

Thirteenth Day.—27th September, 1882.

Present:

Mr. G. W. O'Donnell, Mr. George Morris, D.L., and Mr. R. W. A. Holmes.

Inspector James Smith, G (Detective) Division, Dublin Metropolitan Police, examined.

(Also present: Acting Inspector Andrew Morrow (twenty-two years' service); Sergeant James Murphy (eighteen years' service); Acting Sergeant Patrick Gorman (eighteen years' and a-half service); First-class Constable John Dowd (fifteen years' service); and Constable Michael M'Nally (nine years' service)—all of the G (Detective) Division, Dublin Metropolitan Police.)

Inspector James Smith.

27 Sept., 1882.

2928. *Chairman.*—What is your name?—James Smith.

2929. Your position is that of Inspector of the Detective Department?—Yes, Sir.

2930. How long have you been in your present office?—Since March 1882.

2931. How long have you been in the force?—Nineteen years.

2932. How long have you been in the detective department?—Since January 1865—for nearly seventeen years.

2933. Be good enough to state what you desire to bring under the notice of the Committee—dealing with the several heads of your grievance in what you consider to be the order of their importance?—We have asked in our Memorial for an increase of pay. We ask to be put upon a scale proportionate to the scale of the corresponding branch in London—the Scotland Yard officers. We are the only branch in the Dublin police corresponding to the Scotland Yard men. Their pay stands to ours as 69 is to 33. It is more than double.

2934. You seek to be placed on an equality with the London detective force?—Not exactly; we will allow for the fact of their being employed in the capital of the world, we might say; but we think our pay is not in proportion, or has not reached the point it ought to reach, as compared with theirs. We think we should not be left with pay which is less than half theirs. Theirs on an average is 196*l.* a-year, and ours on an average is only 93*l.* They have all inspectors, and we have only one inspector.

2935. *Mr. Holmes.*—When you say the average pay of the London detectives is 196*l.* a-year, do you include the salary of the Chief Superintendent?—We do, Sir, and we include the salary of ours of his corresponding rank here—Mr. Superintendent Mallon.

2936. What increase do you seek?—Well, we don't name any sum, but we think we ought to be paid in proportion to the same service in London.

2937. It is simply your wish to be placed on an approximate footing with the London men?—Yes, on an approximate footing with the Scotland Yard force.

2938. *Mr. Morris.*—Will you take each rank of the London detective branch and mention the salary, and also mention the salary of the corresponding rank here, and then suggest what proportion your pay should bear to the pay of the London force of detectives?—The Chief Superintendent in London—if my Return is correct—receives a minimum pay of 150*l.*

2939. Beginning at 150*l.*, he rises by 10*l.* annually to 250*l.*?—Yes. I believe he is at present drawing his maximum pay; and the pay of the officer in the corresponding rank here is only 250*l.*

2940. *Mr. Holmes.*—That is Superintendent Mallon?—Yes. There are of chief inspectors three, who draw each a maximum of 350*l.* There is only one in the corresponding rank here—the Inspector of the Detective Department—and his pay is 180*l.*, just about half. In reference to the other inspectors of the London detective force, we have no corresponding grade here to them; but I take it that the men who do the same duty—the acting inspectors with us—should correspond in pay, or get an approximate pay. The London men of that class of inspectors draw a minimum pay—in fact, it commences at the maximum; the pay is 150*l.* a-year.

2941. There is one thing I would point out to you. There is only one inspector at the salary you have just named. I would not refer to him. I would rather take the second-class inspectors in London, of whom there are seventeen, and whose pay begins at 150*l.*, and rises by 5*l.* to 180*l.*?—Yes, Sir. That is the pay of a first-class inspector here, while the corresponding grade of men doing similar duty—the acting inspectors—only receive 93*l.*, 1*s.* 6*d.* exactly, as compared with the 150*l.* of the men in London.

2942. Then are the acting inspectors of the detective force here better paid than the acting inspectors of the other force in Dublin?—They have 1*s.* 6*d.* a-week more. They receive 2*l.* 0*s.* 7*d.*, together with allowances, weekly. Outside they receive 1*l.* 16*s.* 9*d.*

2943. Proceed with your comparison now. You have stated the salaries of the acting inspectors?—They have in London no corresponding grade to our acting inspectors.

2944. They have sergeants?—But they are local grades.

2945. No, in the Criminal Investigation Department, according to the Return which I have before me, there are first, second, and third class sergeants.—I think you will find that they are local men working in union with other men that belong to other divisions; and they have men taking charge of the office at night. They are local sergeants, and some of them are third-class inspectors.

2946. Then you are aware that there are no sergeants in the detective branch proper in London; you have ascertained that as a fact?—Yes, from a Return in which I have only twenty-six in the detective department proper, and all those are inspectors.

Inspector James Smith.

27 Sept., 1882.

2247. From what source have you got that Return?—From a printed form supplied to me by the Chief Commissioner, and I have copied it, and I also hold it in my hand in print.

2248. That is the Return that was handed in by Mr. Superintendent Walker, of the London metropolitan police?—Yes.

2249. I think that without explanation from some officer in London we cannot adopt this Return from which you have quoted as giving the necessary information to us of the state of the detective branch in London?—I understand it is taken from properly authenticated documents.

2250. Kindly proceed with your comparison. You may assume that we will make inquiries as to the numbers, ranks, and pay of the detective branch in London before we conclude our Report, and compare them with yours?—Yes. Well, even assuming that there are lower grades than that of inspector, the corresponding grades here are not paid in proportion. I have quoted the pay of the superior ranks and the pay of the corresponding ranks of the Dublin force, and I have shown that here the pay is far smaller; in fact, less than half.

2251. Taking the class of constables, how does the pay of the Dublin men compare with the pay of the London men?—I think there are no constables in the detective department in London, Sir. I know that very recently we had an inspector over here, and he had a local inspector with him who had only three years' service in the force, and the local man was working in union with the other. These local men would compare with the men appointed on special duty by the other outside superintendents here to act with our men, but they would not compare with our men, with the detective men proper here. We are asking to be put on a fair footing, as compared with the detectives proper in London—with the Scotland Yard men, because the duty deputed to us corresponds exactly with the duties deputed to them, except in this, that ours are far more difficult.

2252. If there are no sergeants or constables in the detective branch proper—in the branch with which you wish to compare yourselves—how do you propose to compare the pay of the constables and sergeants here?—We ask, Sir, to have some of our men of inferior grades promoted, because we say that one inspector is not quite sufficient.

2253. You want to have more inspectors for the detective branch here, and you are ready to give your reasons for that by-and-by?—Yes.

2254. *Mr. Morris.*—What is the entire strength of your department?—Forty-four men, including the superintendent and inspector; forty-two men, and a superintendent and an inspector.

2255. *Mr. Holmes.*—Will you now give us the numbers of the various ranks?—There is 1 superintendent, 1 inspector, 13 acting inspectors, 1 sergeant, 6 acting sergeants, and 19 constables.

2256. Do you consider that nineteen constables require a larger force of officers than you have enumerated?—They do, Sir, in this particular department, because each man has to do the work of an officer outside. He has to do, in fact, more critical work than is done in the station by an officer. A constable is sent out on a most critical inquiry—perhaps an inquiry from England or America, or elsewhere.

2257. Then, in point of fact, you would like to have the whole force composed of officers?—Yes; officers of certain grades, of course. We do not want to make an exorbitant demand, but, as I have said, we wish to have something approximate to what is in London. The reason for asking that is that, firstly, our pay is out of proportion to the London pay; and, secondly, the facilities in London given to the men doing duty are obstacles here.

2258. *Mr. Morris.*—Let me call your attention to the fact, that the proportion of officers to men in your force is as twenty-five is to nineteen?—Yes, that that is so in our department; but there is no man next to us who has not either peculiar fitness, or fitness combined with experience of police duty. Out of the forty-four at present, we have thirty-two who are men of over fifteen years' service; and then all these men, or nearly all, would hold a higher grade outside the detective department.

2259. *Mr. Holmes.*—That is to say, if they had not joined the detective branch, but had remained in the general force, they would have attained a higher rank, and therefore higher pay, than they are in receipt of now in their present position?—They would.

2260. Do not you think that that is more an argument for raising their pay than for making more officers than a proportion of twenty-five to nineteen?—If you will allow me, Sir, I will show you the necessity for having more officers, because I, for one, am supposed to be at all times in the detective office. Persons coming in to make inquiries—critical or private and confidential inquiries—will always wish to communicate with the inspector. It cannot naturally be expected that I can be always there, and, if I am not there, they will not wish to confer with any one else. The superintendent cannot be always on the spot, and if the superintendent is absent I have to act for him. There is no inspector then, so that I have to act either in duplicate, or the duties are done defectively. The duties are, too, very important. We have often to do duties in connection with the seizure of arms which can only be done, according to law, by an inspector. When that duty has to be done by our department, it has to be sent to a divisional inspector, who is not so conversant with the matter; and I need hardly say that the fact of a man making an inquiry, or doing political or confidential duties—the fact of such a man having the rank of an inspector is a great facility to the proper performance of that duty, because people will tell an inspector more than they will tell a constable.

2261. *Chairman.*—The law requires that certain duties in connection with the seizure of arms shall be done by an inspector?—Yes.

2262. And then, you having only one inspector, an outsider must be called in?—Yes.

2263. *Mr. Holmes.*—When you say "the law," to what Act do you refer?—I refer to the present Arms Act. All confidential and important duties under it are to be done by an inspector, and there is no inspector in the place to do them. I would desire to say that there are very many confidential duties that require to be performed in our department by the inspector only. He is very frequently absent, and then there is no inspector there to do those important duties.

2264. *Chairman.*—Then, as I take it, as regards the public convenience and the public service, an additional inspector or inspectors would be required?—Yes; an additional inspector or inspectors would be required to perform the duty properly.

2265. *Mr. Holmes.*—Do you propose to appoint more than one additional inspector?—We do, Sir.

2266. How many?—We would look for four, at least, for the detective department alone; and I can show you afterwards that the carriage department should be conducted by an inspector.

2267. Is the carriage department part of the detective work?—Yes; it is a branch of the detective department.

2268. *Mr. Morris.*—When you mention the "carriage" department, do you also refer to the work in relation to the registration of cabs and cars?—Yes; that is what we call the carriage department—the office having the supervision of all the thousands of vehicles. I may tell you that another reason why we require an additional inspector is that, at present, I cannot get my proper vacation. I have not had one vacation this past twelve months but last Sunday. The duties are more critical and responsible than those of a station inspector outside. The latter are only routine and formal. And our duties are not confined to particular hours; we must be always there, night and day, and very frequently are called in the middle of the night, in reference to telegrams

Inspector John Smith.

17 Sept., 1882.

in cypher, which no one can read, or could have the facilities for reading. And the inspector in our department requires a knowledge of all the ports in the kingdom, and to have intelligence to communicate with them.

2969. *Mr. Holmes.*—I presume the detective force generally have no definite hours of duty like the other men?—They have not, Sir. We wished to mention that in asking for extra pay.

2970. *Chairman.*—You must be always on duty in fact?—You must be always available.

2971. *Mr. Holmes.*—As I understand you, you propose that there should be four inspectors instead of one?—Yes.

2972. What proposition have you to make with regard to the acting inspectors?—To further urge our claim for additional inspectors I think I could mention other matters to show that even compared with other divisions our department requires other inspectors—requires an additional number of inspectors. Now, there is an inspector in charge of a store where he has nothing to do but to put in figures, which is done by a clerk; there is an inspector in the carriage department whose duties are merely departmental, and there is an inspector for the troop, and surely his duties are not so responsible as the duties of the carriage department. There is an inspector for the veterinary department at the North Wall, where the supervision is conducted by constables, and there is an inspector for the mere totting up of statistics—of tables which are furnished and completed from other departments. We have an officer having charge of the carriage department, in which is carried on the licensing of 2,000 and upwards of vehicles, and more than that number of men, and the proper registration of those should be carried on by an officer whose rank should be at least that of an inspector.

2973. He is now, I presume, an acting inspector?—He is only a sergeant.

2974. *Chairman.*—Would you transfer the useless inspectors, as you would call them, to your department?—No, Sir; we would rather expect or wish that the officer who knows the business and fills the position at present in the junior rank should be promoted.

2975. *Mr. Holmes.*—Now, take the case which you have just mentioned. You say that the head of the carriage department is a sergeant. Would you propose that he should be made an inspector, or would you give the post to one of the present acting inspectors, of whom there are thirteen?—We would propose that the person holding the position should be an inspector, and that therefore the person holding it at present should be appointed an inspector.

2976. Then you would wish to put a man who holds only the rank of sergeant over the heads of thirteen acting inspectors?—But we would expect that out of the thirteen acting inspectors there would be made four inspectors.

2977. In addition to having the sergeant made an inspector?—Yes.

2978. Then you would have six inspectors, including yourself?—Yes, Sir; we would expect that the inspector having charge of the department in the absence of the superintendent would be the chief inspector, and that he should have four under him to take charge of criminal and important duties outside and inside the office.

2979. If I understand you, you wish, in addition to the four under him, another inspector to be in charge of the carriage department?—Yes.

2980. So that, including the chief inspector, there would be six inspectors, there being five under him?—Yes, six entirely.

2981. Other witnesses have told us—in fact, Superintendent Carr told us yesterday, that the duties of the acting inspectors throughout the service are precisely the same as those of the inspectors, and altogether as responsible, but I presume from your statement that the duties of the acting inspectors of the detective branch are not as responsible as yours, or as onerous?—Well, they are not, Sir, at present. Of course, they do not take charge of the office, except two members of the department who take charge in conjunction with me in turn every alternate week; but they take part in the performance of very critical duties and enquiries in very important criminal matters through the city. They are deputed to follow up very critical cases, and of course they must be intelligent men, and men of long-standing in the service. In fact, there are some of those longer in the service than a great many inspectors, and passed examinations with men who are long since inspectors outside. I may tell you that at present out of thirteen acting inspectors—I am satisfied that there are only twelve now, there being a vacancy—there are eight of them who passed examinations before superiors now who are now inspectors outside, and who passed at those examinations.

2982. That is when those acting inspectors belonged to the general force?—Yes, when they were outside.

2983. *Chairman.*—But then they made their own election to join the detective department rather than remain in the ordinary force?—Some of them were sent for and brought into the department without any selection on their part—for instance, the present Acting Inspector Morrow, and he has a brother in the outside force who is an inspector.

2984. Have you anything further to add on that head?—Well, no, Sir, I think nothing else.

2985. Kindly deal now with the case of the sergeants?—The same applies to the sergeants. The sergeants have to take their turn. Of course, promotion is very slow at present in our department.

2986. *Mr. Holmes.*—How are men selected for the detective branch?—They are selected by the superintendent consulting other superintendents as to the most steady men they have.

2987. Is it necessary that a constable should be a certain time in the service before he is selected, and is it customary that he should have attained a certain class?—Well, it is not exactly necessary now, because if a man of two or three years' service is met with who is considered a smart likely man to turn out a good detective—an intelligent man—he is taken on, but he has to undergo a course of training, and if he does not turn out what was expected he is sent back to his division.

2988. Have you done with the question of pay now?—Yes, Sir.

2989. Well, what is the next subject?—We ask for extra pay next, Sir.

2990. When you say "extra pay," do you refer to the three months' gratuity given to the Royal Irish Constabulary?—Yes, Sir; that is included in the extra pay for extra duty actually performed, except when it is only inconsiderable and too small; but where a man has undergone a good deal of hardship over his regular time we think he should be paid for it. For instance, if a man is out at night after serving the whole day before, as is generally the case, we think he should receive some consideration for it.

2991. *Chairman.*—Is not your application for additional pay founded upon the number and importance of your duties?—Oh, yes, Sir.

2992. Assuming that you got that additional pay, and are put in a better position, do you think you have any right to ask for extra pay for extra work?—I don't think the claim for extra pay for extra work would be pressed if our general pay was increased.

2993. And who is to be the judge of the extra work except the superintendent who sends the men out on the extra duty?—We don't want it for every one.

2994. *Mr. Morris.*—Do you think that the detective force should be paid by the hour during the time they are sent on extra duty?—I think they are paid elsewhere for extra duty. Perhaps our reasons for asking for extra pay would rather support our claim for an increase of pay, if you allow us to put them forward in that view.

2995. Certainly?—We do not care whether it is

Inspector James Smith.

27 Sept., 1882.

put in as extra pay or any other pay. If we are given the London scale of pay, or approximate to it, we will be satisfied. We do not like to be exorbitant in our demand; we only want what is reasonable; but our duties are certainly very weighty, and we are very often engaged on such arduous work that we are not at times even allowed the opportunity of getting a meal. We are obliged to turn out, and perhaps men are sent to a distant part of the country, and they may have to go there and remain perhaps without an opportunity of changing their clothes.

2996. What the Chairman meant to ask you by the question he put to you was this. You put forward your demand for better pay than the corresponding ranks of the force, on the ground that your duties are more important. Well, assuming that you do get that additional pay, have you any right to ask for extra pay for extra duty when you are already better paid than the corresponding ranks. Do you understand?—Yes, I do, Sir; but we thought that our request for extra pay was for our ordinary duty alone; it being so important that we thought we were entitled to it.

2997. Could you by any possibility, as detective men, draw the line between "ordinary" duty and "extraordinary" duty? Don't you see yourself, as a member of that body, that from the very fact of yours being a detective force, you will find it impossible to draw the line between what is your "ordinary" and what is your "extraordinary" duty? My idea is, that the very business of a detective officer is nearly always on "extraordinary" duty?—Yes, Sir; it must be at all times. We must be ready to turn out at a moment's notice.

2998. I think that is a very good ground to put forward for higher pay; but I do not think it is a ground for asking for extra pay for extra duty?—The reasons, doubtless, do more properly apply to an application for an increase of the ordinary pay, and I think we may waive the application for extra pay if we are given a reasonable increase of pay.

2999. *Chairman.*—If you have dealt sufficiently with that subject, would you pass on to the next topic of your evidence?—Well, in reference to our expenses; we often incur expenses in the performance of our duties that are never repaid, and that cannot be included in any of the accounts of the department. We think we should receive some consideration when those circumstances arise. We would also ask for an increased allowance for plain clothes.

3000. *Mr. Holmes.*—What are your allowances at present, might I ask?—2s. 7d. a-week for plain clothes; the superintendent and inspector nothing, except an allowance for uniform which they must get, although they do not wear it; 8s. for gloves, and 7d. for boots.

3001. *Mr. Morris.*—Well, what do you suggest?—We ask to be put on the pay, and to be given the allowances that the men have who are in a position corresponding to ours in London.

3002. How much have they?—1s. a-day, and superintendents and inspectors, 15l. a-year.

3003. The constables have more than the officers under that head?—They have. I think that that is given in lieu of lodgings. I don't know why; we thought that.

3004. You suggest that all classes below that of inspector should receive 1s. a-day?—Yes, we do.

3005. And that the inspector should receive what?—15l. a-year; what they have in London. We have to dress as well. The men of the detective department must dress respectably, and they cannot appear always in the same dress; in fact, if they did, they would be conspicuous by their appearance. They have to attend meetings, races, bazaars, balls, flower shows, regattas, and other places of public amusement, and, of course, they must appear at those places suitably dressed. They are required to have portmanteaus ready for journeying at any time, and their outfit must be as costly and equal to a gentleman's.

3006. *Chairman.*—And they must have varied costumes?—Yes, Sir, which must be very costly; and they cannot get the care of a gentleman's, because they have to often wear them in all weathers and for days without taking them off; or, at least, a day and a night often.

3007. What is the next head of your evidence?—We compare unfavourably in the rewards given to our men compared with those given to men in other divisions. We have known men in other divisions to get 10l., 5l., and even 20l. prize rewards for mere duty acts. Very frequently we get flattering remarks from Judges and grand juries, but the commendation amounts to nothing beyond that except 10s. or so.

3008. The rewards given to the outside force are larger than those given to your department?—Much larger, and entirely out of proportion.

3009. What subject do you next wish to bring before the Committee?—Well, I think we have nearly all exhausted, except that relating to the pensions. We don't press much for the pensions, except in this, that we know it would tend very much to pacify the young men if the Act of 1867 could be so amended as to give them a better pension. It is, of course, a great cause of discontent.

3010. *Mr. Holmes.*—Are you aware of what the London scale of pensions for the metropolitan police force is?—Yes, Sir; we believe it to be the same as the 1867 Act here.

3011. No, it is not; it differs somewhat. It is somewhat better. It is the same as your Act of 1867 in from fifteen to twenty years, but from twenty to twenty-five years the increments are by two-fiftieths instead of one-fiftieth, so that the London man is in the same position after twenty-five years' service as the Dublin men are after thirty years' service. Then, from twenty-five to twenty-eight years' service, the increments go on by one-fiftieth, to the maximum rate, namely, two-thirds of the pay?—I think that would satisfy our men.

3012. I don't know whether you are aware that there was a Bill before Parliament last Session for the purpose of applying that scale of pensions to the police force in England and Scotland. That Bill will probably be introduced next Session, and if it passes in that form I suppose the men here could hardly expect that they will be given a better scale of pensions than the scale for England and Scotland?—I don't know, but I think not. I think not. They would not ask anything unreasonable, but we expect it would give great satisfaction to have whatever pension that would be given by Act of Parliament granted without being curtailed or cut down in any way. We know the pensions in the service to have been curtailed very much, and we ourselves have had instances of it in the same way, where men of excellent character retired and their pensions were reduced. I think the Chairman knew two of them—Connell, who was cut 5l. a-year, and Raftery, who was cut 8l., for retiring after losing their health. I may add that Raftery was discharged in consequence of serious injuries received by him while arresting a notorious burglar.

3013. Was the curtailment of their pensions in consequence of their having unfavourable records against them?—Connell was a man of excellent character, and so was Raftery. I never knew a report against them in our department.

3014. *Chairman.*—You think the men would wish to have the full amount of their pension without its being affected by previous black marks or punishments?—Yes, Sir.

3015. *Mr. Morris.*—Upon that subject I wish to ask you one or two questions. Suppose two constables to have served twenty-five years both in the force, and that one constable has a great many records of punishment against him, and that he has been fined several times, and that he has, perhaps, been reduced in grade; and suppose the other constable has never during the twenty-five years had a single black mark or bad mark against him, and has never been degraded, do you think that those two men, upon leaving the force, should retire on the

Sergeant James Smith.

27 Sept., 1882.

same pension?—Yes; if they held the same rank on retirement, because the man fined was punished for his offence, and generally men are very severely punished.

3016. Do you think that when a man is fined and reduced that punishment should be sufficient, provided his conduct is subsequently good, that he should get a clear receipt?—Yes, Sir.

3017. You think the punishment should be sufficient and final?—Yes. Generally speaking, it is sufficient. Generally speaking, it is very heavy.

3018. Do you think that when a man is reduced—say, from the rank of sergeant to that of constable—for some offence, that reduction should be only for a period of, say, three years, and that if his conduct was good during three years—exemplary and good in the force—that man should, as a matter of fact, and without any favour, go back to the position he originally occupied, that he should be, in other words, reinstated?—Well, that more applies to the divisions outside than to us; but still we are of opinion that he should be reinstated, because reduction for a year, or two or three years, would be a considerable punishment.

3019. Do you think it would be conducive to the good discipline of the force to have that rule, and that it would be a kind of encouragement to men to work back again; whereas if degraded altogether, and having no chance, they might become reckless?—I think it would give satisfaction, Sir.

3020. But do you think it would work for the benefit of the force; which way do you think it would work. Do you think it would work more for the benefit of the force?—I could not be prepared to speak on that point, because we have no experience of it. In our division it seldom or ever occurs.

3021. No experience of what?—No experience of reductions in our department; but as to how men get on after reduction, I can say that I know myself a few men serving outside in other divisions who were reduced, and still remain reduced as constables, and I know their character to be excellent since they were reduced, and the offences of which they were accused were very doubtful.

3022. How long have they been reduced?—I know some of them have been reduced.

3023. *Chairman.*—For trivial offences?—Yes; for some offences on the complaint of a civilian, who may be is not sufficiently corroborated; and it is the belief of the service that many of the offences are not so aggravated as to entitle the offenders to the punishment they receive. I may mention that this applies more to discipline, which was spoken of more by the other men. An offence that is considered to be rather severely punished is going into a public-house off duty. I think that the men reduced do often turn out exemplary characters, and it is a pity to have them reduced for the remainder of their service, because they are not only punished during their service, but they are punished for life in their pensions.

3024. *Mr. Holmes.*—And I suppose such punishment very often makes a man become reckless?—Well, it does, Sir; they despair.

3025. Taking into account the general severity of the punishments, you think it would be quite sufficient by itself, without affecting the pension?—I think so, Sir. The punishment during the reduction is sufficient, without affecting the pension; what they have lost while they remained reduced should be sufficient.

3026. And then when a man is reinstated you would have all punishments wiped away, and permit him to start with a clean sheet?—Yes, I would, Sir.

3027. *Chairman.*—Is there any other subject in relation to which you wish to give evidence?—We would ask to be allowed to retire at twenty-five years' service, especially in our department this applies, and that the retirement should be compulsory after thirty years.

3028. Voluntary at twenty-five and compulsory at thirty?—Yes. In our department the vigorous campaign that we must perform for twenty-five years must necessarily impair a man's health and mind too, as is frequently the case, fighting against odds after thieves. It would also prevent the superior posts being kept for life and for many years by inactive and inefficient men, as is the case, and those posts we would expect should be left compensatably to the men best fitted for them.

3029. It would act as an incentive to promotion?—Yes, to the higher grades; because when a higher grade is reached, the person who has been fortunate enough to attain to it will remain there for life if he is not compelled to retire, and his duties are very frequently performed by those under him.

3030. But would you compel all ranks, and even the ranks of officers, to retire after thirty years' service?—Yes, Sir; it is the officers that we would expect should be compelled to retire. Of course, it would apply to all who retained important posts, to the higher officers, because great dissatisfaction is occasioned when such posts are retained by inactive men. Of course, as a matter of fact, those posts cannot be attained to while they are held by ineffective men, and, as is generally the case, the younger officers are naturally more effective and more active men. When in that way posts in the higher grades are kept blocked by ineffective men it creates dissatisfaction.

3031. *Mr. Holmes.*—But take the case of a man who joined the force at 18 years of age, he would be only 48 after thirty years' service, and he might be a strong, hale man, with a great deal more work in him; would it not be hard to compel such a man to retire?—It might in any other position, but in the Dublin metropolitan police force I don't think it would. The doctor of the service gives it as his opinion that a man is more or less injured after seven years' service; on oath he said so before the Commission. His duties call him to the worst portions of the city, especially in our department, to the haunts of thieves in the worst parts of the city frequently, and often with much fatigue and abuse as well, physically.

3032. Do you think that the force generally would approve of any such hard-and-fast rule as that all men should retire compulsorily after thirty years' service?—I am sure the force desire it as a body.

3033. But if they knew that the highest pension that they would get after thirty years' service would be only two-thirds of their pay, do you think they would desire it then?—I think the force in general would. Those holding important positions I suppose would not; but if after thirty years' service they would get as much as they would at forty, I don't see why they should not retire.

3034. But still a man might have a great deal of work in him after thirty years' service—he might be able to work on until he was forty years in the force, and would it not be hard to compel him to retire?—I don't know, I think not, and I think he should be willing to leave the post to some one else better than him.

3035. *Mr. Morris.*—Suppose a man was to get three-fourths of his pay after serving thirty years, and that he would then have the power of retiring if he liked upon three-fourths; but suppose he was to get full pay by remaining—do you think he would lose a fourth of his pay by retiring into idle life—what would you expect the majority of men to do?—The majority of men would.

3036. Would forfeit a fourth of their pay and retire into private life?—Yes; I think that a man having active duty to do would understand that he would not be fit for it. A man having a quiet position would not do that, because I daresay he would wait ever longer.

3037. *Chairman.*—Would you now, if you desire to do so, proceed to the next subject of your evidence?—We have not much to say about discipline at present, but there is one matter we would wish to mention. We know of a few instances where men were punished, or rather men were complained of, by persons who, when they had to swear before a magistrate on those complaints, failed to obtain convictions against the parties or officers complained of; and we think that persons bringing complaints against men in the service before the Commissioners—whether an officer or a civilian—should be obliged to give their evidence on oath.

3038. In all cases?—Yes; in all cases.

3039. Mr. Morris.—And to personally appear to substantiate the charge?—Yes, Sir.

3040. Are there any cases—without mentioning any particular case—are there any cases of your own knowledge in which the Commissioners have decided upon a case without the person making the complaint appearing?—I don't remember of my own knowledge.

Acting Inspector Mercer, examined.

Mr. Morris.—There is no case in the detective force in which the Commissioners have adjudicated upon a complaint made by letter or otherwise, without the person making the complaint appearing to substantiate that complaint?—Yes; I know a case in the detective division. I know a case in which a man went to his bed at 6 o'clock in the morning, unaware that he had committed any offence. At 11 o'clock he was called out of bed and brought before the Commissioners on that report, and reduced. Afterwards, through the influence of the inspector in charge of the division, and other senior officers of the department, that man was allowed off with a fine of 2*l*. That was on the report of an officer in the department, and the case was not stated on oath.

3042. Do you know any case in connection with the detective department—confine yourself to that—in which the Commissioners have fined or reduced an officer of the detective force upon a written or verbal complaint, without the person making the verbal or written complaint appearing before them to substantiate the charge?—There is no case, I believe, on record in which that was done, but there are cases on record where men were reported by their own officers.

3043. I did not at all allude to them. I am alluding to the public?—But what I, Sir, feel strongly on, and many men more with me, is that in the case of a man whose character is liable to be taken away the investigation should be on oath, and that a policeman should not be placed in a less enviable position than the commonest felon outside. When we go to the courts, such as before the Judges, and the Magistrates, and the Recorder to prosecute, the inquiry is always conducted on oath, the policeman or officer must be sworn, and then the Court commands respect. We therefore think that in inquiries before the Commissioner, a policeman should not be placed in a less enviable position than a felon on the street. I would wish it, and I have heard the men discuss it, and I am sure it is also their desire, that a man making a charge against them should do so on oath, the same as is done before the Magistrates, Recorder, and the Judges, and these Courts always command respect.

Inspector Smith, re-examined.

3044. Chairman.—Is there anything else that you wish to add?—The married men would like to have some allowance given to them for lodgings. They understand that it is given in London.

3045. Mr. Holmes.—I was just going to ask you in reference to that. As a matter of fact, it is not given in London; but there are blocks of buildings attached to some of the police-stations in London where married men are accommodated, for which they are required to pay for the accommodation a reasonable rent?—We need not urge it when it is not given to the London men.

3046. Acting Inspector Mercer.—But it comes very hard on the married men serving in Dublin, especially belonging to the detective department, that they should be put to so much expense under the head of lodgings, as they cannot live in the localities they were accustomed to among the humbler people, and they must take more expensive lodgings necessarily.

(Examination of Inspector Smith resumed.)

3047. Chairman.—What additional evidence have you to offer to the Committee?—I have nothing to add except a word on the question of increase of pay. It is publicly known that the people are opposed to us; in fact, by the public speakers we are denounced as the people's enemies, and it is very difficult to perform our duties at present. We have had experience, some of us, of the duties in London. They are only a pleasure there, for they are assisted there by the public, the most respectable people assist them and the humble people assist them, and they can do their business in any house they go into. Of course, the more respectable people and the well-disposed are not against us.

3048. Mr. Morris.—As a matter of fact, I believe the police in Dublin, generally speaking, both the detective and the other branch of the service, get less assistance from the public than in England?—Much less, Sir. It requires great perseverance and intelligence to succeed in a critical case of either an inquiry as to a criminal offence, or the detection of a crime; and although our number seems large as compared with the London force, it is small when divided into its proper posts. We have several departments to carry out. I may mention as a matter of fact, that matters affecting the Commissioner when the Commissioner has left his office, and the superintendent of my division has also left, I have to attend to. I have to receive communications, no matter how confidential, and act upon them in their absence, and, no matter who the chief superintendent is, a great deal of the correspondence in the chief superintendent's office comes to us—is sent over to us. We are responsible, as I said before, for the carriage department, although the carriage registry office is occupied and resided in by one inspector, and the registration is carried on by another inspector, outside our department, and, although we have to pay for the cleaning and coaling, repairing and supplying of that office, it is an officer outside who occupies it.

3049. Mr. Holmes.—How do you mean that you "pay"?—We pay for the cleaning of it, we pay the servant who is attached to our building, and it is in our accounts.

3050. Do you mean that there is a deduction made from your pay for it?—Oh, no, Sir. The superintendent has to keep the accounts, and to apply to the Board of Works for repairs and supplies of furniture,

Inspector [illegible].

27 Sept., 1883.

and such things. In fact, we are responsible for the duties performed in it, although it is occupied by an officer outside; and we are responsible that each licensed owner of vehicles and licensed driver lives in the address for which he is registered, yet we are not allowed possession of the registry, and were not until after the Phoenix Park murders, when the necessity was seen, allowed access to the registry. When there were so many inquiries made in reference to vehicles it was ordered to be left with us each evening.

3051. The authorised list of vehicles?—The registry book in which all the licensed parties are registered. We are also responsible for the licensing of all pawnbrokers, and at present there are fifty-seven in the city, and we have to carry out the Habitual Criminals' Act in Dublin, and there is a very large number of habitual criminals in Dublin: since 1871 there were 8,175 living in the city, and on an average there is always at a time about fifty living in this city. Then we have out of our number two men for staff duty—they are always required; we have two clerks out of our strength, and we have a number of men appointed for special duties—staff duty, for keeping the division supplied with coal, and such things. We have to watch the arrival and departure of boats at the North Wall; there are always two men about at that.

3052. Are not these duties which you have just now mentioned part of the ordinary duties of the detective force?—I think not, compared with the corresponding detective force in London. I don't think they employ men for that purpose.

3053. I allude to what you have just mentioned about the men having to watch the arrival and departure of boats at the North Wall?—Oh, yes, that is.

3054. That is clearly part of the ordinary duties of a detective?—Yes; I did not mention those as being an imposition on the division. I only mentioned them to show that a great many extraneous matters do come to us when the chief superintendent does not belong to the department. Before that the chief superintendent did belong to the department. Official documents coming to the chief superintendent, if they require critical handling—or delicate matters of any kind—they would come to the detective department; in fact, everything of a doubtful meaning or character would be sent to the Superintendent of the Detective Department, and in his absence I have to act. All telegrams come to us, and all communications from abroad come to us.

3055. And is it the case that the chief superintendent was always, until the last appointment, a member of the detective force?—No, Sir; but the chief superintendent before the present was, but his predecessor again was not. But we feel at all times, when the chief superintendent does not belong to us, that we get a great deal of business which, properly speaking, should be transacted by the chief superintendent.

3056. *Mr. Morris.*—Well, now leaving out small matters, and supposing you confine yourself to the three particular grievances—if I may call them so—of which you complain. I suppose you consider that one of these would be that you ought to have received some consideration for your extra work during the last three years?—Yes, Sir.

3057. Another is that the Pension Act of 1867 ought to be amended?—Yes, Sir.

3058. And the third is that the detective force ought to receive somewhat better pay than the ordinary force?—Yes.

3059. *Chairman.*—And more rapid promotion?—Yes.

3060. These are the principal things you complain of?—Yes; in fact, they might be called the three "P's"—increase of pay, extra pay, and promotion. The men have mentioned to me, some of them, that they consider, in reference to the question of promotion, that I did not dwell sufficiently upon the fact of the slowness of promotion in the department; and as an example of that, I may tell the Committee that there are some men in our department now who passed examinations and were acting as clerks in our department before men who are at present inspectors outside. For instance, one of these men, Murphy, acted as a clerk in our department prior to the man who succeeded him, and that man is an inspector outside for some time, because he left our department. Intelligent men coming into our department expect that they will be benefited, but after a time they get dissatisfied on finding that promotion is so slow, and it is not a sufficient inducement to retain intelligent men after they have learned their duties as detective officers.

3061. *Mr. Morris.*—Don't you think, supposing the pay of the detective department was increased, it would meet that case?—It would, Sir, along with promotion. We would expect some more inspectors appointed in the department. Of course, the appointment of additional inspectors will affect the other men, in that it will take from some of the lower grades. Of course, that will create a wholesome current of promotion.

3062. *Mr. Holmes.*—You want an increase of pay and more rapid promotion, by the appointment of additional inspectors?—Yes; we have some very intelligent men in the department who are fifteen years in the service, and yet they are only constables; promotion is so slow with us.

3063. Does it often happen that when a man has joined the detective force he leaves it in consequence of the promotion being so bad?—It does, Sir.

3064. And does he go back to the general force?—He does.

3065. Or does he leave the service?—He goes, as a rule, back to the general force.

3066. Can you give us any instance of that?—We can. We know at present a man in the general force, stationed at Kingstown, named Kennedy, who left that way.

3067. He left your force?—He did, Sir.

3068. What rank did he hold?—That of constable.

3069. And what rank has he now?—He is a constable still, Sir.

3070. *Mr. Morris.*—The proportion of officers in London in the detective department stands as 185 is to 63?—If I am right, all the members of that department are inspectors in the detective department proper, and they have local men along with them.

3071. Of first, second, and third class constables there are 63; of sergeants there are [illegible]; of inspectors there are 15; and of superintendents 1?—Yes, Sir.

3072. That is, 185 officers to 63 men?—But they do not correspond with us. We correspond only with the Scotland Yard men. There are men from local divisions included in the numbers you have named. I think we have now given all our reasons for an increase of pay and for promotion, and I do not think there is anything else that I would wish to add to the evidence I have already given.

3071. And do you wish that case brought forward which occurred before the time of the present Commissioners?—In justice I think it should be brought forward. I cannot see what objection a man making a complaint can have to making it on oath. I know the case of two men who were brought before the Commissioners, and fined on the complaint of their superintendent. These men would not get any hearing in their defence, but afterwards the fines had to be cancelled, for the men took other remedy in the matter. Those fines were remitted in consequence of the steps they took. The superintendent, finding that he could not stand by his conduct after getting the men fined, had to bring the sheet and also the men back again, and they went before the Chief Commissioner, Colonel Lake, the same men, and the pay sheet, and those fines were cancelled.

3073. What was the amount of the fines?—10s.

3074. What is the remedy that you would suggest for that?—The remedy I suggest for that is that any man who makes a complaint against another man should do so on oath, the same as in a Court of Justice.

3077. *Mr. Morris.*—Would you have the inquiry held privately before the Commissioners, or in open court before the public?—Before the Commissioners if they like. I hold that no man has a right to be fined, reduced, or degraded unless the evidence convicting him is on oath. The Commissioners [illegible] much the same as a court. I hold that a great deal of these reports would never occur if they had to be proved on oath. There is a strong feeling also, I wish to add, that promotion in the detective department should be by seniority when qualified.

3078. And you think that is the opinion of the force?—Yes, I can prove it. I am allowed by thirty-four men out of the detective department to give it as their opinion unanimously that promotion in the detective department should be made by seniority.

3079. *Chairman.*—Without examination?—There is no necessity for an examination if a man is proved qualified. It is an understood thing that there is no man in the detective department but is qualified for promotion, and it ought not at the same time to be left to pick and choose.

Acting Inspector Morrow, Sergeant Murphy, Acting Sergeant Graham, First-rate Constable John Dowd, and Constable Michael M'Nelly having each been asked by the Chairman whether they concurred in and whether they wished to add to the evidence given before the Committee by Inspector Smith, replied that they entirely concurred in it and regarded it as amply sufficient, as putting forward their case.

[The Committee then adjourned to Tuesday, the 3rd October, 1882.]

Fourteenth Day.—3rd OCTOBER, 1882.

Present:

Mr. J. W. O'Donnell, Mr. George Morris, D.L., and Mr. R. W. A. Holmes.

Captain J. W. Nott-Bower, Chief Constable of Liverpool, examined.

3080. *Chairman.*—Where do you reside?—At Liverpool; I am chief constable there.

3081. How long have you been in that position?—I have been for a year there. Prior to that I was for three years chief constable at Leeds.

3082. *Mr. Holmes.*—Captain Bower, we have already had before us District Superintendent Walker, of the London metropolitan police, with the view of instituting a comparison between the police system here and the police system in London. But it has since occurred to us that probably a more fitting comparison would be between the police force of a city like Liverpool and the police system here; and on that ground we requested the authorities here to ask the Watch Committee of Liverpool to allow you to attend to give evidence at this inquiry. Well, we would like that you should give us some information upon the following matters—the number and organisation of the police force in Liverpool; from what sources of taxation its cost is maintained; the rates of pay; the rates of pension; the manner in which promotion is regulated, and the manner in which discipline is enforced, and matters of that kind. We would be glad if you would kindly commence by telling us the number and organisation of the force under your control?—The present number of the force is 1,[illegible] men. It is constituted, as you may be aware, under the Municipal Corporations Act, and the responsible body for it are the Watch Committee of the Corporation. They, however, delegate the whole of their powers in matters of discipline to me. I have the selection of candidates for the force, and I have all promotions and appointments to the highest ranks, and all punishments, in fact, discipline generally, in my hands.

3083. When you say that the management of the force is controlled by the Municipal Corporations Act, may I ask you, is that a special Act for Liverpool?—No, it is not.

3084. Then to what Act do you refer?—5 & 6 Wm. IV, cap. 76, as amended last Session.

3085. Can you give us the numbers of the various grades in your force?—If I may commence at the bottom of the force, I may say that we have 1,148 constables, and they are divided into five classes of variable numbers. A constable on joining is appointed as a fourth-class constable, and his pay is 24s. 6d. We have the 6d. specially added in order to meet the superannuation stoppage—for which there is a special vote from the Corporation—so that the man receives his 24s. clear. After one year's service in that class with good conduct a man is promoted to the rank of third-class constable, and he then receives 27s. 10d. a week—the 10d. being the superannuation stoppage. After two years' total service with good conduct, and one year in the third class, a man is promoted to the second-class, and receives 29s. 10d. a week. The rank of first-class constable a man attains after seven years' service.

3086. *Chairman.*—That is seven years from their joining the force?—Yes; the conditions for promotion to the rank are that they must have seven years

Captain J. W. Nott-Bower.

[illegible]

service, and five years of that must be free from any reports for misconduct of a serious nature, and they must be efficient constables in the discharge of their duty. We are very particular about that. A man is not considered to have any claim to go to the first class unless he is reported on by his superintendent as being thoroughly efficient. Then there is one other higher class that we call the merit class.

3087. *Mr. Morris.*—You say seven years' service in the second class?—After seven years' total service.

3088. And after five years without any misconduct he gets promotion to the first class?—Yes.

3089. May I ask you if getting drunk is considered a bar to promotion in the force?—Yes, if within the prescribed period.

3090. If he got drunk within the period of five years that you have mentioned—that would be a bar?—Yes, that would stop his promotion.

3091. *Mr. Holmes.*—One offence of drunkenness would stop his promotion?—Yes, that would stop his promotion. In fact, a first offence of any kind, if it were sufficiently serious to be entered in his conduct-book, would stop a man's promotion. In reference to the merit class, I may mention that it is a class to which I promote men if they have done something peculiarly meritorious, and its peculiar nature and limited extent may be learned from the fact, that out of the whole number of constables in the force there are only eight constables in the merit class. They receive an extra allowance of 1s. 6d. a-week, which brings their total actual pay up to 30s. 6d. They receive 31s. 4d.; but the 10d. is stopped for the superannuation allowance.

3092. I perceive that the number of constables in your force bears a very large proportion to the number of the whole force?—Yes, it does. We have no sergeants.

3093. Will you now kindly give us the numbers in the other grades?—I think that perhaps with regard to the officers I had better begin at the top, with the next officers in rank to myself. There are two chief superintendents, and those two chief superintendents are in charge of four divisions. Each of these takes charge of one "Dock" and one "Town" Division. There are the North Town and the North Dock Divisions, and the South Town and South Dock Divisions. They have each charge of two divisions. One of them receives 300l. a-year, and the other receives 275l. a-year. Then there is another chief superintendent of the detective department. His pay is 300l. a-year.

3094. Have they any allowances?—None of them have. The next highest rate of pay is in the case of the Chief Clerk in my office. He is rated as a police constable, he ranks really as a chief superintendent, but his title is that only of Chief Clerk, and he receives 250l. a-year. The clerk in charge of the accounts gets 225l. a-year. The next in rank is the Superintendent of the River Police. He has charge of an independent division of river police, and his pay is 275l. a-year.

3095. *Chairman.*—Is he the Chief Superintendent?—Well, we rate him as superintendent, but he has the chief charge of his own division. The next officer is the Superintendent of the Police Fire Brigade, at 250l. Then comes an officer that we call the Detective Storekeeper. He is, practically, the Chief Clerk of the Detective Department, and he has also charge of any valuable property which comes into the hands of the detectives. His salary is 200l. a-year.

3096. *Mr. Holmes.*—Would you allow me to mention to you that our inquiry here is only concerned with the force proper, and not with the clerical staff?—The reason I was mentioning these different officers was, so that you would not be under a misapprehension as to the total number of our force, and its actual constitution; because in the numbers I have given you all these officers are included.

3097. *Mr. Morris.*—And then probably if there was any change contemplated in the constitution of our police force, it might be useful to have these details recorded?—Quite so. Then there are six superintendents, and they receive 180l. a-year each; and I should here say, with regard to them, that their position is a peculiar, if not a unique, one, for I don't think there is another police force in existence that has officers in an exactly like position. There are three of these under each of the chief superintendents, and they do duty in both the Dock and Town Divisions. We carry on our work on an eight hours' system, and each of the superintendents goes on with the men for an eight hours' turn of duty, during which time each takes charge of, and is responsible for, his divisions to the Chief Superintendent. Then there are two detective inspectors who receive the same pay as the superintendents, 180l. a-year. There is the Governor of the main bridewell—which is certified as a gaol for three-day prisoners, which is also peculiar to Liverpool. He has a salary of 180l. There is a storekeeper at 140l. a-year; a coroner's bailiff at 140l.; two public-house inspectors at 130l.; an inspector of hackney carriages at 130l.; a deputy-superintendent of the fire brigade at 110l.; three detective inspectors at 120l., and an inspector of cabs at 120l. These may be said to be all the special ranks. Then we have eight first-class inspectors at 120l. each; twenty-seven second-class inspectors at 111l.; twenty-four third-class at 40s. 1d. a-week; thirty-five fourth-class at 36s. 6d.; seven detectives at 37s. 4d.; nine detectives at 31s. 8d.; fourteen bridewell keepers at 34s. 2d.; twenty-one bridewell keepers at 31s. 10d.; seven detectives at 30s. 10d.; and six assistant clerks at 28s. 10d. I think that completes the constitution of the police force of Liverpool.

3098. *Mr. Morris.*—About how many is the number of your detective force—officers and men?—The number of the detective force varies in Liverpool, because we have a large number of men whom we employ temporarily, but I think, speaking roughly, that it would be about fifty or sixty men. Of course, there is very heavy detective work in Liverpool.

3099. Is the detective force in Liverpool a separate force?—Oh, no; it is simply a separate department.

3100. I mean, it is a separate department of the force?—Yes, it is a separate department; we have a certain number of officers, as I mentioned in the list I gave you just now, who are receiving special rates of pay, and in addition to that we take men out of the ordinary ranks of the force and put them, when required, into the detective department to aid in carrying on its work.

3101. *Mr. Holmes.*—Do they get additional pay?—They receive no additional pay; they get an allowance for plain clothes while employed on detective duty. They are put on the strength of the detective department, and in that way we are afforded a means of testing their capacity, and if they are found efficient, smart, intelligent men, they succeed to permanent positions in that department when vacancies occur, with, of course, higher rates of pay.

3102. How many divisions are there in the Liverpool police district?—Six divisions.

3103. Are these divisions distinguished by letters, as is the case here and in London?—No, they are not; we have the North Town Division and the South Town Division; and the North Dock Division and the South Dock Division; the river police and the departmental staff, which includes the detective force, the officers of the fire brigade, and others employed on miscellaneous duties.

3104. I presume that the fourth-class inspectors correspond with our sergeants here, that they are the active officers of the force?—Yes, they do, except that their sections would be larger, and there would be a larger number of men under each section inspector; as you have noticed before this, the number of superior officers is rather small.

3105. Then do your first-class constables correspond more to the sergeants?—We have really no officers that correspond with your sergeants; our inspectors do the same duty that the sergeants do, in so far as that they have charge of a section; but the sections are very much larger, and of course they are not able to exercise so close a supervision over the men as the sergeants would do.

3106. Would you kindly state how many barracks or station-houses there are in Liverpool?—We have twenty police stations, but there is only one of these where single men live; but we have bridewell keepers, and they can bring in other men of the force and keep them as lodgers. These bridewell keepers are, as a rule, married men, and occasionally they take in policemen as lodgers.

3107. Where are the other single men accommodated?—They are accommodated in the central station section-house or in private lodgings.

3108. *Mr. Morris.*—How many have you living in the section-house?—At present there are fifty-nine men living there, but we have accommodation for seventy.

3109. *Mr. Holmes.*—Where do the rest of the force live?—The rest of the force live in private lodgings and private houses.

3110. What is the population of Liverpool within the police area?—At the last census it was 548,619. I suppose that we might add somewhere about 5,000 or 6,000 since the census was taken.

3111. Are the men in your force allowed to marry at any period of their service?—They are.

3112. Is a large proportion of the force composed of married men?—Yes, a large proportion are married men.

3113. I think you said that only about fifty men are accommodated in the central station section-house?—Well, the average is larger than that. I mentioned fifty-nine as the present number.

3114. Are they charged rent for their accommodation?—Yes, they are charged rent. They pay 1s. a-week.

3115. *Chairman.*—What does the accommodation consist of?—The 1s. a-week provides them with nothing but lodging, coal, and light.

3116. And has each man more than one room?—No; they are accommodated in dormitories.

3117. *Mr. Holmes.*—Are the rest of the married and single men not provided with accommodation?—No.

3118. And are they granted no lodging allowance?—None whatever.

3119. Must a man who is in a particular division live within his district or section?—Well, we have no hard and fast rule to that effect. The orders are that every man is to report his residence, and he is to live in such a place as I may direct. As a matter of fact, I may state that we do not allow the men to live at inconvenient distances; but, as I have said, we have no hard and fast rule that they are to live in their sections or divisions.

3120. Do you inspect the lodgings or houses where your men live?—No, I do not; but by having a registry of their houses I have a check on them, and can see that they live in respectable streets. If a man went to live in a street, and I did not approve of the place, I should order him to change his place of lodging.

3121. I suppose that every man who conducts himself well can expect to rise from the lower ranks to, at any rate, the rank of a first-class constable?—Certainly.

3122. Are men promoted from the ranks of constable to the higher ranks?—They are. With one exception, all the superior officers have risen from the ranks of the force.

3123. But in consequence of the great number of constables of course a large number of men who join, no matter how well they conduct themselves during their service, must be content to remain first-class constables until they retire?—Clearly.

3124. And therefore it comes to this—that most of the men of your force are practically content to remain in the service with a pay of 29s. 10d., that is to say, unless in the case of an exceptionally intelligent man?—Quite so.

3125. How is the cost of maintaining the Liverpool police force provided—is it entirely from local funds, or is it aided by the State?—The cost of the maintenance of the force falls primarily on the local rates; but on the certificate of efficiency from the Home Secretary, granted on the Report of the Government Inspector of Police for the Northern Division, the Treasury refunds half the total expenditure in pay and in clothing of the town force.

3126. Are you able to say what the total amount of the cost of the maintenance of the force came to last year?—I am not at present. I will forward it to you.

3127. *Mr. Morris.*—But then, practically, one-half is borne by the ratepayers and one-half by the Government?—That is so. Yes.

3128. Do the hackney carriage licence fees go in aid of the local taxation in Liverpool?—I conclude they do, but that is not within my knowledge, as the hackney carriage department is separate from the police in Liverpool. Though we have a police inspector of cars, there is another inspector superior to him who is not a policeman at all. It is a separate department under the Corporation.

3129. Does the amount received for the licences of hackney cars go in aid of the maintenance of the police force?—It is not credited in any way to the police force.

3130. *Chairman.*—You have no police carriage department?—Not solely police.

3131. *Mr. Morris.*—Does the sum received from pawnbrokers' licences also go in aid of the local rates?—I believe so.

3132. *Mr. Holmes.*—As the men, for the most part, have to provide their own lodgings, I presume you can give us very little information as to their cost of living?—I think I can give you the average cost of the lodgings, as I happen to have made some inquiries on the subject some short time ago. I find that for the ordinary cottage in which a constable resides—a four-roomed cottage—the rent is from 5s. 6d. to 7s. 6d. a-week, free of taxes. Rents are very high in Liverpool. I also find that a single constable has to pay for lodging accommodation—for one room and the ordinary attendance—from 3s. 6d. to 4s. 6d. a-week.

3133. Now, if a constable took a whole house, would he be allowed to let part of it to lodgers?—Yes, he would.

3134. Can you give us any idea of what the cost of living would be. Of course, as the men do not live together, you cannot say anything about the cost of messing, except of the single men who are at the Central Station?—No; except, as you say, in the Central Station. I can tell you what the cost of messing is there. The lodging, of course, I have mentioned as coming to 1s. a-week. There is a charge of 9d. a-week for servants. I take these figures, I may mention, approximately, or, rather, from the cost of one week, but that week would present a fair average of the cost. A charge of 1d. for washing, 1d. for newspapers, 1d. for mess utensils, and 5s. for a week's messing, that is, for dinner only. The men have their own lockers, and they provide themselves with their own breakfasts and teas, for which meals the men get whatever they like. The total cost for a week in the section-house was as follows:—For fifty-nine men to the City Treasurer, 2l. 19s. for lodging; 2l. 11s. 6d. for servants' wages; 5s. 6d. washing; 3s. 5½d. cleaning material; 5s. 2d. newspapers; mustard, pepper, &c.; fish, &c.; potatoes, vegetables, &c., 1l. 5s.; and meat, 17l. 17s. 10½d. At the present time they are paying 8d. a pound for beef, and 9d. a pound for mutton. Vegetables, of course, just now are very cheap, and they are buying potatoes at 1s. a score of pounds, while they are at other times as from 2s. to 3s.

3135. Does that estimate include the entire cost of living?—No; it does not include the cost of breakfast and tea, because each man gets what he likes for those meals himself.

3136. *Mr. Morris.*—What is the total cost for fifty-nine men per week?—19l. 18s. 5d.

Captain J. W. Nott-Bower.

8 Oct., 1889.

3137. *Mr. Holmes.*—And that includes rent of barracks, cost of servants, and of the men's dinners? —Yes, and their coal and lights; and it also includes the washing of the sheets and table-cloths, but not the men's private washing.

3138. Are the men required to provide themselves with plain clothes?—They are; yes.

3139. At their own cost?—Yes; that is, with the exception of the men employed in the detective department or on duty in plain clothes, when they get a special allowance.

3140. Can you tell me what the amount of that allowance is?—In the case of constables on special duty and the clerks it is 3s. a-week.

3141. In addition to their pay?—Yes.

3142. Their pay is the same as that of the other constables?—Yes; and detective officers receive 4s. a-week.

3143. *Chairman.*—When on or off duty?—Yes, when on or off duty. If they do not receive uniform they receive a payment in lieu of uniform. I ought to have mentioned that all ranks of the force receive 6d. a-week in lieu of boots, detective and uniform officers alike.

3144. *Mr. Holmes.*—Do you think that that sum is sufficient to provide boots?—It is not sufficient.

3145. *Chairman.*—Is that 4s. to detectives on or off duty permanent?—Yes; if they do not get uniform they receive the allowance I have mentioned the same as if it were pay.

3146. *Mr. Holmes.*—I presume that the men of the detective force proper are not supplied with uniform? —They are not.

3147. And that 4s. is in lieu of uniform?—Yes.

3148. Well, with reference to that allowance, do you think it is sufficient to meet their wants in the supply of plain clothes?—I think it is sufficient to meet their wants in lieu of uniform. Of course, other men have to be provided with plain clothes as well. We only consider it sufficient to clothe them while they are on duty, and it is not of course intended to meet the cost of the whole of their clothing.

3149. Of course, all men requiring to wear uniform are supplied with that uniform free of cost?—Yes.

3150. Will you now kindly tell us what they are supplied with in the way of uniform?—They are supplied with one tunic, two pairs of trousers, great coat, a helmet, and a mackintosh cape; that would be the whole of the annual issue of clothing.

3151. How many pairs of boots do you suppose that a constable, on an average, would use in the year?—I think two pairs of good boots.

3152. And what would be the cost of a pair of good boots in Liverpool?—Well, I should say 17s. or 18s.

3153. And, of course, a man would have to pay for the repairing of them?—Yes, certainly.

3154. Do you think that the 6d. a-week is sufficient?—It does not meet the whole cost. Until quite recently boots were supplied to the men, and, of course, buying them by contract, they were obtained more cheaply; but the men, when it was put to them, preferred procuring their own boots and getting the allowance, and it was accordingly given to them.

3155. Now, as we have begun evidence on the question of allowances, we may as well complete that subject; and, first of all, I would ask you, are the men, single or married, who live in lodgings, given any allowance for fuel and light?—No, none. We have a certain number of men who receive free residences. There are a certain number of the superior officers who receive them, the two chief superintendents, three superintendents, the superintendent of the fire brigade, the Governor of the bridewell, and the resident bridewell keepers—that is, about one-half the total number of bridewell keepers who receive free residences, including coal and gas.

3156. Are the residences found for them, or do they receive an allowance?—The residences are found for them, and the officers of the same ranks who do not receive residences get no allowance, for it is considered that the officer who lives in a station is doing a certain amount of extra duty to the public which compensates the public for the expense of the lodgings.

3157. Will you now kindly mention the allowances given to the men in addition to their pay?—There are really no allowances of any importance. The superintendents receive two guineas a-year for hats and boots. That allowance seems to be given in pursuance of an old custom. That is the only allowance that I could mention.

3158. Perhaps you will now give an account of the duties of the men—of the duties which are performed by the constables who form the great majority of the force?—They do eight hours a-day duty.

3159. That is to say, the day is divided into three tours?—Yes; it is divided into three tours, of eight hours each tour.

3160. *Mr. Morris.*—Does a man continue on duty for the whole eight hours without any intermission? —Yes. We have, I may mention, an arrangement by which we just allow them to draw off into one of the stations to get some refreshments when they are on duty, at about the middle of the tour of duty, but that amounts to only a few minutes. Practically, they are on duty for the whole eight hours.

3161. *Mr. Holmes.*—When a man is off duty can he regard his time as his own, or must he hold himself in readiness for any emergency?—He can call his time his own in the city, but he is not allowed to leave the city without permission. He can wear plain clothes, and go where he likes in the city, or he can stop in his own house; but he is not permitted to leave the city without special leave.

3162. But it does practically amount to this, that when a man has put in eight hours duty, he can look upon the remaining sixteen as his own?—Yes.

3163. And if a married man, he can go to his home without having practically any call upon him, or being expected to turn out for duty again for sixteen hours? —Yes.

3164. Do they take the duty alternately day and night?—Of course, some men have to do more night duty than others, because we have a certain number of men on detective duty who do, practically, nothing but day duty; and we have also a certain number of picked men, called day sections, who are picked, steady, and experienced men, whom we require for duty in regulating the traffic and doing work of that important nature in the streets. An ordinary constable on joining would have more night duty than day for some time; but as far as possible every man gets his turn of day and night duty, and we have a system by which the tours are changed.

3165. But you have not alternate months of day and night duty?—No.

3166. When a policeman makes an arrest or arrests, and has charges to bring before a magistrate, is it in his own time he has to follow those charges to the magistrate's court?—We allow him time off for that—that is, a policeman on a night beat.

3167. When does the night beat commence?—At 9 o'clock.

3168. And when does it end?—At 5 o'clock. In the case of a man who has to appear at court in the morning—the magistrates sit at 11 o'clock—the inspector of his section would send him off duty at 3 o'clock, and by that means give him an opportunity of resting before he goes to the court; and the man on the adjoining beat has to take charge of the absent man's duty. He has to what we call "double" his beat. That is, for instance, if that man would, in walking his beat, pass a certain point once on a half-hour beat, he would, when his beat would be "doubled," only pass that point once an hour instead.

3169. *Chairman.*—Of course, when a constable brings a case to the police-court, he has to wait until that case is disposed of, temporarily or permanently?—Yes.

3170. How many courts sit in Liverpool?—There are generally three courts sitting. There is only one stipendiary magistrate, but there are three magistrates' courts sitting every day.

3171. Separate courts?—Yes. In one court the stipendiary magistrate sits; in another, the coroner always sits. He is a borough magistrate, and acts. He is a solicitor also. He acts as a deputy stipendiary magistrate. He sits every day, and takes all the drunken cases. Then there is a third court, which sits under the presidency of two local magistrates, and they dispose of summons cases.

3172. Are they lawyers?—No.

3173. How many assaults are there before the stipendiary magistrate, on an average, every day?—Last year there were 64 assaults on women and children, 698 assaults on the police, and 1,013 common assaults.

3174. Is that in one court?—No, that would be in the three courts. I could not distinguish the numbers that go into each court.

3175. That number is for the three courts, you say?—Yes.

3176. What would be the average period of detention of a constable who has charges to be disposed of by the magistrates?—I should think about two hours would be the average time.

3177. But I suppose a man has often to remain longer than that?—Yes, he might; but, on the other hand, he might occasionally get away after waiting only half-an-hour or so.

3178. What hours do the magistrates sit?—From 11 o'clock until the business is disposed of.

3179. Is there no fixed hour for rising?—No, Sir; there is no fixed hour for rising.

3180. *Mr. Holmes.*—From what class do the recruits of your force principally come?—Well, from almost every class. We get a very large number of men—and very good men, too—from the fishermen of the Isle of Man. We have a great number of the sons of small Scotch farmers, from the northern parts of Scotland, and also fishermen from Shetland. Of course, we have a large number of English labourers, artisans, and soldiers. I have had a great number of soldiers. There are, I think, about 350 Irishmen in the force.

3181. Have these Irishmen been in the police forces of this country?—Some of them have, but I have been refusing them within the last year. I have been refusing men coming from the police forces in Ireland unless I have received some very good reason for their leaving. I have had quite a number of applications within the last few weeks.

3182. Does admission to the force rest with you?—Yes, it does, entirely.

3183. Do you find that soldiers make good policemen?—I find this in the case of a soldier, that if I can get him to keep sober for about twelve months, he will turn out an excellent man. I find, generally, that soldiers are either very good or very bad. A great number of soldiers join, and I find that the extra amount of freedom they get, through not being so constantly watched as when in the army, makes many of them come to grief in a very short time, through taking to drink.

3184. Do the men as a rule look forward to making the police service their home; I mean in the way of a permanent occupation; or do they simply join it with the intention of leaving it in a little while?—I am afraid a great many do the latter, especially artisans—Englishmen who have got good trades. I am afraid they do join the police service with a view to simply tiding over a slackness of work. But the other men I have mentioned—the fishermen and small farmers, or the labouring men—they generally join with a view to sticking to the force, and on that account, though more trouble in training, I prefer getting them.

3185. In the hope that they intend to make the force their means of livelihood?—Yes.

3186. From your experience, when would you say that men cease to be efficient policemen—after how many years' service?—I would put it down at twenty-five years as the most you could expect.

3187. *Chairman.*—No matter at what age a man might join?—No matter at what age a man might join. When I say that, I do not, however, refer to those men who may have been fortunate enough to rise to the higher ranks of the service. I have been speaking of the ordinary constable who walks the street, and I find that by the time he gets to twenty-five years' service—even though he joins at 20 years of age—he is an old man. Captain J. W. Nott-Bower.

3 Oct., 1882.

3188. *Mr. Holmes.*—Have you any experience of the duties of the police in Dublin?—I have not.

3189. I presume that Liverpool being a seaport town, there are a large number of rough elements amongst the population, and that therefore the duties of policemen are, comparatively, hard duties?—They are very hard. The men get a very great deal of knocking about, and they have a very rough time indeed in some parts of the town.

3190. Are the wives of the married men allowed to pursue a trade?—No.

3191. Why is that restriction imposed?—Well, I think myself that it would be very undesirable that they should be allowed to do so. They would, if so allowed, become interested, I am afraid, in certain people in the town—the people who might deal with them, and the husband would not be able to act in an impartial manner to those members of the public.

3192. Are they allowed to pursue any calling—putting aside the question of trades?—None.

3193. A policeman's wife would not be allowed to make her livelihood as a dressmaker?—Well, it would not be allowed, but it is a thing very difficult of ascertainment sometimes. We would not certainly allow a woman who was a policeman's wife to keep a shop as a dressmaker. She might take in work; that is a thing that we could not prevent.

3194. Would a policeman's wife be allowed to take in washing?—Well, yes; I don't think I would interfere with that.

3195. Are they allowed to have a plot of land on which to grow vegetables, or anything in the shape of a garden?—They could not have that convenience in Liverpool, owing to the densely-populated nature of the town.

3196. Can you now give us some information respecting the discipline of the force. How are charges preferred against the men, and how are inquiries conducted—have you Courts of Inquiry?—No, we have not. The whole discipline of the force rests in my hands, and I look personally into every case. As a rule, of course, the cases are brought before me on report from the inspector of the section, or through the superintendent who parades the men for duty. The case comes before me then on the following day. I am always at my office at 11 o'clock every day to inquire into offences against discipline. The superintendent brings his witnesses, and the accused brings his witnesses, and I inquire into all the circumstances of the case just in the same manner as would a magistrate in open court. I hear all the evidence on both sides, and then give my decision.

3197. *Chairman.*—Is the evidence always given upon oath?—No. I give the man accused of course the opportunity of cross-examining the witnesses against him, and then I decide on the case, and pronounce the penalty.

3198. Do you allow him to bring up any witnesses?—Oh, yes; with the exception of the evidence not being on oath, I conduct the inquiry in almost an exactly similar manner to that in which it would be conducted in the police-court. I allow the accused man to call any witnesses he pleases, whether policemen or civilians. I do not restrict him; and of course any complaints that are brought by civilians against policemen I hear in exactly the same way. If I get a letter from a civilian making a complaint against a policeman, there is promptly a reply sent that I shall be glad to take the charge on the following day at 11 o'clock, and requesting him to attend with his witnesses.

3199. *Mr. Holmes.*—Have you complete discretion

Captain [illegible].

2 Oct., [illegible].

as to your decisions?—Yes; but of course the punishment is limited by Act of Parliament to a week's pay.

3200. What is the average fine that you would inflict for a first case of drunkenness, or would you inflict any fine at all for a first offence of that kind?—I fine a man 10s. for the first case of drunkenness.

3201. In a second case of drunkenness what would occur?—If a second case occurred after a short time, I would reduce a man a class.

3202. But if he was in the lowest class at the time, what course would you adopt?—Well, in that case I would fine him 20s., and if another case occurred after that, I think it would be a proper case for the dismissal of the man; for I think that any man who would get three drunk in one year would not be fit for retention in the service.

3203. For a third offence of drunkenness committed by a man who had previously been reduced, would you dismiss him from the force altogether, or what fine would you inflict?—It may be certain that that would depend upon his length of service and general conduct. If a young constable, I should dismiss him; if he had a considerable length of service, I should probably degrade him another class. I generally adopt another measure also in the case of old constables. If a man has been brought before me three times for drunkenness—that this is his third case—in addition to the fine I impose I warn him that he will be dismissed on the occasion of the next offence, and there is an entry made in his book at the time to this effect—"Reduced second time (or third time as the case may be), and warned."

3204. If, however, a man, after having been reduced, conducts himself properly for a certain time, would you reinstate him to his former position?—When a man is reduced, say from the second to the third class, he is then in exactly the same position as the constable first appointed to that grade. He has to serve for one year from the date of his reduction, and on the completion of that period of service with good conduct he gets his promotion as a matter of course.

3205. Do you think it is prejudicial to the discipline of the force to reinstate a man to a high rank where he would be in command over others, when that man had been convicted of an offence—I mean to say, is it not possible that he would lose his proper influence and control over his subordinates by reason of the idea of his having been reduced, and that they might throw in his teeth the fact of his having been reduced for drunkenness?—Do you mean years before?

3206. Yes, years before?—No; I don't agree with that view at all. I do not think that that would be so. My opinion is, that after a certain lapse of time, if a man conducts himself well, the former offence should be forgotten and not remembered against him. I have myself seen an instance where that has been done, and to my mind most properly done. I have myself promoted a man to an inspectorship, and that man is one of the best inspectors I have. He had been reduced, having been previously an inspector, and was reduced for very great misconduct a considerable number of years ago; but he was a man who served afterwards with most excellent conduct, and he is a man whom ever I consider fully deserved the promotion that has been given him, and I do not think that that man's prior misconduct has in any way interfered with his maintenance of discipline.

3207. You do not think that the men under him would be disposed to throw in his teeth the fact that he had been degraded?—Not at all. I don't think they would at all. I know also of a case of a soldier, who, after being tried by court-martial and sentenced to a term of imprisonment, was four years afterwards a sergeant and discharged with a good character. Also a case of a constable (of the Royal Irish Constabulary), who, after bad conduct in his early service, was promoted on my recommendation, and is now a very valuable officer. I think it right to state that with reference to what I said as to a third offence, I do not go back to look for previous offences beyond two years. I think if a man spends two years free from the offence, say of drunkenness, I ought to look upon his next offence as a first offence.

3208. Are the men of your force allowed to go into public-houses when off duty?—Yes, in plain clothes; but not when off duty in uniform.

3209. I suppose offences of drunkenness are the most serious with which you have to deal?—Well, I consider myself that the offence of going into a public-house when on duty is a more serious offence than that of drunkenness, because I consider that a man who is guilty of that offence, and who habitually goes into a public-house on duty, is perfectly useless; besides, he is absolutely leading the publican to break the law; moreover, much of police drunkenness is traceable to this offence. Then there are the offences which I consider more relate to matters of discipline, such as offences of insubordination, which we have to deal with sometimes. But of course drunkenness is the most serious of the general offences that a man in my position has to deal with. The men have the right of appeal in case of dismissal from my decision—they have the right of appeal to the Watch Committee—and it is a source of great satisfaction to me that they have that right. I should be very sorry if that right of appeal was taken away from them, because I find that the Watch Committee are always ready to support me, and I have never yet had a decision reversed. I never dismiss a man unless I am compelled to do so, but it is satisfactory to know that if one does make a mistake there is a means of correcting it.

3210. For what offence have they the right of appeal?—For any offence for which I dismiss a man.

3211. Are the Watch Committee elected every year by the ratepayers?—They are elected every year by the Town Council.

3212. What position do the members of that Committee generally hold?—A good number of them are magistrates. There are fifteen members of that Committee, and I think that ten or eleven of them are magistrates, and the others are members of the Town Council, and very respectable men.

3213. How is the appeal from your decision in a case of dismissal conducted?—The case comes up on report from me on a written letter of the constable applying to the Committee to reconsider his case, and asking to be reinstated. The Committee then hear the evidence just in the same way as I did, and the man is allowed to say what he wishes, and to examine his witnesses, and then the parties are all ordered out. I am present, and I hear the whole case, and the Committee ask me my opinion on it, and my reasons for coming to my decision, and they then decide the matter by vote. Cases have arisen in which the original decisions have been reversed. During the long tenure of office of the late Chief Constable there may have been one or two decisions of his reversed, or perhaps I should more properly say modified, but that is a circumstance that very rarely occurs.

3214. May I ask you, have you statistics that would enable you to tell us the amount of the fines levied last year?—No, I am afraid I have not. The amount of the fines goes into the superannuation fund, and I could get the particulars you require for any number of years back. I shall be happy to send them to you on my return.

3215. Now, will you kindly give us some information on the question of drill? May I ask you, are the men of all ranks required to put in a certain amount of drilling during the year?—Yes.

3216. And what is the extent of the drill that they have to undergo?—We have no fixed amount of drill—there is no number of days fixed on which drill is required. Every recruit who joins is drilled until he is reported as efficient, and he has practically little drill after that. There is no drill done by the men except in the spring of the year, just about a month before the Government inspection. Then we have drills, beginning with squad drill and company drill, up to battalion drill, and the Government inspection, as it were, finishes the drill for that year, and they do no more drill then—the transit then—for another twelve months. Practically, they do about two days a-week for a month in the year, and that is really all the drill they do.

3217. How long are they drilled each day?—One hour each day. That would be about the average, but we have no fixed time. It depends upon the amount of notice we get of the inspection.

3218. Is the time during which they are drilled included in their hours of duty?—No, it is not.

3219. *Mr. Morris.*—Can you furnish us with the average number of cases of drunkenness that have occurred in the Liverpool police for the last three or five years?—Yes, I will do so; but I have not the statistics at hand that would enable me to do so now.

3220. But you will kindly make a note of it, and send it to us when you return?—Yes.

3221. And also the fines?—Yes.

3222. You could not form any opinion as to what percentage they might be from recollection?—In the police force?

3223. Yes?—I should say, just from recollection and speaking roughly, that I have about two or three cases a-week of it.

3224. That would be about 150 cases in the year?—Yes, that would be it—from 100 to 150 in the year.

3225. *Mr. Holmes.*—Out of a force, practically, of 1,113 constables?—Yes.

3226. Because, of course, cases of drunkenness would be confined to that body?—Yes. It would be about 12 or 13 per cent.

3227. In hearing charges against the men, when any offence against discipline is being investigated, are you the sole arbiter in those cases?—I am.

3228. *Chairman.*—Do any of your superintendents sit with you?—No. They are in the room as a rule, but they take no part in the inquiry.

3229. How many of them do you have in the room?—As a rule, there is the superintendent of the man's division, and the inspector, who brings the charge.

3230. But you are not assisted in any way by them?—I am not assisted in any way. I may add that the two chief superintendents are usually in the room.

3231. *Mr. Morris.*—And I suppose you would just refer to those superintendents as to the general character of the man, and so forth?—Yes. I refer to them on matters of character, and there is also a clerk in the room who has charge of the conduct books, so as to be ready to read out any previous records that may be referred to having reference to the man whose case is being investigated. On hearing the evidence in the case I decide, and I say, "I am satisfied that you are guilty of the offence that is charged against you." I then turn round to the clerk and say, "What is the man's conduct?" and he turns up the place in the book and reads out, "He was fined"—on such a day—"for being drunk," or whatever the offence may have been, and I then decide upon what penalty I shall inflict.

3232. *Mr. Holmes.*—When you speak of the previous records against the man, you allude only to records within the two years previously?—Yes.

3233. He might have had a bad account before two years, but that had been wiped out?—Yes.

3234. *Mr. Morris.*—He gets a clean bill of health after two years?—Yes, he does. Of course, I have had occasionally to look back beyond that period when there is any peculiar offence charged against a man, because it may be important to know whether that man has done anything before of that kind. But practically, records are wiped out after two years for all ordinary offences, and for such an offence as drunkenness I never look back beyond two years.

3235. *Mr. Holmes.*—You told us just now that the fourth-class constable can rise, after certain fixed periods, up to the position of first-class constable, assuming that he has conducted himself well. Would you please tell us now how promotion is regulated from the rank of first-class constable to the merit class, and, I presume, from the merit class to the rank of inspector?—Well, the merit class are men, as a rule, who are old constables, and who are not eligible for promotion. Promotion to the rank of inspector takes place almost entirely from the rank of first-class constables, and it is entirely by selection, and I am altogether responsible for the selections I make; and I select the men and practically appoint them.

3236. *Mr. Morris.*—Are you of opinion that it would be impossible in the police force to have men promoted by seniority?—Utterly impossible.

3237. In fact, it would not work?—It could not work.

3238. And that there is no other way, except by selection, of promoting men?—I can see no other available way of doing it.

3239. *Mr. Holmes.*—In making your selections, may I ask you what principles you go upon?—Well, I have a list of all the first-class constables, and I work down, all the while paying as much attention to seniority as I reasonably can. I begin at the top of the list, and I see a man's name. I have the superintendents in and I say, "What sort of a man is that?" and we talk over the question of that man's fitness, and then, if he cannot get promotion, we work down the list in that way until we find a man suitable for promotion, and I promote him. Of c[illegible] I have to pass over men who, although estimable constables, have not education and intelligence enough to make them eligible for promotion to the higher ranks.

3240. Have you any kind of examination for the men before you make your selection for promotion?—I have no examination. I have each of the men before me, and I get him to write a report of an ordinary police case in order that I may judge of his intelligence, and I see if he can write English and spell well; but there is no formal examination.

3241. And I presume that the only literary examination you have is really to see, when the men join, whether they can read and write?—Yes, when joining; and as I have said, when I am making a man an inspector, I like to see whether he can write a report of an occurrence in fair English in such a way as that any one could read and understand it.

3242. Do you require constables to attend school?—No.

3243. You allow them to educate themselves as best they can?—Yes. On joining I always warn recruits as to the amount of education I expect for the higher ranks of the service. I appoint recruits every week, and see every recruit after he is appointed. I impress upon him all the points of duty, and also the importance of education,—I say that I hope, in the case of every man who is entering the force, that it is his intention to qualify himself for the higher ranks, and I point out that, in order to qualify himself, he must have a certain amount of education. I impress upon recruits that a certain standard of education is indispensable for promotion, and that their upward progress in the service will depend upon their own application to education, so as to make themselves eligible for promotion.

3244. Has a first-class constable any authority over constables of the lower ranks?—None at all, unless he is acting for an inspector who is away on leave. Sometimes we have to appoint a first-class constable to act as acting inspector. He receives no additional pay, but it is one of the ways we have of testing a man's fitness for promotion.

3245. And if that man conducted himself properly, and showed fitness, he would be promoted?—Yes.

3246. When a vacancy arose?—Yes.

3247. *Mr. Morris.*—What amount of leave in the year do inspectors get?—Fourteen days.

3248. And what leave is granted to constables?—Constables get seven days' leave with pay.

3249. Do they get any other leave?—They get a day off in every twenty days. Every twenty days a

Captain J. W. Nott-Bower.

8 Oct., 1882.

Captain J. W. Nott-Bower.

6 Oct., 1882.

man gets a beat off, and then his beat is performed by another man who does a double beat.

2750. That would be about eighteen more days in the year?—Yes, about that.

2751. Eighteen and seven days are the periods of leave given to constables; so that, in fact, a constable gets twenty-five days' leave in a year?—That is so. But we do not call those that I have last mentioned days' leave, because a man cannot go away; but he is off duty.

2752. Practically, it comes to about twenty-five days off duty?—Yes; and then we have, of course, gradations of leave beyond the rank of constable, who, as I have said, get seven days; the bridewell keepers get ten days, the inspectors fourteen days, and the superintendents and some of the senior inspectors—the detective inspectors and others—get twenty-one days' leave, and the chief superintendents get one month each.

2753. Chairman. With pay?—Yes, with pay.

2754. Mr. Morris.—Supposing a man is ill, is his pay stopped?—Two-thirds of his pay is stopped, except in a case in which a man is injured on duty, and in that case he gets full pay.

2755. But is there two-thirds of the full pay stopped when a man is sick?—Yes; but the men themselves have a sick club, which they manage for themselves entirely, and what it would give them makes up the total pay to something over 1*l.* when they are sick; but in the case of a man who has 27*s.* a-week there would be 18*s.* stopped, but he would get 12*s.* a-week from the police sick fund; but that, as I have said, is a fund maintained by the men for themselves.

2756. Voluntarily?—Yes; by an average subscription of about 4*d.* per week.

2757. But suppose a man got a bad cold, and was unable to go on duty for a week or a fortnight, would he lose two-thirds of his pay?—Yes; he would lose two-thirds of his pay for that time.

2758. Is there a medical officer appointed to the police force?—Yes; there are two doctors, one to each of the large divisions. One takes the whole of the North Dock and North Town Divisions, and the other takes the whole of the South Dock and South Town Division.

2759. Do they attend the men gratis?—They attend the men if they are injured on duty, and they also have the examining of candidates for the force, the examination of the men who are applicants for pension, and such others as I may send to them.

2760. But are not the men attended, when sick, at their own homes by those doctors?—The men, when sick, are attended by the doctors of their own sick club; and there are two of those doctors; one for the North Division, and another for the South Division.

2761. And they are paid by the men?—Yes; and not by the Corporation.

2762. Chairman.—Has there ever been any protest against the reduction, when sick, of two-thirds of their pay?—No; none. I wish to tell you, with regard to this matter of the sick fund—I am speaking now my personal views—that I am not in favour of that system, and I think it a bad one. I think the sick club is a bad system, and I should prefer myself instead that the men were not stopped two-thirds of their pay, but only one-third; that they should have medical attendance, and that the sick club should be abolished; for we have to take the certificate of the men's own surgeons where sick leave is requested, and I am aware—of course, I do not mean for a moment to reflect on the surgeons themselves, for they are very respectable men—but I am aware that there is a great amount of pressure put upon those doctors by the men to give certificates in cases where they ought not to give them, and the doctors have been greatly troubled by the men, who have threatened to scandal them about their business if they did not give them certificates.

2763. Mr. Holme.—But suppose there was no pay stopped from the men: from your knowledge of the force and of human nature, don't you think there would be a very large increase in malingering?—I am sure there would; and I am afraid that even with the stoppage there is still a certain amount of malingering. I think a stoppage is absolutely necessary in the rank of constable. I do not think it is in the higher ranks.

2764. What is the proportion of inspectors to men?—There would be, roughly speaking, about 65 inspectors to 1,036 constables on the ordinary effective strength, making the average number of beats in each section about seventeen.

2765. What are the duties performed by the inspectors?—An inspector is in charge of a section. The unit division we have is a beat. Each constable has a beat—a certain number of streets and houses to look after.

2766. Can you tell me how many square miles are within the police district of Liverpool?—The area is 5,200 acres.

2767. Can you give us roughly what would be the extent of a beat?—I could not; it varies so much, according to the nature of the property to be looked after. The beats vary from a beat that would take half-an-hour to walk round to one that would take a man an hour and a-half to walk round. An inspector is in charge of a certain number of those beats, we might say roughly fifteen to twenty, as an average. He is responsible for all that goes on during his eight hours' tour of duty in his section, and his duty is to visit the constables on the beats, and at the same time he acts as a patrol, and an additional man walking round his own section.

2768. Then he has to work, too, for eight hours at a time?—Yes. Then, in charge of the whole division for the eight hours is the superintendent, who parades the whole of the men for duty, and who dismisses them at the expiration of the tour of duty, and who, during the eight hours he is on duty, has to be constantly in his division, and who visits inspectors and constables, and who is, in fact, patrolling about his division and visiting the police stations of his division during his eight hours' tour of duty.

2769. And is the policeman obliged to report to the inspector everything that occurs when he meets him?—Yes.

2770. Is he obliged to report cases where there are nuisances?—Yes, he reports all those things; in fact, everything that occurs on the beat.

2771. Knockers broken off; have they to be reported?—Yes.

2772. And I presume that, if he does not report those things, and if it is afterwards reported to you that he has neglected his duty in that respect, he is fined?—He is brought up before me for neglect of duty by his inspector (for all the reports come in from the inspectors); the reports that come in to me are sent to me in the name of the inspector of the section, through the divisional books.

2773. Are they made directly to you or to the superintendent?—They come through the superintendent of his division, and he then brings it to me.

2774. You say that the superintendent parades his men, and afterwards, at the close of the tour of duty, dismisses them?—Yes.

2775. Where does he parade and dismiss them?—He parades them at the chief station of the division—the central station of the division.

2776. When you say the central station, you do not refer to the section-houses?—No; there are two stations. One is called Seel Street Station, and the other Rose Hill Station—one is in the south and the other in the north of the town, and all the men for duty are paraded at those stations by the superintendent.

2777. And they have to go there to be dismissed?—Yes.

2778. And I suppose a man has to go from his beat to the station-house?—Yes, he has.

2779. About what time would it take a man who is on a beat situated at the most remote point to walk to the station-house?—It would not take a man any great length of time, because the area of the city is not very large, and I should think that half-an-hour would be as long as it should take any man.

2780. With regard to the duties of the superintendent, do they take the charges at those station-houses?—No; the charges are taken by the bridewell keepers. There is a keeper constantly on duty in every bridewell in the borough, and the charges are made to him.

2781. How many police-stations are there?—There are eleven bridewells, but there are some stations that are not bridewells.

2782. What is the distinction between a bridewell and a station?—The bridewells are the stations with cells for the detention of prisoners, and an office where charges are taken.

2783. *Mr. Morris.*—In fact, to take the charges is the bridewell keeper's particular duty?—Yes, that is his particular duty.

2784. Is he under the control of the superintendent?—Yes.

2785. *Mr. Holmes.*—And he is a police officer proper?—Yes.

2786. And does he follow the charges into court?—Yes, he attends in court with his own charges. The bridewell keepers never go out during their tour of duty. They do twelve hours' duty each day in the bridewell, and that is their only duty. There are ten or eleven bridewell keepers doing duty at the main bridewell.

2787. *Chairman.*—I understood you to say that there was some test examination made when a constable joins the force?—There is no test. The only test is the written application made by the men themselves. Each man makes a written application, and I judge of his handwriting and spelling roughly from that.

2788. And the subsequent promotion of that individual up to the rank of superintendent rests with you alone?—Yes; of course, the legal responsibility rests with the Watch Committee.

2789. And you examine candidates for promotion as you think fit?—Yes.

2790. And the Watch Committee act upon your recommendation?—Yes; it practically rests with me.

2791. And you examine as you think fit?—Yes.

2792. *Mr. Morris.*—As I understand it, they hold you accountable and they have the responsibility, but they hold you accountable all the same?—Yes.

2793. *Mr. Holmes.*—I presume that in addition to the ordinary duties which policemen have to perform, the police of Liverpool have to perform all the duties thrown upon them by various Acts of Parliament?—Yes.

2794. *Mr. Morris.*—Although the police are on "active" duty, if I may use the expression, eight hours out of the twenty-four, are they not always in readiness if called upon in case of fire or emergency of that kind?—Oh, yes.

2795. Or of a riot in the street, or of a bad assault where a number of people are concerned?—Yes; a man is bound to be in readiness if called upon at any hour to serve, and he has no claim for any extra time put in.

2796. And have the Liverpool police ever put forward a claim for extra pay for such services as I have described, which must have been rendered by them at some time or other?—Oh, no.

2797. Or suppose there was a regatta at Liverpool, would the police consider it "extra" duty to attend it?—I hardly think they would. I don't think if they did there would be very much attention paid to it.

2798. Suppose policemen in Liverpool were called out suddenly owing to the fact that there was a fire in a street a short distance away from their station, and that on the way to that fire they received an intimation that as the fire had been in the meanwhile put out their services would not be required, and that they could return home—do you think that they would regard an occurrence of that sort a case for extra pay?—Such a case as that is one of constant occurrence with us, because our men have to work the fire brigade as well. They would never think of making extra pay for it.

2799. And that is part of their special duties?—Yes, it is.

2800. *Mr. Holmes.*—I think we will now proceed to deal with the question of pensions and gratuities. Can you tell us what is the scale of pensions under which the members of your force retire?—We have a local Act in Liverpool. We are not under the General Act. It is the "City Police Superannuation Act of 1881" that our men are superannuated under.

2801. Under an Act passed so recently as that?—Yes. It is an amendment of the old Act. It is practically the same as the old Act. There are only one or two small matters in which a change has been effected by it.

2802. Can you give us from that Act your superannuation scale and your gratuity scale?—Yes. After fifteen years' service a pension of not more than half nor less than three-eighths of the pay, and the calculation in reference to pay is based on the average of the pay received during the last ten years of the man's service. After twenty years not more than two-thirds nor less than half the average pay on the last ten years of service, but in both cases it is provided that the age of the man must not be under 57, if below the rank of superintendent, or under 60 if of the rank of superintendent or above it. Of course, that is provided the man is not certified as medically unfit. Of course, a man may be pensioned under that age if he is worn out.

2803. Supposing a man is declared medically unfit after fifteen years' service, would he get the pension that you have just mentioned?—He would get the pension I have mentioned, but it is discretionary with the Watch Committee, who delegate their power to a sub-committee of three or four members, and they give something between three-eighths and one-half.

2804. If a man is worn out, I suppose there is a careful examination by a medical board; indeed, I suppose the medical board is very stringent in its examinations?—Very stringent. There are two police surgeons certifying, and they are very strict.

2805. *Mr Morris.*—In considering with the Watch Committee the subject of a man's pension, and whether you would give him three-eighths or one-half, would you take into consideration the character of the man while he was in the force in fixing the pension at the higher or lower rate?—They would consider his particular service. A man might be in the service between fifteen years and twenty years. Of course, if a man had nineteen years' service, they would give him nearer to the maximum than a man who had only fifteen years' service, and they would consider also his character during the last ten years—during the time that they take the average of his salary. They look back at his character during that period.

2806. And his character is some guide to the pension?—Yes.

2807. Either in lowering or increasing it?—Yes.

2808. *Mr. Holmes.*—When you say they look back for ten years, how does that occur, when you told us, in another part of your evidence, that unfavourable records did not count against a man's promotion or position after two years? I was speaking of that simply in regard to punishments in my own case; but I may say that if there was only one record against a man I do not think the Committee would allow it to weigh with them. I feel it, however, difficult to speak on this subject, for this reason, that we have a committee which is a varying body. We have one committee one year and one committee another year, and both deal with the pensions, and deal with them differently. It is, therefore, difficult to speak on the subject of the way in which they are acting, because some of the

Captain J. W. Nott-Bower.

9 Oct., 18[illegible].

members are inclined to give a man the maximum, while others would give him no more than the minimum, and that is a state of things that has caused dissatisfaction through the English police forces generally.

2309. If a man was fined and reduced, but was afterwards reinstated and was for years well-conducted, would the former [illegible] affect against that man's pension?—Well, I don't think it would to any great extent, as a rule; but I must add, it would depend very much on the gentlemen who happened to be considering the case.

2310. But as a matter of fact, whether it militates against him or not, his character in the force is always inquired into when he is retiring and receiving his pension?—Yes. Then the only other clauses that we have are that after ten years' service if a man is bodily unfit, certified as unfit, he is entitled to a pension not exceeding three-eighths or less than one-fourth. That is a pension that he cannot apply for; that must be simply on the certificate of the surgeon; and after five years' service a man is entitled, under like conditions, to a gratuity of twenty days' pay for each year's service. And then there is another section of the Act which gives power to the committee, if men are rendered unfit from injuries received in the execution of their duty, to give such men two-thirds of their pay, no matter what their service.

2311. Is there any regulation which entitles a policeman to retire on pension after any certain number of years' service?—Not until he attains the age of 5[illegible] years.

2312. *Mr Marra.*—Suppose a man joins at 20 years of age, then he is obliged to serve, if he is in good health, thirty-seven years before he can get out on pension?—That is so.

2313. I think you said that your experience was that, as a rule, after twenty-five years' service, a man was actually worn out?—Yes.

2314. Don't you think it would be for the benefit of all police forces that men should, after serving twenty-eight or thirty years at the outside, be entitled to retire on whatever scale of pension applied to the force to which they were serving?—I think so; indeed, I have a very strong opinion on the subject. I am of opinion that the superannuation system at present in force in England is very disadvantageous to the forces. The matter, as you are probably aware, is under the consideration of the Government at the present time, and a Bill was introduced last Session for the purpose of dealing with the question.

2315. Do you consider that, at all events, a man after serving from twenty-eight to thirty years should be entitled to retire upon whatever scale of pension is fixed?—I am very strongly of opinion that after twenty-five years' service a man should be entitled to retire under the scale of pension fixed for the service. I am now alluding to every man who has not attained a rank higher than that of constable. If a man has attained a higher rank than that I would be inclined to increase the period of service to twenty-eight years, but I think that twenty-five years' service is the most you can get out of men who are obliged to do duty on the streets.

2316. I presume you consider the Liverpool scale a favourable scale?—It is decidedly more favourable than the General Act, which applies to all the other forces in the country.

2317. In your opinion, do you think that the maximum pension ought to exceed two-thirds of the pay?—No.

2318. But you would alter the periods of service? —Yes. I am of opinion that the scale recommended by the Select Committee in 1875, and which was virtually adopted by the Bill which Sir William Harcourt introduced this Session, would be a very fair scale of pension, and I do not think a more liberal scale should be expected. Of course, in a matter of this kind, it is not what the men ask for but what is just that should be considered, and I do not think that the scale I have mentioned should, if adopted, leave them any just grounds for complaint.

2319. Are you aware that in the Bill you have referred to the maximum cannot be attained until after twenty-eight years' service?—Yes, I am.

2320. Would you amend that by giving to them two-thirds after twenty-five years' service?—Yes.

2321. And you think that the scale should be amended in that way?—Yes.

2322. And that if it were so amended justice would be done?—Yes.

2323. And you think the men of the force would be satisfied?—Yes. Of course, they ask more. I have plainly spoken to the men on the subject, and I fancy that, though when they are assembled together they ask more, when you get them individually they seem satisfied.

2324. And you consider the granting of a pension such as you have stated fair and reasonable treatment of the men?—Yes, quite.

2325. Don't you think if a man is entitled to two-thirds of his pension after twenty-five years' service, provided he has the doctor's certificate of unfitness, that that is an inducement to a man to get ill?—I am afraid sometimes it is. I have had a case in Liverpool where a man has been pensioned on a high scale, though the doctors would hardly certify him. The man said he could not do duty and didn't do duty, and he applied time after time for pension and so harassed the doctors, that he made them give a sort of certificate and the Committee gave the pension.

2326. Are pensions borne by the local rates?—They are paid out of the superannuation fund, and a stoppage is made from the men's pay of a certain percentage of the pay.

2327. Will you kindly tell us what deduction is made from the pay of the men in reference to pensions? —It is a stoppage amounting to 3½ per cent. That is a very large deduction made at Liverpool.

2328. Is it not the case that the Corporation add that 3½ per cent. to the pay of the men, so that, practically, there is no deduction from the pay?—That is so in the case of the classes of constables, but not in the case of superior officers. In their case the 3½ per cent. is deducted.

2329. And is that deduction made from all ranks of officers?—Yes.

2330. *Chairman.*—Still?—Yes; and it virtually makes the Government contribution of one-half. They find half the pay, and therefore really half the deduction that is paid into the superannuation fund.

2331. *Mr Nelson.*—Do you find that the deduction is sufficient to meet the pensions?—Certainly not, alone.

2332. To what extent is it supplemented?—It is supplemented by various amounts. Amounts for the service of summonses and the execution of warrants, and they bring in a large sum of money; and then the amounts of the fines imposed on the men, and the sums realised by the sale of old clothing and cast stores,—all these amounts are paid into the fund. There is nothing borne directly from the rates—there is no payment directly from the rates to the superannuation fund. Of course, the amounts of the fees, &c., that I have named, would be paid to the rates if they were not diverted to the superannuation fund, but there is no direct contribution from the rates to the fund.

2333. Supposing that Sir William Harcourt's Bill becomes law next Session, either in its present form or modified, do you think that the Liverpool municipal body, or rather the Watch Committee, will adopt its principles?—Really, I could hardly speak as to that. I can only say this, that if they did not it would cause very great dissatisfaction in the police force, and I feel sure the Committee would weigh the matter very carefully, and take everything into account before refusing to adopt it.

2334. Is not the Liverpool scale more favourable? —No, I don't think it is. You may take the average age of a constable on joining as being about 25 years; well, the present regulations necessitate a man's remaining in the force, if he has health to serve, for thirty-two years, before he can get his pension.

3335. *Mr. Morris.*—Before you leave the question of pensions, permit me to ask you a question as regards the wives and families of men who die in the service, who are not killed while on duty in the force, but of men who die in the service. Is there any provision for the wife and family of such a man?—There is.

3336. To what extent does it go?—It is left entirely in the discretion of the Committee; they can give anything they like. The section of the Act of Parliament says:—"The Watch Committee may from time to time make such allowance to the widow and child or children of any person who joined the force after the passing of this Act, and who died whilst serving in such force, as the Watch Committee, in their discretion as to amount and the continuance thereof, may think fit."

3337. But that allowance does not extend beyond the wife and children?—It is only to the wife and children.

3338. It has been suggested by some of the witnesses examined before us that an allowance should be given to what they called "the next-of-kin" of policemen dying while in the service. Do you believe it possible to carry out that suggestion?—I don't think it is; unless in the case, perhaps, of an old mother, or some one dependent on the man. Under any other circumstances, I cannot see the justice of it.

3339. But suppose it was put as broadly as "the next-of-kin," and you had to advertise for the next-of-kin of the man who had died. Do you think such a suggestion could ever be carried out?—Well, I think it would be very difficult, and I think also undesirable. And in speaking of that, I may state that I think the men of the police are rather acting under a mistaken impression as to what the superannuation fund is, because they seem to think that the money they have paid into the superannuation fund is their own absolute property. I have, however, tried to impress it on them that it is more in the nature of an insurance, and that they have a legitimate right to receive the insurance themselves, and that that is the bargain; but that they have no right to look to get those benefits—which are more than they could have obtained by investing their own money—and also the right to get their own money back again, which some of the men seem to think they have a right to do.

3340. Do the men who subscribe to the superannuation fund pay anything on behalf of an allowance to their widows and children?—No; 2½ per cent. covers all the superannuation.

3341. *Mr. Holmes.*—Are the men in the Liverpool police force content with their rates of pay?—I think they are quite content.

3342. And you consider that the rates of pay are quite sufficient to keep up the efficiency of the service?—Certainly. I have a very large number of applicants. I can always get suitable men.

3343. *Mr. Morris.*—In considering the pay of the Liverpool police, would it ever enter into your head to take into account what a policeman was paid in San Francisco, or New Zealand, or Australia?—No, it would not.

3344. I presume that it would be more probable and more appropriate that you would compare it with the rate of wages that labour receives among the class of men you would get either in England, Ireland, or Scotland?—I think so, certainly.

3345. But you would never even think of inquiring what rate of wages policemen receive in Australia?—No; and were I asked by any of my men to institute such a comparison, I should feel inclined, I think, to tell that man to go to Australia.

3346. And supposing that a policeman under your jurisdiction came to you and informed you that he had received a letter from his brother in Australia, stating that he was in receipt of half again as much pay as the policeman under you in Liverpool, I suppose, on that ground, you would not consider it necessary to increase the pay of the men under you?—No.

3347. *Mr. Holmes.*—Some of the witnesses before this Committee, and before the present Constabulary Inquiry Committee, have represented that the pay given to the police forces in England does not represent the total income of the men, and have insinuated—and, indeed, alleged—that the men were in the habit, in the police forces in England, of receiving "tips" and gratuities from the public for doing certain services for the public and such-like things. Is that the case, so far as you know, with regard to the police forces of Liverpool and Leeds?—Not to any great extent in either Liverpool or Leeds. Gratuities are given to the police for certain services, and those gratuities they report to the Chief Constable, and if he thinks that there is nothing improper in the man's conduct, and that the gratuities may be fairly allowed to be retained, he gives authority to the men to retain them.

Captain J. W. Nott Bower.

3 Oct., 1882.

3348. For what services?—Well, I could hardly say for what services. A man might give a reward for anything that he had lost being found and restored to him by the police. Or if a policeman found a house or shop left open and closed it, and reported to the owner that he had done so, he might receive a gratuity.

3349. Upon an average, what would a man receive from such sources during the year?—It is very difficult to give an average, but I should be surprised if a man would make 10s. a-year.

3350. I think, Captain Bower, you told us that before you became Chief Constable at Liverpool, you filled a similar position for three years at Leeds. Perhaps you could kindly, from your recollection, give us some information respecting the rates of pay, and other matters in relation to the police force there?—The force there numbers 400 men. There are 5 superintendents, 15 inspectors, 54 sergeants, and the balance is made up of constables.

3351. Can you tell us the rates of pay of the various classes?—The superintendents receive 150*l.*, after five years, 175*l.*; and one of the superintendents is on a special rate of 200*l.*; that is one of the five. The inspectors, on appointment, receive 38*s.*; after three years' service they get 41*s.*; and there are three inspectors, who receive 114*l.* a-year. The sergeants receive 33*s.* a-week, and the constables, on appointment, receive 24*s.*; after six months, 25*s.*; after eighteen months, 26*s.*; after three years, 27*s.*; after five years, 27*s.* 7*d.*; and after seven years, 28*s.* The promotions in all classes of constables are regulated in the same manner as I have mentioned in the case of Liverpool; they are consequent on good conduct.

3352. And do a large proportion of the men remain constables all their lives?—Yes.

3353. What is the population of Leeds?—320,000.

3354. Are the superannuations according to a graduated scale?—They are according to the scale laid down in the General Act.

3355. May I ask you, without going into particulars, is it higher or lower than the scale you have given for Liverpool?—It is different. There is more left to the discretion of the Committee than there is under the Liverpool Act.

3356. Well, without going into details, do you think it is pretty much the same?—Well, there are two-thirds given after twenty years' service; and there is one-half given after fifteen years' service. There is a maximum, but it is entirely optional with the Committee to grant anything up to the maximum, no matter how low, and there is no appeal.

3357. Can you give us any further information as to the police forces in other towns?—I can give you the rates of pay of the City of London force. The constables there on appointment receive 24*s.*, and after one year's service they are raised to 26*s.*, and after three and a-half years' service the men may attain to 31*s.* 6*d.*, but the numbers of that class are limited. I cannot, I am sorry to say, give you the number of men in the force.

3358. When you say that Leeds is under a General Act, to what Act do you refer?—The 22nd and 23rd

Captain J. W. Nott Bower

9 Oct., 1902.

Vict., cap. 22. I should like, if you will permit me, to make some further observations on the question of pay. A great deal depends on the amounts that men have to pay for their lodgings in the town in which they are serving. About six months' ago I had occasion, in consequence of a communication from the Home Office, to make inquiries into our rates of pay, as to how they compared with the rates of pay in Manchester. The Home Office apparently considered that the Liverpool rates were rather excessive. However, when I came to compare them closely I found, in the first place, that our average rate of pay was not very much greater than that of Manchester, though the initial rate is much greater; and in the next place, I found that whereas our married men for four-roomed cottages were paying from 5s. 6d. to 7s. 6d. a-week, in Manchester for similar accommodation the men were only paying from 4s. 6d. to 6s. Then in the case of the single men, I found that every single man in Liverpool was paying from 3s. 6d. to 4s. 6d. for lodgings, while the single men in Manchester for the same accommodation were paying from 2s. 6d. to 3s. I made three inquiries through my detective department, so that I am satisfied of the correctness of them, and the representations made to the Home Secretary showing all these points satisfied him, and he allowed the rates of pay to remain as they are.

3359. Do the married men ever complain that they are not given any lodging allowance?—I don't think any such idea has ever entered their minds as that they should have a lodging allowance at all. It never has been done in England. We have no lodging allowance given to any of our men, married or unmarried, and if they go into barracks they pay rent, and if they live out of barracks they pay for their own lodgings, and they do not consider that they have any claim for a lodging allowance.

3360. The rent they pay in barracks is very much less that they pay out?—Yes, because they don't like living in barracks. The men, as a rule, prefer getting out of barracks and paying a larger rent. But we, on the other hand, make up a certain number always living in barracks, because we always desire to have a number of men at hand in case of an emergency—a certain number of men ready to be called out. The men don't like it themselves, because they are more subject to discipline, having to keep closer hours of course, and if we charged them an amount for rent similar to what they would have to pay in private lodgings, the grievance of which they would have to complain would naturally be much greater.

3361. *Mr. Holmes.*—They gain by it in money, and you gain by that arrangement in having the men always at hand?—Yes.

3362. On the question of lodgings for married men, I should like to have your opinion if you would kindly give it. It has been represented to us by some of the men that it would be for the advantage of the force and for the advantage of some of the men if there were blocks of buildings erected by the Government, or hired and let at moderate rents to married men; while other men have stated that, in their opinion, they would rather live separately and at lodgings than with a number of other married men and their families living in the one large block. What would you think of such a plan as that, as a matter of your own opinion?—As a matter of opinion, I don't think my men would like it. I think they would prefer being able to get their own accommodation. Of course, it is very difficult unless one has an accurate knowledge of Dublin to say how it would answer here. Of course so much depends on the nature of the accommodation and the number of the men who have to pay for it, that it is difficult to say whether it would be a consideration for them to have quarters provided by the Government.

3363. Don't you think it would be some advantage in this way? Supposing, in the case of having a number of married men as at your station; if those blocks were provided at a fair, moderate rent for the accommodation of a certain number of married men and were so used, you would also know where to go for a number of men in any emergency?—Yes.

3364. You could readily put your hands upon them?—Yes.

3365. *Mr. Morris.*—Of course, you can only give us the information that you think the Liverpool men would dislike such an arrangement?—I don't think the Liverpool men would like it as a rule. I find that it is the feeling in the police that they wish, at all events, to be made as little military as possible. They do not like being treated so much like soldiers, and when they are off duty they like to consider themselves as civilians and their own masters, and I fancy that if they were compelled to live in buildings provided by the Government they would consider it a hardship.

3366. Then, on the other hand, don't you consider that it is better in some ways that the police should live scattered about, because in that way they have facilities for observation, and for acquiring information?—That may apply to the detective department, but I do not think there is any practical advantage derived from uniformed men in the force living scattered about.

3367. *Mr. Holmes.*—From what you have told us, I presume, from your experience, that the police in England feel that their rates of pay have been fixed at a standard that will give them remuneration for their services as policemen, not with a view to enabling them to marry; and if they marry they must count the cost and be prepared to take the consequences of such a step the same as other people?—Yes, certainly. I consider the pay in Liverpool has been arranged fairly, and is sufficient to enable a man to live respectably in the class of life from which most of the men are taken. In the case of every man who is a bachelor joining the service, I think he can, and does, as a rule, save money. It has never occurred to any man in the Liverpool force to expect that the force should provide for him lodging accommodation on getting married.

3368. Are you of opinion, from your experience, that heavy fines are necessary for the maintenance of discipline?—No, I am not. In fact, I have a very strong opinion to the contrary. I consider that heavy fines impoverish a man's family, and frequently land him in difficulties from which he can never extricate himself. The ultimate punishment in every police force is dismissal, and I believe that if it is understood by the men that a fine of, say, 1*l.*, is a warning, that the next offence (if within a short period) would involve dismissal, the moral effect is as good as would be produced by a fine of, say, 5*l.*, without having the disadvantages I have alluded to. I think dismissal is preferable to a heavy fine.

[The Committee adjourned until Friday, the 10th October, 1902.]

FIFTEENTH DAY.—6TH OCTOBER, 1882.

Present:

MR. J. W. O'DONNELL, MR. GEORGE MORRIS, D.L., and MR. R. W. A. HOLMES.

MR. ALEXANDER MCCALL, Chief Constable of Glasgow, examined.

Mr. Alexander McCall.

6 Oct., 1882.

2369. *Chairman.*—What is your name?—Alexander McCall.

2370. What position do you occupy?—That of chief constable of Glasgow.

2371. How long have you been chief constable of Glasgow?—I have been chief constable for the last twelve years, since May 1870.

2372. Of what length is your connexion with the Glasgow police force?—I have been connected with the Glasgow police force for thirty-two years, since 1850, and my first position there was as inspector of the Detective Department.

2373. What is the population of Glasgow?—The population of Glasgow at the present time is 520,000.

2374. *Mr. Morris.*—About what is the area or extent of the police district?—The area would be about 10 square miles.

2375. What is the organization of the system of the Glasgow police force?—The Glasgow police force is organized under the provisions of the Glasgow Police Act. Under that Act the magistrates and Council are required to provide a police force. They fix the number, the various grades, and the amount of pay.

2376. Does the number fluctuate?—Yes, the number fluctuates; that is to say, it is always increasing, because the population is always increasing. It has increased since December last, one detective officer and six constables. Then the Council is required to appoint a chief constable, and his appointment is made by the Magistrates' Committee, which is a statutory Committee of the Council for police purposes. That Magistrates' Committee and the Sheriff of Lanarkshire appoint the chief constable, and they may also dismiss him. If there is any diversity of opinion between the Magistrates' Committee and the Sheriff of the county in regard to the grounds of dismissal, then there is an appeal to the Lord Advocate.

2377. *Mr. Holmes.*—What is the date of that Act?—It is of 1866, but that is merely a continuing Act. The Act has existed in its present form since 1847, but the Glasgow police force was organized at least 100 years ago under a Police Act. Then having appointed a chief constable, the chief constable appoints every man in the service, and he also dismisses every man excepting those of the rank of superintendent and lieutenant, the two higher grades of the service. There are seven superintendents and twenty-three lieutenants. That number the chief constable cannot dismiss.

2378. By whom are they dismissed?—The dismissal is in the hands of the Magistrates' Committee, and they can only inquire into the conduct of those men that are supposed to be deserving of dismissal, provided that the chief constable has in the first place suspended them from duty. They cannot make any inquiry into the conduct of any man in the service under me until after I have suspended those two ranks.

2379. What is the annual cost of the maintenance of the force?—The annual cost will be about 74,000*l.*

2380. And is that altogether derived from local taxation?—It is paid from local taxation, and there is one-half repaid by the Government.

2381. *Mr. Morris.*—The cost is paid in the first instance, and then you receive a refund of about one-half?—Yes. I may give you the exact amount. The estimated amount for next year is 84,404*l.*

2382. *Mr. Holmes.*—Could you give us the amount raised by local taxation?—The cost of the force is defrayed by a police rate upon an assessment of the rental of the city. The police rate at the present time is 1s. 2d. in the £, but that not only pays the police expenses, but does also pay the expenses of the fire brigade and lighting and cleansing of the city.

2383. *Mr. Morris.*—And then a rate of 1s. 2d. in the £ pays for the police, for the lighting of the city, and the cleansing of the city?—Yes; but of course there is a payment back by the Government of somewhere about 35,000*l.*

2384. *Mr. Holmes.*—Can you say what that police rate of 1s. 2d. in the £ amounted to in the year?—What it amounted to last year, no, I could not. I have not the material for doing so beside me.

2385. Perhaps you will now give us the various grades in the force, and the numbers in each grade?—There are seven divisions altogether in the Glasgow police force, A, B, C, D, E, and F, and the marine is the seventh. There is a chief constable, 7 superintendents, 23 lieutenants, 1 inspector of the detective department, 36 detective officers, 40 inspectors, 80 sergeants, and 841 constables. The scales of wages of constables are as follows:—Of the fifth class the pay is 22s. weekly, and there are 133 men drawing that pay. Then the fourth-class pay is 24s. per week; there are 148 men of that class. There are 200 upon 25s., 294 upon 26s., and 94 upon 27s. This 27s. class is termed the merit class, and it is restricted to 100 men. The 26s. class is the first-class.

2386. I presume, Mr. McCall, owing to the large number of constables as compared with the other ranks, a great number of men who join your force, no matter how good their conduct is, must be content to remain in the rank of constable all their lives?—Oh, yes.

2387. And, in point of fact, the maximum rate of pay which most of the men can expect to receive is 26s. a-week?—Yes.

2388. That is the salary of the second-class?—Yes.

2389. Could you tell us what proportion of the men in the constable class remain constables throughout their service, owing to the want of vacancies?—The percentage of men that are promoted from the rank of constable to the higher grades is very small, but I cannot say how much it is. I may say, for instance, that five of the superintendents that I have just now mentioned have gained their positions from the grade of constable.

2390. Can men rise in your force from the rank of constable to the highest grades of the service?—There is nothing whatever to prevent them. It is a matter altogether of selection by the chief constable.

2391. How long does a man remain in the fifth class before he rises to the fourth?—He remains one year.

2392. And how long is he in the fourth before he rises to the third, and so on?—During the first year's service a man receives 22s. per week. After one year's service, the latter three months of which must have been free from misconduct, and the constable otherwise considered eligible, he receives 24s., and then 25s. after two years' service under the same conditions.

2393. When you say two years' service, do you mean two years' service in the fourth-class?—No.

2394. You mean including all service?—Yes. After three years' service he is eligible for the 26s. class, provided that the latter nine months of that year has been

Mr. Alexander McCall.

4 Oct., 1892.

free from misconduct, and that the man is otherwise considered eligible. And then the fourth class, which is restricted to 160 men—that is after four years' service, from joining I would say—the latter twelve months of which must have been free from misconduct, and that the constable is otherwise considered eligible.

3395. Then in all cases of promotion, the latter period of time must be free from misconduct, and the constable must be otherwise fit?—Yes. In the lowest class it is three months, in the next class it is six months, in the next class nine months, and the next class is twelve months, and those periods must have been free from misconduct.

3396. But owing to the small number of men in the fourth class, a great number of the men who join can never rise beyond the second-class?—Not beyond the first class. The first-class 27s. a-week is open to them from length of service.

3397. I thought you said that the merit class was the first-class?—No; it is distinctly the merit class. The [illegible] class is the first-class.

3398. Then, not counting the merit class, you have only four classes of constables?—Certainly.

3399. As you have now given us the pay of the various classes of constables, will you tell us how many classes of sergeants there are, and what their pay is?—There are three classes of sergeants. The third-class receive 30s.

3400. How many men are there in that class?—Eight. The second-class receives 31s.

3401. How many men are there in the second-class?—There are eight. Then the first-class has 32s.; and there are forty-four in that class. As to those sixteen men in the two lower classes—they are in progress to the first-class, but they have to serve a certain time.

3402. On appointment, and during his first year of service, the sergeant has 30s. per week; during the second year the sergeant has 31s., and after the second year the sergeant has 32s.—those are the three classes?—Yes.

3403. Chairman.—And is the salary increased, whether there be a vacancy or not, after the periods of service?—Yes; that is to say, it does not matter whether there are vacancies or not, they go on by rotation.

3404. Mr. Holmes.—The increase of pay depends upon the length of service, and not upon the vacancy?—Yes, upon length of service. He acquires a title to his pay, from the length of his service and good conduct.

3405. Now, kindly go to the rank of inspector?—In the case of the inspectors, there are three classes of them, and the lowest class has 34s. per week.

3406. How many men are there in that class?—There are five at the present time. Then the next class has 35s.

3407. Is that the second-class?—Yes. After the first year's service the inspector has 35s. a-week.

3408. How many men are there in that class?—There are six in that class at present. Then after the second year's service as inspector the pay is 36s. There are twenty-nine of those. I might add that there are exceptional cases in which some inspectors receive additional pay. For instance, there is one of them who has 4s. a-week extra for acting as drill instructor, and then there is another one has 1s. extra as [illegible] and cab inspector.

3409. Chairman.—They each get 4s. weekly for those duties?—Yes. And then there is one of them also who is inspector of hackney carriages, and he has 4s. a-week added to the highest class pay.

3410. Mr. Holmes.—Now, will you be good enough to proceed to the class of lieutenants?—Yes. There are twenty-three lieutenants altogether. The maximum pay of the lieutenants in the A Division is 1[illegible]l. per year.

3411. How many lieutenants are there upon that pay?—There are three lieutenants receiving that pay just now.

3412. And are they all of the A Division?—Yes, all in the A Division. Then in the case of the lieutenants in the other districts, not the A district, their maximum pay is 160l.

3413. When you say "maximum" pay, what do you mean?—It is the highest pay that I can promote them to.

3414. Does the lieutenant commence at that figure?—No, not at 160l. I might begin him at 100l. when he commences his duty as a lieutenant.

3415. Does the minimum rate depend upon what you fix?—Yes. Just now there are 2 lieutenants receiving 190l.; 1 at 170l. There are 3 at 160l.; 4 at 150l.; 7 at 140l.; 6 at 130l.; 1 at 120l.; and 4 at 110l.

3416. Mr. Munro.—And the fixing of the maximum down to the minimum rests with you?—The maximum is fixed by the magistrates and Council, but the minimum is very much at the disposal of the chief constable when he is promoting a man to the grade of lieutenant or considering what he is worth.

3417. Mr. Holmes.—Upon an average, what might you say would be the minimum rate of pay of a lieutenant, taking the average of your promotions?—I very frequently begin lieutenants at 100l. per annum, and increase them, perhaps, 10l. per annum, until once they reach the maximum.

3418. Will you now proceed to deal with the class of superintendents?—There are seven superintendents; four of them have 250l. per annum, one has 230l., one has 270l., and one 260l. The maximum of the superintendents in all the divisions, except the A Division, is 310l. The maximum of the superintendent of the A division is 350l.; but at the present time he is only in receipt of 300l., because it is not long since he was appointed. He will be promoted at the rate of 10l. per annum until once he reaches 350l.

3419. Are the minimum rates of pay in the class of superintendents fixed by you?—Not exactly; not in the case of the superintendents. The minimum rate for superintendents would now be about 250l., I think.

3420. And what is the amount of yearly increment both in the case of superintendents and in the case of lieutenants?—Well, it altogether depends upon the recommendation of the chief constable when he brings up the list once every year—at the beginning of the financial year, as it were, of men who are receiving salaries, and who have not reached the maximum of the grade that they fill, and with a recommendation that the increment should be the 10l., 20l., or 30l.

3421. According to conduct and merit?—Yes, exactly. The pay of the chief constable is 700l. per annum; that is the highest rank.

3422. Now that you have gone to the rates of pay in the various ranks, will you say how promotion is regulated from the rank of constable to that of sergeant?—That is entirely a matter in the hands of the chief constable. If a vacancy was occurring in the rank of lieutenant——

3423. In the rank of sergeant; we will take that rank first?—Oh, in the rank of sergeant. He would look about him as to who was the best constable in the service to fill that vacancy of sergeant. He would fortify his own opinion by an inquiry of the superintendent who had immediate charge of the man, and ascertaining really the man's abilities, and then he would promote him to the rank of sergeant. The same method would be adopted throughout every grade in the service.

3424. In looking at a man's qualifications, do you look more at his qualifications as a policeman proper, or do you require that he should have some literary qualifications?—If you take the rank of lieutenant, their duties are almost entirely of a clerical character, preparing charges, receiving charges at the various police offices against parties brought to the offices by the police; and those men as a rule—at least in a great many cases—they are young men who have passed through the years' offices. I find that almost essential, unless he has been a man of very long experience in the police service as a sergeant or inspector, in order to promote him to the rank of lieutenant. He requires some legal knowledge to prepare and frame charges, for some of those are pretty intricate in the Scotch

[illegible] that these are the best men for the [illegible].

[illegible] I presume there are very few men pro- [illegible] make to be lieutenants?—Not a few; [illegible] many now promoted from the ranks.

[illegible] have been constables at the earliest [illegible] service?—Yes; who may have been [illegible] one time, but who must have occupied [illegible] superior prior to their promotion to the [illegible].

[illegible] it often happen that a young man who [illegible] writer's office would join as a constable?

[illegible], then, in the case of these men, you [illegible] them directly from the writer's office?—

[illegible] you require a man, upon presenting [illegible], to pass an examination in some [illegible]—for instance, reading, writing, and [illegible]. The first thing a man has to do who is [illegible] appointed as constable is this; He is [illegible], a copy of which I have in my hand, [illegible] answer the questions in that schedule, [illegible], name, occupation, and whether he has [illegible] service before; and there he has to [illegible] at least that he can read and write, [illegible], I can judge from looking at the schedule [illegible] write well or indifferently. He has to [illegible], which has his name and residence, [illegible] with the parish, town, and county, and [illegible] or married, and, if married, the number [illegible].

[illegible] has to fill up that in his own hand- [illegible].

[illegible] you do not require any special examina- [illegible] are satisfied with the way in which the [illegible] been filled up, the man is admitted?—

[illegible] do not require attendance at school?— [illegible] no school of education. Every man [illegible] the service gets a fortnight's instruction [illegible] instruction is, of course, the reading by [illegible] him of the conditions of the service and [illegible] regulations, giving him some instruction [illegible] perform his duty.

[illegible] if a man wishes to rise in the ranks, and [illegible] self for the higher posts, which, of course, [illegible] amount of education, he must get his [illegible] can be can in his leisure hours?—Well, he [illegible] his education if he can. A number of [illegible] a good education as constables. Perhaps [illegible] from the highlands of Scotland, whose [illegible] have been small "crofters," or something [illegible] who may have given their boys a good [illegible] education.

[illegible] as I understand, there is no compulsory [illegible]?—There is no compulsory literary [illegible] every man must be able to read and [illegible].

[illegible] what classes of the community do your [illegible] chiefly come?—The majority are drawn [illegible]," or perhaps what you would call in [illegible] farmers, the sons of small farmers, game- [illegible] gillies, farm-servants—these are the [illegible] supply most of the men of the Glasgow [illegible].

[illegible] they come, I suppose, principally from [illegible] counties?—Yes. I may add that, at the [illegible] the force consists of—I am speaking in [illegible] the strength was 1,088. There were [illegible], 770 Irishmen, 65 Englishmen, and [illegible]. There are, perhaps, a couple of Swedes, [illegible] Belgian.

[illegible] course you have no difficulty in getting [illegible], one just now.

[illegible] you find that the rates of pay are ample [illegible] attract sufficiently good men?—Well, the [illegible] sufficiently good to attract them, but, I am sorry [illegible] can keep them. The most important of [illegible] in my force are among men who have [illegible] years' service. The average service of the [illegible] eight years.

3139. Then you lose a man just when he becomes a serviceable policeman?—Very often.

Mr. Alexander McCall.

6 Oct., 1882.

3140. Do you attribute that to the fact that the pay is not sufficiently good, or that the prospects in the force are not sufficiently good?—I think a good deal of it is owing to the fact that the prospects are not sufficiently good to keep men in the service. For instance, during last year (1881) 111 resigned. Well, 16 of them were under one year's service, 30 were under two years' service, 41 were under three years' service, 16 were under ten years' service, 8 were under fifteen years' service, and 1 was under twenty years' service, and 3 under thirty-five years' service. Then in the rank of inspector there was 1 under twenty years' service, who resigned and 1 under forty years' service. In the rank of sergeant there was 1 under fifteen years' service, making, in all, 111; 40 were dismissed, 4 deserted, and 15 died, making altogether 170 changes in the force in the year.

3141. What occupations do men who leave the force generally take up?—Well, a great many of them emigrate to America, Australia, New Zealand, and the Cape of Good Hope. I suppose, with the object of following agricultural pursuits. Some of them go into the business of a publican.

3142. Will you now tell us what are the duties of a constable? For how many hours is he out on duty during the day?—Well, one-half of the whole force is upon night duty, and that portion begins duty at 9 o'clock at night and continues on duty until 5 o'clock in the morning—nine hours. Besides th[illegible] men have to be at the station a quarter of an hour before the hour for duty, and they are there for at least a quarter of an hour after duty, for inspection and anything of that sort.

3143. And they are on beat duty throughout these nine hours without being relieved at all?—Yes, without any relief.

3144. I suppose these men are on night duty month about?—No. They are permanently upon night duty, but, as vacancies occur in the day portion of the force, they are drafted—the most suitable men are drafted on to the day duty.

3145. Then, I suppose, when a man joins the force first, he is put upon night duty?—Yes; he is always put upon night duty. Then the day relief begins at 5 o'clock, and ends at 9 o'clock at night. It is divided into two halves. One half begins at 5 o'clock, and continues on the streets until 8 o'clock in the morning. He goes off duty at 8 o'clock and returns at 2 o'clock in the afternoon, and continues on duty until 9 o'clock at night.

3146. That is also a nine hours' beat?—Yes. The other half begins at 8 o'clock in the morning, and continues on duty until 2 o'clock in the afternoon. It returns at 5 o'clock, and continues on duty until 9 o'clock, so that, from 5 o'clock in the afternoon until 9 o'clock at night, I have the full strength of the day division on the streets—that is to say, the night portion and the day portion being equal halves, the streets are covered by one-half of the whole force from 5 o'clock in the afternoon until 5 o'clock the next morning.

3147. Now, will you tell us what are the duties of sergeants? How many hours are they on duty, and what exactly are the duties which they perform?—They have precisely the same hours of duty as the constables. The inspectors have the same, and a sergeant will have an average of fourteen men allotted to him, and those fourteen men are laid out upon beats, and it is his duty to go round them continually during his hours of duty to see that the men are attending to their duties, and that they are sober and correct. Then the inspector again, he is also upon street duty; he supervises, perhaps two sergeants, with the men under those two sergeants.

3148. And the lieutenants, what are their duties?—The lieutenants, as I said before, are very much confined to office work. If there are three in the one division, the one that is upon outside duty for the day also takes the supervision of the streets and the men on the beats, but it is of very small extent that. Then

Mr. Alexander McCall.

6 Oct., 1888.

the superintendents are also required to go about their districts and to look after the inspectors, lieutenants, sergeants, and constables.

3449. I think there are, you said, seven divisions?—Yes.

3450. And there are, I presume, seven superintendents?—Yes.

3451. A superintendent for each division?—Yes.

3452. Having told us about the pay, will you now be good enough to tell us what allowances, if any, are given to the men in addition to their pay?—Every man up to the rank of inspector, and including that of inspector, is allowed 6d. per week for boot money, and free uniform clothing, which consists of one tunic in the year, two pairs of trousers, and a helmet and a top-coat every two years. These are the only allowances that they have.

3453. Do the men consider that the 6d. a-week is sufficient for their boots?—Well, I have had no grumbling from them on that account. It amounts to 26s. a-year.

3454. *Mr. Morris.*—Do the Glasgow police wear capes?—Yes; they wear capes and leggings during the winter.

3455. *Mr. Holmes.*—What would be the cost of a pair of boots in Glasgow?—I think they would get a good pair of boots for 12s. They would have enough to provide themselves with two pairs of boots in the year. The cost of each pair would be from 12s. to 13s.

3456. Are those the only allowances they receive?—Yes.

3457. Are there any deductions made from the pay of the men?—Every man is required to become a member of a sick friendly society—for sickness and death—and to that society he contributes 1s. a-month.

3458. May I now ask you, are your men accommodated in barracks, or are they allowed to live where they like?—Well, I have seventy-seven unmarried men accommodated in what we call a section-house—you may call it barracks if you choose. In one house attached to the A Division I have forty single men who are upon day duty. In another house in the same division I have twenty-three men who are upon night duty. Well, in reference to these forty day men, in the event of any emergency taking place during the night, I can lay my hands upon these forty men, because there they are in bed just inside the police office. Then I have, as I have said, twenty-three single men in the other house who are on duty at night, so that in the event of any disturbance taking place, or any emergency through the day time, I can get these men out of their beds in a few minutes, because they are sleeping during the day. And then I will have about, I should think, seventy more—married men—spread throughout the various divisions, and occupying houses that form part perhaps of the police buildings or fire-stations.

3459. And are they accommodated in those places rent free?—No. They pay rent according to the accommodation that they have, according to the size of the house. Those single men pay 1s. 6d. a-week for their accommodation in the section-house, for which they are supplied with bed and bedding and water, gas, and coal. There is a mess cook for the forty men. There are two women for cleaning their dormitories and making up their beds. Each man has a dormitory for himself.

3460. And this deduction of 1s. 6d. goes to pay for the mess cook and the cost of service—covers everything in that way in fact?—Yes.

3461. Well, now, with the exception of those men that you have in those two section-houses, and with the exception of the married men that you have attached to the various police-stations, are all the rest of the force living through the town where they like and as they please?—Not exactly as they like. Every man must live within the division in which he is stationed, and as near to the police office as he can procure a house; that is the only regulation.

3462. *Mr. Morris.*—Is his lodging inspected?—Those houses that the men rent from the magistrates and Council are inspected at least once a-month. The section-houses again, they are perhaps inspected once or twice every week, where the young unmarried men live.

3463. But are the lodgings where the married men or the single men reside subject to any kind of inspection?—Not unless the place in which they live is property belonging to the magistrates and Council.

3464. Are there any restrictions against men in the force taking lodgers. Supposing a man takes a small cottage or house, can a constable take in a lodger?—Oh! he is perfectly free to do so. There is nothing to prevent that.

3465. No regulation?—No; and I may add in reference to that that those married men who are living in houses belonging to the magistrates and Council are encouraged to take in young unmarried constables as lodgers with them; so that it strengthens the force by adding to the number of men who are living together, and who can be easily had in case of emergency.

3466. Is a policeman in your force allowed to carry on a trade?—No.

3467. Is his wife allowed to carry on a trade?—No.

3468. Would she be allowed to carry on the occupation of dressmaker?—This is the rule applicable to that:—"Each member of the force shall devote his whole time to the police service, and he is not to carry on any trade, either by himself or by his wife."

3469. Well, as regards the question I asked you as to whether a policeman's wife might follow the calling of a dressmaker. Suppose it was brought under your notice that such was the case, would you pass it over or would you consider that it fell within the rule?—Well, I don't think I would; I would rather not know of it, as it were.

3470. You would wink at it?—Yes. It is not an occupation where she could incur debt rapidly, or that would involve herself or her husband in difficulties. But if she kept a shop, such as a grocer's, for instance, where she might run up debts against her husband, I would certainly consider that undesirable.

3471. Is that the only objection to a policeman, either by himself or by his wife, carrying on a trade, namely, that they might incur debt?—No, it is not the only objection. I think there are probabilities that if a policeman was carrying on trade by his wife, the hours that he would be off duty he would be assisting his wife very likely, and possibly during those hours when he should be in his bed refreshing himself with sleep; and it would also probably bring him in contact with people he should not know.

3472. And subject him to influences from the public?—Exactly.

3473. Now, when a policeman in your force is off duty, is he free to go where he likes? Supposing he keeps within his district, can he do what he likes?—He has practically liberty to go to any place within the city, but he is not entitled to leave the city without he has obtained permission to do so.

3474. Well, the remaining fifteen hours that he is off duty he can call them his own?—Yes.

3475. Subject to his being called upon, of course, in the event of an emergency?—Exactly. And, of course, he has to turn out to perhaps a dozen drills in the course of the year in the summer months; and then he has to turn out for an hour once a month to hear the rules and regulations of the service read over to him. Then he has to attend courts during his own time, and if there were any extensive public meetings—for instance, such as we had yesterday, when Sir Stafford Northcote visited Glasgow—the probability is that the night men would have to turn out to assist the day service, so as not to strip the streets of too many of the day men.

3476. When a man is required to do any extra duty of that kind, is he compensated for such extra duty on another occasion—would he be let off a certain amount of duty on another occasion?—No. The superintendent, however, if he found a man that should be off duty from 5 o'clock in the morning until 6 o'clock in the evening attending court from 6 o'clock in the morning until 1 or 2 o'clock, he might say to that man, "Instead of coming out to-night at 9 o'clock, you need not come out until 10 o'clock." That would be two hours' compensation for him. But if he was there merely for a couple of hours, from 9 until 11 o'clock, he would not get any recognition of that sort at all.

3477. *Chairman.*—How many courts have you in Glasgow?—There are seven courts sitting every morning; one in each division.

3478. And who presides in those courts?—In the central court—that is, the court of the A Division—there is a stipendiary magistrate. In the other six, citizen magistrates preside.

3479. Are there any particular descriptions of offences in these courts?—Every offence. Every crime or offence comes first before a police magistrate.

3480. Before the stipendiary?—No; before the magistrate sitting in the court of the district in which the man has been apprehended.

3481. And is that magistrate a mere civilian, or does the stipendiary hear the case throughout as well?—The citizen magistrate hears the case throughout, and he has sitting along with him an assessor, who is a legal man. Each citizen magistrate has a legal assessor sitting along with him.

3482. And is that assessor paid?—Yes.

3483. And has he a permanent appointment?—Yes, he has a permanent appointment practically, but he is appointed annually.

3484. What is his salary?—350*l.* is the salary of each assessor, and there are four of them.

3485. And who appoints them?—The magistrates and Council.

3486. And what may be the average number of charges disposed of each day?—I can give you the number of persons apprehended in the course of the year.

3487. In reference to the attendance at the police-courts of the men of the force, I wanted to know the number of charges on an average?—Well, I should suppose that on a Monday morning the number of charges might run up to 350, and from that to 400, all over the city. That, of course, you might say would be a double day, because there has not been a court sitting from Saturday until Monday morning. On other days, maybe 150 charges would be the average.

3488. I wanted to know that in reference to the length of attendance of the police at the police-courts. When does the court sit?—The central court sits at 10 o'clock. Well, upon a Monday the magistrate may be sitting until 3 o'clock in the afternoon.

3489. And how long are the other courts sitting, as a rule?—In the district courts the magistrates should be, perhaps, about one hour in each. The one magistrate officiates in two courts. He would go to B court, and after spending an hour's time there in disposing of the cases he would proceed from that to the other court, and spend another hour there, or until he finishes the cases in that court.

3490. Then, in point of fact, for the six courts there are only three magistrates?—Yes. There is the stipendiary's court, and then there are four courts divided amongst two magistrates; and there is a special magistrate for the marine court, and he only officiates in the marine court.

3491. Well, supposing a man is arrested by a constable before he goes off his beat at 5 o'clock in the morning, how long should that man be detained prosecuting that charge in the police-court?—Well, that night constable might return at 10 o'clock, and remain in the court until 3 o'clock in the afternoon; and he might not be detained an hour.

3492. But what is the average?—Well, I should think it would not be less than an hour—any man having to attend court.

3493. If, in case of their remaining until 2 or 3 o'clock in the afternoon, are they allowed any compensation?—Well, as I said before, the superintendent might say to that man, "Seeing that you have been so long at court, instead of going out at 9 o'clock you may turn out at 10 o'clock."

3494. But there is no rule on the subject?—No.

Mr. Alexander McCall.

4 Oct., 1882.

3495. I suppose the assaults and other crimes of violence on the police are heard in the A Division?—Yes. The strength of that division is greater than any of the rest.

3496. What is the average number during the year of assaults on the police?—Well, my statistics do not show the number of assaults upon the police during a specified period. They do not show that; but I should think I would be able to show that there is ½ per cent. of the force off duty throughout the course of the year—of men who have been injured and rendered unfit for duty.

3497. In discharge of their duty? ½ per cent. of the force?—½ per cent.

3498. Permanently disabled?—Well, disabled for a time.

3499. *Mr. Morris.*—That would be about ten or twelve men in the year?—About six.

3500. *Chairman.*—No more than that?—No more.

3501. *Mr. Holmes.*—What is the Irish population in Glasgow?—The Irish population—that is say, of Irishmen born in Ireland—I should say there would be 100,000 in Glasgow. But if you take again the children of those parties, born in Glasgow, and who rank as Scotchmen or Glasgow men, you would have about 140,000 or 150,000 of a population.

3502. *Chairman.*—Nearly one-third of the whole population?—Yes.

3503. *Mr. Holmes.*—Do the married men complain that they are not allowed lodging allowance?—No.

3504. You have never heard complaints of that kind?—No. When they enter the service they know the conditions that are applicable to them, and the houses are generally cheaply rented, as the magistrates and Council do not wish to make any profit out of them.

3505. *Chairman.*—They fix the rents?—Yes. They are rather inclined to make them a little easy, so far as the rent and the accommodation given is concerned.

3506. *Mr. Holmes.*—With reference to the men who are not accommodated in these houses, what would you suppose that married men would pay for their accommodation?—I think that the rent of a constable would be about 15*s.* per month; a rent of 8*l.* or 8*l.* 10*s.* per annum.

3507. Single men would, of course, pay considerably less?—Of course. They might get lodgings outside at 1*s.* 6*d.* a-week, just what they are paying in the section-house, or perhaps 2*s.*

3508. Then the cost of lodging is moderate in Glasgow?—Yes; I think a young man might accommodate himself very cheaply in Glasgow in the way of lodgings.

3509. You have told us all about the pay, allowances, and duties of the general force; will you now kindly tell us something about the detective force. I see there is one detective inspector and thirty-six detective officers. Does that include the whole of the detective force?—Yes, that includes the whole of the detective force. The thirty-six includes the whole of the detective force, with the inspector.

3510. *Mr. Morris.*—And do you consider that a sufficient detective force for such a city as Glasgow?—Oh, well, I consider so; and within the last three months I have got a grant of an additional detective, as I thought another one was required.

3511. The reason I ask you that is, that in Dublin the force numbers forty-four, as well as I remember, with a much smaller population?—I may state, in reference to those detective officers, that they are not all in one division. Each division has a certain number. For instance, take the B Division; there are two detective officers in that division. In the C Division there are three; in the D Division there are four; in the E Division there are three; in the F there is one; in the marine there are two; and in the central division there is one inspector, three sub-inspectors, and seventeen detectives. That is in the A Division.

3512. *Mr. Holmes.*—When you say the central division, you mean the A Division?—Yes.

Mr. Alexander McCall

8 Oct., 1881.

3513. *Mr. Morris.*—What is the pay of the detective force?—The salary of the detective inspector just now is 180*l.* per annum, but he is eligible for 190*l.*, inasmuch as that is the maximum salary of the situation, but he is merely drawing 180*l.* just now.

3514. There is one Inspector?—Yes, only one. There are seven sub-inspectors. One of the sub-inspectors has 45*s.* per week, two have 38*s.* per week, and four have 36*s.* per week; twenty-six of the detective officers have 34*s.* per week, and two have 32*s.* per week. The standard scale, however, of a detective officer's pay, is 34*s.*

3515. What do you mean by the "standard" scale?—That is the fixed maximum scale of pay that he is entitled to; but you will observe that two only draw 32*s.* These are men that have been constables, and they have been promoted to be detectives, and they commence at 30*s.* per week; but in a few months, if they show efficiency, I will perhaps raise their pay to 32*s.*, and then, in a few months more, they will reach the 34*s.* class, and then they will have got all they can get in that grade.

3516. With the exception of the detective inspector, all the other officers of the force in the detective department are called sub-inspectors?—Yes.

3517. And in the absence of the inspector, which must occur sometimes, who takes charge of the detective department?—Well, the inspector has three clerks. They hold the rank of detectives, but they are assisting him in the clerical duties in his office. They have been well-trained under him, and they become able to fill up his place in the event of a gap of that sort.

3518. Are these three clerks included in the thirty-six detective officers?—Yes.

3519. *Chairman.*—Do they get any extra salary?—No.

3520. *Mr. Holmes.*—Do they receive an allowance for plain clothes?—The detective officers, both sub-inspectors and detectives, get 10*l.* per annum for clothing.

3521. *Mr. Morris.*—In the detective force there are eight officers, and twenty-eight men?—Yes. These sub-inspectors, although they are called so, are really detective officers with long service; and to make a distinction in a way, they have been called sub-inspectors, together with a slight increase of pay.

3522. *Chairman.*—What is the maximum salary of the others?—34*s.* 34*s.* is the maximum pay of a detective officer. A detective officer is, I should say, about equivalent in rank in the service to an inspector—fully more than a sergeant. Each of these men receives 10*l.* per annum in lieu of clothing.

3523. Does the detective inspector receive the same allowance for clothing?—He does not receive it in money. He is supplied with clothing once every year, consisting of a surtout, two pairs of trousers, and a vest and hat, together with 2*l.* for boot money. The superintendents have the same as that officer.

3524. *Mr. Holmes.*—The seven superintendents?—Yes; the seven superintendents and all the lieutenants have the same as the detective inspector.

3525. They get an allowance of clothes and 2*l.* for boot money?—Exactly.

3526. Do they receive any lodging allowance?—No; nothing of that kind.

3527. *Mr. Morris.*—I presume that you, as chief constable, consider that eight officers is quite a sufficient number to have over the men of a force consisting of an entire body of thirty-six?—Oh, well; while they are ranked as sub-inspectors, and receive a little more pay as detective officers, they are scarcely officers in a sense. Their advantages are given more for the purpose of recognising their efficient services than anything else.

3528. *Mr. Holmes.*—And to give them prospects of promotion?—Yes; and, of course, if these men find the detective officers doing anything that is discreditable, and not attentive to their duty, the inspector would look to them to report those matters to him.

3529. *Mr. Morris.*—No doubt it might appear strange that I should have put the question to you, but the reason I did so was because I find that the detective force in Dublin consists of a body of forty-four, with a very much smaller population than that of Glasgow, and out of that body of forty-four there are twenty-five officers and only nineteen men; and it has been put forward before the Committee that there is not a sufficient number of officers in the Dublin detective force. I suppose, judging by your management of the Glasgow Detective Department, you, at all events, would consider that a force of forty-four men, having twenty-five officers, had quite a sufficient strength of officers?—I should think so; but perhaps they are called officers merely in the sense of these sub-inspectors to whom I have made reference.

3530. I shall read the list of them for you. There are thirteen acting inspectors, four sergeants, six acting sergeants, and nineteen constables, who, with a superintendent and an inspector, constitute a detective force of forty-four men?—I do not see how, so far as Glasgow is concerned, so many officers should be required.

3531. And you would not consider, as an abstract proposition, that the number of these officers should be increased?—That depends very much upon the quantity of duty that they have to perform, and the quality of it. Perhaps the detective duty in Dublin may be much more arduous than it is in Glasgow.

3532. And they may be peculiar?—Yes; there may be peculiarities in the duties of the Dublin detective force that do not exist in Glasgow.

3533. Are the detective duties of your department very much confined to Glasgow itself?—Yes, unless they are sent out of the city. If they are required to make an investigation, they have to go to any place to which they may be sent; but they are entirely confined to the city so far as duty is concerned.

3534. They have no correspondence with other parts of the country?—The detective department has correspondence all over the country, and all over the Continent of Europe, and with America and Australia.

3535. Have you a large criminal population in Glasgow?—No. It is not a large criminal population—that is to say, of people who are entirely confined to crime, but there is a considerable population of pilferers, as opportunity may arise, when they can deprive their neighbours of some property.

3536. Have you many ticket-of-leave men there—convicts?—Of ticket-of-leave convicts in Glasgow there were, at the commencement of the year 1881, 96 males; came from prison during the year, 79 males; transferred from other places to Glasgow, 11; total in Glasgow during the year, 186 males and 40 females. And the corresponding numbers of females are—In Glasgow at the commencement of the year 1881, 18; came from prison during the year, 20; transferred from other places to Glasgow, 2; total in Glasgow during the year, 40; gross total, 178.

3537. *Mr. Holmes.*—Have the detective force in Glasgow a headquarter's station of their own?—The head-quarters are in the central or A Division police office.

3538. Of the detective branch?—Yes. Each of the divisions, as I have shown you, has either two or three detectives attached to it, and they just have their office in the police building of the district. It is not a separate branch, as it were, of the service at all. It is not a distinct branch.

3539. Each ward is represented by a certain number of men, and they go to the central office on duty in the morning, and arrange their business?—No. In the case of those men in the various districts, it is their business to inquire into all reports made of crime occurring in their divisions. Well, the number of reports in each of these divisions where there are only three detectives is, perhaps, in proportion to the central district, where a large number of detectives are on account of the large number of reports and the large number of crimes that are committed in that district. Of course, if there was a weakness of efficiency or an emergency arising in any of those districts, or if it was a very important crime that had been committed—either a murder or a very extensive robbery—the probability is that there would be some detectives sent from the central office to supplement the district detectives, and to strengthen them for the time being.

3540. What may be the area of the central division as compared with the others?—The area is small as compared with the other districts, but the population is dense, and the business, as you may see, that is carried on in the A Division, is very heavy.

3541. How many station-houses are there in Glasgow at which charges are taken?—There are seven police offices.

3542. One for each division?—Yes; and then there are seven substations in these divisions—making in all fourteen places where there is an officer on duty and a policeman to take charges.

3543. And the officer engaged in such duty is called a lieutenant?—No; in these sub-stations he will most likely be an inspector—one of the inspectors. Under the provisions of the Police Act, I cannot put an officer in charge of a police-station under the rank of an inspector, and in these sub-police-stations he is quite sufficient of that rank to discharge any duty that is required.

3544. How many hours would a lieutenant be on duty at a time taking these charges—I think you said me that the lieutenants take the charges, do the clerk's work, as a rule?—In these sub-stations he will be twelve hours on duty—one during the twelve hours of the day and another during the twelve hours of the night. They may change the duty, and probably they change all over the divisions once a month from day to night duty, and vice versâ. In the central police office there are three lieutenants for duty inside. They take twelve hours on duty and twenty-four hours off; but the work is very heavy there.

3545. *Chairman.*—As a rule, the inspectors patrol and the lieutenants take the charges?—Yes.

3546. *Mr. Morris.*—In considering the wages paid to the men of your force, I suppose you would never think of taking into account, as some of the witnesses before us have done, what was the pay of police in California, San Francisco, New Zealand, or any of these distant places?—Well, I have that information in statistics, but I do not see what relation it has to the pay of police in Glasgow. I know, for instance, that in New York, where I have been myself, that a police constable there has about as much as one of my superintendents. He would be worth about 200*l.* a-year.

3547. But that would not guide you as to what you would get a good man for in Glasgow?—No; certainly not.

3548. Suppose one of your sergeants came up to you and proposed to read a letter that he had received from his brother, stating that in New Zealand that brother was getting twice as much as he was getting in Dublin, would you consider that a reason for raising his wages?—No; but I would recommend him just to follow his brother. I think when a man joins the force, he does it voluntarily; he comes for his own benefit. He is told when he comes, "These are the conditions of the service—these are your emoluments. If you are not pleased, do not come to the force." And then, of course, if he joins, and that he will become such a valuable man that there is not promotion for him, or that his wages are not sufficient, let him take his services somewhere else, and get as much pay as he can.

3549. *Mr. Holmes.*—I think, if you have nothing further to add on this point, that it would be desirable that we should now come to the question of discipline. How is the matter of discipline regulated in the Glasgow police force—how do you deal with offences?—That is against the men—where the men offend—offences committed by the men?

3550. Yes?—Well, take, for instance, we will say, drunkenness, which is perhaps the most prevalent complaint that is against police constables. If a sergeant finds a man the worse for liquor on his beat, he takes him off his beat to the officer upon duty at the station, who enters there his charge against him. That constable is brought up the next morning at 10 o'clock before his superintendent. That officer has power to inflict a fine not exceeding 10*s.* on any constable, but he must report the fine inflicted to the chief constable immediately thereafter. The chief constable may, if he thinks fit, if he thinks that the superintendent has been too severe or too lenient, he may revise the case, and either remit part of the fine or increase it.

3551. With reference to the infliction of fines. Has the chief constable absolute discretion, or is he limited in any way?—The chief constable, if he is going to inflict a fine, cannot impose a penalty of more than 1*l.*

3552. For drunkenness?—For anything. The rule in reference to that is: "The chief constable shall have power to impose a fine not exceeding 20*s.* on any constable under the rank of lieutenant whom he does not consider it necessary to dismiss." If it was the first offence against a man, the superintendent would very likely deal with it by inflicting a fine of half-a-crown or 5*s.*, and if the man was to offend again he might also fine him again, and the probability is that the third time he would send him to the chief constable, who would consider whether he should inflict a fine then on the scale of 20*s.*, or whether the man should be dismissed as one unsuitable for the service.

3553. That is after how many offences?—Three I should say. It would depend on the length of the service, and whether the three offences came immediately one after another, or once in a year.

3554. Is it the custom to reduce men for the offence of drunkenness, or for grave offences?—Well, the merit class of constables and the first class of constables stand in this relation, that the merit class is a step added to the promotion of a first-class constable. In other words, the constable is first a first-class man, and then a merit-class man. I have deprived the superintendents of dealing with any complaint against these grades of men, for I wish to deal with them with a kind of uniformity. When I put them in the position of first-class or merit-class constables they are told that the stripes put upon their arm are indicative of their being experienced, well-conducted men, and that they can retain them only as long as their conduct is in keeping with that profession, and whenever a man in either of these classes is found offending—and it might be a trivial offence as far as a constable of a lower grade might be concerned—I deprive him of that stripe and reduce him to a lower class.

3555. Supposing he conducted himself well for a period in the lower class, would you allow him to regain his former position?—Yes.

3556. Within what period?—I give them to understand that they will receive back the stripe again provided they conduct themselves well for a twelvemonth, but they are also told that if they have to be reduced again they will never be reinstated; that they had better leave the service and find something where they will have better prospects.

3557. And after a period of one year the unfavourable record is wiped out?—It is, by his promotion to the rank that he had lost. I tell them I will not reduce them twice.

3558. I suppose you find that admonishing and speaking to them in that way has a very good effect?—Yes. When a young man comes from the country, and is thrown into a large populous city such as Glasgow, with the immense temptations around him of a police constable, he has a great chance of falling into some trifling offence, perhaps of taking a little too much spirits, and I make up my mind to expect that in a good many cases; but when a man has had experience, and sees the temptations he is subjected to, I then deal with him in a different way altogether.

3559. Well, now, in the case of a first offence, if a man is brought before you, would you admonish him privately and point out to him the error of his ways, and urge him to a better course of conduct, or would you speak to him in the presence of other men?—It would in all probability be in the presence of the officer who made the complaint against him, and the probability is, that I would have the officer who complained describe what the conduct had been. If he was a young man with only a few weeks' service, I would very likely admonish and advise him to give up

Mr. Alexander McCall.

4 Oct., 1882.

Mr. Alexander McCall.

6 Oct., 18[illegible].

taking drink altogether while he was on duty; and then see whether that course had a good effect or not.

3560. And within your good experience, do you find that a gentle exhortation of that kind has its effect, and that men turn over a new leaf?—Oh, very frequently.

3561. And, in your opinion, an exhortation of that kind is far more effectual than a system of heavy fining?—I look upon heavy fining as useless. When you come to fine heavily, that man has reached a stage of [illegible], for the constant would have been very indifferent, and you had better be relieved of a man of that sort and dismiss him. Besides, very frequently you are only inflicting punishment upon his wife and his family.

3562. Are the men of your force allowed to go into a public-house when off duty and in plain clothes?—Yes; there is no restriction in that respect.

3563. Are they allowed to do so in uniform when off duty?—Well, there is a rule in the service that a man should never be out of his uniform unless he has permission; but that is not very strictly enforced, and while a man is off duty and in uniform I do not think I would have any reason to complain against him, supposing he was going to have refreshment in a public house.

3564. But I suppose on no account are men permitted to go into a public-house on duty?—He is not entitled to enter a public-house unless there is good cause while in discharge of his duty.

3565. *Chairman.*—As I understand you, the maximum fine is 1*l.*?—It is very rarely inflicted. I am sure I have not inflicted it once during my chief constableship.

3566. Well, the alternative usual punishment with that fine is dismissal?—Yes. The chief constable, under the Police Act, might dismiss any man he thinks fit, without assigning any reason for it.

3567. But you think a fine of 20*s.* so very severe that it must be a grave offence, and so grave that the alternative punishment would be dismissal?—Yes.

3568. *Mr. Mercer.*—And in fact, in your judgment, you think it is better to dismiss a man, and get a better man, than to continue a course of excessive fines?—Yes.

3569. *Mr. Holmes.*—In the case of a long interval elapsing between a first and second or third case of drunkenness, would you be disposed to regard that more in the light of a first offence, or would you take into account the fact that he had been drunk on two former occasions, notwithstanding the length of the intervals between those occasions?—I would deal very much with that as a first offence, if it had arisen after a lapse of two or three years. I would deal very much with a man so offending in a lenient way.

3570. As a kind of first offence?—Yes, as an accidental mistake of a man. But if drunkenness was recurring so month after month in a man, then I would say to him, "You are unsuited for the police service; you are evidently not able to withstand the temptations that surround you; therefore you are unfit for the service, and you had better find something else to do."

3571. *Chairman.*—Then as I take it, for the first offence, and for the second and third offences also, you generally caution—you lecture the man in the first instance, and then if there is no interval between the second and third offences you put upon him a nominal penalty?—Yes.

3572. *Mr. Morris.*—Suppose a policeman was dismissed for insubordination, and that he was subsequently pardoned and let back into the force, and then suppose that a month after his reinstatement he got drunk, would you consider that that man was fit for the police force?—No; I would look upon that man's first dismissal as well deserved, and that, having shown him this kindness, and enabled him to return to his position, it would only convince me that he was incorrigible, and that he should not have got the chance of being restored.

3573. *Mr. Holmes.*—You said just now that the men were always required to be in uniform unless they got special leave to be in plain clothes. Do you require your men to provide themselves with plain clothes?—No. Of course, they have plain clothes when they enter the force, and it is generally found, and it is expected, that they will keep up a suit of plain clothing for themselves.

3574. *Chairman.*—I should like to have a comprehensive statement as to the exact course pursued in your force in cases of offences of drunkenness?—In the case of the first offence there is a warning, in the case of the second a small penalty is inflicted, and the third offence may be a heavier fine, or in an aggravated case dismissal; but there are cases in which for the first offence I have thought it necessary to dismiss men—if there is interference with the citizens.

3575. *Mr. Holmes.*—I think we have now gone through nearly every matter I can think of in connection with the force and we come to the final question of all—that of pensions. What is the scale of pensions under which your men retire?—I can answer that question very shortly. There is no such thing as superannuation for the Glasgow police at all. There is a power under the Police Act that the magistrates and Council can grant an allowance to a man on leaving the service, but it is a permissive thing entirely, and that is all; and at the present time the whole sum that is being paid by the community in the way of these allowances is 387*l.* 5*s.*

3576. A year?—Yes, a year; and that is paid amongst eleven decayed men of the service, ten of whom have been constables, and one of them was a sergeant.

3577. Do you consider the fact that the men cannot look forward to pensions accounts to a great extent for so many men leaving your service after a short period?—I think that it undoubtedly is. I think that is certainly the case.

3578. Assuming that the Bill that was before Parliament last Session becomes law next year. I presume that it will extend to Scotland—that the provisions of that Bill in reference to pensions will extend to Scotland?—That was included in the Bill of last Session.

3579. And do you think that with the scale of pensions contemplated by that Bill, and with the present rates of pay, that you will be able to retain the services of men longer than you do now?—I would expect so. I have no doubt it would increase the average length of service of the men.

3580. Do you think that if the men could look forward to fair pensions upon retiring after good service, that they would be content with the existing rates of pay?—I should think so.

3581. And, in your opinion, the present rates of pay are sufficient?—I think they are.

3582. Now, according to your experience, after how many years' service does a policeman, as a general rule, cease to be efficient?—Well, that would depend upon when he entered the service. A man, for instance, I should say, after he reaches 50 years of age, is not likely to be an efficient constable.

3583. But take the case of a man joining at 20 years of age, do you think that, after 25 years' service, there would be much left in him?—That would bring him to 45 years of age. Well, I do not see anything in the service, provided that that man was a healthy man and of good constitution when he joined at 20 years of age; I do not know of anything in the service that should work that man out at the age of 45. I think he should be an efficient man after that for some time.

3584. *Mr. Morris.*—Do not you think that a man serving in the rank of constable, and never reaching a higher grade, after thirty years' service night and day, is pretty well worn out?—Well, if a man joined at 25 years of age, or from that to 30 years of age, I think he would; but if he joined at 20 or 19 years of age, as was contemplated in the Act, after thirty years' service I do not consider that he should be inefficient or wrought out.

3585. In considering the pension list, and the time of service of a policeman, do you consider that it would be desirable to allow a man to retire on whatever pension would be due after he had served twenty-eight or thirty years, without having to undergo a medical examination?—I think it is desirable that there should be a fixed age at which a man should claim his discharge, provided he has served the period that entitles him to the pension, say, twenty-five or twenty-eight years' service; but it would be well to fix the age when he would be entitled to claim his discharge, but I do not know that it would be fair to the public funds that a man, we will say, of 45 years of age, should be allowed to withdraw from the force at that age.

3586. Supposing him to have joined at 20?—Yes; I think that man should be perfectly able for some years after that to discharge the duties of a police constable, and to throw a man of 45 years of age upon the superannuation fund, who may live until he is 70 years of age or more, would be taxing this fund very seriously during a long number of years.

3587. I believe, as a rule, that a Scotchman would take a more practical view of this kind of thing than an Irishman would?—Well, even as a police officer myself, I would have some hesitation in giving a man a pension that he could claim at any time after a certain service; I think it should be accompanied by some restriction as to age or health.

3588. *Chairman.*—How do you deal with violations of discipline in the case of superior officers?—Well, I explained that I have not the power of dismissing a superintendent or a lieutenant. The magistrates' committee are vested with that power, but they cannot even dismiss a superintendent or a lieutenant until I have, as an initiatory step, suspended them from duty. Then the committee is entitled to dismiss officers of either of those ranks if they think fit.

3589. In the case of sergeants and sub-inspectors, in whose power is it to dismiss men of those ranks?—In their cases dismissal is entirely in my hands.

3590. Do you fine them in cases of justifiable complaint against them?—Well, it is rarely that I have any complaints made against men of those ranks. I have had complaints against a sergeant or two, and I prefer more to suspend them, perhaps, for a week or a fortnight, and I then give them time to think over their conduct than to inflict a money fine.

3591. *Mr. Morris.*—And does the fact of suspension stop their pay?—Yes.

3592. Well, that in itself amounts to a fine?—Yes; a severer fine than the 1l. that I could inflict, and no man with me draws any pay when he is off duty, even when sick.

3593. And if a man gets a bad cold, or a fever, owing to the severe strain of night duty, and is laid up for a month, does he receive no pay during that time?—No.

3594. Supposing he is a married man with a family, how is he to support himself?—He has just to throw himself upon his club friendly society.

3595. Which the men subscribe to themselves?—Yes. If he is hurt upon duty, rendered unfit for his duties by having been injured or hurt in the execution of his duty, then he receives his pay.

3596. Suppose a single man, living in barracks, dies, or is removed to hospital, say, and dies in a few days, is there any allowance for his interment?—His relatives would receive one from his friendly society.

3597. But is there any allowance from the public funds for that purpose?—No. "No work, no pay" is the motto adopted.

3598. Because they are allowed 2l. 10s. 6d. in the Dublin force for the burial of a single man who dies, and they wish that was increased to 3l., I think; but then you are aware, I suppose, that we have such things as wakes in Ireland?—Yes, and we have them in Glasgow, and there are rare lively scenes when they do take place.

Mr. Alexander McCall.

6 Oct., 1882.

Colonel John Augustus Connolly, V.C., Assistant Commissioner, Dublin Metropolitan Police, examined.

3599. *Chairman.*—What is your name?—John Augustus Connolly.

Colonel John Augustus Connolly.

6 Oct., 1882.

3600. You are the Assistant Commissioner of the Dublin metropolitan police force?—Yes.

3601. When, may I ask, were you appointed?—I was appointed in October 1877.

3602. *Mr. Holmes.*—I don't know whether you are aware of all the matters which the men have brought under our notice during the course of this inquiry. I may mention to you the most important of them, and I have no doubt that during your examination we will call your attention to others as they occur to us. I think that perhaps the three most important matters are as follows: and taking them in their order, I may tell you that the men feel very much dissatisfied at not having received the grant of three months' pay for extra duty, such as the Royal Irish Constabulary received; secondly, they think that perhaps the reins have been drawn somewhat too tightly in matters of discipline; and, thirdly, they complain of the scale of pensions. Besides these things, they have brought many other matters under our notice, but I think, and I think the Chairman and Mr. Morris will agree with me, the three subjects I have mentioned are the most important of them. Now, I would like to ask your opinion with reference to the first, namely, the dissatisfaction that the men feel at not having received the three months' gratuity. Do you think that that dissatisfaction is well grounded?—I am not in the least surprised at the extreme dissatisfaction of the force at the way in which they have been left out in the cold.

3603. As regards the gratuity of three months' pay?—Yes. I think that they are certainly entitled to the whole period, and to receive it in precisely the same manner as the Royal Irish Constabulary.

3604. I don't know whether you are aware that it transpired, in the course of the evidence before the Constabulary Committee that sat at the beginning of this year, that a great number of the men belonging to the Royal Irish Constabulary were seriously out of pocket by reason of the agitation. For instance, men were ordered away from their stations, and they were charged such exorbitant prices for their lodgings and for food, that the allowances that they then received were not sufficient to meet those charges, and men who had previously saved money in the force were obliged to spend their savings in order to meet the deficit on those charges?—I never was aware in the slightest degree of that fact.

3605. Well, that was the case, and I believe it formed the strongest reason for giving that grant of three months' pay to the men. Do you think that any of your men were out of pocket from the causes that I have just mentioned as arising in the case of the constabulary?—Not to my knowledge.

3606. *Chairman.*—But you think there was ample grounds for discontent?—Yes.

3607. *Mr. Morris.*—We have had, Colonel Connolly, from men who have been examined, instances, I might almost say we had examples, of men in the Royal Irish Constabulary quartered, say in Belfast, or the County Down, or Bray, where none of the disturbances that existed in other parts of the country was witnessed, receiving this gratuity, while the men of the Dublin force were excluded from it. These Dublin policemen considered that they had a great deal more trouble from the Land League agitation for the last three years than these men of the constabulary in Belfast and Bray. Don't you think that, viewing it in that way, it was enough to create some discontent?—Oh, quite so, without even going into detail with reference to the work.

3608. Don't you think, without going into detail, that the Land League agitation, with all its concomitants,

Colonel John Augustus Connolly.

6 Oct., 1883.

[illegible] the arrests of certain men, and the suspects who were imprisoned here, and the rioting in the city, added considerably to the work of the police on duty in Dublin?—Yes; certainly it did.

3809. *Chairman.*—And curtailed the time of the dismissal of the men?—Certainly it did.

3810. *Mr. Morris.*—The men have also stated to the Committee, without going into particulars, that although not actually on active duty, they were frequently kept for many hours ready to be sent out into the streets?—That is perfectly true.

3811. And they also told that when these suspects—and they gave these as instances of their extra work—were being brought up to Dublin, either to a Dublin prison, or some northern prison, that they were ordered, often out of their beds, to the railway stations, and obliged to attend there for hours if the trains were late, awaiting the arrival of these suspects, and thus there was a great deal of extra duty put upon them, arising out of the Land League agitation; is that not so?—Certainly.

3812. Do you agree with that view?—Certainly.

3813. *Chairman.*—And I think, if my recollection is right, that we had it from some of the constables that they had been put to expense out of their own pockets in going from place to place, and that they were not recouped for that?—Well, I was not aware of that.

3814. *Mr. Holmes.*—They gave instances of this kind. When a telegram would come to the police authorities during the day, to the effect that a number of suspects were to arrive in Dublin by a certain train, of course directions were immediately sent to have a number of policemen assembled in the neighbourhood of the railway station at which these suspects were expected to arrive, and if men were sent by their superintendent or sergeant, they were ordered to go to the Kingsbridge or Broadstone, or other railway station, and told to be there at a certain hour; and their statement was, that they frequently had to take cars to reach the railway station in time, and that they therefore lost money in that way?—Well, I do not exactly understand how they had to pay for those cars. The cars are, as a rule, paid for if the men send in a statement of their expenses. If they send in a statement that the car has been hired for their duty to convey them from one place to another, it is allowed.

3815. And if, in the opinion of the Commissioners, it is a proper and legitimate expense?—Certainly. At the same time, there are expenses to meet which, when the call for their attendance at the railway stations first began, there was no fund set apart, as there is now, for special purposes. Since the Phoenix Park murder there has been a large sum of money laid out, it may be described as for personal defence of individuals, and all expenses connected with that. I do not think that there was any fund set apart before the Phoenix Park murder for special expenses.

3816. *Mr. Morris.*—Well, then, as the Committee understand, we suppose you, to a large extent, coincide with the views put forward by the men, that they were entitled to some consideration with the rest of the police who got gratuities?—Yes.

3817. *Chairman.*—And to the same extent?—Yes; to the same amount.

3818. *Mr. Holmes.*—The next question which the men brought under our notice, and seemed to set the most importance upon, was the question of discipline. They alleged generally, and also went into some cases in support of their allegation, that the fines were excessive; that the men were reduced, as they thought, for trivial offences; and that, after a man had been reduced, he had no chance of retrieving his position; in point of fact, that an unfavourable record—to repeat the expression that the men used—"stared a man in the face" to the end of the chapter, and that there was no locus pœnitentiæ given to the men. Now, that was their general statement. They supported this general statement by referring to a number of cases. I think that we have sent you over an extract of a series of cases to which the men had drawn our attention, in order that you, if you thought fit, might have an opportunity of giving a different colour to the stories which the men represented.

3819. *Mr. Morris.*—I wish to supplement Mr. Holmes' observations before entering into the evidence on the question. What the men appeared to me to feel, as well as I could collect their opinions, was that, suppose a man was reduced from being a sergeant to a first-class constable, they wished to have some kind of rule established by which he should, say, after a year, or two, or three years, if he was of good character, and with no black mark against him during that time, go back to his former grade or position. I am merely bringing the matter under your notice in order that you should understand that was very much the view they put forward; instead of being obliged to go to school to work up again as a young recruit would have to do, a man if he were reduced from being a sergeant or a constable might after three years, if his conduct was good, step back to his former position. We have had Mr. Walker, the District Superintendent of the London metropolitan police, before us, and he has been examined on that particular point, and I merely wish to point out, before you enter on the subject, that he appears rather to favour that view?—I do not know the circumstances under which Mr. Walker works, or by whom he is surrounded. As a rule, I think, it could not be adopted; as an exception, certainly. As a rule, I think, it would be unjust. It would be unjust, because a man has once held the position of sergeant, to prefer him again at the end of any particular time over the heads of others. He has had his chance; he has forfeited the confidence of his superiors, otherwise he would not be reduced. He has had his trial. He has failed; and it is only right—it is only just—that others junior to him should then take theirs. At the same time, it is in the power of the Commissioners to recognise in any individual case special services. If he is a man who has distinguished himself, and has been exceedingly efficient in the performance of his duties as a sergeant, we will say that that man should then, if there is an opening, and it there happens to be no man sufficiently or equally worthy with him, that that man might be brought forward again before his time; but I would make it an exception.

3820. It is the rule in England?—Well, I don't think it is just.

3821. And that there should be a limited period of reduction?—Well, that is part of a system, but I do not think that that is just. I think that there are many others—I know that there are in our force many others looking forward to promotion, and I think it would be an unjust thing to prefer a man who has already failed over their heads.

3822. *Mr. Holmes.*—Colonel Connolly, we have already examined before this Committee District Superintendent Walker, of the London metropolitan police force, Captain Nott-Bower, chief constable of Liverpool, and Mr. McCall, chief constable of Glasgow, and the evidence which they have given us on this matter is to this effect, that if a man is reduced he is only reduced for a limited period, and if he behaves himself well during that period, he is reinstated to his former position. Do I understand you to say that you consider that that rule would act unjustly in the case of the Dublin metropolitan police?—I do say that, certainly; I think that in the face of it it is an injustice, and it is no encouragement to men to work up for a rank when they see that a man who has already failed is preferred over their heads.

3823. Take the case of a man in the rank of sergeant who has never been previously convicted of any offence, and who is brought before you on a first charge against him of drunkenness, would you in that case reduce him as a matter of course?—Certainly.

3824. And would you do that even though he had been in the force ten years, and that was his first offence. Would you not think it would be rather that that man should be shut out from any hope?—Oh, he is not shut out.

3825. Or from having any chance of being again promoted?—He can rise of course, and again obtain pro-

sation if he makes the effort so to do. The same abilities which made him attain the position of sergeant in the first instance will be also of advantage to him in attaining it again.

3626. Would you not, in the case I have just instanced, in taking into account his first offence, consider the terrible punishment that reduction was; and would you not be inclined to prefer a small fine, accompanied by admonition and exhortation?—As a rule, no. The men who are called upon to perform the duties of sergeant, and who disgrace themselves in front of their men, do so to such an extent that they damage the discipline that should exist throughout the service for the benefit of the service. A man who is drunk on duty in front of his men is a man who is, I think, unfit to hold the position of a sergeant.

3627. Though it is his first and a casual offence?—Though it is his first offence. You take an exceptional case to raise. I say I am open to make allowance for a case in an exceptional case, and perhaps a man who has a great many years' service, and who is a man who has always been an extremely efficient sergeant, I think the Commissioner is bound to take those points into consideration for the advantage of the service, and then he sets aside the actual justice of the case, and promotes that man again to his former position for the advantage of the service. Where the two things are presented to us as alternatives, we say the advantage of the service is a very important consideration.

3628. I presume that, in cases such as I have instanced, you consult the Chief Commissioner before inflicting the punishment?—Certainly; in all cases of reduction. It is looked upon as a very serious punishment to inflict in the reduction of an officer from his rank, and in all cases of reduction the Commissioners are amalgamated I may say. In all serious cases where there are vexed or complicated points—cases where the award would be rather difficult—as a rule the Commissioners join together.

3629. Then, if I understand you rightly, your evidence is that reduction would be unlimited in point of time?—The reduction would go on to the usual course; it would be unlimited. I do not mean, however, to say by that that a man never would rise to be a sergeant again.

3630. But the reduction would be unlimited in the first instance?—Yes, unlimited; but not necessarily. We have men of various ranks; we have the rank of inspector, and of course it would be hard to reduce an inspector to be a constable, and we take those things into due consideration, although I think, looking at discipline in point of discipline, an inspector should be reduced.

3631. *Mr. Morris.*—We have had some evidence upon this point, and it is one on which I should like to have your opinion recorded, Colonel Connolly, that in some of the forces in England and Scotland the chief constables there think it is almost better to discharge a man from the service altogether, after a certain number of punishments have been inflicted, if his conduct does not permanently improve?—That depends very much upon the man—the disposition of the man. If a man is brought up upon a charge, and it is proved against him, and the man considers that he is not unjustly punished, I do not see why that man should not remain in the service; but if a man, no matter how completely the offence is proved against him, or how just the punishment given, considered that he was unjustly treated, I would certainly not be in favour of making an effort to retain such a man in the force.

3632. Do you find, from your information and knowledge of the force, that a great number of men—if I may use the term to describe it—persuade themselves that they are innocent of the offences for which they are punished?—I don't know; I have no opportunity of knowing that.

3633. *Chairman.*—But don't you think that making the degradation unlimited leads to discontent or to despondency on the part of the men, and to their giving up all hope of a more successful career?—I don't know; I have never heard of it except from you.

3634. *Mr. Holmes.*—Are you not in the habit of always inflicting a fine for the first offence of drunkenness in the case of a constable?—No.

3635. How would you deal with a first case of drunkenness?—I would consider his character, and the punishment suitable for his particular case. With some men it would be the most advantageous course to administer a fine the first time, because it would cure them at once. If I understood from the character of the man, as given by his officers, that he was a man who was always going about tippling and being on the verge of being unfit for duty, and that he was now caught actually unfit, I would be very much inclined to give that man a smart fine for the purpose of deterring him and for his own advantage.

3636. When you say a "smart" fine, what amount would you consider a "smart" fine?—10s.

3637. When you inflict a fine for the first time upon a constable for a case of drunkenness, what does it usually amount to?—About 15s.

3638. And for a second offence occurring within a short period?—1l. 10s., or reduction to inferior rate.

3639. And for a third offence?—Reduction, to inferior rate.

3640. I may mention to you what Mr. Morris has already mentioned, that the chief constable of Glasgow, in a case of that kind, told us where there would be a third offence of drunkenness occurring within a short period, he would consider a man, in whose case that occurred, as unfit for the service, and he would dismiss him?—Well, we should dismiss him for the fourth.

3641. *Mr. Morris.*—Don't you think that heavy fines tend to "knock a man out of time," if I may use the expression, and prevent him meeting his expenses. I allude, of course especially to the case of a married man?—Well, it depends upon what you consider a heavy fine.

3642. I would call a heavy fine 2l., or, indeed, 1l.?—Well, considering the man's pay, it has been represented to me that in some of the forces the Commissioner is limited to a week's pay. In the case of a man who is married, the chances are that he would be a first-class constable, and that man gets 30s. a-week. That would be the very fine I would award him. A fine of 1l. would be very little for that man.

3643. *Mr. Holmes.*—You are quite right in referring to the limitation that is imposed by the General Police Act in England in the case of fining men. The fine cannot exceed a week's pay, and the chief constable of Glasgow tells us to-day that he is limited to 1l.—that is the maximum fine that he can inflict. Now, do I understand you to say that the Commissioners of Police in Dublin have unlimited discretion as regards the amounts of the fines?—I think so. There is no limit.

3644. Then, in holding an inquiry into the conduct of a policeman, what means do you take to satisfy yourself as to the charges?—The evidence brought forward against a man is either by civilians, or by his own officers, or by the joint evidence of the two, sometimes civilians and officers together; sometimes by other constables.

3645. In holding an inquiry of that kind, are all the parties present?—Certainly.

3646. In case a complaint is made by a civilian against a constable, or a policeman of any grade, is the civilian obliged to attend?—Certainly.

3647. And to prosecute his case?—If he does not attend the case is dismissed. But there may be more than one charge. Cases arise usually in this way. A complaint is made by a civilian that he is either assaulted or has suffered some injury, or something of that kind, at the hands of a policeman. The letter is generally sent to the superintendent of the division to which the constable belongs for his report on the matter. His report then comes to the Commissioner, and after that report is received, an answer is sent to the civilian who complains to such and such an effect; and if the Commissioner thinks it is a case in which it is necessary to have an investigation, he tells the civilian, "If you attend my office between such and such hours on such and such a day, your case shall be investigated." Well, he comes, and he brings in a number of witnesses, who

Colonel John Augustus Connolly.

4 Oct., 1882.

support his allegations, and the case is gone into before the Commissioners and decided.

3548. Then, as I understand you, there is no cross-examining of the witnesses, or anything of that sort, before the Commissioners?—No.

3549. It is all statement?—It is voluntary statement.

3550. And you have to judge very much of the probabilities of the stories, naturally?—Yes, a good deal.

3551. And do you consider that it would be an improvement if those inquiries were held before the Commissioners on oath?—No; but when the civilian element comes into the matter, it differs from the element in which the police officers only are concerned; but in cases where the evidence brought to support a case is that of policemen—where the evidence is police evidence—I should object very strongly to sworn testimony, because I think it would be tantamount to saying that you could not believe the statement of a police officer.

3552. You being, as we all know, a distinguished military officer, can answer the question quite readily: in the cases of all courts-martial held, are not the witnesses sworn?—Yes, all sworn.

3553. Do you think it would act injuriously to the force to have a sworn investigation instead of an oral one?—The cases which are tried before the Commissioners are not similar to those that are tried before a court-martial. The cases tried before a court-martial are always cases requiring a very heavy sentence—they are all of a very serious nature. The cases in all regiments that are similar to those cases tried by the Commissioners are tried in the orderly-room of the force before the commanding officers upon testimony which is not sworn.

3554. *Mr. Morris.*—Are you aware of any cases within your time of complaints made by civilians against policemen, I presume in writing, in which the decisions were given without bringing the party complaining forward before the policeman and before the Commissioners?—None. The course which I have pointed out to you and described to you is the invariable rule.

3555. *Mr. Holmes.*—I think we furnished you with some notes of particular cases that have been brought under our notice. Did you think it was worth your while to look into them, or have you any observations to make to us in reference to them,—I need hardly say to you that we do not ask you to do so unless it is your perfect pleasure to do so?—I don't know whether it would be advisable to give the particulars; I have the particulars here if you like to have them published and printed. I do not see the slightest objection to giving you the fullest particulars; the only thing would be the question of names.

3556. We should prefer not having the names?—I think you can ascertain the points in dispute quite well without the names.

3557. The Commission would very much like to impress upon you, Colonel Connolly, that we are not deputed by His Excellency to make any inquiries into the discipline of the force, and that it is neither our wish nor intention to do so; but as His Excellency desired that our inquiry should be full and complete, we were obliged to listen to evidence upon certain matters. To the best of our ability we prevented men from going into particular cases, and we endeavoured to restrict them to general statements. In some instances, the witness who gave the evidence happened to be the person who had been fined or reduced, and in cases of that kind we were not able, of course, to exclude the evidence. With these observations, I would again like to ask you whether, now that you were furnished with particular cases, you wish to, as it were, defend or justify your conduct, or do you wish to show that the representations which the men made admit perhaps of a different interpretation?—I wish to give the full particulars.

3558. Do you think that we have sufficiently conveyed to you, by these observations, that we were most careful not to put you under any kind of examination?—Perfectly.

3559. You are quite satisfied?—Yes. I am only called on to give you my own explanation of certain special cases that came under your notice; I am not speaking as to the system.

3560. The first case in the summary which we supplied to you appears to be that of a man reduced to the bottom of the fourth rate and fined 20s. for smoking at 2 o'clock in the morning, when on duty at the police barrack gate?—I remember the case to which you refer. The real charge brought against this man was "for smoking a pipe while on duty at Kevin Street barrack-gate, between 12 and 1 a.m., on the 20th September, 1879; also, inattention to duty by allowing the foot-way to be used as a urinal within a few yards of him." Now, my own observations on this case, I would add, if you wish—"This constable was very often punished; the above is a very gross case."

3561. Do you remember for what offences he had been punished?—Oh, many; he was very often punished; the offences were, I think, as far as I can remember, inattention to duty, constant inattention to duty.

3562. In what class of constables was he?—In the fourth. It was only a question of degree on the rate; he was not reduced a rate.

3563. Well, the second case appears to be that of the gaoler of Newmarket, who was fined 10s. for smoking in the reserve room at 12 o'clock noon?—The case is, that he was fined 2s. 6d., not 10s., for smoking in the inspector's office, which is a very different place from the reserve room, at Newmarket police-station, contrary to Commissioners' orders, while on duty. My observations on that are—"I consider that a light punishment."

3564. Now, the third case appears to be one in which a number of men were fined for not observing, on their beat, that a knocker had been wrenched off a door. The fines imposed amounted to 1*l*. 7*s*. 6*d*. I have a perfect recollection that no fines were given in this case, so that you can refer to that as you like?—The charge stated, I think, is correct in this case: "For not observing that a knocker had been stolen off the hall door of the house, 111, Grafton Street." The fines were divided. The sergeant was fined 7*s*. 6*d*., the acting sergeant was fined 5*s*., two constables were fined 5*s*. each, and one constable was fined 2*s*. 6*d*. My observations upon the case are—"I consider them fair punishments." The total is 1*l*. 5*s*., instead of 1*l*. 7*s*. 6*d*.

3565. By whom was it discovered that the knocker had been wrenched off?—I could not tell you that.

3566. I presume by the inspector?—Generally speaking, when the men are fined for not discovering and not reporting a thing of that kind, the report usually comes from the owner of the house, who misses his knocker.

3567. The next case is that of a placard that was alleged to be seditious, but subsequently, the witness said, held not to be so. Thirty-four officers and men were fined for not observing it posted on the 10th January. The fines imposed amounted, in all, to 46*l*.?—The fines amounted, in all, to those concerned in this matter, to 24*l*. 10*s*., and the offence was—"For not observing and reporting that placards of a seditious nature were posted conspicuously throughout many places in those avenues and sub-divisions."

3568. Then it was not the case of one placard?—Oh, no, it was the same placard posted in many places. And the fines were: An acting inspector was fined 2*l*., one sergeant and fourteen acting sergeants were fined 1*l*. 10*s*. each, and one constable was fined 1*l*. My remarks upon the case are—"At this time the Land League was very active, and the first notice that the Commissioners had of these placards was being called upon by the Under-Secretary to explain a paragraph in the newspapers announcing that they had been posted. I consider these cases of serious neglect of duty, without excuse of any kind, and the fines in some of the instances too heavy."

3569. *Mr. Morris.*—Before leaving that case, I should like to ask you a question about it. The man who put forward that case, told us that at first these were considered seditious placards, but afterwards were declared not to be so. I suppose it was immaterial to the Commissioners whether the fine point of law, seditious or not seditious, was determined one way or the other; the fines were inflicted for the fact of the police not having reported them?—Yes; and it was part of the charge that the placards were of a seditious nature, which they most decidedly were.

3670. And though they might be held afterwards not to be of a seditious nature, it was the duty of the policemen to have reported them, and not to raise any question about them?—Quite so. As far as the judgment of the police were concerned, they were evidently of a seditious nature.

3671. *Mr. Holmes.*—The next case is that in which two officers, one an acting inspector, and the other a full sergeant—one in plain clothes off duty, and the other in uniform off duty—for going into a respectable public-house. One was fined 7*l.*, and the other was fined 5*l.*?—Yes. The charge in this case was—"For being in a public-house in George's Street, Kingstown, the acting inspector, on duty and in uniform, and the sergeant in plain clothes, and on the sick report." The fine is stated correctly to be 7*l.* for the acting inspector and 5*l.* for the sergeant. My remarks on this case are —"The acting inspector should have been reduced; he should have reported the sergeant instead of drinking with him. The sergeant was fairly punished; he might have been reduced for such an offence."

3672. *Chairman.*—Then the fines were not, in your opinion, excessive?—No. The acting inspector should certainly have been reduced; and it was a very great error indeed that he, on duty and in uniform, should go into a public-house with the sergeant, who was equally culpable for going into a public-house when he was on the sick report.

3673. *Mr. Holmes.*—The next case appears to be one that occurred in 1878, and has reference to a pane of glass which was broken in a house in William Street. The house was alleged to be in off the street. Eleven men, among them four acting sergeants, were fined, the latter 1*l.* each and the constables 10*s.*, for not observing it and reporting it. It was alleged in this case that the men were not allowed to make any defence?—Well, that is not true. The charge was—"For not noticing and reporting that a pane of plate glass, valued at 3*l.*, had been broken in a window in William Street, the constables being on the beat, and the acting sergeants in charge of the section. The fines were: the two acting sergeants, 1*l.* each; the five constables, 10*s.* each." My remarks are—"In this case the house was not off the street. It is a large house, and a well-known house in William Street. The fines are heavier than usual, in consequence of previous reports for the same offence."

3674. Against these particular men?—Not against these particular men.

3675. Then why should they be fined for other people's negligence?—Because all the punishments are published in orders. The men were perfectly aware that these punishments had been inflicted upon other men for not discovering glass broken and reporting it. These punishments had not been previously inflicted upon these men; but we have to deal with officers in the district. There was a previous case where twenty-one panes of glass were broken, and not reported, on the 20th July of the same year, 1878; and there were eight panes of glass broken and not reported on the 6th September, 1878, and twenty panes of glass broken and not reported on the 15th September, 1878. The usual defence was called for from the men.

3676. How do you mean?—Every man was asked if he had anything to say in reference to the case, and the 10*s.* fine was imposed for the sheet of plate glass that they did not report.

3677. I presume that it is a special part of a policeman's duty to observe and report upon such matters?—Yes; a special part of their duty, and they are invariably punished for neglecting it.

3678. Was there any reason to suppose that these men were aware of all these previous breakages of glass?—They must have been aware, because an account of it was all published in orders.

3679. The next case is that of a constable having omitted to go into College Street police-station from where he was stationed, at the College, and, having reported himself to the officer in the station, was fined 10*s.* for being absent from his beat. It is also stated in this case that no excuse was taken from the man?—The charge in this case is being absent from a fixed point—College Green—in consequence of which a sergeant had to arrest a drunken man who was found lying on the footway opposite to Trinity College. My observation is—"If the constable had shown that he had reported himself to the officer on duty at College Street police-station, he would not have been reported." In reference to the statement that no excuse was taken, I may say that constables charged with an offence are invariably asked for their defence.

3680. *Chairman.*—Have you any recollection that that was done in this case?—It is the regular thing; it is always done.

3681. *Mr. Holmes.*—In the next case, the witness gave his name, but as the evidence is not before me I cannot tell you what it is, but when we asked him who the man was that was fined, he said himself. It is the case of a man on duty at Westland Row, it being half-past 6 o'clock in the morning, reported for having one glove off, the charge being—"Walking on beat in a slovenly manner." The man was fined 1*l.*, and, although on the approved list for promotion, was kept back for six months?—That case was—"For being slovenly on his beat, having his hands in his pockets while on duty at Westland Row." He was fined 20*s.* My observations are—"This is a very important post, requiring activity and attention constantly; he has a long defaulters' sheet, and I consider the fine a fair one."

3682. You do not consider it excessive?—I do not.

3683. *Mr. Morris.*—What is the meaning of a long defaulters' sheet. Had he been fined before?—I can show you the sheet. I am certain he had; a great many times.

3684. For the same offence?—I could not answer that without the sheet; but if you would like to see the sheet I can easily get it for you.

3685. *Mr. Holmes.*—The next case is that of a man on duty at an out-station, and who was fined 10*s.* for losing a key?—The case is this: he was charged with neglect of duty in not coming to Chapelizod station to see two constables relieved off duty, and into barracks at 2 a.m. on the 19th September, 1879; also absenting himself from the principal part of his section from 11 o'clock on the 18th until 2·30 a.m. on the 19th September, 1879, and not regularly visiting the constables of whom he had charge, and also losing the key of the barrack door. He was fined 30*s.* My observation on this case is—"I consider this well-deserved punishment."

3686. The next case is that of a man who prevented a woman from the Northern police-court twelve months' since, and who was reduced from first to second class at a loss of 1*s.* 6*d.* per week ever since, notwithstanding the statement of Dr. M'Blain and others, that no unnecessary violence was used, and it is alleged that the woman was not called to substantiate the statement contained in her letter of complaint?—The charge was this—"For refusing to admit a witness into the police court on the 18th August, 1881, and assaulting her when she endeavoured to enter. Also seizing and dragging her out of court when she succeeded in getting in by the opposite door." He was reduced from first to second rate.

3687. *Mr. Morris.*—Did the woman come forward?—She and her sister were both present at the inquiry.

3688. And he was also present?—Yes. My observations on that case are—"In this case the Commissioners considered that the constable acted for the purpose of preventing witnesses giving evidence in a case against a solicitor connected with the court." The accusers were both present at the time of the investigation.

Colonel John Augustus Connolly.

8 Oct., 1882.

Colonel John Augustus Connolly.

6 Oct., 1882.

2689. *Mr. Holmes.*—The next case is that of the same constable who was fined on another occasion for having a glove off. This man, it is stated, was never fined for drunkenness, but he had been previously fined for selling plain porter instead of "XX" to the constables at Kilmainham barrack?—There is no record of this man having been fined for having a glove off, we cannot find any record of that. But the same man was fined 20s. for selling plain porter instead of "XX" to the men in Kilmainham barrack, when he was acting as canteenman. The men found that they were getting bad porter, and they reported him. My remarks on that case are—"This is a case of imposition on the men, and a well-deserved punishment."

2690. The next case is that of a man degraded for the first offence of drunkenness after fourteen years—the reduction continuing since 1877—and fined 20s. for not being in his division in proper time, though he declared that he had received no instructions to do so, and for being in another division at the time?—His case is as follows—"Reduced to first-rate constable for being unfit for duty from the effects of liquor while on duty at Queen Street, on the 5th February, 1877." My remarks on this case are—"A well-deserved punishment."

2691. Was it the first offence of drunkenness, as alleged?—That I could not tell without looking at the sheet; but we can refer to the sheet.

2692. And was he fined 20s. also?—Not for that offence.

2693. The next case is that of a man who was fined 15s. for smoking in Bull Lane at half-past 11 o'clock at night?—That is the same man; and previously to that he was fined 2*l.* for being in a public-house, off duty, and in uniform. That charge was—"Being in a public-house on the 22nd June, 1880, off duty, and in uniform. Fined 2*l.* and removed from the advanced class." My remark is—"This I consider a fair punishment." The next offence to which you have just called my attention occurred in the case of the same man, it was—"For smoking while on duty in Bull Lane, between 11 and 12 p.m. on the 27th July, 1880." He was fined 15s. My remarks are—"This is a most important post, requiring great steadiness and activity. Properly fined." There is another case brought forward by the same man. It goes back as far as 1876. For questioning the decision of the Commissioner about his not removing into his division, and being insubordinate before the chief superintendent. He was fined 20s. My remark is—"Properly fined."

2694. The last case of all on the list which we have given you appears to be the case of a man in June 1880, engaged in the collection of agricultural statistics, who was fined 2*l.* for entering a public-house after his duty was completed?—That is the same man whose offences I have just described, and the reason that that man was removed from the advanced class was because there was an Order that if any man in the advanced class was guilty of a serious offence he was to be removed from it.

2695. Colonel Connolly, you clearly understand the circumstances under which we have brought these cases under your notice, and that it was not with any intention, I need hardly say, of questioning your decisions in any one case, but because we thought it fair and right that as these matters have been brought forward on oath, you should have an opportunity of stating why you so acted?—Certainly.

2696. *Mr. Morris.*—It has been represented, Colonel Connolly, here by some of the men—I think, the greatest number of them—as a grievance, that they are not allowed to go into a public-house when off duty and in plain clothes. I know perfectly well the difficulty of forming a very positive opinion upon that; but I should like very much to hear your view upon it, whether it would be for the benefit of the force, or otherwise, that the present rule should be relaxed. We should be glad if you would give your opinion whether you think it would be likely to lead to intemperance in the force by lending men, while off duty and in plain clothes, to go into public-houses and tipple, and being obliged at a certain hour to go in uniform and take their turn of duty, they might have just a little drop too much?—My opinion is formed very much from the history of the restriction. At one time in the force, up to the year 1840—the force was formed in 1837—the men were allowed to go into public-houses in plain clothes; but that privilege was so abused, that men were constantly found playing cards and drinking in public-houses. Then Mr O'Farrell issued an Order in 1842, and that Order—I have not got a copy of it, but the Chief Commissioner will give you a copy of it when he is examined—will show you how very much he regretted being obliged to issue the Order, but how absolutely necessary it was, from the way in which the privilege had been abused. My own experience is that the men of any force are unfortunately liable to be addicted so very much to drink, that I do not think that regulation could be relaxed as a rule; but I think that some exception might be made to it, and I think that an official permission, if given to men under certain circumstances, when they had a party of friends with them, or anything of that sort, to go into public-houses, might be granted without danger to the force—if it was a sort of temporary relaxation.

2697. *Chairman.*—But if any change was made in the rule, and it was found to work unsatisfactorily, it could be reformed again?—I think it would be very unwise to relax the rule generally.

2698. But the men of the police forces in London and Glasgow possess the privilege of entering public-houses?—I should be very averse to relaxing the rule generally; but, except casually, I think it might be done.

2699. *Mr. Morris.*—Then, as regards leave. The men have put forward a claim for extension of leave beyond the periods that they are in the habit of getting now. I forget exactly the scale they put forward. They put forward a different scale for an inspector, and for a sergeant, and for a constable. The higher grade was to have a longer period. They say that at present the leave is too short, and they also complain that, owing to the state of affairs in this country for the last few years, that they did not get even that leave. They put forward—at any rate, a constable put forward—the suggestion that he ought to be entitled to a fortnight or three weeks' leave in a year, and then that he ought to get two days' leave in the month in addition?—They now get one day in the month and ten days at a run, and I doubt whether you could give them more.

2700. But is it the fact that for the last two or three years they have not got their leave, and that it has been necessary, owing to the state of the country, to keep them on duty?—I have no doubt that it has been necessary to restrict the amount of leave given.

2701. Then they put forward the claim that, unless they are given the leave, whatever it may be they are entitled to, they ought to receive extra pay for the time that they are kept on duty?—I think that pay for leave would not do. Leave is always considered as a privilege, and if because you do not grant a privilege you are to pay for it—I think that is an unreasonable way of looking at it—and the leave was not granted I am sure because the work has been increased; therefore that makes their demand for the three months' gratuity all the more tenable. I consider that the greatest possible attention should be given by the officials to giving the men their leave if possible.

2702. We have had before us the chief constable of Glasgow, and we have also had the advantage of having before us the chief constable of Liverpool, who was the chief constable of Leeds for some years before, and, comparing the population of Glasgow and Liverpool, and finding that it is certainly one-third higher than that of the metropolitan district of Dublin, while the number of police is pretty much about the same, may I ask you, do you consider that the strength of the Dublin metropolitan police force is sufficient in point of numbers?—Considering the nature of the crime that usually we have to deal with in Dublin, I think the force is sufficiently strong.

Colonel John Augustus Connolly.

6 Oct., 1882.

3703. *Mr. Holmes.*—Upon this general question of discipline I would like to ask you, Colonel Connolly, as an Irishman, and a very distinguished Irishman, whether you do not think from your experience that the Irish are very susceptible to the influence of kindness; and whether you think, perhaps, upon mature consideration, that the discipline might have been as easily maintained by adopting a somewhat less severe system of fining, and adopting instead a system of exhortation and dissuasion?—The Commissioners have had to deal with the curse of drunkenness to a very deplorable extent. I would prefer not giving the statistics as to drunkenness for the sake of the force.

3704. *Mr. Morris.*—The complaints that have been made here and pressed are that the discipline of the force is very severe, and that the fines are extraordinarily heavy; I therefore consider it a necessity that you should give any statistics, or any explanation that is in your possession, as to the general question of the discipline of the force, and particularly as to the cause of drunkenness?—I might say here that these statistics will clearly shew the extent to which drunkenness had arisen, and the extent at which it now stands, and that the cases of insubordination in the force and of assaults upon civilians, have decreased exactly in the same ratio as the drunkenness has decreased.

3705. Will you now just read for us those statistics?—The statistics come down to the present day, and begin in 1873; I did not become Assistant Commissioner until 1877. In 1873 the percentage of drunkenness for constables was 39·7; in 1874, 38·0; in 1875, 41·2; in 1876——I wish to make a short statement here. In the year 1876, Sir Henry Lake wrote a very remarkable Order with reference to the intemperance of the force that then existed and was increasing each year, which Order will be given to you by the Chief Commissioner. In 1876 the percentage was 39·8; in 1877 it was 31·1; in 1878 it was 24·6; in 1879 it was 20·2; in 1880 it was 17·4, in 1881 it was 17·4; and up to the present day it is 6·7. The cases of insubordination I was going to give you for the same years. The cases of insubordination for 1873 were 37; for 1874, 40; for 1875, 56; for 1876, 31; for 1877, 27; for 1878, 27; for 1879, 17; for 1880, 18; for 1881, 11. Now, the number of assaults on civilians in 1873 was 40; in 1874, 43; in 1875, 45; in 1876, 29; in 1877, 26; in 1878, 13; in 1879, 13; in 1880, 7; in 1881, 9; and up to the present, in 1882, 4.

3706. Do you consider, Colonel Connolly, that inflicting those large fines and reducing men in grade led to that reduction in the number of cases of drunkenness and insubordination?—I should think so.

3707. I wish to ask you whether this reduction in offences was contemporaneous with the heavy system of fining?—Certainly.

3708. *Mr. Holmes.*—Would not this be the time after so marked a diminution of drunkenness to maintain that diminution by appealing to the men and trying to restrain them by kindness?—The extreme punishments have ceased because the offences have ceased. There are now very few cases, according to the statistics which I have read to the Committee. The percentage of drunkenness for this year, from having been as high as 41 per cent., is now down to 6, so punishments have been reduced to a very considerable extent.

[The further examination of Colonel Connolly was then adjourned until next day.]

SEVENTEENTH DAY.—7TH OCTOBER, 1882.

Present:

Mr. J. W. O'DONNELL, Mr. GEORGE MORRIS, D.L., and Mr. R. W. A. HOLMES.

Examination of Colonel CONNOLLY, Assistant Commissioner, Dublin Metropolitan Police, resumed.

Colonel John Augustus Connolly.

7 Oct., 1882.

3709. *Witness.*—In continuation of the evidence which I gave the Committee yesterday, I wish to add that it will be seen from the figures which I have given the great extent to which drunkenness had risen. After many years of a system of exhortation and mild punishments, the order of the late Chief Commissioner of 1876 clearly shews how he recognised the fact of the increasing drunkenness in the force.

3710. *Chairman.*—Was that Colonel Lake?—Yes, Sir Henry Lake. Severe punishments were necessary if they succeeded in reducing the evil, and as the drunkenness diminished the punishments have been relaxed.

3711. They have been, as a matter of fact, relaxed?—Yes; as a matter of fact they have been relaxed. The figures shew that drunkenness has fallen from a figure of 41 per cent. to 6 per cent.; that offences of insubordination and assaults on civilians have fallen nearly in the same proportion; and that reports of all kinds have also greatly diminished.

3712. *Mr. Holmes.*—You told us yesterday that the cases of drunkenness amongst the constables amounted, some years ago, to over 40 per cent.?—Yes, to 41 per cent.

3713. In arriving at this percentage, have you reckoned each case as a separate case irrespective of whether it might not have been the one constable's second or third offence?—Yes; the cases were taken irrespective of the individuals guilty.

3714. Perhaps I have not conveyed to you with sufficient clearness what I mean. Take the case of a constable who had been in any particular year convicted of three offences of drunkenness. In arriving at a percentage, would the state of things I have put be reckoned as three cases or one case?—As three cases.

3715. Would that be fair to the force?—I think it is unavoidable. I do not see how you could bring it home otherwise. Would it be fair to calculate it the other way, as one offence?

3716. Would not the outside public, if they heard that 40 per cent. of the constables in a particular year had been convicted of drunkenness, be led to regard that statement as conveying that forty in every hundred constables had been convicted of that offence?—That might be, but how could you take it the other way?

3717. *Mr. Morris.*—At all events, you believe that, under the circumstances mentioned by Mr. Holmes, three offences would be counted?—Certainly.

3718. *Mr. Holmes.*—But does it not amount to this, that a few black sheep might cause a very unfavourable impression upon the whole body of constables?—That

Colonel John Augustus Connolly.

7 Oct., 1883.

is the case. That I can assure you is the case, that there are a great proportion of men who have perhaps one case of drunkenness against them, and there are a great number with none at all.

3719. Then, in the interests of the force itself, would it not be better to dismiss these men rather than inflict heavy fines upon them?—Well, one does not like to dismiss a man without giving him one other chance of redeeming. You will see the force of that in a moment. A question was put to me yesterday, to this effect: "In the first instance of drunkenness what punishment do you impose?" and my answer was: "That depends on the character of the man." If he is a man likely to get drunk again, I would give him a very sharp punishment, and try to put a stop to it at once. If he is a man who has a good steady character, I would, in all likelihood, let him off with a "stand over," or a very small fine; but it entirely depends on the character which is given of the individual by his officer.

3720. In measuring the amount of the fine, do you take into account the fact of whether the man is married, or that he has a large family?—I think not, sir. I think once you are aliud to that. I do not consider that that is any business of ours. I think that we have a right to look upon the discipline of the force, and the advantage of the force, in the punishments we administer.

3721. If the punishment is severe, say more than a sovereign, it must affect his pay to a serious extent?—He should consider that before he commits the crime; we cannot go into that, I am afraid, and that has not been in my mind. Speaking of what passes in my mind, I always say, "I am sorry for you, but you should have considered, before you committed the offence, what the result would be."

3722. When you inflicted the fine of 2*l.* upon the acting sergeant who went into the public-house when on sick leave, did it occur to you that that fine amounted to nearly 8 per cent. of his income?—I never measured it in that way; I might have reduced him for the offence.

3723. When you look at it in that way, don't you think it was a very severe fine for an offence of the kind?—No, I do not. I think it was a very proper fine. I look upon the offence as one of a most serious character, considering the man's rank, and the position in which he was placed; and the fine of 2*l.* to the man of superior rank would show you how the increased sum is given to the man with the highest pay.

3724. *Chairman.*—We have had evidence of the systems under which the London and Liverpool police forces have been managed, and in connection with those systems there are no such heavy fines as those that are inflicted on the men in the Dublin force?—In London and Liverpool they have not, I believe, had the same experience with regard to drunkenness that we have had here, and we have always been led, and Sir Henry Lake before us, to consider that going into public-houses was the first step towards that evil.

3725. As a matter of fact, are the punishments in the Dublin force less severe now than they were formerly?—They have been reduced in consequence of the reduction in the number of reports. There are so few reports of any kind that it is not at all necessary to inflict severe punishments of any kind now.

3726. Then, as a matter of fact, severe punishments are not inflicted now?—No.

3727. Within what period has that been the case?—Within the last year. I have already explained to the Committee that as the drunkenness diminished the punishments have been relaxed.

3728. Is the scale of punishments nearly similar to what it had been in Colonel Lake's time?—Very nearly.

3729. *Mr. Morris.*—I was desirous of asking you, Colonel Connolly, more for the purpose of eliciting your opinion than anything else, this question: Suppose there were blocks of buildings built by the Government for the accommodation of the married men of the force, and that there were got clean and comfortable lodgings at a fair and moderate rent, do you think that the married men would take advantage of such accommodation, and that they would like to live in such blocks of buildings, because some of the police whom we have examined were very much in favour of such a plan, while others, I thought, rather doubted whether the men would like to herd together in barracks?—I am aware that the Chief Commissioner has placed such a scheme before the married men of the force, and that on the whole, I may say, they showed a decided reluctance to take advantage of any steps [illegible] in that direction. The Chief Commissioner had communications with the Artizans' Dwellings Company, and with the promoters of other undertakings of that kind and he also made proposals to the Government.

3730. So that in fact your opinion, formed from knowledge of the force, is that they would not like to live in such buildings?—Well, you see, things change so much that I would scarcely like to say that. At the time it was tried there was a reluctance, but I think that that reluctance proceeded, to a great extent, from a good number of the men who would be affected by its being addicted to drink, and not liking any supervision, or as little as possible. That may have been the case, but that that reluctance existed I am aware.

3731. Of course, if they were living in blocks of buildings of that kind they would be more under supervision, whether on or off duty?—That is so.

3732. *Mr. Holmes.*—As to the present rates of pay which constables, sergeants, and inspectors receive—you are aware, of course, that it is only ten years since they were very largely increased?—Yes; it was improved in 1872.

3733. Have any of the men complained to you of their pay being insufficient for the reasonable support of their families?—Never.

3734. And up to recently did they at all grumble, or were they perfectly satisfied with it?—I never heard a word on the question of money, until recently. The discontent in the force originated with the men feeling that they were coming under the action of the new Act of Parliament with reference to pensions. That was the beginning of it. We heard nothing of discontent in reference to money, or pay, or anything of that sort until the men were coming under the operation of this new Act.

3735. Is it a fact that when men joined the force since 1883, under that new Pension Act, they were made aware at the time of joining the force of the alteration in the scale of pensions—are recruits made aware of that?—That I am not quite sure about.

3736. *Mr. Morris.*—One other question I wished to ask you was this: Some of the men represented rather strongly to the Committee, and I think, probably, with a good deal of reason, that when they go out on pension they scarcely ever get employment from anybody. They stated also that their sons find it very difficult to get employment; in fact, that artizans and other people of that class won't work with policemen's sons, and that though a respectable employer might be very glad to employ a policeman's son, the other men in the establishment won't work with him, and the police are thus boycotted. Have you ever heard any complaint of that kind?—Never. From my knowledge of the way in which men are employed in the country, the policeman, I think, is generally acceptable.

3737. Do you apply that observation to the men of the Dublin metropolitan police?—To any policeman. "He is the son of a policeman; the policeman has retired upon such and such a pension," that is a good thing to say.

3738. Do you know of your own knowledge if many of the men of the Dublin police force who have gone out on pension ever get employment?—No, I do not.

3739. *Chairman.*—You do not know, one way or the other?—No. I can, I may say, only speaking generally, from my knowledge of friends of mine who have had recommendations to make of sons of policemen, and particularly if the father had a pension; it was always taken as a creditable point in the case.

3740. There was one matter that was pressed strongly upon us, and that was the return to the Board consisting of the two Commissioners and the seven superintendents—the latter as referees of character—in investigating complaints against the constables, and the object appeared mainly to be that the seven superintendents should be there to give evidence as regards the men who have been transferred from their own to other divisions?—I think the representations that have been made before you on that subject have been made by a section of the men in the force who are, to a certain extent, discontented, and that this is a point which can be very easily met by the manner in which the cases are tried in the present instance, in this way: if a man has been in another division from that in which he is at the present moment, he has nothing to do but to say, "I wish the superintendent of such and such a division to give me a character." In no one case has that been said, and in no one case has any constable so situated or complained that the superintendent of his old division was not present. It has not been done, and any man are reluctant, as a rule, to make any complaint to the Commissioners; but in a case of that sort you can understand how easily a man who is accused of a certain offence, if he liked, could say, "I wish to have a character from my superintendent." That has never been done. If it had been done, I need hardly say that the Commissioners would freely have adjourned the case to the next day for the character asked for by the accused man.

3741. *Mr. Holmes.*—Another question that was brought before us was that of the expenses of married men when they are transferred from one division to another; they are of course obliged to break up their establishments, and they say they are allowed nothing for the expenses to which they are put?—I believe there is no provision for that, but if the cost was inquired into it would not be found, I should think, to amount to much. Certainly it is the fact that these transfers entail occasions, that married men are transferred from place to place, but the cost of that transfer, I should think, would be something very small.

3742. There was one instance of that kind in which nineteen officers and men were transferred on the one occasion?—A good many transfers have been necessary in the force, but that applies more to officers than men, on account of the telegraphic system being adopted. A great many inspectors have been transferred from one station to another.

3743. *Chairman.*—There were nineteen transferred on one occasion?—But that referred to inspectors.

3744. Yes?—That is the reason; it was a special reason, and there is no fund from which we can defray expenses of that kind.

3745. Might it not be desirable to have a fund out of which expenses of that kind could be defrayed?—Yes; it might be a question for consideration.

3746. *Mr. Holmes.*—I presume you would not transfer a married man without some special cause?—No, certainly not; and it has always been extremely difficult to transfer some of the officers, because they have got their houses and establishments, and all these things, and they have not been transferred on account of their having had so much property in one place. That excuse was allowed to effect their remaining stationary until a crisis occurred like that of the introduction of the electric telegraph to certain of the police-stations, when we were obliged to transfer the most intelligent officers to the police telegraph stations. You asked me, Mr. Morris, a question just now as to a state of things that the men had to contend with then connected to boycotting?

3747. *Mr. Morris.*—Quite so?—I do not know as to that, except by reports which have come up to the office of the Commissioners, and which would show that some of our men did not want to go on leave to their homes, because they would be slighted and sneered at during the late agitation of the Land League by their friends belonging to the Land League. Anybody belonging to the police force, or the army, or belonging to any force which had connexion with the Government, was sneered at, and it was said of such a man, "What can you expect from him? He belongs to the Government!" or something of that sort. That was only a passing thing that belonged to the Land League agitation, but that certainly came under my notice as a report.

3748. *Mr. Holmes.*—Upon the question of pay, as I understand you, you never heard of any complaints amongst the men of the insufficiency of their pay until the other day?—Never.

3749. Do you believe that the men seriously think that their pay is insufficient?—No, I do not. I do not see how they can think so.

3750. Are you aware that the second and third class constables here are better paid than the corresponding ranks of the London force?—I am not.

3751. Are you aware that the third class inspectors here are very much better paid than the men of the London force in a similar position?—I happen to know that, but I could not tell you how much better paid they are. I have been under the impression that this force has been better paid, on the whole, than the London force, but I could not give you the figures.

3752. Now, if there was any class that had any ground for complaining of the insufficiency of their pay, what rank would you say it was?—The acting inspectors.

3753. And is it the case that the duties of the acting inspector are as onerous and as responsible as those of the inspector?—Not exactly. But they are very important, meaning that he is called upon to perform all the duties which the inspector performs except the duty at times of taking charge of a division, which is the duty that sometimes a full inspector is called upon to do.

3754. *Chairman.*—And do you consider their pay inadequate?—Yes, I do. I consider that it is the only rank in the service that is so.

3755. *Mr. Holmes.*—Can you suggest how an improvement might be made in their pay without adding to the cost of maintaining the force?—Yes; I can suggest that the pay of the fourth-rate men should be reduced. When they first take up their duty I consider that their pay is too high.

3756. Do you think that there are more sergeants in proportion to constables than are necessary? By sergeants I include acting sergeants?—No, I do not.

3757. How many constables do you think sergeants ought to be responsible for on beat duty?—Well, I do not think you could hold a sergeant responsible for more than five or six men; but it depends upon the beats, where they are stationed. The beats of six men would cover a very large district.

3758. Upon an average, what would be the length of a beat?—Well, they vary very much. At Kingstown they are different from here, and frequently we are obliged only to have a limited number of men on the beats, and make them extend them further. It really varies very much, according to the number of men that we have for the duty.

3759. In fact, you could hardly strike an average?—I do not think you could; but if I give you the number of men, if I say six constables to one sergeant on duty, and that sergeant can exercise a useful supervision over it, would give you an idea of the average size of the beat. You can imagine how far a sergeant could go round so as to exercise his supervision.

3760. And is it from the larger number of constables in the force, and the comparatively small number of officers, that many a man, no matter how well conducted he may be while in the force, can never expect to rise beyond the rank of constable?—That depends, you see, so very much upon the men who are pensioned off and the men who are reduced. But it is a wide question, and I think, up to this, as far as we have gone, that the promotions have been rather rapid.

3761. How is promotion regulated in the rank of constable? I mean to say—take the case of a man upon joining, a well-conducted man—how long must he remain in the fourth grade before he can rise to

Colonel John Augustus Connolly.

7 Oct., 1882.

Colonel John Augustus Connolly.

7 Oct., 1882.

the third, and so on to the first?—Fourth rate, about one year; third rate, about five years; and the second rate, about two years.

3762. Then a well-conducted man might expect to rise to the first rate of constable after seven years' service?—After eight years' service.

3763. There are no fixed periods?—That is the average.

3764. Could it be arranged that well conducted men might rise from rank to rank after certain fixed periods in the service?—Cases have occurred where, upon a man distinguishing himself very much, and being a man of extremely good character, that man has been granted his rate.

3765. I may tell you that in the Liverpool and Glasgow police forces a well-conducted man remains only for a certain fixed period in each rank, and he knows that if he is well conducted, he may, after that fixed period, rise to the higher rank. It is not a matter of uncertainty; it is a matter of absolute certainty?—The rates with us are controlled now by examinations.

3766. In the rank of constable?—In the rank of constable. Examinations are held; they are not severe, and very few men miss. They are so regulated that, unless a man is extremely illiterate, he would be able to pass; and out of seventy examined, I may had the whole pass out from the fourth rate to the third.

3767. And is there an examination to rise from the third to the second, and from the second to the first?—Yes.

3768. In what subjects do you examine the men?—Duty, arithmetic, and geography—a few simple questions in geography, or something of that sort. But once a man has done the paper to get out of the fourth rate, it is almost a certainty of his disposing of the others. Of course there are some old constables of the fourth rate who have refused to compete, and who would find a difficulty in passing the examinations I have named, but, generally speaking, the men get through.

3769. But I suppose that, from the want of the necessary ability, and not from any lack of good conduct, some men can never expect to rise to the rank of sergeant—that they remain, in point of fact, constables all their lives?—Well, I should say that a man, if he wishes to get upon what is called the advanced class—that is the first for promotion, and there is an examination for it specially—any man who wishes to put his name down for that examination, if he is a man of good character, he is put upon that advanced class after a trifling examination, and from that advanced class the promotions are made. It is taken for granted that every man does not wish promotion if he does not go in for the advanced class.

3770. May the men of all the grades of constables belong to that advanced class?—Yes, any grade, provided that a man is six months doing duty.

3771. *Chairman.*—Does it take much of a man's time to prepare for the examination?—Oh, no. There is a regular school always going on at Kevin Street barracks, and if the men attend there, they pass the examination.

3772. Is there compulsory attendance?—No. Oh, no; voluntary attendance; but it has been very much interfered with. At one time I remember the school being filled by the men of the force. At that time seventy were passed out of the fourth rate; but since then some insubordination got in amongst the men, and it has shown itself in an organised reluctance to go to the school, and a complaint against examinations of all kinds.

3773. *Mr. Holmes.*—To rise from the rank of constable to that of acting sergeant what examination is requisite—how do you make the selection—by examination in what subjects?—Well, the examinations are rather more increased in difficulty for that rank than for the advanced class. Of course, if a man has been in the advanced class for some time, and still goes for instruction to the school, when he comes to be examined for the rank of acting sergeant the test appears to be slightly more difficult, but not to any extreme extent.

3774. To rise from the rank of acting sergeant to the grade above do you require an examination?—Oh, yes, there is an examination for every grade above. The examination for the grade of inspector is more difficult again, because taking charges and questions of law are involved in that duty, and they are also called upon to have an accurate knowledge of station-house duty, but the examination would not be considered difficult for any of the positions.

3775. *Mr. Munro.*—In reference to the reluctance that the men have to attend the school, do you think it is a reluctance to attend that particular school, or a reluctance to be brought in contact with the people who teach there?—Well, I will tell you what has taken place.

3776. Or do you think it is a kind of feeling of independence?—It is a work of independence. The case with reference to the teachers was this: the Chief Commissioner had two teachers. He had one teacher for geography and for arithmetic, and for subjects apart from police duties; and the other teacher was a police officer, who instructed in all police duties——

3777. And was the teacher of arithmetic and geography a policeman?—No.

3778. He was a schoolmaster outside?—He was a schoolmaster paid by the Chief Commissioner out of the Police Fund, and with a view to giving the most complete opportunities to these men to qualify themselves, as they were compelled, to pass examinations.

3779. And do you think, in the abstract, that giving young constables an opportunity of getting themselves up—even if they were pretty well up when they came, to prevent them getting rusty on those subjects—do you think an institution of that kind is a useful one for the force?—Very useful. I think it would not be fair to call upon these men to pass examinations unless you had complete facility for them to do so. And so they would, if they were let alone, attend the school regularly.

3780. *Mr. Holmes.*—Turning to the question of pensions, you are aware of the two scales of pensions under the 1847 and 1867 Acts?—Yes.

3781. As regards the pension scale of 1847, I suppose you are aware that it is the most favourable Pension Act that any official could ever expect to retire under?—Certainly.

3782. Well, as regards the Pension Act of 1867, have you yourself considered the subject, and could you give any recommendations as to the alteration of that system?—Yes, I have considered the subject, and I recognise the fact that it is very different from the other.

3783. Between the 1847 and the 1867 Acts?—Yes; there is a wide difference between those Acts, and when the men come to realise the very wide difference between those Acts, of course it creates a proportionately strong feeling; and, in addition to that, the pensions under the 1847 Act were, I rather think, intended to apply to, or to be calculated upon, the old rate of pay, whereas the fact is that they have been calculated upon the new rate of pay. The consequence is that men receive a far higher pension than I believe it was intended by the Act that they should receive.

3784. *Chairman.*—And is the old scale of pensions struck under the new scale of pay?—Yes, and there is a very wide difference. I was going to explain that that makes the feeling against the new Act very much stronger, because they have been receiving really, I believe, a higher rate of pension than was contemplated by the Act by the way in which it has been worked out.

3785. *Mr. Holmes.*—But as regards the Pension Act of 1867, and not placing too much weight upon the fact of the Pension Act of 1847 being so good and exceeding only what would be a fair pension, in what way would you improve the Pension Act of 1867?—I would only suggest one improvement, and that is that the pensions awarded to our men should be in every instance the same as those awarded to the London force. That is the only remark I have to make on that question.

3786. And you think that that would meet the justice of their case?—Yes.

3787. You are aware that there was a Bill before Parliament in the last Session, the object of which was to extend the London scale of pensions to the police forces of England and Scotland?—Yes.

3788. I believe that that Bill will be again introduced, and I presume that the reasonable men of the force can hardly expect to receive a better scale of pensions than the men of the other police forces of Great Britain?—Well, I hope so.

3789. *Mr. Morris.*—As regards the time for a man receiving a pension do you think that if a man served from twenty-eight to thirty years—that instead of being obliged to go before a doctor, or go to hospital, or to do anything which would be an encouragement to malingering—it would be a better plan that, after a man had served a certain number of years, he would be entitled to receive the pension laid down by Act of Parliament, and that he would be entitled to retire from the police force; various dates have been fixed, twenty-five, twenty-eight, and thirty years; have you formed any opinion on that point?—Yes; I believe that the question rests in a very great degree with the men themselves as to whether they will be able to continue in the service after twenty-five years' service, or even after thirty years' service. It is quite possible, I think, that in a great number of cases, if the men are prudent and take care of their health, even with the very great amount of work that they have to do in all weathers—and most trying work it is—that these men will complete their service of thirty years and be well able to come to that. In considering a matter of this sort, you must take into account the character of the men and their conduct, and the fact that many of them are careless and improvident in the matter of clothing. The consequence is, if they neglect wearing warm clothing—and they seem to take a pride in going out in all weathers without sufficient regard to the warmth of their clothing—they are very liable to catch cold; and when they do get cold they are careless about it, and I have in that way known the finest men of the force to go in ten months.

3790. *Mr. Holmes.*—When you say that they take pride in going out in all weathers, is it not a fact that they are obliged to go out in all weathers?—Yes; but I mentioned the fact that they did so without the proper clothing that they could put on. I have always exhorted the men to have two flannel shirts, because I know that there are nights that even with two flannel shirts it would give them as much as they could do to keep warm. And a great many of them have no flannel shirts at all. Can you believe that men would be so foolish as that?

3791. Now, having regard to the ordinary life of a policeman, would you not say that a man who had not risen from the rank of constable or sergeant would be well nigh worn out after thirty years' service?—Well, I should, speaking generally, but I should say that thirty years is good service, and that it should go down to a man's credit having gone through thirty years' service, and I would only make this restriction, that in giving the pension I would not give him the option of going on pension, but would give the Commissioner the power of compelling him to go.

3792. *Mr. Holmes.*—Is it not the case that under the Act of 1867, a man can retire after thirty years' service without a medical certificate?—I think not. However, I think the less said about the medical certificate after thirty years' service the better. At the same time, I would not relax altogether the medical certificate. My opinion is that a man if he does good service has a right to his pension after thirty years; it is a long time.

3793. *Mr. Morris.*—One other matter with reference to pensions. It has been represented to the Committee that a hardship exists in reference to them, that when two men retire on pension at the same length of service, and one man has got several black marks against him during the period of twenty or thirty years that he has been in the force, and the other man has not got so many, or perhaps none, there is a difference made in the scale of pension unfavourable to the first-named man; don't you think that when a fine or punishment is inflicted upon a constable or a sergeant, that it should not be carried on, at all events so far as to be taken into consideration against him in his pension?—Well, it seems hard that it should be taken into consideration at the end of all things, but there are cases where you cannot pass over it; and there are cases that come prominently before the medical officer in which he is obliged to inform the Commissioner of the character and effects of the man's habits of life, and their result. Looking at the man's sheet, you may find that, taking the first ten years of his service, he was a sober man, but that in the next ten years he got drunk four or five times, and then in the last ten years of his service he was frequently drunk. It becomes a question, then, to any man—to any doctor—whether this man has not seriously impaired his health by drink, and in a case of that sort it would be impossible to pass over it. But there is such a variety of cases of that kind that it is impossible to lay down a definite rule concerning them. But suppose there was a man who, during the first ten years of his service, offended so frequently that he has been on the point of dismissal for drink, but that in the last twenty years he has not had a single case against him, I would blot out all his back records altogether. That is the way in which I look at the question.

3794. Don't you think, looking at the uncertainty of pensions, and the insecurity of them, through their being liable to reduction by reason of previous punishments which have been suffered—don't you think that that is calculated to cause great discontent and dissatisfaction in the force?—I think that that is a matter for the consideration of the individual. I must apply, in short, the same answer that I gave with reference to another question that I had to reply to just now. I say that men should consider these things before they commit the offence.

3795. *Chairman.*—When they commit offences and are punished for them in London and Liverpool they, after a certain period, get a clean bill of health and start again?—For pension?

3796. Yes; for pension. The previous punishments are never taken into account when the men of those forces receive pension?—Never?

3797. Never?—Well, then, according to that plan you would give a man who has never been drunk, and has been of most exemplary character during the thirty years of his service—you would place him on a par with a man who has had twenty cases of drink against him.

3798-9. But he has already been punished for these offences?—Yes; that is one way of looking at it, but I don't think it is the correct way.

3800. Don't you think that such a system as that in force in the Dublin police, contradistinguished as it is from the systems in operation in London and Liverpool, is likely to cause discontent and dissatisfaction?—I don't think it ought where men know that it will be so before they enter the service.

3801. *Mr. Holmes.*—As a matter of fact, before a man can get his pension at all the Commissioner must sign a certain certificate to the effect that that man has served with fidelity and diligence?—Yes. It appears to me that the whole of the pensions, as a rule, are subject to the opinion of the medical officer; and if the Commissioner is going to discharge a man on pension, he is obliged to look at all the circumstances, as he is directed by the Act of Parliament to do, and in taking into account these circumstances he cannot shut his eyes to the fact of that man having damaged his health and rendered himself unfit for the service by drink.

3802. *Chairman.*—Then, if that be so, the medical officer is the official who fixes the amount of the pension?—The medical officer has to give his opinion on that point.

3803. It strikes me as being very anomalous that there should be a different system in Dublin from that which prevails in Liverpool and London?—It would be a very anomalous thing to discharge two men on an equal pension of 30*l.* a-year each, the one having been twenty times drunk, and the other not having been drunk at all.

Colonel John Augustus Connolly.

7 Oct., 1882.

Colonel John Augustus Connolly.

7 Oct., 1882.

3604. *Mr. Holmes.*—Is it not the fact that under the Act of 1847 the Treasury cannot give a pension unless the application for it is supported by a certificate of the Chief Secretary to the Lord Lieutenant that the person entitled to it has served with diligence and fidelity?—Yes; with diligence, zeal, and fidelity.

3605. So that, in point of fact, if a man had not, in your opinion, conducted himself with due diligence in the force, you could not, as a conscientious man, give him the certificate?—Certainly not.

3606. And occasional reports for drunkenness—would they preclude you from giving the certificate?—I do not say an occasional case. I have explained as clearly as it is in my power my views in respect to that. If a man who has been guilty of drunkenness for the first five years of his service reformed during the next twenty years, I would not consider his former conduct at all. The last five years would be forgiven and forgotten.

3607. *Mr. Harris.*—As I understand, it appears to me the way you put it is this; that if two policemen, say, serve twenty-five years in the force, and they both retire on the same day, with the same service; and that one was an excellent policeman, zealous, sober, and with no complaint against him; and that the other had several complaints, and had been fined, and had not been, on the whole, a satisfactory man—you consider that it would not be equal justice for these two men to go out of the service upon exactly the same pension?—I would go a little further into that statement, and I would qualify it by saying that the offences should have been offences of drunkenness. And for this reason; that a man is not, to my mind, performing his duty with fidelity to the service who abuses his health, and a man who is guilty of getting drunk time after time is, beyond doubt, abusing his health. We have a punishment for a man who abuses his rest, because he is supposed to have a certain number of hours' rest in the day, and if he chooses to go out and amuse himself without taking his proper amount of rest, there is a punishment, recognising the fact that that man has not performed his duty with fidelity.

3608. And, in fact, if that man does not take rest, in the position of a policeman it renders him unfit for his duty?—Yes, just as much as the man who drinks, looking at it from that point of view.

3609. And I presume, if a policeman conducted himself properly during the greater part of his service, you would not remember the offences of his youth, but you would give the required certificate, as if he had conducted himself throughout as he should have done?—Certainly. As the men have, I understand, complained about having to attend drill, I wish to state to the Committee that, with reference to the drill of the force, it is so arranged that each man has thirty-two hours' drill in a course of four months.

3610. And no drill for the other eight?—No drill for the other eight; and for that time given to drill he is allowed forty-eight hours off duty.

Captain GEORGE TALBOT, Chief Commissioner, Dublin Metropolitan Police, examined.

Captain George Talbot.

7 Oct., 1882.

3611. *Chairman.*—What is your name?—George Talbot.

3612. You are the Chief Commissioner of the Dublin Metropolitan Police?—Yes.

3613. How long have you held the appointment?—I came to the force as Assistant Commissioner in 1873—in July 1873—and was promoted Chief Commissioner in August 1877.

3614. Will you tell us what are your views in reference to the men being paid a gratuity of three months' pay, similar to that awarded to the Royal Irish Constabulary, as some consideration for their extra duty during the past three years?—Well, with regard to the gratuity of three months' pay, I think the great majority of the force deserve it, and I cannot see my way to make any distinction. I am not aware whether it has yet been paid to the Royal Irish Constabulary, or whether any distinction has been made, but there can be no doubt that during the winter months of last year and 1882 the men had a very considerable amount of extra work to do. And I may say it was not confined to last year, but ever since the land agitation began in Dublin that they have had many of them—a great many extra hours of duty, and they have always performed it with the greatest cheerfulness and good-will.

3615. Then you are in favour of their receiving the three months' gratuity the same as the Royal Irish Constabulary?—Yes, certainly, exactly under similar circumstances to the Royal Irish Constabulary.

3616. *Mr. Holmes.*—Are you aware, Captain Talbot, that in the case of the Constabulary it came out in the course of the evidence taken before the Committee that out at the beginning of the year that a great many of the men were seriously out of pocket during the recent agitation? Men were ordered away frequently from their stations, and, owing to the fact of their being charged exorbitant prices for nights' lodging, food, and other necessaries, the allowances they received were not able to maintain them?—I was not aware of it; but I have just heard it.

3617. Do you consider that any of your men lost money by the recent agitation?—No, I do not. But if you will allow me to give you another reason why I think that my men deserve it under the circumstances, is that they have, I may say, nearly double work to do to what the London policemen does, and I took the trouble of making a comparative statement of the figures. If this will assist you—I do not know whether it will or not—but it relates to the London metropolitan force, and also to my own force. It is a Comparative Return of the persons taken into custody by the London and Dublin Metropolitan Police Forces during the years of 1880 and 1881, and is as follows:—

CRIMINAL STATISTICS.

COMPARATIVE Return of Persons taken into Custody by the London and Dublin Metropolitan Police Forces during the Years 1880 and 1881.

Years.	Arrests. London Metropolitan Police.	Arrests. Dublin Metropolitan Police.	Total Number of Arrests by London Metropolitan Police.	Strength. London Metropolitan Police.	Strength. Dublin Metropolitan Police.	[illegible]	Average Arrests by each Man in— London Metropolitan Police.	Average Arrests by each Man in— Dublin Metropolitan Police.	[illegible]
1880	73,490	22,5[illegible]	96,0[illegible]	10,041	1,1[illegible]	9,[illegible]	7	19	10
1881	77,277	20,[illegible]	97,673	11,234	1,1[illegible]	10,1[illegible]	7 nearly	18 nearly	11

Metropolitan Police Office, August 23, 1882.

Captain George Talbot.

7 Oct., 1882.

Now in London the number of arrests, as compared with the strength of the force, is an average of 7 per cent. of the force, while the arrests made by the Dublin metropolitan police amount to nineteen. Now that is in 1880, and in 1881 the percentage is the same in London, and 18 in Dublin. Now when you take into consideration that the man making the arrest has to get up in the morning—the arrest being generally made at night—and attend the magistrate's office, it does entail a very large amount of duty upon the constable. And again, in London, as you can well imagine, arrests are made with a good deal of facility—the public generally render every assistance in their power; in Dublin your own experience will tell you that it is not so easy to make an arrest or to get assistance from the public, as the assaults upon the police will show you.

3818. From what Returns do you get that information?—From the Blue Book of the London Metropolitan Police, and from my Statistical Returns.

3819. We have examined District Superintendent Walker, of the London metropolitan police force, and the Chief Constables of Liverpool and Glasgow, and we gathered from their evidence, I think generally, that when a constable in London, Liverpool, and Glasgow has finished his tour he is, practically, his own master. He cannot go exactly where he likes, but still within reasonable limits he can do what he likes, and go where he pleases—so that the eight or nine hours which represent his tour of duty conclude his day's work. Now is that the case with a Dublin policeman—that when he has finished his tour of duty he is practically his own master?—No; when he has finished his tour of duty—that is his day duty—he must remain in his barrack unless he gets leave, but he is never refused leave if he asks for it.

3820. What I mean is, can he call the sixteen hours his own after he has performed his eight hours' duty?—No, certainly not.

3821. What I wish to convey to you is this: You have just compared the arrests in proportion to the force in London and in Dublin. Now what I want to ascertain from you is, whether the greater number of arrests in Dublin in proportion to the force do not require a large number of constables after they have done their duty—their beat duty—to attend at the police-courts?—Of course it does.

3822. And that therefore that takes away from their leisure hours?—Of course it takes away from their leisure hours.

3823. In other words, if the city was quieter and there were fewer arrests, the constable would have more time to himself?—Exactly.

3824. Do you try by arrangement to compensate a constable who has been detained for a long time at the police-court by giving him less duty at another time?—Certainly, those are the orders. As far as I know, I never heard a complaint of it. The superintendent of the division is emphatically directed to carry out these orders. He gets time off for that. The reason why he has not got time of his own is that he must be bound to take his natural rest. If he was allowed to go out of course at any time he pleased, he would go off and amuse himself for a great part of the time, and he would be utterly unfit for duty the next day. When he asks for leave he has nothing to do but to write on a bit of paper for plain clothes, and he is allowed plain clothes, and allowed to go out where he pleases. Married men are, of course, their own masters entirely. Here is another Return which may be of use to you, and which I would put in. It is a Comparative Return of the arrests connected with the last subject, for assaults committed on the London and Dublin metropolitan police during the years 1880 and 1881; and it will support the last Return in showing that the responsibility in Dublin is very considerably more than it is in London. The Return is as follows:—

COMPARATIVE Return of Arrests for Assaults committed on the London and Dublin Metropolitan Police Forces during the Years 1880 and 1881.

Years.	Assaults on London Metropolitan Police.	Assaults on Dublin Metropolitan Police.	Strength of London Metropolitan Police.	Strength of Dublin Metropolitan Police.	Average Arrests for Assaults on Police by each man in London Metropolitan Police.	Average Arrests for Assaults on Police by each man in Dublin Metropolitan Police.
1880 ..	3,521	764	10,915	1,134	0·33	0·67
1881 ..	3,471	676	11,334	1,134	0·31	0·59

Metropolitan Police Office, Dublin Castle, October 9, 1882.

3825. Have assaults on the police increased much within the last few years?—Well, I have not gone back beyond 1880, so that I cannot exactly answer that question; but in this Return it would appear that in 1880 the average arrests by each man for assaults on the police in the London metropolitan police was 0·33, while the average arrests by each man for assaults on the police in Dublin was 0·67; showing a very considerable increase on 0·33. Similarly, in 1881 in London it was 0·31, and in Dublin it was 0·59, and it was nearly double in each case.

3826. It appears to us from the evidence that has been given that the two questions which weigh most with the men are the questions of discipline and of pension. As regards the question of discipline, the men, while recognising the fact that discipline must be enforced, and not bringing any personal complaints against either of the Commissioners, allege that the fines have been frequent and excessive, and that the punishments altogether, not only as regards fines, but as regards reductions, have been inflicted for what they allege to be somewhat trifling offences; that is practically the gist of their complaint?—If you ask me separately questions in reference to those points, I shall be happy to answer them.

3827. *Mr. Morris.*—Have you instituted any comparison between the fines and the punishments that were inflicted in recent years, and those inflicted in former years?—Certainly.

3828. And taking into account that policemen are now receiving, I suppose, fully one-third more than they used to receive previous to 1872?—One-third more pay, certainly.

3829. And therefore probably that might be a reason for the fines being a little heavier when they could better afford to pay them. In instituting that comparison, can you say, as Mr. Holmes has put it, that you have satisfied yourself sufficiently on those points to put forward the comparison which you have made, or is it not for general reasons?—I carried out the discipline under Sir Henry Lake's administration, and the pay was very bad in those times. The fines were, consequently, not so severe as they were in the years 1878 and 1879, because

George Talbot,
7 Oct., 1880.

the men would feel it much more severely than if I chose to inflict smaller fines, their means being smaller, particularly the married men.

2830. It was about three years that the number of cases of drunkenness was so very large in the force?—I presume that Colonel Connolly has given you the statistics on that point; if he has not given you the statistics of the force, I am prepared to give them, but I do not wish that they should be published if possible. But for the fines inflicted I could not have been responsible for the discipline then, when drunkenness amounted to the very heavy extent that it did—in one year, since 1877, to 30 and 35 per cent. It has gradually decreased to 6 per cent.

2831. Can you state if from Returns, or in any other way, you have satisfied your own mind, or come to the conclusion that about those years of 1878 and 1879 there was a very large amount of drunkenness in the Dublin metropolitan police force—a great number of cases—without giving the particulars?—Certainly. There was a very great amount of drunkenness in the years 1878 and 1879, and I have satisfied myself that it was necessary for Colonel Connolly to inflict more severe punishments than he would have been justified in doing under ordinary circumstances.

2832. And, in your opinion, has the infliction of those fines resulted in the cases of drunkenness being greatly decreased?—Since the year 1878, in consequence of Colonel Connolly's action, drunkenness has decreased from 23·6 per cent. to 6·7 per cent., for the same months of the present year. Similarly have the assaults on civilians decreased from 1878, similarly have cases of insubordination decreased from twenty-seven to eleven last year.

2833. *Mr. Holmes.*—I asked Colonel Connolly whether, in reckoning these cases in any particular year, he reckoned each of the cases as a separate case, irrespective of whether it might not have been the same constable's second or third offence, and he was not able to say?—I do not exactly understand you.

2834. What I mean is, take the case of a constable who had been convicted three times in the year of drunkenness, would you reckon that as three separate cases of drunkenness or one case?—I should represent that as one case of drunkenness; but the Return to which I have just been referring does not represent the men that were drunk. It represents the fact of drunkenness, whether it occurred in the case of three, or one, or two constables.

2835. As I asked Colonel Connolly, so I will ask you—is that altogether fair to the force, and might it not be that a few black sheep would bring the force into very great discredit, whereas the great majority of the force might not have been guilty of those things at all?—You are quite right; it would not be fair to the force to take that high average altogether; but there would not be perhaps more than a dozen men who would be drunk three times in one year, for the simple reason that they would be dismissed. If a man was three times drunk in one year, he would not appear the next year, he would not be in the force to contribute to the drunkenness of the next year. And if you were to take a dozen from that it would not take down the percentage by more than 2 per cent.

2836. When you were Assistant Commissioner, how were you in the habit of dealing with the first offence of drunkenness?—The first offence of drunkenness I should reprimand.

2837. In the case of a second would you inflict a heavy fine?—In the case of a second I should possibly under some circumstances—it all depends on the circumstances of the case very much—as to whether or not the man was on duty; and it would also depend upon his number of years' service. If it was a second offence, and he was a young man, and there was a reasonable time between the offences, I should probably put on a fine. If he was a man of longer service, say six or seven years, and there were already three cases—you are speaking of the second offence—as to whether I should fine?

2838. To what extent would you fine?—That must also depend on the circumstances of the case.

2839. But what would be the average fine?—I should say the average fine would be one of 2*l*. or 3*l*. for the second offence.

2840. *Chairman.*—And that would have been the practice in Colonel Lake's time?—Yes.

2841. *Mr. Holmes.*—Are you aware that under the provisions of the 22nd and 23rd of Victoria, cap. 32, the Chief Constable and the Watch Committee in England and Wales are precluded from inflicting a higher fine than that of one week's pay?—I do not know the Act, but I was informed that such was the case only the other day.

2842. The Chief Constable of Liverpool and the Chief Constable of Glasgow both told us that they were limited to the infliction of a fine of 1*l*., and the Chief Constable of Liverpool said he didn't think that he had ever inflicted that fine during the time he was Chief Constable, and that if a man's conduct required him to be fined to such an amount, it was better to dismiss him. What are your views both as to the limitation under that Act and as to the practice of those Chief Constables?—If that were the case in Dublin, I could not be responsible for the discipline of the metropolitan police; and I am further of opinion that you would have no policemen left except a few of good character. I know that when I administered the discipline many of the men who came before me have said, "Fine me 5*l*. if you like, but do not reduce me;" and yet some of those men I have known to be drunk six, seven, and others of them eight times.

2843. *Chairman.*—Eight times in a year?—Eight times in a year! Oh, no, eight times in their service.

2844. *Mr. Holmes.*—Why should it be necessary to resort to fining more in the case of the police in Dublin than in the case of the police forces that I have just mentioned?—Simply because the only way of bringing down to what it is—to the percentage that you have seen it brought down—and diminishing the cases of drunkenness from 203 in 1879 to 60 in the nine months of the present year; the only way I can account for that being so is by the punishments that have been put upon them. If your Committee would allow me, I would read you the opinion of a man whom the force seemed to look up to, and who thoroughly approved of my discipline when I carried it out under his direction, and that is Sir Henry Lake. I believe that his opinion is considered by even the men of the force a very valuable one. This is an order of the 23rd February, 1876, that was when Sir Henry Lake was in office, and the year before he left. It is as follows:—

"*Police Orders, 23rd February, 1876.*

"With reference to several orders issued from time to time on the subject of intemperance, more particularly to one which appeared on the 21st instant, the Commissioner thinks it right that he should notify to the force a circumstance which has recently occurred, so that hereafter it cannot be said that any officer or constable indulges in habits of intemperance in ignorance of the consequences which will inevitably ensue.

"A member of the force who had served upwards of nineteen and a-half years, and had attained the rank of sergeant, lately appeared before a medical board, and was pronounced unfit for further service under ordinary circumstances. Provided that man had become incapacitated by fair wear and tear of constitution, the Commissioner would have felt himself bound to recommend him to

Government for the maximum pension to which, by his length of service, he would have been entitled, namely, 61l. per annum. It having, however, been brought to the notice of the Commissioner that this man's ill health had been considerably aggravated by too frequent indulgence in intoxicating liquors, he felt it his bounden duty to recommend a certain reduction in his pension.

"When the case came before Government they felt very much inclined to refuse any pension whatever, but after frequent reference to and much correspondence with the Police Department, they have at length, but almost reluctantly, granted the pensioner an allowance of 20l. per annum, being less than half of the amount which might have been allotted to him.

"The Commissioner desires it to be understood that it is not only reduction in pension, or total loss of it, which awaits members of the force as a punishment for intemperate habits. Henceforward he has determined on promoting no officer or constable to any higher rank or even higher rate whose character will not bear the strictest scrutiny, more particularly sobriety, and for this purpose all who come up for examination as to their literary qualifications will be previously inspected by the medical officer of the force, who will report whether they are physically qualified for promotion, and whether he considers any of them have injured their constitutions by irregular habits, even though they may not have been found at any time by their superiors sufficiently under the influence of liquor as to be actually unfit for duty.

"The Commissioner cannot conclude this order without once more urging upon every member of the service, for his own sake as well as for the credit of the force to which he should consider it an honour to belong, the necessity, not only of abstaining himself from an over-indulgence in drink, but of setting a good example to his comrades, for the Commissioner begs to assure the force at large that while he will ever use his best exertions to promote the welfare and happiness of the officers and men under his command, he is determined to use every means in his power to put down with a strong arm a pernicious habit which he is sorry to say has, of late years, very considerably increased in the force, and which has led to the ruin of many an otherwise respectable young man, and would, if persisted in, sooner or later bring the metropolitan police into bad repute."

This is the order which Sir Henry Lake issued, and to which I referred. At the time he issued it, it was just after the close of the year 1877, when they had had no less than 347 cases of drunkenness, or 31 per cent. for the year to which I alluded.

There is an order connected with pensions, and as it has reference to the subject with which you are now dealing, I cannot do better than read it for the Committee. It states:—

"*Police Orders, 21st February, 1878.*

"In accordance with instructions from Government, the Commissioner of Police notifies to the force that the medical officer has been directed in every case of sickness of a member of the force in which the disease is in any degree produced by or can be traced to intemperance, to make a special note of the fact in the sick list, and bring such case specially under the notice of the Commissioner.

"The medical officer will also specially report whether any candidate for promotion is addicted to tippling or is a makegever, and in any case in which unfitness for further duty is produced, hastened, or aggravated by intemperate habits, a special report will be submitted to Government, and the grant of any pension, however small, will be exceedingly doubtful in such a case."

3545. *Chairman.*—What is the date of that order? —The 21st February, 1878, and it is followed by the order which I have just read. So much was Sir Henry Lake impressed with the amount of drunkenness in the force then that he found it absolutely necessary to issue the order I have laid before you. And I may tell you that, nevertheless, although men were fined 2s. and 3s., and that reduction was inflicted, the men still got drunk, and that is my answer to your question in reference to the practice in England when I say that a fine of 10s. would not be effective here in checking the offence.

Captain George Talbot.

7 Oct., 1882.

3546. *Mr. Holmes.*—Do you think that if the men knew for certain that the third offence of drunkenness, occurring within a certain time, would entirely and absolutely lead to dismissal, that that would be as effective as the adoption of a system of heavy fines?—I don't think so.

3547. You think, I suppose, that of the two courses, fining is the more merciful?—I think that fines really have very little effect upon drunkenness, no matter how heavy they are, because the men have so much to spend over and above their needs; but what they do feel is reduction.

3548. Don't you think that these heavy fines must tend to hamper and embarrass married men very much? In the case of a married man with a large family, would not the infliction of a fine of 2s., 5s., or 1l. have the effect of disturbing his arrangements altogether, and of making him despair of ever being able to keep his head above water?—A fine would naturally be more severe upon a married man than it would be upon a single man; but, at the same time, I consider it would be unjust, and it would decidedly be considered unjust, to the men if a more lenient fine was given to a man because he was married than would be imposed if he were unmarried.

3549. I may mention that Colonel Cobbe, who is one of Her Majesty's Inspectors of Constabulary for England, and who gave evidence before the Constabulary Commission, used a very expressive phrase when dealing with that question. "We never like to touch the men's pockets," said he; "we always think of their wives and families"—and I am bound to say that both that gentleman and the Chief Constables of Liverpool and Glasgow concurred in that view. They said, "If a man is incorrigible, and that a reasonable fine has no effect, why, we get rid of him." Don't you think that a system such as I have pointed out as being adopted in England would work better than the system that seems to have been adopted here?—Well, I have already answered that question—that I consider that the punishments that were administered were absolutely necessary for the discipline of the force, and a more lenient scale would not have effected the object in view, viz., of decreasing the extraordinary amount of drunkenness.

3550. And you felt that where the only alternative was to fine or else to dismiss, it was more merciful to fine heavily than to turn a man out of the force?—I consider that the men—the great majority of the men—prefer any fine that I could put upon them sooner than reduction or dismissal.

3551. *Chairman.*—With the gradual decrease of drunkenness and offences against discipline the fines decreased?—With the gradual decrease of drunkenness and of offences against discipline the fines decreased in proportion. I may tell you that in February 1880 I issued an order to the force in which I stated that drunkenness had reached a pitch that could no longer be tolerated, and that, therefore, any man committing himself would be severely punished.

3552. *Mr. Morris.*—And that notice was published in the orders?—That notice was read to all the men in the force.

3553. And published in orders?—Yes; I may submit it to you, it is not very long. It is as follows:—

Captain George Talbot.

7 Oct., 1882.

"Standing Order, 20th February, 1880.

"The amount of drunkenness in the force has now reached a point which, notwithstanding the punishments given, can no longer be tolerated; during the past year it has reached a high figure. The force is informed that constables hereafter reported for being drunk on duty, and having already a drunken report or reports against them, will unhesitatingly be dismissed, regardless of their number of years' service. Many young constables of hardly a year's service have lately been reported for intoxication. The Commissioner attributes this entirely to the bad example shown them by their senior comrades. These young constables are informed that if reported they will meet with the severest punishment, if not dismissal. The number of men reported for drunk exceeds that of any police force in the world, and disgraces its annals. It is well known to the Commissioner that men reported for being drunk on duty never pay for their drink; it is obtained in a low underhand manner from publicans and others, whose only object is to get the sergeants and constables of constables in their power, thus rendering it impossible for them to perform their duties. It shall not be said that the Dublin metropolitan police are hand and glove with the liquor trade, or, in other words, in their power. For this reason, the offence of entering public-houses (except on legitimate business, which duty will have to be substantiated by summons or arrest, as the case may require) will for a first case be punished by reduction, and for a second or subsequent offence by dismissal. It may be remarked, in justice to the great majority of the force, that this mass of crime is due to the repeated offences of a certain section, and this is the greater reason that superintendents, inspectors, and sergeants should use increased exertion and supervision over their men in order to eradicate from its ranks this disgraceful and, to themselves, ruinous vice."

They were consequently well enough informed of the whole of the consequences, and yet drunkenness continued. That was in 1880, and then in 1881 there was a decrease of 8 per cent. in drunkenness amongst the constables. But in the officers it had amounted to the very large number of 6 per per cent. In 1881, on the 6th April, drunkenness having considerably decreased, I issued instructions to Colonel Connolly that, owing to the great decrease in the number of cases of drunkenness, he will relax the fines and punishments, and consequently the fines and the punishments were relaxed since then by him.

3854. What was the date of that?—That was on the 6th April, 1881. I have got before me a Return of the fines that were inflicted, and since I became in command the highest amount of fines inflicted that was known since I have known the force was inflicted in 1875, and Sir Henry Lake's order in 1876 was issued in consequence of the great amount of drunkenness of that year of 1875, when the fines amounted to 564*l.* In 1876, owing to the order, the amount went immediately down to 297*l.*; there was a reformation then. In 1877 the drunk began again, when it was 21 per cent., and 455*l.* was the amount of the fines. In 1878 the amount of the fines was 497*l.*, and drunkenness had risen to 23 per cent. In 1879 the amount was 435*l.*, and drunkenness had decreased to 20 per cent. In 1880 the amount was 331*l.*, and drunkenness had decreased to 14 per cent.; and in 1881, after my order which I have just read to you, the amount levied in fines had decreased to 180*l.*, and the drunkenness had then decreased to 18 per cent.; and up to the nine months of this year the amount paid in fines was 97*l.* 14*s.*, and drunkenness had decreased to 6 per cent. You will find that according as punishment was administered the drunkenness was decreased, and when there was no cause to inflict such severe punishments I issued my order of 1881 to hold the hand quiet, to be milder, and so the punishment was milder on the men, and the amount levied in fines came down from 331*l.*, when there was no further occasion for it, to 180*l.* and 97*l.*

3855. And, as a matter of fact, there has been a decrease?—Yes; for the last three years the amounts paid in fines being respectively 331*l.*, 180*l.*, and 97*l.* No man parted with more than 6*d.* or 1*s.*, even the worst character in the force.

3856. *Mr. Holmes.*—If a constable is reduced for an offence, do you allow him to regain his former rank as a matter of course after a certain period, provided his conduct has been good during that period?—If a constable is reduced from the third to the fourth rate, being a young constable, he goes to the bottom of the fourth rate, and he must rise up in seniority until he goes to the third; it generally takes him a year. If he was a senior constable, that is, a first-class constable, I used, when I administered the discipline, to reduce him to the next lowest grade, which would be the second—10, 20, or 30 steps, as the case seemed to me just, so that he might regain his rate after six months or nine months, as the case might be.

3857. *Mr. Morris.*—And did you find that answer satisfactorily?—Yes.

3858. And you would approve of such a system?—It had this effect, that it made him pay the fine by very small instalments of so much, deducted each week. He would only lose the difference between the first rate of pay and the rate to which he had been reduced, and it would come easier upon him as a married man than otherwise it would if I fined him 3*l.*

3859. *Chairman.*—It came out of his pay?—In fact, instead of receiving first rate, he would receive second-class rate.

3860. Is that habit continued?—I believe Colonel Connolly has had recourse to it, but I leave it entirely to him. I give him a general support, but I do not go into every individual case that Colonel Connolly decides; but I believe he pursues that.

3861. As I understand you, Colonel Connolly generally carries out the discipline of the force. But in any important case, or if a man wishes an appeal, has he the right to go before you?—A man is informed in the Instruction Book that if he has any complaint to make he can always at any moment see the Chief Commissioner. I have received no such complaint for five years.

3862. In fact, there has been no appeal from Colonel Connolly's decision for five years to you?—No.

3863. Although it is published in the Regulation Book of the police that they can do so?—Yes, against any officer in the force they can have access to me. It is published in orders always that the Chief Commissioner is open to hear any complaint the men may have to make, and in visiting the barracks I ask them invariably, "Have you any complaints to make?"

3864. *Mr. Holmes.*—Now, we will take the case of a sergeant who is reduced. Supposing his conduct is good for a certain period, would you allow him, as a matter of course, to resume his former rank?—It would depend.

3865. Well, for a grave offence?—If a sergeant was drunk on duty, and was charged with insubordination or other grievous offence, such as an assault upon a civilian—if he is reduced to the ranks, he cannot be restored to his original rank without going up again through the proper form as laid down in the Instruction Book, and reach his former grade through the several lower ranks. If a sergeant, he should have to become from a first-rate constable an acting sergeant, and then in his turn be again promoted to the rank of sergeant.

3866. *Mr. Morris.*—In fact, he should have to work up again in the same way as he has worked up before?—Yes, in the same way as before.

Captain George Talbot.

7 Oct., 18[illegible].

2867. *Mr. Holmes.*—Does it often happen that a man who has lost his rank regains it again?—Yes, certainly.

2868. Often?—No; it does happen, but I won't bind myself to say often, because I should have to refer to statistics; but I have known cases of it, and there are now men in the force who have regained their former rank.

2869. Do you find, as a rule, that when a man loses his rank he conducts himself well in the hope of regaining it, or do you find that he loses his sense of self-respect, and goes from bad to worse?—Well, I speak from memory when I say that the men who have been reduced have not become worse upon reduction; rather, many of them have gone on, and nearly all aspire to the rank. In cases that are not so serious, such as a breach of discipline or a neglect of the rules of the service, I have restored men to their former rank. I can give instances of it. Men get married without leave; one did so the other day. He was an acting inspector. He married, and after six months or seven months he came and he made a confession that he had married without leave. There are certain regulations to be gone through before a man can marry. One is that his wife is a respectable person, of good moral character, and the other is that there is some little money, like 40*l.* That is the regulation, for the purpose of insuring that the policeman is not marrying a pauper, so that he can keep his wife, and continue to be a respectable member of the force.

2870. When you say a sum of 40*l.*, do you mean that he should have saved that amount, or that his wife should have it?—That they must have it between them; that they should have 40*l* for the purpose of furnishing their little home, and living in some degree of comfort, which is necessary for his health, in order that he should be able to perform his duty. This acting inspector having married without leave, reported it to me that he had done so. To vindicate a breach of discipline like that—having previously punished men for the same offence—I thought it my duty to reduce him to the rank of sergeant; but at the end of six months, he being a man of good character, and having memorialised, I restored him to his previous rank of acting inspector.

2871. Now, may I ask you, do you find that, as a rule, when a man marries, 40*l.* has been saved by himself while in the force?—In many cases it is saved; but in most cases it is not.

2872. In most cases the wife brings the money?—Yes.

2873. *Mr. Morris.*—Or a portion of it?—Yes, or a portion of it; and I have great difficulty in ascertaining that the sum *bonâ fide* belongs to the bride. There is a very considerable desire in Dublin to marry the metropolitan police, and I am averse to allowing a greater proportion of married men than at present exists.

2874. May I ask what the proportion is?—I think it is about one-third that are married. It is absolutely necessary, under the circumstances in which Dublin is situated, to keep two-thirds of the force at least to meet all the casualties and to perform the duties which they may at any moment be called upon to do.

2875. *Mr. Holmes.*—In other words, you feel it necessary to have a certain proportion in barrack?—Yes.

2876. And those men must be single men?—Yes.

2877. *Mr. Morris.*—And owing to there not being any married quarters?—Yes. If men were required for any emergency it would be impossible to collect the married men within any reasonable time to bring them together.

2878. *Mr. Holmes.*—As you have touched upon this question of married men, and have shown that the exigencies of the City of Dublin require that there should be a great number of men living in barracks, and therefore unmarried, may I ask you, have you ever thought whether it might not be of great service to the force to have blocks of buildings near the station-houses for the accommodation of married men?—Four years ago I entered into that subject fully with the late Under-Secretary, and I advocated strongly the building of rows of cottages in the several divisions of the metropolitan police district for the purpose of accommodating married men. I represented that if the Government would advance money they would be at no loss, as the excessive rents charged to my married men, if reduced to a just and fair rent, would amply compensate the Government for the outlay. Mr. Burke advocated the subject, and a piece of ground was bought next to Mountjoy Prison for the purpose of giving a site for the cottages I proposed, and also a station and barrack, which would be worked by the married men who lived close by the station in a row of cottages. No money could be had, but I am happy to say that this day I have received from the Board of Works intimation that the station is to be built, but it omits to say whether the cottages are to be built; but I hope that as the site has been purchased, my original design of building a row of cottages—fifteen or twenty cottages—for married men may be carried out as the beginning of what I think ought to be throughout the force.

2879. Supposing the cottages were built, would you allow the married men of any division to live there, or would you restrict the occupation of them to the men of the particular division in which the cottages are situated?—To its own division. I wish it to be done on the same principle as the coast-guard cottages are done; that is, some fourteen or fifteen cottages, and a superior one for the inspector, who would live at the end house, and see that everything was kept in order, and that no irregularity took place.

2880. Now that you have mentioned the coast-guards, are you aware whether they are charged a rent for the cottages in which they live?—I believe they are.

2881. And, while upon this question, could you tell us about what rent upon an average a married man has to pay for his lodgings—what weekly rent?—I believe that they get very indifferent lodgings indeed for from 6*s.* to 7*s.* per week; but I will furnish you with the exact amount paid in each division. I know that in London lodgings are built for them, and then they are charged a moderate rent.

2882. Have you any idea of what percentage of the married men in London are accommodated in those blocks of buildings?—No, I have not.

2883. Well, I have a return before me from District Superintendent Walker, of the London metropolitan police, and you will be surprised to hear this, that only 3½ per cent. are accommodated; so that, practically, the married men in London are not accommodated?—I thought they would be accommodated.

2884. *Mr. Morris.*—Do you think the married men would like this system of being accommodated in blocks of buildings, or a system of cottages?—I have reason to know that if the men were consulted it would not be a popular movement, as they do not wish to be under supervision.

2885. You mean constant supervision?—Yes, constant supervision. I endeavoured to set up a scheme, by the aid of a few pounds I have saved for the men from the canteen in the depôt barrack, of taking lodgings from the Artisans' Dwellings Company for my married men, and to let them to them at a lower rent, but I found that the movement was so unpopular that if I had taken the cottages they would have been left on my hands. But what the men want is an allowance in money as a lodging allowance.

2886. Do you think that it would be fair to draw the line and to give a man a lodging allowance because he was married, and that if another man does not choose to marry he is not to get a lodging allowance?—No, I do not think it would be fair, because I think it would put a premium on marriage in the force, and as I have stated before, the ladies of Dublin are only too anxious to marry policemen, and we could not have all married.

3887. *Mr. Holmes.*—Are you aware that a lodging allowance is not given to married men in the police forces in England?—Yes, I am aware of that.

3888. And therefore it would be next door to impossible to give it to the men here?—It would be impossible.

3889. As we are upon the subject of barracks, and of accommodation for the men, I presume you are aware that the station-houses in London are accommodated with libraries and reading-rooms, and where there is more than a certain number of men in a station-house, with even billiard-rooms. Are the barracks in Dublin provided with any such attractions for the men?—We have not received any sum or gratuity from the Government towards either libraries or amusements of any sort. With the aid of a small sum at my disposal, the savings of the very small canteen in the Kevin Street barrack, I have already purchased for the service close on 100*l.* worth of books, and have distributed them in cases to each barrack and station-house, so that the men have at their disposal, at all events, some twenty or thirty in each case, purchased by this money, for their amusement, but we have received no aid whatever from the Government.

3890. Do you think that if the barracks were accommodated with reading-rooms, libraries, billiard-rooms, or such like attractions, it would have the effect of weaning the men from public-houses, and make them fonder of police life?—Well, I think it is worth trying, but I have grave doubts of its success in Dublin. I think the men are more disposed to play cards than any other games, and I doubt if billiards would be at all to their taste. They do play draughts, which they are allowed to do; but card-playing led to quarrels, assaults on each other, and fighting, so much so that I had to forbid it; and it also led to gambling and betting, which was highly objectionable in a barrack.

3891. *Chairman.*—Now, Captain Talbot, the Committee would be glad to learn your views in reference to pensions?—Well, my opinion in reference to the question of pensions is that the Pension Act of 1867 is totally inadequate, particularly now, when we have a number of men retiring upon the old scale at the same time that the first are retiring under the new scale. Perhaps a man under the old Act will retire to-morrow, and so will a man under the new Act, and when they begin to compare the amounts received, he, naturally, is not contented; that is the man who retires under the Act of 1867.

3892. *Mr. Morris.*—But, then, is it not the case that men now retiring under the 1867 Act would only be retiring after fifteen or so years' service?—Quite so.

3893. Whereas the men who would be retiring under the old Act would be retiring after thirty years' service?—But that does not weigh with them. They only calculate it as bulk money in their hands, and that makes them complain.

3894. And do you think that this question of the scale of pensions under the Act of 1867 is a very burning question with the men?—Yes, I think it is, with the men. I believe that the young men never consider the question of pensions; but when a man reaches five, six, or seven years' service, he then begins to think what his fate will be, and then he calculates whether it is worth his while to continue in the service with the prospect of such a small pension as is given under the Act of 1867, or whether he can better himself. It was then that the men resigned—the number that did resign to go to Australia; the cause of that being that two or three went out first, and they happened to get into the mounted police in Australia, and wrote home glowing accounts of what they were receiving, and sending their photographs in magnificent uniforms, and all these young men thought that they would naturally appear to being officers in the Australian police instead of constables in the Dublin metropolitan police, and that is the secret of the exodus to Australia.

3895. The intended exodus?—It actually took place. I forget the number of men that went. But with regard to the pensions, the Dublin metropolitan police must abide by whatever pension is settled for the whole of the other police forces, therefore I consider there is not much use my forming an opinion on the subject. I have not given it much consideration, or, indeed, any, as to what it ought to be. There is no doubt that others who are wiser men will settle what the scale should be, and the whole must be satisfied with what is settled in London.

3896. *Mr. Holmes.*—And I presume that the majority of the men of your force are reasonable enough to see that they cannot be put under a better scale?—Quite so.

3897. *Chairman.*—The men complain very loudly that offences for which they have been punished either by fine or reduction affect the amount of their pension?—Well, with regard to that, it would be manifestly unfair to give the same pension to a man who had been reported for six, seven, and eight, and, as I have known, for ten times, for being drunk in his career, and with a long defaulter's sheet, to give that man the same amount of pension for the same number of years as I would give to an exemplary character without a stain on his sheet; otherwise there would be no incentive whatever to good behaviour.

3898. Are you aware that in the London and Liverpool police, when a man has been fined or reduced, the sentence or punishment is final, and is never brought into account as affecting his pension?—I do not know what takes place in other police forces, but I know what I am forced conscientiously to do in this, and the object of the pension is not that he shall receive the maximum that he is entitled to, but that he shall receive that which under all the circumstances of the case shall be deemed just. Those are the terms of the Act of Parliament, I think.

3899. *Mr. Holmes.*—And, moreover, is it not the case, Captain Talbot, under the Act of 1847, that you are absolutely required to give a certificate that the constable has served with diligence and fidelity?—Yes.

3900. And, as a conscientious man, you could not give that certificate unless you believed that he had fulfilled all those conditions?—Certainly not. And it is not only that, but I produce to you the form which I have to sign, and also the forms that have to be filled up by the medical officers, and I will give you the headings of those forms. And while we are on this subject, as it is a very important one, I shall have to trouble you at a little length with another of Sir Henry Lake's orders, and he was looked upon, as I have already said, as a model Commissioner. This is an extract from the Report of Sir Henry A. Lake, dated the 25th February, 1876, and it is about pensions. This is as follows:—

"In accordance with the annexed Minute of the Under-Secretary, received 11th instant, referring for report Mr. Leagon's letter of the 10th January last, relative to the proportion now borne by non-effective expenditure to total cost, both in the Constabulary more than 16 per cent., and in the Dublin police 21 per cent., as compared with kindred forces in England, the Commissioner of Police begs to submit the following statement:—

"In recommending pensions to be granted by

Government under this Act to the Dublin police, the Commissioners did not at all interpret the Act according to the letter of these provisions. Had they done so, the Dublin police pensions would be now several thousand pounds in excess of the present total cost.

"It may be observed, in proof of this, that men appointed before the Act was passed, as a rule, the Commissioners only recommended full pay for and after twenty-five years' service, thus requiring one-fourth longer service than the law required. In like manner, as a rule, the Commissioners endeavoured carefully to discriminate in recommending retiring allowances under the other terms of service prescribed by the Act. They accordingly established a graduating scale, under which an increased amount of pension was awarded for each additional year served, in this way interpreting the spirit rather than the letter of the Superannuation Act.

"It is no doubt quite true that the amount now payable for pensions forms a large part of the total expenditure of the force, but when the arduous and unremitting nature of police duty in so variable and trying a climate as this is borne in mind, it will not appear unreasonable that sixteen or twenty years of such duty, notwithstanding the admittedly superior strength and physique of the Dublin police, should be found to render a large number of its members unfit through ill-health for further service. Nine hours on night duty out of every twenty-four, exclusive of attendance at the police-courts to prove charges every second month, as had formerly for many years been the rule of the service, must necessarily have caused a great wear and tear of the stoutest constitutions; indeed, to such an extent that, but for the prospect of a pension, the Commissioners would have found it most difficult to keep the force together. And the Under-Secretary is aware that among other causes this severity of the service made known in the provinces by retired policemen operated before the increase of pay to render it all but impossible to procure recruits for the force.

"Political combinations in this county, amongst them, at the latest, the Fenian confederacy, have also not failed to contribute their quota to the pension list, many members of the force from time to time having lost their health owing to the harassing duties which they had to undergo in connection with such confederacies.

"The Commissioner trusts he may venture to submit that the pressure of the Dublin police pensions on the Imperial Exchequer is about one-third less than those of the Royal Irish Constabulary, the constabulary force being almost wholly maintained from the Consolidated Fund, while the local income of the metropolitan police amounts from taxation, &c., to about one-third of the whole.

"It may further be observed that the metropolitan police service being a service of much greater severity than the constabulary, the pensions of the former must necessarily bear a larger proportion to the total expenditure than the pensions of the latter.

"The Commissioner of Police has now only to state, in conclusion, that the most scrupulous care is now taken in considering claims for pension. Every circumstance bearing on the case is carefully weighed, and in any instance in which intemperate habits are found to have accelerated or aggravated the cause of unfitness, a large reduction is made in recommending the amount of pension to be granted.

"The Under-Secretary is aware that a special order was recently issued to the force to the effect that any member of it whose cause of unfitness could be traced to intemperate habits would run the risk of not being granted a pension at all. Instructions have also been given to the medical officers of the service to make a special note in the sick report of the case of any man appearing before him whose illness had been in any degree caused by intemperance, and further to report any such case specially to the Commissioner.

"Further, the habits of all men are carefully inquired into, and their physical capacity medically tested before promotion; indeed, nothing is left undone to prevent abuse, and the utmost possible care shall not fail to be taken to prevent the grant of a pension to any man (the physical cause being determined by a medical Board specially summoned periodically for the purpose) except under circumstances perfectly fulfilling all the requirements of the law."

Captain [illegible]

7 Oct., 18[illegible]

I mention this to show you the pressure that was brought to bear on Sir Henry Lake when Chief Commissioner, and on myself subsequently, not to grant pensions to men who had been guilty of offences. And, further, that in the forms to be filled up by the medical officer he is to state whether the constable is wholly incapacitated, or whether he can partially supplement his pension by other civil employment, and he is also to state that he is unfit, and that he never will be fit for service in the Dublin metropolitan police again; and he is also to state the cause which has contributed to the disease for which he is invalided, and whether he has in any way contributed towards it by intemperance or other practices.

3901. *Mr. Holmes.*—Now, before we leave the question of pensions, may I ask you do you happen to know whether pensioners of the Dublin metropolitan police force find it easy to get employment?—They do find it easy to get employment, and I know of instances where employment has been kept open for them, so that when they retire they may avail themselves of it. I know also of a case where a man who had served for thirty years, and, although it was reported by the medical officer that he could find no disease in him, he was in a few months afterwards—rather than dismiss him for malingering—he was struck off the service, and he immediately entered upon an extensive and active dairy trade. That is one of the instances in which employment can immediately succeed being struck off.

3902. *Chairman.*—Is that so at present?—That is so.

3903. *Mr. Holmes.*—Because we had it in evidence that not only policemen themselves would not be employed, but their children would not be allowed in tradesmen's shops with other boys in consequence of the hostility of the people towards them?—In my answer to the previous question I alluded to years before the last two years. It is quite possible what you say may really be so, and I know that policemen in the country, from the fact of their being policemen, have been shunned, and, to use the new word, "Boycotted"; and that many of them have not asked for the annual leave, not wishing to go to their relatives in the country on that account.

3904. *Chairman.*—Are you speaking of the constabulary?—No; of my own men.

3905. *Mr. Morris.*—A great many of the men who were examined here put forward a claim that they should be paid extra pay for extra work, as they called it, and, when questioned on the subject, they described what they meant by that claim in this way—that the men ought to be on duty for a certain number of hours—eight hours, I think, some of them fixed as the amount of duty—but that if a man was called out after that, excepting in some great case of emergency, or if he was to be kept longer on beat, or if he was to be detained in court, that he was to get some extra pay. They also stated that they were entitled, according to the rules, to a certain number of days' leave in the year and also in the month; and they put forward what appeared to me to be rather, at all events, a liberal scale of leave for themselves, by which they were, I think, to get, some of them a fortnight, some of them three weeks, and some as much as a month, in addition to two days for every month in the year, which would in reality come to a very long period, and they wished that in case they could not get this leave that they should be paid double pay for the time that they were kept from their leave, and one of the grounds of their seeking this double pay was that they would be sure to get their leave if you were obliged to pay them double while you kept them?—With regard to the first part of your question, which relates to extra pay for extra work, if you take extra pay for extra work as meaning that if a man was one or two hours on duty one hour more than at another time, it would be practically impossible to calculate the extra pay for extra work in the force; but, practically, extra pay for extra work already exists, inasmuch as when a man performs extra duty he is put upon the sheet for reward, and he receives sometimes 1*l.*, sometimes 2*l.*, and often as much as 3*l.*, and the rewards have gone for extra pay for extra duty up sometimes to no less than something like 1,000*l.* in one year, or from 800*l.* to 1,000*l.* in one year—that is, for extra pay and rewards. So that, practically speaking, if a clerk is kept in his office more than two or three hours he is put upon the sheet at the end of every quarter for reward, and he is granted an amount that is equivalent to the number of hours that he is on.

2906. *Mr. Holmes.*—May I ask you first, if a man is required to attend in the police-court after his ordinary tour of duty, does that attendance count as extra work for which there will be extra pay?—If they got extra pay for that they would be receiving payment of two kinds, because they get off duty for every hour they spend at the police-court, or nearly so.

2907. For what class of extra work is the extra pay given in the shape of these rewards—what is the nature of the extra work?—Rewards are granted by the Commissioner to the police for brave or meritorious conduct in the discharge of their duties. When any of the police have done any act beyond the ordinary police duties, or have skilfully conducted a case to a successful termination, the superintendent may recommend them for a reward, giving all the required particulars on the minuting report, in red ink. The Commissioner considers each case on its merits, and awards such sums as he deems adequate. The men's names and the amount awarded appear in police orders.

2908. What is the nature of the extra work for which men receive extra pay in the shape of these rewards?—Well, if they have been on any particular duty they receive it for extra police duty. Say a man is sent out on protection duty, and that instead of being so engaged for eight hours he is twelve hours, he is put on the sheet and he is rewarded for that. If a man is sent on any particular duty which takes up more of his time than ordinary duty, he receives extra pay for that—extra pay which is distinct from reward. If a man performs a gallant act, he is put upon the sheet and rewarded for diligence; but extra pay for extra work means for extra time given to police duty. Besides that, if he has to use his plain clothes, he is compensated for that by money for his plain clothes.

2909. *Mr. Morris.*—But I suppose if any man gets extra pay for extra work, he must do some substantial work, he must do something that would occupy him some substantial time—you would not calculate that if a man was half-an-hour longer than his usual time on beat that he would be entitled to get extra pay?—No. He is put down upon the sheet for extra police duty, and during the month we cannot calculate it by the clock, or by the second or by the hour, but we say, "This man has diligently performed during the month a certain amount of extra duty," and the Assistant Commissioner measuring [the] amount of reward, [he] says, "This is a man of good character, and he has done extra work," and he is put down for, say, 2*l.*, but he does not measure the time, nor does he pretend to calculate between the man and the State how the man has spent his time.

2910. In fact, your business could not be carried on in any other way?—Moreover, it should be borne in mind that the condition upon which a man enters the police force is that he devotes the whole of his time to his duty.

2911. *Mr. Holmes.*—And is it not the case that his pay is calculated on the assumption that the man gives his whole time to the service?—"I shall devote my whole time to the police service"—that is the oath he takes. With regard to the leave, that is the second part of Mr. Morris' question, that is distinctly laid down in the Instruction Book. With regard to the leave of absence, one day's leave of absence in the month is to be granted to every man—one Sunday or one week-day—and also annual leave as follows: Superintendents, 28 days; inspectors, 28 days; acting inspectors, 21 days; sergeants, 21 days, acting sergeants, 14 days, and constables, 10 days. Full pay is allowed for these periods, and if a man writes to me from the country asking for an extension of his leave upon any reasonable ground whatever, I never refuse it to him if it is brought under my notice. Moreover, any man belonging to any religious persuasion other than the Roman Catholic is entitled on the Sunday to have his leave whether he be on duty or not, for the purpose in the evening of attending his place of worship, and he always, as I am informed, avails himself of it.

2912. Has the state of the country during the last two or three years interfered with the men's leave at all?—During the last winter I certainly refused leave, but during the spring I never did, nor during the last summer; but where the men were short, and when there was hardly a man for duty in the streets, I have refused leave, and, as I venture to think, properly refused it. But I can relax that at any moment. Besides this, the superintendents have power to give an afternoon's leave, and they have directions to give an afternoon's leave to any man applying for it, if he can be spared from duty. Before we leave the question of pensions, I would like to refer to the question of the gratuity under fifteen years' service. I think that this is a just grievance, namely, that if a man dies in the service before he has time to have his papers made out granting him the gratuity, the gratuity is lost to him or his heirs. This matter was fully considered by one of the present Lords Justices of Appeal, Lord Justice FitzGibbon, when he was Solicitor-General in 1878, and I cannot explain the matter better than by reading you his Lordship's observations on the subject. Lord Justice FitzGibbon's Minute, when he was Solicitor-General, on the subject is as follows:—

"*Memorial of ex-Constable Bri[illegible] for Gratuity.*

["*Copy of Minute of G. FitzGibbon, dated*
"*September 14, 1878.*

"Mr. Burke,

"I have no hesitation whatever in saying that the practice disclosed on this file is irregular, and an evasion of the law. The practice has no doubt been forced upon the Department by the extreme hardship of individual cases, but it would be most desirable to deal directly with such cases, either by granting pensions or allowances to widows or children, as was done in the case of A. S. Carberry, or if there be no legal warrant for that course, by obtaining a like statutory power for the Royal Irish Constabulary and Dublin Metropolitan Police as that existing in London under 34 & 35 Vict., c. 104, sec. 6. I think it would be well to consider whether a general power of giving an allowance to a widow or children,

Captain George Talbot.

7 Oct., 1882.

irrespective of the constable's death having been caused by injury received in the discharge of duty, would not be advantageous, otherwise there will be constant cases, such as that of Constable Malins, where either a very charitable construction must be put on the limitation, or great hardships inflicted. In any event, I am afraid the practice of hurrying dying constables off of the force before they depart this life in order to secure an allowance which is to be paid after their deaths to their relations cannot be defended. The three cases cited have each its irregularity, for in No. 1 a man wholly insensible and with his skull fractured is supposed to have put his mark to the necessary receipt, and this was affixed by somebody who probably would not like to consider how his act was to be distinguished from forgery, but that it was done from charitable motives. In No. 2 a sanitary inspector was not reached in time to get his signature before he died, and his widow (in all respects as meritorious an object as the widow of No. 1) seems not yet to have got even an acknowledgment of any one of her three memorials. In No. 3 the constable, who was supposed to be dying, seems to have lost his pay for the eleven weeks during which he was recovering after his last discharge, and having elected to give up the allowance and go back into the force, has since been dismissed, and has forfeited all pension, but does not appear to have got his eleven weeks' pay. It may be added, too, that this practice can't be applied at all to cases of over fifteen years' service."

3913. Has this opinion been acted upon?—No; because we have not the power. However, so it is understood so far.

3914. *Mr. Morris.*—With reference to retirement on pension, some of the men suggested that they should be entitled to get a sum of money instead of pension; have any cases of that kind come before you?—No.

3915. You don't know any case in which a man retired after, say, twenty or twenty-five years' service and received a sum of money instead of pension?—Whether he can receive his gratuity in lieu of pension?

3916. Yes?—I think such cases have occurred.

3917. Is there any objection to that course, do you think?—There could be no objection to that course as long as the State deals with him, and that he has no further claim whatever as a pensioner. But that would be a matter entirely of finance, and not for me. The Commissioner could express no opinion on this matter. It is one for the consideration of the the State, to deal with a man and to see whether they can make a bargain that suits each party best.

3918. But from a police point of view you see no objection?—No. With regard to the question of permission to enter public-houses, I wish to lay before the Committee an order that was issued prohibiting the men from entering into public-houses, and one that was not originated with me, but was considered necessary by Mr. O'Ferrall and Sir Henry H. Lake and Colonel Browne, for an order was issued prohibiting the men of the force from entering public-houses, and it is dated the 18th January, 1840. It is as follows:—

"The sergeants and constables of the force have hitherto considered themselves at liberty to drink in public-houses when off duty; but the Commissioners are now under the necessity of forbidding this practice, and in future any men who are found in public-houses must be reported for disobedience of orders. Policemen cannot be too temperate; but those men who are disposed to refresh themselves moderately must, if married, drink in their lodgings; if single, in their section-houses. Card-playing cannot be permitted, and will be severely punished. The police are expected not only to be active in apprehending offenders against the laws, but to set an example in their own persons of propriety of conduct, and the Commissioners will consider those men who are found drinking and card-playing in public-houses unfit to belong to the force."

3919. And has that ever since been acted upon?—Yes, it has ever since been acted upon, and found that it would be, in the opinion of Sir Henry Lake, impracticable to allow the men to enter public-houses, either on or off duty. But I am willing to make this offer, that if a man wishes to entertain his friends who come from the country he will have nothing to do but ask permission from his station-house officer—the inspector on duty—to be allowed for the afternoon to spend it with his friends, and to resort to any respectable establishment.

3920. *Mr. Morris.*—You would just place upon him the simple restriction of asking leave to do so?—Yes.

3921. *Mr. Holmes.*—Are you aware that the police in England, including the London metropolitan police, are allowed to go into public-houses when off duty, whether in or out of uniform?—I am aware that they are allowed to go into public-houses off duty. I am also aware that they are punished very severely, comparatively for their scale of punishment, for entering public-houses on duty, and the publican is also punished for having given them or allowed them to drink on his premises. But in the London police they have no liquor or porter or beer allowed in the barrack, beyond that which they can send for to a shop round the corner; but in my barrack the men are supplied with any amount of porter they choose to drink, and I am sorry to say that the consumption is very large indeed.

3922. Then you think, having regard to the different circumstances that exist in Dublin, as compared with London and the other cities in England, that it would not be desirable to allow your police to go into public-houses even off duty and in plain clothes?—I have another reason, and it is this: that some four years ago this force was branded very unjustly with being entirely in the publicans' interest; and I maintain that if the men were allowed indiscriminately to go into public-houses that certain-thinking people in Dublin would renew that attack upon them with some fair sense, and nothing would persuade the public but that the constable who frequents public-houses was in the interest of the publican, and that he could not be expected to perform his duty with that impartiality which he can show now through not being allowed to enter a public-house.

3923. And you, in point of fact, think that the duties which a constable has to perform in connection with the Licensing Acts are incompatible with his being allowed to go into a public-house?—Yes; I think that if he was allowed to frequent public-houses it would be certainly prejudicial to his performing his duty. I do not say he would not perform his duty, but I mean to say that the present state of things furnishes an incentive to his performing his duty.

3924. *Mr. Holmes.*—We will now come to the question of promotion. I will ask you, Captain Talbot, to explain to us how a man rises from grade to grade, first of all in the rank of constable, and so on through the service. Take the case of a well-conducted man joining the force; how long would he remain in the lowest grade of constable before he rises to the next highest grade?—When a constable first comes as a recruit he goes to the depôt, where it takes him from three to four months to learn his duty before he can be sworn in as a constable. He is then sworn in, and becomes a fourth-rate constable. He remains in that grade the average time of one year.

3925. When you say "the average time," do you mean to say that his promotion to the higher grade depends upon whether there is any vacancy in the higher grade?—It depends upon vacancy. There is no fixed time. He is then promoted to

Captain [illegible] Talbot.

[illegible] Dec., [illegible]

the third rate, upon which he remains about five years. He then is promoted to the second rate, upon which he remains for two years, and then he becomes a first-rate constable.

3826. Then upon an average a man takes eight and a-half years to rise from the bottom of the fourth rate until he comes to the bottom of the first rate?—Yes.

3827. I presume that a good number of the men who join the force must, in the absence of special intelligence, and owing to the fact that there are not very many higher posts, be content to remain constables all their lives, no matter how well-conducted they are?—Yes, certainly—those without intelligence; now, if you will allow me to go on I will give you the man's rise throughout. Being a first-grade constable, the next grade is that of acting sergeant. This promotion was previously made by Sir H. Lake by selection and good character, together with a very easy examination in reading, writing, and figures. I, however, thought it fairer to throw it open to the whole service by competition. In order to do that I established what I call an advanced class, consisting of forty members; and all first-rate men were allowed to compete for a place upon this class. The examination was a very easy one of reading, writing, and of the first four rules of arithmetic. If a man failed the first time to get on it, he could try it as often as he pleased. When there were two or three vacancies amongst the acting sergeants, I allowed some eight or ten of the advanced class—first the seniors—to go up and compete for the vacancy—the examination is perhaps a little more severe in the way of arithmetic and figures, the papers were sealed up by the superintendent, who remained in the room all the time, they were corrected by Colonel Connolly, the marks were given by him, and the order of merit was given to me. If the man's character was still good, he went up into his seniority of place, according to the order of merit. That was the system that was carried out. From the acting sergeants to the sergeants a similar process took place—so many seniors who were acting sergeants were allowed to go up, and competed for the rank of sergeant, and in their order of merit they were similarly promoted.

3828. But of course you laid special stress upon knowledge of police duties?—Oh, yes, we laid special stress upon knowledge of police duties, and the higher the grades the more we were exacting in our examination in police duties, so that of those men on the advanced class all the acting sergeants were allowed several chances, and to go up as often as they pleased to compete for a vacancy. It was necessary in order to retain his place on the advanced class that he should attend school a reasonable number of times when his duty permitted him, and I inspected that school, took the attendance of the men, and when I saw that a man who is not employed on duty that prevented his attending school so as to advance himself, I then struck his name off the advanced class. I also thought that it was desirable that before a man received extra pay there should be some test of his having a better knowledge of his duties, and in order that he should have every facility in that way, I reorganized the school, and gave them every facility for attending it as they were there. They made considerable progress, and within the last six months the attendance was very large indeed, in fact, it was overcrowded, but since the agitation in reference to the three months' pay began, the school was completely deserted.

3829. May I ask you was the school only for the advanced class of constables?—It was open to the whole service, but the advanced class had it at particular hours to themselves, where they could receive instruction of a superior nature than that which was open to ordinary constables. A very easy examination was required by each constable before he was promoted to his superior rate. Thus the constable who may be tolerably low upon the rate might get up to the next rate in a much better place if he knew his duties better than his comrades. The attendance at the school, however, gave such dissatisfaction, as they thought it was compulsory when not compulsory, that I abolished the examination for rates, and now they are promoted by seniority. I would wish to say this, that the duties that I wish to insist upon, and which I think necessary, are a knowledge of reading and writing—to enable them to take down the numbers of cabs or of houses in streets—to know their public-house duties, or the breaches of the law between the spirit grocer and the publican, and to know the Traffic Act and the car fares. I think these are branches of knowledge that are absolutely necessary to a good policeman.

3830. *Mr. Morris.*—The Chief Constables that we have examined from Liverpool and Glasgow, and I think Mr. Walker, of the London metropolitan police force, also stated it would be impossible to have promotion by seniority in the force. I suppose you concur entirely in that view?—How do you mean—promotion by seniority?

3831. That when there was a vacancy for a sergeant the senior constable should be made a sergeant?—It would be unpracticable, perfectly impracticable.

3832. *Mr. Hobart.*—Is it necessary for a sergeant to pass an examination before he can be made an acting inspector?—Certainly, the promotion is competitive to the rank of acting inspector from that of sergeant.

3833. And from acting inspector to inspector?—Yes, from acting inspector to inspector.

3834. But I presume not from the rank of inspector to that of superintendent?—That question I have not yet decided.

3835. How was it regulated in the past?—They had no examination.

3836. Were examinations always necessary for promotion from rank to rank?—Since I have joined the service they were, but in a very minor degree. There was no system. They existed in a minor degree, but the examination was more a test examination, and was not competitive, that is what I mean to convey. But I laid no intention on the promotions, the man's character must always have been good.

3837. Don't you think that a man might be a first-rate policeman without being able to pass a competitive examination, and that your system might deprive you of the best men?—I think that my system is the best, and even with all the safeguards with which I have surrounded the examination, there are many sergeants now doing station-house duty who would prefer to go the rounds all night than remain in the station-house, lest a difficult charge or a complicated case might come before them which they found themselves incompetent to decide; although these same officers may be very good officers to detect crime in the streets.

3838. We have not asked you yet, Captain Talbot, what your opinion is as to the sufficiency of the rates of pay in the various ranks. I may tell you that all the witnesses nearly asked that their pay should be increased, and complained that it was not sufficient, but at the same time they left the general impression on the minds of the Committee that they did not attach as much importance to this question as to the others that they brought before us?—Yes, I believe that to be their opinion.

3839. Now, what is your general opinion with reference to the sufficiency or insufficiency of the pay?—I think the pay of all ranks is very fair, and I do not believe that the men complain—really complain—of it, with the exception of the acting inspectors, and I think the acting inspector's is a rank that is underpaid.

3840. Well, now, are the duties of the acting

inspector as responsible and as arduous as those of the inspectors?—The duties to a great extent are similar and as responsible, but he has not the responsibility which may often occur to an inspector of having to take charge of the division in the superintendent's absence.

3941. That is a duty, I presume, that is not often likely to arise?—On many occasions I have to send even a third-class inspector to take charge of a division in the superintendent's absence on leave, or on other duty. When he is at the Commission or any other place, the inspector has a very responsible post and very responsible duty, which does not devolve to the acting inspector—which does not fall on the acting inspector. At the same time, I consider him underpaid, and a very deserving class of officer.

3942. Can you suggest how his pay might be made better without increasing the present cost of the maintenance of the force—can you suggest any rearrangement of the rates of pay?—Well, I merely throw this out for your consideration. It is difficult to find money without taking it from some one; but to put it in a fair way, it is the young men who can best afford to lose. A man coming in on the fourth rate receives, I think, 1*l.* 3*s.*, and after one year he receives the largest increase of any, that is 3*s.*, to 1*l.* 6*s.* Now, I think it would not be a great hardship if the man on the fourth rate was kept on it for six months or eight months more before he was promoted to third rate. By doing that you would obtain, I think, that amount of money which would be necessary to increase the pay of the acting inspectors.

3943. What increase would that give per week?—I have not calculated it, and I just merely throw it out to you, that you could do it in this way:—We will say there are 100 men upon the fourth rate, you could, instead of making their pay 1*l.* 6*s.* by promoting them to third rate at the end of a year, you could keep them on the fourth rate at 1*l.* 3*s.* a week for six or eight months longer, and by doing that you would thus slightly retard the promotion of those men, which would, of course, be money in the department to pay the acting inspectors. That is a calculation you could easily make, and I merely suggest the matter as one way out of the difficulty.

3944. Can you say why it was, when fixing the rates of pay in 1873, the pay given to the third-class inspectors here exceeded so much the pay given to the third-class inspectors in London?—No, I cannot. In those days I was Assistant Commissioner, and Sir Henry Lake was entirely consulted with regard to that. I was never even examined with regard to the pay.

3945. *Mr. Morris.*—If you turn your attention for a moment to the detective department, which I understand consists of forty-four men all told, one superintendent, I think, and then several grades of officers, I may inform you they have put forward a claim here to be better paid upon many grounds which it is unnecessary to enter into, you, of course, knowing the working of the force. They have put forward, as grounds in support of their claim for extra pay, that their allowance for clothes—being always in plain clothes, and with continued wear and tear—is small, comparatively speaking; and they put forward various other grounds that it is not necessary to enter into. They also put forward the complaint, I think, that promotion was rather slow. However, it struck me that as there were twenty-five officers and only nineteen men, I was really tempted to ask them did they all want to be officers. They put forward a claim that there should be at all events one additional inspector appointed. I think these are the grounds that they put forward specially, and it struck me that probably they ought to be a little better paid than ordinary policemen, and that, perhaps they ought to have a more liberal allowance for clothes, but I should like to have your opinion on these points?—While under my command, I must say that they were a most excellent body of men, but as their direction has been taken out of my hands, I should not like to answer the question. With regard to the drill, it is alleged that the men have been subjected to harassing drills. I can only say that for a considerable time past they have not been drilled at all, but when in the drill season of the year, which consists of four months, a drill-roll is kept in each barrack, and every man is bound to have one hour's drill in each week, allowing him another hour to go to Kevin Street to the drill and back. He is allowed three hours off duty for the two hours that he has been in the week at drill. Thus, a man only receives during the year sixteen hours' drill—during the whole year—for which he receives twenty-four hours of duty. The drill consists merely in forming fours from the left to the right, or left and rear, and forming to the front, right, left, or rear. It is absolutely necessary that an officer shall be able to move a body of men in some order, and therefore I consider it desirable that before he comes up for examination for promotion that he should show that he is able to move his men through the streets of Dublin without bringing ridicule upon them, and that is why it is that he has to pass a short examination in the subjects of drill I have already mentioned.

3946. Taking into account the extent of the Dublin metropolitan police district, and taking into account the state of affairs in this country, is it your opinion that there is quite a sufficient number of men in the police force?—For the last four years I have constantly represented to the Government, and lately more so in particular, that the numerical strength of this force is totally inadequate to the duties it is expected to perform. I ask for an increase of 250 men at least, and no less will make it efficient. I can give you Returns on Monday showing the comparative strength of the police in the populous districts of London as compared with those in the Dublin metropolitan police district, and from those Returns it will be seen that the London force has at least four times as many men in the populous divisions as we have here. It must also be remembered that we—on account of the unfortunate state of affairs lately in the city—have to double our men on their beats, and, consequently, our force must be diminished, for the purposes of ordinary duty, by one-half. We have also a number of men on protection duty.

3947. Were you obliged to double them on all the beats?—On all the beats in most parts of the city, and particularly so in the rural districts, as on lonely roads a man's life might be exposed to very great danger.

3948. *Mr. Holmes.*—And you consider it essential that the beats should all be doubled?—I do.

3949. *Mr. Morris.*—In the present state of affairs?—Yes, in the present state of affairs I would not undertake the responsibility of sending men singly upon the beats. With reference to the fines, in justice to Colonel Connolly, I think it right to mention this, that when the fines were heavy for what might appear to others to be trivial offences, such as not taking notice of windows that had been broken, knockers wrenched, open gratings, and doors left open, that we have had constant complaints from the citizens of Dublin saying that their glass had been broken, that their areas had been opened, and the padlocks on valuable warehouses wrenched off, and it was then that it became absolutely necessary, in order to make the men more cautious in the discharge of their duty, to put more severe fines on them at those times when there were so many more complaints against them than others, against whom there were probably no complaints. I think it is due to Colonel Connolly to state that.

3950. Then, in fact, at that time you were receiving so many complaints from the citizens of

Captain George Talbot.

7 Oct., 1882.

Dublin that you were led to think that there was neglect of duty on the part of the police?—Certainly. There were constant complaints of knockers wrenched, of glass broken, and of padlocks having been wrenched from stores, and it is a very serious offence that when a policeman is going along a street where a great quantity of valuable grain is deposited, and he sees a padlock wrenched off, and if the place has been entered, and a considerable amount of property stolen, that yet it has never been reported to the Commissioner of Police at what hour that place has been entered.

3851. And there is no way of enforcing information from a policeman except by making him report?—No; and when the final intimation of such an occurrence as I have referred to is, instead of from the policeman, from the person who has lost the property, it is most reprehensible.

[At this stage of Captain Talbot's evidence, the Committee adjourned until the following Monday.]

Seventeenth Day.—OCTOBER 9th, 1882.

Present:

Mr. J. W. O'Donnell, Mr. George Morris, D.L., and Mr. R. W. A. Holmes.

Examination of Captain George Talbot, Chief Commissioner, Dublin Metropolitan Police, resumed.

3852. *Mr. Holmes.*—You told Mr. Morris on Saturday that in your opinion the Dublin metropolitan police is under-manned, and that you require it to be strengthened by the addition of about 150 constables?—Yes.

3853. And you also stated that the proportion of the police to the population in some parts of London was greater than it was here. You did not, I presume, intend to say that the proportion of police to the entire population in the case of the London metropolitan police is greater than the proportion of police to the population here?—The strength of the Dublin metropolitan police in proportion to the area in square miles is greater than that of the London metropolitan police, the proportion being, as far as I am able to calculate it, in London, to an area of 688 square miles, 15·2 to each square mile, in Dublin, to 38 square miles of an area the proportion is 31·8, more than double.

3854. I do not question the accuracy of these figures, but, speaking roughly, the police force in London is about ten times the number of the police force in Dublin?—Yes, about that. I can give you the accurate figures; the strength of the London metropolitan police is 10,484, while the strength of the police force in Dublin at the present moment is 1,116.

3855. Then the London police force is not quite ten times as numerous as the Dublin force; it is about nine times as numerous?—Yes. I was going to give you the calculation as to population.

3856. Are you aware that the population of London within the metropolitan police area is over 4,580,000?—No; it is 3,810,744.

3857. I speak from the evidence given by District Superintendent Walker?—I speak from the Blue Book published by Sir Edward Henderson in 1881.

3858. What is the population of Dublin within the Dublin metropolitan police area?—349,648; the calculation with regard to that in ratio with the London population is 2·25 to every 1,000 of the population, and that of Dublin is 3 for every 1,000 of the population.

3859. Is not a very large police force quite necessary in London, where the wealth of the world is collected, for the protection of property alone?—It is double care; but it is more essential for the protection of life in Dublin. If you will allow me in relation to the subject to compare one of the most populous divisions in London with a similar one in Dublin, I shall take the B or Westminster Division, which has an area of 3 miles and 32 yards. The number of men for police duty within that is 558, being a percentage of 239·65 to the square mile. If you take the B Division in Dublin, which is similarly constituted as to area, &c. —1 mile 319 square yards, I have only 290 men to do the duty, which gives a percentage of 168·78.

3860. What part of Dublin is comprised in the B Division?—The B Division is bounded by the canal on the east side as far as Camden Street. It is bounded on the north by the River Liffey, on the west by Camden Street down to the Castle, including the Castle yard, and down to the River Liffey at Essex Bridge. It is entirely in the centre of the city, and similarly constituted in every respect as the B or Westminster Division would be in London.

3861. Do you know that Glasgow, with a population of more than 500,000, including over 130,000 Irish, has a less numerous police force than Dublin?—I am not acquainted with any statistics connected with the Glasgow police.

3862. Or are you aware that Liverpool, with a population of more than 550,000, including a population of over 120,000 Irish, has only 1,229 men, all told, in its police force?—No; I have not studied the positions of any other police forces, so convinced was I of the absolute necessity of an increase of the force in Dublin. The numerous duties that are put upon us at the present moment of protection, &c., render the force totally inadequate to meet any emergency should a series of burglaries or a series of serious robberies take place.

3863. Do you suppose it would be necessary to increase the force if you gave up the system of doubling the beats?—I think still the present force would be inadequate to the duties. In relation to this, would you allow me to hand you in a Return in which eight or nine of the London divisions are compared to the Dublin divisions, and in which it is shown that the percentage of policemen to the area of each is nearly three-fold in London to that which it is in Dublin. That Return is as follows:—

COMPARATIVE RETURN of the Number of Men for Duty in London and Dublin in Areas of a proportionate size.

London				Dublin			
Division.	Miles.	Men.	Percentage.	Division.	Miles.	Men.	Percentage.
A, or Whitehall ..	1·41	683	471·47	A (partly rural) ..	8·232	180	16·52
B, or Westminster ..	2·24	556	238·45	B	1·319	238	164·79
C, or St. James' ..	0·79	546	436·31	C	1·091	730	814·33
D, or Marylebone ..	1·26	553	227·56	D (partly rural) ..	6·120	194	31·27
E, or Holborn ..	1·23	631	410·23	E (partly rural) ..	9·095	140	15·35
G, or Finsbury ..	2·07	557	256·02	F (rural) ..	15	111	15·05
S, or Hampstead ..	84·89	560	6·64				
T, or Kensington ..	75·49	770	10·21				
X, or Paddington ..	76·46	695	9·16				

3964. Do you know whether in any parts of London it is considered necessary to double the number of men on the beats?—I am not aware.

3965. *Mr. Morris.*—As I understand, Captain Talbot, your connection with the force commenced in 1873?—I joined the force in July 1873.

3966. In giving the opinion which you have stated as to the increase of the strength of the police force in Dublin, I presume your experience for that period of time, coupled with the situation in Dublin, leads you to the conclusion that, upon the whole, some increase of the police force is necessary?—Certainly.

3967. May I ask you when the last increase was made, and what the numbers were before that increase?—I am not prepared to give you the numbers that we had been increased by. We have received no substantial increase, unless you call it an increase where extra duties have been put upon us, such as giving men to the Corporation.

3968. Could you, without much trouble, furnish the Committee with a Return as to what was the strength of the force—say on the 1st January, 1851; the 1st January, 1861; on the 1st January, 1871; and on the 1st January, 1881?—I shall be very glad to send you such a Return for every ten years.

3969. From and including 1851, 1861, 1871, and 1881?—Yes, and giving the authorised strength on the 1st January in each of those ten years; but it will be necessary for me, in case you observe an increase, to give you the reason of that increase in the Return.

3970. Will you please make a note of the fact as to that reason?—Yes. For this reason, that when we gave fifteen men to the Corporation for sanitary duty we were allowed to recruit up fifteen men. But that was no increase of the force, it was simply to provide the Corporation with sanitary police.

3971. And do the Corporation pay for those police?—Yes. The Corporation pay for those men. Similarly, when we had to supply men to the Science and Art Department, we were allowed to recruit up men to supply their requisition.

3972. *Chairman.*—About an equivalent number to those you gave away?—Yes.

3973. *Mr. Holmes.*—I would like to ask you, are the duties which the police have to perform in the suburbs of Rathmines, Rathgar, Sandymount, Dalkey, and Killiney as troublesome or as hard upon their health and constitution as the duties that they have to perform in the City of Dublin?—I consider that their being sent to the rural districts is a privilege, and it is often recommended by the medical officer of the force.

3974. Now, what districts within the metropolitan police area would you term for the purposes you have mentioned rural districts?—I term the F Division entirely a rural district, with the exception of one or two streets in Kingstown. I call the E Division to a great extent rural, Rathmines being the only populous part of it that can be at all termed as town—the townships of Rathmines and the Pembroke township. The D Division, which is situate in the Phoenix Park, is partly rural; the A Division, having Kilmainham in it, is partly rural; but the greatest extent of the A Division is in the city, including within it St. Patrick's Cathedral and the Coombe. The B Division and the C Division are exclusively city divisions.

3975. Can you say why it was when the police force was formed that it was considered necessary to include the suburbs and such distant places as Killiney and Dalkey within the metropolitan police area, more especially when at Dundrum, which is nearer to Dublin than either Killiney or Dalkey, you have the peace maintained by the Royal Irish Constabulary?—I cannot form any idea why that was considered necessary.

3976. *Mr. Morris.*—The men have complained, when examined here, of the hospital accommodation, of their being put into the ordinary wards, and I would ask you, Captain Talbot, if you could suggest any remedy, or if you would approve of a separate ward being put aside at one or two hospitals especially for the purposes of sick policemen owing to the present state of affairs in Dublin?—I have had frequent conversations with Dr. Nedley, who so ably carries out the very important duties of medical officer of this force, and we both were strongly of opinion, and that opinion we have constantly urged, that our men should have a separate ward for themselves. We have had considerable difficulty very often during the last year in getting accommodation for our men in the Government hospitals, and Dr. Nedley has submitted to me a Report, and I have had a long correspondence with the Government on the subject. I cannot too strongly impress upon the Committee the belief that it is perfectly shameful that our men should be allowed to be put into a ward lying alongside of possibly, to say the least, an indifferent character, if not very many times worse, and that I cannot too strongly advocate that we ought to have a separate ward to ourselves.

3977. *Chairman.*—Then you coincide with the opinions given here?—Yes, I do. As I have said, it is really necessary.

3978. *Mr. Holmes.*—I believe you have had great experience of the detective force?—Up to the month of June last the detective department was entirely under my control. Now it is not so.

3979. I presume that the duties that the detective force have to perform are of a very responsible and perhaps of a dangerous character, and that they require for their proper discharge no ordinary intelligence and peculiar qualifications?—The G Division are by far the most respectable, well-conducted, and energetic body of men I have ever had the honour to command. Their duties are often of a dangerous character, and always require great intelligence and tact. I have not known of any officer of the G Division having been punished even by reprimand for the last six or seven years.

3980. Do you consider that the present rates of pay and the prospects of promotion in that particular division are adequate to attract to it the best men in the general force?—I do not consider that they are sufficiently paid—I mean the constables, in a certain respects—that is, in regard to the allowance for plain clothes. I think they ought to be put on a footing with the divisional detective constables in London

3881. *Chairman.*—As regards clothes?—As regards the allowance for plain clothes.

3882. *Mr Holmes*—That is, that they should receive 7s. per week?—Yes; making their pay and allowances equal to the London divisional detective constable. Irrespective of pay, I have always found the men anxious to enter the G Division; they are proud to belong to that division.

3883. Then, in point of fact, you think the G Division contains, so far as intelligence is concerned, the best men you have in the force?—I consider that the men of the G Division are the most intelligent and best conducted I have in the force

3884. *Chairman.*—They are the picked men?—Yes

3885. *Mr Holmes*—Several of the witnesses whom we examined belonging to the G Division told us that men whom they had beaten at examinations when they belonged to the general force had now been promoted over their heads, and they instanced cases of several men who had become inspectors while they were still sergeants or acting sergeants?—That may be so, and I have no doubt it is; but men that enter into the G Division must abide by their luck in reference to promotion in the G Division

3886. *Mr Morris.*—When some of the detective force were under examination, they stated that they thought that the G Division, being a body of forty-four men, would require more officers in it. I took the trouble of asking how many officers and how many men there were in that force, and I found out that the body entirely consisted of forty-four; that there were nineteen constables and twenty-five officers, including sergeants, inspector, and superintendent. As you have suggested that the rest of the force should be increased in number, and as I am more in accord with you on that, I am desirous of asking, do you consider that the detective force requires any larger number of officers than a proportion of twenty-five officers and nineteen men?—I am aware that at the present moment the G Division is undergoing a complete reorganization, under the direction of the Assistant Under-Secretary for Police and Crime, and I should not, therefore, wish to give any opinion upon what he considers, or may consider, right in the matter. I have heard that at the present moment some of the Royal Irish Constabulary are doing detective duty within the metropolitan police districts in concert with the men of the G Division

3887. Is there anything else, Captain Talbot, that strikes you which would give the Committee information for his Excellency, or any suggestions which you would like to make?—There are a few subjects on which I wish to supplement my evidence of last Saturday. In reference to the lodging allowance, with regard to the senior officers, the superintendent and inspectors have to pay from 30*l.* to 40*l.* a-year for a house with adequate accommodation for their families, and their allowances are 20*l.* and 30*l.* The men for suitable lodgings would have to pay for two rooms from 7s. to 8s., and for very indifferent lodgings, from 4s. to 7s. per week. There is another matter of very small amount which I should think ought to be granted to the men—the remission of barrack stoppages.

3888. What do they include?—They include, I think, 1s. a-week; they come to about 1s. 6d. per week

3889. When living in barracks?—For barrack and extra coal. With regard to the discipline, it was suggested that the only punishments given by the directors of some of the police forces in England are small fines, limited to a certain amount, or dismissal

3890. *Mr Holmes.*—And reduction for a limited period?—And reduction for a limited period. I would wish to point out that this country, and particularly Dublin, is in a different condition entirely from any of the police forces that have been compared with the discipline of this, and I do not consider that any comparison could be held. I produce to you a document by which it can be seen that in the year 1844, when the police force was administered by two of the ablest Commissioners, Mr O'Ferrall and Colonel Browne,—that it was the invariable practice to reduce, only in a few cases for limited periods, for all offences, the reductions being in those days tantamount to double or treble the heaviest fine that has been put on the men for the last forty-five years. That document is as follows:—

Some Reductions by Commissioners in 1844.

Date			Name.		Offence.	Commissioners' Decision.
January	13,	1844	Pensionable Constable	Porter	Drunk on beat	Reduced from 2nd to 3rd class.
—	19,	—	—	Lacy	Loitering on beat and omitting to patrol a portion of it	— — —
February	6,	—	—	Moore	Being under influence of liquor when for duty	— — —
—	7,	—	—	Fagan	Slightly under the influence of liquor	— — —
—	8,	—	—	Steward	Ditto	Reduced from 1st to 2nd class for six months.
—	14,	—	—	London, D.	For writing on a newspaper while on duty in [illegible] O'Connell's office	Reduced from 2nd to 3rd class.
—	14,	—	—	Lafferty	Slightly under the influence of liquor	— — —
—	16,	—	—	Gorman	Ditto	— — —
March	12,	—	—	Hamilton	Neglecting to attend a drunken man from a [illegible] and bringing him to the station	Reduced from 1st to 2nd class.
—	19,	—	—	Healy	For taking no steps in the above case	— — —
—	25,	—	—	Coogan	Drunk when for duty	Reduced from 2nd to 3rd class.
April	4,	—	—	Boyd	Being under the influence of liquor when off duty	— — —
—	7,	—	—	Kennedy	For leaving his night duty trousers in bad repair	— — —

It would appear by the records of that year that the Commissioners invariably reduced constables, &c., for any offence in connexion with drink, and also for other offences. The fines imposed during the year and a [illegible] that period were few and light.

(Signed) [illegible] Carr,
Chief Superintendent.

F. W. D. Marshall, Esq.,
&c. &c. &c.

January 25, 1883.

Captain George Talbot.

9 Oct., 1882.

With regard to the extra pay and rewards, of which I promised to furnish you with a Return, I now hand it in. It is as follows:—

RETURN of Rewards, Extra Pay and Allowances for wearing Plain Clothes during the last Two Years.

Quarter to—	Monthly Rewards.		Total Quarterly Rewards.	Monthly Extra Pay.	Total Quarterly Extra Pay.	Monthly Clothing Allowance.	Total Quarterly Clothing Allowance.
		£ s. d.	£ s. d.	£ s. d.	£ s. d.	£ s. d.	£ s. d.
November 30, 1880	September ..	19 19 6		..		15 0 0	
	October ..	21 17 6	63 4 6	3 6 0	11 16 0	15 0 0	45 10 0
	November ..	22 14 6		7 10 0		15 10 0	
February 28, 1881	December ..	29 17 6		..		16 10 0	
	January ..	38 19 6	108 0 6	5 0 0	35 15 9	31 16 9	63 6 9
	February ..	39 18 6		30 15 9		15 0 0	
May 31, 1881	March ..	68 19 6		20 14 9		18 0 0	
	April ..	63 5 0	169 15 0	11 0 6	39 14 10	16 14 6	51 9 11
	May ..	37 19 6		4 3 7		11 0 5	
August 31, 1881	June ..	65 2 6		21 17 5		14 5 0	
	July ..	35 19 0	136 9 0	8 5 11	39 4 1	10 10 9	41 6 0
	August ..	34 17 6		6 19 9		10 10 0	
November 30, 1881	September ..	29 3 0		4 19 1		10 15 6	
	October ..	33 17 6	170 8 0	10 0 4	27 5 1	10 5 0	30 10 6
	November ..	115 0 0		12 2 0		11 0 0	
February 28, 1882	December ..	70 5 0		9 16 4		16 15 0	
	January ..	47 0 0	173 12 6	19 12 10	67 19 0	19 0 0	55 6 0
	February ..	56 7 6		29 5 10		19 10 0	
May 31, 1882	March ..	71 7 6		25 10 0		21 0 0	
	April ..	73 0 0	190 10 6	17 7 7	65 15 6	17 5 0	70 16 9
	May ..	46 5 0		21 17 11		22 5 0	
August 31, 1882	June ..	91 12 6		7 9 1		23 10 0	
	July ..	51 15 0	204 17 6	10 13 8	33 8 0	19 0 0	64 10 0
	August ..	65 10 0		10 0 5		23 0 0	
Totals for two years ended August 31, 1882			1,311 9 6	..	310 9 6	..	393 17 8

From that Return it will be seen that from the 31st November, 1880, to the 31st August, 1882, no less a sum than 1,311*l.* 9*s.* 6*d.* was paid to the men as rewards, and 310*l.* 9*s.* 6*d.* as extra pay, and 393*l.* 17*s.* 8*d.* in mere clothing—allowances for plain clothes.

3991. *Mr. Holmes.*—From what fund are these rewards paid?—From the Departmental Fund; from the vote.

3992. Is there a deduction made from the pay of the men to meet them?—Certainly not.

3993. Or to provide for them?—No, certainly not.

3994. *Chairman.*—I take it that you recommend the abolition of the barrack stoppages?—I would suggest that that might be considered as a boon to the men if you could see your way to do away with barrack stoppages.

3995. *Mr. Holmes.*—But you are aware of course that in London a similar deduction is made?—To speak candidly, I am not aware of that. I thought it was a very small allowance. Now the last subject which I would wish to bring before you, and which you drew out by a question, was that of amusements for the men. We are perfectly destitute of any, and I should strongly recommend that some small sum should be allowed to the men for the purpose of establishing, at all events in the largest barracks, a reading room and some recreation room, something to divert the men, if possible, from the public-house, or to cheerfully occupy their time.

3996. Would you suggest billiards or ball-courts?—In the way of ball-courts, they have ball-courts in nearly all the barracks, but I would rather, as they have the ball-courts, suggest reading, or something that would tend to improve their minds.

3997. *Mr Morris.*—To counteract the cards and the public-house?—The little experience I have made have been accomplished through any saving I can possibly make out of the very small canteen in Kevin Street barracks. I should be anxious to show out of that private fund what has been done. The recruits are clothed on arriving in Kevin Street barracks out of this very small fund at my disposal, and I would ask the Committee to suggest that the recruits in the depôt should receive suitable clothing—such as that with which I now furnish them—at the expense of a fund from the Government. It would be rather disreputable to see young men—some in corduroy trousers, some in rags—drilling about for nearly four months on the square at Kevin Street, and so I have to provide them with a suitable uniform at a very trifling expense.

3998. *Mr. Holmes.*—And you provide the cost of that out of the canteen fund?—Yes.

3999. And you ask that it should be now provided by the Government?—Yes, I ask that the Government should supply them with a similar uniform at a similar expense.

4000. *Chairman.*—What would be the cost?—I can let the Committee know what it would cost. I suppose it would cost about 20s. a suit.

4001. *Mr Morris.*—Upon the whole, do you think that the school and the canteen are useful institutions?—The school I consider the most useful institution that I have been able to form. In London they are obliged to attend it and pay for it; here it is free, and unless in future the Commissioner dispenses with examinations, and has promotion by interest instead of competition, the school is absolutely necessary, because men must know how to do their duty, and constantly I find in the case of young men who could hardly write at the time they joined the force, that when I examine their writing after attending the school for several months there is a great improvement in it.

4002. *Chairman.*—The attendance at school is not compulsory?—No. There is only one thing more I wish to say; I don't know whether it exists in any other police force, but it was done by me, and I think Dr. Nedley will support me in what I say—that it has tended greatly to the health—to the small sick list, the very small sick list of my men, and that is, that every man on night duty has liberty now for a quarter of an hour throughout the summer, and particularly in the winter, when it is so useful to him, to get his hot cup of coffee, which is provided for him for 1*d.*, and he can remain and take his coffee in the station.

4003. At every station?—Yes.

4004. And who pays the expense of that?—There is a little mess fund, and for the sum of 1*d.* he is given a cup of hot coffee or cocoa, as he pleases, and can then go out on his beat again.

Dr. Thomas Nedley.

9 Oct., 1882.

4006. *Chairman.*—Your name?—Thomas Nedley.

4007. What is your position?—I have been since December 1865 medical officer to the Dublin metropolitan police.

4008. *Mr. Holmes.*—We have before us the very valuable evidence you gave before Lord Monck's Committee, and also details of the results of the inquiries you made into the English and Scotch police forces. I now propose to obtain from you similar information, and to ask you some questions touching the material comforts of the men, their food, their health, and in the case of the married men their lodgings. We will commence with their food, the cost of living. Now, I find that you told Lord Monck's Committee that, in consequence of their low rate of pay, the constables in Dublin could not afford to buy a good breakfast. Have you a different story to tell us now?—I am under the impression that the men now are very well fed—that they live well. I occasionally, after the change of pay, made inquiries into the subject of their mode of living as regards breakfast, and I learned that they commenced on that occasion to take a much better breakfast than they had been in the habit of doing.

4009. They had an improved diet?—Yes; after the increase of pay. I have never read the evidence which I gave before Lord Monck's Committee since I gave it, but I am under the impression that then I stated that one of the causes of dyspepsia in young constables was the fact of their eating a great deal too much for their dinner.

4010. Yes; you said that the result of their not being able to buy a good breakfast was that they ate voraciously at dinner, sometimes to the extent of 2 lbs. of meat being consumed by one man, and you added that afterwards many of the men became dyspeptic, and they had very frequently to be placed on the sick list in consequence. Is that the case now?—No. Our health statistics have been improving every year since then. I have written a short report, which has been attached to the annual report that the Commissioners issue each year—in which I have given the progressive improvement on the score of health of the men from that day to this. Have the Committee seen any of these reports?

4011. *Mr. Morris.*—We have not. Probably if you refer to those reports you can give us evidence on the points with which you are now dealing?—Yes, I give every year the number of men that are sick each day—in a Table—from the 1st January to the 31st December.

4012. And these details have been separately kept since 1872?—Yes. I have in my hand the report of the medical officer on the health of the force for the year 1880. Each annual report of the Commissioners, as I have already stated, contains my report on the health of the force; and there is given in each of those reports a Return showing the number of men sick on each day from the 1st January to the 31st December. In my Report for the year 1877 I say—"I have the great satisfaction to report that the health of the metropolitan police, which has shown of late a progressive annual improvement, reached during the year 1877 the highest standard it has attained since the amalgamation of the force. In the year 1865 there were 5 per cent. on the sick list each day. In 1867, the second year of my service, the daily percentage had declined to 4·059, whilst in the tenth following year, that just passed, it reached only 2·675, probably the smallest number of any large city police force in the empire."

4013. *Chairman.*—That is the average daily sick?—Yes.

4014. *Mr. Holmes.*—Whereas in the evidence you gave before Lord Monck's Committee you stated that there were then more men on the sick list in the Dublin force than in any other force in the United Kingdom?—Yes, and I think there are least now.

4015. And you attribute that wonderful change to the increased rates of pay—to the fact that the men can live better than they did before?—Chiefly to that; and also to improvements in the ventilation and sewerage of the larger barracks, and to the supply of hot coffee at the stations for men on night duty. Captain Talbot established this, and ordered time to be given to the night men to avail themselves of such wholesome refreshment. An additional important factor was our strictness in preventing malingering, after the increase of pay. There used to be a feeling of pity for men with large families and small pay coming before me. Oftentimes, without actually showing positive symptoms of any delicacy, there was a suspicion that the men were frequently weak from want of sufficient nourishment, and we would then let them rest for two or three days on the sick sheet.

4016. *Mr. Morris.*—All that has ceased, I presume, now, doctor?—Yes, all that has ceased now.

4017. *Mr. Holmes.*—We will now deal with the case of the single men accommodated in barracks. Can you tell us, approximately, what a single man has to pay for his dinner during the week? I presume that the cost differs in every barrack, and that there is not anything like a fixed rate?—There is a slight difference, but there has been so little complaint with reference to food of late years, and the ailments and diseases from which the men suffer have had very little connexion with the subject of nourishment, that I have never felt the necessity of making inquiries on the subject.

4018. I find that in the evidence given before Lord Monck's Committee Colonel Lake said that the cost of messing came to about 6s. 6d. per week in Dublin, and that you replied that in London the cost came to from 5s. 3d. to 6s. 6d.; now do you think that the present cost in Dublin is more than 6s. 6d.?—From the inquiries I made by chance as to the cost of messing, I am under the impression that a single man expends in breakfast and in dinner at present about 12s. 6d. a-week.

4019. I suppose we may assume that 13s. a-week ought fully to cover their cost of living, for breakfast, dinner, and supper?—Certainly.

4020. We will take the case of a fourth-rate constable, whose net pay is 23s. per week. Do you consider that that man, if he chooses to live prudently, might live very comfortably within his pay?—Certainly.

4021. Provide himself with the requisite food and requisite clothing, and everything that a man in his position requires?—Certainly. It is more than an acting sergeant got before the increase of pay, and the sergeant generally had a family, and had to pay rent, which a fourth-class constable is saved from, as he lives in barracks.

4022. We might now deal with the case of the married men. Have you any idea what on an average they have to pay for their lodgings per week. I suppose it varies much according to the district in

Dr. Thomas Nedley.

9 Oct., 1882.

which they are required to live?—I believe that all round the married police constable or sergeant has to pay more than 4s. a-week for his lodgings.

4023. Over 4s.?—Yes, I think more than 4s. It was clear to me in the examination that I personally had the opportunity of making into the working of the various police forces in England and Scotland, that the cost of lodging was less in each of those places that I visited than it is in Dublin.

4024. Did you make any inquiries in Liverpool, because Chief Constable Nott-Bower, whom we examined, states that the cost of lodging in Liverpool is dear, and that is one reason why the pay of the men there is better than it is in Manchester and Glasgow, where lodging is very cheap?—That did not obtain when I was there. I am certain I made every inquiry, not only as to that, but as to other matters upon which I sought information. But twelve years may make a great difference, for that period has elapsed since I was there. The population of Liverpool is increasing very much, and the increase is principally, I believe, amongst working men. That will naturally set up the cost of lodging. I can have accurate details of the cost of lodging, as well as the cost of living, prepared.

4025. I presume, before the increase of pay was given to the force in 1872, the condition of the married men was miserable, especially if they had large families?—Miserable.

4026. But do you think that the position of the married men, as a whole, is now fairly comfortable, if the men live with common prudence?—They have never complained to me that during their illnesses or their debilities they were not able to afford themselves sufficient nourishment and comfort.

4027. *Mr Morris.*—I presume that previous to their pay having been increased, they had made complaints to you?—Before their pay was increased every married man was put on full pay, which was a privilege that was not given in any other force, I believe, in the empire.

4028. *Mr Holmes.*—You mean while sick?—Yes; while sick we almost invariably put the married men on full pay.

4029. *Mr. Morris.*—Previous to the pay being increased?—Yes. That system was changed after the increase of pay, and from that day to this, I scarcely ever heard a complaint on the part of married men as to the stoppage of 1s. a-day. In every case where the illness is prolonged, or likely to be prolonged, and where there is a large family, the Commissioners allow me to recommend the man for full pay.

4030. *Mr. Holmes.*—Then, in point of fact, in every case of *bonâ fide* illness, especially where that illness is contracted by men while on duty, you do not make the deduction?—Attached to each division there is an officer who is called the staff sergeant. These staff sergeants come to the Castle every day at 11 o'clock. Every man who states he is unfit for duty in consequence of ill-health either appears before me, or gives to me through the staff sergeant, if he is unable to appear, the character of his illness. The staff sergeant is acquainted with the family and condition of each married constable and officer, and I encourage him to tell me any instance in which, according to his knowledge of the man's circumstances or surroundings, it would be wise or prudent to give the man full pay. I generally attend to that recommendation on the part of the staff sergeant; and the staff sergeants, as a class, are most reliable, intelligent, and conscientious men.

4031. Then, in point of fact, Dr. Nedley, the 1s. a-day is only deducted when you have reason to believe that——?—That it can be afforded. In every instance in which I recommend full pay, or prolonged sick leave, or extension of sick leave, the Commissioners evince the greatest readiness to accede to any relaxation of the written rules of the force in favour of the patient, either as regards pay or leave.

4032. What is your opinion, Dr. Nedley, as to the propriety of the rule which requires married men to live within the divisions in which they are stationed?—That is more a matter of discipline than of medical supervision, but, from my knowledge of the force, I believe it would be conducive to the welfare and to the discipline of the force if married officers were obliged to live in their divisions. Whenever a change of residence from town to country would be of importance to the health of the constable I always recommend it, and the Commissioner, except it happens to be very inconvenient, acts in accordance with that recommendation of mine.

4033. I understand that there is a rule in the force preventing men from marrying until they have been five years in the service. At that time a well-conducted man ought, at any rate, to have reached the position of a third-rate constable, whose pay is 24s. a-week. Do you think that a man marrying upon that rate of pay could with economy and prudence live within his pay?—I do.

4034. I believe that there is a rule now restricting married men from letting part of their houses—supposing that a married man could take a house—in lodgings. But don't you think that if they were allowed to let a portion of their houses to lodgers, it might enable them to take a better class of houses than that in which they live now. Do you see any reason why they should be prevented from taking lodgers?—I have never heard that fact before. I see no objection to it. I would recommend that married officers be allowed to let their houses in lodgings for the purpose of adding to their incomes; but it appears to me that the Commissioners should know the character of the lodgers. Upon the question of the stoppages during sickness, I would like to make this addition to what I have already stated; that our sick men are in many respects exceptionally well treated compared with those in any other police force with which I am acquainted. In the London metropolitan police—which resembles our force more than any other—full pay is not given for injuries received on duty except they are of rather a severe character. In every case of injury sustained by a policeman on duty in the Dublin force, no matter how slight the injury may be, there is no stoppage. In the London metropolitan police, whilst they are treated in hospital for injuries, the 1s. a-day is stopped. It is never stopped from our injured constables whilst in hospital. We do not give full pay, neither is it given in any other force, for an injury sustained by the constable in consequence of his own carelessness. If a man slips and sprains his ankle, we do not give him full pay; but if he gets a kick, or if a car strikes him, or if he receives an injury in any way that he could not prevent, he invariably gets full pay, whether in hospital or not. As regards sick leave in the London metropolitan police, the surgeon can only recommend for sick leave for the space of twenty-eight days. At the end of that period, if further leave is required, it must be with the sanction of the Secretary of State. It is then called "detached sick leave," and a new man, of the same rank and class, takes the constable's place. Our Commissioners grant extension of leave very frequently of one month, occasionally of two months or even three months, if, in my opinion, the nature of the case requires it.

4035. *Chairman.*—As regards the pay, what is done in a case of that kind?—The pay varies. If the case be that of a married man with a family he would, under such circumstances, almost certainly get full pay.

4036. *Mr. Morris.*—Upon this subject of illness in the force I wish to ask you a further question. You are aware, doubtless, that we have had a good young men—constables, sergeants, and so on—up before us for examination, and one of the matters to which they alluded in their evidence, and one which they regarded as one of their grievances, was the present arrangement as to hospital accommodation for the force. They represented that when they are sent to different hospitals, and you know them, I presume, that they are put into the ordinary ward with other patients, and that sometimes they are in the same room with other patients who are people that have very little sympathy indeed with them. Some of the lower classes perhaps in Dublin are in the same ward with them; and the men suggest that if there could be some arrangement for a special ward for the police in one or two hospitals in the city where they would be by themselves, that it would be more comfortable, and that they would be less troubled. Can you suggest any remedy or offer any suggestion which could be carried out to meet their wishes; or would you state the arrangements that are at present made, and then give any suggestion so as to meet their wishes, if possible, upon such a question as that?—For many years in my annual Report submitted to the Lord Lieutenant I have introduced this question of hospital accommodation. In my Report for the present year I state: "I must again call attention to the pressing necessity which exists for a change in the character of the accommodation afforded to our sick in the hospitals of the city. As a general rule, this is below the standard which I consider requisite for our men, both as regards food and lodging. The former, in my opinion, should not be allowed to be supplemented through the agency of the nurse at the expense of the patient, and in reference to the latter they should be freed from the immediate propinquity of that class of our fellow citizens, by no means a small constituent of our hospital population, who regard the policeman as their natural enemy. We are supposed to have the right of admission to the hospitals of the House of Industry, as they are supported exclusively by a Parliamentary grant; but our men are almost systematically refused a bed in the chronic medical wards at a time of year when they are most urgently required." That is last year, and I have had to repeat over and over again my protest every year. I have made some representations, but they are never heeded and never acted upon, and Captain Talbot has frequently represented it.

4037. *Chairman.*—And you think that a well-founded grievance?—Yes. These remarks of mine are made in my Report of 1887.

4038. *Mr. Morris.*—I would wish you to give in evidence that extract from your Report which I see you made for the year previous, as a suggestion which you would now offer?—Yes; I shall give the Committee the extract from my Report of 1880 as my suggestion now: "I would recommend also that a ward in each of the chronic hospitals of this institution" (the House of Industry) "should be set apart for the exclusive use of the metropolitan police." During epidemics, or the more unhealthy seasons of the year, we should require hospital accommodation for about twenty men, taking in town and country, and for half that number at other periods. Of these, cases of accident and of sudden urgency will be generally sent to the nearest Infirmary, and of fever always to a fever hospital. Besides, a man may be sometimes allowed to make a selection. Independently of all these, we require for our general run of cases beds for at least twelve men, eight medical and four surgical patients. For these we should have two wards for our exclusive use, and these, in my opinion, ought to be easily secured in the Richmond and Whitworth Hospitals, when it is remembered that they are supported solely by an annual Parliamentary grant. While on the subject, I would also strongly recommend that, in the hospitals where the sick of the metropolitan police are treated, the constables should not be exposed as clinical specimens for the instruction of the large classes of medical students which frequent them.

4039. *Mr. Holmes.*—I see, Dr. Nedley, that in the valuable Table with which you furnished Lord Mayo's Committee, showing the strength, pay, and cost of living of certain police forces in England, you stated that the section houses of the London metropolitan police force are fitted up with libraries, billiard-rooms, and reading rooms, and I think you stated, in the course of your evidence, that it would be a great matter if such attractions were provided for the men in Dublin. Has any step been made since 1878 to carry out your wishes?—None, excepting in the depôt. There have been improvements in the depôt at Kevin Street. The condition of the recruits as regards amusement and general treatment has been considerably improved under Captain Talbot's administration.

4040. Do you think that if the larger barracks were provided with libraries and every barrack with a reading-room that it would have the effect of making the men fond of barrack life, and keep them from frequenting the public-house?—I am quite sure it would have a very important tendency in that direction. The station-houses of the English forces, generally speaking, are far and away superior to ours.

4041. *Chairman.*—In the way of comforts?—Yes, and conveniences. There are waiting-rooms, and there is a comfortable, nice room for the inspector on duty to stay in. He has a nicely furnished apartment, and he has, besides that, another waiting-room, in case that there should be any charge brought by respectable people, where there might be some delay in investigating the nature of the charges brought, at any hour of the day or night. In our station-houses there is not a single room where any respectable person can go to who is preferring a charge. It may take a considerable time to have a charge properly investigated by the officer on duty; and there is scarcely a chair for them to sit on. A person will have to give the charge in an outer room, where probably there are a number of people—many of them half drunk.

4042. *Mr. Holmes.*—Are the dormitories of the men comfortable?—Well; none of the large barracks have been built originally for the purpose. There are a great many improvements that might be easily made, and that would have a very good effect upon the health and comfort of the men; but the ventilation has been considerably improved within the last few years.

4043. *Mr. Morris.*—Then, on the whole, I think your evidence comes to this—that the pay of the men is adequate; that they are well fed—well enough; I am now speaking of the single men—but the accommodation might be improved, and made more in accordance with modern ideas?—Yes, certainly. My recollection of the barrack accommodation of the station-houses in England is, that it is far superior to what it is here.

4044. Do you anticipate any difficulty in keeping up the strength of the force?—No. We are always sure of getting suitable recruits. For the first seven months of the present year we accepted 102. Within the last ten weeks we have got ninety healthy young countrymen—the latter period embracing the time of discontent, resignations, strike, and newspaper exaggerations of the general discontent.

4045. The recruits are at Kevin Street, and is not the canteen there also?—Yes; there is a canteen in every barrack.

4046. There is a canteen at Kevin Street?—Yes.

4047. As regards the recruits, Dr. Nedley, does it strike you that perhaps it might be wiser if there was no canteen, or, at all events, no strong double X porter at the barrack where those young men are—those recruits?—I have no hesitation in stating that the habit of giving XX porter in any quantity, however small, to our recruits, is injurious to their health, and is pernicious in its influence otherwise. I have frequently represented this.

4048. Don't you think it leads up sometimes to men contracting the habit?—Yes. As regards the health of young agriculturists, who have been generally fed on farinaceous food and potatoes, they have suddenly commenced to eat animal food every day in the week. This in itself is a very great change, and yet at the same time they commence to take this highly nutritious food they have opportunities, which they always avail themselves of, of drinking the strongest kind of porter which is brewed, and which they never had an opportunity of tasting before. The result is, that they feel a still greater want of stimulant when they commence to undertake the arduous duty of a constable on the streets.

4049. Are you in favour of the abolition of the canteen at all the barracks?—I should not abolish the canteen at all.

4050. You think it is a good system?—I think it is a system that prevents the excess of going out into the public-house.

4051. But you would have the drink of less strength?—You can command the recruits; and I would place a positive interdict on any kind of drink, except the mildest beer or porter, and I would have in every canteen at all times light porter and beer, that the men might have those liquors in case they preferred them.

4052. Are you aware, Dr. Nedley, that in London, and I may say in the police force generally in England, the police are allowed to enter public-houses when off duty, whether in plain clothes or in uniform. Would you be in favour of allowing the police force here to enter public-houses under such conditions?—I do not consider myself in a position to answer that question straight off; but I believe that there are very good reasons why that subject should be approached more cautiously as regards the Dublin police than the police in any other city in the empire.

4053. *Mr. Holmes.*—Captain Talbot told the Committee, when examined to-day, that, in his opinion, the police force in Dublin was undermanned, and I find that you told Lord Monck, in 1872, that, in your opinion, the force at that time was not sufficient. Do you now concur with Captain Talbot?—Oh, I do concur with him; and then, again, the area of the town has been very much increased. There have been new districts created about Drumcondra, and in other places. Miles upon miles of streets have been built there, and also in the neighbourhood of Haytesbury Street, and the South Circular Road, and Portobello. If the increase were necessary ten years ago, it should be so much more substantial now.

4054. But when you say that the force is insufficient, do you mean to say that the men are obliged to do more duties than they ought to do, or that it is insufficient, looking at it in the interests of the population?—In the interests of the population.

4055. Not as regards the men themselves?—No; not as regards the men themselves. I was going to remark generally upon the discipline of the force, as I served under Mr. O'Farrell and Colonel Lake, as well as under Captain Talbot and Colonel Connolly. I may very safely say this from my own personal experience, that for years before Mr. O'Farrell died he was in failing health—that for years before Colonel Lake retired he was for several months every year in a very delicate state of health, and that as a matter of fact, according to my own observation, the discipline of the force became in many respects somewhat lax, and that I believe there was a good deal of uphill work necessary to be done by Captain Talbot before he was able to remedy some of the abuses that certainly were in existence when he came into the command.

4056–9. *Mr. Morris.*—Will you excuse me asking you a few questions personal to yourself? You have stated that you are a long time connected with the police force, I forget how many years?—Seventeen years.

Dr. Thomas Nedley.

9 Oct., 1882.

4060. May I venture to ask what your salary is?—My salary is 240*l.* a-year. It was supplemented at the time of the great increase, after the Commission of 1872, by an allowance of forage for one horse.

4061. May I ask you, do you happen to know what the medical man, filling the same position that you here occupy, in London receives?—The salary of the chief surgeon of the London metropolitan police is 800*l.* a-year. His duties are to attend once a-week at Scotland Yard; and in consultation with the divisional surgeons whenever they consider it necessary.

4062. How many divisional surgeons are there do you know?—There are 183.

4063. Divisional surgeons?—Yes.

4064. And how are they paid?—They are paid from 20*l.* to 144*l.* a-year. Their collective pay is 3,280*l.* That is the collective pay of the divisional surgeons.

4065. Then the total cost is something like 4,000*l.*?—Yes. I am allowed one assistant, Dr. Long, who receives 73*l.* a-year.

4066. And the total cost here is 350*l.*?—The total cost here is under 400*l.* When I speak of the duty of the chief surgeon in London, I may tell you that I am obliged to attend at the Castle every day.

4067. For about how long?—That varies very much at the Castle on account of the number of patients I may have to see. I may have to go over to give evidence at the police-court, or to go to Richmond Hospital to see a case, or to go to Kilmainham, the Grange, where there is a barrack, or to Chapelizod or Dalkey or Glasnevin.

4068. Then it would appear to me that while complaints have been made by the police force of being underpaid, that you are about the worst paid man in it?—Well, I think I am.

4069. *Chairman.*—This is not within the scope of our inquiry, but I am very glad the matter has been brought under our notice, and I trust that it will meet with consideration in the proper quarter?—As I have spoken of the general discipline of the force, I may state that whilst some few, very few, cases of severe punishment have been brought forward with reference to the Commissioner's action, some of the men seem to have forgotten the number of instances in which men, according to their own acknowledgment, deserved dismissal had their delinquencies not been condoned or pardoned by the Chief Commissioner. I do not like to allow this opportunity to pass without giving opinions on matters perhaps not strictly within my own official duty, but from my long experience in connexion with the force, and from the great interest I take in the welfare of its members, I feel bound to record my opinion of the high character of the men as a body, of their docility, truthfulness, and strict integrity, and also my personal experience of the anxious interest that the Commissioners have taken in the welfare, comfort, and well-being of the entire force.

4070. *Mr. Holmes.*—I will ask you a question before you go, that I ought to have put to you before—in your opinion, after what period of service does a policeman in the lower grades, upon an average, cease to be effective?—I would allow every man to retire at twenty-five years' service, but I would give him an interest in remaining until thirty.

4071. Then, in your opinion, speaking as a general rule, a policeman ceases to be effective and fit for active duty after twenty-five years' service?—After twenty-five years' service, if a policeman has no hope of promotion he is worthless in the force; if he has a chance of getting promotion, he is frequently as good a man as before. As a general rule, a man

Eighteenth Day.—October 21st, 1882.

Present:

Mr. R. W. A. Holmes.

Peter Hughes, Acting Inspector, Dublin Metropolitan Police, *examined*.

Acting Inspector Peter Hughes.

21 Oct., 1882.

4073. What is your name?—Peter Hughes.

4074. What rank do you hold?—I am an acting inspector.

4075. How long have you been an acting inspector?—Since the 5th September, 1879.

4076. When did you join the force?—On the 10th May, 1867.

4077. You gave such useful evidence before the Constabulary Committee on the question of the duties of the force that I thought it right that you should have your evidence upon that question formally recorded before this Committee, and, therefore, in the absence of my colleagues, I have asked you to attend here to-day. Before, however, asking you any questions respecting the duties of the force, I will put to you a few general questions. How many constables are there?—[illegible]

4078. How many in each class?—248, first rate; 132, second rate; 383, third rate; and 251, fourth rate.

4079. How long is a man generally detained at the depôt before he is considered fit for street work?—Sometimes six months or thereabouts. Latterly they have been brought out before that time, the men being scarce on the streets. They were brought out recently at the expiration of about two months, but I would average the time at four months.

4080. I presume that while in Kevin Street they are principally engaged in drill and learning their duties?—Yes, Sir, in drill and learning their duties, together with improving their literary knowledge.

4081. How long does a man remain in the fourth class on an average before he is promoted to the third?—About one year.

4082. Is his promotion certain after that period, or does it depend upon whether he can pass an examination or upon whether there is a vacancy in the class at that time?—When vacancies occur promotion depends upon competition, subject to character.

4083. Are those numbers that you gave me just now the fixed numbers for each class?—Yes, they are the numbers authorised by Government.

4084. For each rate?—Yes.

4084*. Do I understand you to say that as long as there are 383 men in the third grade of constables no man can be promoted from the fourth grade?—Certainly not, Sir.

4085. How long is a man on an average in the third grade before he can be promoted to the second?—About five and a-half years.

4086. And how long on the second before he can be promoted to the first?—About two years.

4087. Then, upon an average, a man does not attain the first rate until after eight and a-half years' service?—Yes, that is about the average.

4088. What proportion of constables can rise to the rank of sergeant?—About 15 per cent. That is the chances are 17 to 3, or about 6 to 1 against them.

4089. Then, about 85 per cent. of the men who join the force can never expect to rise beyond the rank of constable?—Yes, that is the case, Sir.

4090. And that, therefore, the maximum pay of a constable represents the maximum amount which 85 per cent. of the men who join can expect to receive?—Yes, Sir.

4091. The maximum of that pay is, I believe, 28s. a-week?—Yes, being 72*l*. 16*s*. 0*d*. a-year.

4092. How is promotion regulated from the rank of constable to that of acting sergeant?—They are first examined and placed on what they call the "advanced class," in order of merit. A sufficient number—say twelve or fourteen—are again examined periodically, and are put on an "approved list" in order of merit, from which promotions to the rank of acting sergeants are made as vacancies occur.

4093. Is that class open to all the constables?—It is open to those of the first and second rate as a rule, but some third rate men, a few, have been put upon it.

4094. Upon an average how many men are promoted each year to the rank of acting sergeant from the rank of constable. That is to say, how many vacancies upon an average are there each year in the rank of acting sergeant?—I would average it at eighteen. There have been only thirteen promoted up to the present this year, and there is no vacancy at present on that rank.

4095. About eighteen?—Yes.

4096. How many acting sergeants are there?—Ninety-four.

4097. How long upon an average is a man an acting sergeant before he rises to the rank of sergeant?—About four and a-half or five years.

4098. Do all acting sergeants become sergeants?—No, about half, or 50 per cent.

4099. Then, is that in consequence of the paucity of vacancies in the rank of sergeant?—Yes, of course, they cannot be promoted until there are vacancies for them. Some of them may be pensioned off in the interval, others may die, and others again may be reduced.

4100. But, as I understand you, about 50 per cent. of the acting sergeants never rise beyond that rank?—Yes, Sir.

Acting Inspector Peter Hughes.

24 Oct., 1882.

4101. Are the duties of the acting sergeants as responsible almost as those of the sergeants?—The same.

4102. There is no difference between them?—Their duties are even more arduous, inasmuch as they seldom get any special duties, such as races, or the like. The acting sergeant is certainly a hard-worked man.

4103. Has a sergeant authority over an acting sergeant?—Yes, certainly. Every higher grade has authority over a lower grade, with the exception of one constable over another. The senior constable, if they are out together, is held the most responsible.

4104. Then the duties of a sergeant are more responsible than those of an acting sergeant so that he has authority over the acting sergeant?—Yes, inasmuch as he is responsible for the acting sergeant as well as the constable that is the acting sergeant he has on duty immediately under him.

4105. How is promotion regulated from the rank of acting sergeant to that of sergeant?—By competition, subject to character. That competition consists of a knowledge of duties and literary qualifications. They are also subjected to a medical examination as well, and an examination in drill.

4106. Before a constable can be promoted to the rank of acting sergeant, is he examined medically?—Yes, Sir; and in drill also.

4107. Before a constable of one rate can be promoted to a higher rate, is he also examined medically?—Some time ago that was the practice; it has been discontinued latterly.

4108. How many sergeants are there?—Seventy-two.

4109. What proportion of this class can look forward to promotion to the rank of acting inspector?—I would say about half, or 50 per cent.; the same as the others.

4110. How is promotion regulated from the rank of sergeant to that of acting inspector?—By competition, subject to character and medical and drill examinations.

4111. Upon an average, how many vacancies are there in the rank of sergeant in the year?—I would say about ten or twelve.

4112. How long does a man remain a sergeant before he is promoted to the rank of acting inspector—speaking roughly?—I would average it at five years, or it may be less.

4113. Then, upon an average, a man is more than eighteen years in the force before he attains the rank of acting inspector?—It is difficult to form a correct average, in consequence of the manner in which promotion varies; but I would average it at between sixteen and eighteen, or about seventeen years.

4114. How many acting inspectors are there?—Fifty-one. One of these is paid as sanitary inspector by the Corporation. Fifty is the authorised strength.

4115. What percentage of this rank can look forward to promotion to the higher rank—to the rank of third-class inspector?—I would give the same answer as in the other cases—in or about 50 per cent.

4116. How long, upon an average, does a man remain an acting inspector before he is promoted?—I have known some to go ten or eleven years, and others have got promotion in four or five years, and a few in even less than four years.

4117. How is promotion regulated?—By competition, on the same principle as the sergeants and acting inspectors, the examination, of course, being more difficult.

4118. Then it might happen that one who had only just attained the rank of acting inspector might, by attaining the highest place at the examination, be promoted at once to the rank of third-class inspector, over the heads of other acting inspectors?—Oh, no; there are only a few seniors—say about eight or ten of the seniors—examined. In examinations they always take the seniors on the list, except some who decline. Of course, the man who takes the first place would pass over the head of his competitors.

4119. Upon an average, how many vacancies occur in the rank of third-class inspector annually?—About five on an average; certainly not more.

4120. How many third-class inspectors are there?—Ten.

4121. How is promotion regulated from the third class to the second class?—By seniority.

4122. Without examination?—Yes, without examination.

4123. Upon an average, how long does a man remain a third-class inspector?—I would say about three years—perhaps less.

4124. How many second-class inspectors are promoted annually?—I would average it at four.

4125. And how many first-class inspectors are promoted annually?—I would say about three.

4126. How many second-class inspectors are there?—Eight.

4127. And how many first class?—There are eight, but one of these belongs to the detective department, and he is promoted first class at the date of his promotion, and it does not tell in the service with respect to classes.

4128. I see that you belong to the B Division; therefore, I will ask you to give me the duties performed by a constable of that division; but, first of all, will you tell me what part of Dublin is comprised in that division?—The boundary of that division is as follows: From the corner of Fishamble Street, at Essex Quay, to Castle Street, Castle Steps, Ship Street, Whitefriar Street, Redmond's Hill, Wexford Street, Lower and Upper Camden Streets, South Richmond Street, Charlemont Mall, along the canal to the "Ironbridge" east end of Great Brunswick Street, by the gas works to Hanover Quay, by said Quay and Great Britain Quay to the point of the wall, thence by Sir John Rogerson's Quay and the southern quays to the point where it commenced at Fishamble Street.

4129. How many barracks are there in the division?—Strictly speaking, there are only two, but some constables reside in College Street police station.

4130. Where are these two barracks?—At the Castle and Lad Lane.

4131. What is the total of the force of all ranks comprised in the B Division; give each rank?—The chief superintendent, 5 inspectors, 7 acting inspectors, 10 sergeants, 15 acting sergeants, 181 constables, total 219; that is the B Division.

4132. How many men are there in each of these barracks?—The single men stopping in each of the barracks in the B Division are as follows: In Castle barracks, 103, in Lad Lane barracks, 45; in College Street (which is both a station and a barrack), 18; that gives a total of 166 single men of all ranks.

4133. How many married men are there in the B Division?—52 of all ranks, and that number, with the number of single men already given, makes a total of 218, and there is one vacancy at present in the division, which would complete the authorised total of 219 men of all ranks.

4134. How many station-houses are there in this division?—Three.

4135. Where are they?—College Street, Lad Lane, and Clarendon Street; Clarendon Street is an auxiliary station, in charge of one acting inspector only.

4136. What do you mean by an "auxiliary" station?—It is not a principal one; it is open only from 9 P.M. to 6 A.M.

4137. Then Lad Lane is not only a barrack, but a station-house as well?—Yes.

4138. Now, will you proceed to give me an outline of the duties performed by a constable of the B Division; we will take the case of a constable who is belonging to the barrack in the Castle yard?

Acting Inspector Peter Hughes. [illegible], 1882.

—I will give you the day duty first. He is called at 5 o'clock A.M.; he prepares for duty, and goes to College Street station, where he parades at a quarter to 6, and is marched on duty at 6 A.M., and he is posted—we will suppose that this man is on a special post, and is not on beat duty, and that he is, say, in front of Trinity College—where he remains until 9 A.M. This being a fixed point, he patrols for 100 yards on each side of his post. He then returns to the station at 9 A.M., and is dismissed off duty by the officer on duty in the station, who may be an inspector or acting inspector. He then returns to barrack and takes his breakfast. Except that he has a summary or a summons case in the police court, where he must attend, his time is his own until after 2 o'clock, when he dines and again prepares for duty. He then proceeds to his station, where he must parade at 2.45 P.M. sharp. After being paraded and inspected by the officer on duty, he is marched to his beat at 3 P.M. sharp. We will take a beat, for instance, in Dame Street, where he must patrol a certain distance, say, every thirty minutes from that until 9 o'clock P.M. If, during this period, he has occasion to arrest a prisoner, he brings him to the College Street station, where the charge is entered by the officer on duty, and he then returns to his beat. At 9 o'clock he reports himself at his station going off duty. After being inspected by his sergeant, or the officer on duty, he returns to his barrack, after which hour his time is his own except a fire should break out, or any emergency arise, when he must turn out, even if he were in bed. On the next day he gets up at 7.30 A.M., and prepares for duty, breakfasts, and proceeds to his station, where he parades at 8.45 A.M., and is marched to his beat at 9 A.M.; he remains on duty until 3 P.M., when he returns to the station, reports himself, and is dismissed off duty. He returns to barrack, dines, and his time is his own until about 6 o'clock, when he must again prepare for duty, proceed to his station, and parade there at 6.45 P.M. He is marched on duty at 7 o'clock, and remains on duty until 9 P.M., when he returns to the station, reports himself to his officer, and is dismissed off duty. The duty I have described is taken alternately each day for one month, Sunday included. There is no relaxation of duty on Sunday. I now come to the night duty, which is taken each alternate month. A man goes on duty from 9 P.M., and remains on duty until 3 A.M.—six hours, with an additional quarter of an hour for parade, irrespective of the time to prepare for duty. At 3 A.M. he returns to his station, reports himself, when the whole relief is assembled, and they are marched to barrack by a sergeant, except in cases of necessity, when some must remain out until 6 o'clock, making the tour of duty nine hours, which often occurs. That man goes then to bed, and if he has not to attend the police court with a prisoner, or to prosecute in a summons case, he is not called upon again for duty until 10.15 P.M. the next night.

4159. Does it frequently happen that a constable engaged upon night-duty is obliged to attend the police-court on the next day?—Constables on regular street-duty within the city very frequently have to attend the police-court, sometimes three and four times a-week, and oftener.

4160. We will suppose, then, that this constable has had to make an arrest during his tour of duty; when would he be obliged to attend at the police-court, and how long would he probably be detained there?—He must get up not later than 9 o'clock, be at the station at a quarter to 10, to take up his prisoner or prisoners, see that their property is restored to them by the officer on duty, in whose custody that property remains after they are searched. He then escorts them to the police-court, and there hands them over to the constable in charge of the cells until the arrival of the magistrate, which, as a rule, is about 10.40 A.M. each day. The cases are then called by divisions. The prisoner or prisoners having been placed in the dock, the constable is sworn, and prosecutes. He listens attentively to the decision of the magistrate, and if he fines, the constable is responsible that the fine is paid by the prisoner, or that he is held in the cell. If committed, he is equally responsible that his prisoner or prisoners are left before in the cells, and he is responsible for their custody in the meantime. He is able to return to barracks generally about noon. If he has to prosecute in a summons case, as a carman, or in a case of nuisance, or of a violation of the Traffic Act, &c., he must be at the court at 11 o'clock, where he may be detained until after 1 o'clock. We now come to the man's next tour of duty. He must prepare for duty and parade at his station at 10.15 P.M., after hearing orders and "routes," &c., and being instructed in his duty.

4161. What do you mean by "routes?"—Reports of stolen property, or descriptions of persons who have committed serious offences, but who have not been made amenable. The constable is marched on duty at 10.30 P.M., and remains on his beat until 6 A.M.—that is, seven and a-half hours, with an additional quarter for parading, making seven and three-quarter hours that this man is actually on his feet. He is equally open to the chance of having to attend the police-court on the following day. That is a short outline of the hours of duty of a constable; but I would prefer referring you to a detailed account which I hand in (see Appendix). As a constable must perform his duty in all weathers, and is never allowed to sit down, or take any rest while on his tour of duty, except fifteen minutes that is allowed them to take coffee each night while on night duty, I need hardly say that the severity of such duties may be easily imagined.

4162. Now, will you give us an outline of the duties performed by a sergeant; we will take the case of a sergeant belonging to the B Division?—The duties of a sergeant or acting sergeant in charge of a section. Their tours are the same both by day and by night as that of a constable, as already detailed; but their tour is even more severe, inasmuch as they must be in the station-house first, in order to see that their men assemble, and must remain until all are gone, in order to see that they go off duty sober and correct; they must post up their "state"—that is a document on which every man is accounted for—and make a report in writing of all occurrences that come or are brought under their notice during their tours. They must also enter in the public-house book all cases made by them for breaches of the licensing laws during their tour of duty, and must attend the Police Court to prosecute the same, in addition to their regular duties. When on duty they must visit their men regularly, and are held responsible for their good conduct and sobriety. They are also responsible for the order of their section, and for the suppression of all irregularities that may arise in public-houses, spirit groceries, beer-houses, and unlicensed houses.

4163. You said just now that the sergeant is in charge of a section. How many beats are comprised in a section?—Three, four, and five; they vary.

4164. That is to say, that the number of constables under the charge of a sergeant varies from three to five?—It is always more than that, inasmuch as there are constables at special points, and where the beats are doubled, the men will be twice that number, and it often occurs that a sergeant or acting sergeant will have charge of two, and even three, sections at the same time.

4165. Into how many beats, sections, and subdivisions is the B Division divided?—Into two subdivisions, eight sections, and thirty-one beats.

4166. Proceed now to give me an outline of the duties performed by the acting inspectors?—If you permit me, I will read a memorandum on the subject which I have prepared, and that comprises a list of the duties of acting inspectors and inspectors as station-house officers. These duties may be divided into station-house and street duties. We will begin with the station-house duties:—

"Day tour—From 10 A.M. to 8 P.M., ten hours duty in the station and patrolling.

"Night tours—From 8 P.M. to 3 A.M., first night, seven hours; from 8 P.M. to 10 A.M., second night, fourteen hours—each alternate night. Average night's tour, ten and a-half hours.

"Tour of duty changes every week from day to night, the week beginning on Friday.

"In addition to the above tours, the officers must be at their respective stations at least 15 or 20 minutes previous, to take over an account of all occurrences for the preceding tour from the officers whom they relieve, and must remain in the station often as long as two hours after their nominal tour of duty, to make up special reports, put occurrences in the book, and send a copy of same to superintendent's office, and complete all 'routes,' and wire same to G, or Detective Division."

I may add that when there is a full complement of officers attached to each station for the due performance of the duties, there should always be an inspector and an acting inspector on duty together, the one patrolling the sub-division, the other inside the station at the clerical duties. That would take two inspectors and two acting inspectors to properly discharge the duties of the station-house. The full complement is seldom present, in consequence of having to attend to special duties, and sickness, leave, &c. There are stations in rural districts in which the full complement is not maintained, nor is it necessary. For instance, in the E and F Divisions, which are rural districts, there is only one inspector in each station, the remaining number being generally made up by sergeants, and sometimes acting sergeants in cases of necessity. There are also two stations in the F Division, viz., Booterstown and Kill-o'-the-Grange, each in charge of an acting inspector.

4147. When the exigencies of the service render it impossible to maintain the full complement of inspectors and acting inspectors at the city station-houses, I presume that sergeants are employed to do the work of acting inspectors?—Just so, Sir; the senior or most intelligent being selected.

My memorandum then proceeds:—

"First day patrol from 10·15 A.M. to 1·45 P.M.: three and a-half hours.

"Second day patrol from 5 P.M. to 7·45 P.M.: two and three-quarter hours.

"First night patrol from 8·15 to 11·15 P.M.: three hours.

"Second night patrol from 12 night to 3 A.M.: three hours.

"A sergeant goes the third night rounds, being called in off the section for the purpose."

4148. We will take the case of an inspector and acting inspector being on duty at College Street police-station, and their tour of duty commencing at 8 P.M. and ending at 10 A.M. Will you give me an outline of the duties performed by the inspector and acting inspector during that time?—After being fifteen minutes in the station together, one—the inspector, for instance—makes his entry in the occurrence book, noting the time, for the information of his superior officers, that he leaves the station-house to patrol, being 8·15 P.M. He remains patrolling until 11·45 P.M.: three hours and a-half.

4149. Does he patrol his subdivision more than once during that time?—He is not confined to any particular part of his district, but he must see every sergeant and constable under him during that time, except those that are absent legitimately in connexion with their duty. He then returns at 11·45 P.M. to the station, making an entry in the occurrence book, noting the time, stating fully if any sergeant or constable was found absent, and stating fully the cause; also reporting elaborately any occurrence that may come under his notice while out on patrol. Should any occurrence be of any magnitude, it must be entered on a report for the information of his superintendent, and transmitted in the morning, and also reported by wire to the G, or Detective Division. The acting inspector goes out to patrol at 12 o'clock at night, and remains on patrol until 3 A.M.: 3 hours, when he returns to the station and makes an entry similar to that made by the inspector. After completing his reports he then makes a second entry, noting the time that he goes off duty. A sergeant is then called in to perform the morning patrol, the inspector remaining on duty in the station-house until 10 A.M.

4150. Then, as a matter of fact, the sergeant who was called in has to patrol the sub-division from 3 A.M. until 10 A.M.?—No, he only patrols up to 6 A.M., the sergeant in charge of the section being responsible up to 10 A.M., when the inspector and acting inspector commence their tour of day duty. These tours are taken alternately, the next night the acting inspector performing the fourteen hours. The memorandum I have already referred to then continues:—

"While out on patrol they must visit every sergeant and man in their sub-division, and see that they are sober and every way correct. They must also see to the good order and regularity of licensed traders in their districts, and are responsible for the suppression of all irregularities.

"While in the office they must take all charges, all reports of felonies, larcenies, stray children, stray animals, &c.; these they must enter in a book, wire copies to G Division, and send a copy of same to superintendent's office. They must also attend the police-court when there is any case of importance to be heard, and to prosecute their own complaints. They must also attend the superintendent's and Commissioner's office to give evidence in cases of breaches of discipline, and coroners' inquests. If off duty on such occasions, they generally have to perform their regular tour of duty besides."

In dealing with the duties of the various grades of the service I have only spoken of ordinary occasions, and have not taken into account where extra duty is performed in consequence of political disturbances or other cases of emergency.

4151. You have used the phrase "political disturbances." May I ask you, do you think from your own experience that the members of the Dublin metropolitan police force have had, during the last three years, a great amount of extra and harassing duties to perform?—They had a very great amount. I may add that I have known instances where officers and men applied for the annual leave of absence, to which they were entitled, and had to be refused in consequence of the severity of the duties and exigencies of the service, and I know it to be a fact that the members of the force generally, for more than the last three years, have had to perform an extraordinary amount of extra duty.

4152. Have you reason to believe that the police of Dublin have been put to extra expense by the recent agitation?—Certainly all extra duties entailed an amount of expense.

4153. In what way?—For refreshments, and sometimes for car hire.

4154. And when you are obliged to take cars on the public service, are you not reimbursed the amount?—In some instances we are; but if a constable is fatigued by reason of his extra work, and has to take a car, he is never reimbursed. Absence from barracks beyond the usual tour of duty necessarily entails extra expense, for which the men are not recouped. I may add as an instance of the hostility shown to the police by a section of the people latterly, that it is a notorious fact that a member of the service must pay more for his lodgings than an ordinary member of the community, and in some instances it has been known that where men went in uniform to seek lodgings they were

Acting Inspector [illegible]

[illegible] Oct., [illegible]

Acting Sergeant Percy Hughes.

22 Oct., 1888.

refused, although the lodgings were to let, simply because they were policemen.

4155–6. Are there any deductions made from the pay, and, if so, for what purpose?—Is. 3d. per week is deducted—2d. for lodging and 1d. for coal.

4157. What advantages are included under the head of lodging?—Barrack accommodation, with bedding, only. The servants who cook and clean the rooms are paid by the men, a sum varying from 6d. to 1s. being collected from them weekly, according to rank.

4158. Who pays the caterer?—He is a constable detailed for this duty for a certain time in barracks where the number of men is large; where the number of men is small, the man who acts as caterer performs part of his regular duty besides.

4159. *Mr. Holmes.*—I have to thank you very much, Mr. Hughes, for the very valuable evidence you have given me to-day.

[This concluded the evidence taken by the Committee.]

APPENDIX.

LIST OF PAPERS IN THE APPENDICES.

MAPS.

Map of the Dublin Metropolitan Police District.
Map of the City portion of the District on a larger scale.

Appendix I.

MINUTE OF THE UNDER-SECRETARY, AND CORRESPONDENCE RELATIVE TO THE SCOPE OF THE INQUIRY.

(No. 1.)

Minute.

THE Lord Lieutenant appoints a Committee, consisting of Mr. J. W. O'Donnell, late Chief Magistrate (Chairman); Mr George Morris, D.L., of the Local Government Board; and Mr R. W. A. Holmes, Treasury Remembrancer, to inquire into representations made to the Government in certain Memorials recently addressed to his Excellency by the Dublin Metropolitan Police Force.

His Excellency instructs the Committee to inquire fully into the various matters referred to in these Memorials, and to take such evidence respecting them as they may think necessary.

The Chief Commissioner of Police will arrange for the attendance before the Committee of any members of the force whom they may desire to examine, and the services of a short-hand writer will be placed at their disposal.

Mr. Mitchell, of the Paymaster-General's Office, will act as Secretary.

His Excellency particularly desires that the Committee will commence their inquiry forthwith and that they will furnish their Report with the least possible delay.

(Signed) R. G. C. HAMILTON, *Under-Secretary.*

Dublin Castle, August 30, 1882.

(No. 2.)

Sir, *Dublin Castle, September 5, 1882.*

I AM instructed by this Committee to request that you will be so kind as to ascertain from his Excellency the Lord Lieutenant whether it is his wish that the Committee should strictly confine their inquiry to the matters embraced by the Memorials which have been referred to them, or should be at liberty to receive evidence in connexion with any other causes of complaint which the men may like to submit.

The Committee feel it necessary to ask this question, because, in the first place, the Memorials on the face of them, do not appear to be representative, and, again, they cannot shut their ears to the common report that they do not, as a matter of fact, represent the wishes of the force generally.

I should add that the Committee appointed to inquire into the complaints of the Royal Irish Constabulary are not restricted in the scope of their inquiry, and this Committee are strongly of opinion that the Dublin Police Force ought to have the same liberty in representing their grievances which has been accorded to the other force.

I have, &c.

(Signed) F. W. D. MITCHELL,
Secretary to the Committee.

R. G. C. Hamilton, Esq., Under-Secretary.

(No. 3.)

Sir, *Chief Secretary's Office, Dublin Castle, September 9, 1882.*

I AM directed by the Lord Lieutenant to acknowledge the receipt of your communication of the 5th instant, asking, by desire of the Dublin Metropolitan Police Inquiry Committee, whether they should strictly confine their inquiry to the matters embraced in the Memorials which have been referred to them, or be at liberty to receive evidence in connexion with any other cause of complaint which the men may wish to submit.

In reply, I am to inform you that, as his Excellency explained to the Committee when they had an interview with him on the 7th instant, he desires that their inquiry should be searching and complete.

Matters of a purely personal nature should not be received or inquired into; and if in the course of the inquiry matters of discipline should be raised upon which the men entertain strong views, but respecting which the Committee may feel a difficulty in advising, it will be sufficient that in their Report the attention of his Excellency should be called to such matters.

I am, &c.

(Signed) R. G. C. HAMILTON.

F. W. D. Mitchell, Esq.,
Secretary to the Dublin Metropolitan Police Inquiry Committee.

Appendix II.

SCALES OF PAY OF THE POLICE FORCES OF THE UNITED KINGDOM IN 1881.

Arranged in Ten Classes according to the Mean between the Highest and Lowest Rates of the Pay of the Constables in each Force.

NOTES.

1. [illegible]
2. [illegible]
3. The "Model Scale" [illegible]
4. "Mean Classes" and "Mean Rate" [illegible]
5. [illegible]
6. The rates of pay of the English and Scotch counties and boroughs are taken from the Parliamentary Returns for the year 1881. [illegible]
7. The numbers of Inspectors and Sergeants [illegible] of Constable.
8. Summary.—The total number of Constables included in the List being [illegible], the percentage in each of the Classes was as follows:—

Class I. [illegible]	[illegible]	Class VI. [illegible]	13·1
" II. [illegible]	[illegible]	" VII. [illegible]	[illegible]
" III. [illegible]	[illegible]	" VIII. [illegible]	[illegible]
" IV. [illegible]	[illegible]	" IX. [illegible]	[illegible]
" V. [illegible]	[illegible]	" X. [illegible]	[illegible]

Counties and Boroughs.	Pay of Superintendents. (Annual.)	Pay of Inspectors. (Annual.)	Pay of Sergeants. (Weekly.)	Pay of Constables. (Weekly.)	Mean Pay of Constables. (Note 2.)	No. of Inspectors and Sergeants.	No. of Constables.

Counties and Boroughs	Pay of Superintendents. (Annual.)	Pay of Inspectors. (Annual.)	Pay of Sergeants. (Weekly.)	Pay of Constables. (Weekly.)	Mean Pay of Constables. (Note ?)	No. of Inspectors and Sergeants.	No. of Constables.
8. [illegible], County	[illegible]	[illegible]	[illegible]	[illegible]	[illegible]	[illegible]	[illegible]
10. Truro	[illegible]	[illegible]	[illegible]	[illegible]	[illegible]	[illegible]	[illegible]
11. [illegible]	[illegible]	[illegible]	[illegible]	[illegible]	[illegible]	[illegible]	[illegible]
12. Abingdon	[illegible]	[illegible]	[illegible]	[illegible]	[illegible]	[illegible]	[illegible]
13. Pembrokeshire	[illegible]	[illegible]	[illegible]	[illegible]	[illegible]	[illegible]	[illegible]
14. Sutherland	[illegible]	[illegible]	[illegible]	[illegible]	[illegible]	[illegible]	[illegible]
15. Arbroath	[illegible]	[illegible]	[illegible]	[illegible]	[illegible]	[illegible]	[illegible]
16. [illegible]	[illegible]	[illegible]	[illegible]	[illegible]	[illegible]	[illegible]	[illegible]
17. Maldon	[illegible]	[illegible]	[illegible]	[illegible]	[illegible]	[illegible]	[illegible]
18. Inverness, Burgh	[illegible]	[illegible]	[illegible]	[illegible]	[illegible]	[illegible]	[illegible]
19. Forfar, Burgh	[illegible]	[illegible]	[illegible]	[illegible]	[illegible]	[illegible]	[illegible]
20. Leominster	[illegible]	[illegible]	[illegible]	[illegible]	[illegible]	[illegible]	[illegible]
21. Elgin, County	[illegible]	[illegible]	[illegible]	[illegible]	[illegible]	[illegible]	[illegible]
22. [illegible], Burgh	[illegible]	[illegible]	[illegible]	[illegible]	[illegible]	[illegible]	[illegible]
23. Perth, Burgh	[illegible]	[illegible]	[illegible]	[illegible]	[illegible]	[illegible]	[illegible]
24. Plymouth	[illegible]	[illegible]	[illegible]	[illegible]	[illegible]	[illegible]	[illegible]
25. [illegible]	[illegible]	[illegible]	[illegible]	[illegible]	[illegible]	[illegible]	[illegible]
26. [illegible]	[illegible]	[illegible]	[illegible]	[illegible]	[illegible]	[illegible]	[illegible]
27. [illegible]	[illegible]	[illegible]	[illegible]	[illegible]	[illegible]	[illegible]	[illegible]
28. Banff, County	[illegible]	[illegible]	[illegible]	[illegible]	[illegible]	[illegible]	[illegible]
29. [illegible]	[illegible]	[illegible]	[illegible]	[illegible]	[illegible]	[illegible]	[illegible]
30. [illegible]	[illegible]	[illegible]	[illegible]	[illegible]	[illegible]	[illegible]	[illegible]
31. Cornwall	[illegible]	[illegible]	[illegible]	[illegible]	[illegible]	[illegible]	[illegible]
Totals						319	1,262

Class II.—[*Mean Pay of a Constable* [illegible] *and under* [illegible].]

Counties and Boroughs	Pay of Superintendents. (Annual.)	Pay of Inspectors. (Annual.)	Pay of Sergeants. (Weekly.)	Pay of Constables. (Weekly.)	Mean Pay of Constables.	No. of Inspectors and Sergeants.	No. of Constables.
1. [illegible]	[illegible]	[illegible]	[illegible]	[illegible]	[illegible]	[illegible]	[illegible]
2. Isle of Ely	[illegible]	[illegible]	[illegible]	[illegible]	[illegible]	[illegible]	[illegible]
3. [illegible]	[illegible]	[illegible]	[illegible]	[illegible]	[illegible]	[illegible]	[illegible]
4. Chipping Wycombe	[illegible]	[illegible]	[illegible]	[illegible]	[illegible]	[illegible]	[illegible]
5. [illegible]	[illegible]	[illegible]	[illegible]	[illegible]	[illegible]	[illegible]	[illegible]
6. Montrose	[illegible]	[illegible]	[illegible]	[illegible]	[illegible]	[illegible]	[illegible]
7. Argyle	[illegible]	[illegible]	[illegible]	[illegible]	[illegible]	[illegible]	[illegible]
8. [illegible]	[illegible]	[illegible]	[illegible]	[illegible]	[illegible]	[illegible]	[illegible]
9. Perth, County	[illegible]	[illegible]	[illegible]	[illegible]	[illegible]	[illegible]	[illegible]
10. [illegible]	[illegible]	[illegible]	[illegible]	[illegible]	[illegible]	[illegible]	[illegible]
11. [illegible]	[illegible]	[illegible]	[illegible]	[illegible]	[illegible]	[illegible]	[illegible]
12. Suffolk, E.	[illegible]	[illegible]	[illegible]	[illegible]	[illegible]	[illegible]	[illegible]
13. —— W.	[illegible]	[illegible]	[illegible]	[illegible]	[illegible]	[illegible]	[illegible]
14. Devonport	[illegible]	[illegible]	[illegible]	[illegible]	[illegible]	[illegible]	[illegible]
15. [illegible]	[illegible]	[illegible]	[illegible]	[illegible]	[illegible]	[illegible]	[illegible]
16. Aberdeenshire	[illegible]	[illegible]	[illegible]	[illegible]	[illegible]	[illegible]	[illegible]

Counties and Boroughs.	Pay of Superintendents. (Annual.)	Pay of Inspectors. (Annual.)	Pay of Sergeants. (Weekly.)				Pay of Constables. (Weekly.)							Mean Pay of Constables. (Note 2.)	No. of Inspectors and Sergeants.	No. of Constables.
	£ s. d. £ s. d.	£ s. d. £ s. d.	s. d.	s. d.	s. d.	s. d.	s. d.	s. d.	s. d.	s. d.	s. d.	s. d.	s. d.	s. d.		
17. Clackmannan	..	..	[illegible]	..	..	[illegible]	[illegible]	..	..	..	..	[illegible]	[illegible]	[illegible]	1	8
18. Chichester	..	..	[illegible]	..	..	[illegible]	[illegible]	..	..	..	..	..	[illegible]	[illegible]	1	4
19. Wisbech	..	..	[illegible]	..	..	[illegible]	[illegible]	..	..	..	..	..	[illegible]	[illegible]	[illegible]	[illegible]
20. Wigtown	1?? 0 0 and house	..	[illegible]	..	..	[illegible]	[illegible]	..	..	..	[illegible] 6	21 6	[illegible]	[illegible]	[illegible]	14
21. Canterbury	..	74 15 0 —	[illegible]	..	..	[illegible]	[illegible]	..	..	..	..	[illegible]	[illegible]	[illegible]	4	17
22. Stirling, Burgh*	..	—	[illegible]	..	..	[illegible]	[illegible]	..	..	..	..	[illegible]	[illegible]	[illegible]	[illegible]	13
23. Ayr*	1?? 0 0 and lodgings	..	[illegible]	..	..	[illegible]	[illegible]	..	..	..	..	[illegible]	[illegible]	[illegible]	1	4
Home Department Scale (No. 1)	150 0 0—180 0 0	105 0 0—90 0 0	[illegible]	[illegible] 3	[illegible] 0	[illegible]	[illegible]	..	[illegible]	[illegible]	[illegible]	[illegible] 0	[illegible]	[illegible]	..	..
24. [illegible]	1?? 14 10—1?? 14 10	—	[illegible]	..	..	[illegible]	[illegible]	[illegible]	[illegible]	[illegible]	[illegible]	[illegible]	[illegible]	[illegible]	[illegible]	[illegible]
25. [illegible]	—	?? 4 0—?? 1 ?	[illegible]	[illegible]	[illegible]	[illegible]	[illegible]	..	[illegible]	[illegible]	[illegible]	[illegible]	[illegible]	[illegible]	11	[illegible]
26. [illegible]*	1?? 0 0 —	?? 1? 0 —	[illegible]	—	..	[illegible]	[illegible]	..	..	..	..	[illegible]	[illegible]	[illegible]	[illegible]	[illegible]
Totals	..	..	..	..	..	..	..	..	..	..	..	..	..	..	165	437

Class III.—[*Mean Pay of a Constable 22s. and under 23s.*]

Counties and Boroughs.	Pay of Superintendents. (Annual.)	Pay of Inspectors. (Annual.)	Pay of Sergeants. (Weekly.)				Pay of Constables. (Weekly.)							Mean Pay of Constables.	No. of Inspectors and Sergeants.	No. of Constables.
1. Tenby	..	..	..	..	..	..	[illegible]	..	..	..	..	..	[illegible]	[illegible]	..	[illegible]
2. Brecon	..	..	[illegible]	..	..	[illegible]	[illegible]	..	..	..	..	..	[illegible]	[illegible]	[illegible]	[illegible]
3. [illegible]	..	..	[illegible]	..	..	[illegible]	[illegible]	..	..	..	..	..	[illegible]	[illegible]	[illegible]	[illegible]
4. Renfrew, County	1?? 0 0 —	?? 0 0—?? 0 0	[illegible]	..	..	[illegible]	[illegible]	..	..	..	[illegible] 6	[illegible]	[illegible]	[illegible]	[illegible]	[illegible]
5. Colchester	..	?? 0 0 —	[illegible]	..	..	[illegible]	[illegible]	..	..	..	..	[illegible]	[illegible]	[illegible]	[illegible]	[illegible]
6. Johnstone*	1?? 0 0 —	?? 0 0 —	[illegible]	..	..	[illegible]	[illegible]	..	..	..	..	[illegible]	[illegible]	[illegible]	[illegible]	[illegible]
7. Port Glasgow*	1?? 0 0 —	?? 10 0 —	[illegible]	..	..	[illegible]	[illegible]	..	..	..	..	[illegible]	[illegible]	[illegible]	[illegible]	[illegible]
8. Galashiels*	1?? 0 0 —	..	[illegible]	..	..	[illegible]	[illegible]	..	..	..	[illegible]	[illegible]	[illegible]	[illegible]	[illegible]	[illegible]
9. [illegible]	..	..	[illegible]	..	..	[illegible]	[illegible]	..	..	[illegible] 6	[illegible]	[illegible]	[illegible]	[illegible]	[illegible]	[illegible]
10. Kirkcaldy	1?? 0 0 —	..	[illegible]	..	..	[illegible]	[illegible]	..	..	..	..	[illegible]	[illegible]	[illegible]	[illegible]	[illegible]
11. [illegible]	..	..	[illegible]	[illegible]	[illegible]	[illegible]	[illegible]	..	..	..	..	[illegible]	[illegible]	[illegible]	[illegible]	[illegible]
12. [illegible], Burgh	1?? 0 0 —	..	[illegible]	..	..	[illegible]	[illegible]	..	..	..	..	[illegible]	[illegible]	[illegible]	[illegible]	[illegible]
13. [illegible]	..	..	[illegible]	..	[illegible]	[illegible]	[illegible]	..	..	..	..	[illegible]	[illegible]	[illegible]	[illegible]	[illegible]
14. Newport, I. W.	..	..	[illegible]	..	..	[illegible]	[illegible]	..	..	..	[illegible]	[illegible]	[illegible]	[illegible]	[illegible]	[illegible]
15. Norfolk	1?? 0 0—1?? 0 0	?? 0 0—?? 0 0	[illegible]	..	..	[illegible]	[illegible]	..	[illegible]	..	[illegible]	[illegible]	[illegible]	[illegible]	[illegible]	[illegible]
16. Bute	..	..	[illegible]	..	..	[illegible]	[illegible]	..	..	..	..	[illegible]	[illegible]	[illegible]	[illegible]	[illegible]
17. Fife	1?? 0 0—1?? 0 0	?? 0 0—?? 0 0	[illegible]	..	..	[illegible]	[illegible]	..	..	..	..	[illegible]	[illegible]	[illegible]	[illegible]	[illegible]
18. Ipswich	?? 1? 0	?? 0 0 —	[illegible]	..	..	[illegible]	[illegible]	..	..	..	..	[illegible]	[illegible]	[illegible]	[illegible]	[illegible]
19. Haddington	1?? 0 0 —	?? 0 7 —	[illegible]	..	..	[illegible]	[illegible]	..	..	..	[illegible]	[illegible]	[illegible]	[illegible]	[illegible]	[illegible]
20. Sussex, E.	1?? 0 0—1?? 0 0	..	[illegible]	[illegible]	[illegible]	[illegible]	[illegible]	..	..	..	[illegible]	[illegible]	[illegible]	[illegible]	[illegible]	[illegible]
21. [illegible]	..	?? 0 0—?? 0 0	[illegible]	[illegible]	[illegible]	[illegible]	[illegible]	..	..	..	..	[illegible]	[illegible]	[illegible]	[illegible]	[illegible]
22. Buckinghamshire	1?? 10 0—1?? 0 0	1?? 0 0—?? 0 0	[illegible]	[illegible]	[illegible]	[illegible]	[illegible]	..	..	..	[illegible]	[illegible]	[illegible]	[illegible]	[illegible]	[illegible]
23. York, E. Riding	1?? 0 0—1?? 0 0	1?? 0 0—?? 0 0	[illegible]	[illegible] 7	[illegible]	[illegible]	[illegible]	..	..	[illegible]	[illegible]	[illegible]	[illegible]	[illegible]	[illegible]	[illegible]
24. Montgomeryshire	..	?? 0 0 —	[illegible]	..	..	[illegible]	[illegible]	..	..	[illegible]	[illegible]	[illegible]	[illegible]	[illegible]	[illegible]	[illegible]

Counties and Boroughs.	Pay of Superintendents. (Annual.)	Pay of Inspectors. (Annual.)	Pay of Sergeants. (Weekly.)	Pay of Constables. (Weekly.)	Mean Pay of Constables (Weekly.)	No. of Inspectors and Sergeants.	No. of Constables.
[illegible]	[illegible]	[illegible]	[illegible]	[illegible]	[illegible]	[illegible]	[illegible]
Home Department Scale (No. II)	[illegible]	[illegible]	[illegible]	[illegible]	[illegible]	..	..
[illegible]	[illegible]	[illegible]	[illegible]	[illegible]	[illegible]	[illegible]	[illegible]
Home Department Scale (No. III)	[illegible]	[illegible]	[illegible]	[illegible]	[illegible]	..	..
[illegible]	[illegible]	[illegible]	[illegible]	[illegible]	[illegible]	[illegible]	[illegible]
Totals	..	..	..	..	..	[illegible]	[illegible]

Class IV.—[Mean Pay of a Constable [illegible], and under [illegible].]

Counties and Boroughs.	Pay of Superintendents. (Annual.)	Pay of Inspectors. (Annual.)	Pay of Sergeants. (Weekly.)	Pay of Constables. (Weekly.)	Mean Pay of Constables (Weekly.)	No. of Inspectors and Sergeants.	No. of Constables.
[illegible]	[illegible]	[illegible]	[illegible]	[illegible]	[illegible]	[illegible]	[illegible]

Cities and Boroughs.	Pay of Superintendents. (Annual.)	Pay of Inspectors. (Annual.)	Pay of Sergeants. (Weekly.)	Pay of Constables. (Weekly.)	Mean Pay of Constables.	No. of Inspectors and Sergeants.	No. of Constables.
6. Denbigh, County	[illegible]	[illegible]	[illegible]	[illegible]	[illegible]	[illegible]	[illegible]
7. Bedford	..	[illegible]	[illegible]	[illegible]	[illegible]	[illegible]	[illegible]
8. Northamptonshire	[illegible]	[illegible]	[illegible]	[illegible]	[illegible]	[illegible]	[illegible]
9. [illegible]	[illegible]	[illegible]	[illegible]	[illegible]	[illegible]	[illegible]	[illegible]
10. [illegible]	[illegible]	..	[illegible]	[illegible]	[illegible]	[illegible]	[illegible]
11. Peterborough	..	..	[illegible]	[illegible]	[illegible]	[illegible]	[illegible]
12. Royal Irish Constabulary Proposed rates, 1883	—	[illegible]	[illegible]	[illegible]	[illegible]	[illegible]	[illegible]
		Head Constables	Constables and Acting Constables	Sub-Constables			
13. Beverley	..	..	[illegible]	[illegible]	[illegible]	[illegible]	[illegible]
14. Guildford	..	..	[illegible]	[illegible]	[illegible]	[illegible]	[illegible]
15. [illegible]	..	..	[illegible]	[illegible]	[illegible]	[illegible]	[illegible]
16. Brighton	[illegible]	[illegible]	[illegible]	[illegible]	[illegible]	[illegible]	[illegible]
17. Reigate	..	..	[illegible]	[illegible]	[illegible]	[illegible]	[illegible]
18. Cardiganshire	[illegible]	..	[illegible]	[illegible]	[illegible]	[illegible]	[illegible]
19. Reading	..	[illegible]	[illegible]	[illegible]	[illegible]	[illegible]	[illegible]
Home Department Scale (No. IV)	[illegible]	[illegible]	[illegible]	[illegible]	[illegible]	..	..
20. Hereford	..	..	[illegible]	[illegible]	[illegible]	[illegible]	[illegible]
21. [illegible], County	[illegible]	[illegible]	[illegible]	[illegible]	[illegible]	[illegible]	[illegible]
22. [illegible]	..	[illegible]	[illegible]	[illegible]	[illegible]	[illegible]	[illegible]
23. St. Alban's	..	..	[illegible]	[illegible]	[illegible]	[illegible]	[illegible]
24. Hertfordshire	[illegible]	[illegible]	[illegible]	[illegible]	[illegible]	[illegible]	[illegible]
25. Ipswich	..	[illegible]	[illegible]	[illegible]	[illegible]	[illegible]	[illegible]
26. Cambridgeshire	[illegible]	[illegible]	[illegible]	[illegible]	[illegible]	[illegible]	[illegible]
27. [illegible]	[illegible]	[illegible]	[illegible]	[illegible]	[illegible]	[illegible]	[illegible]
28. Berwick	[illegible]	..	[illegible]	[illegible]	[illegible]	[illegible]	[illegible]
29. Bridgnorth	..	..	[illegible]	[illegible]	[illegible]	[illegible]	[illegible]
30. [illegible], County	[illegible]	[illegible]	[illegible]	[illegible]	[illegible]	[illegible]	[illegible]
31. Edinburgh, County	[illegible]	[illegible]	[illegible]	[illegible]	[illegible]	[illegible]	[illegible]
32. [illegible]	..	..	[illegible]	[illegible]	[illegible]	[illegible]	[illegible]
33. Hull	[illegible]	[illegible]	[illegible]	[illegible]	[illegible]	[illegible]	[illegible]
34. Essex	[illegible]	[illegible]	[illegible]	[illegible]	[illegible]	[illegible]	[illegible]
35. Leith*	[illegible]	[illegible]	[illegible]	[illegible]	[illegible]	[illegible]	[illegible]
36. Dundee*	[illegible]	[illegible]	[illegible]	[illegible]	[illegible]	[illegible]	[illegible]
37. Southampton	..	[illegible]	[illegible]	[illegible]	[illegible]	[illegible]	[illegible]
38. Oxford, City	..	[illegible]	[illegible]	[illegible]	[illegible]	[illegible]	[illegible]
39. Weymouth	..	..	[illegible]	[illegible]	[illegible]	[illegible]	[illegible]
40. Dover	..	..	[illegible]	[illegible]	[illegible]	[illegible]	[illegible]
41. [illegible]	..	..	[illegible]	[illegible]	[illegible]	[illegible]	[illegible]
42. Wolverhampton	..	[illegible]	[illegible]	[illegible]	[illegible]	[illegible]	[illegible]
Totals	..	..	..	..	..	[illegible]	[illegible]

Cities and Boroughs.	Pay of Superintendents. (Annual.)	Pay of Inspectors. (Annual.)	Pay of Sergeants. (Weekly.)				Pay of Constables. (Weekly.)							Mean Pay of Constables. (Article 2.)	No. of Inspectors and Sergeants.	No. of Constables.
	£ s. d. £ s. d.	£ s. d. £ s. d.	s. d.	s. d.	s. d.	s. d.	s. d.	s. d.	s. d.	s. d.	s. d.	s. d.	s. d.	s. d.		
Class V.—[Mean Pay of a Constable, 24s. and under 25s.]																
1. Lichfield	[illegible]	[illegible]	[illegible]	[illegible]	[illegible]	[illegible]	[illegible]	[illegible]	[illegible]	[illegible]	[illegible]	[illegible]	[illegible]	[illegible]	[illegible]	[illegible]
2. Roxburgh?	[illegible]	[illegible]	[illegible]	[illegible]	[illegible]	[illegible]	[illegible]	[illegible]	[illegible]	[illegible]	[illegible]	[illegible]	[illegible]	[illegible]	[illegible]	[illegible]
3. Selkirk?	[illegible]	[illegible]	[illegible]	[illegible]	[illegible]	[illegible]	[illegible]	[illegible]	[illegible]	[illegible]	[illegible]	[illegible]	[illegible]	[illegible]	[illegible]	[illegible]
4. Partick	[illegible]	[illegible]	[illegible]	[illegible]	[illegible]	[illegible]	[illegible]	[illegible]	[illegible]	[illegible]	[illegible]	[illegible]	[illegible]	[illegible]	[illegible]	[illegible]
5. Renfrew, Burgh	[illegible]	[illegible]	[illegible]	[illegible]	[illegible]	[illegible]	[illegible]	[illegible]	[illegible]	[illegible]	[illegible]	[illegible]	[illegible]	[illegible]	[illegible]	[illegible]
6. Peterborough, Liberty	[illegible]	[illegible]	[illegible]	[illegible]	[illegible]	[illegible]	[illegible]	[illegible]	[illegible]	[illegible]	[illegible]	[illegible]	[illegible]	[illegible]	[illegible]	[illegible]
7. Kendal	[illegible]	[illegible]	[illegible]	[illegible]	[illegible]	[illegible]	[illegible]	[illegible]	[illegible]	[illegible]	[illegible]	[illegible]	[illegible]	[illegible]	[illegible]	[illegible]
8. Greenock	[illegible]	[illegible]	[illegible]	[illegible]	[illegible]	[illegible]	[illegible]	[illegible]	[illegible]	[illegible]	[illegible]	[illegible]	[illegible]	[illegible]	[illegible]	[illegible]
9. Govan	[illegible]	[illegible]	[illegible]	[illegible]	[illegible]	[illegible]	[illegible]	[illegible]	[illegible]	[illegible]	[illegible]	[illegible]	[illegible]	[illegible]	[illegible]	[illegible]
10. Maryhill	[illegible]	[illegible]	[illegible]	[illegible]	[illegible]	[illegible]	[illegible]	[illegible]	[illegible]	[illegible]	[illegible]	[illegible]	[illegible]	[illegible]	[illegible]	[illegible]
11. Glasgow	[illegible]	[illegible]	[illegible]	[illegible]	[illegible]	[illegible]	[illegible]	[illegible]	[illegible]	[illegible]	[illegible]	[illegible]	[illegible]	[illegible]	[illegible]	[illegible]
12. Edinburgh	[illegible]	[illegible]	[illegible]	[illegible]	[illegible]	[illegible]	[illegible]	[illegible]	[illegible]	[illegible]	[illegible]	[illegible]	[illegible]	[illegible]	[illegible]	[illegible]
Home Department Scale (No. V)	[illegible]	[illegible]	[illegible]	[illegible]	[illegible]	[illegible]	[illegible]	[illegible]	[illegible]	[illegible]	[illegible]	[illegible]	[illegible]	[illegible]	[illegible]	[illegible]
13. Newcastle-under-Lyme	[illegible]	[illegible]	[illegible]	[illegible]	[illegible]	[illegible]	[illegible]	[illegible]	[illegible]	[illegible]	[illegible]	[illegible]	[illegible]	[illegible]	[illegible]	[illegible]
14. Ayr, County	[illegible]	[illegible]	[illegible]	[illegible]	[illegible]	[illegible]	[illegible]	[illegible]	[illegible]	[illegible]	[illegible]	[illegible]	[illegible]	[illegible]	[illegible]	[illegible]
15. Rutlandshire	[illegible]	[illegible]	[illegible]	[illegible]	[illegible]	[illegible]	[illegible]	[illegible]	[illegible]	[illegible]	[illegible]	[illegible]	[illegible]	[illegible]	[illegible]	[illegible]
16. Denbighshire	[illegible]	[illegible]	[illegible]	[illegible]	[illegible]	[illegible]	[illegible]	[illegible]	[illegible]	[illegible]	[illegible]	[illegible]	[illegible]	[illegible]	[illegible]	[illegible]
17. Radnorshire	[illegible]	[illegible]	[illegible]	[illegible]	[illegible]	[illegible]	[illegible]	[illegible]	[illegible]	[illegible]	[illegible]	[illegible]	[illegible]	[illegible]	[illegible]	[illegible]
18. Surrey	[illegible]	[illegible]	[illegible]	[illegible]	[illegible]	[illegible]	[illegible]	[illegible]	[illegible]	[illegible]	[illegible]	[illegible]	[illegible]	[illegible]	[illegible]	[illegible]
19. Carmarthenshire	[illegible]	[illegible]	[illegible]	[illegible]	[illegible]	[illegible]	[illegible]	[illegible]	[illegible]	[illegible]	[illegible]	[illegible]	[illegible]	[illegible]	[illegible]	[illegible]
20. Bath	[illegible]	[illegible]	[illegible]	[illegible]	[illegible]	[illegible]	[illegible]	[illegible]	[illegible]	[illegible]	[illegible]	[illegible]	[illegible]	[illegible]	[illegible]	[illegible]
21. Warwickshire	[illegible]	[illegible]	[illegible]	[illegible]	[illegible]	[illegible]	[illegible]	[illegible]	[illegible]	[illegible]	[illegible]	[illegible]	[illegible]	[illegible]	[illegible]	[illegible]
22. Pontefract	[illegible]	[illegible]	[illegible]	[illegible]	[illegible]	[illegible]	[illegible]	[illegible]	[illegible]	[illegible]	[illegible]	[illegible]	[illegible]	[illegible]	[illegible]	[illegible]
23. Margate	[illegible]	[illegible]	[illegible]	[illegible]	[illegible]	[illegible]	[illegible]	[illegible]	[illegible]	[illegible]	[illegible]	[illegible]	[illegible]	[illegible]	[illegible]	[illegible]
24. Staffordshire	[illegible]	[illegible]	[illegible]	[illegible]	[illegible]	[illegible]	[illegible]	[illegible]	[illegible]	[illegible]	[illegible]	[illegible]	[illegible]	[illegible]	[illegible]	[illegible]
25. Congleton	[illegible]	[illegible]	[illegible]	[illegible]	[illegible]	[illegible]	[illegible]	[illegible]	[illegible]	[illegible]	[illegible]	[illegible]	[illegible]	[illegible]	[illegible]	[illegible]
26. Glossop?	[illegible]	[illegible]	[illegible]	[illegible]	[illegible]	[illegible]	[illegible]	[illegible]	[illegible]	[illegible]	[illegible]	[illegible]	[illegible]	[illegible]	[illegible]	[illegible]
27. Newport, Mon.	[illegible]	[illegible]	[illegible]	[illegible]	[illegible]	[illegible]	[illegible]	[illegible]	[illegible]	[illegible]	[illegible]	[illegible]	[illegible]	[illegible]	[illegible]	[illegible]
28. Carlisle	[illegible]	[illegible]	[illegible]	[illegible]	[illegible]	[illegible]	[illegible]	[illegible]	[illegible]	[illegible]	[illegible]	[illegible]	[illegible]	[illegible]	[illegible]	[illegible]
29. Lancaster	[illegible]	[illegible]	[illegible]	[illegible]	[illegible]	[illegible]	[illegible]	[illegible]	[illegible]	[illegible]	[illegible]	[illegible]	[illegible]	[illegible]	[illegible]	[illegible]
30. [illegible]	[illegible]	[illegible]	[illegible]	[illegible]	[illegible]	[illegible]	[illegible]	[illegible]	[illegible]	[illegible]	[illegible]	[illegible]	[illegible]	[illegible]	[illegible]	[illegible]
31. [illegible]	[illegible]	[illegible]	[illegible]	[illegible]	[illegible]	[illegible]	[illegible]	[illegible]	[illegible]	[illegible]	[illegible]	[illegible]	[illegible]	[illegible]	[illegible]	[illegible]
32. Maidstone?	[illegible]	[illegible]	[illegible]	[illegible]	[illegible]	[illegible]	[illegible]	[illegible]	[illegible]	[illegible]	[illegible]	[illegible]	[illegible]	[illegible]	[illegible]	[illegible]
Home Department Scale (No. VI)	[illegible]	[illegible]	[illegible]	[illegible]	[illegible]	[illegible]	[illegible]	[illegible]	[illegible]	[illegible]	[illegible]	[illegible]	[illegible]	[illegible]	[illegible]	[illegible]
33. Ramsgate?	[illegible]	[illegible]	[illegible]	[illegible]	[illegible]	[illegible]	[illegible]	[illegible]	[illegible]	[illegible]	[illegible]	[illegible]	[illegible]	[illegible]	[illegible]	[illegible]
34. Lewes	[illegible]	[illegible]	[illegible]	[illegible]	[illegible]	[illegible]	[illegible]	[illegible]	[illegible]	[illegible]	[illegible]	[illegible]	[illegible]	[illegible]	[illegible]	[illegible]
35. Berwick?	[illegible]	[illegible]	[illegible]	[illegible]	[illegible]	[illegible]	[illegible]	[illegible]	[illegible]	[illegible]	[illegible]	[illegible]	[illegible]	[illegible]	[illegible]	[illegible]
36. [illegible]	[illegible]	[illegible]	[illegible]	[illegible]	[illegible]	[illegible]	[illegible]	[illegible]	[illegible]	[illegible]	[illegible]	[illegible]	[illegible]	[illegible]	[illegible]	[illegible]
37. Halifax	[illegible]	[illegible]	[illegible]	[illegible]	[illegible]	[illegible]	[illegible]	[illegible]	[illegible]	[illegible]	[illegible]	[illegible]	[illegible]	[illegible]	[illegible]	[illegible]

Cities and Boroughs.	Pay of Superintendents (Annual).	Pay of Inspectors (Annual).	Pay of Sergeants (Weekly).	Pay of Constables (Weekly).	Mean Pay of Constable.	No. of Sergeants.	No. of Constables.
38. [illegible]	[illegible]	[illegible]	[illegible]	[illegible]	[illegible]	[illegible]	[illegible]
39. Derbyshire	[illegible]	[illegible]	[illegible]	[illegible]	[illegible]	[illegible]	[illegible]
Totals	...	...	...	...	...	826	2,077

Class VI.—[Mean Pay of a Constable 30s. and under 32s.]

Cities and Boroughs.	Pay of Superintendents (Annual).	Pay of Inspectors (Annual).	Pay of Sergeants (Weekly).	Pay of Constables (Weekly).	Mean Pay of Constable.	No. of Sergeants.	No. of Constables.
1. Cardiff	...	[illegible]	[illegible]	[illegible]	[illegible]	[illegible]	[illegible]
2. Windsor	...	...	[illegible]	[illegible]	[illegible]	[illegible]	[illegible]
3. Northampton	...	[illegible]	[illegible]	[illegible]	[illegible]	[illegible]	[illegible]
4. Great Grimsby	...	...	[illegible]	[illegible]	[illegible]	[illegible]	[illegible]
5. Macclesfield	...	[illegible]	[illegible]	[illegible]	[illegible]	[illegible]	[illegible]
6. Cumberland and Westmorland	[illegible]	[illegible]	[illegible]	[illegible]	[illegible]	[illegible]	[illegible]
7. Hastings	...	[illegible]	[illegible]	[illegible]	[illegible]	[illegible]	[illegible]
8. Salford	[illegible]	[illegible]	[illegible]	[illegible]	[illegible]	[illegible]	[illegible]
9. Northumberland	[illegible]	[illegible]	[illegible]	[illegible]	[illegible]	[illegible]	[illegible]
10. Cambridge	...	[illegible]	[illegible]	[illegible]	[illegible]	[illegible]	[illegible]
11. Hartlepool	...	...	[illegible]	[illegible]	[illegible]	[illegible]	[illegible]
12. Chesterfield	...	[illegible]	[illegible]	[illegible]	[illegible]	[illegible]	[illegible]
13. Tunbridge Wells	...	...	[illegible]	[illegible]	[illegible]	[illegible]	[illegible]
Home Department Scale (No. VII)	[illegible]	125 0 0—150 0 0	[illegible]	[illegible]	[illegible]	...	...
14. Bedfordshire	[illegible]	[illegible]	[illegible]	[illegible]	[illegible]	[illegible]	[illegible]
15. [illegible]	[illegible]	[illegible]	[illegible]	[illegible]	[illegible]	[illegible]	[illegible]
16. Montgomeryshire	[illegible]	[illegible]	[illegible]	[illegible]	[illegible]	[illegible]	[illegible]
17. Banbury	...	[illegible]	[illegible]	[illegible]	[illegible]	[illegible]	[illegible]
18. Walsall	...	...	[illegible]	[illegible]	[illegible]	[illegible]	[illegible]
19. Coventry	...	[illegible]	[illegible]	[illegible]	[illegible]	[illegible]	[illegible]
20. Leicestershire	[illegible]	[illegible]	[illegible]	[illegible]	[illegible]	[illegible]	[illegible]
21. [illegible]	[illegible]	[illegible]	[illegible]	[illegible]	[illegible]	[illegible]	[illegible]
22. South Shields	...	[illegible]	[illegible]	[illegible]	[illegible]	[illegible]	[illegible]
23. Lincolnshire	[illegible]	[illegible]	[illegible]	[illegible]	[illegible]	[illegible]	[illegible]
24. Lincoln, City	...	[illegible]	[illegible]	[illegible]	[illegible]	[illegible]	[illegible]
25. Huntingdon	[illegible]	[illegible]	[illegible]	[illegible]	[illegible]	[illegible]	[illegible]
26. [illegible]	[illegible]	[illegible]	[illegible]	[illegible]	[illegible]	[illegible]	[illegible]
27. Chester	...	[illegible]	[illegible]	[illegible]	[illegible]	[illegible]	[illegible]
28. Stockport	...	[illegible]	[illegible]	[illegible]	[illegible]	[illegible]	[illegible]
29. Wakefield	...	[illegible]	[illegible]	[illegible]	[illegible]	[illegible]	[illegible]
30. Glamorganshire	[illegible]	[illegible]	[illegible]	[illegible]	[illegible]	[illegible]	[illegible]
31. Hull	...	[illegible]	[illegible]	[illegible]	[illegible]	[illegible]	[illegible]
32. Tynemouth	...	[illegible]	[illegible]	[illegible]	[illegible]	[illegible]	[illegible]
33. Newcastle-on-Tyne	[illegible]	[illegible]	[illegible]	[illegible]	[illegible]	[illegible]	[illegible]
34. Dumbarton, Burgh	[illegible]	...	[illegible]	[illegible]	[illegible]	[illegible]	[illegible]

[0118]

Cities and Boroughs.	Pay of Superintendents. (Annual.)	Pay of Inspectors. (Annual.)	Pay of Sergeants. (Weekly)				Pay of Constables. (Weekly.)							Mean Pay of Constables. (Note 2.)	No. of Inspectors and Sergeants.	No. of Constables.
	£ s. d. £ s. d.	£ s. d. £ s. d.	s. d.	s. d.	s. d.	s. d.	s. d.	s. d.	s. d.	s. d.	s. d.	s. d.	s. d.	s. d.		
52. Portsmouth	[illegible]	[illegible]	[illegible]	[illegible]	[illegible]	[illegible]	[illegible]	[illegible]	[illegible]	[illegible]	[illegible]	[illegible]	[illegible]	[illegible]	[illegible]	[illegible]
56. [illegible]	[illegible]	[illegible]	[illegible]	[illegible]	[illegible]	[illegible]	[illegible]	[illegible]	[illegible]	[illegible]	[illegible]	[illegible]	[illegible]	[illegible]	[illegible]	[illegible]
57. [illegible]	[illegible]	[illegible]	[illegible]	[illegible]	[illegible]	[illegible]	[illegible]	[illegible]	[illegible]	[illegible]	[illegible]	[illegible]	[illegible]	[illegible]	[illegible]	[illegible]
58. Bradford	[illegible]	[illegible]	[illegible]	[illegible]	[illegible]	[illegible]	[illegible]	[illegible]	[illegible]	[illegible]	[illegible]	[illegible]	[illegible]	[illegible]	[illegible]	[illegible]
59. [illegible]	[illegible]	[illegible]	[illegible]	[illegible]	[illegible]	[illegible]	[illegible]	[illegible]	[illegible]	[illegible]	[illegible]	[illegible]	[illegible]	[illegible]	[illegible]	[illegible]
60. [illegible] (See Note 3)	[illegible]	[illegible]	[illegible]	[illegible]	[illegible]	[illegible]	[illegible]	[illegible]	[illegible]	[illegible]	[illegible]	[illegible]	[illegible]	[illegible]	[illegible]	[illegible]
61. Stalybridge	[illegible]	[illegible]	[illegible]	[illegible]	[illegible]	[illegible]	[illegible]	[illegible]	[illegible]	[illegible]	[illegible]	[illegible]	[illegible]	[illegible]	[illegible]	[illegible]
62. Scarborough	[illegible]	[illegible]	[illegible]	[illegible]	[illegible]	[illegible]	[illegible]	[illegible]	[illegible]	[illegible]	[illegible]	[illegible]	[illegible]	[illegible]	[illegible]	[illegible]
63. York, W. Riding	[illegible]	[illegible]	[illegible]	[illegible]	[illegible]	[illegible]	[illegible]	[illegible]	[illegible]	[illegible]	[illegible]	[illegible]	[illegible]	[illegible]	[illegible]	[illegible]
64. Sheffield	[illegible]	[illegible]	[illegible]	[illegible]	[illegible]	[illegible]	[illegible]	[illegible]	[illegible]	[illegible]	[illegible]	[illegible]	[illegible]	[illegible]	[illegible]	[illegible]
Totals															[illegible]	[illegible]

Class VII.—(*Mean Pay of a Constable* 27*s. and under* 28*s.*)

Cities and Boroughs.	Pay of Superintendents. (Annual.)	Pay of Inspectors. (Annual.)	Pay of Sergeants. (Weekly)				Pay of Constables. (Weekly.)							Mean Pay of Constables. (Note 2.)	No. of Inspectors and Sergeants.	No. of Constables.
1. York, City	[illegible]	[illegible]	[illegible]	[illegible]	[illegible]	[illegible]	[illegible]	[illegible]	[illegible]	[illegible]	[illegible]	[illegible]	[illegible]	[illegible]	[illegible]	[illegible]
2. Derby	[illegible]	[illegible]	[illegible]	[illegible]	[illegible]	[illegible]	[illegible]	[illegible]	[illegible]	[illegible]	[illegible]	[illegible]	[illegible]	[illegible]	[illegible]	[illegible]
3. [illegible]	[illegible]	[illegible]	[illegible]	[illegible]	[illegible]	[illegible]	[illegible]	[illegible]	[illegible]	[illegible]	[illegible]	[illegible]	[illegible]	[illegible]	[illegible]	[illegible]
4. [illegible]	[illegible]	[illegible]	[illegible]	[illegible]	[illegible]	[illegible]	[illegible]	[illegible]	[illegible]	[illegible]	[illegible]	[illegible]	[illegible]	[illegible]	[illegible]	[illegible]
5. London Metropolitan Police	[illegible]	[illegible]	[illegible]	[illegible]	[illegible]	[illegible]	[illegible]	[illegible]	[illegible]	[illegible]	[illegible]	[illegible]	[illegible]	[illegible]	[illegible]	[illegible]
6. York, North Riding	[illegible]	[illegible]	[illegible]	[illegible]	[illegible]	[illegible]	[illegible]	[illegible]	[illegible]	[illegible]	[illegible]	[illegible]	[illegible]	[illegible]	[illegible]	[illegible]
7. Doncaster	[illegible]	[illegible]	[illegible]	[illegible]	[illegible]	[illegible]	[illegible]	[illegible]	[illegible]	[illegible]	[illegible]	[illegible]	[illegible]	[illegible]	[illegible]	[illegible]
8. Middlesbrough	[illegible]	[illegible]	[illegible]	[illegible]	[illegible]	[illegible]	[illegible]	[illegible]	[illegible]	[illegible]	[illegible]	[illegible]	[illegible]	[illegible]	[illegible]	[illegible]
9. Leamington	[illegible]	[illegible]	[illegible]	[illegible]	[illegible]	[illegible]	[illegible]	[illegible]	[illegible]	[illegible]	[illegible]	[illegible]	[illegible]	[illegible]	[illegible]	[illegible]
10. Durham, County	[illegible]	[illegible]	[illegible]	[illegible]	[illegible]	[illegible]	[illegible]	[illegible]	[illegible]	[illegible]	[illegible]	[illegible]	[illegible]	[illegible]	[illegible]	[illegible]
11. Bristol	[illegible]	[illegible]	[illegible]	[illegible]	[illegible]	[illegible]	[illegible]	[illegible]	[illegible]	[illegible]	[illegible]	[illegible]	[illegible]	[illegible]	[illegible]	[illegible]
12. Gateshead	[illegible]	[illegible]	[illegible]	[illegible]	[illegible]	[illegible]	[illegible]	[illegible]	[illegible]	[illegible]	[illegible]	[illegible]	[illegible]	[illegible]	[illegible]	[illegible]
13. Oldham	[illegible]	[illegible]	[illegible]	[illegible]	[illegible]	[illegible]	[illegible]	[illegible]	[illegible]	[illegible]	[illegible]	[illegible]	[illegible]	[illegible]	[illegible]	[illegible]
14. Wigan	[illegible]	[illegible]	[illegible]	[illegible]	[illegible]	[illegible]	[illegible]	[illegible]	[illegible]	[illegible]	[illegible]	[illegible]	[illegible]	[illegible]	[illegible]	[illegible]
15. Durham, City	[illegible]	[illegible]	[illegible]	[illegible]	[illegible]	[illegible]	[illegible]	[illegible]	[illegible]	[illegible]	[illegible]	[illegible]	[illegible]	[illegible]	[illegible]	[illegible]
16. Barrow	[illegible]	[illegible]	[illegible]	[illegible]	[illegible]	[illegible]	[illegible]	[illegible]	[illegible]	[illegible]	[illegible]	[illegible]	[illegible]	[illegible]	[illegible]	[illegible]
Totals															[illegible]	[illegible]

Cities and Boroughs.	Pay of Superintendents. (Annual.)	Pay of Inspectors. (Annual.)	Pay of Sergeants. (Weekly.)	Pay of Constables. (Weekly.)	Mean Pay of Constables.	No. of Inspectors and Sergeants.	No. of Constables.
CLASS VIII.—(*Mean Pay of a Constable* [illegible] *and under* [illegible].)							
1. Huddersfield	[illegible]	[illegible]	[illegible]	[illegible]	[illegible]	[illegible]	[illegible]
2. Manchester	[illegible]	[illegible]	[illegible]	[illegible]	[illegible]	[illegible]	[illegible]
3. Lancashire	[illegible]	[illegible]	[illegible]	[illegible]	[illegible]	[illegible]	[illegible]
4. Rochdale	[illegible]	[illegible]	[illegible]	[illegible]	[illegible]	[illegible]	[illegible]
5. Leeds	[illegible]	[illegible]	[illegible]	[illegible]	[illegible]	[illegible]	[illegible]
6. London City	[illegible]	[illegible]	[illegible]	[illegible]	[illegible]	[illegible]	[illegible]
Totals						[illegible]	[illegible]
CLASS IX.—(*Mean Pay of a Constable* [illegible] *and under* [illegible].)							
1. Liverpool	[illegible]	[illegible]	[illegible]	[illegible]	[illegible]	[illegible]	[illegible]
2. Preston	[illegible]	[illegible]	[illegible]	[illegible]	[illegible]	[illegible]	[illegible]
3. Ashton-under-Lyne	[illegible]	[illegible]	[illegible]	[illegible]	[illegible]	[illegible]	[illegible]
4. Stockport	[illegible]	[illegible]	[illegible]	[illegible]	[illegible]	[illegible]	[illegible]
5. Nottingham Town	[illegible]	[illegible]	[illegible]	[illegible]	[illegible]	[illegible]	[illegible]
Totals						[illegible]	[illegible]
CLASS X.—(*Mean Pay of a Constable* [illegible] *and upwards*.)							
1. Birkenhead	[illegible]	[illegible]	[illegible]	[illegible]	[illegible]	[illegible]	[illegible]
2. Bolton	[illegible]	[illegible]	[illegible]	[illegible]	[illegible]	[illegible]	[illegible]
Totals						[illegible]	[illegible]

Appendix III.

STATISTICS OF DUBLIN METROPOLITAN POLICE.

(1.)—Return showing the authorised Strength of the Dublin Metropolitan Police Force (exclusive of G Division), with Pay and Allowances.

Ranks.	Divisions. A.	B.	C.	D.	E.	F.	Total.	[illegible]	Weekly Pay. £ s. d.	[illegible] d.	Total Weekly. £ s. d.	Yearly Pay. £ s. d.	Yearly Allowances. £ s. d.	Total Yearly. £ s. d.
Chief Superintendent	..	1	..	..	..	..	1	..	..	..	..	[illegible] 0 0	105? 0 0	[illegible] 0 0
Superintendent	1	..	..	..	..	..	1	..	..	..	..	[illegible] 0 0	[illegible] 0 0	[illegible] 0 0
Ditto	..	..	1	..	..	..	1	..	..	..	..	[illegible] 0 0	[illegible] 0 0	[illegible] 0 0
Ditto	..	..	..	1	..	..	1	..	..	..	..	[illegible] 0 0	[illegible] 0 0	[illegible] 0 0
Ditto	..	..	..	..	1	..	1	..	..	..	..	[illegible] 0 0	[illegible] 0 0	[illegible] 0 0
Ditto	..	..	..	..	..	1	1	..	..	..	..	[illegible] 0 0	105? 0 0	[illegible] 0 0
Inspectors—														
1st Class	1	1	1	..	..	1	[illegible]	..	..	..	..	[illegible] 0 0	[illegible] 0 0	[illegible] 0 0
2nd Class	[illegible]	1	1	1	1	..	[illegible]	..	..	..	..	[illegible] 0 0	[illegible] 0 0	[illegible] 0 0
3rd Class	[illegible]	1	1	[illegible]	[illegible]	[illegible]	[illegible]	..	..	..	..	[illegible] 0 0	[illegible] 0 0	[illegible] 0 0
Acting Inspectors	[illegible]	[illegible]	4	6	[illegible]	[illegible]	[illegible]	..	1 16 0	[illegible]	1 [illegible] [illegible]	[illegible] 17 7	[illegible] 16 [illegible]	[illegible] [illegible] [illegible]
Sergeants	11	[illegible]	9	16	11	11	[illegible]	..	[illegible]	[illegible]	1 [illegible] [illegible]	[illegible] [illegible] [illegible]	[illegible] 1[illegible] [illegible]	[illegible] [illegible] [illegible]
Acting Sergeants	20	18	13	14	[illegible]	16	[illegible]	..	1 [illegible] [illegible]	[illegible]	1 [illegible] [illegible]	[illegible] 16 [illegible]	[illegible] 16 [illegible]	[illegible] [illegible] [illegible]
Constables—														
1st Rate	44?	34?	43	[illegible]	[illegible]	31?	[illegible]	..	1 [illegible] [illegible]	[illegible]	1 [illegible] [illegible]	[illegible] [illegible] [illegible]	[illegible] [illegible] [illegible]	[illegible] [illegible] [illegible]
2nd Rate	[illegible]	[illegible]	16	[illegible]	[illegible]	9	[illegible]	..	1 [illegible] [illegible]	[illegible]	1 [illegible] [illegible]	[illegible] [illegible] [illegible]	[illegible] [illegible] [illegible]	[illegible] [illegible] [illegible]
3rd Rate	[illegible]	[illegible]	74	[illegible]	[illegible]	[illegible]	[illegible]	..	1 [illegible] [illegible]	[illegible]	1 [illegible] [illegible]	[illegible] [illegible] [illegible]	[illegible] [illegible] [illegible]	[illegible] 10 [illegible]
4th Rate	[illegible]	[illegible]	[illegible]	16	24?	18	[illegible]	..	1 [illegible] [illegible]	[illegible]	1 [illegible] [illegible]	[illegible] [illegible] [illegible]	[illegible] [illegible] [illegible]	[illegible] [illegible] [illegible]
[illegible]	[illegible]	1	[illegible]	1	..	..	[illegible]	..	..	..	..	..	..	..
Supernumeraries	..	..	..	..	..	..	..	[illegible]	0 [illegible] [illegible]	..	..	[illegible] 0 0	..	..
Total	[illegible]	219	[illegible]	196?	141?	139?	1,1[illegible]	..	..	..	..	..	..	..

Note.—Superintendents commence at [illegible]l., and rise by an increment of [illegible]l. per annum for five years, until the maximum [illegible]l. per annum.

[illegible]d. per week allowed to members of the troop for spurs and gloves.

[illegible]l. a year for lodging and [illegible]l. for uniform is allowed to Inspectors.

[illegible]d. per week is allowed to all ranks under Inspector for boots and making of uniforms.

(2.)—Return showing the authorised Strength of "G" or Detective Division, with Pay and Allowances.

Ranks.	Division. G.	Weekly Pay. £ s. d.	Weekly Allowances. s. d.	Total Weekly. £ s. d.	Yearly Pay. £ s. d.	Yearly Allowances. £ s. d.	Total Yearly. £ s. d.	
Superintendent	1	..	..	..	[illegible] 0 0	[illegible] 0 0	[illegible] 0 0	
Inspector	1	..	..	..	[illegible] 0 0	[illegible] 0 0	[illegible] 0 0	Resides in barracks; only draws [illegible]l. of the allowance.
Acting Inspectors	[illegible]	1 19 0	[illegible]	[illegible]	[illegible] [illegible] [illegible]	[illegible] [illegible] [illegible]	[illegible] [illegible] [illegible]	
Ditto	[illegible]	1 [illegible] 0	[illegible]	[illegible]	[illegible] 1 [illegible]	[illegible] [illegible] [illegible]	[illegible] [illegible] [illegible]	
Sergeants	[illegible]	1 [illegible] [illegible]	[illegible]	1 17 [illegible]	[illegible] [illegible] [illegible]	[illegible] [illegible] [illegible]	[illegible] [illegible] [illegible]	
Acting Sergeants	6	1 [illegible] [illegible]	[illegible]	1 [illegible] [illegible]	[illegible] 0 0	[illegible] [illegible] [illegible]	[illegible] [illegible] [illegible]	
Constables—								
1st Rate	[illegible]	1 [illegible] [illegible]	[illegible]	1 [illegible] [illegible]	[illegible] [illegible] [illegible]	[illegible] [illegible] [illegible]	[illegible] [illegible] [illegible]	
2nd Rate	1	1 [illegible] [illegible]	[illegible]	1 [illegible] [illegible]	[illegible] [illegible] [illegible]	[illegible] [illegible] [illegible]	[illegible] [illegible] [illegible]	
Total	[illegible]	..	..	..	..	..	..	

Allowances to Superintendents:
- [illegible]l. per annum for a horse.
- [illegible]l. — for forage.
- [illegible]l. — for a servant man.
- [illegible]l. — for office and stable, where accommodation is not given.
- [illegible]l. — for clothing.
- [illegible]s. per day car hire to Superintendents of D and E Divisions.

(3.)—RETURN showing the Number of Officers and Men serving in the above Force on the 31st October 18[illegible], and their respective Periods of Service.

	Superintendents.	Inspectors.	Acting Inspectors.	Police Sergeants.	Acting Police Sergeants.	Constables.	Total.
Under 1 year	..	..	..	..	..	[illegible]	[illegible]
1 year and under 2 years	..	..	..	..	..	[illegible]	[illegible]
[illegible]	[illegible]	[illegible]	[illegible]	[illegible]	[illegible]	[illegible]	[illegible]
	1 (Chief)	..	..	..	..	..	[illegible]
Total	[illegible]	[illegible]	[illegible]	[illegible]	[illegible]	[illegible]	1,14[illegible]
Vacancies	..	..	[illegible]	[illegible]	..	..	3
Appointed strength	[illegible]	[illegible]	[illegible]	[illegible]	[illegible]	[illegible]	1,14[illegible]*

* 1,1[illegible], excluding vacancies.

(Signed) J. A. CONOLLY, Commissioner.

Appendix III.

(4.)—RETURN showing the Number of Persons charged and the Number of Charges refused in the several Stations of the above-named District during the Month of October 1882.

Divisions and Stations.		Persons Charged.			Refused Charges.			Remarks.
		Males.	Females.	Total.	Males.	Females.	Total.	
A	Chancery Lane	117	97	214	1	2	3	
	Newmarket	61	29	90	2	2	4	
	Kilmainham	45	19	64	1	..	1	
B	College Street	179	46	225	4	[illegible]	4	
	Lad Lane	41	14	55	1	..	1	
	Clarendon Street	27	22	49	3	..	3	Open from 9 P.M. to 6 A.M. only.
C	Store Street	117	66	183	2	..	2	
	Summer Hill	45	44	89	1	..	1	
D	Green Street	94	54	148	1	..	1	
	Bridewell Lane	95	49	144	..	..	..	
E	Rathmines	30	18	48	1	..	1	
	Donnybrook	70	8	78	..	..	..	
	Irishtown	55	12	67	1	..	1	
F	Kingstown	46	24	70	2	..	2	
	Blackrock	19	4	23	..	..	..	
	Booterstown	7	1	8	..	..	..	
	Dalkey	9	1	10	2	1	3	
	Kill-o'-the-Grange	2	..	2	..	..	..	In charge of the Acting Inspector only, who is also in charge of the sub-district.
Total		999	379	1,379	20	9	25	

(Signed) RICHARD CORR, *Chief Superintendent.*

(5.)—RETURN showing the Station-houses in the above District at which Charges are taken and Prisoners confined.

Division.	No.	Station.	Remarks.
A Division	1	Chancery Lane	Off Little Street.
	2	Newmarket.	
	3	Kilmainham.	
B Division	4	College Street	
	5	Lad Lane	Off Baggot Street.
	6	Clarendon Street.	
C Division	7	Store Street.	
	8	Summer Hill.	
D Division	9	Green Street.	
	10	Bridewell Lane	Off Church Street.
E Division	11	Donnybrook.	
	12	Rathmines.	
	13	Irishtown.	
F Division	14	Kingstown.	
	15	Blackrock.	
	16	Dalkey.	
	17	Booterstown ..	Each in charge of an Acting Inspector.
	18	Kill-o'-the-Grange ..	
Total	18		

No. 6. Clarendon Street is only open from 9 P.M. to 6 A.M. each night, in charge of an Acting Inspector.

(Signed) F. A. CONOLLY, *Commissioner.*

(6.)—RETURN of the Number of Candidates who presented themselves from 1872 to 1882, the Number admitted, and the Number rejected.

Years.	Total Number.	Number Admitted.	Number Rejected.
1872	152	140	12
1873	[illegible]	[illegible]	[illegible]
1874	[illegible]	[illegible]	[illegible]
1875	[illegible]	[illegible]	[illegible]
1876	[illegible]	[illegible]	[illegible]
1877	[illegible]	[illegible]	[illegible]
1878	[illegible]	[illegible]	[illegible]
1879	[illegible]	[illegible]	[illegible]
1880	[illegible]	[illegible]	[illegible]
1881	[illegible]	[illegible]	[illegible]
From 1st January to 11th September, 1882	[illegible]	[illegible]	[illegible]
Total	2,415	1,365	1,050

(Signed) F. M. HINDS, *Secretary.*

September 11, 1882.

(7.)—RETURN of Removals from the Force from all causes from 1872 to 1882.

Year.	Deaths.	Pensioned.	Discharged with Gratuity.	Voluntary Resignations.	Compulsory Resignations.	Dismissals.	Discharged unfit for further Duty, Under Five Years' Service, Sickness.	Total.
1872	10	[illegible]	15	73	..	47	..	168
1873	4	[illegible]	9	10	..	[illegible]	1	[illegible]
1874	5	[illegible]	[illegible]	[illegible]	..	[illegible]	..	[illegible]
1875	5	[illegible]	11	[illegible]	..	[illegible]	..	[illegible]
1876	7	[illegible]	6	[illegible]	..	[illegible]	1	[illegible]
1877	6	[illegible]	5	[illegible]	..	[illegible]	[illegible]	[illegible]
1878	11	[illegible]	5	[illegible]	..	[illegible]	[illegible]	[illegible]
1879	[illegible]	[illegible]	[illegible]	[illegible]	[illegible]	[illegible]	[illegible]	[illegible]
1880	6	[illegible]	[illegible]	[illegible]	[illegible]	[illegible]	[illegible]	[illegible]
1881	[illegible]	[illegible]	[illegible]	19	[illegible]	[illegible]	[illegible]	[illegible]
1882 (portion of) ..	7	[illegible]	[illegible]	[illegible]	[illegible]	[illegible]	1	[illegible]
Totals	[illegible]	[illegible]	[illegible]	[illegible]	[illegible]	[illegible]	[illegible]	[illegible]

NOTE.—Of the number [illegible] in 1882, there are 17 men [illegible] who attended the meeting in contravention of orders.

(Signed) F. M. HINDS, *Secretary.*

September 11, 1882.

(8.) - *INSPECTOR'S UNIFORM.*

	£	s.	d.
Undress patrol jacket	3	15	6
Great coat	[illegible]	10	6
Cape and cover	0	16	[illegible]
Undress trousers	[illegible]	[illegible]	[illegible]
[illegible] and belt	[illegible]	[illegible]	[illegible]
Sword knot	[illegible]	[illegible]	[illegible]
Dress tunic	[illegible]	[illegible]	[illegible]
Dress trousers	[illegible]	[illegible]	[illegible]
Helmet	1	12	[illegible]
Total	[illegible]	[illegible]	[illegible]
Undress, constantly in wear	12	[illegible]	[illegible]
Dress uniform, only occasionally worn	[illegible]	[illegible]	[illegible]
Total	[illegible]	[illegible]	[illegible]
Allowance in Dublin—			
Inspector	[illegible]	0	0
Superintendent	[illegible]	0	0

A full suit of inspector's uniform, dress and undress, costs about 22*l.* it appears. The attached list specifies the articles and the prices. The present allowance of 5*l.* per annum fully covers the total expenditure on account of his uniform by an inspector during the whole term of his service in that rank; but his difficulty is to find the money to buy the suit on his appointment as inspector.

The undress suit, which costs about 12*l.*, lasts from one and a-half to two years; the dress suit, which costs about 10*l.*, is worn only occasionally, and should last the entire service of an inspector as such.

(Signed) GEORGE TALBOT, *Chief Commissioner.*

(9)—Duties performed by Constables on ordinary Occasions.

Day Duty.	1st Tour.	2nd Tour.	Time actually on the streets.	Parade at Station 15 minutes before being marched on duty.	Total time actually on their feet.	Remarks.
1st relief ..	6 a.m. to [illegible] a.m.	[illegible] p.m. to [illegible] p.m.	[illegible] hours	¼ hour	[illegible] hours	Taking each alternate day.
2nd relief ..	9 a.m. to 3 p.m.	[illegible] p.m. to [illegible] p.m.	[illegible] hours	¼ hour	[illegible] hours	

Constables on day duty are *actually on their feet* an average of nine hours daily, irrespective of preparing for duty, and proceeding to and returning from their respective stations.

Night Duty.	Tour.	Time on the streets.	Parade at the Station 15 minutes before being marched on duty.	Time that they are actually on their feet.	Remarks.
1st relief	9 p.m. to [illegible] a.m.	[illegible] hours	¼ hour	[illegible] hours	Taking each alternate night.
2nd relief	10 30 p.m. to [illegible] a.m.	[illegible] hours	¼ hour	[illegible] hours	

Night duty men perform an average tour of seven hours *actually on their feet*. The time spent in preparing for duty, proceeding to and from their respective stations as a rule entails two hours by day and one when on night duty, in addition to the tours of duty.

Constables on street duty in Dublin seldom—even at the most peaceable times—perform a tour of duty without having to arrest a prisoner, whom they must escort to and prosecute at the police courts, or without having a summons case. This they invariably do in addition to performing their ordinary tours of duty.

In the event of a fire breaking out, or any emergency arising, all men off duty in barracks are turned out—if required, or as many as are required—and no matter how long so employed, must turn out for duty at the time appointed for their respective reliefs.

When constables are acting on night duty they are often called upon to perform nine hours each night.

Constables on duty, particularly in rough parts of the city, are invariably met with hostility from the crowds when making arrests, often assaulted severely, and not unfrequently with fatal results.

---

(10)—Return showing the Number of Married and Single Officers and Men in the Force in October 1882.

Division.	Superintendents.	Inspectors.	Acting Inspectors.	Police Sergeants.	Acting Police Sergeants.	Constables.	Total.
Town A ..	1	[illegible]	[illegible]	[illegible]	[illegible]	[illegible]	[illegible]
Town B ..	1	[illegible]	[illegible]	[illegible]	[illegible]	[illegible]	[illegible]
Town C ..	1	[illegible]	[illegible]	[illegible]	[illegible]	[illegible]	[illegible]
Town D ..	1	[illegible]	[illegible]	[illegible]	[illegible]	[illegible]	[illegible]
E ..	1	[illegible]	[illegible]	[illegible]	[illegible]	[illegible]	[illegible]
F ..	1	[illegible]	[illegible]	[illegible]	[illegible]	[illegible]	[illegible]
G ..	1	..	[illegible]	[illegible]	[illegible]	[illegible]	[illegible]
Total married ..	7	[illegible]	[illegible]	[illegible]	[illegible]	[illegible]	[illegible]
Single	..	[illegible]	[illegible]	[illegible]	[illegible]	[illegible]	[illegible]
Vacancies	..	..	[illegible]	1	..	..	[illegible]
Authorised strength ..	7	[illegible]	[illegible]	[illegible]	[illegible]	[illegible]	[illegible]

(Signed) J. A. CONOLLY, *Commissioner*.

(11.)—RETURN showing the Number of Officers and Men residing in the several Barracks in the Dublin Metropolitan Police District.

Division.	Barracks.	Married men residing in Barracks.				Single men residing in Barracks.				Total.
		[illegible]	[illegible]	[illegible]	[illegible]	[illegible]	[illegible]	[illegible]	[illegible]	
A.	[illegible]	..	..	..	..	..	[illegible]	[illegible]	[illegible]	[illegible]
	Kevin Street?	..	..	..	..	..	[illegible]	[illegible]	[illegible]	[illegible]
	[illegible]	..	..	..	..	..	..	[illegible]	[illegible]	[illegible]
	[illegible]	..	..	..	..	..	[illegible]	[illegible]	[illegible]	[illegible]
B.	The Castle	..	..	..	..	[illegible]	[illegible]	[illegible]	[illegible]	[illegible]
	Lad Lane	..	..	..	..	[illegible]	[illegible]	[illegible]	[illegible]	[illegible]
	College Street Station	..	..	..	..	..	[illegible]	..	[illegible]	[illegible]
	[illegible] Street Station	1	..	..	..	..	..	..	[illegible]	[illegible]
C.	[illegible] Street	..	..	..	..	..	..	[illegible]	[illegible]	[illegible]
	Store Street	..	..	..	..	..	[illegible]	[illegible]	[illegible]	[illegible]
	Summer Hill	..	..	..	..	[illegible]	..	[illegible]	[illegible]	[illegible]
	Capel Street	[illegible]	..	..	..	[illegible]	..	..	[illegible]	[illegible]
D.	[illegible] Street	..	..	..	..	..	[illegible]	[illegible]	[illegible]	[illegible]
	[illegible]	..	..	..	..	..	[illegible]	[illegible]	[illegible]	[illegible]
	[illegible]	..	..	..	..	..	[illegible]	[illegible]	[illegible]	[illegible]
	[illegible]	..	..	..	..	[illegible]	[illegible]	[illegible]	[illegible]	[illegible]
	[illegible]	..	..	..	..	..	[illegible]	[illegible]	[illegible]	[illegible]
E.	[illegible] Street	..	..	..	..	..	[illegible]	..	[illegible]	[illegible]
	[illegible]	..	..	..	..	[illegible]	[illegible]	[illegible]	[illegible]	[illegible]
	Donnybrook	..	[illegible]	..	..	[illegible]	[illegible]	[illegible]	[illegible]	[illegible]
	[illegible]	..	..	..	..	[illegible]	[illegible]	..	[illegible]	[illegible]
	[illegible]	..	..	..	..	..	..	[illegible]	[illegible]	[illegible]
	[illegible]	..	..	..	..	..	..	[illegible]	[illegible]	[illegible]
F.	Kingstown	..	..	..	..	[illegible]	[illegible]	[illegible]	[illegible]	[illegible]
	Blackrock	..	..	..	..	..	[illegible]	[illegible]	[illegible]	[illegible]
	Dalkey	1	..	..	..	[illegible]	..	..	[illegible]	[illegible]
	Booterstown	..	..	..	..	[illegible]	..	[illegible]	[illegible]	[illegible]
	Kill-o'-the-Grange	..	..	..	..	[illegible]	..	[illegible]	[illegible]	[illegible]
G.	Exchange Court	..	..	..	..	[illegible]	[illegible]	[illegible]	[illegible]	[illegible]
	Total ..	[illegible]	[illegible]	..	..	[illegible]	[illegible]	44	[illegible]	[illegible]

Inspectors [illegible], are also provided with lodgings in police premises.

(Signed) J. A. CONOLLY, *Commissioner*.

(12.)—AUTHORIZED Strength of the Dublin Metropolitan Police for Ten Years, 1873–82?

Year.	Superintendents.	Inspectors.	Acting Inspectors.	Sergeants.	Acting Sergeants.	Constables.	Total.	Remarks.
1873 ..	[illegible]	[illegible]	[illegible]	[illegible]	[illegible]	[illegible]	[illegible]	
1874 ..	[illegible]	[illegible]	[illegible]	[illegible]	[illegible]	[illegible]	[illegible]	
1875 ..	[illegible]	[illegible]	[illegible]	[illegible]	[illegible]	[illegible]	[illegible]	
1876 ..	[illegible]	[illegible]	[illegible]	[illegible]	[illegible]	[illegible]	[illegible]	
1877 ..	[illegible]	[illegible]	[illegible]	[illegible]	[illegible]	[illegible]	[illegible]	
1878 ..	[illegible]	[illegible]	[illegible]	[illegible]	[illegible]	[illegible]	[illegible]	
1879 ..	[illegible]	[illegible]	[illegible]	[illegible]	[illegible]	[illegible]	[illegible]	
1880 ..	[illegible]	[illegible]	[illegible]	[illegible]	[illegible]	[illegible]	[illegible]	
1881 ..	[illegible]	[illegible]	[illegible]	[illegible]	[illegible]	[illegible]	[illegible]	
1882 ..	[illegible]	[illegible]	[illegible]	[illegible]	[illegible]	[illegible]	[illegible]	

The twenty constables in 1877, and the acting inspector, four sergeants, and two acting sergeants in 1878, were added in lieu of equal numbers employed on sanitary duty, at the Four Courts, at North Wall (on cattle plague duty) and General Post Office, they being paid by the Departments employing them.

The eight constables in 1878 were added in lieu of a similar number employed in Museum and Royal College of Science.

The eight constables in 1879 added in lieu of eight additional men sent on sanitary duty.

The three constables in 1880 in lieu of three additional men to Museum.

The twelve men added in 1881 in lieu of those employed inside of Kilmainham Gaol.

(Signed) RICHARD CORR, *Chief Superintendent*.

(13.)—Return of Pay and Allowances to the Force, disbursed out of the Vote for the Year 1881-82, showing the Proportions borne respectively by the Imperial and Local Revenues, and the sources of the latter, and Amount derived from each in the Year.

Total Pay and Allowances to the Force.	Proportion borne by Imperial Revenue.	Proportion borne by Local Revenue.
£	£	£
[illegible]*	[illegible]*	[illegible]*

* Shillings and pence omitted.

Local Income for the Year 1881-82.

Sources.	Amount derived from each.
	£ s. d.
Police tax ..	[illegible]
Carriage licenses, &c. ..	[illegible]
Publicans' fees ..	[illegible]
Fees, fines, and penalties ..	[illegible]
Pawnbrokers' licenses ..	[illegible]
Miscellaneous (sale of old stores, forfeited property, &c.) ..	[illegible]
Total ..	[illegible] 19 [illegible]

(Signed) George Talbot, *Chief Commissioner*.
Metropolitan Police Office, Dublin Castle, December 1882.

(14.)—Area and Population of the Dublin Metropolitan Police District as per Census, 1881.

District.	Area in Statute Acres.	Population in 1881.		
		Males.	Females.	Total.
Dublin City ..	[illegible]	[illegible]	[illegible]	[illegible]
Rural district ..	[illegible]	[illegible]	[illegible]	[illegible]
Total district ..	[illegible]	[illegible]	[illegible]	[illegible]

(Signed) Richard Corr, *Chief Superintendent*.
Chief Superintendent's Office, November 30, 1882.

(15.)—Rates of Pay before 1857.

	Annually. £ s. d.	
Chief Superintendent ..	[illegible] 10 0	
Superintendents ..	[illegible] 0 0	Before increase in [illegible].
Inspectors, 1st Class ..	[illegible]	
" 2nd Class ..	[illegible]	
" 3rd Class ..	[illegible]	

The pay of superintendents commenced at [illegible] yearly, and rose by a yearly increment of 5*l.* to [illegible], the maximum.

	Weekly Pay before Revision in 1857.	Remarks.
	£ s. d.	
Acting Inspectors ..	[illegible]	Previous to 1857 good-conduct pay was added to a man's ordinary pay when he arrived at certain periods of years of service, his conduct being considered. By the revised scale, which commenced the 1st April, 1857, this good-conduct pay was abolished, a few pence were added to the weekly pay of some ranks, and to other instances (as in the case of a few constables of the G Division) a reduction was made, to equalize all pay for the same rank, and the three classes of constables were made into four [illegible], the yearly rates [illegible] the [illegible] increment.
" ..	[illegible]	
Sergeants ..	[illegible]	
" ..	[illegible]	
Acting Sergeants ..	[illegible]	
" ..	[illegible]	
Constables, 1st Class ..	[illegible]	
" " ..	[illegible]	
" 2nd Class ..	[illegible]	
" 3rd Class ..	[illegible]	
" ..	[illegible]	

		£	s.	d.	
1	Superintendent	[illegible]	0	0	annually.
1	Acting Inspector	1	[illegible]	[illegible]	weekly.
1	"	1	[illegible]	[illegible]	"
1	"	1	4	10	"
10	"	1	[illegible]	[illegible]	"
	Acting Sergeants	1	1	10	"
1	Constable	1	1	[illegible]	"
1	"	1	0	10	"
2	"	0	19	11	"
4	"	0	19	[illegible]	"
1	"	0	13	11	"
1	"	0	16	[illegible]	"
1	"	0	16	[illegible]	"

Notes.

Before 1867 there was no inspector, and there were no sergeants in the G Division.

All the members of the G Division, being employed on detective duty, wore plain clothes, for the purchase of which no allowance was given to them.

Metropolitan Police Office,

September 16, 1882

(16.)—Detective Division.—Carriage Duty, &c.

Memorandum by Superintendent Mallon.

Sergeant on carriage duty	[illegible]
Constables on carriage duty	[illegible]
Constable as messenger	[illegible]
Constable looking after barracks, &c.	[illegible]
	10
Constables on pawn-office duty	5
	15

They should not be regarded as detective officers and provided for as such.

The carriage men and pawn duty men might, if eligible, pass into the detective department.

The barrack men and the messenger might be effective men of any division.

JOHN MALLON,

Superintendent.

December 7, 1882.

(17.)—Return showing the Number of Persons taken into custody for Assaults committed on the Dublin Metropolitan Police in each year from 1872 to 1881, inclusive.

Years	Number of Prisoners arrested.
1872	[illegible]
1873	[illegible]
1874	[illegible]
1875	[illegible]
1876	[illegible]
1877	[illegible]
1878	[illegible]
1879	[illegible]
1880	[illegible]
1881	[illegible]
Total	[illegible]

J. A. CONOLLY,

Commissioner.

Appendix IV.

STATISTICS OF THE LIVERPOOL CONSTABULARY.

Population 548,649

Area ... ... [illegible] acres.

(I.)—LIVERPOOL CONSTABULARY.

Ranks.	Number.	Rates of Salaries and Pay.	Rates of Deduction for Superannuation Fund.
Head Constable	1	£ 750 per annum	2½ per cent.
Chief Superintendent	1	[illegible] "	
" " Detective	1	[illegible] "	
Chief Clerk	1	[illegible] "	
Assistant Clerk	1	[illegible] "	
Superintendent River Police	1	[illegible] "	
" Fire Brigade	1	[illegible] "	
[illegible]	[illegible]	[illegible] "	
Superintendents	[illegible]	[illegible] "	
Inspectors, detective	[illegible]	[illegible] "	
Governor of Main Bridewell	1	[illegible] "	
Bridekeeper	1	150 "	
Coroner's beadle	1	[illegible] "	
Inspector, public houses	1	[illegible] "	
" lodging houses	1	[illegible] "	
Deputy Superintendent Fire Brigade	1	[illegible] "	
Inspectors, detective	[illegible]	[illegible] "	
Inspector of carts, &c.	1	[illegible] "	
1st Class Inspectors (including clerks, &c.)	[illegible]	[illegible] "	
2nd "	57	[illegible]	
3rd "	[illegible]	[illegible] 4d. per week	
4th "	[illegible]	[illegible]	
Drummers	7	[illegible]	
"	9	[illegible]	
Bridewell keepers	14	[illegible]	
"	[illegible]	[illegible]	
Detectives	7	[illegible]	
Assistant clerks	8	[illegible]	10d. per week.
Merit Class constables	1,241	[illegible] 6d.	
1st "		[illegible]	
2nd "		[illegible]	
3rd "		[illegible]	
4th "		[illegible]	6d. per week.
Total strength of the force	[illegible]		

Strength of Fire Brigade—	
Superintendent	1
Deputy Superintendents	[illegible]
Engineers	[illegible]
Constables	[illegible]*
Total	[illegible]

* These [illegible] firemen are included in the above five ranks of constables, and get [illegible] per week additional pay.

Constables are promoted from [illegible] to 27s. 10d. per week after twelve months' service; to [illegible] after two years; to [illegible] after seven years (subject to good conduct and efficiency). There is also a higher class for special merit.

Allowances.—The chief superintendents, three superintendents, superintendent of fire brigade, Governor of Main Bridewell, and the resident Bridewell keepers, have a free residence in their respective divisions, and at their stations.

Uniform clothing is supplied; but when not worn by constables on special duty, clerks, &c., an allowance of 3s. (in the case of detective officers of [illegible]) per week is given. An allowance of [illegible] per annum is given in lieu of boots.

Salaried inspectors receive [illegible] per annum in lieu of uniform, and superintendents receive [illegible] annually for hats and boots.

Deductions when Sick.—No deductions from salaried officers. The other officers and men, when sick, have two-thirds of their pay stopped. They subscribe, on an average, [illegible] per week to a sick club, from which they draw 12s. per week when ill, and in case of death [illegible], [illegible], or [illegible] is granted for funeral expenses.

Leave.—Seven days per annum, with pay, to constables, and fourteen days to inspectors; intermediate ranks ten days. Three days on the funeral of a near relative and one day on a constable's marriage. Special leave to constables,—thirty-six hours off about each [illegible] day.

Retiring Allowances from Superannuation.—After fifteen years' service, a sum not more than one-half nor less than three-eighths of average pay (on last two years' service). After twenty years' service, a sum not more than two-thirds nor less than one-half of average pay, provided the age be not under fifty-seven years if below the rank of superintendent, and sixty of or above that rank. After ten years' service, a sum not exceeding three-eighths, nor less than one-fourth, if worn out. After five years, a gratuity equal to twenty days' pay for every year's service. Men disabled by bodily injuries received in the execution of their duty may be allowed an annual sum not exceeding two-thirds

(2.)—ALLOWANCES to Officers of the Detective Department when Absent from Town on Business.

Superintendent	Second-class train fare, cab and bus fare, and [illegible] per day for personal expenses.
Inspectors, constables, &c.	Third-class fare, cab and bus fare, and [illegible] per day for personal expenses.

Day means a day and a night. Less than half a day counted half a day. If journey commenced before midnight and continues during the night, counted as half day. A day of 12 hours counted as half day.

(Signed) J. W. NOTT BOWER,
Head Constable and Director of Fire Brigade.

Central Police Office, August 4, 188[illegible].

(3.)—PAY of Constables—1836 to 1875.

Class.	Merit.	1.	2.	3.	4.	5.	6.
	s. d.	s. d.	s. d.	s. d.	s. d.	s. d.	s. d.
1836	..	18 0	16 0	..	..	..	..
1846	..	20 0	18 0	16 6	..	..	..
1853	..	21 0	20 0	19 0	..	..	..
[illegible]	..	24 6	23 0	21 0	20 0	..	..
[illegible]	[illegible]	[illegible]	[illegible]	[illegible]	[illegible]	..	..
[illegible]	..	[illegible]	[illegible]	[illegible]	[illegible]	[illegible]	[illegible]
[illegible]	..	[illegible]	[illegible]	[illegible]	[illegible]	[illegible]	..
1875	[illegible]	[illegible]	[illegible]	[illegible]	[illegible]	..	..

	Number.	
Merit Class	7	Special merit, irrespective of length of service.
1st Class	511	7 years' service, 2 years' clean books, efficiency.
2nd "	437	2 years' service, clean books, efficiency.
3rd "	92	1 year's service, clean books, efficiency.
4th "	[illegible]	On appointment.
Total	1,[illegible]	Strength not full.

(4.)—STRENGTH and Allocation, 17th November, 188[illegible]

Allocation.	Chief Superintendents.	Superintendents.	Inspectors.	Bridewell Keepers.	Constables.	Total.
Chief Constable's Office	..	3*	[illegible]	..	[illegible]	[illegible]
Messengers	..	..	..	..	6	6
Stores	..	..	2	..	6	8
Detective Department	1	[illegible]	[illegible]	..	[illegible]	[illegible]
[illegible] Department ..	..	..	1	..	[illegible]	[illegible]
[illegible] Act, &c.	..	..	1	..	2	[illegible]
Police Courts	..	..	[illegible]	..	11	[illegible]
Coroner's Court	..	..	1	..	[illegible]	[illegible]
[illegible]	..	..	[illegible]	..	[illegible]	[illegible]
Car Office	..	..	[illegible]	..	[illegible]	[illegible]
Bridewells	..	[illegible]	[illegible]	[illegible]	[illegible]	[illegible]
Fire Brigade	..	1	4	..	10	15
[illegible] Police	..	[illegible]	..	..	[illegible]	[illegible]
Clerks to Chief Superintendents ..	..	..	4	..	..	4
	1	[illegible]	[illegible]	[illegible]	[illegible]	[illegible]
Divisions	[illegible]	6	[illegible]	..	[illegible]	[illegible]
Chief Constable	..	..	..	..	..	1
Total	4	14	[illegible]	[illegible]	[illegible]	1,[illegible]

* Chief Clerk and Accountant Clerk.
Clerks.
Assistant Clerks.
Chief Clerk (Detective Office) and two Detective Inspectors.
Includes four Clerks.
Includes three Assistant Clerks, [illegible] Detective Officers on special pay, and [illegible] Constables temporarily employed as [illegible].
** [illegible] of Main Bridewell.
†† Clerks at Main Bridewell.
‡‡ Temporary Assistance at Main Bridewell.

The designations given to the various ranks in the Table are not those by which the men are, in all cases, locally known. They are, however, for the most part those given in the Government Returns, and the principle adopted is to classify all men with salaries of 160*l.* per annum and upwards as superintendents, those in receipt of from 36*s.* 3*d.* a-week to 150*l.* per annum as Inspectors, and those with pay of less than 36*s.* 3*d.* a-week (excepting the Bridewell keepers) as police constables.

The Main Bridewell (an institution peculiar to Liverpool) is certified as a gaol for the detention of "3-day" prisoners.

(Signed) J. W. NOTT BOWER.

(5.)—NUMBERS of Police on Town, Dock, and River duties.

Town police	[illegible]
Dock	[illegible]
River	19
Total (of all ranks)	1,2[illegible]
Officers—	
In Departments	[illegible]
In Divisions	[illegible]
Total	[illegible]

	On Beats.	On Special Duty.	Total.
Town Constables	773	[illegible]	[illegible]
Dock	[illegible]	[illegible]	[illegible]
			1,1[illegible]
River Police (on boats on Mersey)			17
Total Constables			1,1[illegible]

Constables on Special Duty, and in the Stations.

	Town.	Dock.	Total.
Head Constable's Office	4		
Police [illegible]	4	[illegible]	
Detective Office, &c.	[illegible]		
Police Courts	[illegible]	[illegible]	
[illegible]	[illegible]		
[illegible]	[illegible]		
Coroner's Court	[illegible]		
Main Bridewell	[illegible]		
Fire Station	10		
Total	[illegible]	4	[illegible]

(Signed) J. W. NOTT BOWER.

(6.)—RETURN of the Number of Prisoners and refused Charges for the Month ended 31st October, 1882.

Bridewells.	Prisoners.			Refused Charges.					
				Males.		Females.		Total.	
	Males.	Females.	Total.	Intoxicated.	Others.	Intoxicated.	Others.	Intoxicated.	Others.
Rose Hill	[illegible]	[illegible]	[illegible]	[illegible]	[illegible]	[illegible]	[illegible]	[illegible]	[illegible]
Athol Street	[illegible]	[illegible]	[illegible]	14	[illegible]	[illegible]	[illegible]	[illegible]	[illegible]
Prescot Street	[illegible]	[illegible]	[illegible]	[illegible]	[illegible]	[illegible]	[illegible]	[illegible]	[illegible]
[illegible]	[illegible]	[illegible]	[illegible]	[illegible]	[illegible]	..	[illegible]	[illegible]	[illegible]
Derby Road	[illegible]	[illegible]	[illegible]	[illegible]	..	[illegible]	[illegible]	4	[illegible]
	[illegible]	[illegible]	[illegible]	[illegible]	[illegible]	10	[illegible]	[illegible]	[illegible]
[illegible]	[illegible]	[illegible]	[illegible]	[illegible]	[illegible]	..	[illegible]	[illegible]	[illegible]
[illegible]	[illegible]	[illegible]	[illegible]	[illegible]	[illegible]	..	[illegible]	[illegible]	[illegible]
Argyle Street	[illegible]	[illegible]	[illegible]	[illegible]	19	[illegible]	[illegible]	[illegible]	[illegible]
Warren Street	[illegible]	[illegible]	[illegible]	[illegible]	..	[illegible]	[illegible]	[illegible]	[illegible]
	[illegible]	[illegible]	[illegible]	[illegible]	[illegible]	[illegible]	[illegible]	[illegible]	[illegible]
North Dock	[illegible]	[illegible]	[illegible]	[illegible]	[illegible]	[illegible]	[illegible]	[illegible]	9
South Dock	[illegible]	[illegible]	[illegible]	4	[illegible]	[illegible]	[illegible]	[illegible]	[illegible]
	[illegible]	[illegible]	[illegible]	[illegible]	[illegible]	4	[illegible]	11	[illegible]
Main Bridewell	[illegible]	[illegible]	[illegible]	[illegible]	[illegible]	[illegible]	[illegible]	6	7
Total	1,1[illegible]	1,1[illegible]	[illegible]	[illegible]	[illegible]	[illegible]	[illegible]	[illegible]	[illegible]

CHARGES in the Section-house to each Police Constable.

	£	s.	d.
Lodgings ..	0	1	[illegible]
Servant's wages ..	0	0	[illegible]
Washing sheets and towels ..	0	0	1
Newspapers ..	0	0	[illegible]
Mess utensils ..	0	0	1
Mess (dinner only) ..	0	[illegible]	[illegible]
Total ..	0	[illegible]	[illegible]
[illegible], rent for Section-house ..	[illegible]	[illegible]	[illegible]
Servants' wages ..	[illegible]	[illegible]	[illegible]
Washing for the mess ..	[illegible]	[illegible]	[illegible]
Cleaning materials, &c. ..	[illegible]	[illegible]	[illegible]
Newspapers ..	[illegible]	[illegible]	[illegible]
Mustard, pepper, and barley ..	[illegible]	[illegible]	[illegible]
Salt ..	[illegible]	[illegible]	[illegible]
Potatoes and vegetables, [illegible] ..	[illegible]	[illegible]	[illegible]
Beef at [illegible] and mutton at [illegible] per lb. ..	11	[illegible]	[illegible]
Total ..	[illegible]	[illegible]	[illegible]

(Gas and coals are supplied by the Corporation [illegible]).

	Manchester.	Liverpool.
Cottages in which constables reside ..	[illegible]	[illegible] One of [illegible]
Lodgings for constables ..	[illegible]	[illegible]

(Signed) J. W. NOTT BOWER.

(7.)—STATEMENT of the Number of Police Constables in Liverpool and Manchester, Rates of Pay in each Class, also the average Rate as per Report of Government Inspector for 1880. (Compiled 6th January, 1882.)

LIVERPOOL.

Constables	s.	d.	
[illegible] at ..	[illegible]	[illegible]	Average rate [illegible]
[illegible] ..	[illegible]	[illegible]	
[illegible] ..	[illegible]	[illegible]	
[illegible] ..	[illegible]	[illegible]	
[illegible] ..	[illegible]	[illegible]	
[illegible]			

MANCHESTER.

Constables	s.	d.	
110 at ..	[illegible]	[illegible]	Average rate [illegible]
[illegible] ..	[illegible]	[illegible]	
[illegible] ..	[illegible]	[illegible]	
[illegible] ..	[illegible]	[illegible]	
[illegible] ..	[illegible]	[illegible]	
[illegible] ..	[illegible]	[illegible]	
[illegible] ..	[illegible]	[illegible]	
[illegible]			

(8.)—COMPARATIVE STATEMENT of the Increments of Pay given to Constables in the Police Forces as under. (Compiled 3rd January, 1882.)

	London (A) Metropolitan.	London, City of.	Liverpool.	Manchester.	Birmingham.	Glasgow.	Lancashire (September [illegible]).
	s.	s. d.	s. d.	s.	s.	s.	s. d.
On appointment ..	[illegible]	[illegible]	[illegible]	[illegible]	[illegible]	[illegible]	[illegible]
After [illegible] months' service	..	..	..	[illegible]	..	..	In [illegible] months [illegible]
" [illegible] "	..	..	..	..	[illegible]	..	[illegible] months [illegible]
" 1 year's "	..	[illegible]	[illegible]	[illegible]	[illegible]	[illegible]	[illegible]
" [illegible] years' "	..	..	[illegible]	[illegible]	..	[illegible]	
" [illegible] "	[illegible]	..	..	..	..	[illegible]	
" [illegible] "	..	[illegible] B	..	..	..	..	[illegible]
" [illegible] "	..	..	..	[illegible]	..	[illegible] C	
" [illegible] "	..	..	..	..	..	..	
" [illegible] "	..	..	..	..	[illegible]	..	[illegible] years
" [illegible] "	..	..	[illegible]	..	..	..	[illegible]
" [illegible] "	[illegible]	..	..	..	..	..	
" [illegible] "	..	..	..	..	[illegible]	..	
Merit Class [illegible] ..	Reserve [illegible]	B. Numbers limited.	Merit Class [illegible] Number limited.	1st Merit [illegible], 2nd Merit [illegible] additional.	Merit pay [illegible] additional.	C Merit restricted to [illegible].	[illegible] per week.

(A). Lodgings are provided for a large proportion of single men at 1s. per week. Quarters for married constables [illegible] per week.

CONTRACT PRICES OF PROVISIONS IN 1874 AND 1883.

(I.)—Statement of Contract Prices of the undermentioned Articles in the Years 1874 and 1883 in Ireland (Commissariat Department).

Note.—Where no price is stated no contract existed.

Station.	1874. Meat, lb.	1874. Bread, 4 lbs.	1874. Milk, gallon.	1874. Potatoes, cwt.	1874. Oatmeal, cwt.	1874. Rice, cwt.	1874. Sugar, cwt.	1874. Tea, lb.	1874. Coffee, lb.	1883. Meat, lb.	1883. Bread, 4 lbs.	1883. Milk, gallon.	1883. Potatoes, cwt.	1883. Oatmeal, cwt.	1883. Rice, cwt.	1883. Sugar, cwt.	1883. Tea, lb.	1883. Coffee, lb.
	d.	d.	d.	s. d.	£ s. d.	£ s. d.	£ s. d.	s. d.	s. d.	d.	d.	s. d.	s. d.	£ s. d.	£ s. d.	£ s. d.	s. d.	s. d.
Dublin district—																		
[illegible]	[illegible]	[illegible]	[illegible]	[illegible]	[illegible]	[illegible]	[illegible]	[illegible]	[illegible]	[illegible]	[illegible]	[illegible]	[illegible]	[illegible]	[illegible]	[illegible]	[illegible]	[illegible]
Athlone	[illegible]	[illegible]	[illegible]	[illegible]	[illegible]	[illegible]	[illegible]	[illegible]	[illegible]	[illegible]	[illegible]	[illegible]	[illegible]	[illegible]	[illegible]	[illegible]	[illegible]	[illegible]
[illegible]	[illegible]	[illegible]	[illegible]	[illegible]	[illegible]	[illegible]	[illegible]	[illegible]	[illegible]	[illegible]	[illegible]	[illegible]	[illegible]	[illegible]	[illegible]	[illegible]	[illegible]	[illegible]
[illegible]	[illegible]	[illegible]	[illegible]	[illegible]	[illegible]	[illegible]	[illegible]	[illegible]	[illegible]	[illegible]	[illegible]	[illegible]	[illegible]	[illegible]	[illegible]	[illegible]	[illegible]	[illegible]
[illegible]	[illegible]	[illegible]	[illegible]	[illegible]	[illegible]	[illegible]	[illegible]	[illegible]	[illegible]	[illegible]	[illegible]	[illegible]	[illegible]	[illegible]	[illegible]	[illegible]	[illegible]	[illegible]
Birr	[illegible]	[illegible]	[illegible]	[illegible]	[illegible]	[illegible]	[illegible]	[illegible]	[illegible]	[illegible]	[illegible]	[illegible]	[illegible]	[illegible]	[illegible]	[illegible]	[illegible]	[illegible]
Boyle	[illegible]	[illegible]	[illegible]	[illegible]	[illegible]	[illegible]	[illegible]	[illegible]	[illegible]	[illegible]	[illegible]	[illegible]	[illegible]	[illegible]	[illegible]	[illegible]	[illegible]	[illegible]
[illegible]	[illegible]	[illegible]	[illegible]	[illegible]	[illegible]	[illegible]	[illegible]	[illegible]	[illegible]	[illegible]	[illegible]	[illegible]	[illegible]	[illegible]	[illegible]	[illegible]	[illegible]	[illegible]
[illegible]	[illegible]	[illegible]	[illegible]	[illegible]	[illegible]	[illegible]	[illegible]	[illegible]	[illegible]	[illegible]	[illegible]	[illegible]	[illegible]	[illegible]	[illegible]	[illegible]	[illegible]	[illegible]
[illegible]	[illegible]	[illegible]	[illegible]	[illegible]	[illegible]	[illegible]	[illegible]	[illegible]	[illegible]	[illegible]	[illegible]	[illegible]	[illegible]	[illegible]	[illegible]	[illegible]	[illegible]	[illegible]
Curragh	[illegible]	[illegible]	[illegible]	[illegible]	[illegible]	[illegible]	[illegible]	[illegible]	[illegible]	[illegible]	[illegible]	[illegible]	[illegible]	[illegible]	[illegible]	[illegible]	[illegible]	[illegible]
Dublin	[illegible]	[illegible]	[illegible]	[illegible]	[illegible]	[illegible]	[illegible]	[illegible]	[illegible]	[illegible]	[illegible]	[illegible]	[illegible]	[illegible]	[illegible]	[illegible]	[illegible]	[illegible]
Galway	[illegible]	[illegible]	[illegible]	[illegible]	[illegible]	[illegible]	[illegible]	[illegible]	[illegible]	[illegible]	[illegible]	[illegible]	[illegible]	[illegible]	[illegible]	[illegible]	[illegible]	[illegible]
[illegible]	[illegible]	[illegible]	[illegible]	[illegible]	[illegible]	[illegible]	[illegible]	[illegible]	[illegible]	[illegible]	[illegible]	[illegible]	[illegible]	[illegible]	[illegible]	[illegible]	[illegible]	[illegible]
[illegible]	[illegible]	[illegible]	[illegible]	[illegible]	[illegible]	[illegible]	[illegible]	[illegible]	[illegible]	[illegible]	[illegible]	[illegible]	[illegible]	[illegible]	[illegible]	[illegible]	[illegible]	[illegible]
[illegible]	[illegible]	[illegible]	[illegible]	[illegible]	[illegible]	[illegible]	[illegible]	[illegible]	[illegible]	[illegible]	[illegible]	[illegible]	[illegible]	[illegible]	[illegible]	[illegible]	[illegible]	[illegible]
Longford	[illegible]	[illegible]	[illegible]	[illegible]	[illegible]	[illegible]	[illegible]	[illegible]	[illegible]	[illegible]	[illegible]	[illegible]	[illegible]	[illegible]	[illegible]	[illegible]	[illegible]	[illegible]
[illegible]	[illegible]	[illegible]	[illegible]	[illegible]	[illegible]	[illegible]	[illegible]	[illegible]	[illegible]	[illegible]	[illegible]	[illegible]	[illegible]	[illegible]	[illegible]	[illegible]	[illegible]	[illegible]
Maryborough	[illegible]	[illegible]	[illegible]	[illegible]	[illegible]	[illegible]	[illegible]	[illegible]	[illegible]	[illegible]	[illegible]	[illegible]	[illegible]	[illegible]	[illegible]	[illegible]	[illegible]	[illegible]
[illegible]	[illegible]	[illegible]	[illegible]	[illegible]	[illegible]	[illegible]	[illegible]	[illegible]	[illegible]	[illegible]	[illegible]	[illegible]	[illegible]	[illegible]	[illegible]	[illegible]	[illegible]	[illegible]
Mullingar	[illegible]	[illegible]	[illegible]	[illegible]	[illegible]	[illegible]	[illegible]	[illegible]	[illegible]	[illegible]	[illegible]	[illegible]	[illegible]	[illegible]	[illegible]	[illegible]	[illegible]	[illegible]
Naas	[illegible]	[illegible]	[illegible]	[illegible]	[illegible]	[illegible]	[illegible]	[illegible]	[illegible]	[illegible]	[illegible]	[illegible]	[illegible]	[illegible]	[illegible]	[illegible]	[illegible]	[illegible]
[illegible]	[illegible]	[illegible]	[illegible]	[illegible]	[illegible]	[illegible]	[illegible]	[illegible]	[illegible]	[illegible]	[illegible]	[illegible]	[illegible]	[illegible]	[illegible]	[illegible]	[illegible]	[illegible]
Newbridge	[illegible]	[illegible]	[illegible]	[illegible]	[illegible]	[illegible]	[illegible]	[illegible]	[illegible]	[illegible]	[illegible]	[illegible]	[illegible]	[illegible]	[illegible]	[illegible]	[illegible]	[illegible]
[illegible]	[illegible]	[illegible]	[illegible]	[illegible]	[illegible]	[illegible]	[illegible]	[illegible]	[illegible]	[illegible]	[illegible]	[illegible]	[illegible]	[illegible]	[illegible]	[illegible]	[illegible]	[illegible]
[illegible]	[illegible]	[illegible]	[illegible]	[illegible]	[illegible]	[illegible]	[illegible]	[illegible]	[illegible]	[illegible]	[illegible]	[illegible]	[illegible]	[illegible]	[illegible]	[illegible]	[illegible]	[illegible]
[illegible]	[illegible]	[illegible]	[illegible]	[illegible]	[illegible]	[illegible]	[illegible]	[illegible]	[illegible]	[illegible]	[illegible]	[illegible]	[illegible]	[illegible]	[illegible]	[illegible]	[illegible]	[illegible]
Sligo	[illegible]	[illegible]	[illegible]	[illegible]	[illegible]	[illegible]	[illegible]	[illegible]	[illegible]	[illegible]	[illegible]	[illegible]	[illegible]	[illegible]	[illegible]	[illegible]	[illegible]	[illegible]
[illegible]	[illegible]	[illegible]	[illegible]	[illegible]	[illegible]	[illegible]	[illegible]	[illegible]	[illegible]	[illegible]	[illegible]	[illegible]	[illegible]	[illegible]	[illegible]	[illegible]	[illegible]	[illegible]
[illegible]	[illegible]	[illegible]	[illegible]	[illegible]	[illegible]	[illegible]	[illegible]	[illegible]	[illegible]	[illegible]	[illegible]	[illegible]	[illegible]	[illegible]	[illegible]	[illegible]	[illegible]	[illegible]
Tullamore	[illegible]	[illegible]	[illegible]	[illegible]	[illegible]	[illegible]	[illegible]	[illegible]	[illegible]	[illegible]	[illegible]	[illegible]	[illegible]	[illegible]	[illegible]	[illegible]	[illegible]	[illegible]
[illegible]	[illegible]	[illegible]	[illegible]	[illegible]	[illegible]	[illegible]	[illegible]	[illegible]	[illegible]	[illegible]	[illegible]	[illegible]	[illegible]	[illegible]	[illegible]	[illegible]	[illegible]	[illegible]
Cork district—																		
[illegible]	[illegible]	[illegible]	[illegible]	[illegible]	[illegible]	[illegible]	[illegible]	[illegible]	[illegible]	[illegible]	[illegible]	[illegible]	[illegible]	[illegible]	[illegible]	[illegible]	[illegible]	[illegible]
[illegible]	[illegible]	[illegible]	[illegible]	[illegible]	[illegible]	[illegible]	[illegible]	[illegible]	[illegible]	[illegible]	[illegible]	[illegible]	[illegible]	[illegible]	[illegible]	[illegible]	[illegible]	[illegible]
[illegible]	[illegible]	[illegible]	[illegible]	[illegible]	[illegible]	[illegible]	[illegible]	[illegible]	[illegible]	[illegible]	[illegible]	[illegible]	[illegible]	[illegible]	[illegible]	[illegible]	[illegible]	[illegible]

[illegible]

Station.	[illegible] Meat, lb.	Bread, 4 lbs.	Milk, gallon.	Potatoes, cwt.	Oatmeal, cwt.	Hay, cwt.	Sugar, cwt.	Tea, lb.	Coffee, lb.	[illegible] Meat, lb.	Bread, 4 lbs.	Milk, gallon.	Potatoes, cwt.	Oats, cwt.	Hay, cwt.	Sugar, cwt.	Tea, lb.	Coffee, lb.
	d.	d.	s. d.	s. d.	£ s. d.	£ s. d.	£ s. d.	s. d.	s. d.	d.	d.	s. d.	s. d.	£ s. d.	£ s. d.	£ s. d.	s. d.	s. d.
Belfast Command—																		
Armagh	[illegible]	[illegible]	[illegible]	[illegible]	[illegible]	[illegible]	[illegible]	[illegible]	..	[illegible]	[illegible]	[illegible]	[illegible]	..	..	..	..	..
Ballyshannon	..	..	..	..	..	..	..	..	..	[illegible]	[illegible]	..	..	..	..	..	..	..
Belfast	[illegible]	[illegible]	[illegible]	[illegible]	[illegible]	[illegible]	[illegible]	[illegible]	..	[illegible]	[illegible]	[illegible]	[illegible]	[illegible]	[illegible]	[illegible]	[illegible]	..
Belturbet	[illegible]	[illegible]	[illegible]	[illegible]	[illegible]	[illegible]	[illegible]	[illegible]	..	[illegible]	[illegible]	..	..	..	..	..	..	..
Carrickfergus	..	[illegible]	..	..	..	..	..	..	..	[illegible]	[illegible]	..	..	..	..	..	..	..
Cavan	..	..	..	..	..	..	..	..	..	[illegible]	[illegible]	..	..	..	..	..	..	..
Drogheda	[illegible]	[illegible]	..	..	..	..	..	..	..	[illegible]	[illegible]	..	..	..	..	..	..	..
Dundalk	[illegible]	[illegible]	[illegible]	[illegible]	[illegible]	[illegible]	[illegible]	[illegible]	..	[illegible]	[illegible]	[illegible]	[illegible]	[illegible]	[illegible]	[illegible]	[illegible]	..
Enniskillen	[illegible]	[illegible]	[illegible]	[illegible]	[illegible]	[illegible]	[illegible]	[illegible]	..	[illegible]	[illegible]	[illegible]	[illegible]	[illegible]	[illegible]	[illegible]	[illegible]	..
Ports on Lough Foyle ..	..	[illegible]	..	..	..	..	..	..	..	[illegible]	[illegible]	..	..	..	..	..	..	..
Ports on Lough Swilly ..	[illegible]	[illegible]	..	..	..	..	..	..	..	[illegible]	[illegible]	..	..	..	..	..	..	..
[illegible]	..	..	..	..	..	..	..	..	..	..	..	..	..	..	..	..	..	..
Londonderry	[illegible]	[illegible]	[illegible]	[illegible]	[illegible]	[illegible]	[illegible]	[illegible]	..	[illegible]	[illegible]	[illegible]	[illegible]	[illegible]	[illegible]	[illegible]	[illegible]	..
Monaghan	[illegible]	[illegible]	..	..	..	..	..	..	..	[illegible]	[illegible]	..	..	..	..	..	..	..
Newry	[illegible]	[illegible]	[illegible]	[illegible]	[illegible]	[illegible]	[illegible]	[illegible]	..	[illegible]	[illegible]	[illegible]	[illegible]	[illegible]	[illegible]	[illegible]	[illegible]	..
[illegible]	[illegible]	[illegible]	..	..	..	..	..	..	..	[illegible]	[illegible]	..	..	..	..	..	..	..
Omagh	..	[illegible]	..	..	..	..	..	..	..	[illegible]	[illegible]	[illegible]	[illegible]	[illegible]	[illegible]	[illegible]	[illegible]	..

(Signed) J. LESLIE ROBERTSON, *acting for Commissary-General in Ireland.*

Dublin Castle, 8th September, [illegible]

(2.)—Return showing the Contract Prices of certain Articles of Diet in the undermentioned Prisons during the Years 1874 and 1883 respectively.

No.	Article.	Quality.	Rate of price.	[illegible] 1874.	[illegible] 1883.	[illegible] 1874.	[illegible] 1883.	Belfast. 1874.	Belfast. 1883.	Cork. 1874.	Cork. 1883.	[illegible] 1874.	[illegible] 1883.	Londonderry. 1874.	Londonderry. 1883.	[illegible] 1874.	[illegible] 1883.	Tralee. 1874.	Tralee. 1883.	[illegible] 1874.	[illegible] 1883.
1	Bread, white	[illegible]	[illegible]	[illegible]	[illegible]	[illegible]	[illegible]	[illegible]	[illegible]	[illegible]	[illegible]	[illegible]	[illegible]	[illegible]	[illegible]	[illegible]	[illegible]	[illegible]	[illegible]	[illegible]	[illegible]
2	Bread, brown	[illegible]	—	[illegible]	[illegible]	—	[illegible]	—	[illegible]	[illegible]	[illegible]	[illegible]	[illegible]	[illegible]	[illegible]	—	[illegible]	[illegible]	[illegible]	[illegible]	[illegible]
3	Oatmeal	[illegible]	Cwt.	[illegible]	[illegible]	[illegible]	[illegible]	..	[illegible]	[illegible]	[illegible]	[illegible]	[illegible]	[illegible]	[illegible]	[illegible]	[illegible]	—	[illegible]	[illegible]	[illegible]
4	New milk	[illegible]	Gallon	[illegible]	[illegible]	[illegible]	[illegible]	[illegible]	[illegible]	—	[illegible]	[illegible]	[illegible]	[illegible]	[illegible]	[illegible]	[illegible]	[illegible]	[illegible]	[illegible]	[illegible]
5	Tea	[illegible]	Lb.	—	[illegible]	[illegible]	[illegible]	—	[illegible]	—	[illegible]	—	[illegible]	—	[illegible]	—	[illegible]	—	[illegible]	—	[illegible]
6	Coffee	[illegible]	„	—	[illegible]	[illegible]	[illegible]	—	[illegible]	—	[illegible]	—	[illegible]	—	[illegible]	—	[illegible]	—	[illegible]	—	[illegible]
7	Sugar	[illegible]	Cwt.	—	[illegible]	[illegible]	[illegible]	—	[illegible]	—	[illegible]	—	[illegible]	—	[illegible]	—	[illegible]	—	[illegible]	—	[illegible]
8	Rice	[illegible]	„	—	[illegible]	[illegible]	[illegible]	—	[illegible]	—	[illegible]	—	[illegible]	—	[illegible]	[illegible]	[illegible]	..	[illegible]	—	[illegible]
9	Beef	[illegible]	Lb.	[illegible]	[illegible]	[illegible]	[illegible]	—	[illegible]	[illegible]	[illegible]	—	[illegible]	—	[illegible]	[illegible]	[illegible]	—	[illegible]	[illegible]	[illegible]
10	Mutton	[illegible]	„	[illegible]	[illegible]	[illegible]	[illegible]	—	[illegible]	[illegible]	[illegible]	—	[illegible]	—	[illegible]	[illegible]	[illegible]	—	[illegible]	[illegible]	[illegible]
11	Potatoes	[illegible]	Cwt.	[illegible]	[illegible]	[illegible]	[illegible]	—	[illegible]	[illegible]	[illegible]	[illegible]	[illegible]	[illegible]	[illegible]	[illegible]	[illegible]	[illegible]	[illegible]	[illegible]	[illegible]

(Signed) GEO. SPRUDE, *Superintendent of Stores.*

General Prisons Board, Dublin Castle, September 8, 1883.

(3.)—Summary of Commissariat and Prisons Board Returns, showing Average Contract Prices of Provisions in 1874 and 1883.

		1874. Average for Local and Convict Prisons in Dublin.	1874. Average for Seven Provincial Prisons in Ireland.	1874. Commissariat Average for about Sixty Towns in Ireland.	1883. Average for Local and Convict Prisons in Dublin.	1883. Average for Seven Provincial Prisons in Ireland.	1883. Commissariat Average for about Sixty Towns in Ireland.
		s. d.	s. d.	s. d.	s. d.	s. d.	s. d.
Beef	Per lb.	[illegible]	[illegible]	..	[illegible]	[illegible]	..
Mutton	„	[illegible]	[illegible]	..	[illegible]	[illegible]	..
"Meat"	„	..	..	[illegible]	..	..	[illegible]
Bread	Per 4lb.	[illegible]	[illegible]	[illegible]	[illegible]	[illegible]	[illegible]
Milk	Per gallon	[illegible]	[illegible]	[illegible]	[illegible]	[illegible]	[illegible]
Potatoes	Per cwt.	[illegible]	[illegible]	[illegible]	[illegible]	[illegible]	[illegible]
Oatmeal	„	[illegible]	[illegible]	[illegible]	[illegible]	[illegible]	[illegible]
Rice	„	[illegible]	[illegible]	[illegible]	[illegible]	[illegible]	[illegible]
Sugar	„	[illegible]	..	[illegible]	[illegible]	[illegible]	[illegible]
Tea	Per lb.	[illegible]	..	[illegible]	[illegible]	[illegible]	[illegible]
Coffee	„	[illegible]	..	[illegible]	[illegible]	[illegible]	..

Appendix VI.

THE Dublin Artisans' Dwellings Company (Limited) was established in the year 1876, under the provisions of "The Companies Act, 1862," with an original capital of 50,000*l*., subsequently increased to 100,000*l*., divided into shares of 10*l* each.

The leading objects for which the Company was established were:—

1. The acquisition of lands, houses, and other property, within the city and county of Dublin.
2. The erection of dwellings or places of residence for artisans and others.
3. The acquisition of existing buildings, and their adaptation as dwellings for artisans and others.
4. The letting of the property so acquired.

The Company was started on strictly commercial principles, but with the intention and belief, which experience has confirmed, that beneficent results would follow its action. The rate of dividend is limited to 5 per cent.; 4 per cent. has been regularly paid up to the present, the preliminary expenses have been cleared off, and a reserve fund has been established. The following Table will show in detail the progress and the present position of the Company:—

Locality.	Number of Houses or Tenements.	Number of Rooms and particulars of Rents charged in each locality						Number of Occupants …	Cost of land and of Buildings.
		One Room.	Two Rooms.	Three Rooms.	Four Rooms.	Five Rooms.	Six Rooms.		
Buckingham Street	[illegible]	[illegible]	[illegible]	[illegible]	[illegible]	[illegible]	[illegible]	[illegible]	[illegible]
[illegible]	[illegible]	[illegible]	[illegible]	[illegible]	[illegible]	[illegible]	[illegible]	[illegible]	[illegible]
[illegible]	[illegible]	[illegible]	[illegible]	[illegible]	[illegible]	[illegible]	[illegible]	[illegible]	[illegible]
[illegible]	[illegible]	[illegible]	[illegible]	[illegible]	[illegible]	[illegible]	[illegible]	[illegible]	[illegible]
The Coombe	[illegible]	[illegible]	[illegible]	[illegible]	[illegible]	[illegible]	[illegible]	[illegible]	[illegible]

Of the five areas mentioned in the preceding Table, four were acquired from private individuals, and one (The Coombe) from the Corporation of Dublin, who, under the provisions of the Artisans' Dwellings Act, are empowered to clear unhealthy areas, for the improvement of the dwellings of the poorer classes, and to dispose of such areas, when cleared, for the purpose of the erection of suitable residences in substitution for those displaced.

The capital expenditure of the Company up to the present time amounts to 63,770*l*., which includes 7,840*l* borrowed from the Board of Public Works in Ireland, repayable, by half-yearly instalments, within a period of forty years, at a rate of 4 per cent. per annum interest.

The residences provided by the Company are in request; the rate of mortality which prevails contrasts most favourably with that of Dublin, and more especially so with the localities in which are situated the dwellings of the humbler classes.

The rents charged, which in proportion are lower than those paid for the wretched accommodation which existed previously, are regularly paid; there is a visible improvement in the manner and appearance of the inhabitants, and the sites adjoining begin to show progress in order and civilization—results fairly attributable to example.

An extension of the operations of the Artisans' Dwellings Company is urgently required. There are numerous sites which, in the interests of civilization and sanitation, are capable of being made available for the purpose. Negotiations for purchase of three, comprising an area of some 13 acres, are in progress.

The subject of the residences of the married constables of the Metropolitan Police is likely to receive the attention of the Committee now investigating certain complaints made by the force, and it deserves consideration whether the Dublin Artisans' Dwellings Company may not be availed of as an existing organization capable of supplying a requirement in the direction.

The centres in which the greatest requirement for improved accommodation exists are those in which, generally stated, law and order least prevail. The constable when off duty, although divested of his uniform and baton, is nevertheless a symbol of respectability and order, and his presence has a moral effect desirable to be secured. It has been justly observed that a policeman in his private residence forms the centre of a peaceful nucleus.

One of the most important functions of a constable is that he should know the greatest number of people in the locality in which he resides, and that he should, in fact, possess as much as possible of the knowledge qualifying him to discharge detective duty.

The objects of the Artisans' Dwellings Company bring it within the principle which sanctions the advance of public money for the general good. By enabling it to obtain money for the purposes of the acquisition of sites and the erection of residences on the most favourable terms upon which money is advanced by Government, for any public purposes, its sphere of usefulness would be extended, and in return it could secure, under suitable arrangements, a stipulated amount of accommodation at a rental to be agreed on. Provision could be made under which, out of any profit to be derived by the Company from the advance of money at the low rate of interest, a portion could be set aside until an adequate amount had accumulated to meet depreciation by wear and tear, and thus prevent the possibility of pecuniary loss in respect of the advances.

(Signed) E. O. ARMSTRONG,

Director of the Dublin Artisans' Dwellings Company, Limited.

Dublin, December 1882.

Appendix VII.

RATES OF WAGES, 1882.

(1.)—*Wages paid by the Alliance Gas Company of Dublin.*

	s.	d.	
Stokers ..	[illegible]	[illegible]	a-day, seven days per week.
Assistant stokers	[illegible]	[illegible]	„ „
Barrow-men	[illegible]	[illegible]	„ „
Foremen ..	[illegible]	[illegible]	„ „
Tallymen	[illegible]	[illegible]	„ „
Scrapers ..	[illegible]	[illegible]	„ „
Coal-heavers	[illegible]	[illegible]	„ „
Gate-porters	[illegible]	[illegible]	„ „
Cabin-boys	[illegible]	[illegible]	a-day, six days per week.
Labourers	[illegible]	[illegible]	„ „
Tradesmen	[illegible]	[illegible]	to [illegible] per week of [illegible] days.

Note.—The stokers work in turn on alternate nights.
The working hours are from 6 a.m. to 6 p.m., with one hour allowed for breakfast and one hour for dinner. On Saturdays the hours are from 6 a.m. to 4 p.m.

(2.)—*Wages paid by Midland Great Western Railway of Ireland.*

	s.	d.	
Policemen ..	17	6	a-week, with clothing.
Porters ..	13 to 17	0	„ „

(With, in most cases, cottages or apartments, rented at 2s. a-week).

(3.)—*Great Southern and Western Railway of Ireland.*

	£	s.	d.	
Inspectors ..	1	15	0	per week.
Watchmen ..	0	17 to 15	0	„
Gangers .. (With a gratuity at Christmas of [illegible])	0	17	0	„
Pilgmen .. (With a gratuity at Christmas of [illegible])	0	14	0	„
Guards (passengers), [illegible] a-week, and after five years (With an allowance of [illegible] a-week for lodgings).	1	[illegible]	0	„
Guards (goods), [illegible] a-week, and after five years (With [illegible] a-week for lodgings).	1	1	0	„
Signalmen, [illegible] a-week; after three years, [illegible]; and after five years	1	1	0	„
Porters (goods department)	0	15	0	„
Porters (coaching department)	0	14	0	„

(4.)—*London and North Western Railway.*

	£	s.	d.		£	s.	d.	
Guards ..	1	[illegible]	0	to	[illegible]	[illegible]	0	per week.
Porters ..	0	[illegible]	0	–	1	[illegible]	0	„
Signalmen ..	1	0	0	–	1	10	0	„

Note.—The ordinary hours of labour are sixty-six per week. No lodgings are provided.

(5.)—*Dublin Port and Docks Board.*

	£	s.	d.	
Superintendent of harbour police ..	1	10	0	per week.
Sergeant	1	1	0	„
Constables—				
1st Class	1	0	0	„
2nd Class	0	17	0	„

Note.—They are supplied with uniform, and are paid for one day extra when on duty on Sunday, and the same when occasionally placed on special night duty.

(6.)—*Dublin Corporation Fire Brigade.*

Firemen—	£	s.	d.	
1st Class	[illegible]	[illegible]	[illegible]	per week.
2nd Class	[illegible]	[illegible]	[illegible]	"
3rd Class	[illegible]	[illegible]	[illegible]	"
4th Class	[illegible]	[illegible]	[illegible]	"

(Promotion after one year in each class. Uniform, clothing, and lodgings are provided.)

(7.)—*Dublin United Tramways Company.*

	£	s.	d.	
Conductors, 3s. to 3s. 6d. per day	[illegible]	[illegible]	[illegible]	per week.
Drivers, 3s. 6d. to 4s. per day	[illegible]	[illegible]	[illegible]	"
Timekeepers	[illegible] to [illegible]	[illegible]	[illegible]	"
Traffic Inspectors	[illegible]	[illegible]	[illegible]	"

Note.—Drivers and conductors are allowed every tenth day off, and receive half-pay for that day. Timekeepers have every tenth day, and receive full pay.

(8.)—*Building Trades.*

(Copy.)

Meade and Son, Builders, Dublin, December 3, 1882.

Dear Sir,

The following are the rates of wages of the different classes of workmen in the building trades.

Yours faithfully,

(Signed) JOSEPH MEADE.

F. W. D. Mitchell, Esq., Secretary to the
Dublin Metropolitan Police Committee of Inquiry.

	Per Day.	Per Week.
	s. d.	s. d.
Carpenters	[illegible]	[illegible]
Bricklayers	[illegible]	[illegible]
Stone cutters	[illegible]	[illegible]
Plasterers	[illegible]	[illegible]
Sawyers	[illegible]	[illegible]
Plumbers	[illegible]	[illegible]
Painters	[illegible]	[illegible]
Labourers	[illegible]	[illegible]

Appendix VIII.

SCALES OF PENSION.

(1.)—London Metropolitan Police.

Scale of Pensions granted to Police who joined the Service prior to 1862.

All pensions for life.

After 15 years' service	[illegible] of salary.
„ 20 „	[illegible] „
„ 21 „	[illegible] „
„ 22 „	[illegible] „
„ 23 „	[illegible] „
„ 24 „	[illegible] „

No pension to exceed [illegible] of full pay except for injury on duty.

Scale of Pensions granted to Police who have joined since 17th March, 1863.

All pensions for life.

After 15 years' service	[illegible] of pay.
For each additional year from 15 to 20 years	[illegible] „
After 20 years' service	[illegible] „
For each additional year completed, from 20 to 25 years	[illegible] „
After 25 years' service	[illegible] „
For each year completed, from 25 to 28 years	[illegible] „
After 28 years' service, the maximum pension of [illegible] or	[illegible] „

(2.)—Dublin Metropolitan Police.

1. For men appointed before July [illegible], [illegible], [illegible] & [illegible] Vict., cap. [illegible]—

For 15 to 20 years' service	[illegible] of pay.
For over 20 „	Full pay.*

* A pension not exceeding full pay [illegible] pension, a man was required to serve [illegible] years for full pay.

2. For men appointed after July [illegible], [illegible], [illegible] & [illegible] Vict., cap. [illegible]—

For 15 and under 20 years' service	[illegible] pay.
„ 20 „ 25 „	[illegible] „
„ 25 „ 30 „	[illegible] „
„ 30 years and upwards	Full pay.

3. For men appointed after August [illegible], [illegible], [illegible] & [illegible] Vict., cap. [illegible]—

For 15 years' service	[illegible] of pay
For every additional year from 15 to 30 years	[illegible] „
For 30 years completed, the maximum pension of	[illegible] „

(3.)—Scale of Pension proposed for the English and Scotch Police Forces in the Bill introduced into Parliament in 1882.

After 15 years' service completed	[illegible] of pay.
For each year from 15 to 20 years	[illegible] „
After 20 years' service completed	[illegible] „
For each year, from 20 to 25 years	[illegible] „
After 25 years' service completed	[illegible] „
For each year, from 25 to 28 years	[illegible] „
After 28 years' service, the maximum pension of [illegible] or	[illegible] „

Appendix IX.

MEMORANDA RELATING TO LONDON METROPOLITAN POLICE.

(1.)—Accommodation in Barracks for Married Men.

Extract from a Letter to Mr. Holmes from Sir E. Y. W. Henderson, K.C.B., Commissioner of the London Metropolitan Police.

We have only 359 married men living in quarters, and 7,305 in private lodgings, the former, no doubt, have an advantage, as their rent is less than what they would have to pay elsewhere. The Police Fund loses considerably on those quarters; but it is money well spent, and I should gladly see the system greatly extended. The great difficulty in the interior divisions is that of land, which is is very difficult to get, and the prices asked enormous. No doubt the married men are heavily handicapped.

Replies given by Chief Inspector Cutbush, of the London Metropolitan Police, to Questions sent him by the Committee.

Q. 1. What would you say is the average weekly rent paid by the married men for their lodgings when they are not accommodated in the blocks of buildings?—*A.* The average weekly rent paid by each rank throughout the service is as follows:—Inspectors, 10s. 6d.; sergeants, 7s.; constables, 6s.; with a tendency to increase.

Q. 2. Would this rent be in excess of the rent he would have to pay for the same number of rooms in the blocks of buildings?—*A.* Yes. The following scale being the highest rate paid by each rank occupying married men's quarters:—Inspectors, 5s. 6d. per week; sergeants, 4s per week; constables, 3s. per week; for which one sitting-room, two bed-rooms, with kitchen or scullery are provided. Any married man desiring an extra room is charged for same at the rate of 6d. per week for every 50 superficial feet.

Q. 3. *If a married man takes a house, is he at liberty to let part of it to lodgers?*—*A.* Yes.

Q. 4. What percentage of the force are married, approximately?—*A.* About 73 per cent. of the whole force are married.

Q. 5. What percentage of the married men are accommodated in blocks of buildings?—*A.* About 31 per cent. of the married men are accommodated in police quarters.

(Signed) C. H. CUTBUSH, *Chief Inspector.*

(2.)—Fines.

Memorandum by District Superintendent Walker.

The Assistant Commissioners limit their fines to 20s., or, in cases of serious misconduct, reducing rank, or placing upon a lower or the lowest class, such as from 1st to 3rd.

(Signed) R. WALKER, *District Superintendent.*

(3.)—Detective Division.

Memorandum by Chief Superintendent Williamson.

December 6, 1882.

The organisation of the detective force of the London Metropolitan Police consists of a Chief Superintendent and a certain number of inspectors at head-quarters at Scotland Yard. The inspectors are divided into chiefs and first and second class.

In the police divisions there are attached to each a local inspector, and so many sergeants and patrol police constables as are considered necessary for the requirements of the district in which they are stationed.

The sergeants are divided into first, second, and third class, and when they obtain the second-class rank their pay increases by annual increments until the maximum of each rank is reached. The whole of the department is under the control of the Director of Criminal Investigations, and necessarily form one department.

A Return of the number of each rank, and their pay, is attached.

The supervision of hackney carriages forms no part of detective duties in London.

The "local detectives" are as much a part of the detective force as the men at Scotland Yard.

FRED. WILLIAMSON,
Chief Superintendent.

(4)—Mess Expenses in Barracks.

Memorandum by District Superintendent Walker

The caterer is a policeman, who takes the duty in turn without payment. Bedmaking, cleaning and coal are paid for by the Government, and covered by the 1s. a-week deducted for lodging.

The cook's services and cooking utensils cost each man 1s 3d. a-week; the average cost of mess besides is 5s 3d., making, with 1s. for lodging, a total payment of 7s. a-week for barrack charges.

The town mess is cheaper than the suburban, on account of the greater number of men.

(Signed) R. WALKER, *District Superintendent.*

Appendix X.

Extracts from the Evidence given by Colonel C. A. Cobbe, Inspector of Constabulary for the Eastern Counties, Midland and North-Western District of England, before the Royal Irish Constabulary Commission of Inquiry, 188[illegible].

(1.) Pay.

8306. Can you tell us whether the men in the force are able to save money?—No. I do not think they can in the lower grades.

8307. When you say the lower grades, what ranks do you mean?—Constables and sergeants.

8308. Do they make their inability to save money a ground of complaint?—No.

8309. How do you account for their not attempting to save money?—A happy-go-lucky disposition. They do not think of it, like many of us. For the first four or five years they do not think much of pensions, but it is the prospect afterwards of pension, when they begin to settle down and think a bit, that relieves their minds; and pension, after all, is a sort of deferred pay.

8310. *Mr. Holmes.*—When you say that constables as a rule do not save, do you allude to constables in receipt of such high weekly wages as 28s. and 29s.?—Yes.

8311. And you say that sergeants do not save either?—A few sergeants here and there do, who have got a little private money of their own, and add to it. I have known one or two constables who saved money, but they starved themselves.

(2.) Lodgings of Married and Single Men, &c.

7929. *Chairman.*—I now come to allowances of another kind. Is there any allowance made to the constabulary of your district for the purpose of lodging?—A great number of the head constables are provided with residences at the police offices.

7930. The head constable being what answers for the purposes of town duty to the chief constable in the county?—Yes, the chief officer of police.

7931. But for the inspectors, sergeants, and constables, is it customary to make any allowance for lodging?—No. There is no such thing as an allowance with regard to the boroughs, unless the house happens to be there.

7932. Are the men ever provided with lodgings in barracks in the boroughs?—Yes.

7933. Generally, or only in some cases?—It is very exceptional. It is the case in Birmingham, Wolverhampton, and a few other places.

7934. When that provision is made by Birmingham, Wolverhampton, and some other places, is there a corresponding deduction made from their pay in respect of it?—The men pay 1s. a-week for the lodging allowance. That is a deduction, but they get for it lodging, clean sheets, and washing, as an equivalent.

7935. *Mr. Harrel.*—Does it include cooking and the providing of mess materials?—I am not sure of that. I think the mess is separate.

7936. *Mr. Holmes.*—When the men are provided with accommodation in barrack, are they also provided with fuel and light?—Yes, for that money. They have gas in barrack.

7937. In Birmingham are most of the men accommodated in barrack?—All the single men are, to the number of about 200. I think there are about thirty men, more or less, in each of the six stations.

7938. *Chairman.*—As a rule, then, do the married men in Birmingham live out of barrack?—Yes.

7939. *Mr. Holmes.*—Are there any men not accommodated in barrack?—Not in the town.

7940. *Chairman.*—Married men living outside barrack in Birmingham get no allowance for lodgings corresponding to the actual provision made for their single comrades?—Nothing at all.

7941. Then he gets nothing?—He is free from barrack life, and has his own house. Boroughs will not entertain the question of paying extra rent like the counties.

7942. Passing to the counties, tell us what provision, if any, is made for lodging accommodation in counties?—In counties, at every station-house one or two officers live.

7943. Do the officers pay anything for the accommodation they get there?—Yes, on a fixed scale for grade.

7944. The fixed scale of the particular grade to which they belong?—Yes.

7945. *Mr. Harrel.*—What is a station-house?—Where there are cells.

7946. *Mr. Holmes.*—And where charges are taken?—Yes; and generally where there is a petty sessions town.

7947. *Chairman.*—Are those men who so reside in the station married men?—The officer is generally a married man. There is always a married man in the station-house.

7948. Take the men who do not reside in the barrack, but outside, what allowance is made for them?—In some counties all rent above [illegible] is paid by the county, but the house must be taken with the sanction of the chief constable.

7949. Above 2s. a-week ?—Yes.

7950. It is, perhaps, a very difficult question to answer: What is the average cost of lodgings of the unmarried constables in your district ?—2s. 6d. per week for lodgings in a village, and 1s. more for washing.

7951. *Mr. Herral*.—Then, in point of fact, for lodging alone the county would only contribute 6d. of the 2s. 6d. ?—I was talking of single men; but where the county pays the excess of 2s., it is in the case of a house taken for a married constable.

7952. *Chairman*.—Is this allowance of money paid over 2s. confined either theoretically or practically to the case of married constables living outside ?—Yes; to married men.

7953. And single men do not get it if they have a house ?—Single men do not get it at all. How can they ? They only pay 1s. for barrack accommodation.

7954. *Mr. Herral*.—Then the instance you gave us of 2s. 6d. a-week paid by a single man is all out of his own pocket ?—It is out of his own pocket, but he gets cooking done. If he lives in the barrack room belonging to a station in the county he pays 1s., but living as a single man he pays 2s. 6d., for which he gets a lot of advantages in the way of housekeeping.

7955. But the single man gets no allowance for it ?—No.

7956. The married man gets anything he pays in excess of 2s. ?—In some counties. There are no coals.

7957. *Chairman*.—Does the allowance paid over the 2s. in the case of married men extend to the majority of the counties in your district ?—It exists in many, Leicester and some others. They are considerate, generally speaking, about it. You want a good man down at a place. You take him from a quiet place and send him to this, and he is a loser, having perhaps to pay a heavy rent. So it is necessary to do something of that sort. I think the system exists in almost all the counties, but I should not like to state that it does.

7958. *Mr. Holman*.—Take the case of a man who pays 5s. a-week; would the county pay the difference ?—Oh, yes.

7959. Then, in point of fact, you assume that any man in the force, whether married or single, should at least pay 2s. a-week for his lodgings, but that if he has to pay more, whether married or single, he will receive the difference from the county ?—The county will pay, but we should never press a single man for more than 1s., which is as much as he ought to pay. Then 2s. for the married man, 2s. 6d. for a sergeant, and 3s. for an inspector. You cannot send a man to a place and have him out of pocket by it.

7960. Do any such cases arise of single men being sent to places where an allowance has to be made for lodgings ?—No.

7961. *Chairman*.—Are there any other allowances ?—The chief officer or head constable of the borough gets coals and gas sometimes.

7971. Are the separate police establishments of those towns more highly paid than those of the counties in which they are situated ?—Generally. In the counties sometimes there is an allowance made for high rent. In the towns there is none, and the men have to pay their rent, which is higher than in the counties.

7972. *Mr. Holman*.—Practically, does it come to this, that the higher rate given in the towns is to compensate the men for the absence of lodging allowance ?—Yes; rents are higher. In many of the counties—it is not universally the case—when the rent is above 2s. a-week the county will pay out of the rates the difference beyond 2s. In the boroughs there is never such a thing known.

7973. *Chairman*.—Do you think the difference of pay given in the towns over the rates of pay in the country was intended to meet that ?—Not entirely; but it is a matter of great consideration no doubt.

7974. *Mr. Holman*.—Suppose the counties adopted the Government scale of pay, would they continue to pay the lodging allowance where the rent was over 2s. ?—Oh, yes.

7975. It would come to this, that where a town adopted the Government scale, a man in the town would be worse paid than in the county, because in the county he would be getting a lodging allowance over and above 2s. ?—The county of Cambridge has adopted one of these scales, 21s. 7d.; but in the borough of Cambridge, where they have higher rents, the pay begins at 23s. 7d., and goes up to 26s. 8½d.

7976. *Chairman*.—Take the case of a member of the county constabulary, where he has to get lodgings in a town, he gets whatever is over 2s. ?—The excess of 2s. in his rent; but the expense of living is not so much in towns. It is more than that in certain places in the counties where it is desirable to have a policeman, and you cannot have him there unless you pay for the house. But the house is taken with the approval of the chief constable. This is the rule in many counties. I can ascertain all if you wish. In boroughs no such arrangement is made, and consequently rent is a consideration in rates of pay.

(3.) Deductions for Sickness and for Superannuation.

7962. Be kind enough to tell us whether there are any deductions made from the pay ?—From the pay of everyone there is a deduction of 2½ per cent. for the superannuation fund. The rules as to sickness are very irregular.

7963. *Mr. Holman*.—Is that deduction contemplated in the Bill before Parliament ?—It is, and it is in force now.

7964. *Chairman*.—You were proceeding to speak about the rules as to sickness ?—The custom with regard to sickness is varied. In some places a small subscription is paid by the men to a fund.

7965. They pay in sickness and health ?—Right through, like a club.

7966. Is that a voluntary proceeding on the part of the men, or is it under regulations?—It is done voluntarily.

7967. Then the authorities do not provide a man with medical assistance?—No. In most cases they do, but where they do not this has been done by the men themselves.

7968. Is the tendency to provide them with a medical attendant?—Yes.

7969. *Mr. Harrel.*—And without deduction?—Yes. They sometimes stop 1s a-day pay from a man when he is sick; but in England we have sick clubs, and almost every man in the borough belongs to those clubs. It is a very good provision if he becomes sick, for his pay is, say, 3s a day, and he gets 2s. out of that, or 12s. a-week for being sick, besides the allowance from his sick-club. He is well off for being sick, but they keep a great watch on that.

7970. *Chairman.*—You say they stop 1s a-day. Do you mean the authorities stop it?—Yes, and that goes to the superannuation fund.

7971. That is not turned to the purpose of curing him?—No.

7972. *Mr. Harrel.*—And where that rule is enforced, is the pay stopped every day a man is sick?—Yes.

7973. Or is it after a certain interval elapses?—In a case like that it is very much discretionary with the authorities. There is no fixed rule applying to all forces alike, but they have the power of doing it.

7974. *Chairman.*—Is that power by local arrangement or by Act of Parliament?—The Act says a provision for superannuation is to be made by stoppages from men during sickness.

7975. Is there any definite period of sickness after which the authorities think it necessary to raise the question of the fitness of the continuance of a man in the force?—No.

7976. Suppose a man is sick for six months, do they begin to consider whether he is fit to remain in the force?—If the report of the medical officer is of a nature that his illness is going to be permanent, then his case is brought forward.

7977. *Mr. Holmes.*—Take the case of a man who has contracted serious illness in the discharge of his duty—for instance, small-pox—would the deduction be made?—Not at all, if there is the least excuse. There is the greatest liberality about it if there is the least excuse in the world.

7978. It is only to prevent malingering that the stoppage is made?—That is it.

---

(4) Wives' Industries and Trades.

8088. Has he a right to avail himself of his leisure time, or of the sixteen hours you have spoken of, for any industry?—No constable, by Act of Parliament, is allowed to follow another pursuit for hire or gain.

8089. Is he allowed to cultivate a garden?—We do not object.

8090. Is he allowed to keep a pig?—It is a matter in the chief constable's discretion. We do not allow pigs at a police-station, but we do not object in the case of a constable with a cottage.

8091. If he be a married man, are there any regulations controlling the occupation of his wife?—None.

8092. As a rule, do the wives of the men employ themselves as laundresses, or for any other purpose?—Not much.

8093. They confine themselves to their domestic duties?—Yes.

8094. *Mr. Holmes.*—Is the wife of a constable allowed to keep a shop?—It is a questionable point. I would not allow it.

8095. *Mr. Harrel.*—In fact, you would not allow the wife of a constable to engage in any occupation which would bring her on such terms with the general public as might influence her husband in the discharge of his duty?—I would not. I think my feeling would be that it ties a man too much to the place in case you want to move him.

8096. *Mr. Holmes.*—Then, it is your opinion that the rule prohibiting a constable from keeping a shop is not for the purpose of preventing his having too close relations with the people of the locality, but so as to admit of his being moved about readily, and that he may not become too attached to the district?—A little bit of both—partly both.

8097. I want to know whether the reason is to prevent contact with the people?—So far as we have gone yet, it is not to prevent contact with the people; it is more to keep them independent altogether.

8098. You say, then, the reason is this, that you might wish to move a man from one district to another. If he kept a shop, he would be, of course, loth to leave; and it was more on that account the rule was made than to prevent his having too intimate relations with the people?—Yes.

(5.) Gratuities received from the Public.

8163. *Chairman.*—Now, please, pass to the extraordinary duties of the town policeman?—Where constables are wanted for theatres, shows, and things of that sort, there is an allowance of about 6d. an hour made. This is generally given to a tired policeman, that is to say, a man who has done his eight hours, so that his work shall not be thrown upon the other men.

8164. *Mr. Harrel.*—How are these men selected?—By the direction of the superintendent. He selects the most suitable men.

8165. In point of fact, it is during the period of a man's resting hours he is able to earn this 6d. an hour?—Yes. There is also a little money allowed for what is called "knocking" in the morning. That gives a benefit to the man. The local authorities allow it.

8166. Is that a general allowance all over your district?—It is limited to large towns. The "awaking" allowance is only in the large towns.

8167. Each man makes his bargain with the person he awakes as to what gratuity he gets?—It is a half-penny a-morning, or a half-penny a-week. I am not sure.

8168. Is that allowance earned to any great extent by the force in large towns?—It helps very considerably some of the men in Birmingham.

8169. That is confined to the working classes?—Yes.

8170. *Mr. Holmes.*—About how much would it add to a constable's weekly pay?—About 2s. or 3s. a-week.

8171. Would that apply to a great number of the force?—No, only to a picked lot. It is not always satisfactory, as producing a little favouritism.

8172. *Chairman.*—With whom does the selection rest?—With the officer of a division, not of a beat. He is put on the beat and has the benefit of awaking. It is a little matter of favouritism, but you cannot help that.

8173. We have been spoken to about constables in England getting what are called "tips" for various things besides "awaking." I suppose that system is forbidden by the regulations?—They are obliged to report those things in the county forces. I do not think the rule is so strong in the towns, but in the county forces they insist upon always reporting such a thing, and the chief constable says either "Yes" or "No" whether the man may keep it.

8174. But is there a system of gratuities common in the county forces?—No.

8175. What class do these gratuities come from?—From gentlemen chiefly.

8176. *Mr. Holmes.*—Under what circumstances are gratuities given?—For instance, finding a dog and taking it home to its master; or, if a policeman is employed by a gentleman, say, at an auction, the gentleman would probably give him a small present, and if he did not, the man would be entitled to certain extra pay from his own authorities, and the bill sent to the gentleman.

8177. *Mr. Harrel.*—When a policeman receives a gratuity is he obliged to make a report of it?—Yes.

8178. Can he receive it without permission?—No.

8179. Then he is obliged to obtain permission before he can receive it?—Before he can hold it.

8180. He receives it subject to permission?—Yes.

8180*. *Mr. Holmes.*—Are we to understand, then, that the policemen in England, as a rule, add somewhat to their recognised incomes from other sources?—No.

8181. Not as a rule?—No. You cannot call that adding to their income for the special duty I have mentioned, it is all expended in the allowance. With regard to "tips" and gratuities, they are so very trifling. I suppose there are not ten men who get 1s. a-year.

8182. You say there are not ten men who get 1s. a-year; do you mean ten men in your whole district?—In my whole district. Indeed, we set our faces very strongly against such a system, and there is no reason to believe it is carried to any great extent.

8183. *Chairman.*—Are there any other duties in towns you wish to refer to; church duties?—None.

(5.) Recruits.

8184. Will you tell us, please, from what rank of life, as a rule, the constables are taken in your district?—Generally from the agricultural.

8185. In the towns, do they come at all from the artisan class?—Yes, but not to any very great extent.

8186. Where they do come from the town, do they come from the labouring classes of the town, or the skilled artisan classes, as a rule?—From both. They come from all sorts.

8187. I believe there does not exist to the same extent in the midland counties in England that there does in Ireland the class of peasant farmers?—I think not. There are a great number of the police who had been farm bailiffs, and they are very good men, too.

8188. But not many come from the farming class?—The men are farmers' sons, some.

8189. Farmers' sons?—Yes. The ones are farm bailiffs. A farm bailiff is the headman; he is really a farmer, and educated.

8190. *Mr. Holmes.*—Having regard to the high wages given for skilled labour, you get very few recruits from that skilled class?—Comparatively we do. We prefer the agricultural classes. I would say eight-tenths of the force were of the agricultural class.

8191. In point of education and intelligence, what are the characteristics of the force?—They are very well educated indeed. They must all read and write, and I am surprised sometimes to see how well they can do so. We do not take any who cannot read and write.

8192. But apart from their knowledge of reading and writing, would you say, as a rule, they are intelligent men?—Generally they are. Every now and then you come across a man who may appear somewhat less intelligent than others, but he works round.

8224. *Mr. Harrel.*—On the subject of recruits and recruiting, what form is a man obliged to go through before being received as a probationer into a police force?—On applying for admission, a paper is sent from the chief constable to the candidate, who has to fill up answers to a number of questions, and these are to be certified by a number of resident people who have known his character for the last five years of his life. There is a medical certificate at the bottom of that, and then the man's own signature that it is correct. He is then called upon to join or not, according to the vacancies there may be.

8225. Is there any difficulty in obtaining recruits for the different forces in your district at present?—Not at present. At times there has been very great difficulty.

8226. Is there any standard as to height and chest measurement?—The rules laid down by the

Secretary of State require that the man shall not be less than 5 ft. 7 in. in height. As a rule we do not take men of less than 5 ft. 6 in. in height, and 36 in. chest.

8177. Is there any means by which candidates of the several forces are registered so as to be called when wanted?—Yes; there are plenty of candidates at present, but if a candidate be not taken on soon he seeks employ elsewhere.

8178. At present, every man who wished to join one of those police forces might not be able to do so until after a considerable interval of time?—For a selected force he might have to wait, but we could get him appointed in some force if he wished.

(7.) Marriage, Permanence &c.

8193. *Chairman.*—Passing from that, are there any regulations limiting the right to marry in the force?—No.

8194. Do you take married men as recruits into the force?—We take them in preference to single men in the counties.

8195. Are there any rules in large and highly organized forces like the Birmingham town force with reference to restriction of marriage?—Only to getting a certain number of single men in to fill up the barracks. There are large barracks for twenty or twenty-five men.

8196. That is to say, you will place some limit to the number of married men you take in as recruits?—Yes.

8197. *Mr. Holms.*—When you say you prefer married men in the counties, is that because they are likely to remain in the force?—Yes; and they are better men, more competent, and generally a little older.

8198. *Chairman.*—Do you find men who, in consequence of the size of their family, are unable to live on their pay, leave the force?—No. They cling to it. The larger the family the more they cling to the force.

8199. Speaking first for the rural, and afterwards, if necessary, for the town districts, tell us at what age the English policeman generally marries?—I could not give you a definite answer. Some come in at 22 and 23, and others hang on to 30, and they marry at those ages.

8200. Is it a usual thing to find a policeman unmarried at any particular age?—No; they are generally married.

(8.) Fines and Punishments.

8210. Passing from that, will you be kind enough to tell us about punishments—for what men are punished, by what authority, and how they are punished?—In counties the chief constable has the power of punishing the men up to a certain amount, which is limited by Statute. In towns the Watch Committee have the power.

8211. *Mr. Holms.*—When you say limited by Statute, to what Act do you refer?—We have only four or five Acts of Parliament that concern us. It is the Act of 1859 which regulates the scale of punishment.

8212. *Chairman.*—In the county the chief constable, in the town the Watch Committee, have power to punish, I suppose in both cases on the report of an intermediate officer?—Yes.

8213. What are the offences?—Neglect of duty, drunkenness, and breaches of discipline—everything.

8214. And insubordination?—We have not much of that.

8215. Tell us the nature and scale of punishments?—Under the 22 and 23 Vict., cap. 32, sec. 25: "The chief constable of any county police force, and the Watch Committee of any city, borough, district, or place, is and are hereby empowered to suspend any constable within their respective jurisdiction whom he or they shall think remiss or negligent in the discharge of his duty, or otherwise unfit for the same, and the said chief constable or Watch Committee is and are hereby also empowered at his or their discretion to fine any such constable in a sum of money not exceeding one week's pay, and to reduce the said constable from a superior to an inferior rank, such fine and reduction in rank to be in addition to any other punishment to which the said constable may be liable; and all punishments, penalties, and fines such as above enumerated, heretofore imposed or inflicted under rules framed under and by virtue of the 3rd section of the Act 2 & 3 Vict., cap. 93, shall be deemed to have been legally imposed or inflicted."

8216. Then the limits of punishment for each offence are limited by the second rule?—Yes, the maximum.

8217. Tell us what effect, if any, these punishments have on the promotion or pension of the men?—In the present state of the Superannuation Acts, I am sorry to say they have a very bad effect. They tell in the case of pension to the man's disadvantage.

8218. Will you tell us, please, whether the Bill lately before Parliament contemplates any change?—Yes; by allowing men to claim for length of service instead of leaving it discretionary with the authorities.

8219. Without being affected by any punishment?—Yes; by any entries in the conduct book. That is what we have been aiming at all through.

8220. But with regard to promotion, tell us what would be the effect of these punishments and their record?—I think they would have a salutary effect with regard to promotion.

8221. But do they influence promotion at present?—I think they do slightly in the towns—in the counties the chief constable knows his man, whether it is an accidental fault or habitual.

8222. There is no hard and fast regulation, by which a man's records, either in town or county, are barriers to his promotion?—No.

8223. *Mr. Heard.*—In point of fact, notwithstanding records, promotion is within the discretion of the superior officer?—Yes; in counties, and Watch Committee in boroughs, influenced by the report of the chief officer.

8224. *Chairman.*—Of course, degradation from inspectorship is one of the modes of punishment? —Yes.

8225. When you degrade a man from inspectorship, do you reduce him to constableship?—You usually let him down by steps.

8226. And if he conducts himself well in the step to which he has been reduced, has he a fair prospect of being restored?—He has a chance again according to what his real value is, and his subsequent conduct.

8227. *Mr. Holmes.*—Is a man generally fined for a first offence of drunkenness?—No; he is reprimanded.

8228. What is usually the amount of a fine for drunkenness where there is a fine imposed?—It varies so much, I could not possibly tell you, but it is a very severe punishment, indeed, to be more than 10s. I should consider 5s. a full fine unless under aggravated circumstances. We do not touch their purses in England if we can help it to any extent that can be a hardship to the men.

8229. Then, do you think that efficient discipline can be maintained without resorting to a system of fining?—Without resorting to severe fining. It stands to reason that, if you throw a man into debt to pay a big fine, he is a sore man for ever, and always working against his collar.

8230. *Mr. Harrel.*—I take it for granted the circumstances under which the offence may have been committed will be always taken into account in measuring the punishment?—Always.

8231. And that a man who commits an offence by drunkenness on duty adds greatly to that offence?—Yes; we consider drunkenness on duty aggravates the offence.

8232. *Mr. Holmes.*—And it would be for a case of drunkenness on duty that the fine of 10s. would be imposed?—Yes.

8233. *Chairman.*—Is there anything corresponding to the Irish Constabulary Court of Inquiry for dealing with charges against the men?—I do not know what that Court is.

8234. *Mr. Harrel.*—When a man is reported for a breach of discipline, is that report made on paper?—Yes.

8235. Is that paper put into the hands of the man so reported?—Yes, and he writes what he has to say upon it.

8236. In the event of his denying the accuracy of it, how is the propriety of the charge determined?—By personal investigation, either by a superintendent or the chief constable.

8237. I take it that he puts upon that paper the result of his inquiry?—Yes.

8238. Is that final?—The chief constable has all the power in himself. He records upon the paper, "I award so much," and then it is put into the general orders.

8239. Is there no appeal to any one from that?—No appeal. With the Watch Committee it is somewhat of the same form, but the inquiry is personally gone into.

8240. In towns the Watch Committee exercise the powers which in counties are exercised by chief constables?—Yes.

(2.) PROMOTION.

8241. *Chairman.*—Please to tell us what the general principles are on which promotion is conducted in the force?—Every force has a certain staff of officers, and, as vacancies occur, the best men are selected from the grade next to fill them up.

8242. Are the selections irrespective of seniority?—If two men are equal, the senior man would get the advantage; but it is done by selection.

8243. Is the selection made by examination?—No, not generally. In one force I think they do examine.

8244. In literary subjects?—In writing, calculation or arithmetic, keeping the pay-sheet, burglary, and sheep-stealing cases. In Yorkshire, I made every candidate for promotion send in an imaginary case of sheep-stealing, burglary, and pay-sheet.

8245. Then, in the main, the fitness of a man for the discharge of his duty is the ground of selection?—Always always.

8246. Who has the voice in the selection?—The chief constable in the county.

8247. According to your experience, does the chief constable make himself so personally acquainted with the merits of the men, as to be able to form a good judgment?—Yes; he does it through the superintendent of the district and personal knowledge.

8248. What I want to know is, whether his personal knowledge is brought much into play in the matter?—All promotion is with the knowledge of the chief constable.

8249. Does he himself know personally of the merits of the candidates, or is he guided by the experience of the superintendent?—In the smaller forces he does it all himself.

8250. How often does the chief constable see the men as a rule?—It is hard to say; he has to go over the district.

8251. How often does the chief constable of a county (who is analogous to our county inspector) see every man?—He does not assemble every man. He goes to petty sessions generally every three months, and he sees the men very frequently. There is no fixed rule about it.

8252. He goes to petty sessions every three months?—He does generally. He goes to every station once in three months in many places. No man could do it so often in Yorkshire.

8253. In your capacity of chief constable in Yorkshire, you were bound to depend to a large extent on the representations of your superintendents?—Very much.

8254. Are the men satisfied with the system of promotion?—Yes.

8255. Are you aware whether there is any idea that favouritism prevails? I do not ask you whether it does prevail; but whether such a feeling at all exists among the men?—I do not think the feeling exists openly, or is talked about much, but I have no doubt there are a great number of men dissatisfied, who think they ought to have been selected.

6256. I suppose in all the forces you have to deal with the position of inspector is filled by men raised from the ranks?—Yes.

6257. Is the position of superintendent also?—Mostly. There are a few exceptions.

6258. Where are the exceptions?—In two or three counties. Some few are from the outside—military and naval men.

6259. Is the fancy to employ outside men an old fancy, or one that has grown of late?—I do not think it is increasing. It has always been so in my experience.

6260. Does that produce any dissatisfaction in the force?—I think it does, as a matter of opinion.

6261. Do you think the dissatisfaction it produces is calculated to deteriorate the force?—No.

6262. It is mere sentiment?—Yes. I do not think the constables and sergeants of the divisions under these officers object.

6263. Will you be kind enough to tell us what the rule is with regard to borough head constables?—They are advertised for and appointed by the Watch Committee, generally from outside the force.

6264. These men hold a position similar to that of the chief constable in the county?—They are chief officers of the local police. They have not the power of punishing; they are entirely under the Watch Committee.

6265. Would you then consider their position as somewhat analogous to that of a superintendent in a county?—Yes; that is what it is.

6266. Except that probably in the case of a large town like Birmingham they have a larger body of men under their control than an ordinary superintendent?—Yes.

6267. Are the head constables taken from the inspectors?—Never, or very rarely from the force to which they are appointed, but generally from men who have gained experience in other forces.

6268. Do the inspectors who rank next to these head constables discharge duties at all similar to the duties of superintendent in the counties?—No; they are more like upper sergeants.

6269. In point of fact, there is no analogy between the inspector in the town and the superintendent in the country?—None.

6270. He ranks more like the inspector in the county?—Yes.

6271. Do you approve of the system of selecting the head constable in boroughs from outside the force?—Yes, for the sake of *fresh blood* it is almost a necessity.

6272. Do you think he obtains greater deference from the men, and maintains greater discipline among them, than a man chosen from themselves would do?—Much more so; he is free from all [illegible].

6273. Do the duties of a superintendent in the country bring him into contact with the magistracy of the county to any extent?—Yes, a great deal.

6274. Are the men now holding the position found to discharge such duties satisfactorily?—They give satisfaction to the Justices with whom they are connected. I think there could be fewer superintendents with greater benefit to the service.

6275. *Mr. Herrick.*—Do you think that a system by which a fewer number of men of a higher class were engaged in the position of superintendent would be better than the present one?—I think so.

6276. The excessive number of superintendents arises from the large number of separate police establishments?—Yes.

(10.) Travelling Allowances and Transfers.

6277. *Chairman.*—Be kind enough to tell us what particular allowances are made for absence from quarters or marching?—They vary. There is no allowance for superintendents marching from their quarters. Do you mean superintendents only?

6278. The lower ranks?—There is a special duty allowance granted to all who are absent for the night.

6279. I suppose these special duty allowances are contained in certain regulations?—Yes.

6280. *Mr. Holmes.*—And I suppose they are intended to cover the cost of living and providing them with a night's lodging when absent from their district?—That is what the allowances are for.

6281. *Chairman.*—Are there allowances for absence a certain number of hours in the day-time. Say a constable is absent 10 or 12 miles from his village from 6 o'clock in the morning until 6 o'clock in the evening?—That would be case for special consideration.

6282. But as a rule, would he get any allowance?—The railway fare is paid, 1d. a mile.

6283. I suppose these things are regulated in each force by the chief constable?—Yes.

6284. In the case of transfer does a man get any allowance?—If not ordered away for misconduct he gets a travelling allowance varying according to the discretion of the chief constable.

6285. If a married man is transferred, is the expense of the removal of his family taken into account?—It is quite in the discretion of the chief constable.

6286. From your own experience as chief constable, can you say whether a large family was made the ground for expecting more?—I gave it in Yorkshire on removals.

6287. You generally gave more in such cases?—Yes, for good conducted men on transfers.

6288. *Mr. Holmes.*—When a man is obliged to break up his house, being ordered elsewhere for the good of the service, and no fault of his own, are the expenses which he has to incur taken into account?—Speaking from my own experience, I did not let a man lose for the benefit of the service; but if a man was misconducted I took that into consideration.

6289. *Chairman.*—If a man gets married in the force, is he removed to another place from where he happens to be stationed at the time?—He is, to some other part of the county, away from his relatives and his wife's relatives.

---

(11) Popularity of Policemen, and Employment of Pensioners

8289. *Chairman.*—Be kind enough to tell us whether, as a rule, the constables of the police forces in your district are popular with the people, and in ordinary times get on well with them?—In ordinary times they are as popular as anybody in the village, a bootmaker, or any one else.

8290. You told us if a policeman was popular in a village he was really a big man?—Yes; he is a great man and looked up to. He is a "Mister."

8291. When he retires from the force does he find it easy to get employment?—If he is sound he gets employment immediately.

8292. *Mr. Holmes.*—What kind of employment?—As night watchman. They jump at him in every direction, such as the coal and gas works, &c.

8293. *Chairman.*—Does he get charge of public buildings?—Yes. I do not think they find any difficulty in getting employment if they are sound; but up to the present we have very few men in our forces fit for work, being superannuated in consequence of their being detained till they are so old there is no more work to be got out of them.

8294. *Mr. Holmes.*—What rate of wages do these men expect when they go out retired and get situations; would they be satisfied with 10s. or 12s. a-week?—Yes, having their pension too.

8295. It is employment yielding something like that they would be fit for?—Yes, some quiet work.

8296. Would a retired constable be glad to get any employment?—He would not take garden work or hard labour work. He has not it left in him to do such work. You must remember we squeeze the orange terribly at present.

8297. *Chairman.*—Would the men, as a rule, take to labour after leaving the force?—No; they are not fit.

8298. Do you think that, having held such a dignified position as you describe in the villages, they would, if they could, settle down as agricultural labourers?—I do not think they would. They might till their own garden. A retired constable has got a little money; he has his pension.

8299. His pension, of course, is considerably less than his pay?—Yes.

8300. Is he able, as a rule, by what employment adds to his pension, to live pretty comfortably?—Pretty well, if he is in good health. The doctor's bill would hurt him.

8301. *Mr. Holmes.*—Would a police pensioner object to driving a cart or van?—Oh, dear, no; but he would not do such a thing as pick stones.

8302. *Mr. Herrel.*—Would he look upon employment as keeper of a gate lodge, in livery, as suitable?—Yes; a sort of watchman, that is.

8303. *Chairman.*—Suppose he retired as an inspector?—An inspector would not take it. He has been "Sir" and "Mr." for many years.

8301. Do the men save money?—I have known some policemen make money.

8302. Do you find that, owing to the provident habits of men when they marry and the necessities of their family, they underfeed themselves?—I have seen such cases.

8303. *Mr. Holmes.*—Do you find that men who were able to live and save some money whilst single make complaints when they are married that they find their pay insufficient to keep them and their families?—No; we do not find any complaints of that sort.

8304. *Mr. Herrel.*—Married policemen and their families mix and associate on equally advantageous terms with the people of the locality?—Oh, yes; that is one of the advantages of the married policemen.

8305. They are received among the people?—They are quite amongst the people. That is the peculiarity of the English system, that they are part of the people representing order. In country villages a policeman is a great man. He goes into the market town for petty sessions, and he has the commissions of his village friends to buy groceries and look up things. He is a great man.

8306. *Mr. Holmes.*—When you say he gets commissions to buy groceries and things of that kind, is he paid for them?—Oh, dear, no! He is above that. He is a great man.

---

(12) Drill and General Discipline

8329. *Mr. Holmes.*—As a final question, I would like to ask you whether the men are fairly satisfied with the scales of pay to which you have drawn attention?—They are, with little variations, which are easily remedied.

8330. *Chairman.*—Is it your experience in England that you require a different class of discipline and management for a large town force like that of Birmingham to that required for a county force?—I think different management is required.

8331. *Mr. Herrel.*—But, after all, in speaking of the discipline of any police force, it must generally be different in its character to the discipline of a military force?—Altogether. We do not attempt severe discipline.

8332. A policeman renders the most valuable service acting on his own responsibility?—Exactly, and if with a cheerful will.

8333. And with a cheerful will. And, consequently, the enforcement of military discipline, which would convert him into a machine, would render him useless as a policeman?—For our English service entirely.

8334. And unless a man is fitted for, and prepared to take, separate individual responsibility, he is of no use whatever?—He is of no use whatever. We would a great deal sooner get rid of a man than to be bothered with discipline, such as having always to be watching him.

8335. Of course, perfect obedience to his superiors is absolutely necessary in every instance?—Absolutely necessary. Whatever order is given must be obeyed by the subordinate.

8312. *Chairman.*—Be kind enough to tell us what the nature of the discipline is, whether it is of a military character?—It is not.

8313. But it is of a character peculiar to the police?—Peculiar to the police.

8314. Be kind enough to state its general features?—I do not know how to put it, except that you tell a man to do a thing and he does it.

8315. Are the men drilled?—They are drilled a little during the summer months in the little drill they require so as to aid in four-deep, and so on. I never allow men to exhibit drill to me more than four-deep. If there was a row, it would be necessary to make large bodies of men to get them into sections. Police should never be in larger sections than of two men. Therefore, what is the use of drilling fifty and sixty men as a body? It is only waste. They are drilled about two months at head-quarters to out four-deep, two-deep, and single rank. Then they go out to a division. Perhaps they are paraded twice a-month, and they are assembled for drill in the summer months for about an hour.

8316. Are they paraded before superintendents?—Yes.

8317. *Mr. Harrel.*—At what periods?—Generally in the summer.

8318. Twice a-month?—Yes; they generally assemble together twice a-month in the summer.

8319. Are they ever drilled to use fire-arms?—No.

8320. Are they drilled to use swords?—In some forces they are, and in others they are not. All have cutlasses in the station houses, but no shooting arms or practice.

(13.) Leave.

8321. *Mr. Holmes.*—Is a policeman entitled to any vacation?—Yes, but not as a right. In every force a man will get seven to ten days, as much as he wants.

8322. *Mr. Harrel.*—Is there any stoppage of pay on leave?—No, except for staying beyond leave.

(14.) Retirement and Length of Service.

8013. At what period of service do you think it desirable that men should retire from the force, as a general rule?—I should say twenty-five years' service. The men will vary so much; you may get one or two, but very few, among the men fit beyond that. The upper officers are often quite fit after twenty-five years' service.

8207. *Chairman.*—Taking constable, sergeant, and inspector all round, what is the average length of service of the English policeman?—About twenty-two years, as given in evidence by Dr. Power.

www.ingramcontent.com/pod-product-compliance
Lightning Source LLC
Chambersburg PA
CBHW020827230426
43666CB00007B/1138